JOHN KEATS

Robert Gittings was born in Portsmouth in 1911, the son of a naval surgeon. He was educated at St Edward's School, Oxford, and Jesus College, Cambridge, where he was Research Fellow, and later an Honorary Fellow.

Between 1940 and 1963, Dr Gittings was a producer and writer of features and educational scripts for the BBC. He was then a Visiting Professor at several universities in the USA. He had many volumes of his own verse and verse dramas published during his lifetime, and his *Collected Poems* appeared in 1976.

His books include *John Keats* (1968; Penguin, 2001); *Young Thomas Hardy* (1975) and *The Older Hardy* (1978), published together in one volume in Penguin in 2001; *The Nature of Biography* (1978); *The Second Mrs Hardy* (with Jo Manton, 1979); and *Dorothy Wordsworth* (with Jo Manton, 1985).

Robert Gittings was awarded the CBE in 1970, and he also received many literary and academic awards, including the Annual Award of the Royal Society of Literature in 1955 and the W.H. Smith Literary Award for 'the most outstanding contribution to English Literature' in 1968 for his biography *John Keats*. He also won the Christian Gauss Award of Phi Beta Kappa in 1975 for *Young Thomas Hardy*, while *The Older Hardy* received the James Tait Black Memorial Book Prize for the best biography of 1978 and the prize of the Royal Society of Literature for 1979. Robert Gittings died in 1992.

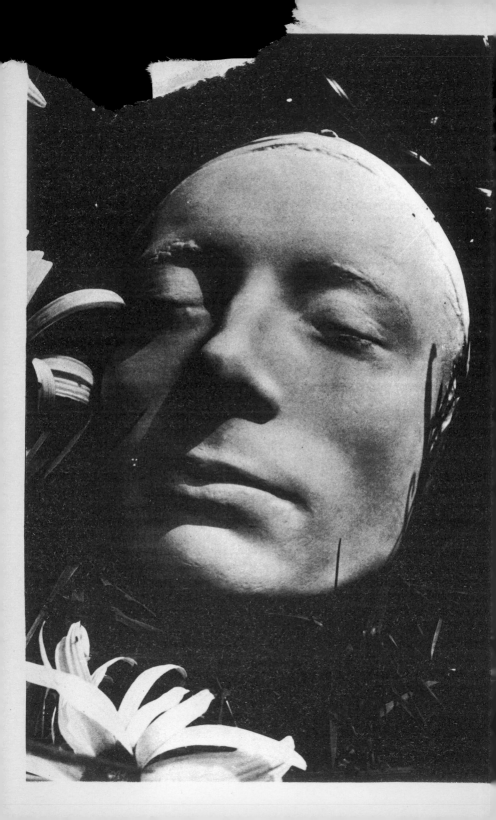

JOHN KEATS

BY ROBERT GITTINGS

PENGUIN BOOKS

PENGUIN BOOKS

Published by the Penguin Group
Penguin Books Ltd, 27 Wrights Lane, London w8 5TZ, England
Penguin Putnam Inc., 375 Hudson Street, New York, New York 10014, USA
Penguin Books Australia Ltd, Ringwood, Victoria, Australia
Penguin Books Canada Ltd, 10 Alcorn Avenue, Toronto, Ontario, Canada M4V 3B2
Penguin Books India (P) Ltd, 11, Community Centre, Panchsheel Park, New Delhi – 110 017, India
Penguin Books (NZ) Ltd, Private Bag 102902, NSMC, Auckland, New Zealand
Penguin Books (South Africa) (Pty) Ltd, 5 Watkins Street, Denver Ext 4, Johannesburg 2094, South Africa

Penguin Books Ltd, Registered Offices: Harmondsworth, Middlesex, England

First published by Heinemann 1968
Reprinted as a Classic Penguin 2001

1

Copyright © Robert Gittings, 1968
All rights reserved

Printed and bound in Great Britain by The Bath Press, Bath

FOREWORD

In the past thirty years, three great scholarly critical biographies of John Keats have appeared, all American, the works of Professors C. L. Finney, W. J. Bate and Aileen Ward. Any English writer on the subject is at once in debt to these authors; if he is lucky enough, as I have been, to enjoy their unique and generous friendship, he is fortunate indeed. This foreword is, in part, a dedication of my own book to these three leaders in the field.

Though there have been excellent biographical and critical studies by English writers in the same period, none has approached these three in thoroughness and scope. It is against the background of these American works that I present my own attempt at the first fully comprehensive English biography of the poet. What is there to say that they have not already said? The answer is to be found in one of the most curious paradoxes of literary history. For various reasons, the greater part of what Keats's hand put on paper, manuscripts of poems, letters, marginalia, is now in the United States of America, and readily available to anyone resident there. Yet the evidence for most of the facts of his life, and even more, the living origin of much of his work, remains in England, not easily available to American scholars, except on a prolonged visit, since it requires close research in public, local and private collections.

Thanks to advantages, which I have gratefully acknowledged elsewhere, I have enjoyed the best of both these worlds: that is, time and opportunity to research deeply in England, and also to examine the great American collections at first hand. I have personally seen more of the original sources for a life of Keats than anyone now living. As a result, this book contains much that has not appeared before, and often differs from accepted accounts. Where there are serious differences with other authorities, and where these authorities differ among one another, I have tried to provide footnotes to explain how misunderstanding may have arisen. I have also tried to subject my own previous books to the same kind of scrutiny. If this is on many counts a new view of Keats, it is because I have attempted everywhere to seek the oldest sources of reliable evidence.

* * *

This book is indebted to a great number of people and organizations. I have tried briefly to list as many as possible, and I must apologize for any inadvertent omissions.

Work of this nature is impossible without financial help. The Phoenix Trust by its major award in 1963 made it possible for me to undertake and start the book. A Leverhulme Research Award assisted me with its central stages. That the book was ever completed, in the way it has been, is due to Arthur A. Houghton Jr. Scholars throughout the world are indebted to Mr. Houghton's magnificent contributions to the Keats Collection in the Houghton Library, Harvard University; it gives me great pleasure to record my own personal and inestimable debt. I must also thank warmly the Henry P. Kendall Fund.

Space forbids personal mention of all archivists and librarians; but I must make an exception with Dr. W. H. Bond of the Houghton Library, Harvard University, who spared no trouble to give me ideal working conditions, and who incidentally provided me with three delightful and efficient graduate helpers, Robert Kirkpatrick, David Riggs, and Patricia Onion. To Dr. Bond, and the staff of the Houghton Library, I am specially grateful.

I also owe thanks for much help to the County Archivists and staffs of the County Record Offices of Berkshire, Buckinghamshire, Cornwall, Cumberland and Westmorland, Devon, Dorset, Essex, Middlesex, Somerset, and West Sussex; the Archivists and staff of the Greater London Record Office, the Borthwick Institute of Historical Research (the University of York), the Bristol Archives Office, the Commonwealth Relations Office, St. George's Hospital, London, and the Diocesan Record Office, Salisbury; the Curators of the Hunterian Museum (Royal College of Surgeons), the Wisbech and Fenland Museum, and the Berg Collection of the New York Public Library; the Librarians and staffs of the following libraries: West Sussex County Library, King's College, Cambridge, Magdalen College, Oxford, Cambridge University Library, the London Borough of Camden, the Metropolitan Borough of Chelsea, the Corporation of London, Guildhall Library, the British Museum, the Wellcome Historical Medical Library, Stepney Borough, Boston (Massachusetts) Public Library, Lambeth Palace, Royal College of Surgeons of England, Wills Library, Guy's Hospital, Yale University, Borough of Reading, City of Exeter, Wiltshire Archaeological and Natural History Society, Royal Army Medical College, Brighton Public Library, Westminster Public Library. I am indebted for additional information to the Clerk of the Chamberlain's Court, Guildhall, A. C. Cole, Windsor Herald, the Town Clerk of Wells, Somerset, the Medical Superintendent, Graylingwell Hospital, the Honorary Secretary of the London and Middlesex Archaeological Society, the Keeper of Printed Books, Department of Printed Books, Bodleian Library, and the Registrar, St. Gregory Seminary, Cincinnati, Ohio. The Curator of Keats-Shelley Memorial House, Rome, Signora Vera Cacciatore, and the Assistant Curator of Keats Memorial

House, Hampstead, Mrs. Christina M. Gee, accommodated my work in those buildings and gave me invaluable help, while Russell A. Fraser, formerly Chairman, Department of English, Vanderbilt University, Tennessee, afforded me generous facilities at that University. I also thank the incumbents of the parishes listed in my footnotes and appendices.

Among many who have helped with advice, knowledge and material are Edmund Blunden, Cleanth Brooks, Arthur Crook, Sir Claude Elliott, the Master Heward, Ian Jack, Sir George Mallaby, Eleanor Nicholes, Sylva Norman, Noel Poynter and J. H. Walter. The late Nicholas Ross gave me the advantage of his loving study of many out-of-the-way details about Keats. Living relatives of persons in the Keats story include the Very Reverend the Dean of Durham, for Severn material, Richard Carr Taylor and his sister Mrs. Eileen Shorland, and the many charming American descendants, young and old, of George Keats, particularly Miss Ella Keats Whiting. The interest shown by my fellow members of the Committee of the Keats-Shelley Memorial Association has been greatly appreciated, as has been the kindness of the President and the Secretary-Treasurer of the Keats-Shelley Memorial Association of America.

I have already recorded my virtual dedication of this book to those great American scholars, Professors C. L. Finney, W. J. Bate and Aileen Ward. Apart from my appreciation of their books and scholarship, I wish here to set down my deep personal thanks and regard in more detail. Professor Finney provided me with full access to his unique collection of pootostats of Keats' material, probably the finest in private hands in the world. Though I have now seen the originals of most of these, some—e.g. the material in the Pierpont Morgan Library, New York—I owe entirely to Professor Finney. I regard myself, as generations of others have done, as his pupil, and indeed it is from him that I learnt Richard Woodhouse's method of shorthand. Professor Bate has provided more instances of kindness and generosity than one could imagine, until one came to know how habitual this is with him. Before I had even arrived at Harvard, he had made himself effectively my host at that University, and the pleasure and success of my stay there was largely due to his unfailing thoughtfulness and care. His encouragement and help has extended to reading and commenting on the manuscript of this book, and to furthering its progress in every way that real altruism could suggest. With Professor Aileen Ward, I have a long and happy history of fruitful and informed discussion both in this country and in America, and an exchange of ideas that has even taken the form of a joint broadcast. To her, my family and I owe some of our most pleasant introductions to American life, and to a background of thought and opinion that has been one of the most stimulating factors for this book.

Finally, the book has been helped to what completion it possesses by the following people. Morton Marrian has given indefatigable assistance towards

Appendix 2, and Robert Fichter contributed much to Appendix 3. The manuscript was expertly typed by Pamela A. Taylor, and the problems of making a workable index were solved by Susan Hibbert. E. S. Peacock, of the Chichester Photographic Service, and Christopher Oxford have photographed the majority of the illustrative plates, while the colour slide for the jacket-design was made by the Cincinnati Art Museum. Christopher Fry, Leslie Norris and Ted Walker read this view of a poet's life with the eyes of practising poets, while Anthony Beal of Heinemann Educational Books has seen it through every editorial stage with sympathetic regard for what Keats's own publisher termed "that problem, the author". My daughter Clare has given me expert advice on Keate monumental brasses, and has rubbed one for the book. My wife, Jo Manton, as well as constant encouragement, has given me the incalculable benefit of her deep insight as a biographical writer, and has both widened the horizon and concentrated the style and arrangement of the whole book.

The quotations from Keats's letters, with his own characteristic variations of spelling and punctuation, follow, in almost every instance, those given in the great edition of Hyder E. Rollins. The text used for the poems is generally that of the second edition by H. W. Garrod (1958), though when poems are quoted from the letters, I have sometimes made an exception in favour of versions appearing there.

CHICHESTER   ROBERT GITTINGS
1963–1968

CONTENTS

PART III

THE LIVING YEAR

PART IV

THE LAST YEAR

APPENDICES

ILLUSTRATIONS

Nos. 4, 5, 7, 8, 15, 17, 19, 20, 21, 24, 25, 29, 30, 35, 36, 45, 47, 50, 51 are photographed by Christopher Oxford, and are reproduced by permission of the Libraries and Art Committee of the London Borough of Camden from the Collections at Keats House, Hampstead.

The frontispiece is photographed by Rodney Symes of the David Paul Design Group.

ABBREVIATIONS
USED IN THE FOOTNOTES

Colvin (1887) – Sidney Colvin, *Keats*, 1887.
Colvin – Sidney Colvin, *John Keats, His Life and Poetry*, (3rd. ed.), 1920.
Lowell – Amy Lowell, *John Keats*, 2 vols., 1925
Hewlett – Dorothy Hewlett, *A Life of John Keats*, 1949.
Ward – Aileen Ward, *John Keats: The Making of a Poet*, 1963.
Bate – W. J. Bate, *John Keats*, 1963.
Finney – C. L. Finney, *The Evolution of Keats's Poetry*, 2 vols., (reprinted) 1963.
JKLY – Robert Gittings, *John Keats: The Living Year*, 1954.
MOK – Robert Gittings, *The Mask of Keats*, 1956.
KI – Robert Gittings, *The Keats Inheritance*, 1964.
KSR – Robert Gittings, "Keats's Sailor Relation", *Times Literary Supplement*, 15 April 1960.
MKO – Robert Gittings, "Mr. Keats's Origin", *Times Literary Supplement*, 5 March 1964.
HBF – H. B. Forman (ed.), *The Poetical Works and Other Writings of John Keats*, 4 vols., 1883.
KC – Hyder E. Rollins (ed.), *The Keats Circle*, 2 vols., 1948.
MLPCK – Hyder E. Rollins (ed.), *More Letters and Papers of the Keats Circle*, 1955.
Letters – Hyder E. Rollins (ed.), *The Letters of John Keats*, 2 vols., 1958.
Garrod, *Works* – H. W. Garrod (ed.), *Keats' Poetical Works*, (2nd. ed.), 1958.
LFBFK – Fred Edgcumbe (ed.), *Letters of Fanny Brawne to Fanny Keats*, 1937.
Haydon – Willard B. Pope (ed.), *The Diary of Benjamin Robert Haydon*, 5 vols., 1960–63.
CLH – Thornton Hunt (ed.), *Correspondence of Leigh Hunt*, 2 vols.
Sperry – Stuart M. Sperry, Jr., "Richard Woodhouse's Interleaved and Annotated Copy of Keats's Poems (1817)", *Literary Monographs*, vol. 1, The University of Wisconsin Press, 1967.
Adami – Marie Adami, *Fanny Keats*, 1937.
Sharp – William Sharp, *Life and Letters of Joseph Severn*, 1892.
E. – *The Examiner*, 1808–1825.
G.M. – *The Gentleman's Magazine*.
Finney, photostat – C. L. Finney, photostats, private collection.
Dilke, ann. – C. W. Dilke's annotations to Milnes's *Life, Letters*, etc. of John Keats.
KHM – Keats House Museum Guide, (6th. ed.), 1966.
KSMB – Keats-Shelley Memorial Bulletin.
KSJ – Keats-Shelley Journal.
G.L. – Corporation of London, Guildhall Library.
P.P.R. – Principal Probate Registry, Somerset House.

PROLOGUE TO BIOGRAPHY

JOHN KEATS died on 23 February 1821. On 4 June, his publishers announced "Speedily will be published, with a portrait, *Memoirs and Remains of John Keats*. Printed for Taylor and Hessey." Although Taylor claimed that Keats himself had wished him to write the poet's life, this announcement seemed premature to many friends of Keats, on whom the memoirs and remains would naturally depend, and they decided not to co-operate. Their self-appointed spokesman, Charles Brown, dismissed Taylor as "a mere book seller".[1] The publisher lost heart, and no one who had known Keats at first-hand ever wrote a full biography. There were, however, biographical jottings of varying natures and values. The earliest were probably the brief notes made by Charles Wentworth Dilke in his copy of *Endymion*.[2] These, though reasonably accurate as far as they go, are very short, a total of less than 1500 words. The quarrel between Dilke and Brown, which developed in the half-dozen years from 1824 to 1830, destroyed all hope that these two friends of Keats's maturity could collaborate.

Meanwhile John Taylor the publisher had not given up hope of completing a memoir himself, and in 1827 he had a stimulating encounter which has influenced, directly or indirectly, nearly all biographers of Keats. Taylor was a freeman of the Girdlers' Company and had been Master in 1825. After Easter, the Court and Livery, that is the whole Company, holds a dinner to which the junior half of the liverymen bring personal guests. As the guest of one of these, a Mr. Macauley, there appeared at this dinner on 19 April 1827 Richard Abbey, who had been trustee and guardian for John Keats. Taylor took the opportunity to question him about the poet's origins and early life, and wrote the results down the next day. This account[3] has almost always been treated as if it were a sober and formal interview conducted in Abbey's counting-house or Taylor's office, though the frequent slips of the pen and misunderstandings that occur in it might make one suspect a morning-after atmosphere. The character of the two men involved has also been misunderstood. Both have been written down as prim, censorious and strait-laced, but there is strong evidence to the contrary. Abbey might occasionally urge restraint in the entertainments of his own City Company, the Patten-makers, of which he had twice been Master, but at other times he is shown as

1. Edmund Blunden, *Keats's Publisher*, 92–94.
2. KHM, No. 52.   3. KC, I, 302–309.

3

sanctioning the liveliest festivities. Taylor, as publisher, certainly held the opinion that too great an emphasis on sexual matters might harm the sale of Keats's poems, but he preserved bawdy verses from a friend among his own private papers,[1] and wrote poems himself which have more than a suggestion of passion. In fact, this meeting of Taylor and Abbey bears all the marks of two middle-aged men of the world—Taylor was 45 and Abbey 62[2]—in a relaxed mood after an extremely good and well-wined City dinner. Their conversation follows a familiar pattern for two middle-class Englishmen on such an occasion, especially as this was the reign of George the Fourth. Its topics, in order, consisted of anecdotes about women and sex, other people's drinking habits, the presumption of the lower orders, the nobility of one's own conduct, and the peculiarity and ingratitude of the younger generation. Under these heads, Keats's mother was an over-sexed and immoral woman, and his father an upstart; both drank. Abbey was a virtuous guardian whose benevolence was not confined to the Keats children, while they, especially John, had treated him with foolish ingratitude. "These are not Materials for a Life of our poor Friend which it will do to communicate to the World" commented Taylor, the publisher once more taking over from the diner-out.

His problem, which he was in no position to analyse, was how much *veritas* there may have been *in vino*. It is a problem which has beset the beginnings of most biographies of Keats; for, in spite of Taylor's comment, the world was presented with a version of these materials rather sooner and more casually than need have happened. In this same year, 1827, Leigh Hunt, fulfilling a promise to another publisher, tried that sure remedy for financial difficulty, a biography of the great people he had known. *Lord Byron and Some of His Contemporaries* came out early in the following year. This book, regarded by some as the blunder of Hunt's life, is certainly hastily and carelessly written. Its opening paragraphs on Keats, obviously derived in part from some passing-on of the Girdlers' dinner conversation, are a masterpiece of inaccurate and unfortunate phrasing:

He was a seven months' child: his mother, who was a lively woman, passionately fond of amusement, is supposed to have hastened her death by too great an inattention to hours and seasons. Perhaps she hastened that of her son.

Mr. Keats's origin was of the humblest description; he was born 29 October 1796, at a livery-stables in Moorfields, of which his grandfather was the proprietor. I am very incurious and did not know this until I was told it only the other day. He never spoke of it, perhaps out of a personal soreness which the world had exasperated.

Although Hunt, on other occasions, wrote perceptively and sympathetically about Keats, practically every statement here is dubious or demonstrably wrong. There were angry protests from Keats's surviving brother and others, while Brown, who commented "I hate Hunt's account of

1. Taylor MS, Bakewell.
2. Faculty Office, Calendar of Marriage Allegations, Lambeth Palace Library.

him", was probably stimulated to write his own fragmentary memoir which remained unpublished for a hundred years. Such an opening, based by his own admission on hearsay, might have led to suspicion of the rest of the account of Keats given by Hunt; yet it is fair to say that this first printed memoir of the poet has coloured all subsequent biography, and has become embedded into a body of Keats legend, which is to this day very difficult to shift. The fable of the poor boy who miraculously makes good was added to the other fable, also started by Hunt and crystallized by Shelley in *Adonais*, of the over-sensitive soul martyred by a harsh world.

Much of this fable still remains. This is not without its benefits; we are attracted by legend to look closer for the truth. Moreover, the life of an intensely creative artist almost naturally carries an element of fable in it, the traces of a primitive meaning which sometimes transcends the facts. Keats himself recognized this when he wrote to one of his brothers, "A Man's life of any worth is a continual allegory—and very few eyes can see the Mystery of his life—a life like the scriptures, figurative—".[1] Yet he himself felt the passion for accurate information and living detail which we all feel about any great and inspiring figure. A few pages later in the same letter to his brother, he described exactly his own physical attitude when reading by the fireside, and added "Could I see the same thing done of any great Man long since dead it would be a great delight: as to know in what position Shakspeare sat when he began 'To be or not to be'."[2]

The "great delight" of literally and exactly reconstructing the day-by-day details of a life such as Keats's must not, of course, be mistaken for an explanation of the life of a poet. His own warning about the allegorical nature of creative life will be remembered. Yet any new biographer of Keats must hope that in exploring the fable, the truth of each actual fact that emerges will be more illuminating than the figurative allegory that has hitherto served. This book is an attempt to find the factual basis for almost every reported incident or event of Keats's life. Such an attempt is by no means new. Thirty years ago, that great scholar Claude Lee Finney attempted, he said, "to reconstruct the environment in which Keats lived and to present and explain the personal, social, political, religious, philosophical and poetical forces which inspired and influenced his poems." He added, "I have made myself acquainted with Keats's friends through the existing records of their lives and I have read the books he read."[3]

Excellent biographies in the past thirty years have greatly enlarged our knowledge and appreciation of the poet, but not always along these lines. They have too often accepted second-hand detail about Keats and his friends, and have sometimes produced interpretations the reverse of the truth. The prologue to any new biography is to find the true origins of even the most often-repeated events and the most familiar story.

1. *Letters*, II, 67.   2. *Letters*, II, 73.   3. Finney, I, Preface.

PART 1

APPRENTICE YEARS

Chapter 1

MR. KEATS'S ORIGIN

"Mr. Keats's origin was of the humblest description."

— LEIGH HUNT

THE NAME Keats has many forms. In the still-unregulated spelling of the eighteenth century it ranged through every possible variant from Kates to Ceates, often in the same family. The most usual version seems to have been Keate. The name probably means a herdsman, and it is no accident that the original centre of the Keate families of southern England was the impressive range of sheep-walks along the north Berkshire Downs between Pangbourne and Wantage. In the Tudor red-brick and half-timber villages tucked away under this escarpment, Keate or Keats still appears in many parish registers. The main branch of this family emerges to gentility early in the sixteenth century, based perhaps on the sheep-farming enclosures of that time; it is on the grazing uplands near West Ilsley, where place-names such as Kates Field still persist, that the family is first centred.[1] Branches soon spread to the sheltered villages below, and occupied manors there, eastward to East Hagbourne near Didcot, westward to East Lockinge, near Wantage, and the punning coat of arms of the Berkshire Keates, three wild cats passant in pale sable, was adopted.[2] The family was prolific and enterprising; it did not stay merely local. By the early seventeenth century migrations had occurred as far as Cornwall,[3] to Exeter and its neighbourhood in East Devon, and to London, some members to the Inns of Court, others to trade. Oxford was the family University, and its roll numbered clergy and lawyers. There was strong family sense. Seventeenth-century wills show Cornish Keates remembering their Berkshire and London cousins and vice versa; Devon Keates come to London to make their fortune with the help of relatives there. A generosity of temperament can be discerned; some Berkshire Keates died, "leaving behind them good fames of hospitalyty & other virtues", as the engraved memorial records. As the obverse of this, and allied to family pride, an impetuous

1. *Visitations of Berkshire, 1532–1666.*
2. W. H. Hallam, *History of the Parish of East Lockinge, Berks.* (1900). Other families, apparently unconnected, in Gloucestershire, Worcestershire and East Dorset bore three Kites' heads, representing a local pronunciation, and were generally written "Keyt".
3. C. S. Gilbert, *An Historical Survey of the County of Cornwall*, II, 168–169.

temper can be guessed. Keate wills have more than their share of children disinherited or left contemptuously small annuities, sometimes with opprobrious reasons for doing so. Long life and virility marked the family. There were numerous second marriages and a multiplicity of half-brothers and sisters.

By the eighteenth century the family of Keate was a vast concern, a microcosm in itself of the gradations of the social ladder. Some members had climbed; others, like one section of a Madron (Penzance) branch, had become the objects of parochial scandal, and had slipped several rungs.[1] By the middle of the century, this family, stretching from Spitalfields to Land's End, ran the gamut of the social scale, from a baronet down to a blacksmith, from an ordinary mariner up to a man of letters. Many kept shadowy connections with one another, though the degrees of cousinhood were by now becoming remote. John (by far the most usual) and George were common Christian names, though West Country baptisms produced local exotics such as Sampson and Shilson, and marriage alliances added their oddities. Hoo was a Keate Christian name in Hertfordshire, and Avery in the London parish of St. Luke, Old Street, close to where Keats's father Thomas lived and worked. Thomas emerges fairly late as a family name, but then becomes comparatively frequent. There was still a high proportion of those who could style themselves gentlemen in the family, and who lived on private means, though many of these owed their fortune to mercantile or property transactions. One of these was the minor poet, painter and connoisseur, George Keate (1729–1797), who lived on the proceeds of a property deal made by his namesake and great-great-grandfather in Spitalfields.[2]

Keats looked like his father Thomas Keats, short, stocky, thick-set, with dark or reddish hair and hazel eyes,[3] and an active, alert, manly bearing. Though his brother George thought that John had a facial resemblance to their mother,[4] Keats looked nothing like his brothers and sisters, to judge by portraits, and his general resemblance to his father struck the only person to have seen them much together.[5] The two were of a physical type common to members of the Keate family. Eye-witness accounts of the surgeon Robert Keate, a contemporary of Thomas Keats, bear a startling likeness to those of Keats and his father.[6] In her old age, and following a tradition which she had evidently believed all her life, Thomas Keats's daughter Fanny said she remembered "hearing as a child that he came from the Land's End." After Keats's death, Dilke stated that "the father was a Devonshire man", and

1. Madron Parish Registers. Richard Keate (born 1692), the last of this branch to claim gentility, co-habited with his deceased wife's sister; their children were baptized as base-born, and appear to have left the parish.
2. *Survey of London* (1957), XXVII, 248.   3. KC, I, 274.
4. KC, I, 288.   5. C. Cowden Clarke, *Recollections of Writers*, 121.
6. Appendix 3.

Brown that he was "a native of Devonshire". Yet this must have been hearsay. Keats himself never spoke of his father's origins, and went out of his way in a letter to launch a violent attack on all Devonshire men. In the year 1773 (or early 1774) when Keats's father was born, there is no recorded baptism of a Thomas Keate or Keats in any parish in either Devon or Cornwall, nor for that matter in any London parish. The only absolutely sure fact about his origins is that he had a female relative called Elizabeth Keats.[1] The only person so far known who fulfils the conditions of this date and this relationship is the Thomas Keats baptized at St. Mary's, Reading, on 21 July 1773, whose father, also Thomas, came from the nearby Berkshire village of Stratfield Mortimer, and was a baker; the mother's name was Elizabeth Davey, and there was a sister Elizabeth.[2] There is evidence that the West Country Keatses kept up their connection with Berkshire, and with Reading in particular.[3] The most likely solution to a problem in which there can be no final certainty is that this Thomas was Keats's father, born like others in the widespread family of his name in one of its traditional centres of occupation, Berkshire, but perhaps later connected with relatives in the West.

Whatever his origins, Keats's father impressed those who met him. Though his eldest son was totally silent about him, a silence even stranger than that which Keats maintained about his mother, there was a family tradition of him "as a man of good sense and very much liked."[4] Lively, energetic and intelligent, he struck those who saw him as something above his reputed position, which has been described in much later accounts as helper, ostler or waiter at his father-in-law's inn and stables. His "excellent natural sense, and total freedom from vulgarity and assumption" in this position becomes more explicable if, as well as sharing a physical likeness with members of the Keate family, he was perhaps a blood-relation in one of its lower branches. Moreover, his financial assets which, by the age of 30, were just under £2000, need not have been, as has been sometimes assumed, solely the result of his fortunate marriage.

His wife was of a totally different physical type, though sharing with him a reputation for extreme good sense and practicality. Handsome, tall like all her family, with a good figure, large oval features and a wide full mouth, she too made an impression, though a mixed one. Charles Cowden Clarke found her manner saturnine, though he afterwards omitted the phrase; Abbey had stronger phrases, and Taylor came away from his evening out with the notion that Keats's mother "was a singular Character & from her he may be supposed to derive whatever was peculiar in his Mind & Disposition"— possibly an injustice to the qualities of Keats's father. Her grandfather, Martin

1. Jean Haynes, "Elizabeth Keats", KSMB, IX, 21.
2. Registers, St. Mary, Reading; Stratfield Mortimer registers; the Diocesan Record Office, Salisbury.
3. Appendix 2.   4. KC, I, 288.

Jennings, who was born in 1696, first appears as being of the parish of St. Botolph, Aldgate, in 1723, when he married Mary Clementson of the same parish, who was two years younger than himself. After two daughters, born in Aldgate, one of whom died young, their son, John Jennings, Keats's grandfather, was baptized in St. Stephen, Coleman Street, on 13 October 1730, and their daughter Mary in the neighbouring parish of St. Botolph Without, Bishopsgate, three years later. The family seems to have settled in the latter parish for this Mary Jennings was married there on 27 March 1758 to Richard Havers, and after his early death she returned there from the nearby parish of Christ Church, Spitalfields, to marry a widower, Charles Sweetinburgh, on 20 December 1768. Sweetinburgh was a victualler, who carried on his business first in Half Moon Alley, off Bishopsgate, and then at the sign of the Camel in Leadenhall Street.[1]

Meanwhile there are no certain records of her brother, Keats's mother's father, until early in 1774, when John Jennings appeared as the occupier of a leasehold stables, the Swan and Hoop, 24 The Pavement, Moorgate, in the parish of St. Stephen, Coleman Street. He also purchased his freedom of the City of London on New Year's Day and of the Innholders' Company on 4 January. He later took a short lease, and in 1784 a 21 year lease, together with that of the Swan and Hoop inn, No. 25. The inn, a busy centre situated on London Wall, was a valuable property, while only just over one year later, in 1785, John Jennings took over the lease of yet another profitable asset close by, No. 22 The Pavement. He let this at a rent which by the end of his life was bringing him £46 a year, and it was sublet in tenements. He also took up mortgages on other people's property, lent money on property security, and invested steadily in Government funds and East India stock.[2]

How John Jennings obtained the money to buy City leases and to carry on a property and loan business to the extent that his executor's accounts reveal remains uncertain. The theory that he once ran a line of coaches does not seem to have any substance in fact. The whole connection of the Swan and Hoop with the coaching business, which has often been assumed as the background of Keats's childhood, is extremely dubious. On the other hand, the Swan and Hoop inn and stables, with two coach houses, a large yard, and extensive stabling for three dozen horses, was most certainly well-placed for a more domestic and perhaps equally profitable use. Business men living north of the City would drive in their coaches as far as London Wall, and then put up their horses at the Swan and Hoop, while they themselves walked through the close narrow streets to their offices. Among the inn's clients were several relatives of Sir Robert Peel.[3] Jennings, like his brother-in-law Sweetinburgh, was a victualler; the inn provided "bait" or refresh-

---

1. Appendix 1.   2. MKO.
3. S. M. Ellis, *Wilkie Collins, Le Fanu, and others* (1931, rept. 1951), 284: Sir L. Peel, *A Sketch of the Life and Character of Sir Robert Peel* (1860), 311.

ment for such customers, and for their coachmen parked there throughout the day. These sturdy characters played a big part in Keats's background. Whereas his descriptions of horses are poor or conventional, one of his liveliest pieces of prose and best bits of comic poetry are about coachmen. "The Coachman's face says eat, eat, eat", he wrote. His own sensuous and almost schoolboy preoccupation with eating and drinking, and his celebration of both in poetry and prose, could have the simple explanation that these were the actual business of his forebears. Those who carry on the victualling trade usually live well themselves. Abbey's after-dinner reminiscences to John Taylor characterized John Jennings as "a complete Gourmand". This has been played down by biographers, unnecessarily sensitive about this aspect of Keats, but it is certain that the proprietor of the Swan and Hoop died of gout, and owing debts for wine and brandy, though there is no such evidence to attribute, as Abbey did, "the love of the Brandy Bottle" to his daughter.

She herself inherited from her mother a North Country shrewdness, whereas her father was remembered as being generous with his fortune to the extent of being gullible. On 15 February 1774, at St. Stephen, Coleman Street, John Jennings had married Alice Whalley, born in 1736 in the parish of Colne, Lancashire.[1] Alice Whalley at her marriage, however, was of the same City parish as her husband. There were plenty of Whalleys in neighbouring parishes; she presumably had Lancashire relatives who migrated to London, as the Peels did, and indeed, it may have been through her that the Peel family patronized the Swan and Hoop. The late marriage of John and Alice Jennings affected their children, none of whom had the long lives enjoyed by their parents. Their eldest child and only girl, Frances, Keats's mother, was baptized on 29 January 1775; then followed the two boys, Midgley John (21 November 1777) and Thomas (4 January 1782). The unusual Christian name of the former is found as a surname in both the Colne and in neighbouring City parishes.

The upbringing of Keats's mother followed the pattern of many City families. Since the reign of Queen Elizabeth, the East End had provided an overspill for the City population. The Keate estate in Spitalfields, dating from 1661, was typical of building operations continually stretching into the green fields of Middlesex and Essex, populated densely with merchants, traders and manufacturers of every sort and nation, including the foreign communities that naturally sprang up near the Port of London. The inner ring of this packed area was already a warren of the poorer classes, particularly in Whitechapel and Spitalfields. The outer suburbia stretching from Bethnal Green, Stepney and Hackney north to Walthamstow, Edmonton and Enfield were populated in a different way. Here the successful City merchant or manufacturer would buy or build a country house in rural surroundings,

1. Phyllis Mann, "New Light on Keats and His Family", KSMB, XI, 33.

and send his sons and daughters to the select schools that had grown up in this area. The heroine of Wycherley's *The Gentleman Dancing Master* (1672) had studied at Hackney School, while with Dissent and trade going together these schools were often of Nonconformist origins or principles. It was a mark of success to move out into the country, sometimes of failure in business to have to return to live "over the shop". On the other hand, some City men with a busy trade preferred to postpone their country house till retirement, while seeking the advantages of a country education for their sons and daughters.

John Jennings, with a busy inn to supervise, chose the latter course, taking a leading part also in the affairs of his City Company, the Innholders, and of his parish, serving as Master in one and senior Churchwarden in the other.[1] His brother-in-law Charles Sweetinburgh, who was ten years older, had by 1790 moved out to Holloway Down, near Stratford le Bow, Essex, after a similar business career, but Jennings evidently preferred to be on the spot. He followed the usual pattern, though, in sending his children out of the City and East End to be educated. It is not known where he sent his daughter Frances, though she was afterwards praised for her talents, sense and deportment. He sent his sons Midgley John and Thomas to Clarke's School at Enfield, taking boys from 6 to 16 years old; John Jennings's sons must have been among the earlier pupils for it was only founded in 1786 by the Reverend John Ryland, a Calvinist minister of Northampton. He had as Headmaster John Clarke, who had married Ryland's step-daughter and come with him from Northampton where he had taught in Ryland's original school, taking over the management of the Enfield school almost from the start.

The background of Keats's mother was therefore one of comfortable affluence and good education. Whether her "singular Character" represented a rebellion against this environment there is not enough evidence to say, but the only daughter of a well-to-do man easily acquires a certain amount of self-will. This appears in the first positive documented action we have of hers. On 9 October 1794, at the age of 19, she married on the other side of London at St. George's, Hanover Square, Thomas Keats, who was only just twenty-one himself.

Though the marriage was by banns, no relative of either the bride or bridegroom witnessed it; it had every indication, like several later actions of Frances Keats, of being a hasty affair. Nor is it certain how and where she met Thomas Keats. The only positive statement that at the time of the marriage he helped in her father's stables is in Abbey's after-dinner reminiscences. Abbey's attempts to make Frances virtually a nymphomaniac—it was, he said, dangerous for a man to be alone with her and she was abnormally fond of displaying her extremely good legs—include the incidental information that she used to go shopping in Bishopsgate, opposite the church of St.

1. Jean Haynes, "John Jennings: Keats's Grandfather", KSMB, XIII, 18–23.

Botolph Without where her eldest son was baptized. Crossing the muddy market thoroughfare, Abbey remarked, she used always to lift her skirts higher than she need have done; Thomas Keats would not have to work at the Swan and Hoop to appreciate her charms. There is no proof that the young couple lived with her parents, nor that their first son John was born at the Swan and Hoop; this, and the statement that he was a seven-months' child, appear solely in Hunt's hasty account which caused Keats's grand-nephew to remark sceptically "Others boldly assert that, like Jesus of Nazareth, the poet was born in a manger."[1] Since his baptism took place in St. Botolph Without, outside the parish in which the Swan and Hoop was situated, on 18 December 1795, and his date of birth was given at the time as 31 October 1795, it is far more likely that he was born in that parish, and that his mother's pregnancy, with a birth over a year after her marriage, was a normal one. Hunt, snatching at journalistic straws, and trying to embroider the account he had just received of Keats's mother as "a lively woman", may have made this assumption of premature birth from the poet's lack of height, not realizing that in this he merely resembled his father.

We have indeed no real knowledge at all how Keats's parents lived and worked during the first seven years of his boyhood. Various other family details emerge. His uncle, Midgley John Jennings, joined the Navy before the mast as a volunteer soon after his sister's marriage, though his speedy promotion makes it clear he had influential friends in this career; his commission as a second-lieutenant in the Marines took effect from 29 April 1796, and he was transferred to a fighting-ship, H.M.S. *Russell*, early in 1797. At the same time Keats's younger uncle, Thomas Jennings, provided a more ominous family note; he was buried in the summer of 1796 having died at the age of fourteen of "a decline"—the familiar name for tuberculosis. Midgley John then went on to do well in the Battle of Camperdown (11 October 1797); though his behaviour there cannot have been as spectacular as the legends afterwards told about it at his old school, it probably contributed to his quick promotion to a first-lieutenancy in 1799, when he was transferred to Chatham Barracks.[2]

Meanwhile, the Keatses themselves had had a move. The inn was still flourishing under the personal management of John Jennings, whose affairs enabled him to take a block of shares in the new Government 1797 5 per cent stock, but there is no sign yet that the Keatses joined him there. Indeed, after a second son, George, was born on 28 February 1797, the Keats family were living north of the City Road in Craven Street, one of the places where the

1. Sharp, 253.
2. KSR. Cowden Clarke's legend that he fought in Admiral Duncan's flagship, *Venerable*, and was singled out there by the Dutch Admiral, de Winter, probably derives from the famous imaginative painting by J. S. Copley, senior. In it, a tall Marine officer is present at the meeting of the Admirals on board *Venerable*. Jennings, however, served on board *Russell*.

genuinely open and green fields nearest approached the crowded hub of City and East End. Although they now lived in a more remote parish, the Keats family kept in touch with the Jenningses, and Keats may have been present at the christening of his small cousin Juliet Sweetinburgh in the Jennings family church of St. Stephen, Coleman Street on 6 April 1800. His own brother Tom had been born a few months before on 18 November 1799. The fact that no Keats child was ever baptized at the Jennings family church perhaps shows that the younger family kept itself fairly independent.

From the time the family went to live in Craven Street, when Keats was just beginning to talk, stories about him as an infant begin. In the next-door house lived a Mrs. Frances Grafty. Meeting George Keats some years later and finding that John had become a poet, she remembered that at this age "instead of answering questions put to him, he would always make a rhyme to the last word people said, and then laugh". Many children do this without becoming poets, but there is no need to doubt this anecdote. From a year or so later, when he was five, comes another story, told by a former servant to his brother Tom. It speaks of him even then as "violent and ungovernable", a description confirmed by eye-witnesses in his schooldays. He got hold of "a naked sword"—not necessarily, as has been thought, a toy—and held his mother prisoner in the house with it. This story, characteristic of all we know later of his possessive and passionate nature, has been thought exaggerated, partly because it was retold by Haydon the painter; but it was written down on a day when Haydon had just been talking to Keats.[1] The much milder version, which portrays Keats as guarding the sick-room of his mother, was concocted[2] from a combination of this story and quite a different anecdote by Haydon. Both Mrs. Grafty's anecdote and Haydon's story contain elements of Keats's essential make-up—playfulness, laughter, rage and the desire for possession.

A fourth boy, Edward, was born on 28 April 1801, and by now the family was on the eve of a change of circumstances. John Jennings, in his late sixties, had served his term as Master of the Innholders Company in the year 1797–1798; from the next year onward, he took less part of the Company's doings, which may mark the onset of ill-health and thoughts of retirement. He had an awkward decision to make about his Moorgate properties. The leasehold of each was due to end in the year 1805, the Swan and Hoop at Lady Day and the nearby tenements at Michaelmas. One solution would be to live there till the leases expired, and then retire to the country. Another would be to rent a country house, not build or buy, and to retain a controlling interest in the public house, stables and neighbouring property until their leases ran out: a semi-retirement rather than a full giving-up of active life. He chose the latter course, and began to look at the country district where he had sent his sons to school. A survey of this district in 1798 remarked that "the entrance to Enfield from the windmill is charming; it abounds with smart boxes of from £30 to £60 a year."[1] One of the smaller of these "smart boxes" would do, for there was only himself, his wife Alice, and their maid Christian Finlayson. In the latter half of 1802, he moved them to a "nice house" at Ponder's End, Enfield, recently built by a Miss Fuller, and let at one of the £30 rents.[2]

John Jennings was able to do this to his satisfaction by putting in his son-in-law Thomas Keats to manage the Swan and Hoop and stables for him, and to keep an eye on the nearby property; head ostler and livery-stable-keeper are later descriptions of Keats's father. The numerous family, with another on the way, moved to live above the inn, their first proven connection with it, late in 1802. Just before the move they had lost one member, the youngest, little Edward Keats, buried in Bunhill Fields on 9 December. Early in the next year, Thomas Keats was admitted to the freedom of the Inn-holders Company, in order to be able to carry on the business of the inn, though John Jennings still retained the lease of the property, and appears to have charged him and Frances a rent of £44. One does not know what arrangement was made about the profits of the business, nor whether when the lease expired, Thomas Keats had any intention of renewing it for himself. Although he had a fair amount of money put away, there are signs that he could not always find cash readily. He now had further obligations. His only daughter Frances Mary was born 3 June 1803, and about the same time, he decided to send his two elder sons to the school their uncles had attended, Clarke's School at Enfield, not far from their grandfather and grandmother. Their mother afterwards said she wanted to send them to Harrow; this could have followed their early schooling at Clarke's, if the family fortunes had improved sufficiently, and it was not an out-of-the-way idea. In spite of Harrow's great reputation it was by no means confined to children of the upper classes or the aristocracy such as Lord Byron; it was still regarded by the trading classes of Middlesex as the local county school.

Keats went to Clarke's School with his brother, after a short period at some local dame school, in August 1803, the school year then having two terms, one from August till Christmas, and the other from January to Midsummer. He was lucky to go when he did for before the end of the school year next Midsummer his whole home life was to undergo a drastic revolution. One or two apparently minor events occurred in this space, to add their weight to later family happenings. At the end of January 1804, his 80-year-old great-uncle Charles Sweetinburgh died and was buried in Bunhill Fields. He had perhaps been much less successful in business than his brother-in-law John Jennings for he had returned to his former City haunt of Old Street—

1. J. Middleton, *View of the Agriculture of Middlesex* (1798), 124.
2. KI, Appendix 4.

sometimes a mark of failure—and he left his wife Mary only £600. John Jennings, who was left a token legacy to buy a mourning ring, was named in his brother-in-law's will as a good friend, perhaps a hint that this friendship should extend to supporting his sister, the widow, in her old age.[1] Then on 12 March, Keats's uncle Lieutenant Jennings married one of the many daughters of a Huntingdonshire clergyman, the Reverend William Peacock. His wife Margaret, with a brood of unmarried sisters left behind at home, was reckoned to be indirectly provided for by her elderly and well-to-do father-in-law.

These possible financial calls on John Jennings, however, were nothing to the personal shocks that soon assailed the whole family. About one o'clock in the morning of Sunday 15 April, John Watkins, a watchman, a mile or so north of the Swan and Hoop, near Thomas Keats's old abode in Craven Street, heard a clatter of hooves and saw a riderless horse go past him. Such a sight, at a time when everybody in City or country could put a leg across a horse and stay on it, was the equivalent of a loose ice-axe slipping down a Swiss mountain. Watkins guessed what it meant, and hurried up the City Road till he came to Wesley's Chapel. It was as bad as he could have feared. Near the Chapel gateway a man lay with his body in the road and his head on the pavement, insensible and covered in blood from a deep wound in the right side of his head. The watchman dragged and carried him to the nearest surgeon in a side road. Half an hour later, having recognized or found out who the man was, he helped to take him to his home, the Swan and Hoop. It was Thomas Keats. He died that morning without regaining consciousness.[2]

1. P.P.R., Heseltine, 136.
2. Jean Haynes, "A Coroner's Inquest, April 1804", KSMB, XIV, 46. The inquest makes it clear, as newspaper reports do not, that all this took place in the early hours of Sunday morning.

Chapter 2

THE INFANT LEGATEE

"In the said cause Rawlings against Jennings the Infant Legatees respective Account and the said Accountant General is to declare the trust thereof accordingly subject to further order of this Court."

– Order in Chancery, 13 February 1810

THE TWO children at home were too young to realize or remember the tragedy and the elder boys, John and George, were at school in the middle of their second half. Thomas Keats, according to one account, had visited them that day.[1] If this is so, it was unlucky that he did not take his wife with him and drive her in the gig, which was their usual way of visiting the boys.[2] Hearsay attributes to him the habit of riding himself "a remarkably fine horse", and fact records that he dined that Saturday in Southgate, halfway between his home and Enfield. The after-dinner verdict of Abbey and Taylor was that he was "most probably very much in Liquor". This is as little capable of proof or disproof as the efforts of some later writers to suggest that he was completely sober. It was not an age when any man was likely to pass the time between dinner, then early in the afternoon, and sometime after midnight without taking on board a certain quantity of drink. On the other hand, such were the habits of the age, this was unlikely to have affected his horsemanship, although it was a showery night and the cobbles slippery. At all events he was dead at the age of thirty, leaving four young children, the oldest of whom, John, was only eight and a half.

His burial on 23 April in the Jennings family vault in the north aisle of St. Stephen, Coleman Street was the last time the Jenningses and the Keatses were to meet as a united family for some years. The events of the next two months were crucial for the children. One fact emerges from this confused time. Their mother seems to have disappeared. When the Poor Rate collector called at the Swan and Hoop, he found someone called Elizabeth Keats in charge.[3] This is the first and last time when anyone on Keats's father's side of the family appears in his story, a curious situation which argues some

1. C. Cowden Clarke, *Recollections of Writers*, 121.
2. KC, II, 146.
3. Jean Haynes, "Elizabeth Keats", KSMB, IX, 21.

unexplained circumstances in the first twenty-one years of Thomas Keats's life. This Elizabeth Keats was possibly a sister who figured in a mysterious incident much later, in 1819, when, according to Keats, writing to George about it, a woman in mourning called at their former lodgings in Hampstead, and, finding Keats was away in the country, "talk'd something of an aunt of ours" to the landlady.[1] This shadowy aunt can only have been on his father's side, and it seems likely that she was the person who appeared at the crisis of Thomas Keats's death, and helped out with the Swan and Hoop.

Her help did not last much beyond Midsummer, for then occurred an action by Keats's mother which will always be the subject of unfulfilled speculation. It is as well to notice the material situation in which Frances Keats now found herself. She took a short lease, in her own name, of the stables, though not of the inn, to begin when her father's ran out on 25 March 1805. Her husband had died intestate, and she in fact took a year to obtain administration of his estate. This amounted to under £2000, a useful legacy but only just enough when invested to pay rent and rates for the Swan and Hoop, let alone support four small children, two of whom were already at boarding school. Whatever Frances's motives may have been—and she was obviously a creature of impulse—she remarried just over two months after her husband's funeral. The name of the man was William Rawlings. According to Abbey, who seems to have repeated the information to Keats's sister, he was a bank clerk; nothing is really known about him except that he paid £1 7s. as subscription to a trade directory in which he described himself as a livery-stable keeper. There is no evidence of his being an innholder or having anything to do with the stabling business. He seems to have been a young man, and the marriage, by a macabre choice, took place at the same church as the widow's first marriage, one of the witnesses being the parish clerk. Again, neither of her parents attended. Mrs. Jennings actively disapproved of the marriage.

The effect of this remarriage on the children must have been profound, especially on John. He was his mother's favourite, and his passionate possessive nature towards her had already shown itself. There is a conflict of opinion over how much the children had to do with their step-father. Writing in her old age, Fanny Keats stated that "My Brothers and myself never lived with them"—her mother and Rawlings—"but always with my grandmother."[2] On the other hand, Abbey stated that this did not take place in the lifetime of their grandfather.[3] The fact that Fanny, who was anyway only one year old at this time, never mentions the house at Ponder's End, while both she and her brother George seem to speak of their grandfather by

1. *Letters*, II, 237.
2. KHM, No. 85. Most biographies follow Adami, 18, in substituting the words, "but went at once to my grandmother".
3. KC, I, 305.

hearsay only, tends to confirm Abbey's account. It must therefore be assumed that the whole Keats family and their new step-father settled down at the inn when John and George came back from school at Midsummer. Mrs. Rawlings certainly took over the management again at that time,[1] paying rent as before to her father out at Enfield. What he thought about her marriage is unknown. He was weakening in health; his will, which he made on 1 February 1805, had many signs of being a hastily-drafted affair, though it is clear he considered in some detail the obligations he felt to various members of his family. In brief, he intended to leave half his fortune, out of a total of about £13,000, to his wife, another third or so to his son, and the rest to provide annuities of £50 and £30 respectively to his daughter and sister, Mary Sweetinburgh. The Keats children were left a lump sum of £1000 between them.

Just five weeks after he had appended a feeble signature to this document, John Jennings died. The inn servants were put into mourning, and he was buried with some expense, as befitted a wealthy and prominent member of the parish, in the family vault in St. Stephen's. Within his family, however, there was at once some uneasiness, especially at the Swan and Hoop, where his lease would run out in under a fortnight. The will had been drafted by an amateur, a local land-surveyor, and it looked likely to be disputed. Two of the three executors were Lieutenant Jennings and the widow, but instead of the third next-of-kin, Frances, John Jennings had nominated as executor a business friend and parish neighbour, Charles Danvers, who seemed from the first unwilling to serve in this capacity. He might well wish to avoid being implicated, for Frances Rawlings felt slighted; her brother and her mother appeared to adopt an evasive attitude to her. They kept the provisions of the will dark, even her own legacy of £50 per annum, and proceeded to prove it without her knowledge, the Lieutenant coming up by coach with his wife and daughter from Hartford, Huntingdon, where his first child had just been born. He then set about dealing with the affairs of the estate in what may well have seemed to his sister a high-handed way, issuing a demand for the last quarter's rent from herself and Rawlings, which they countered by a bill for various sums owed to the inn by her father.

It was a moment of crisis for Keats's mother and step-father. The lease of the Swan and Hoop stables meant that they had to pay a large rent to the City. Rawlings had no assets, and Frances had not yet touched her late husband's capital. Purely fictitious later accounts have imagined that William Rawlings was an adventurer; if he were, of which there is no proof, he had got himself into a singularly unprofitable adventure. Like many people in difficulties, Frances and her husband decided that their position could be improved by going to law. On 6 April 1805, they brought a Bill of Complaint in Chancery against her brother and mother (and the unfortunate Charles Danvers) as

1. She paid the Poor Rate from the third quarter of 1804. G. L. MS 2. 433/12.

defendants. Yet another fiction, invented eighty years later, has represented their action as some sort of test case made by mutual agreement by all parties to clarify the will;[1] but the terms of their Bill bear every mark of a hostile action, as do the defendants' answers. Frances, in short, accused her own brother and mother of concealing the will from her, of administering it to their own advantage, and taking possession of her father's estate for their own use, without even allotting her the rightful legacy of £50 a year; she further put forward the large claim that her father "under the true construction of the will" had intended her to take a third share with the other two of the unwilled part of the estate, which, owing to the ambiguities of the will about capital, might be very considerable, a capital sum of over £3500.

It was a gamble on her part, in more senses than she may have realized. Considering the notorious delays of Chancery, one needed good health and a long life to embark on such a case; Frances might have reflected that one of her family had already died young from tuberculosis. Her own mother now took a step which has been variously interpreted. At Midsummer 1805, she moved from the rented house at Ponder's End to another a mile or so nearer London, at Edmonton, where Thomas Hammond, the doctor who had attended her husband in his last illness, had his practice. She settled in the same road, Church Street, and here at Edmonton, as both Fanny Keats and Richard Abbey remembered, the Keats children went to live with her, and remained under her care.[2] The exact circumstances of this arrangement will never be known. Most accounts assume that she "took" or "removed" the children from her daughter, or even that Rawlings dumped them on her,[3] but these are later inventions. The important fact for the children was that the family split over the will, which may as yet only have been a vague matter of adult talk, was given actual physical form by separation from their own mother. Keats was left with a distrust of people's motives and a deep personal insecurity that followed him all his life. "I scarcely remember counting upon any Happiness", he wrote, and again, "I have suspected every Body".[4]

Any form of personal shock at such an early age has profound effects, and the shock for John Keats took many forms—his father's death, his mother's remarriage, the family quarrel over the will, and the exodus of the children to their grandmother. He needed a huge element of stability to emerge from all this a balanced person. In the event he was left with a "hypochondriasm" or "melancholy", a "horrid Morbidity of Temperament"; the wonder is that

1. The authority on Chancery History, the Master Heward, however, states "these are clearly hostile proceedings of a normal kind", and adds "if the action was a friendly one, merely to construe a will which was doubtful, the executors would have been the plaintiffs and the beneficiaries the defendants" (personal communication). See also KI, 8–15.

2. KHM, No. 82.   3. Adami, 18, Hewlett, 18–19, Ward, 10.
4. *Letters*, I, 186 and 292.

he overcame it at all in a life which continued to have its elements of stress. This argues some exceptionally reassuring and approving side to his childhood, which, denied him by the accidents and actions of his parents and relatives, was provided by his school. It is not too much to say that Clarke's School now became his real home; so many of his characteristic attitudes, habits of mind, ways of looking at life correspond with the spirit that prevailed there. Moreover he himself found an all-important elder friend, guide to taste and sympathetic companion in the son of the headmaster, Charles Cowden Clarke, successively pupil, pupil-teacher and teacher at the school.

Clarke's School had a distinct tone, shared with the liberal and progressive, usually Nonconformist schools of the period, but with personal elements particular to itself and its headmaster. John Clarke anticipated in many ways the more consciously humanitarian and experimental regime of such schools as Hazelwood, which became well-known after the Napoleonic War. In the years from 1803 to 1815, liberal principles everywhere in the country were fighting a rearguard action against the hardening effect of a long and bitter war. The deceptive Peace of Amiens (1802–1803) had only been a prelude to the real and decisive struggle for the country's existence, a struggle not only against Napoleon on the other side of the Channel, but against reaction, which could always claim the sanction of a national emergency, on this side. Up and down the country, small pockets of liberalism kept their integrity and care for human dignity, and in its private way, Clarke's School was one of them, its seventy or eighty boys and masters a miniature of that spirit.

In such a small community, its character derived from its headmaster. John Clarke established a curriculum where "a book of Livy, the 'Bucolics' of Virgil, and the 'Hecuba' of Euripides"[1] were not the sole mental food from nine years old to fifteen, as they were for generations after in the great public schools. The school library was full of history and geography; prizes were given for voluntary translations from Latin and French; the French language was taught by the Abbé Béliard, an émigré, and though Keats objected to the French method of cramming boys like "young jackdaws", he learned to read French with ease, Clarke had influential friends of liberal views in the neighbourhood, and senior boys could meet these. His influence on the school discipline was equally enlightened. In an age when flogging in schools matched the brutalities of the fighting services, Clarke substituted a system of bad and good marks with prizes for the latter. Small dormitories and family surroundings in a converted private house, a rural setting where the boys had their own garden plots, complete an almost idyllic picture.[2]

Clarke, however, did not impose a stamp of likemindedness on his boys; there was full scope for individual bent. One of the pupils, contemporary with Charles Cowden Clarke, was Edward Cowper the inventor. Keats's own

1. Thomas Hughes, *Tom Brown's Schooldays*, chap. 9.
2. C. Cowden Clarke, *Recollections of Writers*, 2–7; *Letters*, I, 155.

contemporaries generally had his own prosperous middle-class background, but developed in widely varied ways, as musicians, artists, writers and lawyers. It was a school where character was appreciated as much as intellect, which accounts for the acceptance of Keats himself for, according to a contemporary Edward Holmes, he was "not in childhood attached to books". His passion was, as several accounts confirm, for fighting, and, as Holmes goes on to say, "He was a boy whom any one from his extraordinary vivacity & personal beauty might easily have fancied would become great—but rather in some military capacity than in literature."[1]

Keats's militant and violent temperament at school, the see-saw of his behaviour, "in passions of tears or outrageous fits of laughter always in extremes" has been variously interpreted; it has been said, perhaps with some truth, that it was meant to compensate for his small size or his instability at home, or both. He had lived his infant life too, and gone to his early dame school before Clarke's, on the fringes of the extremely extrovert and mixed population of London's East End, where, as he himself wrote in later years, "Though a quarrel in the streets is a thing to be hated, the energies displayed in it are fine." The London of Daniel Mendoza, the Jewish boxer and publican of Whitechapel, had been his nursery, where passing gentlemen, for amusement, would put down money to see a likely lad fight with a butcher, then the proverbial type of strong man, and one whom Keats himself tackled in his time. In the quiet reasonableness of Clarke's school, this may at first have been Keats's obvious way of making a mark; he fought, it was said, for the honour of his Naval uncle, promoted more quickly in school legend than his own career to a hero's rank. A fancied injustice to his brother Tom even led John to strike a master. His brother George evidently knew from early days how to deal with "one of his moods"; taller and long-limbed, from their mother's side of the family, he would pin John down till his anger exhausted itself and its obverse of warm affection returned.

The same posture could be observed in the Chancery suit between Keats's mother and uncle, who now had become the main contestants, their mother having sworn an affidavit that she had in no way "intermeddled" with the stock or cash of her late husband's estate. Keats's mother's indignant recourse to the law was halted by the delays of Chancery; her brother replied to her hostile action by a number of unfriendly acts of his own. Although he grudgingly admitted her right to an annuity, he did not release a penny of it from their father's estate. At the same time he was solicitous of their mother, and actually released to her more than she might have been entitled, for with four small grandchildren in her care and school fees for three—Tom had joined his brothers—she needed the money. The legal preliminaries dragged on for over a year until the case came up for hearing on 22 May 1806. Both sides were fully represented—legal fees eventually amounted to 3 per cent of

1. KC, II, 163–164.

the whole estate—and in July judgment was given. It was a complete victory for Keats's grandmother and uncle. They were allotted all the capital they had claimed, she absolutely, he for life, and were to share the cash residue. Keats's mother was excluded from everything except her £50 annuity, and even the time when she should get that was postponed indefinitely, until the claims of her successful relatives should have been satisfied. The action initiated by herself and her husband had utterly failed.

It is clear that her second marriage had failed also. By summer 1806, William Rawlings was living alone at the Swan and Hoop.[1] His wife had left him, and he appears to have disposed of the lease soon after to the new occupier. It is probable, as Abbey told Taylor, that he died within the next few years. Whether the Chancery disaster and the failure of his marriage had any connection is impossible to say. It is also impossible to say what now became of Keats's mother. She had no money, and she could hardly return to her own mother, against whom she had brought a hostile law-suit, still in process of settlement. These circumstances lend more credence than has generally been given to the story that she then lived with another man. Abbey identified him, so Taylor thought, as "a Jew at Enfield, named Abraham". A general muddle of place-names and districts occurs throughout Taylor's after-dinner jottings, and Enfield may have been a mistake for Edmonton, where a J. Abraham had certainly owned property a few years before.[2] According to Joseph Severn, "Keats used to say that his great misfortune had been that from his infancy he had no mother."[3] This implies a long separation, though the cause of it was kept from Keats, who remembered his boyhood as a time when he idealized women.[4] His subsequent disillusion with them, and total silence about his own mother, may reflect some later knowledge of disturbing facts.

Old Mrs. Jennings made great efforts to act as a mother to her four grandchildren. A farmer's daughter, she had a fund of practical wisdom which may account for Keats's frequent use of country proverbs, such as "Many people live opposite a Blaksmith's till they cannot hear the hammer." Her house at Edmonton was a place where Keats could return every holiday to be a more natural though less colourful self than at school. There was no need in the quiet elderly atmosphere to prove himself by aggressive tactics as in the public world of school. He got into the usual scrapes of a small boy, and was threatened with the usual punishments, though of a mild sort such as not being allowed to go to the annual Edmonton Fair when it came round; according to his own doggerel verses, the worst he did, though no doubt a

1. The Church rates, collected some time after Lady Day 1806, show her name crossed out and his substituted as ratepayer. G.L. MS 4489/1.
2. Edmonton rate-books, 1799-1800.
3. *Incidents from My Life*, 1858 (Severn MS).
4. *Letters*, I, 341.

B*

big enough crime in a household ruled by females, was to agitate his grandmother and her maid Christian by filling their washing-tubs with minnows, tittlebats and miller's thumbs which he smuggled in from the neighbouring brook, slipping out of the house before anyone was up. There were the usual pets, cage-birds, mice and goldfish, which did not make for spotless North-country housekeeping.[1] Small brightly-coloured garden birds, tomtits and goldfinches, are lovingly observed and described in Keats's poems, their sharp fluttering movements and flashing wings. In spite of her age, Mrs. Jennings understood children. Keats himself said that he was tenderly attached to her, and she herself put on record her love for all her Keats grandchildren. The memory of their grandmother mixing and baking for them a rich Lancashire cake with raisins and cherries remained with Keats's sister Fanny when she herself was an old woman.[2]

Another element of normal family life for Keats was his small sister. He carried his early sense of responsibility for her all through his life, writing her letters that sound like those of a kind, wise young uncle, without the slightly patronizing tone that George always adopted to her. Competing in kindnesses for her was a civilizing factor for all the boys; as George wrote, they were "always devising plans to amuse you, jealous lest you should prefer either of us to the others."[3] They even took her round the school, where the Headmaster's wife noticed what a sweetly-behaved child she was.[4] Memories of occasions like this and of many other garden moments with her, both at Edmonton and at Enfield, stayed with Keats so that he could remind her of how they promenaded round gardens together "apple tasting—pear tasting—plum judging—apricot nibbling—peach scrunching—Nectarine sucking—and Melon carving".[5] To look after a small sister gave them a shared sense of consideration for her, even down to suggesting remedies for the chilblains that troubled her every winter. They realized that the burden fell more severely on her than on them; she was too young yet for the distractions that school provided to take her mind off the question that must have hung over all of them, the mystery of a mother who was alive and not with them. To care for his small sister was for Keats an exercise of normality to balance the inexplicable contradiction of nature that seemed to surround their mother.

For meanwhile it was not only their mother's absence that affected them; the spirit of litigation she had raised, like the Furies of a Greek tragedy, seemed bent on destroying the whole family. The burden of the complicated estate, every penny of which had to be accounted to Chancery, fell on her brother the Lieutenant. Late in 1807, he went on sick-leave and joined his wife and three children in Huntingdon; soon he was spitting blood. In August 1808 he at last received his legacy from Chancery, the case in which she had involved him having delayed his inheritance for three and a quarter

1. *Letters*, I, 314; II, 46 and 149.   2. Adami, 29.
3. MLPKC, 24.   4. Sharp, 255.   5. *Letters*, II, 149.

years. It was too late; within three months he was dead, the family disease of tuberculosis having been hastened by financial worry and family strife. One of his last acts was to pay, not of his own initiative but by order of Chancery, part of the arrears of his sister's annuity. He had kept her waiting, but she had perhaps helped to kill him. Next year she herself appeared to be, as her Counsel in Chancery claimed, "in great distress". She petitioned her brother's executors for some more of her annuity, which was granted her, not grudgingly, but as "the wish of all parties". This seems to show that after her brother's death a reconciliation had taken place between her and her mother, and makes this the most probable time for her mysterious exile to have ended, and for her return into her children's lives.[1] She was now, however, a sick woman, taking to her bed with something George vaguely named "a rheumatism". She lavished her long-absent affection on her eldest boy, John.

This return, after the comparatively ordered world of Clarke's School in term-time and his grandmother's old-fashioned household in holidays, brought a shock of change into the life of the thirteen-year-old boy which has been variously interpreted. His reticence has left no direct clue what it meant to him; yet, rightly observed in the time-sequence of his adolescence, his mother's reappearance coincides with an event noticed by everyone who knew him then. The culmination of his fits of violent passion at school seems to have come round about the age of thirteen, when he struck the master. That he could be betrayed so far by anger may itself have been a lesson, to be reinforced in him by his Headmaster's gentleness over the offence. Almost immediately afterwards came the death of his uncle, family reconciliation and his mother's return. He began the term in January 1809 with a new resolve, which was to startle everyone by its all-or-nothing thoroughness. From refusing to do anything to please the masters and barely scraping through his lessons, "he determined", as Charles Cowden Clarke remembered, "to carry off all the first prizes in literature". This almost overnight sense of responsibility has one likely cause. He now was the oldest male in the family, and he once more had a mother, in distress, dependent, and approving of everything he did.[2]

The means he used to make up his vast lee-way of inattention were, like everything else he did in his life, extreme. They followed the kind of simple logic that became a mark of his adult years. Since he required all his time for the task, he would give literally all his time to it. He got up before everybody

1. A special Order was made so that the payment of her annuity should jump the queue of "the number of causes that stand in the paper before it". P.R.O. 33, 569, f. 715. The willing co-operation of all parties needed to achieve this is unlike any previous litigation, and would argue a reconciliation at this time.
2. Ward, 17, believes the cause to have been his mother's death; but he won his first prize several months before she died.

else and read; he read all through meals, he worked indoors all through half-holidays. If the masters drove him out to take exercise, he would walk with a book. Even in the evenings, at supper in the school-room, he held a book close to his eyes, groping for the food on the table beyond it. He went through every book in the school library, history, geography, exploration and romance, the same type of mental food that had nourished Coleridge's few masterpieces. Yet all this was only a background. His object was to obtain first prize of the three that John Clarke gave each half-yearly term for translations from French and Latin done voluntarily in the boys' spare time. Fénelon and Virgil were read and translated by him in immense quantities. Greek was not a prize subject, but the needs of classical translation led him to classical reference books in which the Greek myths took their place among their Latin cousins, the *Pantheon* of Andrew Tooke, the *Polymetis* of Joseph Spence, and, above all, the *Bibliotheca Classica* of John Lempriere, which he kept by him all his life. The indirect results of his scheme were therefore much vaster than he can have dreamt then, but its direct result was achieved too. At Midsummer 1809 he won, by a considerable distance, the first prize.

The book chosen for him was C. H. Kauffman's *Dictionary of Merchandize . . . for the use of Counting Houses*. It was a very reasonable choice for the headmaster of a school which catered for the sons of the trading and business classes—two of Keats's exact schoolfellows were the son of an ironmonger and the son of an oil-merchant—to give to a pupil who, however attractive and individual in character, was noted for being "*not* Literary", and who before this term had seemed only interested in fighting, cricket and "a sort of grotesque and buffoon humour". Much later, half-conscious memories of this book were joined perhaps with even earlier ones of the Port and East End of London to emerge as poetry;[1] but for the time it was a symbol of achievement and a spur to further success. He had done what he had set out to do, and in his direct logic there was no reason why he should not do it again on an even larger scale. He set out to make a prose translation of the whole of the *Aeneid*.

It was as well that this new-found outlet for his confidence occupied him so much at school during his second 1809 term, for at home, after the brief summer of his mother's return, the clouds were gathering again. Ill and thankful for small mercies, Keats's mother had abandoned her claim for any capital from her brother's executors, though remaining in the Chancery suit seeking the capital for her own annuity and the legacy to her children, which had still not been allotted by the Court. Her illness was advancing while the Law seemed to stand still, in a way horribly reminiscent of the fate to which she had unthinkingly condemned her own brother. Shortly before Christmas occurred something almost like a blow from his grave. Her brother's widow, Margaret Jennings, petitioned Chancery that all her late husband's capital,

1. Bate, 26, n. 4.

still held by the Court, should be allotted absolutely to their three children, Keats's small cousins. This outbreak of fresh litigation with its threat of further delay may well have accelerated the progress of Frances's illness, now openly showing itself as tuberculosis. When John Keats returned for his Christmas holidays with another end-of-term first prize to his credit, he found his mother gravely ill. The renewal of hope that had helped to launch him on a new phase of life looked like being shattered, almost as soon as it had begun. It is probably this terrible realization to which he referred when he afterwards wrote "I have never known any unalloy'd Happiness for many days together: the death or sickness of some one has always spoilt my hours".[1] Yet he brought to this realization all his newfound purpose and practical application. Hammond, the family doctor in the house up the road, had prescribed the meaningless palliative medicines of the time; John pinned his hope on the proper administration of these drugs, and would allow no one to give them to her but himself. He cooked for her, he put his ruling passion for books at her disposal, sitting up all night in an armchair and reading her novels at all times.[2]

A few weeks after her sons had gone back to school, the sick woman had at any rate some small satisfaction from the Law. On 13 February 1810, capital of £1666 13s. 4d., which would produce her annuity of £50, was at last ordered to be set aside in Chancery for her, and to be allotted to her children after her death. It now looked as if this would be of more use to the children than to herself, especially when joined to their own inheritance; the same Order in Chancery directed that her father's cash legacy of £1000 to them should be invested in 3 per cent Consols and placed in trust to "the infant legatees respective Account" for each one to apply to the Court at 21 "as they shall be advised". The claim of the other infants, her brother's children, was however dismissed, though their mother took half her late husband's capital. The remaining half ultimately found its way to the Keats children. This was a grievance and explains the utter silence by Keats about his Jennings cousins, and theirs about him, so complete that when the daughter of one wrote a family memoir long after Keats's fame was established, she never mentioned that they were related to the poet. The unlucky law-suit had provided yet another element of isolation for Keats.

Litigation and death had been a dominant background to the happiness of his schooldays; the last blow was perhaps the worst. In March, at school, he was told that his mother was dead. He had buoyed himself with hope, and the shock was sudden; at the time it shattered his new self-sufficiency. He gave way to "impassioned & prolonged grief", which overcame him so violently that even in the school-room he had to hide himself in an alcove under the master's high desk, to the sympathy of his school-fellows. On 20 March 1810 he saw her buried in the family vault in the north aisle of St.

1. *Letters*, II, 123.　　2. Haydon, II, 107.

Stephen, Coleman Street, her cause of death recorded, like that of her brothers, as a "decline", the stock term for tuberculosis. One can hardly say, with Hunt, that perhaps she hastened the death of her son, but she had certainly left him in many ways a dubious legacy.

Six years had passed, of almost continuous crisis and change for the observant sensitive boy, open and prodigal of his feelings, as his own brother remarked, whose eye would moisten and lip quiver at the mere recital of others' joy or distress. Many of the results of these six years can be seen quite directly in his later life. Over-shadowing all was the threat of "the family complaint", the disease that had removed his mother and uncles. Believing, as everyone did, that tuberculosis was hereditary, the thought was with him to the last. "It runs in my head", he wrote in the final letter of his life, "we shall all die young". The blows struck in these years had been so many and so swift that he was left with a sense that fate was against his whole family. "O, that something fortunate had ever happened to me or my brothers", he burst out again. More potent even than this was the sense of isolation. His father's death and mysterious family circumstances had left him no relatives on that side; his mother's law-suit had cut him off from any on the other. The uncles and aunts who feature so largely in the memories of many orphan children had no part in his life. He was thrown into an intense relationship with his brothers, "passing the Love of Women" as he said, which often supported him, but which just as often was to distract him from true judgment. In material matters, the outcome of these years was to give him an inheritance in Chancery of just over £800 capital, his mother's and the portion willed direct to him by his grandfather, which he could apply for at 21. Yet the distasteful business of the family litigation had left him a morbid horror of enquiring into even the simplest money matters, which was to handicap his whole adult life. Such things were, as he himself said, "No trouble indeed to any one else . . . to me worse than any thing in Dante." Businessmen and lawyers became ogres to him. "I think we may class the lawyer in the same natural history of Monsters", he wrote, and as such he evidently classed William Walton, his mother's lawyer, who alone knew of his Chancery inheritance. The ultimate enigma of these years was his mother. In an outspoken age, when children were not protected from adult behaviour, his complete silence about her suggests some shattering knowledge, with which, at various times in his life, he can be seen dimly struggling to come to terms. Here was, again in his own words, "a gordian complication of feelings, which must take time to unravell and care to keep unravelled."[1] The spiritual and material legacy left him at fourteen and a half was so complicated that no one could possibly foresee what he might make of it.

1. *Letters*, I, 342.

Chapter 3

THE MOST PLACID PERIOD

"When he left Enfield, at fourteen years of age, he was apprenticed to Mr. Thomas Hammond, a medical man, residing in Church Street, Edmonton, and exactly two miles from Enfield. This arrangement evidently gave him satisfaction and I fear that it was the most placid period of his painful life."

– CHARLES COWDEN CLARKE, *Recollections of Writers*, 125

THE NEXT decisive event in Keats's life took place just three months later. At Midsummer 1810, when he was aged fourteen years and eight months, he left school. This fact, stated in all older biographies and reminiscences by his contemporaries, has been so universally dismissed by modern biography that one must briefly look ahead some years in his life for confirmation. In short, the new Apothecaries Act of 1815, under which he was examined in July 1816, required of its candidates at least five years' apprenticeship to an apothecary, followed by six months' practice at a hospital or nine at a dispensary. Keats began the second half of this qualification by joining the surgical practice of Guy's Hospital in October 1815; by that date he must have served a full five years' apprenticeship, as indeed Charles Brown and Keats's medical contemporary, Henry Stephens, confirm. He therefore began his apprenticeship before October 1810.[1]

In actual fact, fourteen and a half seems to have been a reasonable time for a promising boy to leave Clarke's School. If he were to embark on an apprenticeship of five or often seven years in a non-trading profession, law or medicine, he could hardly afford to hang about till fifteen and a half.[2] The

1. Modern biography has erroneously assumed that the Society of Apothecaries acted under a set of antiquated regulations which could be easily evaded, and that the full term of apprenticeship need not have been served. This ignores the Act of 1815, and the stringent way its regulations were enforced in its first year during which Keats was a candidate, when many applicants were rejected because their apprenticeships were incomplete (Minutes and Reports of Examiners, Society of Apothecaries, G.L. MS 8239/1).

2. Keats's friend James Peachey left to be articled to a solicitor in the previous October when he was fourteen and a half (Baptisms, St. George's, Hanover Square, and G.L.C. F/PEY(1)). This early start was as necessary for Peachey as a solicitor as it was to Keats as a doctor, for he was not finally admitted to the Courts till summer 1819 (G.L.C. F/PEY(2)), when he was twenty-four.

only evidence of his being associated with the school as a regular pupil, later than 1810, is a copy of Bonnycastle's *History of Astronomy* bearing a printed label "Assigned as a Reward of Merit" to him at Midsummer 1811. The differences in wording between this inscription and that of the Kauffman, chiefly in the substitution of the word "Assigned" for "Awarded", seem to show, however, that this was not, as has been thought, a regular school prize. Moreover, all accounts agree that Keats's spectacular industry, love of reading and success in prize-winning did not take place till his last two or three terms at school. He had won his first prize at Midsummer 1809, and so at Midsummer 1810 he must have left. We do not know what prize he received then, but we know what it was for. He had got some considerable way, in spite of the shock and distraction of his home life, with his voluntary translation of the *Aeneid*. He even produced the first example of his penetrating moments of literary criticism while doing this by remarking to Charles Cowden Clarke that there was "feebleness in the structure of the work"; his only other literary opinion from this time is more commonplace—that no one would dare to read Macbeth alone in a house at two o'clock in the morning.[1]

At the same time that her eldest grandson left school, Alice Jennings decided to leave nearly all her fortune of over £8000 worth of stock to her dead daughter's children. Her prime object was to see that no further dispute should put this part of their inheritance back into Chancery. Advised by Walton, the solicitor who had acted for her daughter, and who, after the reconciliation, dealt with her own affairs, she put her entire fortune in trust into the hands of two City businessmen, John Nowland Sandell of Schneider & Co., Russia merchants, 3 Broad Street Buildings, and Richard Abbey, of Abbey, Cock & Co., tea and coffee warehousemen, 4 Pancras Lane. Both men were in their forties. Sandell, the younger, was an extremely prosperous man; his office had at one time been near the Swan and Hoop, and true to the pattern of a well-to-do merchant he had a house out of the City, at Dalston near Hackney. Abbey was also a man of substance; he had a large property called Pindars in Marsh Street, Walthamstow, then described as a populous village which "abounds with the villas of opulent merchants".[2] Though five years older than Sandell, he seems to have been the junior trustee; but owing to various circumstances, he came to play a considerable part in Keats's life.

John Taylor, Keats's publisher, came away from his City dinner with the confused impression that Richard Abbey "had a common Country & Birthplace" with Mrs. Jennings, and came from Colne in Lancashire, though he then went on to speak of him as a Yorkshireman. In spite of its contradictions, this account has been accepted by all biographers, though since Abbey was only a child of nine when Mrs. Jennings married in London, their acquaintance must have begun much later, when he also came to the capital.

1. C. Cowden Clarke, *Recollections of Writers*, 122–124; KC, 147 and 164–165.
2. *The Picture of London* for 1810.

There is nothing which connects Richard Abbey or his family with Colne or Lancashire; he was baptized on 13 August 1765 over fifty miles away, and his parents came of uncompromising Yorkshire stock. The Abbey family were farmers at Healaugh in the Vale of York. Abbey's father Jonathan and his uncle Richard, sons of Richard Abbey of Healaugh, moved further east in the Vale to Skipwith, where Abbey was christened after his grandfather and uncle, being the eldest of six children. Curiously enough, one point in his childhood resembled Keats's own; for when he was only nine or ten, his own father died and was buried at Skipwith.[1] He was evidently left extremely well off, for when only just twenty-one, he appeared in London in charge of his own tea-broking business at 6 Size Lane, off Budge Row.[2] In the same year, 1786, he was wealthy enough to buy his membership of a City Company, the Pattenmakers, and his freedom of the City, and to marry. Surprisingly, he married an illiterate girl—she could not write her own name—Eleanor Jones. Her "ignorant and unfeeling gabble" was later remarked on by Keats. The couple were childless, but had adopted a two-year-old girl, now about Fanny Keats's age, in melodramatic circumstances, if Abbey's account to Taylor is correctly reported.[3]

Much in Abbey's attitude to the Keats children, both now and later, had its roots in his own background. He was not remarkably old-fashioned, as most biographers have thought, but sturdily provincial. The inhabitants of the Vale of York, of which the Abbeys were longstanding members, are notable for their hard-headed attitude in worldly affairs. Scrupulously honest, they combine this with an ability to look after their own interests on every possible occasion, and are openly contemptuous of those who do not. Abbey regarded John Keats, in a purely material way, as a youth placed in very much the position that he himself had been, an elder son whose father and grandfather had died leaving him ample provision, with care and foresight, to make good in the world. For the major part of John Jennings's fortune, which had been rescued from Chancery by Mrs. Jennings, was now safe-guarded for her grandchildren by trust indenture. This indenture of 30 July 1810 handed her capital and cash to Sandell and Abbey "from thence-forth as and for their own Monies and Effects in as full large and ample a manner to all intents and purposes whatsoever as she . . . might or could have

1. Freedom admissions, Chamberlain's Office, Guildhall; parish register transcripts, and wills, York Diocesan Records, The Borthwick Institute of Historical Research, York.

2. G.L. MS 5653/2. A brother, Jonathan, later traded in chocolate at 10 Budge Row.

3. She was the daughter of a young woman from Colne, who also came to London and lived near Mrs. Jennings. One day Mrs. Jennings was summoned to her house, and found her dead, murdered by her husband; a baby boy was first looked after by Mrs. Jennings, and then went to his grandmother in the North, but the girl stayed on with Mr. and Mrs. Abbey, into whose care she had temporarily been put, and was known as Miss Abbey.

done if the said recited Indenture had not been made." In other words, the estate passed completely out of her hands; anyone who made claims on it, for example Mrs. Midgley Jennings, would now have to deal with Sandell and Abbey. Keats's grandmother retained only its interest during her lifetime, and stipulated that the estate should be administered upon "several Trusts" for her grandchildren. The Keats grandchildren were left just over £2000 capital each, with an extra cash legacy of a few hundred pounds for the one girl, Fanny. Mrs. Jennings's will, of the following day, appointed her two trustees also to be her executors and guardians of her grandchildren during their minorities, with power to sell or reinvest stock for their benefit.[1]

This power was almost at once exercised by Sandell and Abbey on behalf of John Keats. Keats had decided on a medical career as a surgeon-apothecary or general practitioner. The legend that this choice was forced on him is widespread, and perhaps was fostered by some of his own remarks, for in later exasperation, he seems to have told at least two friends how much he hated his apprenticeship to a surgeon. This retrospective distaste, which his independent nature would probably have displayed toward apprenticeship in any profession, must not be confused with his choice of this particular career. According to Cowden Clarke, it was his own selection, and one which evidently gave him satisfaction. It was also an extremely natural one. He had just seen his mother die of a disease for which there was no proper diagnosis or treatment. His reaction was to attack the unknown agency of death. The fighting services, for which his friends thought him most fitted, were barred to him by his lack of height, and in spite of his recent reading, he was basically "*not* Literary". One of the books he had read during the past year, the Kauffman, was in fact scientific, and dealt in detail with the processes and by-products of many mineral and vegetable substances. He had no distance to seek for entry into medicine, for Thomas Hammond, his doctor and neighbour, was one of a family firm of surgeons. Its older generation, like himself, were Members of the Corporation of Surgeons, its younger, Members of the newly-established Royal College of Surgeons. Hammond himself was ready to take a pupil. On 17 August 1810, he apprenticed his own eldest son to another surgeon; there were signs, perhaps, that he had quarrelled with the boy. At all events, he had to pay an apprenticeship premium of £210 for him, and welcomed an apprentice himself, for whom he charged exactly the same sum as premium. One fee paid for the other, and Keats's apprenticeship most probably dated from exactly this time. It was not a very good moment for Keats's trustees to sell out stock to pay for this. Wellington's Peninsular campaign looked a forlorn gamble, and Government funds were at a low quotation. Keats must have shown his resolve most

1. KI, 33. Misunderstanding of the terms of the Indenture, set out clearly in P.R.O. C. 33, 616, f. 809, has led Norman Kilgour, KSMB, XIII, 24–27, to put forward a theory of the trustees' dishonesty, which is unsupported by any fact.

strikingly for Sandell and Abbey at once to sell over £300 worth from his inheritance to produce his premium money.[1] No such special treatment was allowed George, who was taken from school at the early age of thirteen and a half to be a clerk in Richard Abbey's business; he was set to work with Cadman Hodgkinson, Abbey's seventeen-year-old apprentice, the son of a City druggist.[2] Tom, only ten, remained for the time behind at school.

The events of this five-year apprenticeship were in total contrast to the turbulent six years before. Apart from one moment of minor drama, they justify Charles Cowden Clarke's verdict "that it was the most placid period of his painful life". All that is really known about this period is that it was spent, or at least begun, in the house called Wilston in Church Street, Edmonton, with a surgery in the garden and a room above the surgery for apprentices to live in. Only one anecdote of his work with Hammond survives, and this simply shows how many apprentices acted as a kind of superior servant for their masters, sweeping rooms or looking after horses. According to a small boy at Clarke's School,[3] he was dared to throw a snowball at Keats while the old boy, famous for fighting, was left minding Hammond's horse in the snow outside. On the other hand, Keats's later record in medicine shows that Hammond taught him well. The real and major influence on Keats's life during the years from fourteen to nineteen was Charles Cowden Clarke. Clarke managed to arrange with his remarkable ex-pupil what amounted, in modern terms, to an unofficial day-release system between apprenticeship and school. About three afternoons every fortnight, Keats would leave the surgery for the two-miles' walk to Enfield, where Clarke made his own free half-days coincide. Keats brought or returned a book, while Clarke always had fresh reading for him. Sometimes it was not a book, but the manuscript of a translation. He went steadily on with his prose version of the *Aeneid*, begun at school, and eventually finished it. In fact, it is clear that, under this arrangement, he was still regarded as in some sense a pupil. It was for this that he was probably "assigned" his copy of Bonnycastle at Midsummer 1811. He was, of course, a pupil with special privileges. He dined with the headmaster, and after dinner in good weather, he and the headmaster's son would go off to the arbour in the big garden and talk undisturbed till dark and the nightingales came, and Keats had to return through the evening fields to Edmonton. It is this period of special and continued education to which Clarke gave the term "placid". If the shocks of early life prepared the ground for poetry, these years of unlooked-for

---

1. KI, 47.   2. G.L. MS 5652/2 and MS 7221/2.

3. R. Hengist Horne, who told slightly different versions to Theodore Watts-Dunton and to Edmund Gosse(*Joseph and His Brethren* by C. J. Wells, with a note by Theodore Watts-Dunton, p. xlvi; Colvin (1887) 11-12). In later editions, Colvin added that a fellow-apprentice said Keats was "an idle loafing fellow, always writing poetry" but cited no source.

security sowed the seed. We cannot even say that Keats would have been a
poet without these evenings with Charles Cowden Clarke, when he

> revel'd in a chat that ceased not
> When at night-fall among your books we got:
> No, nor when supper came, nor after that,—
> Nor when reluctantly I took my hat;
> No, nor till cordially you shook my hand
> Mid-way between our homes:

The naive lines are startling in their sincerity; the deepest feeling can be read
between them.

It was now that the reading of pupil–teacher and ex-pupil began to turn to
literature. Keats's taste for this had been prepared to some extent while still
a pupil at the school by his close friendship with Edward Holmes. This
"intimate school-fellowship and liking" between Keats and Holmes,
attested by Clarke himself, has been too little noticed. Holmes's great love
was music, in which he became a distinguished critic, but his literary taste
was also impressive and must have influenced Keats. Holmes had first won
Keats's respect by proving himself a fighter. Clarke may have first interested
Keats in poetry in a similar way, for among the earliest books they seem to
have read was Edward Fairfax's spirited translation of Tasso's *Gerusalemme
Liberata*, long passages of which describe the deeds of the Crusading army led
by Godfrey of Bouillon. For a boy whose talents appeared to lie "in some
military capacity", this was a natural way into poetry; a copy of this volume
was among Keats's books at his death.[1]

Charles Brown afterwards said that Keats, until the age of eighteen, "had
not been occupied in reading works of imagination", but this must not be
taken too literally to exclude all poetry. Keats had owned a copy of *Paradise
Lost* from the year he left school, 1810,[2] though he did not read Milton
generally until much later, in the autumn of 1817. He said that he learnt from
Cowden Clarke "all the sweets of song", and went on to particularize them—
the sonnet, the ode, the epigram, the epic. Their reading was probably not
as systematic as this catalogue makes it sound, but varied with the fancy of the
two friends. What is significant is Clarke's teaching that the epic "was of all
the king". He was not the last of Keats's friends to encourage him to admire
poetry on a large scale, so that Keats himself could later exclaim "Did our
great Poets ever write short Pieces?" Much can be argued one way and the
other about whether this emphasis on epic was wise for Keats. On the one
hand, the ambition to write a long poem, when he came to writing, provided,

1. KC, I. 253.
2. KHM, No. 16, Volume 2 only. Since Volume 1 is missing, though Volume 2
contains Keats's signature and the date, 1810, it may be that this is the missing school
prize for his first translations of the *Aeneid* at Midsummer 1810.

as he himself said, "a test of Invention", a huge training-ground for his technique; on the other, it led him dangerously near the fallacy of equating size with quality, a tendency which he had in a sense to unlearn all through his poetic career. Meanwhile, to the epic of action, Fairfax's Tasso, and the epic of religious myth in Milton, was added the epic of personal growth of the poet in another poem undoubtedly read by the two friends, James Beattie's *The Minstrel*.

Beattie's fragmentary poem consists of two books only, the second of which was published in 1774. It is a pre-Wordsworthian account of the education of a poet's mind, in a flexible Spenserian stanza; both its tone and its technique were copied by Byron in *Childe Harold*. Its method and its message were adopted by Keats, particularly the latter; in fact, the general idea of the poem is one repeated again and again by Keats in poetry and in prose. It is the theme of the poet's education and quest, a journey of the spirit accompanying a vaguely topographical tour of various types of countryside and person, at once announced in Beattie's lines:

Ah! who can tell how hard it is to climb
The steep where Fame's proud temple shines afar.

This idea of the toil for Fame through poetry, satirized by Byron in the more sophisticated stanzas of *Don Juan*, Canto One, runs through all Keats's writing. The scheme of Beattie's poem is that of a poetic pilgrimage, in which the imagination grows from fancy to knowledge, taught by experience. The "youth" or minstrel, hero of the poem, is the son of a shepherd, "a man of low degree"; he loves nature, he is a "visionary boy", and among his visions is a fairy feast. He listens to the old tales of a "Beldam", he gains inspiration from these and from contemplating enormous cloudscapes, and he becomes a poet. In Book II he meets a hermit who assists his progress by warning him against the imaginary ills of Fancy, and prescribes (as Beattie says in a note) "the influences of the philosophic spirit in humanizing the mind". As the result of this advice, the youth embraces "Science" or "Philosophy", but he does not throw over his instinctive and traditional "Fancy", typified by the folk-lore of the Beldam and his own musings on Nature. He retains his love of Fancy, so that he can turn his new-found science or knowledge into poetry. As a result, he makes his verse less "flowery" and becomes a real poet. The thought of Beattie's poem can be seen in much that Keats wrote in his letters, and runs through many of his poems, up to *The Fall of Hyperion*, with its quest for knowledge and its distinction between the true poet and the mere dreamer.

Clarke gave Keats another theme that runs through all his letters and poetry. This was the radical ideal in politics, and it came from a specific source. Mr. Clarke had taken from its foundation in 1808 Leigh Hunt's radical weekly, *The Examiner*. When its editor and his brother were imprisoned early in 1813 for a libel on the Prince Regent, the Clarke family sent him presents of flowers, fruit and vegetables from the school gardens, and Charles Cowden Clarke, as the bearer of these, soon became acquainted with Hunt. *The Examiner* was read by all the senior boys at the school, and Charles lent it to Keats; he recalled the anecdote that when one of Keats's trustees, Sandell or Abbey—it is always assumed to be the latter—found out about this, he exclaimed that if he had fifty children he would not send one to that school. With Keats, it started the reading-habit of a lifetime; he did not miss a number, and was still subscribing to *The Examiner* within a few months of his death. The result of this weekly infusion of radicalism was a mixed blessing for Keats. It provided a generalized outlet for his passionate sympathies; but it sometimes led him to import into his poetry the crudest political and social propaganda, and into his life excessive and often unjustified outbursts of personal indignation.

There was one such occasion even in this calm period of Keats's apprentice years. Late in 1813 or early in 1814, he quarrelled with Hammond and ceased to live with him.[1] Dilke believed that he had broken his apprenticeship, though there cannot have been a complete legal break in view of Keats's later qualification. There seems general agreement that Keats did not get on personally with his master, and Cowden Clarke, Haydon and J. H. Reynolds all corroborate that there was a break of some sort.[2] Keats's brother George confirmed that owing to the quarrel, Keats ceased to live in with Hammond, and lodged away from the surgery from some time in 1813.[3] Keats in September 1819 said that it was seven years since his hand "clenched itself against Hammond". There have been attempts to explain away this remark, but Dilke wrote of Keats's quarrel with the surgeon as a well-known thing, and emphasized what it meant to Keats in terms of money.[4] To live away from the surgery forced Keats to pay board and lodging twice over; the premium, which Hammond would hardly return, was meant to cover living-in expenses.

Whatever the cause of the quarrel, the later part of the year 1813 marked a new independence in Keats's life and a move into lodgings of his own. According to George, he was joined in these lodgings by their precocious younger brother Tom, who had also tried an office-boy's job with Abbey and left it. Independence brought expense, especially since Keats had an open, prodigal nature, which he seems to have inherited from his grandfather. It is not certain, as George said, that he habitually spent three times the income from his share of his inheritance from his grandmother; but his premium had already depleted the capital, so that while his brothers and sister were due to have a little more than £60 a year interest, Keats from the start had £10 less.

1. Dilke, ann. II, 41.
2. KC, II, 148, 169, 177; KHM, No. 52; Haydon, II, 107.
3. KC, I, 277.   4. KHM, No. 124 and Dilke, ann. II, 41.

Stocks were still extremely low in the long-drawn crisis of the Peninsular War, and any further withdrawals from capital would be on very disadvantageous terms. Estimates that Keats spent about three-quarters of this capital during his medical education have been doubted,[1] but expenses of this order were inevitable.

Independence too may have helped to buy Keats incalculable benefits. In October 1813, he was eighteen years old; and sometime after this birthday he wrote his first poem.[2] Clarke's accounts of what he called "the spark that fired the train of his poetical tendencies" are contradictory. At one time he said that Keats "must have given unmistakable tokens of his mental bent", and at another that he had given till then no idea of his real love of poetry.[3] The spark undoubtedly fell when Clarke, one evening in the old arbour at school, read Keats the *Epithalamion* of Spenser. Keats was so enchanted by this new poet that he took away with him that night the first volume of the *Faerie Queene*, which, said Clarke, "He ramped through . . . like a young horse turned into a Spring meadow." The time that this took place was almost certainly the early Spring of 1814; weather fine enough for open-air reading and the vivid phrase of Clarke's simile both suggest this. Keats was eighteen and a half when he produced his first poem. Poetry was a new extension of the imitative facility he had always shown; he had been known at school as a mimic, and Clarke had noticed his likeness to Edmund Kean the actor. Now, as he read a poetic epithet, he was irresistibly impelled to act it, especially if it had about it an element of one of his favourite aspects of life, the grotesque. Spenser's catalogue of deep-sea monsters, beginning

> All dreadful portraicts of deformitee:
> Spring-headed *Hydraes*, and sea-shouldring Whales,

affected him so much that, as Clarke said, "he *hoisted* himself up, and looked burly and dominant", as he lovingly repeated the last words. From such intuitive, almost physical sympathy, it was only one further step to write himself his *Imitation of Spenser*.

> Now Morning from her orient chamber came,
> And her first footsteps touch'd a verdant hill;
> Crowning its lawny crest with amber flame,
> Silv'ring the untainted gushes of its rill;
> Which, pure from mossy beds, did down distill,
> And after parting beds of simple flowers,

1. Most biographies follow Lowell, I, 48, who mistook the premium of £40 for each year for the whole amount of the premium. Premiums were generally in multiples of £40 to £50 per annum, but could be as much as £100 per annum, e.g. £500 for a five-year apprenticeship.
2. KC, II, 55.
3. Compare C. Cowden Clarke, *Recollections of Writers*, 125 and KC, II, 148.

By many streams a little lake did fill,
   Which round its marge reflected woven bowers,
And, in its middle space, a sky that never lowers.

   There the king-fisher saw his plumage bright
   Vieing with fish of brilliant dye below;
   Whose silken fins, and golden scales light
   Cast upward, through the waves, a ruby glow:
   There saw the swan his neck of arched snow,
   And oar'd himself along with majesty;
   Sparkled his jetty eyes; his feet did show
   Beneath the waves like Afric's ebony,
And on his back a fay reclined voluptuously.

   Ah! could I tell the wonders of an isle
   That in that fairest lake had placed been,
   I could e'en Dido of her grief beguile;
   Or rob from aged Lear his bitter teen:
   For sure so fair a place was never seen,
   Of all that ever charm'd romantic eye:
   It seem'd an emerald in the silver sheen
   Of the bright waters; or as when on high,
Through clouds of fleecy white, laughs the cœrulean sky.

   And all around it dipp'd luxuriously
   Slopings of verdure through the glassy tide,
   Which, as it were in gentle amity,
   Rippled delighted up the flowery side;
   As if to glean the ruddy tears, it tried,
   Which fell profusely from the rose-tree stem!
   Haply it was the workings of its pride,
   In strife to throw upon the shore a gem
Outvieing all the buds in Flora's diadem.

The *Faerie Queene* was only the springboard for this composition, for all
Keats's epic reading is remarkably assimilated in these stanzas. The opening
uses the words and tone of the many invocations of the dawn in Fairfax's
Tasso, while the lake and the island partly derive from Books 15 and 16 of
that work, but more from the Bower of Bliss in Book 2 of Spenser's *Faerie
Queene*, which was also Fairfax's inspiration for his passages. In fact, this
double impact of two epics, whose wording is sometimes identical—Keats's
favourite quotation "Gather the rose of Love" actually comes from both—
accounts for the vividness of the imaginary scene in Keats's mind. Beattie's
The Minstrel contributes characteristically the phrase about the "romantic

eye", while the swan, as was noticed in Keats's own lifetime,[1] swims in from the Eden of *Paradise Lost* Book 7, where she

> with Arched neck
> Between her white wings mantling proudly, Rowes
> Her state with Oarie feet:

Yet the effect is not one of pastiche, but of an individual voice and a realized vision. In a first poem, a poet often displays what he will be more clearly than for several years afterwards. This, for all its immaturity, is a Keatsian poem. From his mature style it lacks—and it is a vital lack—the Shakespearian touch which gave such a "large utterance" to his later work, for in spite of the reference to King Lear, the full impact of Shakespeare on him was yet to come; but its creative vitality can be seen by putting it alongside stanzas by the many other writers who imitated Spenser at this time. Keats's lines, in spite of artificial diction, impress one by their essential sincerity, as of a genuine experience. They have been viewed as an unconscious allegory of his own childhood, and there may be much in that view.[2] What they certainly convey is youth, freedom and a tremendous sense of release, an extension of his joyous ramping through the spring meadows of new experience. This relief may represent his own independence, but it is not fanciful to connect it with the overwhelming sense of escape that was sweeping the whole country at that moment; for in this April 1814, Napoleon had at last capitulated and abdicated. The mood of the country, after virtually twenty years of war, was expressed by Leigh Hunt in his *Ode for the Spring of 1814*, published in *The Examiner*[3] though its author was still in prison. Keats, with his ardent and hopeful liberalism, shared in this mood when, in Hunt's words,

> The green and laughing world he sees,
> Waters, and plains, and waving trees,
> The skim of birds and the blue-doming skies.

In fact, the next subjects on which Keats tried his new-found skill were political ones. In the same month, he wrote his sonnet *On Peace*. Its message is that of Hunt's editorials, an appeal to the crowned heads of Europe to use their victory for general liberty. Keats had seen the illuminations that decorated the buildings of a rejoicing London. His rather clumsy and over-long ninth line

> With England's happiness proclaim Europa's Liberty

1. Sperry, 144–145.
2. Ward, 30–32, where the poetic quality of the verses seems curiously undervalued, as also by Bate, 36.
3. E. No. 329, p. 251.

is practically a translation of the inscription that blazed from Somerset House:

>Europa Instaurata, Auspice Britanniae
>Tyrannide Subversa, Vindice Libertatis.

At the same time, the liberal-minded Duke of Sussex, speaking at the Easter Fete at the Mansion House, struck a warning note. He reminded his hearers that Charles II, on his recall to the throne, had made professions of preserving rights and liberties, but that a few years later he and his successor were "trampling on the rights of the people".[1] This warning, addressed to the restored Bourbons and other crowned heads, seemed only too well-called-for; on May 22 *The Examiner* announced that "good faith and good policy are at once to be set at nought" and on May 29 Keats wrote his dismal and rather damp squib on *the anniversary of the Restoration of Charles the 2nd.*,[2] in which he invoked the heroes of Leigh Hunt's articles, Algernon Sydney, Russell and Vane. However, the "Infatuate Britons" of his epigram continued to rejoice, and Keats undoubtedly joined with them in the City pleasures of that optimistic summer. He saw, in spite of *The Examiner's* sarcasm, the grandiose Jubilee organized by the Prince Regent in the Parks, including a Naumachia or water-battle on the Serpentine, a term which he incorporated later into a satirical poem.

The Examiner, determined to regard all this jubilation as mere bread and circuses for a deluded public, acidly remarked that such vulgar celebrations could hardly hope to provide

>Such sights as youthful poets dream
>On summer eves by haunted stream;

but in fact this was precisely what they did provide for Keats. For the first time in his life he was enjoying the natural freedom of Regency manners in mixed company. The hearty masculine society of Clarke's school, his friendship with Charles Cowden Clarke, the duties of the surgery, his intense reading, the comparative isolation of Enfield and Edmonton, the elderly household of his grandmother and her maid, had left him little opportunity for contact with women, except ideally. "When I was a Schoolboy I thought a fair Woman a pure Goddess, my mind was a soft nest in which some one of them slept though she knew it not."[3] Now they were flesh and blood and all about him. During the Jubilee, in Vauxhall Gardens, he was staggered by the

---

1. E. No. 329. pp. 254–255.
2. Usually dated a year later (Finney, Ward etc.,) but politically far more appropriate to 1814. In 1815 it would have come in the middle of Napoleon's Hundred Days, and would have been topically meaningless. Ward, 418, n. 18, says that in 1814 "Keats was celebrating constitutional monarchy". He was, in fact, warning it.
3. *Letters*, I, 341.

beauty of an unknown young woman, who did not perhaps even notice him. The verses he wrote on this occasion were conventional but the experience was deep. He returned to it three and a half years later to write, with greater mastery, two of his best sonnets still harking back to this encounter. Its strange incompletion is a symbol that recurs in his poetry. His excitement over women, and his social difficulties with them, had some of their source in a sudden change of fashion. English women had for ten years been cut off from Paris. Now, with the peace of 1814, ankles and breasts reappeared overnight; the new muslins, and very little else, clung to the figure, and the waistline ascended to just under the bosom. The breasts and ankles of Keats's early poems are not Cockney vulgarity so much as literal description, while the high waistline made waltzing virtually impossible for anyone his height.

These difficulties were nothing to those of his poetry. Many arts are analogous to forms of physical skill; there is a beginners' luck, followed by a period of self-conscious failure. Perhaps Clarke gave him too systematic a course in poetry, for nearly every poem for the next year was a pastiche of a different poet. The lines after the encounter at Vauxhall resemble Byron's *To a Beautiful Quaker*, and it is no surprise that Keats wrote that winter a sonnet to Byron, echoing *Childe Harold* and inviting him to continue "the tale of pleasing woe". The only poem that touches, though slightly, a real note, was caused by a real and near happening. In the first half of December 1814, old Mrs. Jennings died; she had apparently been failing for some time. Keats wrote a sonnet, at about the time of her burial on 19 December at St. Stephen, Coleman Street. It has spontaneous feeling, but it is padded out with Miltonisms, and comes to a lame conventional ending, very much in the style of James Beattie.[1]

Mrs. Jennings's death did not make much difference in the circumstances of the Keats children, except Fanny, who at the age of ten went apparently to live with one of her guardians, Abbey, at Walthamstow, with visits to the other, Sandell, at Dalston. Yet in the new state of awareness and sensitivity which the pursuit of poetry produces, it reminded Keats of the tragic side of the past. His apprentice poems plunge into gloom, as well as into a bewildering assembly of half-assimilated models. A sonnet to Chatterton early in the New Year tries to import some of the latter's archaisms, but is still Miltonic and has much of Coleridge's monody on the young poet, which Keats found in the preface to Chatterton's collected works. A sonnet written on the day that Leigh Hunt left prison (2 February 1815) is the most Miltonic of all, almost a parody, though Keats evidently thought well enough of it to show it to Cowden Clarke "with conscious look and hesitation", the first time that Clarke realized his young friend was not only reading but writing poetry.

1. The lines *On Death*, a complete pastiche of Beattie, are only doubtfully attributed to Keats. Garrod, *Works*, xlix–l.

About this time he also gave Clarke a sonnet, *To the Moon*, which, like Clarke's own sonnet, *To the Sun*, has not survived.[1]

Materially, Keats had nothing to worry about. His apprenticeship may have been chequered, but it was soon coming to an end. His grandmother's trustees, now his guardians, Sandell and Abbey, busied themselves in collecting some of the debts to her estate, including the capital in Chancery of her sister-in-law Mary Sweetinburgh, who had predeceased her by a year. He was moving in the social circle of his gregarious brother George, and he lived with Tom, who was reckoned to understand him better than anybody. Yet settled gloom and poetic uncertainty deepened. An ode *To Hope* in February was a hopeless performance in every sense. Strongly derivative from Campbell's *The Pleasures of Hope* and other models, it failed to find any voice of its own. Even its burst into politics

> Great Liberty! how great in plain attire!
> With the base purple of a court oppress'd

comes straight from Leigh Hunt's contemporary leaders on the expanded Order of the Bath, "this new badge of the court-disease . . . destructive . . . of that plain unadorned self-respect."[2] Even more derivative, though from another source, was his *Ode to Apollo*, so like Gray's odes as to be again almost a parody.

Keats had invoked Hope to cheer his "morbid fancy", and this is a real description of his state at this time. It is a word constantly applied to him; he called it "horrid Morbidity", his brother George spoke of it as "nervous morbid temperament" and "melancholy and complaining". His neurotic doubts at this time were put in a startling form by Haydon the painter, who spoke of him during this period of his apprenticeship "some times telling his Brothers & in an agony he feared he never should be a Poet, & if he was not he would destroy himself".[3] Biographers have generally ignored or discredited this description of Keats's state of mind, but there is no reason to doubt it. Haydon goes on to insist that George and Tom told him this, and of their alarm. George confirms it by speaking of "many a bitter fit of hypochondriasm" and he goes on to say "he avoided teazing any one with his miseries but Tom and myself and often asked our forgiveness; venting, and discussing them gave him relief".[4] Keats continually spoke of his gratitude to his brothers for seeing him through such crises. It was, in fact, the greatest luck that, with his temperament, he should have had such thoroughly ordinary and commonplace relatives, fully absorbed in their typically lower-middle-class background. George and Tom were like any young clerks in an

---

1. KC, I, 274. See *Letters*, I, 113 where Keats mentions Clarke's sonnet, not, as sometimes thought, H. Smith's *To the Setting Sun*, which was not written till Jan.–Feb. 1817. Essex Record Office, MS D/DR Z11.

2. E. No. 369, p. 49.   3. Haydon, II, 107.   4. KC, I, 284–285.

early novel by Dickens, dandified in dress, ready for a little flutter at cards, or a flirtation with the girls. They carried with them the literacy they had learnt at Clarke's School, and a lively gift of quotation, but any comparison of their letters with John's shows how firmly on the earth their feet were. Even the sister Fanny was a stodgy little person, who turned out to have inherited the financial acumen and persistence of her grandmother. All this was invaluable to Keats. In a later poem describing uncannily his morbid mental state, he clings to

> the sight of well remember'd face,
> Of Brother's eyes, of Sister's brow—constant to every place.

From these despondent and even suicidal moods, it was George's self-appointed mission to relieve Keats by, in his own rather self-congratulatory words, "continual sympathy, explanation, and inexhaustible spirits, and good humour". A further distraction, on a national scale, was Napoleon's escape from Elba and the Hundred Days. There was no poetry from Keats during these days of drama, and when it reappeared, it was of an uncompromising lightheartedness. This once more matched the country's mood after Waterloo, but it had a more domestic cause. George had got into a set of minor poets and poetical young ladies, into which he introduced Keats. The leaders of this set were Caroline and Ann Felton Mathew, the daughters of a wine-merchant, living with their elder sister Jane and younger Helen in Goswell Street, together with a brother Felton, who soon inherited the business. They introduced Keats to their cousin, George Felton Mathew, poet and leader of a poetic circle. He too had several sisters, of whom the youngest, the thirteen-year-old Mary Strange Mathew, kept an album, *The Garland*, in which she copied the poetical effusions of her brother and his friends.[1] Keats was stimulated by their gatherings in Goswell Street or at the house of George Felton Mathew's father, an Oxford Street mercer, the exchanges of poems with writers unknown to subsequent literary history such as Frederick Leffler, and what Mathew called their "little domestic concerts and dances". He admired Mathew's most considerable poem, *Written in the Time of Sickness and addressed to a Friend*, from which he borrowed several phrases and ideas in his own early poems, and he began to write himself with greater freedom.

It is easy now to make fun of the relationship between Keats and Mathew, which even then had an obvious comic element. For one thing, Keats, with his great sense of comedy, reacted in a very natural way to Mathew's pose of the conventional young poet of the Byronic period. Mathew's poems were the stock properties of Gothic romance, abounding in glooms, ruined monasteries and dark woods. He viewed the world, poetically at least, as a vale of tears, and determined to live up to it in his behaviour. He liked to paint himself as "languid and melancholy . . . thoughtful beyond my

1. Finney, photostat.

years", and like his poems he took a high moral tone about life. He was disappointed that Keats never seemed to play up to this, and did not show "the tears in his eyes nor the broken voice which are indicative of extreme sensibility". Had Mathew known it, Keats could be moved in just this way; for, with Cowden Clarke, he had been so affected by the lines from *Cymbeline* where Imogen describes the departure of Posthumus, that his eyes filled with tears and his voice faltered. In Mathew's company, however, Keats acted with self-protective humour; he always took care to appear robust, hearty and confident, full of animal spirits and enjoyment of life.[1]

Yet Keats's reading broadened during his first few months of friendship with Mathew; it brought him back into the main stream of epic, which he had studied with Cowden Clarke before his experiments with more conventional eighteenth-century models. The two friends shared an enthusiasm for Fairfax's Tasso and for the *Faerie Queene*. To these, Mathew and his cousins added modern attempts at epic, William Sotheby's translation of Wieland's *Oberon*, *Psyche, or the Legend of Love*, by Mrs. Henry Tighe, and perhaps the oriental verse-tales of the laureate Robert Southey. The fluency, conventionality and thin texture of such works had at first an unfortunate effect on Keats, and his poetical friendship was celebrated in some of his worst poems. In August 1815, when Caroline and Ann Mathew were seasiding at the newly fashionable Hastings, they sent Keats a seashell and a copy of Thomas Moore's *The Golden Chain*. Keats wrote them and their cousin a poem each in the lilting empty style of Moore, with some appalling rhymes— "smart is" and "Britomartis" was one. About now, he also wrote the three sonnets on Woman, which reach the low-water mark of his poetry, though they were among Mathew's favourites.[2] To Mathew's approval, Keats for once burst into tears,[3] "overpowered by the tenderness of his own imagination", at the lines

> God! she is like a milk-white lamb that bleats
> For man's protection.

The depths of such lines perhaps show that Keats had been too closely protected from life during these five placid years; but he was now on the threshold of a reality, which brought in its turn a revolution in his apprenticeship to poetry.

---

1. C. Cowden Clarke, *Recollections of Writers*, 126; KC, II, 185.
2. Finney, 110-112, believes these were written the following year; but see Ward, 418, n. 14.
3. Sperry, 145.

Chapter 4

NATURE'S OBSERVATORY

"O Solitude! If I must with thee dwell,
Let it not be among the jumbled heap
Of murky buildings; climb with me the steep,—
Nature's observatory—"

JOHN KEATS, *Poems,* 1817

NO ONE knows what Keats or his guardians had in mind for him as he came to the end of his five-year apprenticeship. Up to this point in medical history, it would have been quite possible for him to set up practice as surgeon–apothecary on the strength of this apprenticeship alone. On 12 July 1815, however, the situation radically changed. On that date, the new Apothecaries Act, drawn up after much debate and delay, came into being, "to prevent any Person or Persons from practising as an Apothecary without being properly qualified as such." From 1 August onward, anyone intending to practise in any part of England or Wales would have to pass an examination before the new Court of Examiners of the Society of Apothecaries; he would not even be admitted to the examination unless he had previously served a five years' apprenticeship and at least six months' hospital training. The rules were enforced strictly, and the penalties for disobeying them were severe. Keats would have to add at least six months at hospital to the apprenticeship he was just finishing, in order to gain this new minimum medical qualification.

As the pupil of a Member of the Corporation of Surgeons, Keats may already have been advised to take a hospital training as a preliminary to the further qualification of Membership of the Royal College of Surgeons; but the new legislation made hospital work compulsory even if he wished merely to be a Licentiate of the Society of Apothecaries, the sole difference being that he would have to take a year's hospital training for Membership and six months for the Licentiate. Whichever he was aiming for, Keats certainly registered at the Counting House of Guy's Hospital on Sunday 1 October 1815 for twelve months, paying a preliminary office fee of £1 2s.[1]

1. Confusion exists in many biographies about the length of time for which he originally registered. He comes halfway down a page in which all pupils are registered for "12 Mo.", and his name has "Do" (for "ditto") against it. When he became a dresser (see below, p. 51), the figure 6 was entered against the "Do.", indicating that he took up

This step increased the total expenses of his medical training far more than he or his guardians may have bargained for. Further fees to be registered as a surgical pupil, separate lecture fees for every course he attended, expenses for books, surgical instruments and lodgings near the hospital would now have to be faced. Sandell and Abbey had to sell out still more of Keats's depleted capital in a market at rock-bottom after the panic of the Hundred Days. It is a mark of Keats's determination still to be a doctor that he pressed on at this time. Poetry had not yet been successful or fruitful enough to swing the balance away from the profession he had chosen; on the evidence of the apprenticeship he had served in each, he was better qualified at this moment to be a doctor than to be a poet.

It is difficult to say how much medical knowledge Keats had when he entered Guy's Hospital. He was not unfamiliar either with Guy's or with the standard of teaching at the joint medical school of the United Hospitals, Guy's and the adjoining older foundation of St. Thomas's. His master Thomas Hammond had entered Guy's himself just under thirty years before Keats. He had been dresser to a competent and successful surgeon, William Lucas senior, and he had family connections by marriage on the teaching staff.[1] As well as these links with the United Hospitals, Hammond was a member of a reputable firm of family doctors, and well-qualified himself. Keats was probably better equipped and prepared than some of his fellow medical students. The transfer from apprenticeship to a large teaching hospital was certainly not the leap in the dark for him that has sometimes been represented.

Keats may also have come to the surgical practice of Guy's with some stronger recommendation than we know. One of the earliest events in his career at Guy's certainly suggests that some such influence was at work. The senior anatomy lecturer, the well-known surgeon Astley Cooper, put Keats under the care of his own temporary dresser, George Cooper. This was more than he had done for his own nephew—George Cooper, incidentally, seems to have been no relation—whom he had allowed "to become very intimate with some of the greatest rattlepates in the school". George Cooper lodged at 28 St. Thomas's Street with Frederick Tyrrell, surgeon's apprentice, and he and Cooper took Keats into their lodgings, sharing a common sitting-

---

his dressership after six months. His original registration as a pupil, however, was for twelve months. In the *Register of Pupils and Dressers arranged in alphabetical order*, made later, the entry of six months is made to indicate the period before he became a dresser, and this has been confused in most biographies with the original registration entry.

1. Phyllis G. Mann, "John Keats: Further Notes", KSMB, XII, 23–25, which however confuses William Lucas senior (surgeon 1773–1799) with his son William Lucas junior (1799–1821). Hammond's and Keats's entries at Guy's appear most fully in two volumes of records at Guy's Hospital, *Entries of Physicians' and Surgeons' Pupils, 1778–1813* and *1814–1827* respectively.

2 St. George's, Hanover Square, where Keats's parents were married.

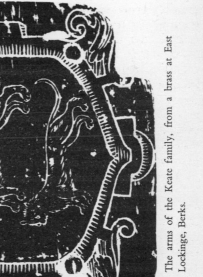

1 The arms of the Keate family, from a brass at East Lockinge, Berks.

3   St. Botolph, Bishopsgate, where Keats was baptised.

4   Edmonton in 1806.

5   The Clarke School at Enfie.d.

6   Charles Cowden Clarke.

8 Tom Keats.

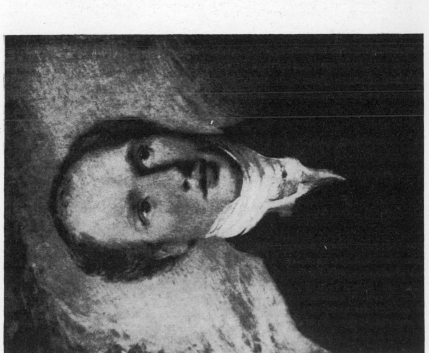

7 George Keats.

9　Guy's Hospital, Borough, with the statue of its Founder.

10　The Operating Theatre of Old St. Thomas's Hospital, 1821, the only early 19th-century operating theatre to have escaped demolition or conversion.

11   Apothecaries' Hall, Blackfriars, where Keats was examined and became Licentiate.

12   A group of waltzers, 1817. The high waistline made waltzing difficult for anyone as short as Keats.

13 James Henry Leigh Hunt, 1815.

14 Benjamin Robert Haydon, 1815.

16 William Hazlitt, 1822.

15 John Hamilton Reynolds. c. 1817.

17   Sketches of Keats by Benjamin Robert Haydon, November 1816.

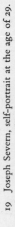

19   Joseph Severn, self-portrait at the age of 29.

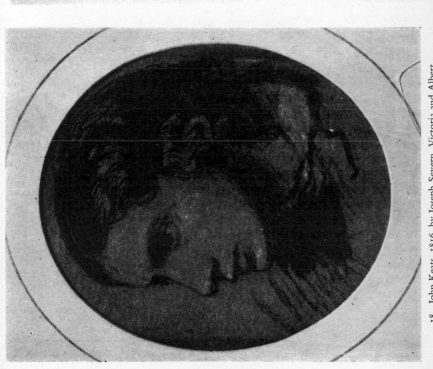

18   John Keats, 1816, by Joseph Severn. Victoria and Albert Museum, Crown Copyright.

20　Charles Jeremiah Wells.

21　Leigh Hunt's Cottage, the Vale of Health, Hampstead Heath.

room.[1] Dressers and surgeon's apprentices were the aristocracy of the hospital students, especially the latter, who paid for the privilege in premiums of £500 and upwards, as Tyrrell's father, the City Remembrancer, had done. Something had marked out Keats specially for Astley Cooper to put him in the company of these privileged older men (Cooper was twenty-three and Tyrrell twenty-two), his own dresser and apprentice. The coincidence that Keats resembled, both in name and in physical appearance, a famous contemporary surgeon is perhaps the most likely cause.[2]

On Monday 2 October, Keats paid the further fee of £25 4s. to register himself as a surgical pupil for twelve months.[3] Then he and the crowd of other students sought out their lecturers. The hospital registration gave a student merely the right to attend the hospital practice and "to make such enquiries" of the surgeons as he could. For him to obtain detailed tuition in the various branches of surgery and medicine there were separate lectures delivered in each subject three times a week. By traditional arrangement, the lectures in anatomy and surgery, and the dissections, took place in St. Thomas's—though the senior lecturer, Astley Cooper, was a Guy's man— and those in the theory and practice of medicine, chemistry, materia medica and other subjects were given in Guy's. Outside the lecture theatre in each hospital was a little lobby in which the students scrambled to pay their fees personally to the lecturers in advance. Keats put himself down for two terms' courses in Anatomy and Physiology with Astley Cooper and Henry Cline, who always took over Cooper's course after the first five or six weeks, two courses in the theory and practice of medicine with Dr. Babington and Dr. Curry, both Irishmen, two in chemistry with Alexander Marcet, an extremely distinguished Fellow of the Royal Society, and one term's course in materia medica with Dr. Cholmeley. The two main lecture terms ran from October to mid-January, with a short Christmas break, and from 20 January to the middle of May, when it grew too hot for anatomy and dissection. There was a short summer term for suitable subjects such as botany. Keats paid out a total of 32 guineas for these courses of instruction. There is no evidence that he took the early-morning midwifery course by Dr. Haighton; it was not necessary for him to do so in order to qualify, and he would have had plenty of obstetric experience while assisting Hammond. He then went to Cox's Medical Library, a few doors from his lodgings, and bought the standard medical text-books, including an anonymous and extremely useful manual, *The London Dissector*, compiled by an assistant surgeon in the Artillery. A

1. C. L. Feltoe, *Memorials of John Flint South*, 51 and 81.
2. Appendix 2. The suggestion that he did it because Keats seemed "lonely" or "not happy" appears in some biographies, but seems to have no foundation.
3. This remaining fee of £25 4s. was recorded in the volume *Surgeons Pupils of Guy's and St. Thomas's Hospitals from Jan. 1812 to separation March 1825.* This volume has been lost; facsimiles of the pages referring to Keats are in the Keats House Museum, Hampstead.

C

case of medical instruments and some 2s. notebooks for lectures completed his equipment for the new life.[1]

It is clear that he took to it and that it was congenial to him. As a boy he had always had an eye for "character", often, as was noticed, of a somewhat grotesque kind. Southwark and the Borough Hospitals abounded with character, good and bad, and always lively. It was a neighbourhood still almost Elizabethan in its lack of what a guide-book called "the progress of refinement". Here Keats attended, just as Shakespeare did, the bear-baitings of the district. Afterwards regaling Cowden Clarke with a description of one of these, he showed his enjoyment and his sense of mimicry by playing the parts not only of the bear and the snapping dogs, but also of the raffish and curious clientele of the establishment. "His comic fancy" said Clarke, describing this, "lurked in the outermost and most unlooked-for images of association";[2] nor was it divorced in any way from his poetic fancy, for Keats even used the imagery of the bear-pit in a cancelled line in *Endymion*. In the same way, the ghoulish though comic assembly of body-snatchers and grave-robbers, who obtained anatomical specimens for the hospital, were indirect material for poetry; Ben Crouch, the hoarse-voiced drunken son of the Guy's carpenter, with his quarrelsome and colourful team of resurrection men, Bill Butler, Jack and Bill Harnett, and Jack, Ben's brother, provided Keats with food for imagination that could later

> Work through the clayey soil and gravel hard,
> To see scull, coffin'd bones, and funeral stole;

The resurrectionists, though, were always careful to leave the shroud behind in the coffin to avoid committing a felony, the disturbance of the grave and taking the corpse being merely a misdemeanour.[3] Pre-anaesthetic operations were a grimmer side of the medal, to which some students never became hardened; the torments of the Titans in *Hyperion* may owe much to these. Hospital experience and Borough life gave a new reality to Keats's poetry.

Hospital life was congenial in itself, to judge by its immediate results. Keats benefited from his contact in lodgings with the two experienced older men. Although a fine new dissecting-room had just been opened in Thomas's, the Guy's apprentices and dressers, like Tyrrell and George Cooper, used a small room in their own hospital. There was a good spirit among students in the United Hospitals and "no lack of well-informed past and present dressers who were always ready to help a junior, and to whom the junior never hesitated to resort", as one of the apprentices noted.[4] Some such help in the little dissecting-room undoubtedly came Keats's way, for he had only been

1. Feltoe, op. cit., 30–31, 37. *The Picture of London for 1815* (16th edition).
2. C. Cowden Clarke, *Recollections of Writers*, 144–145.
3. Feltoe, op. cit., 93–100.   4. Feltoe, op. cit., 126.

four weeks at the hospital when he was accepted for the next vacant dresser-ship. The post would fall due in a few months' time, and it might even be a dressership to Astley Cooper himself. Keats's swift promotion may have been partly owing to his privileged position, but it must also have been the result of hard work. It brought a small immediate reward in material terms; since he would no longer be a surgeons' pupil when he took up his dresser-ship, the office returned to him the difference between his year's fee of 24 guineas as a pupil and the half-yearly fee of 18 guineas, so that Keats found himself credited with a rebate of 6 guineas.[1] This success in his profession would, however, involve him in much greater ultimate expense, for some time next term he would have to re-register as a dresser, and pay the much larger dresser's fee of £50, handing it over personally to the surgeon to whose firm he was allocated.

This early promotion in medicine reflected the merits of his first month's hard study; one of his notebooks has survived from this period, when he noted down the first twelve lectures by Astley Cooper, which were on simple physiology, and a few on bones and fractures, which Cooper also delivered before handing over the course to Henry Cline. Keats was not altogether a good note-taker; as with his appreciation of character, it was the vivid, the picturesque and the out-of-the-way that attracted him. Cooper, a well-prepared lecturer with a racy conversational manner, was full of good phrases which Keats noted in full, perhaps to the exclusion of more weighty matter. His notes on Cooper's tenth lecture, scanty in other respects, record that "The patriot K(oskiusko) having had the Sciatic Nerve divided by a pike wound was a long while before his limb recovered its sensibility" and again that "A celebrated italian put out the Eyes of a Bat and turned it loose into a Room and found that it did not strike itself against the Parieties". Keats found that the best way of remembering the many facts of surgery and medicine was to attach them to concrete and striking examples; he himself once explained to Cowden Clarke the workings of the stomach by comparing that organ to a nest full of young birds. It was not an orthodox way of taking notes, but it accorded with his natural temperament and brought him quick success.

Any such success in a rough and critical community must have a personal basis too; there is no doubt that Keats had an extremely attractive personality at this time. "A painter or a sculptor" as George Felton Mathew remembered, "might have taken him for a study after the Greek masters", and he went on to apply to Keats the lines of Hamlet

> A station like the herald Mercury,
> New-lighted on some heaven-kissing hill.

1. *Surgeons Pupils in Guy's and St. Thomas's Hospitals . . . 1812 to . . . 1825.* Ward, 49, says "beside the October 2 entry of his name was added '6 Mo.' ", but this is a confusion with the 1 October entry (see above p. 47, n. 1).
2. KC, II, 185.

This vivid physical presence added to the advantages he gained from quick wits and hard work; it had the disadvantage, as he was to find later, of sometimes collecting him too many friends, and Keats suffered the experience, familiar in student circles, of meeting a senior student who thought the attractive junior a promising subject for a religious or spiritual conversion. This was another dresser, John Spurgin,[1] who attempted to convert Keats to the doctrines of Swedenborg, and continued to do so by letter when, after a few weeks, he left to study medicine at Caius College, Cambridge. Keats was already in doubts about orthodox Christian belief, after reading *The Examiner* throughout his apprentice days. His scepticism in religion and radicalism in politics had begun to alarm Mathew, who uneasily saw in his poetic friend "a faultfinder with everything established", and began to have doubts about his poetry as well.

For the new reality and wider life of his hospital training was accompanied by nothing less than a revolution in Keats's poetry. For the first time he read the works of a really great contemporary poet. In March 1815, William Wordsworth had brought out his first full collected edition in two octavo volumes. This same autumn Keats obtained these, and they were among his books at his death.[2] Now began the poetic love–hate relationship between Keats and the older poet's works which was a large part of the background of his writing life, the "half of Wordsworth", in his own words, which he never ceased to admire. To judge by the quotations, conscious and otherwise, which permeate Keats's poems and letters, this was literally the half contained in the second volume that he now possessed. The first volume, which has a preponderance of poems of *Lyrical Ballads*, was far less congenial to him, and he seldom mentions its contents unless to satirize or deplore them.

The new and powerful voice of the best of Wordsworth is at once heard in Keats's own poetry. The contrast with what he had written only the previous summer comes almost like a physical shock. Two verses from a summer poem to the Mathew sisters ran

> Yet over the steep where the mountain stream rushes
> With you, kindest friends, in idea I muse;
> Mark the clear tumbling crystal, its passionate gushes,
> Its spray that the wild flower kindly bedews. . . .

1. Guy's Hospital, *Entries of Physicians and Surgeons Pupils*, 1 October 1814; and Edward B. Hinckley, "On First Looking into Swedenborg's Philosophy", KSJ, IX (1960), 15, where Spurgin is incorrectly given as younger than Keats. He had matriculated at Caius College over a year earlier aged 19 (Alumni Cantabrigiensis).

2. Not *Lyrical Ballads*, 3rd ed. 1802 (KC, I, 253 n.) nor *Poems in Two Volumes* of 1807 (Ward). The two–volume octavo edition of 1815 combined the contents of these volumes, and added fresh poems. Keats's own letters and poems contain quotations and reminiscences entirely from the 1815 edition, including echoes of poems that only occur in that edition. The 1807 edition, which Ward thinks identical with the octavo volumes Keats possessed, was in fact a duodecimo.

> For, indeed, 'tis a sweet and peculiar pleasure,
> (And blissful is he who such happiness finds,)
> To possess but a sand in the hour of leisure,
> In elegant, pure, and aerial minds.

This October, using the same idea and even much of the same poetic vocabulary, Keats wrote

> O Solitude! if I must with thee dwell,
> Let it not be among the jumbled heap
> Of murky buildings; climb with me the steep,—
> Nature's observatory—whence the dell,
> Its flowery slopes, its river's crystal swell,
> May seem a span; let me thy vigils keep
> 'Mongst boughs pavillion'd, where the deer's swift leap
> Startles the wild bee from the fox-glove bell.
> But though I'd gladly trace these scenes with thee,
> Yet the sweet converse of an elegant mind,
> Whose words are images of thoughts refin'd,
> Is my soul's pleasure. It certainly must be
> Almost the highest bliss of human-kind,
> When to thy haunts two kindred spirits flee.

The Mathew sisters[1] are once more pictured in country surroundings; yet the verse is totally altered. The words, especially in the sestet, are largely the same, but the whole spirit and movement of the sonnet is different, and essentially Wordsworthian. It is not only that Keats borrows from Wordsworth's *Prefatory Sonnet* the bee and foxglove image

> Bees that soar for bloom,
> High as the highest Peak of Furness Fells,
> Will murmur by the hour in Foxglove bells:

adding probably "the deer's swift leap" from *Hart-Leap Well* in the same volume, but the treatment and phrasing, such as "Nature's observatory", are wholly Wordsworthian. To the new realistic scenery of his working life, "the jumbled heap" of the Borough buildings, he has added a new poetic climate and geography, stronger and more bracing than the popular-romance background of the Mathew poems.

1. The "two kindred spirits" are not Keats and Mathew, as supposed by J. Middleton Murry, *Studies in Keats Old and New*, 1–3, nor George Keats and an unnamed girl of their circle, though Stuart M. Sperry, Jr., *Huntington Library Quarterly*, XXIX, No. 2 "Keats's First Published Poem" has rightly shown that, according to Woodhouse, the poem was written "perhaps . . . *for* his brother". The exact verbal resemblances of the sestet to those of the previous poem make it refer clearly to Caroline and Ann Mathew, perhaps for George to send to them.

There is amusing evidence of this new-found enthusiasm in one of the worst poems Keats ever wrote. Strictly speaking it is hardly a poem, but a poetic document, showing him trying to assimilate the new and unfamiliar influence. Just before the Solitude sonnet, but after beginning to read Wordsworth, Keats wrote another set of jingling anapaests to one of the Mathew girls. It begins "O come, dearest Emma", and has set people searching for a non-existent Emma Mathew. Keats had, in fact, a student friend, Charles Severn, whose sister was a real Emma,[1] but the Emma of the poem is none of these. As a Wordsworth scholar has pointed out, Emma or Emmeline, varying with the exigencies of metre, is the name habitually used by Wordsworth in poems for his sister Dorothy.[2] He addresses her as Emma in the first of his *Poems on the Naming of Places*, which were particular favourites of Keats, and of which the second and third added their influence to the Solitude sonnet, especially recalling Wordsworth's moving description of his sister as

> She who dwells with me, whom I have loved
> With such communion, that no place on earth
> Can ever be a solitude to me.

Keats attempted the more natural manner of the older poet for the first few stanzas, and briefly succeeded in being less stilted than in his summer poems, but the poem ends in bathos, defeated partly by its puerile form. In the Sonnet, form matched content; but *To Emma* is at least an interesting transition.

The first result of this poetical departure by Keats was that George Felton Mathew became thoroughly alarmed. Poems in which his friend addressed one of Mathew's cousins as Emma in homely Wordsworthian style and a sonnet, apparently also referring to them but entirely in the Wordsworthian manner, with images drawn from the Lake District, seemed a false step. Mathew set himself to encourage Keats back into the right romantic path by addressing him in a poem of his own *To A Poetical Friend*. In this he firmly stuck to the metre of Keats's summer poems, and provided Keats with a list of the romantic stock in trade—"knights-errant", "captures and rescues", "wonderful loves"—that the two had shared as fit subjects for poetry. He alluded to their reading in common, to Wieland's *Oberon* and other romance-poems. The sting of this effusion was in its close, when he implored Keats, in his free time from medical study, to pursue not just poetry, but the right kind of poetry.

> And when evening shall free thee from Nature's decays,
> And release thee from Study's severest control,
> Oh warm thee in Fancy's enlivening rays;
> And wash the dark spots of disease from thy soul.

1. KC, II, 256–257.
2. *The Poems of John Keats*, ed. E. de Selincourt, 563.

And let not the spirit of Poesy sleep;
Of Fairies and Genii continue to tell—
Nor suffer the innocent deer's timid leap
To fright the wild bee from her flowery bell.

In other words, he admonished Keats, write in your former romance style and do not follow the homely nature imagery of Wordsworth which you used in the Solitude sonnet.[1] Almost immediately, chance gave Keats time to reply himself in verse to this appeal.

By the second week in November, Henry Cline had begun his portion of the anatomy lectures. "Gentlemen", he announced after his lecture on Wednesday 8 November, "tomorrow there is a very grand civic festival; and, as many of you who come from the country would probably wish to see it, and will not have another opportunity, it has been the custom here to give a holiday, and therefore there will be no lecture tomorrow." The class hooted with pleasure at the prospect of a free day to see the Lord Mayor's procession on the Thames;[2] but to Keats, a Londoner, it was a free day for poetry and poetic company, such as he had asked for in the Solitude sonnet. It was not with the Mathews that he spent it, however; from the next poem he wrote it can be inferred that he travelled out to Enfield to spend it with Cowden Clarke.

Clarke's acquaintance with Leigh Hunt, made during his imprisonment, had ripened into a firm friendship. As some measure of gratitude, the warm-hearted but dilatory Hunt had long promised to send Clarke specially-bound copies of his latest works. These had arrived on 8 November, with a graceful letter from Hunt apologizing for their unintentionally red binding and for the delay in sending them: "You must fancy the books are blushing for having been so long before they came."[3] The volumes were Hunt's grandiose masque, *The Descent of Liberty* and his satire *The Feast of the Poets*, reissued that year with a new preface and accompanied by another poem, *Politics and Poetics*, in which Hunt demonstrated, according to his own sub-title "the desperate situation of a journalist unhappily smitten with the love of rhyme".

Keats spent the holiday with Clarke reading and discussing these new productions by Hunt, and the next poem he wrote, dated November 1815, shows how he assimilated them. It is his verse *Epistle to George Felton Mathew*. When Keats published this poem, over a year later, with two other verse epistles, he headed the group with a quotation from William Browne, the Elizabethan poet, and in the opening of the poem he compares himself and Mathew to Beaumont and Fletcher; it has therefore been assumed that he was reading the Elizabethan poets now, and that his couplets are modelled on

1. Neither J. Middleton Murry, *Studies in Keats* (1930), 4, nor Werner W. Beyer, *Keats and the Daemon King*, 67, realized that these lines are a criticism on Mathew's part. Murry treats the lines as "nonsensical".
2. Feltoe, op. cit., 39.
3. C. Cowden Clarke, *Recollections of Writers*, 193–194.

those of Browne, Drayton and similar poets.[1] In fact, his poem is derived almost entirely from recent reading of living poets, Leigh Hunt and Wordsworth. The whole idea and shape of the poem is based on *Politics and Poetics*, which describes the dilemma of a political journalist who strives vainly to get away for brief moments to write poetry. Substituting his own medical studies for Hunt's political journalism, Keats produced a poem on exactly the same pattern. Like Hunt he seeks a "nook" or "spot" in the country, like Hunt he has a vision of Fairies dancing by moonlight, like Hunt—this time from *The Descent of Liberty*—he has an imagined scene of the bards and liberators of history, including Shakespeare and "four laurell'd spirits"—in Hunt they are named as Pulci, Ariosto, Tasso and Spenser. Like Hunt he finds the pull of his other occupation too strong, and after a graceful but obscure allegorical tribute to his friend, containing allusions which even Mathew found puzzling,[2] he breaks off abruptly, as if, as indeed may have happened, his holiday had ended and lectures or dissections had to be resumed. The couplets move with the easy pace of Hunt's, but they have a certain stiffening which comes from Wordsworth. They resemble the several short epistles, printed for the first time in the 1815 volumes, which Wordsworth had inscribed at various points in Coleorton, the estate of his friend and patron Sir George Beaumont. Wordsworth addresses Sir George, as Keats does Mathew, as a fellow-artist, in this case a pictorial one since Sir George was a painter. Furthermore, he manages to insert complimentary references to Sir George's ancestor Francis Beaumont, giving Keats the suggestion for his own allusions to Beaumont and Fletcher.

In fact, Wordsworth, and not at this time Hunt, remains Keats's idea of a poet; it is the scheme of *Politics and Poetics* that Keats adopted, and not, on the whole, the style. Hunt, in this volume containing his two narrative poems, did set Keats's newfound enthusiasm for Wordsworth along the channels through which it was to run. Yet the discovery of Wordsworth remained Keats's own, and it was a remarkable taste for him to have acquired unaided. It was certainly not one he had shared with Cowden Clarke, who in common with most of the reading public seems to have been ignorant of Wordsworth. The years between Wordsworth's two-volume edition of poems in 1807 and the two-volume 1815 edition which Keats possessed represent the lowest ebb of Wordsworth's reputation. Of the thirteen reviews of the 1807 *Poems*, all were unfavourable except one. Not only the poems were criticized, but Wordsworth's self-conscious divisions of his work into categories such as "Moods of My Own Mind". *The Critical Review* said he should "spend more time in his library and less in company with the moods of his own mind". In 1808 a devastating parody of Southey, Wordsworth and Coleridge appeared, *The Simpliciad*, thought to be by a future Irish bishop, Richard Mant. In 1811 when Hunt first published *The Feast of the Poets* in *The Reflector*, he

1. Finney, I, 84–85.   2. KC, II, 187–188.

took the popular critical line, although he had not read any of Wordsworth's poems. Wordsworth was parodied and utterly ridiculed. In 1814, having read *Lyrical Ballads* and the 1807 Poems in prison, he had undergone a change of heart; while still keeping the satire and parody of Wordsworth's style, he dismissed him from the feast more gently. In 1815, in the version which Keats read at Clarke's, he had become a convert to Wordsworth, whom he had met shortly after his own release from prison. He now allowed him a seat at the feast, a long series of couplets in his praise, and what he called "this inordinate note" on Wordsworth's poetry, twice as long as any other in the book. Echoes of these notes occur throughout Keats's letters and poems, and he read this one carefully, and based much of his own later judgment on it. It begins "If Mr Wordsworth is at present under a cloud, it is one, we see, of divinity's wearing" and continues, "We have had no poet since the days of Spenser and Milton . . . who saw farther into the sacred places of poetry . . . the native region of the first order of poetical spirits." It is immensely to Keats's credit that he had seen in a few months what it had taken his hero, the editor of *The Examiner*, several years to discover. At the same time, his appreciation of Wordsworth was modified, perhaps healthily, by the reservations which Hunt still expressed. Hunt deplored Wordsworth's habit of what he called "making a business of a reverie", and, harping on the 1807 edition, he summed up, "In some of the effusions called Moods of My Own Mind,[1] he mistakes the commonest process of reflection for its result." He also hinted, as he had allowed Hazlitt to hint in *The Examiner*, that Wordsworth was betraying his former radical principles; the kindly 1813 sonnet to the poor mad old king seemed to give special offence in this direction. No review of the 1815 volumes, incidentally, appeared in *The Examiner*, and only a sarcastic footnote by Hazlitt mentioned the new poems. Keats was far ahead of his time and of the most distinguished critics of the day in recognizing Wordsworth.

He was now far ahead of Mathew in every way. His lines in the Epistle, with their firm Wordsworthian ring, demonstrate this, and supplement the Solitude sonnet. It is his first sustained poem, his first handling of the difficult rhymed couplet; again, like many first attempts, it is more successful than much that was to follow. Mathew valued it, but it was the end of their intellectual friendship. The poem contained a would-be complimentary reference to Mathew's longest work, matching the original in its banality:[2]

1. Keats alluded to this note twice in his letters. *Letters*, I, 263 and 287. These references are satirical, like Hunt's, and derived from this note, though Ward, 420, takes them to mean that Keats was using the 1807 volumes.

2. Cf. Mathew's couplet from *Written in Time of Sickness*

> The ruin'd monastery, the waving woods,
> All show more gloomy in the doubtful light.

> *The Garland*, Finney photostat, p. 153

C*

> There must be too a ruin dark, and gloomy,
> To say "joy not too much in all that's bloomy."

Yet Keats by no means renounced his Wordsworthian tendencies in this poem, and indeed his attempts to "moralize on Milton's blindness" echo Wordsworth's sonnets on liberty such as "Great men have been among us". The whole tone was uncomfortably radical for Mathew, with its invocation of some of the political heroes of Leigh Hunt's *The Examiner*. The poetical friends were drifting apart. Mathew made one further effort. He interpolated an extra stanza into his own poem, picking up Keats's references to Milton and Shakespeare, and claiming that they too had nourished their poetry on romantic subjects, so that

> Like theirs, is the cast of thine earlier lay

but the phrase itself shows how much he realized Keats was now out of sympathy with the matter and the manner of this "earlier lay". By the end of the year, Keats had passed out of the Mathew orbit.

This move accentuated for Keats a personal problem. One of the leaders of the Mathew circle was a lively dark-haired girl called Mary Frogley. Mathew wrote poems to her; she herself in middle age spoke of poems "to, and on me" written by Keats,[1] and was spoken of as an old flame of his. Early in 1816, he wrote her a sonnet.[2] This poem beginning "Had I a man's fair form" shows some of the difficulties Keats still found in society, and how self-conscious he felt about his lack of height. Couched obscurely in a style that returns to his romance reading of Spenser and Tasso, the meaning of its octave was clear to Keats's friends; "the author has an idea that the diminutiveness of his size makes him contemptible and that no woman can like a man of small stature."[3] This poem has been taken to show a crisis in his relations with women in general and with Mary in particular, but the evidence for this is sketchy. Certainly the sestet of the sonnet displays quite a different attitude. Keats compares Mary to roses steeped in dew, and says he will gather the roses and the dew "by spells and incantation". Remembering his favourite quotation from Tasso and Spenser, "Gather the rose of love", and the fact that "dew" was a common English symbol in folk-lore and rustic speech for virginity, this part of the sonnet is a confident hope for success in love, which he will achieve, in spite of fancied physical handicap, "by spells and incantation"—that is, by the power of his verse.[4] It is the poetic equivalent of John Wilkes's assertion that in five minutes' conversation with any woman he

1. KC, II, 218.
2. Its close likeness to the Valentine to her of 14 February 1816 seems to indicate the date and the recipient.
3. Woodhouse's annotation to *Poems*, 1817. Sperry, 148.
4. Woodhouse queried the meaning of these lines; but see James Reeves, *The Idiom of the People*, 54–55.

could overcome the initial disadvantage of his ugly face. There is too little here to say how matters stood between Keats and Mary Frogley, though he found time, when deeply distracted three years later, to send his remembrances to her. She was certainly interested enough in Keats to become his staunch defender against critics of his poetry, and to get a cousin of Mathew, one of the Kirkman brothers of Portsmouth, to make her copies of Keats's early poems. She married one of Keats's fellow medical-students, George Neville, but that is not to say she would have married Keats.

What the sonnet also shows is that Keats, in common with other pupils at Clarke's school, used a kind of Elizabethan jargon, poetry or prose, in talking or writing about women. It was a way of expressing what Keats called "my Boyish imagination" about women, and perhaps of protecting it into manhood against some of the real facts, which, in the squalid daily events of a large London hospital, were showing the other side of the picture. According to one of the older St. Thomas's men, Keats composed during lectures a prose passage of this kind, in sub-Elizabethan style, detailing the charms of a sleeping maiden.[1] Similarly to order, he produced a poem full of the same imagery in February 1816 for his brother George to send as a valentine to Mary Frogley. Whether this again represented some love-victory for the younger, but taller, brother is doubtful. Keats composed two other lost valentines, perhaps for the Mathew sisters, at the same time, and his description of Mary's physical charms, largely omitted in the copy George sent, were heightened by William Hazlitt's Round Table essay *On Beauty*, which Keats read the week before in *The Examiner*.[2] When he himself made a copy, he behaved in a light-hearted way that seems to show that the convention of treating young women as subjects of archaic language and sentiment was already wearing thin, in the frank and healthy exchanges of student atmosphere. Across the second sheet of his manuscript,[3] he scribbled an impromptu quatrain of cheerful and slightly bawdy doggerel—

> I am as brisk
> As a bottle of Wisk—
> Ey and as nimble
> As a Milliner's thimble.

Keats was far from being the average type of medical student; his behaviour was so different from many of the rest that it was thought worth remarking that he was "never inclined to pursuits of a low or vicious—Character",[4] though even the pious Spurgin had implied that there were attractive girls

---

1. W. C. Dendy, *The Philosophy of Mystery*, 100, though there is some doubt whether Dendy is reliable.
2. E. No. 423, pp. 77–78.
3. C. H. Townshend Collection, Wisbech and Fenland Museum.
4. KC, II, 210.

at hand in the Borough. Yet his first term at Guy's gave him a broadening of experience, the contact with people of wide ability from all over the country, with backgrounds and education very different from his own. His first really individual piece of reading, his study of Wordsworth, shows him beginning to form judgments for himself; the range of character presented to him by his hospital life was invaluable to him as a poet, and continued to lead him from his late beginnings in literature to an astonishingly quick growth of maturity. "Lord!", he wrote, "a man should have the fine point of his soul taken off to become fit for this world."[1] All that he saw and experienced in the crowded jumble of student life became of intense interest to him, a perpetual speculation into human nature and motive. "This it is that makes the Amusement of Life", he wrote,[2] using the word, as he always did, in its eighteenth-century meaning of "interest":

This it is that makes the Amusement of Life—to a speculative Mind. I go among the Feilds and catch a glimpse of a stoat or a fieldmouse peeping out of the withered grass —the creature hath a purpose and its eyes are bright with it—I go amongst the buildings of a city and I see a Man hurrying along—to what? The Creature has a purpose and his eyes are bright with it.

Such remarks, the fruit of his later mature philosophy, draw on the reserve of early experience which he was acquiring now, and which was to grow almost daily.

1. *Letters*, I, 188.   2. *Letters*, II, 80.

Chapter 5

THE WELL EDUCATED PRACTITIONER

"The Act has already tended to the increase of Industry and application among Students of Medicine, and ... it will eventually be the means of raising up a class of well educated Practitioners in every Part of the Kingdom."

– Minutes of the Court of Examiners.
Society of Apothecaries, 25 July 1816.

NEW YEAR 1816 brought yet another element into Keats's experience. So far his life as a poet and in medicine had been nurtured by helpful and approving groups of people—Cowden Clarke and the school, his brothers George and Tom, the Mathew circle, and senior students like George Cooper, Tyrrell and Spurgin. Now, just before Christmas 1815, Cooper picked up his Guy's leaving certificate, obtained his Licentiate of the Society of Apothecaries, and went off to practise at Brentford. Tyrrell was already doing a course at Edinburgh, Spurgin at Cambridge. Keats was alone in the sitting-room at the St. Thomas's Street digs. The expenses of board and lodging already overdrew his tiny annual income. They cost £63 a year,[1] while he had now at the most £20. In backing him, his trustees had been indulgent, but soon they would have, in the low state of the market, to sell out nearly another £100 of stock to meet the fees of his dressership. Sharing another sitting-room in the same house were two students who had entered at the same time as Keats: Henry Stephens and George Wilson Mackereth. Keats asked if he might join them to save expense, and they agreed.[2] These two men represented, far more closely than the company Keats had kept so far, the average type of medical student, though Stephens had a taste for poetry and the theatre, and a latent turn for invention which was to result in his patent for the famous blue black ink.

Stephens was a little suspicious of Keats, his quick promotion, his association with senior men, and this must be reckoned in the mildly unflattering

1. The cost of lodgings in the Borough had not changed much in the twenty years since William Knighton wrote "I never should have conceived it to be half so expensive ... 60 guineas a Year for my Board". A.N.C. "A Guy's Freshman in 1796", *Guy's Hospital Gazette*, 13 October 1908, 440.
2. KC, II, 207–208. Another student, Frankish, may have shared also.

portrait he has left; but it is probably a fair idea of how Keats appeared "amongst mere Medical students", as Stephens put it. He talked and thought of nothing but poetry, and condemned out of hand not only Stephens's own attempts at verse, but his taste in poetry. Stephens was not an insensitive observer, for his description of Keats's own taste coincides with Cowden Clarke's; he noticed that Keats was fond of imagery for itself and that the most trifling similes seemed to please him. What Stephens evidently could not stand was the uncritical adulation of George and Tom for their brother. They now became regular visitors to St. Thomas's Street, where Keats was taking time off to become much more sociable. Another visitor was a lively Yorkshire student from St. Bartholomew's, Henry Newmarch. He was a family friend, presumably on old Mrs. Jennings's side, and he pitched into Keats and the brothers with the familiarity of old acquaintance.[1] A self-assured young man, he had worked out his career already—an M.R.C.S. and a post as surgeon in the East India Company[2]—and he was equally confident about such matters as poetry. To Stephens's amusement, Newmarch in his turn handled Keats's verse very roughly, though he chiefly had his eye on getting a rise out of Keats's brothers, whom he provoked to frequent quarrels in the poet's defence. This may have been healthy for Keats. There is a lack of surviving verse at this time, which perhaps indicates that he took the criticism to heart and destroyed some.

Another family friend who appeared now was William Haslam, a young solicitor. He was the son of a grocer; some of his family had belonged to the Fruiterers' Company, of which Keats's great-uncle Sweetinburgh was at one time Master. He was about the same age as Keats.[3] Yet another new friend at this time was Joseph Severn, two years older but young in appearance and manner. He was just finishing a wearisome apprenticeship "stabbing copper" for an engraver, and painting water-colour miniatures in his spare time to buy books and painting-materials. Both of these young men seem at this time to have had more contact with George Keats than with Keats himself, and though Severn thought Keats was very intimate with Haslam this close friendship probably grew later. Severn himself, in fact, was very nearly removed from any chance of friendship with Keats, for in May he was almost crushed to death by the crowd at the Haymarket Theatre, where Mrs. Siddons was making one of her returns to the stage.[4] Hearty masculine company put friendship with women into the background, though Stephens

1. KC, II, 208–210.   2. Various sources, India Office Records.

3. Letters, I, 74. Brown thought he had been at school with Keats, KC, II, 52. Keats himself implied that he met Haslam through George. Letters, I, 392.

4. Sharp, 11–17. Severn with his usual vagueness dated his meeting with Keats at various years from 1813 to 1817. Since Keats addressed him as "My dear Sir" late in 1816 (Letters, I, 115) it is probable they did not see much of each other till 1817, though Severn claimed that Keats read him the Solitude sonnet at their second meeting (Sharp, 162).

had opportunity to observe that Keats was gentle and good-mannered to them; he noticed Keats's attitude to them in a way that exactly chimes with the sentiments of the sonnet to Mary Frogley: "He would have been pleased to find himself admired by the Fair Sex, for his Genius, but not for his person."

Work was also an overriding consideration. The second course of lectures had started, and early in March, Keats took up his dressership. This was a drastic change, and went far beyond the ward-duty twice a week when the dresser attended the surgeon on his rounds, carrying the plaster-box as his badge of office, and noting down his master's instructions for each new case admitted to the hospital. His registration as dresser brought him from the crowded student benches at the back of the operating theatre literally into the front line; a contemporary letter defined his new position. "He has the execution of everything but the great operations, the smaller and most frequent ones he is allowed to perform when he has been long enough in train to lose the trembling hand, in short, before the end of the year he becomes, as it were, an Assistant Surgeon, for all the accidents are submitted to his care and judgment, he takes up the vessels after operations, puts on the bandages, and acts a foremost character in the presence of numberless spectators."[1] Nor did his duties end there. He took turns with the other dressers for a week at a time in the sleeping room next to the operating theatre, in the capacity of a House Surgeon. There he had to deal with any haemorrhage, accident or other crisis by day or night on his own responsibility; these emergencies, in the insanitary conditions, were frequent and could be horrific.[2]

His attendance on his surgeon during "the great operations", which he himself was too inexperienced to perform, could be even more nerveracking. In the front three rows with the other dressers and apprentices, he could see everything that went on at close quarters. It was not only the groans of the patients, half-stupefied with rum, or, worse, the cries of the children that could shake one; worst of all was the terrifying lack of skill of some of the surgeons. At this point, luck or influence deserted Keats. Instead of the temporary dressership under Astley Cooper, which Henry Cooper had held and in which Keats had perhaps deputized, he was now appointed to the dressership left vacant by William Bentham Everest under William Lucas junior, the son of Hammond's master.[3] Dogged by ill-health, including premature deafness, "Billy" Lucas had never been fit enough to study anatomy in the unhealthy dissecting-room of his day; but the influence of a successful father proved stronger than this handicap, and in 1799 he duly

1. William Hill, "Richard Bright—a Bio-Bibliography", *Guy's Hospital Gazette*, 1950, 378.
2. B. Golding *A Historical Account of St. Thomas's Hospital*, 125-126.
3. Guy's Hospital, *Physicians and Surgeons Pupils . . . 1814-1827*.

succeeded to the parental position as surgeon in the hospital. Here he began a career of butchery which even his generous colleague, Astley Cooper, was to recall with critical horror: "he was neat-handed, but rash in the extreme, cutting amongst most important parts as though they were only skin, and making us all shudder from the apprehension of his opening arteries or committing some other error."[1] He put students off surgery not, as has been suggested, because he was dull, but because he was dangerous; the person most to appreciate the danger was his own dresser, left to clear up the mess he had made.

At first, Keats faced the now-widening areas of his life and experience with remarkable confidence. He registered as dresser to Lucas on 3 March 1816 for a period of twelve months. This showed that he was intending to take the full year of surgical training that was required for Membership of the Royal College of Surgeons, and that, in spite of the expense, he would prepare for this by attending further courses of surgical lectures in the autumn.[2] The only poem that has survived from this time shows a parallel confidence in its power to assimilate fresh literary experience. The untitled sonnet beginning "How many bards gild the lapses of time" demonstrates a new technique in the individual rhythm of its first line. Its content is equally sure and calm. The great poets, Keats says, who have fed his fancy, come into his mind when he starts to compose, with echoes of their characteristic styles; but this does not cause him any confusion or disturbance. He can assimilate them, and, in his own words, "make pleasing music" of their influences. The poem is a successful example of the theme it propounds. His reading, from Spenser to Wordsworth, is present in it, yet it strikes an individual note. Only a few lines in the sestet sound like plain imitation; they echo Wordsworth's sonnet on Dover, which Keats was later to parody. The total effect was condensed and mature, as some of Keats's earliest critics were to recognize.

Yet now, as spring came, while dissecting-room and operating theatre began to show a noisome contrast with the weather outside, Keats's life in medicine and poetry seemed to lose its way. There was none of the suicidal despair of the previous spring, but a more profound unease. It has been thought that the early psychological divisions of his life were now catching up with him,[3] but there was much in the crowded circumstances of day-by-day existence to disturb him. One of the difficulties of assessing this period in Keats's life is that almost the only witness to it is his room-mate Stephens, remembering it thirty and forty years later, and even he left two accounts which do not always agree. The first he supplied to Mathew in 1847;[4] the

1. Feltoe, op. cit., 52; Wilks and Bettany, *A Biographical History of Guy's Hospital* (1892), 134.
2. H. C. Cameron, *Mr. Guy's Hospital*, 147.   3. Ward, 57.
4. KC, II, 206-214.

second consisted of conversations with another doctor beginning in 1856.[1] Meanwhile, Monckton Milnes's first biography of Keats had come out in 1848, and Stephens's later reminiscences are unconsciously influenced by this; for instance, he told Mathew that he knew absolutely nothing of Keats's parentage, while ten years later he stated that Keats's origins were well-known throughout the medical school, and that he was sensitive about them, an afterthought obviously derived from Milnes's book.

For this, and for other reasons, Stephens is not an entirely good witness, especially in his second account. But through his eyes Keats's behaviour this spring does show certain excesses natural to anyone of his temperament living under considerable strain. Among the rough-and-tumble of hospital life, he now felt it necessary to establish his own identity, and, in a super-ficial sense, to act the poet. "The greatest men in the world were the Poets, and to rank among them was the chief object of his ambition", Stephens noted. Keats decided to make sure he was a poet by dressing and looking like Byron. While George and Tom still wore high collars and neckerchiefs, their poet brother turned down his collar, and wore it open with only a thin black ribbon round his bare neck; he also experimented with a set of Byronic moustaches.[2]

All this was a necessary counterpart to the encroachments of medicine, the long night hours of the dressers' room, the horrible realities of Lucas's surgery, the grind of mechanical memorizing for the Society of Apothecaries examination, with its long lists of drugs from the *Pharmacopeia Londinensis*. Yet these minor affectations reveal an uncertainty in Keats's poetic thought. He was not as confident as his own recent sonnet had made him sound. Nothing was to tell him that he had found a style of his own. He was un-known as a poet, without a line published. In a search for reassurance, he turned to his intellectual touchstone, *The Examiner*, and its poet-editor. Here was poetic success which had endured persecution and prison without compromise. Leigh Hunt had done what Keats felt himself failing to do, and kept poetry alive in a workaday world.

Keats, in a crisis, often harked back to the secure days of school. He turned to *The Examiner* now partly because it had been the inspiration of his thought in his last year at school; then, according to George, he had been "a little infected" by some of Leigh Hunt's affectations,[3] and had often copied his political attitudes. He had shown little or no sign, however, of being influenced by Leigh Hunt as a poet until he had read him with Cowden

1. B. W. Richardson, *The Asclepiad* (1884), 138–155.

2. KC, II, 211; Ward, 62, adds a sailor costume, though it was not till the second half of 1817 that Keats was observed "dressed in a sort of naval costume". W. C. Hazlitt, *The Hazlitt Memoirs*, I, 275.

3. KC, I, 280. George specifically puts this "infection" when Keats was only fourteen or fifteen, and not in his medical student days as supposed.

Clarke in November 1815; even then, it was simply Hunt's problem of how to fit poetry into a working life that he echoed. In this spring of 1816, however, Keats turned for the first time to Leigh Hunt not only as a political exemplar, but as a model for his poetry. *The Examiner* became for him not only a political but a poetic guide. Unfortunately both for its editor and for his yet-unknown protegé, Hunt was printing a great deal of his own occasional verse in its pages at this exact time. The index to the bound numbers for 1816 shows a far larger proportion of "Original Poetry by the Editor" than for any other year. Hunt was working out a poetic creed, and found his own paper a convenient platform for experiment. In his notes to *The Feast of the Poets*, which Keats had read, Hunt hoped that imitation of the best work of Dryden, Spenser and Milton "might lead the poets of the present age to that proper mixture of sweetness and strength", and Keats had fulfilled that hope in his March sonnet. Yet in his own *Examiner* verse, Hunt had not stuck to his own prescription, but had added a fatal element of what he called "an idiomatic spirit in verse". It was his own interpretation of the Wordsworthian doctrine of the use of common speech, and its affectations sprang from his avoidance of what he considered the crudities of Wordsworth. Byron had put his finger on its dangers the previous autumn, when he sent Hunt a friendly warning against "a kind of harsh and yet colloquial compounding of epithets, as if to avoid saying common things in a common way".

It was a stroke of ill-luck, comparable to his dressership to Lucas, which induced Keats to take Leigh Hunt's 1816 productions in *The Examiner* as a poetic guide just at this time. These, and Hunt's *The Story of Rimini*, published in February, chart him as a poet in the next few months. In fact, poems by Keats followed in fairly regular progression similar poems from the editor's pen. The first instance of this was a trivial one but it showed the way the wind was blowing. Early in April Keats read in *The Examiner* Hunt's tripping translation from the 54th Ode of Anacreon.[1] Going into Marcet's chemistry lecture, the rhythm was still in his head; he seized Stephens's notebook, and scribbled in it his own imitation of "Anacreon's sprightly old age", as Hunt had called his effort. Keats's "Give me women, wine and snuff", borrowing a beard from Anacreon and a facetious tone from Hunt, was noted by Stephens as typical of Keats's growing inattention at lectures,[2] but poetically it was a disturbing sign of a new mood. This mood developed to a dangerous pitch in his *Specimen of An Induction to a Poem*.[3] These couplets beginning

> Lo! I must tell a tale of chivalry;
> For large white plumes are dancing in mine eye

1. E. No. 431, p. 203.   2. KC, II, 210.
3. Ward, 65, places the *Induction* later in the summer, but it is closely related to his February valentine poem, and he would not have gone several months before reading *Rimini*.

have no impulse but a desire to do something like Hunt's *The Story of Rimini*. Keats felt he *must* tell a tale of chivalry apparently for no other reason than because Hunt had just done so. The "Induction" thus produced does not lead to a "tale" nor does it feel as if it ever could. In loose repetitive couplets, Keats tried to recapture the scene from Hunt's poem where Paolo rides in cavalcade to meet Francesca. It was, at any rate, the most effective scene in Hunt's poem that had set him off; but once he had exhausted the images of that scene, the plumes, the lance, the knight, the steed, the poem petered out. Instead of any story, Keats ended with an apology to Spenser for having tried to follow

> that bright path of light
> Trac'd by thy lov'd Libertas

—the bright path of light being *The Story of Rimini* and Libertas the name Keats adopted for Hunt. Hunt is not quite the major influence in this fragment; Spenser and Wordsworth are still there, Spenser in chivalric images that recall the poems to Mary Frogley, Wordsworth in an unconscious echo of *Daffodils*. Yet Keats, who in balancing the work of these major poets had seemed to be achieving a style of his own, was now surrendering this maturity, which he had shown in his last sonnet, before the superficially attractive style of Hunt. It is easy to see why Hunt's style fascinated him at this time. At its best, it was a kind of Wordsworth-without-tears, colloquial without the obstinate rural simplicities that alienated even Wordsworth's admirers. To Keats it must have seemed, as Hunt had intended it, an excellent compromise between the virtues of the traditional and the modern poets. Yet the mannerisms by which Hunt tried to get this effect, though he removed a few from *Rimini* after Byron's criticism, were strong enough for Keats to begin to adopt them too. The weak-ending couplets in y and ly and ing, by which Hunt tried to introduce informality of technique into his verses, start to appear in this *Induction*; so, even less fortunately, does the chatty cosiness by which Hunt tried to introduce informality of mood. It was what Keats afterwards condemned as "mawkishness" in himself. At the same time, it would be wrong to regard Hunt as a disaster for Keats's poetry. Keats would not have followed him if he had not fulfilled some need in his poetic life. To follow exclusively the epic Spenser and the philosophic Wordsworth might have been stultifying, and the frank vulgarity of the lightweight Hunt provided a poetic liberation from these mighty but perhaps overweighty champions.

At all events, *Rimini* and Hunt's *Examiner* poems became the food of Keats's inner life this spring and summer. He had ended the *Induction* by hoping that Hunt would plead with the shade of Spenser for Keats's own poems; but, it must have occurred to him, Hunt did not even know of the existence of these poems. *The Examiner* was publishing a particularly large amount of contributors' verses as well as those by its editor. Hunt had been introduced to Wordsworth in the previous year and was now printing some of his sonnets. Byron, about to leave England after the break-up of his marriage, had added to his general unpopularity by contributing some pro-French stanzas to the issue of 7 April, and a fortnight later Hunt reprinted from *The Champion* Byron's private *Fare Thee Well* verses to Lady Byron. It was a natural forum for a young poet who admired both the editor and his distinguished contributors. Occasionally, there was a poem by some lesser-known writer signed with initials. This might be a way of bringing his own poetry to Hunt's notice. He looked through his past poems with evident care, and, with the sound taste of self-criticism which hardly ever deserted him, he chose his most solid and individual production, the *Solitude* sonnet which he had written the previous autumn. He even improved this, substituting "innocent mind" for "elegant mind" in the sestet, and tightening the rhythm of another line; and so, with the initials J.K. attached, he sent it to the editor. When he opened the issue of 28 April, it was not there; but in the little space for editorial announcements, after the bankruptcies and prices of stock, he read "J.K., and other Communications, next week".

He was to be published; for the first time a poem of his was to be circulated not in young women's private albums, but in a public journal. In this rose-coloured mood he read the editor's own verse epistle to *Lord Byron on his departure for Italy and Greece*.[1] This was the first of a number of verse epistles to friends which Hunt was to write and print this summer, and which, in their turn, set off a series of similar poems by Keats. This one had its share of the splendid absurdities from which Hunt's poems were seldom free, but it did not seem so to Keats. He took in his stride Hunt's picture of the Mediterranean full of bathing beauties, white and shapely with bosoms and long arms of snow, assembled there for Byron's benefit,

> To hail the laurell'd Bard, that goes careering by.

In fact, he composed a sonnet on the same theme, imagining himself on a voyage to Italy where he could see such sights

> And float with them about the summer waters.

His self-identification with Byron, in dress and appearance, was now allied to a self-identification with Hunt in manner and sentiment of verse, and this was confirmed by the publication of his *Solitude* sonnet next week on 5 May. *Rimini* and its author were now his poetic guide, and he plunged into the long poem which was to mark the peak of their poetic influence upon him.

It is easy to make both too little and too much of the 160-line fragment *Calidore* which Keats wrote in May.[2] It cannot quite be dismissed as an

1. E. No. 435, pp. 266–267.
2. Ward again believes this to be written later in the summer.

imitation of Hunt. Keats had, after all, read Spenser long before he read *Rimini*, and the poem owes its opening directly to *The Faerie Queene*, from which it also takes its hero. It is certainly disastrously Huntian in some of its descriptions of people and their actions; Calidore goes upstairs "with hasty trip" and "leaps along" corridors in a way that reproduces Hunt's manner in *Rimini* only too faithfully. On the other hand its natural description, its literal observation of the early summer scenery, is Keats's own, the climate of many more mature poems than this. The swallows dipping on and off the water, ruffling the surface with their wings and breasts, phrases such as "spiral foxgloves" or "the nightingale's first under-song", even a cancelled description of laburnums that "bow their golden honours to the ground" have a freshness and strength upon which he continually drew for his best poetry. It is the poetic inheritance of his alert boyhood, into which he plunged back so often and so fruitfully. Yet if youth and natural description are the hall-marks of the poem, they are also its pitfalls. Descriptive passages continually defeat Keats's attempt to start a narrative; they probably represent various takings-up of the theme in the few intervals from medical work. Finally, early in June, still stuck in a picture of moon-rise, Keats gave up and turned the last few lines he had written into a Miltonic sonnet with the very Miltonic opening "To one who has been long in city pent".

This sonnet was, according to George Keats, "written in the Fields". The second course of lectures had just finished, and Keats, when not on duty as a dresser, had more free time to revise and read for his Licentiate of the Society of Apothecaries, which he and Mackereth were planning to take at the end of July. His other room-mate, Stephens, nervous about the Latin he would be expected to translate in the *Pharmacopeia*, was postponing his attempt till a month later.[1] Ever since the incident in the chemistry lecture, he had noticed Keats's growing inattention and tendency to "scribble verses", and he had witnessed Keats's pleasure at the publication of his first poem in *The Examiner*. Now, while they went bathing together in the New River, and read their books in the meadows, he observed that Keats seemed to be paying very little attention to the medical profession.[2] In the sonnet Keats was certainly not reading the *Pharmacopeia*, but "a debonair and gentle tale of love and languishment" such as *Rimini*. In the second of the three linked Miltonic sonnets he wrote during June, he is reading *The Examiner* and trying to write poetry, while the third sonnet is a reminder that the end of lectures meant a renewal of the society of his brothers; it is written to a school-friend of Tom, the attractive but untrustworthy Charles Wells.

These sonnets, composed "in the happy fields" were, however, only offshoots of a long personal poem upon which Keats was now brooding. It is often a poetic process to disguise what has to be said first of all in narrative; then, if narrative does not succeed, to discard it and begin the poem again

1. G. L. MS 8239/1.   2. KC, II, 211.

on a more openly personal pattern. Keats did this later in his recasting of
Hyperion as *The Fall of Hyperion: A Dream*, and on a minor scale he achieved
much the same poetic shift now. The *Specimen of an Induction* and *Calidore*
had failed and hampered him whenever he turned from description to attempt
any sort of story. He decided to try again with no sort of external plot, but,
like Wordsworth, with the internal drama of the progress of his own poet's
mind. This time he began with a piece of frankly personal description

> I stood tip-toe upon a little hill

and proceeded to paint the scene of Hampstead Heath in June.[1] The lightness
and freshness of these opening lines, the sense of youthful and personal
experience, was not achieved without effort, and shows what a conscious and
self-critical artist Keats had already become. The poem had at first started
with a moralizing and impersonal half-line "He who has lingered", which
Keats quickly abandoned for the abrupt and personal opening,[2] and continued, though not without some technical difficulties on the way, into a
picture of his own enjoyment:

> The air was cooling, and so very still,
> That the sweet buds which with a modest pride
> Pull droopingly, in slanting curve aside,
> Their scantly leaved, and finely tapering stems,
> Had not yet lost those starry diadems
> Caught from the early sobbing of the morn.
> The clouds were pure and white as flocks new shorn,
> And fresh from the clear brook; sweetly they slept
> On the blue fields of heaven, and then there crept
> A little noiseless noise among the leaves,
> Born of the very sigh that silence heaves:

His first sixty lines, pursuing this alert and delighted vein, ended with two
couplets, written again, for all their delicacy, with considerable technical
effort, in which the "tip-toe" theme of the opening passes from the poet to
the objects of his pleasure:

> Here are sweet peas, on tip-toe for a flight:
> With wings of gentle flush o'er delicate white,
> And taper fingers catching at all things,
> To bind them all about with tiny rings.

The Wordsworthian transition, from his own feelings to the apparent mood
of natural objects and then back again, was as subtle as his own previous

1. "as he stood beside the gate that leads from the Battery on Hampstead Heath into
a field by Caen Wood". Leigh Hunt, *Lord Byron and Some of His Contemporaries* (1828),
249.

2. Keats Collection, Houghton Library, *59M-143.

attempts at narrative had been clumsy. This form left him free from the temptations of Huntian dialogue and bathos, and in all the sixty lines there are only two *Rimini* phrases, "jaunty streams" and, regrettably, "tasteful nook". Indeed, the only real borrowing from Hunt was a happy one. The lines just after the opening resemble Hunt's charming fragment of translation from Homer, *Mercury Going to the Cave of Calypso*, of which the editor of *The Examiner* had been so justly proud that he had printed it in whole or in part twice in the last few weeks.[1] Wordsworth was the most direct influence on this attempt at poetic autobiography by Keats, both in theme and in actual poetic example. The plan of the poem, a gradual unfolding of an inner development through an outward observation of nature, is completely Wordsworthian. To dwell on a single spot, its flowers and birds and trees, until, as Wordsworth wrote,

> Such place to me is sometimes like a dream
> Or map of the whole world

was Keats's plan too. His whole opening shows the influence of the Wordsworth sonnet, in which these lines occur,[2] and he closely follows Wordsworth's own use of the "tip-toe" theme in the sonnet's

> And wild rose tip-toe upon hawthorn stocks.

The voice of his lines, though, is notably Keats's own; it has a sense of liberation and poetic freedom, an exhilaration matching his own repeated use of the word "tip-toe". It looks as hopefully to the future as the rather stale clutch of Miltonic sonnets had looked back to the experimental past.

The immediate future, however, lay with medicine rather than with poetry, and in July the lines had to be put aside. Keats was now approaching the first stage of professional medical qualification, for which he had undergone such a long and expensive training. He was only just ready for it, and some pressure was probably being put upon him. His trustees, Sandell and Abbey, had spent freely on him, and there is no hint that he had been kept short of money, although each demand he made on them had meant selling in a very unfavourable market. By now, the greater part of his share of his grandmother's capital had gone, and only a few hundreds were left. Sandell, the senior trustee, was a kindly man, if we can judge from a tiny note of heavy-handed mock-humour he had written for Keats's sister Fanny early in the year.[3] In the middle of May, however, he died unexpectedly young.[4] Richard Abbey was now sole trustee. He was not necessarily a sterner customer; there are signs that Sandell had been a little slack in his trusteeship.

1. E. No. 439, p. 330.
2. "How sweet it is when mother Fancy rocks".
3. KHM, No. 80.
4. Norman Kilgour, "Mrs. Jennings' Will", KSMB, XIII, 27.

Probate had not yet been obtained for Mrs. Jennings' will with its small personal estate—her capital was, of course, in the trustees' hands—and some minor debts of the estate had not yet been paid. Abbey set himself to tidy up this, though with almost punctilious legality toward the Keats boys.[1] He also looked with a logical and businesslike eye on the career of John Keats. Over £1500 capital had been a lot to invest in a young man, and there could be some minor retrenchments. The Society of Apothecaries, under its new regulations, charged a higher fee to candidates applying for a licence to practise in London. This seemed an unnecessary expense. Keats could practise where he had family connections, just outside the statutory ten-mile radius, and perhaps rival his former master; it irked Abbey that Hammond had made no attempt to pay back part of the premium after the quarrel.[2]

Keats therefore came up to Apothecaries Hall at Blackfriars as a candidate to practise as an apothecary in the country. He had the minimum qualification of apprenticeship, hospital attendance and lectures. Hammond, in spite of their differences, had given him a satisfactory testimonial, and after the six days' statutory notice in writing, he was accepted by the Court to sit for the examination on 25 July. This was only in four subjects—translation of the *Pharmacopeia* and Physicians' prescriptions, the theory and practise of medicine, pharmaceutical chemistry and materia medica—but in spite of its omissions, notably in anatomy and physiology, it is clear that the syllabus was taken seriously by the Court of Examiners, and was far from being the scrap of paper it has sometimes been represented. In the year that the new Apothecaries Act had been in force, the examiners had considered the claims of 188 candidates. Ten had not even been allowed to sit, owing to inadequate qualifications, usually irregular apprenticeships. Another eleven had been rejected when they came to examination.[3] This meant that one candidate in every nine had been turned down, a formidable failure rate; indeed on this day, one of the seven candidates was ploughed. This was not, however, Keats, but his room-mate Mackereth; it was he who returned to tell Stephens his sad news and the unexpected intelligence that Keats had been examined by Everard Brande and had passed.

It must be emphasized, in view of a tendency to play down Keats's medical ability, what a real achievement this was. Much of the assumption that Keats was not a promising doctor, and did not take his medical training seriously, is due to two accidents, both connected with this Society of Apothecaries examination. The first is that Stephens, when he went up for the same examination a few weeks later, failed it. In his chagrin at having ploughed when Keats had passed at the first attempt, Stephens belittled the standard of the examination, saying that it was not a real test of medical knowledge,[4] in

1. *Letters*, I, 103.
2. Apothecaries Act 1815, Clause XIX: KC, I, 307.
3. G.L., MS 8239/1.   4. KC, II, 211.

spite of all historical evidence to the contrary. He played down Keats's abilities and interest in medicine, and suggested that he got through mainly on his knowledge of Latin. The second accident is that the prime source of general information for the background of Keats's student days, the *Memorials* of John Flint South, a contemporary of Keats at St. Thomas's, has a gap in the manuscript just where South is about to describe the great improvement in the standard of the Apothecaries' qualification.[1] The impression has therefore been left that the examination Keats passed was a merely nominal one. Complete evidence to the contrary comes from Astley Cooper, who in his surgical lectures commented "To the Company of Apothecaries society is much indebted, as to them we owe the Act which makes a certain course of education indispensible for medical students."[2]

Keats's success was also a proof of long study and full apprenticeship. Nothing can have been faked either in his acceptance as a fully-qualified candidate nor as an examinee. That winter, the Court rejected three times the claims of a candidate who had served an irregular apprenticeship, and when at last they reluctantly admitted him to the examination they failed him. Keats had satisfied an exacting body in every way. Indeed, when he and the other new Licentiates had taken a congratulatory tea and left, the Court sat down to pass a resolution recording how much the standard of candidates had improved under the new Act: "they cannot help founding on it a conviction that the Act has already tended to the increase of Industry and application among the Students of Medicine, and that it will eventually be the means of raising up a class of well educated Practitioners in every Part of the Kingdom." One of these well-educated practitioners was now John Keats, Licentiate of the Society of Apothecaries.[3]

---

1. Feltoe, op. cit., 65, where there is a note to this effect.
2. *The Lancet* (1823), I, 7.   3. G.L. MS 8239/1 and 8241/1.

Chapter 6

THE NEW ERA

"The busy time has just gone by, and I can now devote any time you may mention to the pleasure of seeing Mr. Hunt—'twill be an Era in my existence."

-JOHN KEATS to C. Cowden Clarke, 9 October 1816

LONDON was warm and muggy in the summer of 1816. At the lodgings in St. Thomas's Street, which were kept by a tallow-chandler called Markham, Ben Crouch and his body-snatchers had deposited a corpse. This was an order from George Cooper, who wanted to prepare a skeleton to keep up his anatomical studies while in practice at Brentford. The lodgers assisted their landlord to wax the body and despatch it in a hamper by river to Brentford, but long before it arrived, its smell had been the subject of comment by passengers on the boat, who were hardly reassured by the captain's remark that it came "from a tallow chandler's in the Borough, and very likely it is graves".[1] Even without incidents such as these, the Borough and its hospitals were no place to be in August. Lectures had ceased, and although the Friday operations went on, each of the three surgeons had four dressers attached to him, so it was possible for Keats to take nearly two months' holiday if one of the others would do a double duty week. He needed a complete holiday and so did his younger brother Tom.[2] Keats decided to take up the arrangement of living with Tom, which had been broken by his entry to Guy's. He left the lodgings in St. Thomas's Street, with Stephens still sweating over his *Pharmacopeia*, and took Tom off on the steamer to Margate, then at the height of its popularity as a pleasure resort for Londoners. It was a place frankly described by another poet as "a cheshire-cheese full of mites",[3] but as usual in seaside bathing-places, the crowds congregated round the promenade and a few fashionable beaches. Near at hand there were cliff-walks where the ripe corn came right down to the chalk-edge, and one could

1. Feltoe, op. cit., 81–82. Stephens thought the name of their landlady might have been Mitchell. KC, II, 207. "Graves" was a pun on the two meanings of the word—the familiar one and "the refuse of tallow".

2. Lowell, I, 172 and Ward, 66, assume that Tom went abroad to Lyons, possibly for his health, the previous winter; but this clearly occurred in summer 1817, during his visit to France with George. KHM, No. 104, Brown to Dilke, 20 January 1830.

3. R. J. White, *Life in Regency England* (1963), 135.

gaze undisturbed out over open sea. Nor was the company of Tom any distraction: rather the reverse. Like his gifted brother, but without the power of creation, he was beginning to read deeply, and according to George he understood Keats better than anyone else. George himself, the family sheet-anchor, was left behind in London, where he lodged free with Abbey's head clerk Mr. Swan, whom they facetiously nicknamed Wagtail.[1] Contact between the three brothers was closer than ever now that Keats had temporarily relaxed from medicine. Tom's friend Wells, who worked for a London solicitor, had managed to provide the two on holiday with a number of letters "franked" or endorsed with the signature of a Member of Parliament,[2] which, under the unreformed postal system, could be used for free correspondence to any recipient in the kingdom. They used these to keep in touch with George, and Keats used them to send poetry.

He had brought down his manuscript poems for sorting and reflection, including the increasing number left unfinished during the hard work of the last months. New impressions, however, resulted in new poems, or gave a fresh turn to old ones. It was apparently the first time that Keats had lived by the sea; his intense identification of himself with natural objects made it a revelation and a wonder. He at once wrote a sonnet to George in which the main theme was

> The ocean with its vastness, its blue green,
> Its ships, its rocks, its caves, its hopes, its fears,
> Its voice mysterious, which who so hears
> Must think on what will be, and what has been.

Keats's invention stumbled over the ending, which turned out as lamely as some of his Mathew poems, but new inspiration and a family audience had at any rate started him writing again. His unfinished poems still daunted him, as did his whole situation, poised between medicine and poetry; but his fresh surroundings and the sonnet started a liberating idea. Why not write in verse to George *about* his own poetic problems?

It is easy to see how this idea of a verse epistle came to Keats. Almost every other issue of *The Examiner* that summer contained a verse epistle by its editor. His *Epistle to Lord Byron* had encouraged Hunt to launch into a series of these verse letters, some addressed to an imaginary correspondent, "Tom Brown", and others to real friends such as Hazlitt and Charles Lamb.[3] Hunt kept a deliberately light touch in his couplets by writing in a dactylic measure; Keats, for a domestic audience but in keeping with a more serious purpose, stuck to iambics. Yet he used the tone of voice and many of the images from

1. KHM, No. 52; *Letters*, I, 104.
2. Ward, 66, assumes that Wells was with them on holiday, while Bate, 66, assumes that Keats went alone and was joined later by Tom: but see Brown to Dilke, 20 January 1830, KHM, No. 104.
3. E. Nos. 444, 445, 446, 452 in particular.

Hunt's epistles, and his *Epistle To My Brother George* is composed in rough topical paragraphs on the same plan as Hunt's verses. Its first paragraph takes up the theme of his lack of inspiration, which has followed him from hospital even to the countryside. The second provides more hope. From "water, earth or air" he feels new inspiration coming to him, so that he can re-create the mood in which he composed *Calidore*, though unfinished still his most considerable poem to date. A long and less-successful paragraph dwells on what Keats was later to call his "Love of Fame", the desire to leave a body of poetry behind him. He breaks this off to describe himself in the act of writing poetry for George. This, for all its realistic open-air setting, is nearest in actual phrases and detail to Hunt's description of his own rural composition in his first *Epistle To His Cousin Thomas Brown*,[1] yet it has a serious touch, lacking in Hunt. Keats was beginning to write not merely on what seemed suitable subjects for poems, but on subjects that seriously concerned him.[2] He had with him the sixty lines started earlier in the summer. These had been suggested by Wordsworth's sonnet "How sweet it is when mother Fancy rocks" and its "tip-toe" imagery. Looking at the opposite page in his copy of Wordsworth, Keats's imagination had been transfixed by Wordsworth's sonnet of the Shepherd and the Moon, calling to his mind the classical legend of the Moon Goddess and the shepherd Endymion. The moonscape conjured up by Wordsworth in this second sonnet gave a new turn to Keats's ideas about his yet unnamed sixty lines, with their Wordsworthian theme of the poet and nature. Could they be developed, through using the story of Cynthia and Endymion, into a poem with that theme, not just one more verse introduction that got nowhere? He nursed this hope, calling the unfinished poem "Endymion" from now onward in his mind; meanwhile he posted the finished verse-epistle to George.

George kept the poem, under Keats's instructions, so as to make a fair copy of it; Keats may have thought there was some hope of publication, since Hunt seemed so partial to verse epistles. George's letter of reply had its own stimulating news. John Clarke had retired from the school at Enfield, and Charles Cowden Clarke was in London for a long stay with his brother-in-law John Towers, a chemist in Clerkenwell. George was going to see him, and keep Keats in touch with him. In his present mood of reflection and mental stock-taking, this reminder of Clarke's existence had a deep effect on Keats. As he surveyed his own position, he felt he could never have achieved such success, limited as it might be, without his older friend. He had not even dreamt of being a poet when he first became Clarke's pupil; now, though with only one poem published, he could dare to call himself by that name. His verse epistle to George had not entirely satisfied him; perhaps Clarke would inspire him, in spite of their separation over the past months. He began a fresh set of couplets to Clarke.

1. E, No. 444, pp. 409–410.   2. Bate, 70.

He used, perhaps unconsciously, an opening image which had been the most striking single part of the first poem he had ever written, after the arbour readings at Enfield, the picture of the swan ruffling its way through the water, whose drops were as elusive as poetry. He recalled Clarke's poetic preferences, Tasso, Spenser, Shakespeare, and his poetic friendship with the author of *Rimini*. Then came his own debt to Clarke, their wide reading together of every sort of poetry, especially Spenser. Milton appears, less expectedly, in references that perhaps echo a recent eulogy by Hazlitt in *The Examiner*;[1] so does Clarke's introduction of that paper to his pupil. With half the poem gone in this catalogue of gratitudes, it becomes more intimate and personal. Using terms that resembled in many ways Hunt's verse epistle to Hazlitt, but with an undercurrent of stronger feeling, Keats reconstructed his apprenticeship visits to Enfield, the music in the Clarke household, the walks in the Green Lanes, the arbour readings, his reluctant going, accompanied by his friend halfway back to Edmonton. In imagination, he shook hands and parted from Clarke again, and the poem ended; but the scene it had evoked did not leave his mind. His feelings, cramped by the epistolary style, reached out for more freedom. He took down the first sixty lines of his "Endymion" poem, and wrote on. He had left it in a Hampstead setting with June sweet-peas peering over the cottage walls. Now without pause, he carried on where the epistle to Clarke had just ended, on the walk from Enfield, at a spot which Clarke afterwards was delighted to recognize as the bridge over the last brook before Edmonton.[2] Losing the stiffness of the epistle, catching the Wordsworthian emphasis of their sixty-line prologue, the verses took on a new authority. Single lines such as

How silent comes the water round that bend

have a Shakespearian inevitability. The school of minnows in the stream, the flock of goldfinches flirting along the surface become fully realized poetic experiences, a Middlesex counterpart of Wordsworth's Westmorland mountainscapes. Now the Moon begins to dominate all other natural symbols in the poem; and either now or shortly afterwards, Keats wrote a passage that becomes explicitly Wordsworthian, though still in his individual tongue:

> For what has made the sage or poet write
> But the fair paradise of Nature's light?
> In the calm grandeur of a sober line,
> We see the waving of the mountain pine;
> And when the tale is beautifully staid,
> We feel the safety of a hawthorn glade:

In these quiet September days Keats devoted himself to poetry and the

1. E. No. 447, pp. 460–462.
2. C. Cowden Clarke, *Recollections of Writers*, 52 and 138.

materials for poetry in a way he had not found possible for a whole year. The contrast with the Mathew poems of exactly a year ago was the measure of how far he had gone. Keats was absorbed now in thoughts about poetry, just as in his later schooldays he had been absorbed in reading. His intense nature, always in danger of burning itself out in sheer mental effort, had the company of Tom to make it "feel the gentle anchor pull". He was so concentrated on his own poetic problems that he did not realize his brother might have a problem too. Enclosed in letters from Wells, Tom was receiving curious screeds from an unknown French girl. He had never seen her, but she somehow knew of him through Wells, and seemed to be making advances to him. She wrote to him while, it appeared, fighting off the advances that Wells was making to her. It was an intriguing situation, if it were true; but something in the mock-Elizabethan phrasing of the letters, the common language of the Clarke school-fellows, might have warned Tom that there was either more or less behind the obviously-disguised handwriting.[1] Perhaps he was over-susceptible or a little vain, perhaps he had inherited his grandfather's gullible strain. He kept the letters and did not show them to John, nor apparently reveal to his brother the lady's improbably high-sounding name—"Amena Bellefila."

The long holiday was ending, its length a reminder of George's friendly criticism that John and Tom habitually lived far beyond their limited incomes.[2] Keats by now had little left of his grandmother's legacy. He had to find fresh lodgings in the Borough, and enrol for a course of surgical lectures, the famous series on Surgery delivered by Astley Cooper,[3] if he were to take the Membership of the Royal College of Surgeons early next year, the classic progression of "passing the (Apothecaries) Hall then the College", which Stephens, who had failed "the Hall" in August, would now have to make in reverse order. Everyone would expect a man of Keats's ability to take this step. His dressership was daily more onerous, with extra duty-weeks to make up for his leave, and extra responsibility as Lucas now left more and more of the minor operations, as well as blood-lettings and tooth-drawings, solely to him. The first week of October was a whirl of busy and often sordid activity, searching the dirty streets of the Borough to find lodgings in the small intervals from hospital work. He found rooms at 8 Dean Street, a turning joining St. Thomas's Street and Tooley Street, now obliterated by London Bridge Station. The rooms looked gloomily across at a Nonconformist meeting-house. After the revelations of sea and sky at Margate, the Borough seemed to him even more "a beastly place". He no longer had Tom to cheer

1. Hewlett, 377–381.
2. KC, I, 277. Keats, in his turn, told Brown that George and Tom overspent their incomes. KHM, No. 104. In fact, they all did, but George least since he was in regular work.
3. Printed The Lancet, 1823–1824.

him, "being", as Cowden Clarke remembered, "house-keeper and solitary";[1] but any gloom he may have felt was soon lightened by a series of new events. These sprang from Clarke himself. Though in his thirtieth year and no longer a schoolmaster, Clarke regarded his grown-up pupils with a schoolmaster's eye, and continued to do so all his life, handing out praise or blame to them in classroom terms throughout their adult careers. Hearty in all he enjoyed, a loud-voiced singer and handy cricketer like the sporting heroes of the Hambledon Club whom he celebrated, he remained the perpetual teacher, with a soft spot for any reminder of schooldays. Such a reminder had been Keats's verse epistle, and it roused Clarke to an impulse of generous pride in his pupil. In the poem, Keats lamented that his verses hardly seemed adequate for one who enjoyed the friendship of the author of *Rimini*. This struck a spark of warm response in Clarke. He at once got together two or three of the manuscript poems by Keats in his possession, to show to Hunt on his next visit to Hampstead in the first week of October. One of these was a long poem—almost certainly the Epistle itself—and the other two were sonnets, including, luckily, the mature and assured "How many bards".

Their reception was surprising, even to Clarke, who had diffidently introduced them as the compositions of a youth under 21, whom Hunt had already unknowingly published.[2] Hunt began to read the long poem and after the first twenty lines broke into expressions of open admiration. An even more impressive reaction than that of the ever-volatile editor came from another guest who happened to be at the Vale of Health cottage. This was Horace Smith, a contributor to *The Examiner* at this time. A wealthy stockbroker, who had become rich through a shrewd gamble in Government Loans at the time of Waterloo, assisted by inside information from his Civil Servant brother James, he was chiefly known as the joint author with James of a brilliant series of poetic parodies, the *Rejected Addresses*, but he was also a serious poet in his own right, with a partiality for sonnets of a reflective nature. He fastened on Keats's "How many bards", and read it out loud with marked approval, especially the sestet. He repeated the last line but one

That distance of recognizance bereaves,

with special delight, and commented "What a well-condensed expression for a youth so young!" Though his choice of line perhaps showed a more eighteenth-century standard of criticism than Hunt's, Smith had put his finger on the growing sureness in Keats's work. Clarke was questioned about Keats, "with reference to any peculiarities of mind and manner", and as a loyal schoolmaster was able to give him a good reference. He was bidden to bring the young man himself to the Vale of Health.[3] It was gratifying for

1. C. Cowden Clarke, *Recollections of Writers*, 128; Bate, 84, n. 1.
2. C. Cowden Clarke, *Recollections of Writers*, 132.
3. C. Cowden Clarke, *Recollections of Writers*, 133.

Hunt to be the discoverer of yet another promising young poet; only that week he had acknowledged in *The Examiner*[1] a first contribution from "Elfin Knight"—that is, Percy Bysshe Shelley, and he had just received a small book of poems called *The Naiad* by an already-promising writer, John Hamilton Reynolds.

Clarke, delighted with this success, told Keats the news when he called at Clerkenwell. Keats was still harassed with beginning-of-term arrangements, but as soon as these were settled, he wrote to Clarke on Wednesday 9 October. To meet Hunt, he said, "will be an Era in my existence". He already had a good idea of Hunt's taste in poetry, through the lengthy notes to *The Feast of the Poets*, in which Hunt castigated the mechanical couplets of Pope and more recent writers such as Erasmus Darwin. He got out his own verse manuscripts, in anticipation of becoming acquainted "with Men who in their admiration of Poetry do not jumble together Shakspeare and Darwin".[2] Here, however, Keats's own native self-criticism began to take charge of his new enthusiasm. Many of his juvenilia did not seem good enough to show to these sophisticated older critics, both in their thirties. He resolved to burn most of what he had copied—whether he did or not in the end is uncertain— but he made an exception with the *Epistle to George Felton Mathew*, his first couplet exercise which did not have, he may have hoped, "the extreme pitch of sameness" which Hunt had found in Darwin's rhymes.

His spirits rose as he wrote on, inviting Clarke to visit him at Dean Street, giving him his directions through the narrow winding Borough streets after he had "run the Gauntlet over London Bridge" into the wilds of Southwark. When they last met, Clarke had hinted that he had something he wanted to show Keats. It was a book that was going the rounds of the Leigh Hunt circle. Hunt had written in his verse epistle to Charles Lamb, published in *The Examiner* of 25 August, "Of Chapman, whose Homer's a fine rough old wine".[3] A 1616 folio edition of George Chapman's translation of Homer was owned by Thomas Massa Alsager, who was in charge of the musical and financial departments of *The Times*. He was a friend of Lamb, and had helped Hunt in prison. Clarke also knew him, and was known by him to be a lover of Elizabethan poets and a classicist. In some way, probably by Hunt first borrowing it and then lending it to Clarke, Alsager's folio Chapman was now in Clarke's hands. He did not bring it to Dean Street, as Keats suggested; prudence may have warned him that even so sturdy a figure as Clarke, who had been known to outdistance footpads with his "cricketing speed", should not run the gauntlet of the Borough thieves' kitchens with a valuable and borrowed book in his portfolio. Instead, it was the occasion of an all-night session next time Keats came to Clerkenwell, most likely during the week-end of 11 to 12 October, "our first symposium", as Clarke called it, adding "and a memorable night it was in my life's career".

1. E. No. 458.   2. *Letters*, I, 113.   3. E. No. 452, p. 537.

The sole account of this memorable night is Clarke's, though it has often been retold. Its upshot is equally famous. Keats left Clarke at six in the morning, with the long fourteen-syllable lines of Chapman's version of the *Iliad*, the rough rhyming *Odyssey* pentameters, still rolling in his head like breakers on a beach. He composed as he went in the Miltonic or Petrarchan sonnet-form that he had used all summer, but in lines which spoke a different language from all his previous efforts. Once back at Dean Street, he fell on pen and paper, and so that tiredness should not confuse him, marked down the right-hand margin exactly where the sonnet-rhymes should come; then, with only one after-thought of correction, he wrote

On the first looking into Chapman's Homer

Much have I travell'd in the Realms of Gold,
  And many goodly States and Kingdoms seen,
  Round many Western islands have I been
Which Bards in fealty to Apollo hold.
Oft of one wide expanse had I been told,
           deep
Which ~~low~~ brow'd Homer ruled as his Demesne:
  Yet could I never judge what Men could mean,
Till I heard Chapman speak out loud and bold.

Then felt I like some Watcher of the Skies
  When a new Planet swims into his Ken,
Or like stout Cortez, when with wond'ring eyes
  He star'd at the Pacific, and all his Men
Look'd at each other with a wild surmise—
  Silent upon a Peak in Darien.

He sealed the paper in the form of a letter, found an early-morning postal messenger, and despatched it to Clerkenwell, where Clarke, coming down to breakfast at ten o'clock, was amazed and delighted to find the sonnet on his table.[1]

The poem has an authority never heard in Keats before. It is whole in conception and imagery, and carries through its theme to the end; far from weakening in the sestet, as many early sonnets by Keats do, it reinforces the first line's statement of Conquistador discovery with the memorable and exact picture of the Spanish adventurer and the new ocean. It is the first poem by Keats to have the fully free movement of original creation; something may be due here to the extreme physical tiredness under which it was composed. His bodily energies were so restless that they often needed damping-down to allow mental creation; the same type of situation a few

1. C. Cowden Clarke, *Recollections of Writers*, 128–130.

D

years later produced *La Belle Dame Sans Merci*. Three main elements can be seen in the sonnet's composition. First, of course, was the immediate effect of the exact passages in Chapman's Homer that Keats and Clarke read. Clarke detailed these with fewer lapses of memory than he sometimes made. They read mostly in the *Iliad*, choosing, in Clarke's words, "some of the 'famousest' passages, as we had scrappily known them in Pope's version". The one passage from the *Odyssey* that Clarke mentions is the scene of Ulysses's shipwreck from Book 5 which earned, Clarke said, "the reward of one of his delighted stares", elsewhere described as "that earnest stare, and protrusion of the upper lip".[1] Though Clarke implied that the phrase "the sea had soaked his heart through" had this particular effect on Keats—a phrase incidentally not in Homer but introduced by the translator[2]—there is no doubt the poem echoes the beginning of the voyage of Ulysses, with its imagery of stars and ocean:

> He beheld the Pleiades;
> The Bear, surnamed the Wain, that round doth move
> About Orion, and keeps still above
> The billowy ocean.

As Clarke noted, certain passages in the *Iliad* had such a stirring effect on Keats that "he sometimes shouted". These were from Books 3, 5 (not 3 again, as Clarke says) and 13. From Book 3 they read the description of the orator Ithacus

> But when out of his ample breast he gave his great voice pass,
> And words that flew about our eares, like drifts of winter's snow;
> None thenceforth, might contend with him;

From Book 5, another star and ocean simile described the helmet and shield of Diomed as being

> Like rich Autumnus golden lampe, whose brightness men admire,
> Past all the other host of starres, when with his chearefull face,
> Fresh washt in loftie Ocean waves, he doth his skies enchase.

From Book 13 they read the description of Neptune which tells how

> the great Sea-rector spied,
> Who sate aloft on th'utmost top, of shadie Samothrace,

and his journey through his sea-domains, blazing with gold;

> His bright and glorious pallace built, of never-rusting gold;
> And there arriv'd, he put in Coach, his brazen-footed steeds,
> All golden man'd, and pac't with wings; and all in golden weeds
> He cloth'd himself.

1. KC, II, 148.   2. Ward, 74.

Clearly the dominant images of the poem, the "realms of gold", the ocean, the stars and planets, the figure gazing out to sea, and the great voice speaking, form an almost literal survey of the parts of Chapman that Keats had just read.[1]

As well as being an instantaneous response, the poem is a summing-up of much that had accumulated in Keats's life and thought all through his apprentice years. Once again, under deep emotion, he reverted to the events of his schooldays, especially now, as he shared a profound experience with Clarke. Perhaps for this reason, a great deal of his past reading at school fused with his immediate reading that night. Robertson's *History of America*[2] and Bonnycastle's *Astronomy* helped the imagery of Cortez and of the new planet, together with more recent reading in Shakespeare and in Wordsworth. Keats's experience of the sea, and a deeply-seated belief in the inspiration of Apollo, God of poetry and healing, are there too. The poem is an expression of his life at the exact point he had reached. It also expresses his dream of a new life about to open before him on meeting Hunt, the "Era in my existence" he anticipated when he wrote to Clarke.[3] This new era was matched by the new planet and the new ocean of his sonnet. Keats himself stands on the edge of discovery, like the Spanish explorer and the astronomer Herschel.

This same quality of anticipation is vividly described by Clarke in his recollections of the actual day, sometime in the week beginning 13 October, when he and Keats walked out to Hampstead to keep the appointment with Hunt:[4]

The character and expression of Keats's features would arrest even the casual passenger in the street; and now they were wrought to a tone of animation that I could not but watch with interest.... As we approached the Heath, there was the rising and accelerated step, with the gradual subsidence of all talk.

Hunt was also to remember the meeting, not only for the physical impact of the young poet, but for the "sheaf" of poems, including the just-written sonnet that he carried with him. Poems and poet combined for Hunt in

the impression made upon me by the exuberant specimens of genuine though young poetry that were laid before me, and the promise of which was seconded by the fine fervid countenance of the writer. We became intimate on the spot, and I found the young poet's heart as warm as his imagination.[5]

1. Lowell, I, 176–179.
2. From which, as often pointed out, he confused Balboa's first sight of the Pacific with Cortez's first sight of Mexico City.
3. It is generally stated that the meeting with Hunt took place before Keats wrote the sonnet. Hunt himself, however, implies that the sonnet was among a "sheaf" of poems—the fair copies Keats mentions on 9 October—handed to him by Keats. E. No. 466, p. 761.
4. C. Cowden Clarke, *Recollections of Writers*, 133.
5. Leigh Hunt, *Lord Byron . . .*, 247.

Hunt's generosity about other men's work made him the perfect entrepreneur for new poetry, if the financial difficulties of his life and the habitual chaos of his house did not interfere. Although, thanks to the latter, Hunt had completely lost the manuscript of the poem Shelley had just sent him, Keats was more fortunate in the fate of the copies he now handed over. Hunt showed them to all his friends—Godwin, Hazlitt, and Basil Montague in particular—and, he was gratified to find, "they were pronounced to be as extraordinary as I thought them".

"The interview", said Clarke, "stretched into three morning calls", and, he added, "Keats was suddenly made a familiar of the household." This could not possibly be combined with regular attendance at lectures and exacting duties as a dresser at Guy's Hospital, five or six miles away. Clarke probably exaggerated, since Keats certainly attended lectures and fulfilled some duties of his dressership after being absorbed into Hunt's circle; but the real crisis of decision between the claims of medicine and poetry came at this moment. It was a double dilemma, the first part of which had nothing to do with poetry, but with Keats's own temperamental difficulties as a surgeon. Charles Brown later wrote[1]

He has assured me the muse had no influence over him in his determination, he being compelled, by conscientious motives alone, to quit the profession, upon discovering that he was unfit to perform a surgical operation. He ascribed his inability to an over-wrought apprehension of every possible chance of doing evil in the wrong direction of the instrument. 'My last operation', he told me, 'was the opening of a man's temporal artery. I did it with the utmost nicety; but, reflecting on what passed through my mind at the time, my dexterity seemed a miracle, and I never took up the lancet again.'

Keats's dislike of surgery may have been partly temperamental, as he himself suggested, the fault of identifying himself too much with the patients' feelings and the chances of failure.[2] Yet he was by now so experienced as a dresser, with countless minor operations performed, with, in his own words, the utmost nicety and dexterity, that another cause is likely. He had seen too much of the bungling of Lucas, whose own senior colleagues were horrified with apprehension—Keats's own term—when he operated, for fear of his "opening arteries or some other error". Keats must have seen at close quarters Lucas make the mistake of opening an artery instead of performing a simple venesection, or opening a vein to let blood, frequently done from the temple. The fear of doing what Lucas had done communicated itself to Keats.[3] Moreover, that very October, Keats had heard Astley Cooper tell the

1. KC, II, 56.   2. Ward, 59.

3. Brown's slip of memory or lack of understanding substituted what Keats was afraid of doing, "the opening of a man's temporal artery", for what he in fact performed successfully, the opening of a vein; but his account, though confused, points to Keats's area of apprehension.

story of a Guy's dresser, who had made this exact mistake; the patient lost thirty-seven ounces of blood, and died.[1]

The second and much larger decision, to give up medicine generally as a profession, came of his own free will. He again told Brown, "In no period of my life have I acted with any self will, but in throwing up the apothecary-profession." Keats gave this up because he came slowly to feel he should not or could not combine it with literature. This autumn he found he could no longer concentrate on his lectures. "The other day, for instance", he told Cowden Clarke, "during a lecture, there came a sunbeam into the room, and with it a whole troop of creatures floating in the ray; and I was off with them to Oberon and fairyland." A junior demonstrator, Walter Cooper Dendy, claimed to notice that now "in the lecture room of St. Thomas's . . . his mind was on Parnassus with the Muses . . . while the precepts of Sir Astley Cooper fell unheeded on his ear."[2] Yet the medical profession was not distasteful to him in any way; it was only "the Hammond days" of his apprenticeship that he ever regretted. He had found his hospital training interesting and useful. He did not give away his medical text-books, and congratulated himself on having kept them, while at various times in his life, he seems to have contemplated quite readily the idea that he might take up medicine as a profession again.[3] He prescribed and advised medically for his friends and brothers, and was ready with minor first-aid. The best of his poems have an objective exactness which undoubtedly developed through the study of medicine. Even such an apparently imaginative simile as

With the wreath'd trellis of a working brain

from the Ode to Psyche was suggested by medical theories which he read in his text-books or learnt from his anatomy lectures.

The double decision—to give up both the profession of a surgeon and the practice of medicine—could not be put into effect at once. Keats was still a fortnight short of his twenty-first birthday, still legally responsible to his sole guardian Abbey. He was outwardly merely a doctor addicted to poetry, "little Keats", regarded by his fellow medical students as a "cheerful, crotchety rhymester".[4] Yet inwardly the die had been cast for poetry, and the new era in his existence, which he had anticipated, was already beginning.

1. *The Lancet* (1823), I, 4–5. Cooper's introductory Surgical lecture was standard, year by year.
2. Dendy, op. cit., 100. Keats's relatively full notes for his lectures in autumn term 1815 place this anecdote in autumn 1816.
3. *Letters*, I, 276; II, 70, 114, 121, 125, 298.
4. B. W. Richardson, *The Asclepiad*, 139; C. Cowden Clarke, *Recollections of Writers*, 132.

Chapter 7

STANDING APART

"And other Spirits there are standing apart
Upon the Forehead of the Age to come."

– JOHN KEATS, *Poems*, 1817

KEATS, on the eve of his twenty-first birthday, had an extraordinarily attractive physical presence, best described by Severn, though the country walks with Keats, which so impressed the young painter, did not take place till the following summer.[1] Severn noted that although Keats was small, not more than three-quarters of an inch over five feet, he seemed taller, partly because of the erect carriage of his limbs and head, partly because of the perfect proportion of his body, but most of all because of his expression, which Severn described as dauntless, "such as may be seen on the face of some seamen".[2] Only when deep in thought or reading was his tiny stature noticeable. His eyes, hazel and gypsy-coloured, impressed everyone. They seemed to glow and almost to throw out a light of their own in front of him, "just like those of certain birds that habitually front the sun". This eagle or hawklike appearance of Keats was unfortunately softened by Severn in his many portraits, but it impressed the painter strongly during life; this was the quality that made people turn round to look at Keats in the street. His complexion was bright and glowing, his features quivering and mobile. His large pugnacious mouth with jutting upper lip was noted by some of Keats's friends as an oddity, but not enough to spoil the impression everyone had of a head like a Greek god, small, neat and oval. His hair was reddish-gold, wavy and alive; "the silken curls felt like the rich plumage of a bird".[3]

There was another side to this dashing and lively picture. Severn was almost totally unreliable over facts and dates, but visually he was a trained observer. He was one of the few outside Keats's own family to record the reverse of the medal. Keats had moods when all the life seemed to go out of him. When nervous or depressed, he seemed on casual acquaintance to be the opposite of his usual attractive self, loose, slack and insignificant. This sudden change marked the onset of what he recognized as his own black moods, when he would become suspicious, irrational, brooding over small faults and diffi-

1. Not, as often said, summer 1816; see Finney, I, 219 for the correct dating.
2. Appendix 2.   3. KC, II, 268.

culties so that in his own words they became "a theme for Sophocles". At these times, Severn noted, he would answer harshly and coldly or not speak at all, and his eyes, the only part of his face to seem alive, would darken and veil themselves in shadows as if "consumed by some secret and fatal anguish". These depressive swings were sometimes fatal also for friendship. It is a fact that for all his remarkable tolerance, there was hardly a friend of Keats who did not disillusion him at one time or another, or of whom he did not speak with bitterness, though often to retract generously with an apology for what he called his "lunes". His closest friends, like his family, came to accept this as a part of him which did not cloud, and indeed could almost enhance the rest of his nature. These two sides to Keats's life, temporarily masked by the placid period of his apprenticeship, demonstrated in the grown man how deep the divisions of childhood had been.

Few people could have been better chosen to bring out the happy side of Keats's nature than his new friend Leigh Hunt. Himself a lifelong optimist, who, as one of his sons remarked, seldom viewed anything as it really was, Hunt was not without knowledge of the dark side of life; debts, illness and domestic tension haunted his household, and he had just suffered some form of nervous breakdown after his two-year imprisonment. It was his tragedy to have always the air of a child prodigy who had not quite fulfilled his promise, and much of his lightheartedness was whistling to keep his courage up. Through the rosy glow in which he enveloped his own position he could nevertheless see the troubles of others, and he was a particularly good friend in a crisis, as Shelley, just now moving toward one of his inevitable and recurrent collisions with grim reality, was shortly to find. The idyllic setting Hunt had now deliberately given himself, the white-painted cottage in the Vale of Health in the middle of Hampstead Heath, full of music, pictures, busts, flowers and books, disguised at first the chronic disorder of slattern wife, bluestocking sister-in-law, ill-organized children and his own dilettante fecklessness; in fact it charmed those who had lived hard and seriously, to find this oasis where high ideals seemed to be lived lightly. Hunt's professed aims were "to promote the happiness of his kind, to minister to the more educated appreciation of order and beauty, to open more widely the door of the library, and more widely the window of the library looking out upon nature". They found an instant echo in Keats.

Hunt fulfilled at this moment one paramount need in a young poet, the companionship of a professional, practising literary man. On the edge of choosing literature rather than medicine as a profession, Keats needed to discuss the whole basis and nature of poetry, and to weigh the merits of the "many Bards" of his own sonnet. Many of Hunt's tastes, such as the worship of Spenser, already coincided with his own; some were novel, for there is no mention of a new hero, Chaucer, before this time.[1] Some were extended by

1. Cowden Clarke implies that Keats did not begin to read Chaucer till the following

Hunt, who probably introduced Keats to the poem of Wordsworth he came to value most highly, the long philosophic *The Excursion*, published in 1814. This alone would make Hunt one of Keats's highest poetic benefactors. Hunt, according to some objectors, introduced Keats only to one aspect of these poets, stressing the more decorative style and the minor embellishments, and missing the harder core of their work. Such critics fail to realize how far Keats had formed his own tastes before he met Hunt. He was too deeply read in Wordsworth, for instance, to be permanently affected by Hunt's personal domestication of the older poet's rugged philosophy and style, though he may have swung for a few weeks between the original source and its persuasive imitator. It has not been usually noticed that the poems of Keats influenced by the less happy aspects of Hunt's style—*An Induction, Calidore*, the summer sonnets and verse-epistles—were all written before he had met Hunt in the flesh. They are the product of Hunt the editor of *The Examiner* and Hunt the author of *Rimini*, but not of Hunt the professional literary man. Keats needed intensely such a person, after years of well-meant but amateur criticism and appreciation. Mathew, Stephens, his own brothers, even Clarke, were out of touch when compared with Hunt, their tastes conventional to a degree, their reading limited, especially in the moderns. A man who not only wrote poetry and poetic criticism himself, but who knew established modern poets such as Wordsworth, and those not yet established such as Shelley, brought reality and health into Keats's vague idealization of the poetic function. At last he could talk poetry with a poet.

Keats had, moreover, a side that positively enjoyed excess and did not jib at vulgarity. His love of the grotesque persisted all his life,[1] together with other down-to-earth feelings. "I scout 'mild light and loveliness' or any such nonsense in myself", he remarked when an admirer used this phrase about him.[2] If Hunt partly satisfied this side of him, the first friend he was to meet through Hunt in the middle of October 1817 gave him all he could have wished for. Benjamin Robert Haydon the painter was in the middle of a fortnight's holiday from his crowded painting-room at 42 Great Marlborough Street, and had taken lodgings at 7 Pond Street, Hampstead. He had known Hunt ever since the founding of *The Examiner*, to which he contributed articles and reviews on art. During the same time, he had campaigned incessantly on behalf of the Elgin marbles, since 1808 when he was first overwhelmed by their truth and beauty. The culmination of his violent

---

February (*Recollections of Writers*, 139). The parallels between Chaucer and some of Keats's poems written late in 1816, noted by Woodhouse, indicate a slightly earlier familiarity. Sperry, 119.

1. C. Cowden Clarke, *Recollections of Writers*, 114. Keats's anecdote about a pregnant woman (*Letters*, II, 236), often taken as an indication of his ill-health or his friends' bad influence, is an ordinary example of this love of the grotesque and earthy.

2. *Letters*, II, 17.

assertions, against most critical opinion, that these were genuine works of Greek art and should be acquired by the nation, had just come in 1816 with an onslaught on their behalf in *The Examiner* against Payne Knight, a director of the British Institution. Haydon believed, though no one knows the truth, that this finally turned the scale for purchase. This campaign, and his later lectures to working-class audiences in the provinces, constituted his real gift to British art, one which he never fulfilled in his own painting. With an often-admitted preference for words rather than paint as a medium of expression, Haydon obstinately spent his life doing the thing for which he was least fitted. He set his defective sight and excitable brain to the most exacting task he could possibly have contrived for them, the production of huge pictures in the high Renaissance manner. In an era of neat Georgian box-like dwellings, no one except a few owners of large country mansions could afford wall-space. Haydon's life was therefore spent in trying to persuade aristocratic patrons to buy large areas of canvas which they did not really want, and which he had to drive himself to paint. For over two years he had been engaged on a mammoth work, "Christ's Entry into Jerusalem", which took him nearly four more to complete. His gusto for life was voracious, his observation vivid, but his inner thoughts were often on the verge of mania. Huge ghostly figures of Religion, High Art and Sex haunted the private pages of his voluminous journal, in which he had recently recorded that

The three summits of human happiness are first the consciousness of having done your duty & the pious purity that comes over your Soul. The next, success in great schemes, & the third is a lovely girl who loves you, in the dining room of the Star & Garter at Richmond, sitting after dinner on your knee . . .[1]

For Keats here was a grotesque ready-made with the additional attraction of his picturesque gifts of expression. Just as Keats had given "a delighted stare" at Chapman's phrase about Ulysses, "the sea had soaked his heart through", so he responded to this short-legged bull-necked man, who could describe his own sea-bathing at Bo Peep, near Hastings, in the same epic terms, not forgetting indeed to compare himself with Ulysses.[2] There were more solid grounds for the friendship; Haydon also knew Wordsworth, and in fact it was he who had introduced him to Hunt in the summer of 1815. He was a tremendous reader of Shakespeare, whose plays he quoted continually all through his life and literally in his dying moments. He was also an admirer of the younger contemporary poets, and Reynolds had dedicated *The Naiad* to him. Sweeping into Hunt's cottage, where he called nearly every day of the holiday, he seized upon the new young poet, inviting him to dine at Pond Street and meet Reynolds.

John Hamilton Reynolds, whom Keats encountered at Haydon's on Sunday 20 October, was a third and very welcome element in Keats's new life, a young and approachable writer of about his own age, with a growing but not too overwhelming reputation. The two older men, Hunt and Haydon, were essentially set in the mould they would maintain all their lives. Reynolds, for all his sophisticated bearing and dark, fashionable good looks, had an uncertainty in his eyes and an expression that suggested a man who had not yet found his métier. Reynolds's father was a schoolmaster, now teaching at Christ's Hospital, and living nearby in the City with his wife, who was a writer of sorts, and four daughters. John, the only son, had become at sixteen a junior clerk in an insurance office. He had a similar social environment to Keats's and a business experience parallel with Keats's apprenticeship days. As well as being just a year older, he was a quicker developer. At eighteen he had published his first book of verse and *The Naiad*, of which pre-publication copies were now circulating, was his fourth. In spite of this early achievement, he felt an uneasiness about his life and work which showed itself in frequent bouts of worry and ill-health. On the other hand, he was always an excellent companion, with a playful intelligent wit, whose effervescence Keats once compared to ginger-beer. In his search for a congenial career, which would enable him to write, Reynolds was moving away from insurance and towards the Law, which he eventually entered. Keats, having made his own secret decision about medicine and poetry, felt that here for once was someone he himself could help. Their friendship was a steadily-deepening one. It survived the treacherous sharpness of Reynolds's wit, and Keats's later irritation with the cloying sentimentality of Reynolds's sisters and their gushing mother. Much of Keats's deepest thought about poetry was expressed in letters to Reynolds, and it is significant that he could think of bringing out a joint book with him. Reynolds's own letters show him incorporating, almost without realizing it, phrases in poetry and prose from Keats, using them as familiar quotations to people who could not have known their origins.

Reynolds's quicksilver quality, which led Keats to compare him to the god Mercury, showed indeed that he was not a poet but a brilliant imitator. Friends noticed, though he denied it, that the long poem he had in hand resembled Beattie's *The Minstrel*. One early book was an imitation of Byron, just as *The Naiad* imitated Wordsworth. His real genius, like that of Horace Smith, lay in parody, and his skit on Wordsworth's *Peter Bell* is one of the greatest parodies of all time. All Keats's three new friends, in fact, were flawed in ways only the future could show. Hunt ended not altogether unfairly portrayed by Dickens as Skimpole, Haydon in ghastly suicide, and Reynolds, more self-critical, as "that poor obscure—baffled Thing,—myself!"[1]

Within a week, Keats had aroused the interest of these three quite different men. Biographers have dwelt on Keats's need, as an orphan, to find a father figure, or on his role as a "gifted child" to seek the company of older men.[2]

1. KC, II, 231.   2. Bate, 52.

In fact, many of Keats's friends, Reynolds for instance, were only marginally older, and some, like Severn, had considerably less mature temperaments. All, it appears, sought him, rather than he seeking them, and came jealously to regard him as their discovery, a unique being. There was also the detail that Keats appeared in this often-struggling community of artists and writers to be a well-to-do young man. Hunt was doubtless sincere when he wrote, "Keats and I might have been taken for friends of the old stamp, between whom there was no such thing even as obligation, except the pleasure of it"; yet the fact that Keats seemed to have money as well as talent cannot have been overlooked. Keats's money-situation was to cause him so much trouble, and indeed was so extraordinary in itself, that it has often been misunderstood.[1] Now, at his twenty-first birthday, it presented a series of dramatic ironies, stemming from the Chancery case. His grandfather's fortune and the comfortable Edmonton home had given Keats a feeling that there would always be money somewhere; but his revulsion from the family battle over the inheritance had given him a horror of ever enquiring into the details. It is clear that all through his life he automatically shut off his mind when matters of business were mentioned. Such a shrinking from fact was understandable; but, from his twenty-first birthday onward, it was to maim the material side of his life, and plunge him into endless difficulty. His financial position at coming-of-age seemed simple. He was then entitled to possess for himself two trust funds, his grandmother's, now administered by Richard Abbey, and his grandfather's, administered by the Accountant General in Chancery. Of these, his grandmother's had originally been by far the larger, but it had been drained by his six years' professional training. As a result, it was by now the smaller of the two, only a few hundred pounds, while his grandfather's, of about £800 capital, had the advantage of some accumulated cash interest. Prudent advice might have led Keats to transfer the two sets of capital intact to his own name, and reinvest his grandfather's interest. He would then have had about £50 a year to live on while building up a surgical practice.

This advice was never given, and Keats's actions, or lack of action, could not have been more wildly different from this course. On the one hand, after some delay in obtaining proof that he actually was twenty-one, he chose to cash the remnants of his grandmother's capital. His behaviour towards his grandfather's trust fund was startling. He never applied to Chancery for it; it is quite clear that he never knew that it was there, and never made any enquiry to find out. This appears so strange that Richard Abbey has been accused of concealing the existence of this fund. To account for this suppositious and extraordinary action, since Abbey could have benefited in no way from it himself, a motive of Puritanical sadism has been invented. In

1. Dilke claimed with some justice "to know more of Keats's affairs than Keats himself" (Sharp, 199), but even he was ignorant of the full situation.

fact, Abbey, like Keats, was ignorant of the fund, which was no concern of his and which had come into existence at an earlier date than his guardianship. The one living person who knew, and could have set matters in motion, was the family solicitor, Walton; but a busy solicitor with a very large practice, as he had, cannot always be expected to remind his clients when they should take initiative. Keats must have learnt from his grandmother before her death that he had financial expectations, but she had obviously failed to explain that these came from two sources. His morbid reluctance to enquire more closely into his inheritance deprived him of more than half of it. At the same time, the feeling that he had a potentially large inheritance led him to spend and lend what he touched freely. As a result, he never had as much as he hoped for his needy friends, while his well-to-do friends never realized that he could not afford their style of living.[1] Financially he was henceforth at the mercy of a situation he never understood.

These difficult rocks, on which friendship was to founder between Keats and Haydon, were far in the future; Keats was on the crest of the wave of his new relationships all through the rest of October 1816. The first immediate result was a spurt forward with his long Wordsworthian "Endymion" poem, and for a good reason. He was reinforced in his reading of Wordsworth by Hunt's new enthusiasm for The Excursion in general, and Book IV in particular. This was the section, with the significant title "Despondency Corrected", in which Wordsworth extolled the learning and philosophy of past civilizations, and, most especially, the mythology of classical Greece. To Keats, with whole passages of Lemprière in his head, this struck an answering chord. The next eighty lines of his "Endymion" poem, ending with his actually naming his hero, are an entirely Wordsworthian celebration of Greek pantheism. They trace, exactly as Wordsworth had done in this part of The Excursion, the creation of myths to the inspiration of the poet by nature. The poet's vision of nature creates legends of Fauns, Dryads, Pan, Zephyr and Narcissus, looking first of all on natural objects and then, "with small help from fancy", transforming them into these eternal prototypes. Wordsworth seen clear, and not at all weakened through Hunt's intervention, inspires the best section of Keats's long poem.[2] As was his habit while on a long work, he threw off sonnets at the same time. These have a more Huntian ring, or rather they are the type of sonnet Hunt liked to print in The Examiner, domestic and occasional. Two of them, On Leaving some Friends at an Early Hour and its unnamed counterpart beginning "Keen, fitful gusts", were written on two separate evenings at Hunt's cottage. The first, after a dinner with Hunt and Reynolds, which ended in Keats going home in a

1. KI, 36–39. Walton's own will suggests that his faculties were failing.
2. Ward, 424, n. 12 does not see any parallels between Keats and The Excursion until the real Endymion of 1817; but the likenesses between Book IV and "I stood tip-toe" lines 125–204 are too close to be ignored. See Finney, I, 175.

hackney coach,[1] echoes ineptly both his "Endymion" poem and the Chapman's Homer sonnet. The second, describing the long walk back to London through dry rustling lanes under a starry November sky, is more like Wordsworth in its direct and simple opening:

> Keen, fitful gusts are whisp'ring here and there
> Among the bushes half leafless, and dry;
> The stars look very cold about the sky,
> And I have many miles on foot to fare.

More in *The Examiner* manner, and indeed borrowing from Horace Smith's sonnet in the issue of Sunday 27 October,[2] was the sonnet *To A Young Lady who sent me a Laurel Crown*. Laurel crowns were bandied about, both as figures of speech and in actual fact, in Hunt's circle, though this young lady was probably a new addition to the acquaintances Keats continued to make through his brother George. Such introductions tended to fall off, however, from now onward. Keats was becoming more independent of George, less likely to be grateful for the company of poetical tradespeople such as Mathew. George began to get his friends from Keats rather than the other way about, and these friends themselves proliferated. Reynolds alone in the next few months introduced Keats to six lasting friends.[3] Clarke, delighted at his succesful venture, pressed on, and partly engineered Keats's first breakfast at Haydon's painting-room.[4]

This Sunday meeting, on 3 November, to see "this glorious Haydon and all his Creation", as Keats put it in one of his many musical puns, was marked by favourable auspices. Keats was in high spirits, having spent the day before in the country "to look into some beautiful Scenery—for poetical purposes"; many of the lines in "I stood tip-toe", which describe the poet doing this, were probably written that Saturday evening. Then the copy of *The Examiner*, which came out that Sunday, announced the publication on "the earliest opportunity" of the Chapman's Homer Sonnet together with some selections of Reynolds's *The Naiad*. Haydon had also good reason to be pleased with this number of *The Examiner*. It contained a review by William Hazlitt of the Catalogue Raisonné of the British Institution, which, as the writer said, "is pretty well understood to be a declaration of the views of the Royal Academy". To Haydon's delight, the critic pitched into that hated body with all the very considerable invective at his disposal. The Academy was characterized as "a merchantile body, like any other merchantile body, consisting chiefly of manufacturers of portraits". He condemned their work as meretricious, and compared their exhibitions to a brothel. He defined the three requisites for good painting as gusto, the picturesque, and close

---

1. Woodhouse's note, Sperry, 150. 2. E. No. 461, p. 673.
3. Taylor, Hessey, Dilke, Brown, Rice, Bailey. *Letters*, I, 85.
4. *Letters*, I, 114–116.

imitation, and lashed the Academicians for being deficient in all three, ending "The public have seen to the contrary. They see the quackery. . . ."[1]

Haydon, in Renaissance manner, introduced portraits of his friends into the crowd for his painting of Christ's Entry into Jerusalem. Hazlitt sat for his portrait this Sunday, and it was probably at this time in Haydon's studio that Keats first met him.[2] If so, Keats saw the critic at his most expansive, full of ideas for the Round Table essays which were his chief contribution to *The Examiner*. Their meeting was the beginning of an admiration for Hazlitt which Keats maintained all the rest of his life with only minor reservations. There were indeed possibilities of the grotesque in this new acquaintance too, "brow-hanging, shoe-contemplative, *strange*", as Coleridge had called him. Keats was quick to make a friendly parody of his mannerisms, his excited interjections of "By God!" when anything moved him, and his other self into which he would withdraw and say literally nothing but "yes" and "no" for an entire evening.[3] Yet his own moods of elation and deep-set depression made Keats more ready than most of their circle to sympathize with the same manic-depressive swing in Hazlitt's temperament. He could understand the older man's morbid convictions of failure. "How is Hazlitt?" he wrote to Reynolds less than a year after their meeting, "We were reading his (Round) Table last night—I know he thinks himself not estimated by ten People in the world—I wishe he knew he is—".[4] Hazlitt was the only modern writer that Keats quoted at length in his letters, and it is sometimes difficult to disentangle Keats's prose from Hazlitt's, so alike is the style and thought.

How Hazlitt appeared to Keats in the expansive atmosphere of Haydon's studio is described by Reynolds, writing about a similar occasion only a few months later, when the critic was at his remarkable best,

full of eloquence,—Warm, lofty & communicative on every thing Imaginative & Intelligent,—breathing out with us the peculiar & favourite beauties of our best Bards,—Passing from grand & commanding argument to the gaieties & graces of Wit & humour,—and the elegant and higher beauties of Poetry. He is indeed *great* company, and leaves a weight on the mind, which "it can hardly bear." He is full of what Dr Johnson terms "Good talk." His countenance is also extremely fine:—a sunken & melancholy face,—a forehead lined with thought and bearing a full & strange pulsation on exciting subjects,—an eye, dashed in its light with sorrow, but kindling & *living* at intellectual moments,—and a stream of coal-black hair dropping round all.[5]

Hazlitt dashed his conversation throughout, as he did his essays, with "the peculiar & favourite beauties of our best Bards". He and Haydon, once got together, probably produced more quotation from Shakespeare than any other two men of their age, and it is no accident that from this winter

1. E. No. 462, pp. 696–699.   2. Haydon, II, 64.
3. *Letters*, I, 123 and II, 14.   4. *Letters*, I, 166.   5. KHM, No. 155.

Shakespeare becomes the presider above all others in Keats's literary Pantheon. This Sunday was the first of many in Haydon's studio, and he soon grew to quote as exuberantly as his host. Haydon remembered how Keats himself walked up and down the painting-room, "spouting Shakespeare", and then suddenly realized that he was on call at Guy's and dashed from the symposium to Mr. Lucas's unhappy patients and his own duties as dresser.[1]

What the occasion certainly produced was Keats's first, though not his best sonnet addressed to Haydon, and beginning "Highmindedness, a jealousy for good." Though it owes something to Wordsworth's and Hunt's sonnets to Haydon, which had already appeared in *The Examiner*, it owes more to Hazlitt's review of the Catalogue Raisonné. The Academicians were characterized, just as they had been by Hazlitt, as a group of merchants, "A money-mong'ring pitiable brood", and the sonnet's conclusion puts its trust, as Hazlitt had done, in the natural good taste of ordinary inarticulate people, so that

> Unnumber'd souls breathe out a still applause,
> Proud to behold him in his country's eye.

This sonnet also provided further proof that Keats's admiration of Wordsworth was as strong as ever, and had not been in any way diluted by what Haydon called Hunt's "sophistications". Half a line from the octave of the sonnet is an extract in quotation marks from Wordsworth's *The Happy Warrior*, a "singleness of aim", which he applied happily, as the painter doubtless thought, to Haydon's monomania.

Another meeting arranged for Keats by Clarke was with Charles Ollier, who with his brother James ran a bookselling and publishing business in Welbeck Street.[2] Once again, in all probability, Hunt made the introduction, but Clarke clinched it, knowing the procrastinations of Hunt's many-sided life. The Olliers were anxious to do new poetry. Keats began to think in terms of a volume. He also had to think in concrete physical terms of how to organize his life. Winter was coming on, and he could not always be walking the "many miles" of his sonnet between Hampstead and Southwark. Even though a sofa-bed was made up for him in Hunt's library, so that he could stay the night whenever he wanted,[3] there were still his early duties on operation days at Guy's; he had not yet put into practice his secret resolve to break with medicine, for he had only just turned twenty-one, and was still waiting legal proof, from a servant of his parents', that he was of age to come into his depleted inheritance.[4] He would have to be patient for a few more weeks. Meanwhile, to ease the strain, he hit on a compromise, which

1. Haydon, II, 101.   2. *Letters*, I, 115.
3. C. Cowden Clarke, *Recollections of Writers*, 134.
4. Haydon, II, 107.

would have an additional advantage of saving money. About the middle of November, he moved from Dean Street into lodgings at 76 Cheapside with George and Tom. It was one lap on the journey to Hampstead, and not too far from hospital across London Bridge. The lodgings were well placed for three young bachelors. Just at that point an archway led off Cheapside into Bird-in-Hand Court; the Keats boys had rooms on the second floor to the west of the arch, a very short way from Bow Church.[1] In Bird-in-Hand Court itself, there was the Queen's Arms Eating-House, from which dinners and suppers could be sent up "at a short Notice, and at a moderate Expence". The freedom and the intimacy of this setting were touchingly recorded by Keats in the sonnet *To My Brothers*, written there on Monday 18 November, Tom Keats's birthday:

> Small, busy flames play through the fresh laid coals,
>   And their faint cracklings o'er our silence creep
>   Like whispers of the household gods that keep
> A gentle empire o'er fraternal souls.
> And while, for rhymes, I search around the poles,
>   Your eyes are fix'd, as in poetic sleep,
>   Upon the lore so voluble and deep,
> That aye at fall of night our care condoles.
> This is your birth-day Tom, and I rejoice
>   That thus it passes smoothly, quietly.
>   Many such eves of gently whisp'ring noise
> May we together pass, and calmly try
> What are this world's true joys,—ere the great voice,
>   From its fair face, shall bid our spirits fly.

This was indeed a poem "proceeding" as Wordsworth put it, "from sentiment and reflection", based very closely on No. XX of the poems in that section of his own volumes, the unnamed sequence of sonnets beginning

> I am not One who much or oft delight
> To season my fireside with personal talk,—

lines which Keats himself quoted in a letter. It is, in fact, the most Wordsworthian poem that Keats ever wrote, though it still bears his own special stamp. It is interesting too as the last poem written by Keats in Wordsworth's Christian tradition; though noted as a sceptic a year earlier, Keats had not yet allowed Hunt's agnosticism to intervene in his poetry. Yet its main feature is that it celebrates in verse the close-knit empire of the three brothers. Tom and George were to Keats a "fireside divan", as he himself described Wordsworth's circle of approving women, wife, sister and sister-in-law. They performed the same functions, copyists of his poems,—Tom

1. C. Cowden Clarke, *The Riches of Chaucer* (1835), 52.

was now keeping a notebook, in which this sonnet appears—supporters of his belief in himself, and companions with whom he shared his reading and thought. The poem is a reminder of his prose description of their relationship: "My Love for my Brothers from the early loss of our parents and even for earlier Misfortunes has grown into a affection 'passing the Love of Women'."[1]

It is also a reminder how much Keats lacked and needed a stable older person to advise him at this decisive point in his life. His new friends stimulated and encouraged him, and furthered his literary career; but, at twenty-one, he seemed utterly without family connections, an uncle or aunt or any relative of an older generation, who could tactfully have guided his material life without doing harm to his inner genius. The only older person in any way connected with him was Richard Abbey, whose place of business was a few yards away in Pancras Lane. The news he still had to tell his ex-guardian, that he was throwing up the profession for which he had been expensively trained, was hardly going to promote good relations between them, as Keats must have guessed. This curious lack of close relatives, for which his mother's unlucky lawsuit must bear most blame, was underlined by an equally curious circumstance about the new home occupied by the Keats boys. At 74 Cheapside, next door but one, was a prosperous and expanding hat-maker's business. Its owner's name was Joseph Keats. He controlled several hat-making establishments,[2] including probably that of his less reputable brother, Thomas Mower Keats,[3] again only a few doors away at 14 The Poultry, the eastward continuation of Cheapside. Forty years later, these hat-making brothers were claimed as relatives of Keats,[4] and modern writers have pointed out that Richard Abbey at various times suggested that both John and George Keats should go into the hat-making business.[5] Yet exhaustive enquiry has failed to establish any hint of relationship,[6] and indeed all available signs point to this being a pure coincidence. The stay at 76 Cheapside was an extremely social time, when many friends of Keats visited him there, and must have noticed the hat-making business and the coincidence of the name. No one, not even Cowden Clarke, who describes these lodgings minutely, ever mentions the hatter Keatses or suggests a relationship; nor does Keats, when writing of Abbey's plans of employment

1. *Letters*, I, 293.

2. Feltmakers Company Minutes, 1790–1825, G.L. MS 1570/6.

3. He married a Fortnum, but failed to enter their business, failed to pay his dues to the Feltmakers, and went bankrupt.

4. This claim of relationship arises from another Joseph Keats, a bookseller of Chelsea and Brighton, who also claimed to be Keats's second cousin and to have often discussed Keats with Leigh Hunt. Hunt, however, could not remember even meeting him. CLH, II, 261. See Appendix 2.

5. *Letters*, II, 77 and 192.

6. Jean Haynes, "Keats's Paternal Relatives", KSMB, XV, 27–28.

for him and George. Such a concerted silence, from so many sides, suggests that there was no relationship, in spite of the name, and that once again Keats had no blood-relatives to whom he could turn for advice.

With Abbey now so near at hand, the interview about Keats's future could not long be postponed. According to Abbey's own recollections, he himself took the initiative by proposing that his former ward should eventually set up in practice somewhere near Edmonton,[1] where his grandmother had been known and respected, and where the Keats boys still had many friends.[2] The result, copied by Taylor from Abbey's dinner-table conversation, has a ring of truth, typical of both their characters, and probably represents the authentic dialogue:

He communicated his plans to his Ward, but his Surprise was not moderate, to hear in Reply, that he did not intend to be a Surgeon—Not intend to be a Surgeon! why what do you mean to be? I mean to rely on my Abilities as a Poet—John, ~~are you Mad or Silly~~ you are either Mad or a Fool, to talk in so absurd a Manner. My Mind is made up, said the youngster very quietly. I know that I possess Abilities greater than most Men, and therefore I am determined to gain my Living by exercising them.—Seeing nothing could be done Abby called him a Silly Boy, & prophesied a speedy Termination to his inconsiderate Enterprise.

Whether this is a verbatim account or not, it clearly was not the sympathetic discussion Keats might have valued from one of his own stock and temperament. It is easy to make play with Abbey's lack of understanding, but he had received a genuine shock. He and Sandell had supported Keats up to the hilt in the high expenses of training for his own choice of profession. They could not have guessed that he might abandon it at this late stage, when nearly all his grandmother's money had been spent; Abbey himself had made such good use of whatever he had inherited from his Yorkshire grandfather and father that at Keats's age he had been master of his own business, married, and a Freeman of the City. To Abbey, Keats was a young man with only enough cash to last for a year or two, deliberately throwing away his prospects. The irony was that he, like Keats, was ignorant of the further fund in Chancery, though there is no guarantee he would have been any more in sympathy with Keats's project if he had known. The real disaster of this interview was that it deprived Keats of any possible advice, and left both sides touchy and suspicious during the whole of the rest of their association.

Reaction from this scene plunged Keats deeper into poetry, and at once into a sonnet that echoed his assertion to Abbey, "I know that I possess Abilities greater than most Men." On Tuesday 19 November he spent another enthusiastic evening with Haydon, which, in his own words,

1. Probably Enfield, just outside the ten-mile radius. The "Tottenham" of Taylor's account, KC, I, 307–308, must be a slip of the pen, since Keats had no licence to practise there.
2. *Letters*, I, 236.

wrought him up. In the sleepless night that followed, he composed a poem of quiet intensity. Unlike the sonnet it resembled, Wordsworth's "Great Men have been among us", Keats's "Great spirits now on earth are sojourning" looked not to the past, but to the present day. In the octave he celebrated his artistic mentors, Wordsworth, Hunt and Haydon himself; in the sestet he turned to the poets and artists of the future:

> And other Spirits there are standing apart
>   Upon the Forehead of the Age to come;
> These, these will give the World another heart
>   And other pulses—hear ye not the hum
> Of mighty Workings in a distant Mart?
>   Listen awhile ye Nations, and be dumb.

Set off by a line from yet another recent sonnet of Hunt's to Haydon, just printed in *The Examiner*,[1]

> 'Tis like the budding of an age new-born,

this passage clearly points to the aspirations of Keats himself. He echoed it in a conversation with Haydon next spring, and in a meeting at hospital with Stephens soon after, the latter noticed that "he gave himself up more completely than before to Poetry."[2] Haydon added fuel to his fire by proposing to send the sonnet to Wordsworth himself, a prospect which, Keats wrote, "put me out of breath", though Haydon did not actually manage to send it off till the end of the year.[3] More practically, he made one of his few successful critical suggestions about Keats's technique, so that the sonnet is always printed with the last four words of line 13 deleted, a bold technical device which leaves the imagination free to supply the sound "Of mighty Workings", as in some great artistic dynamo.

The sonnet went the rounds of their circle, inspiring a companion piece from Reynolds, whose over-receptive mind was always quick to catch a new tone of voice. To Keats the excitement it generated, in contrast with his dubious material prospects, brought a new hardening of purpose: "I begin to fix my eye upon one horizon—."[4] Meanwhile Hunt provided the final element that was to precipitate and complete the change in Keats's life. The editor of *The Examiner* decided not simply to print Shelley's *Hymn to Intellectual Beauty*, extracts from *The Naiad*, and the Chapman's Homer sonnet, as he had announced; deflected perhaps by having lost the manuscript of the first poem, he decided to work all three up into an article, *Young Poets*, which appeared on Sunday 1 December. Like nearly all Hunt's ephemeral articles, it promises more than it fulfils, and puts off airily to some future date further critical notice which in fact never appeared, though there

1. E. No. 464, p. 725.   2. Haydon, II, 106; KC, II, 211.
3. *Letters*, I, 118.   4. *Letters*, I, 118.

was a substantial quotation from *The Naiad*, and Shelley's poem, recovered, was printed under his own name next January. Keats received better treatment than his companions; Hunt paid tribute to his "ardent grappling with Nature", criticized his sonnet soundly and appreciatively, and printed it in full. The value to Keats was to be publicly recognized as a member of what Hunt called "a new school of poetry", a second wave of the revolution begun by Wordsworth and Coleridge, hailed by Hunt as being more promising than the first. Hunt's generous appreciation did not stop there. On the same day that the article appeared, he wrote a personal sonnet to Keats,[1] addressing his young poet by name, and foreseeing "a flowering laurel" on his brow. This confirmation of his powers, when he most needed it, swept all Keats's doubts away. He showed Hunt's article to Stephens, who remembered vividly the effect it had upon him. "This sealed his fate". From that moment, his apprentice years were over.

1. British Museum, Additional MSS, 33, 515. Garrod's statement, *Works*, lxxxi and 2, that the MS is not in Hunt's autograph, and that therefore the date is unreliable, has misled biographers. The sonnet, with MS alterations and the date, is unmistakably in Hunt's hand.

PART II

YEARS OF TRIAL

Chapter 8

PLEASURE'S TEMPLE

*"It was a poet's house who keeps the keys
Of Pleasure's temple."*

– Sleep and Poetry, lines 354–355

KEATS marked the turning-point in his life by the longest poem he had so far written. It seemed to his friends incomparably the best.[1] Far more coherent and unified than anything he had yet attempted, it was three times the length of any of his verse-epistles, and, unlike any of them, constructed on a logical pattern. Keats called it a "strange assay Begun in gentleness". It began one evening when he lay in the little bed made up for him in Hunt's parlour study. Sleep had been driven out of his head by the talk of poetry; his firelit surroundings continued these ideas. Classical busts and pictures looked down on him from the walls. A print of Poussin's "Empire of Flora" came into his mind, its foreground of Flora and her nymphs, and above them Apollo with his golden chariot; from his bed he could see another, taken from Stothart's picture of Petrarch's meeting with Laura. Everything seemed a symbol of the poetry to which he had just totally dedicated his life. Lines and phrases jumbled themselves in his head all the sleepless night, and when dawn came he rose up full of energy to write.

The plan of the poem was of extreme simplicity. The first forty lines record how sleep was expelled by poetry. The two are opposed; Keats does not yet see what he was later to describe as "indolence" as a necessary state for poetic creation.[2] Sleep may be "more full of visions than a high romance", but Poetry is "higher beyond thought" and can only be described in mysterious hints, such as Wordsworth used of his own inspiration. Keats repeats these in his own self-dedication to poetry in the next forty lines, in the Wordsworthian phrase:

> And many a verse from so strange influence
> That we must ever wonder how, and whence
> It came.

Like Wordsworth, too, he believes that these mysterious promptings must

1. Woodhouse's note, Sperry, 152.
2. Though Ward, 91, believes he already did.

103

be applied to actual life, "the events of this wide world", in order to become immortal poetry.

This point brought Keats up short. What had life so far been for him, but a series of the most violent contrasts?

> Stop and consider! life is but a day;
> A fragile dew-drop on its perilous way
> From a tree's summit; a poor Indian's sleep
> While his boat hastens to the monstrous steep
> Of Montmorenci. Why so sad a moan?
> Life is the rose's hope while yet unblown;
> The reading of an ever-changing tale;
> The light uplifting of a maiden's veil;
> A pigeon tumbling in clear summer air;
> A laughing schoolboy, without grief or care,
> Riding the springy branches of an elm.

For the first time, he saw both the tragic and the joyful, which he had experienced, as complementary to poetry; he developed this idea all through life to his last dying letter[1] where he spoke of "the knowledge of contrast, feeling for light and shade, all that information (primitive sense) necessary for a poem." Yet the famous lines that follow, beginning

> O for ten years, that I may overwhelm
> Myself in poesy;

were entirely free from premonition. He confidently looked forward to writing both pastoral and epic poems, symbolizing them by the garden of Flora and Apollo's chariot from the Poussin picture.

At this point, Keats's first doubts of himself as a poet emerge. His life, in spite of self-dedication, is too full of "stern realities", the tedious material side of the business of living.[2] Unfortunately, he chose to drown these doubts for the next hundred lines by a straight versification of Hunt's critical notes to the 1815 edition of his *The Feast of the Poets*. He had probably meant simply to have a meditation on the theme of Wordsworth's sonnet

> The World is too much with us; late and soon,
> Getting and spending, we lay waste our powers;

for he echoes the sonnet closely. Instead, he chose the easy way, and a second-hand slackness invaded his poem. He echoed Hunt's attack on Pope and the Augustans in the famous phrase

> They sway'd about upon a rocking horse,
> And thought it Pegasus

1. *Letters*, II, 360.   2. Woodhouse's note, Sperry, 154.

though the actual image was from Hazlitt's contribution to *The Examiner*, "On Milton's Versification".[1]

> Dr. Johnson and Pope would have converted his (Milton's)
> Pegasus into a rocking-horse.

Hunt's stricture on the French school of poetry, "Boileau, and their followers" was exactly repeated. Nor were Keats's attempts to refer to the best of modern poetry very happy. After conventional tributes to the early deaths of Kirke White and Chatterton, he praised Wordsworth, not in the resounding terms of his fine sonnet, but only in the tame image of the swan by a lake—singularly inappropriate to Wordsworth—which Keats had used in his own juvenile Byron sonnet. He praised Leigh Hunt in the terms of the latter's abortive masque, *The Descent of Liberty*. He turned to Byron, Wordsworth and Coleridge, and instead of expressing his own sympathy with Wordsworth, with which his own poems were now instinct, he chose to take the line still adopted by Hunt. He stressed and condemned the homely subject-matter of the *Lyrical Ballads* poems at the expense of what, he admitted, "is sweet and strong, From majesty". Romantic poets were to be deplored because of their themes, misrepresented as "Darkness, and worms, and shrouds, and sepulchres";[2] or, as Hunt had more jauntily put it, "thorns and duffel coats absolutely confound you". Even his hopes for the future of poetry, symbolized as a flowering myrtle,[3] only end in Hunt's idea that

> they shall be accounted poet kings
> Who simply tell the most heart-easing things.

Then, suddenly, the true theme of the poem returns. The next section, paying tribute to Wordsworth in almost every echo, is of quite different calibre. It presents

> The shiftings of the mighty winds that blow
> Hither and thither all the changing thoughts
> Of man

with a humility completely different from the previous passage; Keats confesses that he is as yet too inexperienced to sort out "the dark mysteries of human souls". With humility too he looks out over the "ocean dim" of the poetic tasks before him. This vision and its difficulty was too much for him. He broke off and added the epilogue he had perhaps already planned, bringing the poem back to the setting of Hunt's library where it had started.

1. E. No. 399, p. 542.

2. Woodhouse, Sperry, 155, makes this refer only to Byron, presumably for his recently-published *Darkness*, and to Coleridge's *Christabel*; but Wordsworth is also hinted at.

3. "Allusion to the coming age of poetry under the type of a myrtle" (Woodhouse's note, Sperry, 156).

Sleep and Poetry, for all its lapses and occasional loss of direction, had a completeness absent from any previous long poem by Keats. Unequivocally written about those things he had most at heart, literature and poetry, it took what had been the vague theme of the summer epistles and made it the motive force of a whole poem. Its inner intensity arose from Keats's own effort finally to convince himself that, in his own later words, "My occupation is entirely literary".[1] Keats was seeking all through the poem for a guiding principle, something more than merely a chance impulse to write, "a vast idea" through which he would come eventually to understand "The end and aim of Poesy". This idea marks out *Sleep and Poetry* from all his previous verse.

It also probably marks the moment when he realized that the legend of Cynthia and Endymion was too important a poetic symbol merely to be worked into his own "I stood tip-toe". Looking over these lines, jumbled together on various bits of paper ever since he started them in the summer, he began to feel the poem was far too spasmodic and formless for the larger task.

A glance at one of its lighter passages,[2] however, gave him the impetus for a charming personal sonnet at this time. Through George, still a source for friendships of a non-literary sort, he had met a pleasant family living at Westminster, Mrs. Wylie, the kindly widow of an infantry officer, and her three children of about his own age, Henry, Charles and Georgiana. The last-named was nineteen,[3] simple in her dress, shy in manner, warm-hearted like her mother, and—always a recommendation with Keats—not too tall.[4] Sensitive and individual, she was someone with whom Keats felt an instinctive sympathy, especially in her sincerity and genuine originality of mind. He was content to know her, as he afterwards said, for "mind and friendship alone"; perhaps this feeling was made inevitable by the understanding that soon developed between her and George. Yet he wrote her a sonnet, in which she resembles the ideal picture of a young girl he had painted in his "Endymion" poem. It is both a personal portrait and the part-realization of a vision he had not quite yet met in the flesh. The sonnet was written at George's request; yet it seemed something more than a friendly exercise to aid a brother's wooing, and impressed Reynolds so much that he compared the picture it created to the Venus de Medici.

At Hunt's the circle had now expanded to include its most startling member, on the brink of the most devastating experience in a life full of crises. Shelley, separated from his wife Harriet and their two children, was

---

1. *Letters*, II, 176.   2. "I stood tip-toe", lines 93–106.
3. Phyllis G. Mann, "More Keatsiana", KSMB, XIII, 38. The idea that she was only fourteen originates with J. F. Clarke, "Some Account of George Keats", *The Dial*, April 1843. In later life, she seems to have pretended to be younger than she was; hence Clarke's mistake.
4. KC, II, 212.

living with Mary, the daughter of William Godwin and Mary Wollstone-craft, at 5 Abbey Churchyard, Bath, where she was nursing their own baby. Among the complications of his life, which included Mary's step-sister Claire, now with child by Byron, he found time to follow up his large gift to Hunt with a long and generous letter enclosing a small personal present, and announcing himself as "an outcast from human society". This was written from Marlow, where he was staying with Thomas Love Peacock. On Wednesday 11 December,[1] he came up to London for a brief visit to Hunt, not knowing that on that very day an inquest was being held on Harriet's body, found drowned in the Serpentine. Mercifully ignorant, he took pleasure in Hunt's unfeigned admiration and in the company assembled at the Hampstead cottage. Two of its members had met for the first time while waiting for Shelley to arrive from Marlow; these were Keats and Horace Smith. Keats had been hoping to make Smith's acquaintance for the past two months, but the witty parodist, full of a recent reading of Shelley's work, and anxious to see a poet with such a remarkable reputation, seemed hardly to notice the young man whose sonnet he had once picked out for praise.[2] In any case, Shelley, once arrived and introduced, soon began to dominate the conversation, though he seems to have winced politely at some of Hunt's facetiousness. On a walk across Hampstead Heath in the fine weather, Smith deliberately sought out Shelley, and the two tall men, striding out together, soon left Keats and the rest of the company behind.

Shelley returned to Bath, where the appalling news he had missed in London followed him, and Keats was left to ponder the two poems he had left behind with Hunt, the manuscript *Hymn to Intellectual Beauty* and the printed *Alastor*. The first, for all its striking phrases, did not appeal to him; he had little sympathy for a view of human life, lacking its essential poles of light and shade, as a "dim, vast vale of tears", the identical facile generalization Keats himself had rejected in the work of George Felton Mathew. *Alastor* was a different matter, in spite of its extravagant imagery and pervading vagueness. It was on the subject which occupied Keats's own mind, the poet's search for truth and ideal beauty in a world that often seemed to conceal rather than contain these. It was another poem in the direct line of Beattie's *The Minstrel*, in which the poet's quest is symbolized by changing scenery, though Shelley had adopted from Southey more of the fashionable oriental background than would ever have occurred to Beattie, or indeed to Keats himself. Moreover, it was strongly Wordsworthian; a poem which started with an unacknowledged quotation from Wordsworth and ended

1. Not Friday 13 December, as said by Ward, 93. The meeting took place on a fine day; both 12 and 13 December were stormy. G.M. (1816), 574.

2. Thirty years later, he could only remember that Keats already looked consumptive (which seems unlikely) and that "his manner was shy and embarrassed, as of one unused to society, and he spoke little" (*New Monthly Magazine*, Vol. 81, p. 239).

with an open one could not fail to interest Keats. Here, perhaps, was some hint for the long allegorical poem he felt he himself must write. Like Endymion, but to a less happy end, the hero of *Alastor* is haunted by the phases of the moon, whose dramatic going-down is made to coincide with his own frustration and death.

At all events, this complete and highly-finished work, nearly twice as long as anything he himself had done, was a spur to Keats to get his own poems in order for publication. Ollier and his younger brother, with their new shop in Welbeck Street, were anxious to have as one of their first publications a volume by a new poet whose fame had been already prophesied. Keats's self-criticism must have jibbed at some of his own juvenile poems. Among lyrics of the Mathew period, "O come, dearest Emma" was rejected, for George to use it in his addresses to Miss Wylie as "O come, Georgiana", and though many—too many—were allowed to remain, Keats marked them off from the rest of the volume by putting them in a section of their own. Sonnets of all dates, except those on Woman, which were relegated to the juvenilia, had also a separate section. They were strengthened by some improvements on *The Examiner* version of the Chapman's Homer sonnet, but weakened by a new Huntian sonnet based on some lines at the end of *Sleep and Poetry* about Kosciusko and Alfred, whose busts adorned Hunt's study. At the week-end of 14/15 December, Keats went on an expedition which probably involved a discussion of how his book should be printed. He began the Saturday at Haydon's studio, where the painter put him through the minor ordeal of having his life-mask taken. Reynolds sat by and watched while the plaster set and was taken off, a smooth image of the strong face, firm nose and wide, full lips. The weather was fine again, and Keats set off from the Great Marlborough Street studio to walk to Vauxhall. Here he had an appointment with a friend and contemporary at school of Charles Cowden Clarke. Thomas Richards had left Clarke's school at just about the time Keats joined, to be a civilian clerk in the Ordnance Office at the Tower, where his father, John Richards, was in the Royal Coach Department.[1] Richards was a man of wide taste and reading. Clarke acknowledged that it was to him that he owed all his own love of literature.[2] He had another quality equally likely to appeal to Keats, the most out-of-the-way sense of humour combined with an eccentric appearance and utterance; curious accidents were apt to happen as the result of this, such as breaking his leg while romping with his own child, Clarke's godson. Although his love of the grotesque was as strong as ever, it was more to the point for Keats at this moment that this man had a younger brother Charles Richards, who was going to print the new volume of poems for the Olliers;[3] the whole arrangement shows the

1. P.R.O./WO/47/2637.   2. KHM, No. 200.
3. M. Buxton Forman, "Keats and the Richards Family", *Times Literary Supplement*, 26 April 1934.

guiding hand of Clarke, who was fond of trying to make mutual use of the talents of his school-fellows. Keats had ample time for discussing his book, for one of the fierce storms that had plagued the past week blew up, and Richards offered him a bed, which he accepted rather than face the long walk back to Cheapside.

Monday 16 December found him back at home, meeting with Severn. This may have been the time when the painter made his first charcoal drawing of Keats, the only portrait that he did not sentimentalize. The strength and energy of the life-mask are there, quite free from the pudgy complacency of Severn's innumerable later versions. There is also a characteristic feature which the weight of plaster had perhaps flattened out of the mask,[1] the very noticeable and sensitive projection of the upper lip over the lower. This, which occurred even more strikingly in a sketch of Keats, made a few weeks earlier by Haydon on one of the pages of his journal, confirms the visual descriptions of several friends; these two rough sketches are the real Keats, lost in later idealizations.[2] One sees the purpose and even a hint of obstinacy in the powerful features and firm set of jaw. It overcomes any weakness of chin that the curious formation of his mouth might produce. Determination, of a sort, was what he certainly showed on this day, by writing the date firmly that evening at the end of the lines of his rambling "Endymion" poem

> —but now no more,
> My wand'ring spirit must no further soar.—

He would leave the poem purposely unfinished,[3] and reserve his greater project for the future. It must have taken some self-control to do this, and a letter to Clarke, whom he saw with Severn and Reynolds the next day, shows Keats half-inclined to tinker on, a temptation which he rejected.

The poem itself ends, if it can be said to end, in a strange passage where Keats imagines the bridal night of Endymion and his Moon-Goddess as having an extraordinary effect on earth's inhabitants. The healthy seem more than mortal, the long-despaired-of sick are miraculously cured, and all the young give themselves over to love. This ideal vision, or at least the second section of it, has been associated with some memory of his boyhood hopes while nursing his mother,[4] but the passage needs to be taken as a whole. If it has any topical significance, it is surely the liberation Keats himself feels in the unfolding project of his own future poem on the great myth of Endymion, the heightened power he feels in his own life. This heightening marks the

1. Donald Parson, *Portraits of Keats*, 33.

2. To Ward, 89, the Severn sketch is "a falsification", but she does not mention its close likeness to Haydon's sketch.

3. Ward, 422, n. 10.

4. Ward, 59–60, 92 assumes that the passage refers to "a sick woman", but "The languid sick" of the poem are everywhere collective and plural.

final dropping away of his life as a surgeon and physician, and its rebirth as a poet. The picture of the hospitals restoring their patients to friends and relatives, cured without the aids of medicine, is perhaps a symbol of his own final rejection of medicine as a way in which he was to serve life. The dedication of the last six years was ended, and a new one had taken its place, which was to last the rest of his days. It confirms the total creed he had expressed in *Sleep and Poetry*.

This coincided with a shift in Keats's beliefs and opinions which had perhaps been preparing for some time, but which now began to show in his poetry. A reader of *The Examiner*, he was, of course like its editor, a rationalist and a deist, but he did not openly express these opinions in any extreme form; Mathew had found him careful of the feelings of others in religious matters. Nor does Hunt seem to have discussed them with his protegé. Now, visiting Hunt on Wednesday 18 December, Keats found the cottage caught up in a new and agitating atmosphere, created by Shelley. Shelley was everywhere, darting to and fro in the agony of his fears that his dead wife's relatives would withdraw her children from him, or even that some action might be started to deprive him of his child by Mary Godwin. He dashed from Hunt to his lawyers, to Mary's step-mother and back to Hunt again. He guaranteed to marry Mary and to put the children temporarily in the charge of Hunt; in both of these actions he had Hunt's approval and sympathy which, he wrote to Mary, "sustained me against the weight and horror of this event".[1] In some obscure self-defensive way, Shelley felt he was doing battle with Church and State, with religious bigotry and political oppression, over what was a purely personal matter, and this feeling was intensified to certainty when his dead wife's family made the children subject to a Chancery suit. His atheistical anti-clericalism, always militant, was therefore even more strongly expressed than usual at this time; he impressed it on those around him like an obsession, swamping the mild agnosticism with which Hunt used to tease his orthodox friends. Keats never seems to have treated Shelley with anything more than reserve; as one who had early known real tragedies in life, he may well have found Shelley's dramatic attitudes and self-justification hard to take. He could not, however, help catching the tune of the words and expressions that were flying around. His recent sonnet *To Kosciusko* had ended on the most conventional religious note. His next, written on Sunday 22 December, not only had a Shelleyan title—*Written in Disgust of Vulgar Superstition*—but was an attack on the trappings of Christianity, notably the bells of Bow Church near his lodgings, echoing the "gloominess and bad taste" Hunt had noted a year before in an article on Christian funerals.[2] More significantly, as Tom Keats noted, the sonnet was written as a kind of exercise in a quarter of an hour; this shows he had already picked up the

1. F. L. Jones (ed.), *Letters of Shelley*, I, 520.
2. E. No. 411, pp. 732, 733.

dangerous habit from Hunt of the sonnet-competition, reducing poetry to a parlour-game. In Hunt's circle, the pastime of writing sonnets on a set subject with a fifteen-minute time-limit was a well-worn evening sport. In fact, just over a week later, on Monday 30 December, when Shelley was fully occupied elsewhere getting married to Mary, and the atmosphere at the cottage was quieter, Hunt proposed by the evening fireside that he and Keats should compete *On The Grasshopper and the Cricket*. Charles Cowden Clarke, who incidentally saw Shelley's extreme opinions through rose-coloured glasses and refused even to notice Keats's,[1] was there, though not as a time-keeper, as on this occasion there was no limit. Keats certainly finished his sonnet first, and its opening

> The poetry of earth is never dead

brought generous praise from Hunt, as did the specially Wordsworthian tenth and eleventh lines,

> On a lone winter evening, when the frost
> Has wrought a silence,

while Keats, with matching generosity, told Clarke on the way home that he preferred Hunt's effort. Yet for all its good result here, the last-written poem that Keats included in his new volume, it was a dangerously domesticated attitude to adopt to poetry.

Poetry indeed seems to have been pushed into the background during the New Year; with Shelley and his wife now dominant in the circle, conversation was more on ideas than literature. Keats was more often seen not taking part, sitting in his favourite attitude with one leg crossed over the other, and stroking his instep, now and again putting in a quiet remark. On one such occasion, when Clarke himself was playing the schoolmaster, and putting Hunt, Shelley and the fine amateur singer Henry Robertson right about the laws of astronomy, Keats quietly murmured, in a mild Cockney pun, "Charles's wain".[2] He kept himself similarly in the background on a more fiery occasion. Horace Smith had been fascinated by Shelley, his gentlemanly manners, his learned conversation, and he invited him—Mary was assisting Claire's confinement at Bath—to dine at his home in Knightsbridge on Monday 20 January 1817. Other guests were Keats, Hunt with his wife and sister-in-law Elizabeth Kent, and Thomas Hill, a fat little City man who fancied himself as a literary patron, and whose mannerisms were mocked behind his back. To complete the party was Benjamin Robert Haydon. The inclusion of two such emphatic grotesques as Haydon and Hill, the latter well-known for his way of concluding any argument with

1. C. Cowden Clarke, *Recollections of Writers*, 152; Sharp, 257.
2. KC, II, 137. Severn, who tells the story, wrote "Robinson", but no such person is known in Hunt's circle. Hunt had met Henry Crabb Robinson the diarist in 1812, but did not see him again till after Shelley had finally left England.

"Sir, I happen to *know* it!", rouses a suspicion that Smith wanted to provoke an explosion. If so, he was disappointed in Hill, who sat unexpectedly overawed, but he had full value when Shelley, knowing Haydon to be a meat-eater and an over-vehement Christian believer, looked up at the painter from his vegetarian plate, and began in a tone of deliberate mildness, "As to that detestable religion, the Christian religion—". Haydon, seeing Hunt smirk, suspected a trap, though it may have been Shelley who felt defensive; he had just had to answer a Bill of Complaint in Chancery, brought by a legal fiction in the names of his own children, and saying that he had "blasphemously derided the truth of the Christian Revelation and denied the existence of God as the Creator of the Universe". Fresh from what he regarded as a hypocritical plot to separate father from child, Shelley was likely to react strongly to a professed Christian, and when the servants had cleared away, "to it we went like Devils". The Devils of this violent argument quoted for their purpose not Scripture but Shakespeare. Keats heard his favourite *Cymbeline* used as a proof of Shakespeare's Deism, while Haydon countered with *Hamlet* and *Measure for Measure*. More to the point, he heard Haydon refute Shelley's theory of a worship of nature "on the mountains" with forthright remarks that impressed his mind. "Yes", said Haydon, "I go out on the mountains, full of holy feeling— & then an Eagle darts on a lamb, or a Hawk on a lark— & pick it before my eyes!"[1] Part of Haydon's fury was due to his feeling that Shelley and Hunt had been able to indulge sexual appetites which he himself found so difficult to control—"The dreadful lascivious scenes that haunt one's imagination like the sound of a gong on the trembling nerves"[2]—and he relieved his mind afterwards by spattering his journal with suspicions of Hunt's immorality with Elizabeth Kent.

Keats had said nothing, but to Haydon's overheated imagination, he seemed to be in moral danger from such men, including perhaps Smith, who was just writing a series of Deistic sonnets, extolling the worship of Nature.[3] He was joined in this apprehension by Severn,[4] who also claimed to have defended Christianity by Shakespearian quotations on another occasion, and to have worsted Shelley in front of Hunt and Keats. Haydon felt he had a special proprietorial interest in Keats. Pleased with the effect of Hazlitt's head darkly regarding Christ, the painter had this January sketched Keats's vivid features into the background of his great picture, shouting in fervent enthusiasm among the Jerusalem crowd. On New Year's Eve, Haydon had written to Wordsworth about Keats with an air of proud possession, belatedly enclosing the "Great spirits" sonnet; Wordsworth had replied, with cautious appreciation, on the very day of Horace Smith's dinner-party.

1. Duncan Gray and Violet W. Walker, 'Benjamin Robert Haydon on Byron and Others', KSMB, VII, 23.

2. Haydon, II, 78.   3. Essex Record Office, MS D/DR zII.

4. Sharp, 116–117. Severn's claims, however, are always doubtful.

As the entrepreneur of poetry at such a high level, Haydon felt it his duty to withdraw Keats from the "smuggering" atmosphere of Leigh Hunt, who showed himself equally proprietorial to Keats, though in a different way, by giving him the arch nickname of "Junkets".[1] In spite of Haydon's efforts, it was with Hunt that Keats was mostly to be found during the next month, very often in company with Shelley and Mary Shelley, to whom he introduced George. They were evenings of fiercely radical talk. Shelley's hopes of his children by Harriet now depended on the decision in Chancery of Lord Eldon, who, as he too rightly feared, would not be favourable to him. Hunt was attacking the Church thanksgiving that had followed an incident when stones were thrown at the Prince Regent, and, even more bitterly, the suspension of Habeas Corpus that also followed the incident. Keats sat imbibing revolutionary phrases. Little trace remained of the dressership at Guy's, and he can only have carried out his duties there in the most perfunctory way. On 7 February, his friends Henry Stephens and Henry Newmarch passed their examinations to become Members of the Royal College of Surgeons, one to proceed later in the year to a practice on the borders of Bedfordshire and Hertfordshire, the other to sail for India. Keats had not completed the course of surgical lectures that would qualify him to sit, and he did not enter for the examination. Nor was he even writing much poetry at this time, though a week before he had produced a sonnet on a fine day, after a run of ten cloudy ones in a row, beginning, "After dark vapours have oppress'd our plains". Absorbed in new personal impressions, he could only write, as it were, to order. During a party at the Cheapside lodgings, he received from Charles Richards the last proof-sheet of his book, with a note that if there were to be a dedication, it must be sent back at once with the corrected proof. Among the buzz of conversation, he sat down and, using their competition technique, wrote without correction a dedicatory sonnet to Leigh Hunt, handing it for approval to the publisher Charles Ollier, who was one of the party.[2] This facility when pressed, though spectacular, was not altogether a good advertisement for the coming book. His feebler sonnets, such as *Kosciusko* and *After dark vapours*, loyally printed by Hunt in *The Examiner*, aroused doubts in experienced literary friends of Shelley, such as Peacock and Hogg, who next month frankly told Mrs. Shelley that Hunt ought to stop printing them. Sometime too, Shelley himself, on one of their walks on Hampstead Heath, tactfully tried to persuade Keats to delay publication until he had a better collection. The lack of ease that Keats always felt with Shelley, whether it sprang from differences of social status, physique or their views on poetry, made him ignore a suggestion which his own self-criticism must often have put before him. Even

1. "an ... allusion to his friends of Fairy-land". Milnes, I, 44, but also possibly based on Keats's West-country pronunciation.
2. C. Cowden Clarke, *Recollections of Writers*, 137–138.

though, as Hunt said, "Keats did not take to Shelley as kindly as Shelley took to him", there was more self-protection than resentment in the feeling. Keats had been a silent spectator of the way Shelley could turn the lives of others upside-down both in admiration or in opposition. Still unsure of himself and his own poetic achievement, though equally sure that he had something unique to offer, Keats felt it urgent not to be swamped, even by kindness. Shelley had now arranged to rent a house at Marlow, where he had often stayed, and with his fondness of pseudonym was already "The Hermit of Marlow" in a pamphlet printed by the Olliers, henceforth his publishers also. He invited Keats to stay with him there, but Keats refused "that I might have my own unfetterd scope".[1] All the same, Keats was sufficiently influenced by Shelley's criticism to add a last-minute prefatory note to the volume of poems, excusing the juvenilia: "The Short Pieces in the middle of the Book, as well as some of the Sonnets, were written at an earlier period than the rest of the Poems." It also seems[2] that before they parted the two poets agreed to write their next long poems in friendly competition, but on a huge scale compared with the sonnet-bouts at Hunt's, a matter of 4000 lines each. Keats was, of course, to write his long-meditated *Endymion*, Shelley a tale with an oriental and revolutionary setting, embellished with incest.

The Shelleys left London on Thursday 27 February. Some days before they went,[3] Keats wrote his first sonnet for over three weeks. It was another impromptu occasional piece, written in Cowden Clarke's pocket-Chaucer while the latter was asleep after a long walk to Keats's lodgings. It marked Keats's delight in a poem then printed as Chaucer's *The Flower and the Leaf*, which he read for the first time while his friend slept.[4] He was struck by the likeness of some of its early lines, beginning "Upon a certain night", to his own *Sleep and Poetry*. There was still just time to slip in these lines as a motto on the separate title-page of his own poem, though the printer, doing yet one more rush job, left out the vital half-line with which the quotation opened.[5] The sonnet was at once promised publication in *The Examiner*, but a much more important publication was now due. On the week-end of 1 March, the first advance copies of his printed *Poems* were in Keats's hands, bound in grey boards, and priced moderately at six shillings. On the title-page, an engraving of Shakespeare[6] and a motto from Spenser, who had inspired Keats's first poem, introduced the book where that poem and its successors now appeared in print.

1. *Letters*, I, 170.
2. T. Medwin, *Life of Percy Bysshe Shelley*, I, 298; Ward, 423, n. 30.
3. Not the same day, 27 February, as often stated, mistaking the day Reynolds wrote his "Sonnet—to Keats. On reading his sonnet written in Chaucer" for the day Keats wrote his own sonnet.
4. C. Cowden Clarke, *The Riches of Chaucer*, I, 52–53. Clarke later confused matters by saying this was the first time Keats read *any* Chaucer.
5. Sperry, 118–119.   6. Sperry, 120–121 and 140.

Chapter 9

A FLOWERING LAUREL

"I see ev'n now,
Young Keats, a flowering laurel on your brow."

– LEIGH HUNT, *To John Keats*

HIS BOOK was published. The "flowering laurel" Hunt had prophesied for him, and which he had used as a serious image in so many of his own poems, was now firmly on his brow. It is clear that he saw this image in a very different way from Hunt's playful conventional symbol. To Keats, it was literally a sacred mark of his dedication to Apollo, God of Healing and Poetry, whose first attribute he had now rejected for total devotion to the second. It is only in this light that the extraordinary effect of an apparently trivial incident can be explained. It was one of those incidents which, as Keats afterwards said, one remembers with blushing, but it went deeper than that. It marked the turning-point in his relations with Hunt, and it is ironic it should spring from the publication of the book which Hunt had so much helped to encourage and sponsor.

Piecing together various accounts, what seems to have happened was this. On Saturday 1 March, in a spell of beautifully fine warm weather, Keats set out with a copy of *Poems* in his hand to give to Hunt. As he walked up Millfield Lane, Hampstead Heath, beside the Ponds, he met on the wooded path Hunt himself. This seemed to both like an omen. Hunt invited Keats home to the Vale of Health to celebrate the publication. After dinner, the weather was mild enough for them to take their wine in the garden, where the constellation of Orion, the Bull and the Pleiades shone brightly above them. In this starry and inspiring setting, the garden warm with early spring and the book of poems with its vernal promise between them, it seemed natural enough for the two poets to strike a poetic attitude. Shelley was no longer with them to turn the talk to more transcendental matters, and both may have felt the necessary luxury of being a little silly.[1] It was an instance of what Haydon described, writing of another occasion with Keats, as "The excessive mad anticks of people of real Genius when they meet after hard thinking". At all events, Hunt felt moved to embody his admiration by picking and twining a chaplet of laurel and placing it on Keats's forehead;

1. Ward, 423, places the incident later, not realizing Shelley was now at Marlow.

Keats, not to be outdone, wove together strands of ivy and put them on Hunt's head.[1] To Hunt, the next move was obvious. They should each write a sonnet to mark the moment, with a fifteen minute time-limit. He dashed off not one but two. Keats, perhaps feeling his first doubts about the occasion, started slowly and had to bolster his out with lines filched from the sonnets in his own book of poems and with revolutionary phrases heard from Shelley. At that moment, visitors—possibly, though not certainly, the sisters of J. H. Reynolds—were announced. Hunt, quick not to seem ridiculous before women, took off his crown. Keats, in a kind of obstinate self-justification, insisted on keeping his on throughout their stay, and even on writing another sonnet, still weaker, *To the Ladies Who Saw Me Crown'd*.

Keats very soon realized the weakness of the verse, and the silliness of the occasion. What jolted him in the next few days was Hunt's complacency about the matter. Whereas Keats only let one person see his sonnets—Reynolds, whose sisters may have been involved—Hunt circulated his, and, worst of all, published them next Spring, thus providing some of the heaviest artillery for the reviewers' onslaught on himself and Keats.[2] Keats's instinct that he had betrayed the sacred trust of Apollo by indulging in such a mockery was not a reaction as unreal as the occasion that provoked it; it was literally and almost tragically true. He had written himself down as one to whom verse was a mere pastime, the total opposite of the dedicated vessel of the lines in his own *Sleep and Poetry*. All Haydon's warnings and hints rushed back to him, and it was no accident that he spent the next day on an almost holy mission with the painter, a visit to the Elgin Marbles. Here was the true classical spirit he needed to inform his own *Endymion*, not the fake libations and laurels of the previous evening. As if in a penance for his two previous sonnets, he went home to write two sonnets to Haydon and the Marbles.[3] The form is the same, but the change of tone in these sonnets is absolute. He stresses his weakness, his lack of ability to do justice to the subject, everywhere his own insufficiency

Like a sick Eagle looking at the sky

which Haydon, to whom he at once sent the sonnets, thought the finest image of a poet that had ever been written.[4] It was the antithesis of the image he and Hunt had projected the night before.

The official publication day, Monday 3 March, saw a less fanciful celebration at Haydon's studio, with Reynolds and Charles Cowden Clarke. "The first volume of Keats's minor muse", as Clarke put it, "was launched amid

1. Bate, 138–140, gives the best account.
2. J. R. MacGillivray, *Keats: A Bibliography & Reference Guide*, xxii.
3. All four sonnets, in Keats's hand, appear in the copy of *Poems* which he gave to J. H. Reynolds.
4. *Letters*, I, 122.

the cheers and fond anticipations of all his circle". The publisher contributed a stiff sonnet, but he may already have been nervous at his venture. The book was hardly subscribed at all, except for Keats's immediate friends. The Olliers were new at the game, and it must have horrified their hopes, when, in another of Clarke's forthright expressions, "the book might have emerged in Timbuctoo" for all the interest it aroused. They clearly dropped some expressions of alarm or even resentment, for it is an astonishing fact that within three weeks, Keats found himself negotiating with quite a different set of publishers. John Taylor and James Augustus Hessey had been in partnership at 93 Fleet Street for over ten years. Originally booksellers only, they had gradually built up a respectable list of their own publications, mostly of a kind that may be called educational. From this solid foundation, they were now beginning to branch out into modern poetry. A scheme to reprint Leigh Hunt's verse-epistles from *The Examiner* fell through, but in autumn 1816 they had brought out Reynolds's *The Naiad*, and did not seem perturbed when the works of this young poet failed to sell.[1] Both Taylor and Hessey were lively-minded men in their thirties; both were lightly-built, active, sociable, attractive to women. Taylor, slightly the elder, was the son of a bookseller of Scots descent, who had married a Nottinghamshire girl and set up at East Retford in that county; he had the vivid mobile dark good looks often found in Nottingham, especially when he snatched off the silver-rimmed glasses he wore at work. Hessey, equally short-sighted, was in demand at parties for his singing, playing and dancing. He had married a West-country girl, while Taylor remained a bachelor; but Taylor was the consultant and ally of friends and relatives in love, both male and female, and was soon reckoned "so old a Practitioner" that his advice and help was sought in the most complicated affairs.[2] He had been a poet when younger, and still practised that art as well. This, though it led him into an unhappy urge to improve the work of his young poets by corrections in proof, had the advantage that he understood their temperamental difficulties; he himself suffered at this time from some nervous trouble, which, as he had just told his father at Retford, "makes me look pale and poorly when I feel disturbed at anything".

To this sympathetic character Keats was probably introduced by Reynolds, who had been well-treated by the firm. It was a shot in the battle for Keats, in which the parties were defining themselves as Hunt, Shelley and the now dubious Olliers on the one side, and Reynolds, Haydon and some more established publisher on the other; Taylor, who managed the editorial section, while Hessey looked after the business, read Keats's *Poems* with interest, though he was judiciously critical of some parts. Meanwhile, Keats's

1. E. Blunden, *Keats's Publisher*, 40–41.
2. E. Blunden, *Keats's Publisher*, 149; J. Richardson, *The Everlasting Spell*, Appendix V; MOK, 108–114.

Elgin Marbles sonnets had been printed simultaneously on 9 March in *The Examiner* and in the rival radical Sunday paper *The Champion*, edited by John Scott. More to the point, Reynolds, a regular contributor to *The Champion*, had printed there a laudatory review of the book of poems, more notice than Hunt was to manage for nearly three months. Keats was delighted by this friendly act, and in thanking Reynolds spoke darkly of other friends whom it would not please, perhaps already with the rival party in mind.[1] Haydon wrote to Keats a week later, telling him frankly that he once thought he might be led astray, "but the feelings (you have) put forth lately—have delighted my soul—always consider principle of more value than genius—".[2] He offered Keats eternal friendship, which he also confided to his journal. On the same day, Haydon had a rapprochement with Hunt—"I really love him to my heart & only feel panged at his liability to delusive principles"— but in spite of friendship all round, he still did not quite trust Keats to separate the man from the principles. He advised Keats to leave Town in preparation for his "longer sort of poem of Diana and Endymion".

Taylor was extremely interested in the projected poem, the more so when he met the author who was planning it. Keats came to him in the full uniform of a radical poet, which Taylor, who had a gift for sly description, passed on to his provincial relatives, who were duly surprised at "such a singular style of dress".[3] The publisher, though amused, had a talent for looking beyond outward appearance, and for drawing out the inner qualities in a man, even on slight acquaintance. In the open-shirted dishevelled youth he saw, even at this early stage, someone who would be, as he put it quite simply, a great poet; on the business side he also saw that a long poem might catch the undoubted fashion for such things, and bring profit to both poet and publisher. Taylor combined a genuine taste for what was of high quality with a regard for what might attract the public. Just at this time, a bronzed Surrey farmer, who had already published a journal of his tour in France, was setting off for America. Morris Birkbeck, who sailed on 13 March, 1817, was to publish his American journals with Taylor and Hessey, who rightly anticipated that books on the opening up of the Middle West would have a good public; this publication had more consequence than they could have reckoned for the young poet with whom Taylor was now negotiating.

Meanwhile Keats himself stood poised among the various influences at work around him, fully conscious of them. Not only was it an age when people spoke out and let their opinions be known, but he himself was alive to every shade and variation of human life. The currents sweeping around him crossed and recrossed, pulling in different ways while he considered

1. Not "the Abbeys and their friends". *Letters*, I, 123, n. 4.
2. *Letters*, I, 124–125, clearly written the same day as Haydon, II, 101.
3. Blunden, KP, 41.

how to strike out now that his first effort had dropped, almost unnoticed, into the ocean. Haydon might write on Monday 17 March "your Sleep & Poetry—it is a flash of lightening that will sound men from their occupations, and keep them trembling for the crash of thunder that *will* follow", but the plain fact was that, as Keats admitted, his book "was read by some dozen of my friends who lik'd it; and some dozen who I was unacquainted with who did not". Reynolds might review him eulogistically in *The Champion* (though unfortunately, as was his habit, with sneers at other living poets) with the words that "a young man starts suddenly before us, with a genius that is likely to eclipse them all"; yet Hunt, on the same day, instead of following up his *Young Poets* article in any way, had devoted all his energies to trouncing the Government for suspending habeas corpus, lamenting the wretchedness and humiliation of the country, just as if no new young genius had just started up at his elbow. Admittedly when "J.K.'s lines"—the *Flower and the Leaf* sonnet "delayed, owing to the pressure of temporary matter"— were printed in *The Examiner* next week, Hunt managed a brief note to explain who J.K. was, but unaccountably omitted to add the vital information that J.K. had just published a book of poems.[1]

All this, and the Olliers scratching their beards too, might well have made Keats cynical; but all the signs are that he kept the humane and admirable detachment that was to mark him all through his life, the refusal to take sides or be involved in petty literary or personal warfare. He continued to see Hunt, particularly at the Oxford Street house of Vincent Novello, the organist and composer, "who" in Charles Lamb's words,[2] "by the aid of a capital organ, himself the most finished of players, converts his drawing-room into a chapel, his week days into Sundays, and these latter into minor heavens". Clarke would often be there, coming over from his brother-in-law in Clerkenwell, and so would Keats's musical schoolfriend, Edward Holmes, robust company to take a part in the singing and drink the beer that came in with the supper-tray. Hunt contributed his own "joco-serio-musico-pictorio-poetical" side to the entertainment, and was always roused to some of his most facetious puns by the Novello ladies, Mrs. Novello and her sister, whom he christened "Ave Maria" and "Salve Regina".[3] Keats, as usual, sat quietly putting in a word or two here and there. The little daughter of the house, Mary Victoria, looking on at Cowden Clarke, who was later to become her husband, remembered Keats tucked against the organ, listening while Novello played, in the attitude so characteristic of him, with one foot on the other knee. Holmes remembered, though perhaps from a later gathering, that when fugues were being played, Keats, engaging in a verbal battle with Leigh Hunt to describe this type of music, produced the definition that their

1. E. No. 480, pp. 145–147, No. 481, p. 173.
2. Charles Lamb, "A Chapter on Ears", *London Magazine*, March 1821.
3. C. Cowden Clarke, *Recollections of Writers*, 195.

themes interchanging were "like two Dogs running after one another through the Dust".[1]

Keats gave full measure to the somewhat high-flown terms in which Haydon was now addressing him, though, with his shrewd sense of values, he would surely have been amused to learn that the painter, always in debt, had vowed "I only know that if I sell my picture, Keats shall never want". Haydon had confided to him that, on the beautiful evenings they were having this clear and fine March, "as the dusk approached, and a gauzey veil seemed dimming all things" after a hard day's painting, he had seen "the faces of the mighty dead" crowd into the studio to inspire him. Keats too was meditating, as he always did but with even more intensity, on the "mighty dead" of poetry, whom he had so often openly invoked in the poems just published. Could he possibly achieve anything like their standard in the work he was about to begin? He was reading their work passionately. He had borrowed from Clarke an earlier volume in the set of pocket-Chaucer.[2] This contained *Troilus and Criseyde*, which Clarke had just finished reading himself with unbounded enthusiasm, and which Keats marked in his friend's copy. More than all, he now followed one piece of advice Haydon had given him, with his usual whole-hearted literalness: "read Shakespeare".[3] He had, of course, a working knowledge of Shakespeare from his earlier reading with Clarke, and from his visits to the theatre, when the text was illuminated for him by the lightning-flashes of Kean's acting. Yet until this moment, in the middle of March 1817, there is no sign of the appetite, the passion Shakespeare became for him, so that every poem and every casual letter echoed Shakespeare in its rhythms and conscious or unconscious remembrances. Now he decided to take Haydon's advice, and this, for him, meant to read every word. The first open sign of this was a playful parody of Falstaff's "Banish Jack Falstaff" speech from *Henry IV*, Part 1, which he made in a letter of 17 March to Reynolds, for Reynolds too was an ardent appreciator, who always liked, he said, to begin a letter with a panegyric on Shakespeare.[4] Another less obvious sign at about this time was a sonnet written to one of Reynolds's sisters. She had given him one of the moulded paste gems manufactured by William Tassie, which were popular at the time. This one represented the subject of Hunt's recent poem, *Hero and Leander*. Keats replied with a sonnet which, though still strictly Miltonic in form, like all his other early sonnets, had something which they all had so far lacked, distinct

1. Holmes to Hunt, 1823, quoted Blunden, *Leigh Hunt*, 202.

2. Cowden Clarke's set, containing the MS of the *Flower and the Leaf* sonnet, is now in the British Museum, Add. MSS 33, 516. Some volumes of Woodhouse's copy are in Keats House Museum, No. 29. Both these sets are sometimes mistaken for Keats's own copy, which he possessed later, but which has disappeared.

3. *Letters*, I, 135, where Haydon is clearly repeating previous advice.

4. KHM, No. 155, J. H. Reynolds to Mary Leigh.

echoes of Shakespeare, more especially from the play which was to become an obsession with him over the next month, *The Tempest*.[1]

Reading Shakespeare, haunted by the mightiest of "the mighty dead" and the play in which he had bowed himself out of his own time, Keats began to move imperceptibly to the moment when he would begin his own large-scale poem. Now he need no longer interrupt a reading of Shakespeare by hearing the clock strike and realizing that he was late for his duties at hospital. On 3 March, the same day that his own book was published, his hospital appointment had come to an end in official fact, as it had already done in unofficial practice. There was no dramatic leave-taking of the profession. He simply allowed his appointment to die away, and did not collect any form of final certificate from the hospital.[2] From his St. Thomas's Street days, he kept his medical books, and, for a time, at least one medical friend. This was Henry Stephens, who had now gone ahead of him by attending surgical lectures and obtaining his M.R.C.S. Stephens, however, could not legally do the dispensing and other duties of an ordinary practice without the Licence of the Society of Apothecaries, which Keats held and which he had failed to acquire. He was staying up in London to sit for this necessary qualification, which he and George Mackereth at last managed to get on 1 May, and he still came over from St. Thomas's Street to see Keats at the Cheapside lodgings. It is possible he hoped to borrow a little of the Latin, which had steered Keats through the terms in the *Pharmacopeia*. They fell into their familiar habits, Stephens at his texts, and Keats with a poetry notebook in hand. As Stephens had seen him do in their medical digs, Keats curled up in the window-seat, and Stephens remembered how that part of any room had always been known to their fellow-students as "Keats' place". Keats looked up Cheapside, the cobbled streets' noisy traffic now still, into another beautiful gauzy evening with St. Paul's silhouetted against the twilight, a symbol itself of "the mighty dead". He began to write a few lines, and then, according to Stephens's account,[3] stopped, and read out the first line to his companion

A thing of beauty is a constant joy

He asked Stephens what he thought of the line. "It has the true ring, but is wanting in some way", Stephens claimed to have advised him. Keats, with his instinct always to correct at once, worked at the line and then read it again to Stephens,

1. Finney, I, 193. Ward, 169, places the sonnet a year later, but cites no evidence. Its style is quite different from his later sonnets. According to Woodhouse, Keats planned to write a series of sonnets on Tassie's gems, a somewhat juvenile idea.

2. Guy's Hospital, *Physicians and Surgeons Pupils and Dressers, 1814–1827*.

3. B. W. Richardson, *The Asclepiad*, 148. Stephens's story has been questioned, but since he was in London at this time, there is no reason to doubt its essential truth. Richardson also repeated Stephens's story verbally to H. Buxton Forman. HBF, I, 121.

A thing of beauty is a joy for ever

He again asked Stephens what he thought, and this time his friend had no hesitation.

The poem was begun. It was perhaps a curious beginning after the first bold Shakespearian statement of the opening lines. The two-dozen lines which he probably wrote on that occasion sum up what had been passing through his mind over the past weeks, and the influences that had been pulling at him. The pessimistic picture of a world that has lost its nobility in

> the inhuman dearth
> Of noble natures

exactly echoes Hunt's political leader on the degenerate figures of modern government; yet

> Some shape of beauty moves away the pall

from day-by-day life—nature, poetry, and, above all

> the grandeur of the dooms
> We have imagined for the mighty dead;

in Haydon's exact phrase, until all these become

> An endless fountain of immortal drink,
> Pouring unto us from the heaven's brink.

These "essences", as he afterwards added in a short linking passage which joined this introduction to the main poem, are not merely felt for the short twilight hour that induces them; once felt they are with us for ever, just as the idea of his own first line was to haunt his thought, and emerge in various forms at various later stages of his consciousness—"What the imagination seizes as Beauty must be truth"—"Beauty is truth, truth beauty"—"I cannot conceive any beginning of such love as I have for you but Beauty". Keats had not only found a first line and a beginning; he had found a principle that was to maintain him all through his life. "I have lov'd the principle of beauty in all things" was his thought when he faced the implications of his last fatal illness; on this evening in Cheapside, he made his first and perhaps most memorable statement of this creed.

For the present, the lines were to be put on one side; it may even be that Keats did not at first realize they were the start to the poem, but regarded them as a separate meditation. Events now gave him little leisure to meditate. He and his brothers had decided to leave the Cheapside rooms. This move to Hampstead has often been associated with some signs of growing ill-health in Tom,[1] but there is no direct evidence anywhere of this. It has also been said that this was Keats's way of making the move "into the country . . . out

1. By Lowell, I, 465, followed by Hewlett and Bate.

of Town" advised by Haydon,[1] but this is impossible. Haydon would never have advised Keats to move into Hampstead, a district frequented by Leigh Hunt; what the painter was advocating was a complete change of atmosphere far from London and its literary coteries. There were probably a number of factors involved in the move, mostly personal to Keats himself. There was a hint in his letter to Reynolds on Monday 17 March that his own health was troubling him; the parody of Falstaff it contains is on the subject of health, and Keats seems to suggest here, as in so many later letters, that the night air gave him some trouble. Stephens, with a medical eye, had noticed that even when bathing in the summer, Keats "complained after he came out as if the Bathing did not agree with him".[2] This is no more than to say that something in his constitution was susceptible to damp, and there is no doubt that the Cheapside lodgings were full of rising damp. One of London's many underground rivers, the Walbrook, flowed directly underneath the house, and in flood time it made the cellars awash.

There were also temperamental reasons for a move. Although Abbey was no longer Keats's guardian and trustee, he was a presence to be felt, with his counting-house just round the corner. Long ago, Tom had disliked his clerking job with him, and left; George, about now, fell foul of Cadman Hodgkinson, his companion in Abbey's office. This young man had completed his apprenticeship, on the strength of which he was about to obtain his City freedom.[3] The cause of George's quarrel with him is obscure. Possibly both hoped for a junior partnership in the firm, and Hodgkinson, on his slight seniority, got promotion, though there is no evidence he became an official partner. At all events, Keats's loyalty to George was so roused that he never mentions Hodgkinson's name without wishing him some ill-luck or ill-health. Most of all, his own relations with Abbey were worsening. The disapproving merchant was in no mood to help in any way.[4] What stung Keats, however, was not Abbey's disapproval, on which he had always reckoned since their interview about his career, but his attitude to the published poems. In a hope that his ex-guardian would be won over, or at least see he was in earnest and had something to show for it, Keats gave him a copy of the book that March. When they next met, Abbey approached him with heavy-handed humour. "Well, John", he said, "I have read your Book, & it reminds me of the Quaker's Horse which was hard to catch, & good for nothing when he was caught—So", he went on, making sure the

1. *Letters*, I, 125; Ward, 108 and 423 n. 36. Hunt himself used "country" to mean places farther out than Hampstead.
2. KC, II, 211.
3. G. L. MS 5652/2; Chamberlain's Office, Guildhall, Freedom Admissions.
4. Haydon, II, 107. Abbey appears to have been over-punctilious in legal matters. He had only just (4 April 1817) obtained probate of Mrs. Jennings's will, presumably having waited for the exact account of any cash owing to the estate from her late sister-in-law's share from Chancery.

joke was understood, "Your Book is hard to understand & good for nothing when it is understood." This robust Yorkshire humour was hard to stomach. "Do you know", said Abbey, ten years later, recounting the incident to Taylor at the Company dinner, "I don't think he ever forgave me for uttering this Opinion."[1]

On all these counts, and especially now that Keats had severed his connection with the Hospital south of the river, a move to the healthy heights north of London was indicated. Lodgings were dotted all over the Hampstead area. The Keats boys took the first floor in the house of the local postman named Bentley,[2] near the Heath at No. 1 Well Walk, where the lime-trees in the little avenue were just beginning to show pale green buds. In the fine weather they were all out of doors, strolling to friends over the Heath, and it was not until next winter that they realized the lodgings were uncomfortably cramped, that the Bentleys' noisy small boys were difficult to ignore, and that in the little house one became unpleasantly aware of the number of people and compelled, as Keats put it, to "breathe worsted stockings". Yet Bentley was a friendly landlord, his wife a kind and motherly person, particularly attentive to Tom.

The sense of release was shown by Keats in the first light-hearted letter he wrote after the move. Hunt too was more charming than irritating, and Keats picked up some of the old fascination. Yet there was criticism even then in his tone. Hunt was revising *Rimini* for a second edition, and composing a long new poem, on Wordsworth's theme of *The Excursion*, Book IV, called *The Nymphs*. Keats, with the same inspiration for his own just-started poem, saw how Hunt tended to prettify and make quaint the serious vision he hoped his own verse would embody. His facility was alarming, in more senses than one. "Mr. H. has got a great way into a Poem on the Nymphs and has said a number of beautiful things" was Keats's slightly caustic comment, to which he added, with affected casualness, "I have also written a few Lines." In his heart he knew his few lines written at Cheapside were something outside Hunt's scope. However, Hunt's enthusiasms were contagious. Keats was enough involved to write a sonnet on the revised *Rimini*, echoing in it his own "few Lines". He copied it for Hunt into the presentation volume of his own *Poems*.[3] On Wednesday 26 March, he went to Novello's specially to hear Hunt's own composition, words and music, of a four-part hymn entitled "To the Spirit Great and Good", a pleasant little deistic ditty of a kind innocuous enough to seem suitable at the Catholic Novellos.

All the same, Keats had in spirit broken with Hunt, ever since the laurel-crowning incident, which still irked him. The move to Hampstead itself had provided him with new and more solid friends, of Reynolds's introduc-

1. KC, I, 308.   2. Dilke, ann. I, 188.
3. Keats Collection, Houghton Library, *EC 8, K 2262.

tion. Charles Wentworth Dilke and his charming wife Maria lived at the bottom of the Heath near Pond Street. With a friend, Charles Brown, Dilke had built in the year after Waterloo, two small semi-detached houses, Wentworth Place. He lived in one, Brown in the other. A Civil servant in the Navy Pay Office like his father before him, Dilke was also a literary man. He had made a useful six-volume edition of *Old English Plays*, a continuation of Robert Dodsley's *Select Collection* of 1744; Keats's constant reading in these plays dates from his friendship with the Dilkes, and lasted until his death, tempering his own passionate attachment to Shakespeare with examples of lesser drama which he healthily absorbed into his own poetry. Dilke was six years older than Keats, inclined to be serious, dogmatic and orderly. This, and his wife's naturalness and straightforward manner, were a change from the slightly feverish disorder that often reigned at the Vale of Health, where sudden drama was apt to cut across the playfulness, and threats of suicide had been known.

Hunt, in fact, was in some sort of crisis, and had accepted Shelley's invitation to stay at Marlow as an escape. For reasons probably connected with money, he decided to make the stay terminate his tenancy of the Vale of Health cottage. There was therefore an immense amount of accumulated lumber to pack and dispose before Hunt, his wife, sister-in-law and children could take the coach on Sunday 6 April.[1] Keats as a neighbour was called in to help, and he spent the day before the move at the cottage in what even Hunt was forced to describe as "all the chaos of packed trunks, lumber, litter, dust, dirty dry fingers &c.".[2] He had an opportunity to meditate what really lay in more senses than one behind the wallpaper, the busts, the pictures and the prints. Hunt was over a thousand pounds in debt at this time, and there was evidently some financial matter to settle, which Hunt entrusted to Keats. It involved dealings with a bailiff, very likely that "old Wood", whom Keats reported in a letter to Hunt soon after, as "a very Varmant –sharded in Covetousness".[3] Keats was left with a number of papers, probably bills or summonses, which he decided to lock in a trunk, rather than involve himself too deeply in Hunt's tangled finance. The disillusion commenced by the crowning was now complete. Keats felt as dirtied by the whole affair as the bare stripped cottage he had just left, once the goal of his pilgrimage.

Only a day or two later, he was still obsessed by this shabby picture when he went for a walk with Haydon. The painter led him through his favourite country path, past the isolated picturesque farms of the Kilburn meadows, only a mile north of Oxford Street, but the best natural scenery near London.[4]

1. F. L. James (ed.), *Letters of Shelley*, I, 537, n. 1.
2. C. Cowden Clarke, *Recollections of Writers*, 195. Letter of Hunt to Clarke, misdated April 9, See n. 1, above.
3. Ward, 110; *Letters*, I, 137.
4. J. Richardson, *Recollections of the Last Half Century*.

Filling his lungs, and remembering the rubbish, human and material, he had had to sweep up that week-end, Keats suddenly shouted loudly, "What a pity there is not a human dust hole". They had been talking, Haydon said, about "some mean people", but the inference was plain. Keats went on to say, "Byron, Scott, Southey, & Shelley think they are to lead the age, but—". Later hands have removed the last eight or ten words of the sentence, but once again, the meaning can be inferred, for Haydon added, "This was said with all the consciousness of Genius; his face reddened." Reynolds's comparisons in *The Champion* review may have been partly in Keats's mind, but more so was the feeling that with *Endymion* started he too was as he later said, "among the English Poets". The "consciousness of Genius" that Haydon noted was of the same order as the quiet confidence he displayed when the poem was finished, even in the face of the reviews.

Now his mind was finally made up. He would take Haydon's advice, and, with his brothers' half-reluctant urging too, separate even from them to do his great work alone, and to battle it out, as he had never done before, without their support. It would be a test of his faith that he could stand on his own feet as a poet and as a person, unfettered. The Dilkes, whom he had just met, were great lovers of the Isle of Wight, and Dilke's sister had married into a family from the nearest part of the mainland. Keats decided to take himself and his poem there, just as Wordsworth had taken his to the Lakes. His decision was helped by that of John Taylor. Taylor had taken soundings on the *Poems*, perhaps read the opening lines of *Endymion*, and this week he too made up his mind. He would publish *Endymion*, and intended Keats to be one of his permanent authors. He wrote to his father at Retford, "We have agreed for the next Edit. of Keats's Poems, and are to have the Refusal of his future works. I cannot think he will fail to become a great Poet." It was an astoundingly percipient remark. He added, evidently on the strength of recent talks with Keats, that the poet was not likely to repeat such indiscretions as the dedication to Leigh Hunt in any later work. He was right, though Keats still had it in his power to shock publishers. What the Olliers thought, for all that Taylor was a tactful man, may be guessed; they could hardly have been pleased, as they were soon to show.

Decision made, Keats at once acted. Writing his new publishers a brief but warm note of thanks, he prepared to leave London. Shakespeare, which he and his brothers now read incessantly, would be his companion. Seeking for the most portable form, he picked on the duodecimo seven-volume edition published by Whittingham in a handy pocket size in 1814, with neat woodcuts.[1] This version of the plays had been first edited in 1773 by George Steevens, based on Dr. Johnson's edition; it had the advantage of Steevens's very considerable scholarship, though Keats, commenting drily on Steevens's strictures on *The Comedy of Errors*, wrote in his copy "you are too wise or

1. Keats Collection, Houghton Library, *EC 8.

rather otherwise as the old phrase is". The edition was to inspire him for *Endymion*. He packed these volumes near the top of his box, which also contained some prints; in Huntian style, he intended to embellish any lodgings where he stayed with Mary Queen of Scots and Milton grouped with his daughters. There was also an original sketch by Haydon, and, more down-to-earth, a warm woollen plaid scarf for the outside of the coach and to protect his throat from the cold spring nights. Some cups and a basket, perhaps for possible picnics as the weather got warmer, did not arrive in time from the Reynoldses; but with plenty of books, and plenty of paper to cover with poetry and letters, Keats completed his packing. It was the first expedition he had been known to take entirely alone, in itself a symbol of the great enterprise. On the evening of Monday 14 April, travelling on the outside of the coach, he set out for Southampton.

Chapter 10

THE LITTLE BOAT

"And, as the year
Grows lush in juicy stalks, I'll smoothly steer
My little boat, for many quiet hours."

– *Endymion*, I, 45–47

THE COACH carried Keats through suburbs, whose names he never knew, and out into the open heathy country of Surrey and Hampshire. There was white dust on the hedges from the fine dry spring. They passed large houses with classical statues of Nymphs—"N. B. Stone", Keats noted facetiously—and the scenes of rural evening. About halfway, the frost which chilled southern England almost every night this April made Keats feel cold, and he was forced to pay extra to ride inside. He woke at dawn on the borders of West Sussex and Hampshire, where the chalk South Downs are thickly wooded, and the early sunlight shone bright gold on the gorse growing profusely in the yellow sandstone ridges to the north. The coach turned further south, and rattled through the Bargate, with its two stone lions, into Southampton in time for breakfast. At the inn, in a strange town where he knew no one, Keats felt unaccustomedly lonely; he unstrapped his case, took out the first two volumes of Shakespeare, and dipped into *The Tempest* and *A Midsummer Night's Dream*—"There's my Comfort", he told himself, quoting from the former. He went down to the quayside, and finding it was dead low water and the Isle of Wight boat would not leave till 3 that afternoon, strolled about the town. Loneliness began to gain, so he took out some paper, and wrote an account of his journey to his brothers, from whom he was now parted for the first time.[1] He felt lost without their close company, and his first instinct was to speak to them in a letter.

This letter was also the first of the many long descriptive screeds Keats was to write. Unlike his later prose, in which one can hear his tone of voice as though in conversation, it leans heavily on literature. The pictures he paints of the evening countryside are conventional and literary, types rather than observation. "William seeing his Sisters over the Heath—John waiting with a Lanthen for his Mistress" are the rustic figments of theatre and novel, without individual life. What are real to him are books, especially the plays

1. *Letters*, I, 128–130.

from which he quotes almost obsessively, and the small circle of friends and relatives he had just left. "You, Haydon, Reynolds &c. have been pushing each other out of my Brain by turns." The effort of living and thinking on his own was as yet strange to him, and something of a strain, making him feel "rather muzzy". The first real stages of his integration as a person were just beginning. He crossed that afternoon to the Isle of Wight, landed at Cowes and drove to Newport, where he slept at a lodging. Scratched on the window pane was a legend "O Isle spoilt by the Milatary", which confirmed the disgust Keats, in true *Examiner* fashion, already felt at the large barracks planted there during the late war, full of

> The scarlet Coats, that pester human kind.

Turning his back on this "Nest of Debauchery", though not, as he admitted, without a cheering thought that it might have made the Isle of Wight girls "a little profligate" toward a civilian like himself, he set off on a day trip to Shanklin. There the deep wooded cleft of the Chine, the waterfall and the moving sea, and the bald slopes of St. Catherine Down with its chalk cliff all delighted him. The price of lodgings, however, put him off, and he returned to Newport, unfashionable but just as beautiful. Its special attraction was the ivy-covered walls of Carisbrooke Castle, a mile outside the town looking down over a little village of watercress streams, where willows were beginning to show their early colour, and dairy maids, yoke on shoulder, climbed the slope with full creamy pails. This sheltered valley, and indeed all the Island, was full of primroses, and the low-creeping blue birdseye or germander speedwell, though these shut in the cloudy weather, which had temporarily broken the fine spell—"the Rain holds whereby that is Birds eyes abate", as Keats wrote to Reynolds.[1] Keats could also climb the cowslip-sprinkled downs to the north, and get a fine view over the Solent to the "continent" of England, whose inhabitants were still spoken of by the natives of the island as "foreigners". He clinched with some lodgings in Castle Road, which led from Newport to Carisbrooke, where he had a view of the castle itself. There was a kindly landlady, called Cook; what seems to have finally attracted him was a print of Shakespeare in the passage, which he begged from Mrs. Cook to hang over his little library. In spite of this good omen, he was still disorientated; he longed for "the power of seeing how our Friends got on, at a Distance", and he asked them for letters. Change, strain, solitude, the chilly nights made him sleepless. Feeling "narvus" and "all in a Tremble from not having written any thing of late", with the opening of *Endymion* still halfway down his first page, he made matters worse by reading *King Lear*, whose lines obsessed him with haunting significance; his surroundings took on the monster shape of Edgar's huge evocation of cliff and sea in his words to the blind Gloucester. To exorcise this nervousness, he set it to

1. *Letters*, I, 131.

work in a fine sonnet *On the Sea*, which he sent to Reynolds, who immediately quoted it to friends[1] and later printed it in *The Champion*. This gave only temporary relief, but it pointed the way, and on Thursday 18 April, Keats plunged into *Endymion*.[2] Writing swiftly, he poured into the poem all the new sights and feelings that had taken possession of him. He worked through the external impressions of heath, valley and downland, and began to recall the purpose of the poem. It was to be on a grand scale, like the books of *The Excursion* that had given him the idea of embodying life in a classical legend. Indeed, he referred to the poem and the act of poetic composition in the exact terms that Wordsworth used in a long-favourite poem of Keats's, the *Personal Talk* series of sonnets.

> And thus from day to day my little boat
> Rocks in its harbour, lodging peaceably.

So Wordsworth had written of his own inspiration. Keats set out his own poetic ambition in the same image:

> And, as the year
> Grows lush in juicy stalks, I'll smoothly steer
> My little boat, for many quiet hours,

until, as he hoped, autumn

> With universal tinge of sober gold

would see the poem finished. For the moment, his task was to make the most of his spring inspiration, and his almost morbid need to write as a kind of therapy. He composed swiftly,[3] sprinkling his lines with half-unconscious images and epithets from the two Shakespeare plays he had unboxed at Southampton, so that Latmos and the procession of worshippers to Pan, though shot with visual memories of the Pan-Athenean feast from the Elgin Marbles, were presented in terms more suitable to Elizabethan Warwickshire. It could be objected, as Byron objected to Book IV of Wordsworth's *The Excursion*,[4] that every geographical detail in it was false; the fact remains that Keats, with instant sureness, drew on his deeply-felt sense of atmosphere, the half-remembered garden landscape of his childhood, to make a setting in which the reader at once breathes the same air as the simple worshippers of the woodland god. Moreover, the setting acquires a Wordsworthian mysteriousness as it progresses. A haunting line,

1. KHM, No. 155, J. H. Reynolds to Mary Leigh, 28 April 1817.
2. Garrod, *Works*, lxxxix, mistakes Keats's joke to Haydon (*Letters*, I, 141) to mean that Keats did practically nothing for a month. Keats said at that date (10 May), that he was not *halfway* in the poem.
3. There is no reason to believe that Keats did not write at his usual rate of 30-50 lines a day during this week. He describes himself as being "in continual burning of thought".
4. Moorman, *William Wordsworth*, II, 267-268.

The surgy murmurs of the lonely sea

takes its force from his own sonnet and his own loneliness. In writing Keats begins to grapple with his own apprehension of the world around him, in a way that moves toward the creative state of Wordsworth in the *Immortality Ode*, when the older poet had felt and rejoiced in

> those obstinate questionings
> Of sense and outward things,
> Fallings from us, vanishings;
> Blank misgivings of a Creature
> Moving about in worlds not realized,
> High instincts before which our mortal Nature
> Did tremble like a guilty Thing surprised:

Keats was in that state when, on 26 April, he came to write the first great set-piece of his own poem, the *Hymn to Pan*.[1] Its early stanzas, still Elizabethan in feeling, derive not only from Shakespeare, but from Drayton's poem on the same theme, *The Man in the Moone*, from Sandys' Ovid, and from Keats's schoolboy classics such as the two *Pantheon* volumes, classical dialogue encyclopedias by Baldwin (William Godwin) and Tooke.[2] As the *Hymn* progresses, it becomes more and more infused with Wordsworthian authority, until the full note is struck in the final stanza:

> Be still the unimaginable lodge
> For solitary thinkings; such as dodge
> Conception to the very bourne of heaven,
> Then leave the naked brain: be still the leaven,
> That spreading in this dull and clodded earth
> Gives it a touch ethereal—a new birth:
> Be still a symbol of immensity;
> A firmament reflected in a sea;
> An element filling the space between;
> An unknown—but no more:

Keats could not climb any more in this rarefied mental air; he finished the stanza perfunctorily, but for a moment his vision had reached the mountain height of his leader, Wordsworth, and he knew it. The strain of such an achievement, his highest so far, was immense. "Solitary thinkings" and "naked brain" are pointers to his own half-joking, half-frightened confession that "By this means in a Week or so I became not over capable in my upper

1. Woodhouse notes "26 Ap 1817" at the head of the column containing the Hymn to Pan in the Galignani edition given him by Severn in 1832. Keats Collection, Houghton Library *EC 8.2262. He also notes MS variants of the first stanza, not recorded in Garrod, *Works*, 72.

2. Finney, I, 260–268 for an analysis of all these influences.

Stories." The exact date of composition of the *Hymn* links it with this mental state.

Unaccustomed solitude and intense composition left him vulnerable and alarmed. His instinct was to seek a point of familiar safety. He had been happy six months before in his lodgings at Margate with Tom. Like a homing pigeon, he set off on the 150-mile journey along the South Coast. In spite of this sudden exit, he had charmed Mrs. Cook so much that she gave him the print of Shakespeare to keep. Perhaps, he felt, this was a good omen, in the midst of the mental turmoil. He had hoped Tom would join him in the Isle of Wight, where he had bought a copy of *Marmion* for him; but whether the younger brother joined him before or after his move, he was certainly with him at Margate, where they fell into the sympathetic pattern of their earlier days. George, meanwhile, was involved not so happily. Leaving Abbey, after his quarrel with Hodgkinson, he had gone to work for a linendraper at 62 Bread Street; bowing to the customers he served did not suit his temperament either, and he soon gave it up. He then engaged in some scheme of business with a man called Wilkinson, borrowing some of Keats's newly-cashed capital for the purpose; this project too proved abortive.[1] George also took on himself an office which hardly served Keats. Thinking that the Olliers were failing to push the volume of *Poems*, George wrote them a letter from 62 Bread Street whose brash and over-loyal contents can be inferred from the reply they wrote him on Tuesday 29 April. They obviously were smarting from Keats's defection to Taylor, and this gave them an opportunity of washing their hands. "We regret that your brother ever requested us to publish his book" they began, went on to assume George might like to take responsibility for the unsold copies, and, unnecessarily, added that the customers who had bought it were so dissatisfied that one "told us he considered it 'no better than a take in'." Though this may have been exaggerated, the Olliers had some reason for bitter feeling. The demand had been so small, that not only bound copies, but whole sets of the printing, still unbound in quires, remained on their hands. They eventually sold these off to a bookseller, Edward Stibbs, at the minute rate of three-halfpence a copy; he bound them in boards for another twopence-halfpenny, and sold the lot very slowly at 1s. 6d. each.[2] Taylor & Hessey took over some of the bound copies.

Keats was at first unaware of these undercurrents and complications. He resumed his routine of eight hours a day work and study with Tom, and put the finishing touches to the *Hymn to Pan*, which he sent off in the first week

---

1. Ward, 119, confuses George's two projects by assuming that a Thomas Wilkinson, auctioneer, lived at 62 Bread Street, whose occupants were in fact W. G. Taylor, wholesale linendraper, and Walton, Newton and Walton, Manchester warehousemen. Thomas Wilkinson lived at 19 Bread Street. *Johnstone's London Directory*, 1817.

2. W. C. Hazlitt, I, 276, where *Endymion* is an error for *Poems*.

of May to Haydon. The painter, who had already received a letter about Keats's mental doubts and difficulties, and had written an encouraging reply,[1] was able to add a note of real enthusiasm at this evidence of achievement: "I have read your delicious Poem,[2] with exquisite enjoyment, it is the most delightful thing of the time—You have taken up the great trumpet of nature and made it sound with a voice of your own." Haydon's recognition that here, in spite of groping and uncertainty, Keats had found his own voice, was a stimulus to more work. He had already written a classical description of the peasants' games and contests. These, ending in the picture of his solitary hero, also lead to a picture of himself; Endymion, with his alternations of elation and despair, is more and more Keats. Yet he was now beginning to meet the difficulties of construction in his poem. The first four hundred lines, which he had written by the beginning of May, had not touched the core of the story, the love of Endymion and his Moon-Goddess. Lacking Wordsworth's talkative triangle of Self, Wanderer and Solitary from *The Excursion*, Keats sought a way of expounding Endymion's position by giving him a confidante. Noticing in Lemprière that Endymion had a son called Paeon, he invented for his hero a sister called Peona,[3] introduced, somewhat ominously, as "a most tender lass". The next three hundred lines, which he wrote in the first week of May, were so unsatisfactory that when he came to revise the poem for publication, he cut at least a fifth of them. They get Keats through the necessary business of explaining how his hero was visited by the Goddess, and that is the most that can be said for them. Their slackness suggests that Haydon was right when he advised Keats to live away from everyone, even his brothers, while composing. The painter had seized on a vital point for the poet as artist. Keats had outlived the need for support and help from his brothers in his poetic life, though he still craved it personally, and the note of cosy intimacy, which may have come from his association with Tom, was a disaster in the mouths of Endymion and Peona as he wrote on.

Some indications of the rather childish mood he fell into with Tom may be found in the way the two brothers treated Dr. Johnson's critical comments in the Steevens seven-volume Shakespeare[4] Keats was reading. Johnson's own notes, which Steevens generally printed at the end of each play, were handled by Keats with mischievous adolescent humour. He began by

1. *Letters*, I, 134–135.
2. *Letters*, I, 136. The words must refer to the *Hymn*, not to the sonnet, *On the Sea*, as suggested.
3. He was possibly influenced by the brother-and-sister construction of Shelley's poem, *Laon and Cythna*, which they may have discussed before they both left London. In references in Keats's letters he always spells her name Paeona, in accordance with her origin.
4. Keats Collection, Houghton Library, *EC 8, for the volumes marked in Keats's and Tom's hands.

underlining with approval Johnson's remark on *Two Gentlemen of Verona* that "it will be found more credible that Shakespeare might sometimes sink below his highest flights, than that other should rise up to his lowest"; a phrase from Johnson's note on *The Merry Wives of Windsor* also pleased him, but every other note by Johnson Keats either ignored or treated to satirical comment. He usually did this by crossing out the note heavily, and adding an opprobrious quotation from the play just read. Johnson's note on *Twelfth Night* was merely crossed out with no quotation; but at the end of his note on *Measure for Measure*, Keats burst out, from the play,

> But Man! Proud Man!
> Drest in a little brief authority
> Plays such fantastic tricks before high heaven
> As make the angels weep.

He added three exclamation marks to reinforce his scorn, and having once thought of this way to deflate Johnson, there was no stopping him.[1] At the end of *A Midsummer Night's Dream* he wrote "Fie" before the printed name of Johnson, and added no fewer than four quotations or deliberate misquotations from the play, beginning "Such tricks hath *weak* imagination". After *The Merchant of Venice*, he applied the Prince of Aragon's "which pries not to the interior" as a criticism of Johnson's shallow taste. To *As You Like It*, he added a parody of Audrey's remark to Touchstone about poetry, writing "Is *Criticism* a true thing?" At the end of *The Winter's Tale*, he was ready with Paulina's "lo fool again" for Johnson, and after *Macbeth*, two appropriate quotations from the play, "Thou losest labour" and "As the Hare the Lion". To Johnson's note on *Antony and Cleopatra*, he cheekily appended Charmian's

> Your crown's awry
> I'll mend it

while finally, to counter Johnson's suggestion that *Titus Andronicus* was not written by Shakespeare, Keats, stumped for a quotation from the play itself, adapted from *Julius Caesar* in the same volume, the lines

> Ye Blocks! Ye stones! ye worse than senseless things!
> Knew ye not Pompey—

This private attack on the great arbiter of the Augustans was humour very much in the style of Leigh Hunt, to whom Keats had just made another facetious quotation from *A Midsummer Night's Dream* in a letter.[2] It reflects, too, his own lack of mature taste and criticism at this time, even though his

1. Tom, in his hand, added his own would-be satirical quotations from *Love's Labour's Lost*, *As You Like It*, and *All's Well That Ends Well* at the end of Johnson's notes on those three plays.
2. *Letters*, I, 136.

instinctive appreciation of Shakespeare was already great. His one critical note is very unlike his later and deeper insight into Shakespeare. Against Antony's "Fie, wrangling queen", he wrote "How much more Shakespeare delights in dwelling upon the romantic and wildly natural than upon the monumental". He added "see Winters Tale 'when you do dance' &c", a passage he also marked. Yet if in general his markings in this edition concentrate on the "romantic and wildly natural" in Shakespeare, he was absorbing the style and manner deeply. Falstaff had already impressed him, and he noted twice in *The Merry Wives of Windsor* how Falstaff had what he called "a peculiar way" in his prose style, expressive of his character. It was a style and character that Keats adopted in his own prose writings, so that certain passages of his letters read like the great prose outpourings of Shakespeare's creation.

For all this adolescent bravado, he was uneasy about his work. He confessed to Haydon "Truth is I have been in such a state of Mind as to read over my Lines and hate them." It was all very well for Tom to read him couplets from Pope, and agree how much better John's were—"they seem like Mice to mine"—but Keats, with Shakespeare as the imaginary "Presider" over his own verses, had other standards. Haunted still by the passage in *King Lear*, he began to see his task towering above him like a cliff. All that he had done so far seemed insignificant. This feeling was underlined by a letter from Hunt, which had arrived just as he was packing for Margate, and which he had put off answering; for Hunt, cheerfully installed at Marlow, and editing *The Examiner* from there, showed not the least sign of reviewing his poems, but with Shelley at his elbow poured himself into attacks on Church and Government, a "Battering Ram against Christianity". Keats eventually contrived a letter in reply, though, as he confessed to Haydon, he scarcely knew what he said in it. He managed some shrewd criticism of certain passages in Book One of Hunt's *The Nymphs*, which he had seen in manuscript, but Hunt took no notice.[1] Signing himself "John Keats alias Junkets", perhaps as a sop to Hunt's playful patronage, Keats was uncomfortably led to consider his relationship with Hunt. Hunt, he felt, flattered himself "into an idea of being a great Poet". In his own self-critical mood, Keats had uneasy searchings too. The laurel-crowning incident came back to him in all its pretentious absurdity. Snatching a moment from the main poem, he dashed off an abject apology to the "God of the golden bow", Apollo, whom he had insulted on that occasion, and in such a way

> To tie like a madman thy plant round his brow,
> And grin and look proudly,
> And blaspheme so loudly,
> And live for that honour, to stoop to thee now.

1. The three phrases Keats criticized were printed unaltered in *Foliage* (1818).

Yet even now, he caught himself out again "talking like a Madman" in a letter to Haydon.

In this unsettled state, he received on Sunday 11 May an alarming letter from George, "by which it appears that Money Troubles are to follow us up for some time to come perhaps for always". George was apt to exaggerate his financial woes, and he may only have meant that his business scheme with Wilkinson had fallen through, and he could not repay Keats his £40 or £50 loan. There are, however, obscure hints of another kind of inconvenience. Abbey had, of course, ceased to be Keats's trustee, and to have any direct financial control over him, but since Sandell's death he was sole trustee for the other Keats children. There are signs that he co-opted another trustee to safeguard their position and his own, as he had a right to do. Both Dilke and Brown, who never knew Sandell, spoke later of another trustee, who proved unsatisfactory and fled the country to Holland.[1] From later correspondence between Keats and George, his name would appear to have been Fry,[2] but he remains a shadowy figure.[3] He may have served Abbey, however, as a useful excuse for delaying or refusing to cash any of George's capital before he came of age, for which George was eventually grateful,[4] though he felt aggrieved now. Whatever the position, George's feelings, by chain reaction, increased Keats's mood of despondency. This, luckily enough, was the saving of his poem at this point. Shelley had met the disaster of being legally deprived of his children with the philosophy that "all human evils either extinguish or are extinguished by the sufferers", and was extinguishing his by writing his long poem with boundless enthusiasm.[5] Keats too had a philosophy which, as he afterwards expressed, "can bear real ills better than imaginary ones",[6] and he too found a solution in writing them down. His confessed tendency to "a horrid Morbidity of Temperament" found magnificent expression in a passage where his hero analyses just such a state in himself, and it strikes a note of deeper enquiry in the poem which is maintained for some time afterward. In itself, it is a remarkable insight into his own depressive moods, where the familiar world of natural surroundings could become, by a momentary shift of view, full of warning portents:

> Away I wander'd—all the pleasant hues
> Of heaven and earth had faded: deepest shades
> Were deepest dungeons; heaths and sunny glades
> Were full of pestilent light; our taintless rills
> Seem'd sooty, and o'er spread with upturn'd gills

1. KHM, No. 104, Brown to Dilke, 6 Sept. 1824; KC, II, 175.
2. *Letters*, II, 185, 228, 231.
3. Though not, surely, invented by Abbey, as suggested by Norman Kilgour, "Mrs. Jennings' Will", KSMB, XIII, 24–27.
4. KC, I, 278.   5. F. L. Jones (ed.) *Letters of Shelley*, I, 539.
6. *Letters*, II, 186.

Of dying fish; the vermeil rose had blown
In frightful scarlet, and its thorns out-grown
Like spiked aloe. If an innocent bird
Before my heedless footsteps stirr'd, and stirr'd
In little journeys, I beheld in it
A disguis'd demon, missioned to knit
My soul with under darkness;[1]

Nothing could better illustrate the "disguis'd demon" in Keats's own make-up, for which writing was practically the only exorcism. This was matched by a healthy energy in practical matters. Keats whipped off an appeal for an advance to his generous new publishers, and decided that a change of scene from the bleak East Kent coastline would do him good. He picked on Canterbury where "I hope the Remembrance of Chaucer will set me forward like a Billiard-Ball", he wrote to Taylor and Hessey on 16 May, thanking them for £20, and promising them a good "next Month" of writing.

Keats also explored further in the reading of Shakespeare, encouraged by exhortations in letters from Haydon, and by correspondence with George, who had just himself read *A Midsummer Night's Dream*, *The Tempest*, and *King Lear*, keeping in intellectual step with his talented brother. Just before leaving for Canterbury on 17 May, Keats had been reading hard in *Antony and Cleopatra*. Shakespeare's great love-duet began to lend a shape to the theme of his own poem. As well as the self-exploration it had already become, it moved imperceptibly into a commentary upon love and life, a natural train of thought for a young man on the threshold of both. As Keats wrote on, he formulated in the next 150 lines of the poem, permeated with images and situations drawn from Shakespeare's Egyptian tragedy,[2] what he was afterwards to regard as one of the most important elements in the whole poem. As he told Taylor[3]

I assure you that when I wrote it, it was a regular stepping of the Imagination towards a Truth. My having written that Argument will perhaps be of the greatest Service to me of any thing I ever did—It set before me at once the gradations of Happiness even like a kind of Pleasure Thermometer—and is my first Step towards the chief Attempt in the Drama—the playing of different Natures with Joy and Sorrow.

With this exposition of this passage must be set another[4] which clearly refers to the same part of Book One of *Endymion*:

I am certain of nothing but of the holiness of the Heart's affections and the truth of Imagination—What the imagination seizes as Beauty must be truth—whether it existed before or not—for I have the same Idea of all our Passions as of Love they are

1. *Endymion*, I, 691–702.
2. *John Keats: A Reassessment*, 28. See particularly *Endymion*, I, ll. 714, 740–745, 753, 791–793, 817–823.
3. *Letters*, I, 210–218.   4. *Letters*, I, 184–185.

all in their sublime, creative of essential Beauty—In a Word, you may know my favorite Speculation by my first Book. . . .

The "regular stepping" of the passage, to which Keats refers in these later letters, is one familiar in Plato's dialogues. The highest state of mortality is Love, and Love pursued to its utmost is immortal, and at one with all the other "essences" or real ultimates of Truth and Beauty. From these remarks of Keats about this passage, a school of critics has regarded the whole poem as a neo-Platonic allegory, in which Endymion is the Poet searching for Love, Truth and Beauty, typified by Cynthia the Moon-Goddess, which he wins only after the trials of experience. Yet Keats is only talking about this particular passage, as his later comments make clear; he never makes any pronouncement on the whole poem in this way. Moreover, although there is much unconscious neo-Platonism in the passage, influenced not only by *Antony and Cleopatra* but by the great speeches of Berowne in *Love's Labour's Lost* which he was also reading and marking, his comments, which give it such a Platonic interpretation, were both written after he had been led to discuss Plato later in the year.[1]

Keats, in fact, confessed that there was no general plan for the poem as a whole. "Before I began", he wrote,[2] "I had no inward feel of being able to finish; and as I proceeded my steps were all uncertain." More explicitly, he wrote to George at about this time, either late in his stay at Margate or from Canterbury:

Endymion . . . will be a test, a trial of my Powers of Imagination and chiefly of my invention which is a rare thing indeed—by which I must make 4000 lines of one bare circumstance and fill them with Poetry;

and he went on to justify his intention to write a poem of such a length in an image that shows the flowering of his characteristic Falstaffian prose style, as

a test of Invention which I take to be the Polar Star of Poetry, as Fancy is the Sails, and Imagination the Rudder.

None of this, written at exactly the same time as the passage in Book One, shows any sign of a conscious working at any allegory; Keats's emphasis is on what he calls Invention, to take a story and fill it with Poetry. With his deep reading in *The Faerie Queene*, not even suppressed by his new allegiance to Shakespeare,[3] he must have regarded allegory as part of the inventiveness necessary for a long poem, but it was only one element in the complex of his poetic task, the simple but gigantic test of his powers. He ended the letter to George with yet another rueful shrug at his own laurel-crowning episode, and

1. The most helpful analysis of this passage and these various points of view is found in E. C. Pettet, *On the Poetry of Keats*, 123–145.
2. Garrod, *Works*, xciii.   3. *Letters*, I, 170.

to this or another letter from Canterbury, he added the comment "I have forgotten all surgery". It was not that he regretted his medical training; but the step he felt he had taken in formulating and writing this credo now marked him off from his past for ever. Moreover, it looked to the future. "The playing of different Natures with Joy and Sorrow", so evident in his own nature, was to become more and more his poetic concern.

For the moment, this concern was to finish the First Book—he was near his stint of 1000 lines—and set Endymion off on his adventures. The remainder of the Book fell back, as so often, on Keats's boyhood reminiscences and schoolboy scenery. He finished abruptly, with a touch that shows how little logic there was in the poem's construction. Endymion vows to think no more of his strange encounters with Cynthia, and sets off with Peona in their little boat; yet then Peona, unexplained, completely disappears from him, and only returns, equally unexplained, in the very last 200 lines of the whole poem. She, at least, is no part of allegory, though her part as confidante to Endymion may be a parallel to the part played to Keats by the receptive Tom. He now left to rejoin George in Hampstead, while Keats went on to spend Whit-week in a deserved seaside holiday. He went alone to the little coastal hamlet of Bo Peep, west of Hastings, whose name spoke of its smuggling history, and where there was a small inn near the ruins of the wartime barracks. Haydon, who had enjoyed himself hugely there, had probably recommended it.

Keats in a holiday mood may have hoped, as he did in the Isle of Wight, that he would find the girls "a little profligate". Instead, he found himself having an adventure with an enigmatic and mysterious young woman, whose exact status he could never quite make out, but who was to move increasingly in the same literary circle as himself. Mrs. Isabella Jones was beautiful, talented, witty and lively, and about his own age—or so he believed. She was not in the first flight of society, for her name was not listed among the fashionable visitors for the month, but she was in the habit of summering at Hastings with an elderly member of a titled Irish Whig family, Donat O'Callaghan, to whom she was attached in some undefined way. Widely read, though with conventional tastes, she found the attractive young poet interesting in more senses than one, for before they were very long acquainted Keats found that he "had warmed with her . . . and kissed her." This phrase has been taken to mean many things, from the mildest of flirtations to a possible sexual initiation for Keats.[1] What it seems to mean, in the language of the day, is that he was stirred sexually by her, but that he, or more probably she, found it better to "make a full stop at kissing", as he said when discussing sexual matters elsewhere.[2] This is borne out by the

1. See Bate, 167–168, Ward, 121–122.
2. "Warm" certainly had sexual connotations in Regency times, and "kissed" was often used for the sexual act itself, though perhaps not certainly here.

little poem he wrote for her to keep, as a memory of their Whit-week encounter. The second verse is typical:

> You say you love; but with a smile
> Cold as sunrise in September,
> As you were Saint Cupid's nun,
> And kept his weeks of Ember.
> O love me truly!

The half-rueful reference to the ember days on which they were meeting would appeal to Isabella Jones, who among her other accomplishments turned out to be well-up in Church festivals, but it is unlikely that she complied with the passionate requests in the later part of the poem. However, she proved a stimulating experience not only for Keats but for his poetry. The opening of Book Two of *Endymion* begins with a panegyric of romantic love, sets Endymion wandering in a landscape which is unmistakably the coastline near Bo Peep, where he meets an enigmatic nymph in what appears to be the local Hastings beauty-spot, The Fishponds. She offers him comfort, but stops short of love.

These lines were probably written early in June when he had returned to London; he was certainly back in Hampstead by Tuesday 10 June, when his debts made him borrow a further £30 from his publishers. The three summer months of June, July and August are something of a puzzle. In spite of a momentary falter in the middle of May, he had written his long poem well up to the courageous schedule he had sketched in its early lines. Book One was done, Book Two started, and at this rate he was well on the way to the hoped-for completion by the autumn. An average of thirty to forty lines a day was a commonplace to him, in company with both Wordsworth and Shelley; why then did Book Two, which, like Book One, could have taken him only just over a month, take three?

There is an almost complete lack of evidence to suggest an answer; apart from the begging letter to Taylor & Hessey, only one other brief note by Keats this summer has survived. Some lines as he continued *Endymion* suggest a feeling of disappointment and inadequacy. In the poem, he develops his growing philosophy that the disappointments of existence rightly used, are the food of life; yet, significantly, his own hero is unable to make use of this philosophy, although he recognizes its truth:[1]

> But this is human life: the war, the deeds,
> The disappointment, the anxiety,
> Imagination's struggles, far and nigh,
> All human; bearing in themselves this good,
> That they are still the air, the subtle food,

1. *Endymion*, II, 153–161.

> To make us feel existence, and to show
> How quiet death is. Where soil is men grow,
> Whether to weeds or flowers; but for me,
> There is no depth to strike in;

After this fine passage of personal and deep feeling, the poem embarks on a long haul of commonplace in thought and description, which justifies Keats's own dissatisfaction. Some of the disappointments of this time in his life may be guessed. Haydon again was right to hint that Keats involved himself too much in the affairs of his brothers. George's business affairs were becoming as unsatisfactory as Tom's health; he had to eat humble pie to Abbey, and, there is reason to believe, went back to work for him sporadically. Keats took George's humiliation very personally;[1] as for Tom, Keats's medical knowledge, far from being forgotten, cannot have given him much ease. His own plans to visit the Continent that summer on a working holiday to "collect incidents, study characters", as Haydon said, gave way to a similar project for the good of his brothers, involving money he had hoped to spend on himself.[2]

Such vexations were, as he had said, enemies of work, "like a nettle or two in your bed". There were others which struck more directly at the work itself. Apart from a short, friendly anonymous notice in the *Monthly Magazine*, no review had appeared to second Reynolds's praise in *The Champion*. Now, almost at the same time, Keats suffered reviews of a very different nature from two other friends. Returning to London, he encountered[3] George Felton Mathew's review in *The European Magazine* for May, and Leigh Hunt's long-awaited notice in *The Examiner* of Sunday 1 June. Both were staggering in their patronizing attitude. Mathew's review was outrageous to the point of being absurd. He actually jeered at Reynolds's praise of Keats, and perversely only preferred those early poems which Reynolds had found "very inferior to the rest". He pontificated on "the mere luxuries of imagination", and attacked the finest short poem in the book, the Chapman's Homer sonnet. A warning, only too true, that Keats's lines on Pope in *Sleep and Poetry* would cause "ridicule and rebuke" completed his tally of destruction. Yet Hunt in *The Examiner* was, if anything, even more exasperating for a young author. After a pompous start, announcing that "the author and his critic are personal friends", Keats and his poems were never mentioned again. The whole column was devoted to a re-hash of Hunt's views on English poetry from Dryden to Wordsworth, worked up from his notes to *The Feast of the Poets*. Admittedly it promised "to be concluded next week", but "next week" was, in Huntian reality, five weeks ahead. When the review was at last resumed on Sunday 6 July,

1. *Letters*, I, 287.
2. KHM, No. 104, Brown to Dilke, 20 Jan. 1830.
3. Ward, 118, thinks he saw Mathew's review earlier at Margate.

Hunt made some amends by judicious quotation; but a larger part of these two columns consisted in pointing out faults. As the most shattering blow of all, he suggested that Keats had "a tendency to notice every thing too indiscriminately and without an eye to natural proportion and effect" which resembled the poetry of Erasmus Darwin. Not many months before, Keats had looked forward ardently to meeting Hunt as one of those "who in their admiration of Poetry do not jumble together Shakspeare and Darwin". Now, by an irony that he could not possibly have foreseen, here was Hunt jumbling him together with Darwin in just the same way. Even the conclusion of the notice on 13 July, with longer quotations, could not make up for what had gone, or not gone, before. Hunt's preferences, too, were couched in an unhappily domestic language that lent to the poems themselves an atmosphere of absurdity—"a piece of luxury in a rural spot", "a little luxuriant heap" and so on. Keats was led to realize what he afterwards bitterly expressed, that Hunt's praise could be more damning than his criticism. Even an outsider remarked that the review was "done with an air of patronage, not with heart".[1]

Hunt himself, to do him justice, was palpably uneasy. On Wednesday 25 June he had at last returned to Town, staying at first with his brother John in Maida Vale before moving later in July to his new home at 13 Lisson Grove North. Hazlitt and other friends called, but not Keats; on Tuesday 1 July, Hunt wrote to Cowden Clarke with affected jocularity, "What has become of Junkets I know not. I suppose Queen Mab has eaten him."[2] When Keats at length summoned up resolve to go round to Lisson Grove, he seems to have dressed with unusual smartness, a device he always adopted as a cure for disturbed feelings. His well-brushed jacket with its shining buttons gave another young visitor of about his age, the son of C. H. Reynell the printer, the impression that Keats was dressed for the occasion "in some sort of naval costume".[3] What passed between him and Hunt is unknown. Certainly Hunt exerted his habitual charm, for a month or two later, Keats wrote to Reynolds speaking of Hunt's failings, yet admitting "but then his makes-up are very good". However skilfully Hunt made it up at this time, though, Keats's admission of his virtues was only temporary, and he never again wrote of Hunt other than critically. Hunt on the other hand seems to have been reassured. Many of his further actions and references to Keats were extremely generous, and he was genuinely hurt when he found out long afterwards the real state of Keats's feelings toward him.

1. Caroline Scott to B. R. Haydon, 19 July 1817.
2. C. Cowden Clarke, *Recollections of Writers*, 194.
3. W. C. Hazlitt, I, 275. "Naval" costume, hitherto always misquoted "sailor", suggests officer's uniform rather than seaman's dress as has sometimes been assumed; nor did this encounter take place till Hunt had moved to his new home. Hunt emphasizes what care Keats took of his appearance (*Book of Gems*, Vol. 3, 1838) during the time he knew him.

It seems more than likely that these disturbances of personal relationship had to do with the slow progress of *Endymion*. On the other hand, some happier social relationships were probably, in their way, just as much of a stumbling-block. Two friends found a special need for his company this summer, and sought opportunities to be with him; one of these was Severn. This shy, fair youth, with the slightly feminine features, looked and behaved as if he were younger than he was. Anxious to please, accident-prone throughout his life, he was both clumsy and endearing, sometimes irritating, frequently lovable. He kept up a flow of cheerful talk, but worried over trifles. His desire to shine in company led him innocently to claim in later age more than his real acquaintance with famous people and events. All the time Keats was away writing Book One, Severn had pestered George at Hampstead to know when John would be back, and to be reassured that Keats had not forgotten their friendship. Severn found Keats's "taste in the arts, his knowledge of history, and his most fascinating power in the communication of these" an inspiration which opened, as he said, "a new world" to his hopes of being a successful artist.[1] The fashion of painting from literary or historical subjects was at its height, and Severn had already exhibited one picture in this genre. Severn was not very well read, and Keats with his "mental richness" was an endless joy to him. This summer he attached himself like a spaniel to Keats, and in the beautiful weather they went for long walks, not only across Hampstead Heath to Caen Wood, but far into the old Middlesex Forest which still stretched, as it does today, over parts of Highgate Hill. Not only Keats's knowledge of literature but his feeling for nature fascinated Severn, nature in the Wordsworthian sense including human nature in all its aspects and even its by-products of dress and superficial appearance:

Nothing seemed to escape him, the song of a bird and the undernote of response from covert or hedge, the rustle of some animal, the changing of the green and brown lights and furtive shadows, the motions of the wind—just how it took certain tall flowers and plants—and the wayfaring of the clouds: even the features and gestures of passing tramps, the colour of one woman's hair, the smile on one child's face, the furtive animalism below the deceptive humanity in many of the vagrants, even the hats, clothes, shoes, wherever these conveyed the remotest hint as to the real self of the wearer.

Severn is one of the earliest witnesses to the power of Keats to enter into the "identity" of everything he encountered, animate or inanimate. Haydon confirmed this. "The humming of the bee, the sight of a flower, the glitter of the sun, seemed to make his nature tremble!" What Clarke had seen as an aspect of comic fancy and mimicry was now developing into an insight which viewed everything in its poetic aspect, the "essences" of things, their real

1. Sharp, 19.

existence. The haunting image of the sea, begun at Margate the previous autumn, intensified almost unbearably in the Isle of Wight in company with his reading of *King Lear*, made him feel the movement of the summer fields in the Kilburn farms, the full-leaved chestnuts and oaks of the Highgate forest, or even the grassy meadows as an inland sea, akin to the great simile of Wordsworth's *Immortality Ode*. "The tide! The tide!" he would cry, as a wave of wind came billowing across the surface of the land.[1] Severn in turn helped to enlarge Keats's visual sense on their visits to galleries and exhibitions of paintings. Their conversations about the Greek spirit and their enjoyment together of the Elgin Marbles found their way into *Endymion*.[2] It is no accident that Book Two became more pictorial, a series of highly-coloured tableaux, lovingly described, as its hero, bidden to seek his love in earth, water and air, wanders through underground galleries, whose alcoves contain scenes like classical paintings—Venus and Adonis, Alpheus and Arethusa—, their details laid on in Titian colours. One Sunday, Keats read to Severn and Cowden Clarke the whole of the description of Venus and Adonis, with the *Hymn to Pan* from Book One as a companion piece.

Keats's other friend in his walks on Hampstead Heath was Reynolds. Their shared passion was Shakespeare. Keats bought himself a new large copy, a facsimile folio, in which they could read together in the open, instead of peering at the small volumes of his other edition. Reynolds also had personal problems to discuss as they sat on the Heath. After an unhappy first love affair—the girl had died young—he had met in September 1816 some sisters at Sidmouth in Devon called Leigh. They had introduced him to another Devon girl, Eliza Drewe, with whom he was now in love, and who encouraged him in his hopes of marriage. Keats, feeling perhaps that his lively friend might regret being shackled too early, spoke in general terms against marriage; yet he showed Reynolds a few more little love-lyrics, in the style of "You say you love" that he had written himself. They have some connection with the love-passage between Endymion and Cynthia which he had now reached in his poem, and can be regarded as off-shoots from the long work. One of them, however, beginning "Unfelt, unheard, unseen" seems certainly to speak of some actual sexual experience that took place this summer.[3] Reynolds quoted briefly and decorously from it in *The Champion* of 17 August, in which he also printed Keats's sonnet *On the Sea*.

To the preoccupations of old friends was added the acquaintance of two new ones, whom Keats had met very briefly in the Spring, both through Reynolds. The Leighs, even before seeing Reynolds, had heard about him from his friends, James Rice and Benjamin Bailey. Rice, a young lawyer in

---

1. Sharp, 20–21.   2. *Endymion*, II, 250–260.
3. See the penultimate line, "I'll feel my heaven anew". To feel one's heaven, or more usually to feel one's way to heaven, was current usage for beginning the sexual act. Appendix 4.

his father's firm, was incurably ill, visiting Sidmouth for his health; but he made light of his affliction with constant wit and gaiety. Neat and dapper, he had the sufferer's gift of husbanding his energy. Suffering too had given him a wisdom which Keats recognized and admired, saying that he "makes you laugh and think". Concerned for Reynolds's prospects in marriage, Rice was persuading him to become articled to a relative of his own in the law, Frank Fladgate, who formed one of a light-hearted set of professional men living between Oxford Street and Piccadilly. He often did not return from their parties to his home in Poland Street till morning.

Benjamin Bailey was of another type, though biographers have been too ready to agree with the view of the light-weight garrulous Severn, who found him "rather stern". Although an East Anglian, he had relatives in Devon at Colyton near Sidmouth, where he probably first met Rice; later they both introduced Reynolds to the Leighs. With them Bailey had addressed innumerable poems to the Leigh sisters, and was at this time agonizingly in love with Tamsin Leigh, who had just rejected him for a Lieutenant—"flung upon a desart shore after much tossing", as he wrote to Reynolds.[1] Though his own forte was for light verse, he had a passion for philosophy, especially Plato, and an enthusiasm for the great philosophic poets, Dante, Milton, and Wordsworth. Born in 1791 of a family from the isolated fenlands of Lincolnshire though living at this time a few hundred yards within the borders of Cambridgeshire,[2] he had felt the call to serious things comparatively late, and he was 25 when, the previous autumn, he had matriculated at Oxford to read for Holy Orders. This August he was in London, but he intended to spend the second half of the Long Vacation reading in the out-of-term peace of the University. He had been drawn to Keats, both by his looks and his nature, in their brief acquaintance in the Spring, and now he saw him constantly. A voracious reader himself, he was the only person to complain that Keats's reading was not systematic enough. He felt that Keats only knew Milton and Wordsworth in isolated passages of fine poetry, and he found that Keats did not know Dante at all,[3] faults that he set himself to remedy.

Keats responded to the challenge. It came at the right time, for Book Two of *Endymion* had largely gone back to the romance Elizabethan style of his early days, based on Spenser and Sandys' translation of Ovid, and was drawing to a tired conclusion. Its very last line, however, has the sudden

1. KC, I, 6.
2. His baptism on 2 April 1792 shows that his parents lived at French Drove, the northernmost tip of Thorney, the northernmost parish of Cambridgeshire. All the family property was in Lincolnshire, and the Bailey family came from Leake and Wrangle in that county. In Thorney parish they were neighbours of their relatives by marriage, the famous family of Wing, astronomers and mathematicians.
3. The expression 'pure serene' in the Chapman's Homer sonnet has been thought to come from Cary's translation of Dante's *Paradiso* but see Finney, I, 124.

F

sharp isolated echo of the great single lines with which Dante finishes each Canto. Keats's

> He saw the giant sea above his head

does for Endymion what the last line of *Inferno*, Canto 26, in Cary's version, did for Ulysses,

> And over us the booming billow clos'd.

Keats marked this line with approval,[1] and about now he acquired the two-volume 1805 edition of the *Inferno* he kept till his death. He was ready for a change of intellectual climate, and also of scene. Many of his friends, the Dilkes, the Reynolds girls and Haydon were out of Town. Reynolds himself was ill, and Hunt was absorbed in political leaders, warning against any relaxation in the cause of liberty during the parliamentary recess. Finally, George and Tom, on his money, had gone off on the foreign holiday Keats had hoped to take himself. Yet something must be done about *Endymion*, after the slow progress of Book Two; Shelley had written twice as many lines, and was in a fair way to complete his poem. Keats was therefore delighted when Benjamin Bailey suggested he should come back to Oxford with him, and attack Book Three of the poem there. As at many other times in his life, it seemed to him that the change of scene would solve the problems of a poem. Hampstead Heath was beginning to pall, in spite of one dramatic incident when Keats, Cowden Clarke and another friend, probably Reynolds, passed unscathed within two yards of a savage bull, quelling the creature by the power of the human eye.[2] Haydon, whose advice to leave London for the country he had taken in the Spring, had just spent a delightful week in Oxford, and strongly recommended its atmosphere, where "Everybody shewed you Latin & Greek books to explain any question, as if they had been English."[3] Oxford seemed the perfect answer for continuing his classical poem.

1. In the pocket edition, published by Taylor & Hessey next year. For Keats's approval of Dante's account of Ulysses's death, see *The Indicator*, Vol. I, p. 65, KHM, No. 172.
2. Leonidas M. Jones (ed.), *Selected Prose of John Hamilton Reynolds*, 424 and 482.
3. Haydon, II, 126.

Chapter 11

THE CAVE OF QUIETUDE

"a grievous feud
Hath led thee to this Cave of Quietude."
– Endymion, IV, 547–548

KEATS started Book Three of *Endymion* before he left for Oxford. Unluckily it was a false start. These first forty lines,[1] which he let stand in spite of Bailey's disapproval, did him as much harm with the conventionally-political readers of *Endymion* as the Pope passage did with the conventionally-poetical readers of the *Poems*, and for the same reason; both stem directly from Hunt. In a thunderous *Examiner* editorial of 3 August, Hunt pointed out how "the dull and insolent usurpers of the Constitution" had, in nine recent instances, seen the instruments of their attempted oppression turn against themselves;[2] he repeated variations on this theme throughout the month, on the last day of which he turned from London to Paris, satirizing the French clergy for accepting what he called "the Roman purple" of Cardinals' hats.[3] The tone of these articles was exactly and unhappily caught by Keats, who began his Book with an attack on the dull and incompetent rulers of the world's affairs "in empurpled vests, And crowns, and turbans". By a fatal unconscious association, he was echoing the line, "Turbans and Crowns, and blank regality" of his first laurel-crowning sonnet to Hunt, once more "talking like a madman" in some loyal response to Hunt's attractive power. He also seems to have had a genuine feeling that he should not divorce politics from poetry.[4] The impulse that led him to this was better employed in a satirical sonnet he wrote at the same time, "Nebuchadnezzar's Dream".[5] This picked out from Hunt's leader the difficulties of the Government in its proceedings against two radicals, Thomas Wooler, editor of *The Black Dwarf*, and William Hone, editor of *The Reformist's Register*. Hone had published Biblical parodies attacking the Government; Keats's sonnet was a

1. His note "Oxford, Septr. 5" indicates a fresh start at line 41.
2. E. No. 501, pp. 481–482.   3. E. No. 505, p. 551.
4. "K. said, with much simplicity. "It will easily be seen what I think of the present Ministers by the beginning of the 3ᵈ Book."—Woodhouse, note to interleaved *Endymion*, Berg Collection, New York Public Library.
5. Aileen Ward, "Keats's Sonnet, 'Nebuchadnezzar's Dream' ", *Philological Quarterly*, XXXIV, No. 2.

parody of the Book of Daniel, praising Hone and jeering at his prosecutors in the same terms as Hunt had done.[1] He gave a copy to Cowden Clarke, who appreciated it as a regular *Examiner* reader.

Keats and Bailey travelled to Oxford on the Defiance coach on Wednesday 3 September, and Keats at once settled down "among Colleges, Halls Stalls", as he wrote next day to the Reynolds girls, in a wildly facetious letter that carried on his mood of Biblical parody. Always stimulated by a change of scene, he pressed on with the poem, for a classical reference in the same letter chimes exactly with one at line 71 of the new Book.[2] The conditions he found were ideal for poetry. After a June heat-wave, the weather at Hampstead had often been treacherous; now a succession of golden days showed Oxford at its autumnal best. Bailey's rooms were in Magdalen Hall, tucked alongside Magdalen College, overlooking its deer-park, tree-lined grove, and small clear streams, where Keats was able each evening to take the advice given by the historian of Oxford, Antony Wood—"Goe into the Water-walks, and at some time of the year you will find them as delectable as the banks of the Eurotas . . . where Apollo himself was wont to walk and sing his lays." Magdalen Hall itself had a mixed bag of students with a reputation for slackness and drink; only a few years later, half the buildings were burnt down in a fire started in the rooms of a future priest, who had given a dramatic entertainment and a supper there, an event which hastened its move to the site of Hart Hall, where it eventually became the reconstituted Hertford College. Bailey himself, though cramming theology and philosophy, found time both to strike suitable tragic attitudes about his lost Miss Leigh, and perhaps unknown yet to Keats, to be working up a courtship of the second of Reynolds's sisters, Marianne. Bailey's father was a rich land-owner and Justice of the Peace, and he had been brought up in a well-appointed country-house with a fully-stocked cellar; he was undoubtedly the wealthiest of Keats's close friends,[3] living in Mayfair near his brother Edward, who married the publisher John Martin's sister. Perhaps the Baileys were trying that very eighteenth-century solution for the youngest son of a large county family, the Church. His rooms at Oxford were certainly more like a young squire's, with comfortable furniture, snuff, cigars and drinks, and conversation not always on a higher plane. This cheerful yet studious atmosphere in a beautiful city delighted Keats, with his sense of history and fun. Continuing his vein of parody as a happy offset to *Endymion*, he wrote a brilliant thumb-nail sketch of Oxford in the form of a skit on a Wordsworth poem, and sent it to amuse Reynolds during his convalescence. Its last verse described his comfortable surroundings.

1. Compare particularly Keats's description of Daniel, "Good king of cats", and Hunt's satire about the "catspaws" of the Government.
2. "Tellus" is mentioned in both.
3. Will of John Bailey, P.P.R., Herschel, 354.

There are plenty of trees,
And plenty of ease,
And plenty of fat deer for parsons;
And when it is venison,
Short is the benison,—
Then each on a leg or thigh fastens.

Meanwhile, the major work of *Endymion* went steadily on. Book Three was planned by Keats as a self-contained episode, unlike the loosely-connected scenes of the other books. He concentrated on a single myth from Ovid, adapting it to his own story. Endymion, journeying beneath the sea, meets Glaucus, a fisherman who has been made terrifyingly old by Circe, jealous of his love for Scylla. He is surrounded by the bodies of lovers who have been drowned at sea. Endymion, fulfilling a prophecy in a magic book, restores Glaucus to youth and to Scylla, and at the same time revives all the lovers. He is then promised fulfilment of his own love. This episode has perhaps more meaning than Keats's self-confessed task to take yet another 1000 lines and fill them with poetry. Glaucus's story was meant as some parallel with Endymion's, the love of a mortal for an immortal, and some shadowy theme begins to emerge for the whole poem, the idea of regeneration through suffering and experience. Endymion, though in this book only doing what he is told, is made to realize through Glaucus the active trials he may have to suffer before he is worthy of his love, and also the resurrective power of true feeling. Academic life with Bailey helped Keats to inject more meaning into the poem.

Endymion also progressed more regularly through Keats living with someone who had a set task of work to do; Bailey took up his books after breakfast, and Keats took up his pen. He wrote a steady fifty lines a day, and if he fell short, made it up the next day, composing, as Bailey said, "apparently with as much ease, as he wrote his letters". In fact he sometimes finished for the day well before two or three in the afternoon, read through what he had written to Bailey, and then read or wrote letters before they went out for a walk together. He was in splendid health, bathing frequently without ill effects, and hiring a boat on the Isis from the middle of the month onwards. More important even than work or health, he found at this time in Bailey a friend to whom he could talk utterly without reserve. Among other things, he spoke, as he seldom did, of personal and family matters. He revealed to Bailey that he was worried about his sister Fanny, and how fond of her he was. Abbey and the other trustee[1] had apparently shown their disapproval at her seeing too much of her brothers. Keats's reply to this was to send her one of Taylor and Hessey's educational books, and to write to her at her boarding school, Miss Tuckeys', in Marsh Street, Walthamstow, near

---

1. Bailey speaks of "the guardians", KC, II, 279.

Abbey's country house. It was the first of many letters written he said, "in order that I may not only, as you grow up love you as my only Sister, but confide in you as my dearest friend."[1] He ended "You will preserve all my Letters and I will secure yours", a promise she kept, though he did not. In this first one, he told her about Oxford, and, in simple terms, the story of Endymion. He also gave her news of George and Tom, who had written to him from Paris, where they were having what proved to be an expensive holiday. They had seen all the sights, including theatres, and, like the young students in Du Maurier's *Trilby*, "taken them over a set of boxing gloves" for exercise. They had other activities, which Keats did not tell Fanny. One was a trip south to Lyons[2]; the other, probably excited by Haydon's lurid accounts of the place,[3] was a visit to the notorious gaming houses and brothels of the Palais Royal, where they were tempted to play and lost money, "far too much for their circumstances".[4] Keats seems to have confided this news, and perhaps other details, to Bailey, for the latter's verdict on Tom, whom he never met, was that "from his character he must have lived a life of discomfort to himself & those with whom he was connected, if the character I have heard of him be just".[5] This pronouncement, in view of the French journey, may not be so self-righteous and unfeeling as it appears, especially as Tom was said to be in eager search of the mysterious French girl Amena; Reynolds also made a cryptic remark about Tom, suggesting that he had burnt his fingers in some way.[6]

Keats not only spoke to Bailey of personal problems and affairs; he felt free to range with him over the whole wide field of thought and discussion. Though their temperaments were very different, it was not so much an attraction of opposites as has sometimes been made out. Circumstances were to part them in the near future, but during this month of seclusion they drew very close together in a real relationship. Bailey's genuine and almost naive interest in things of the mind and spirit appealed to Keats; in a letter to the Reynolds girls, he thanked them and their brother for having introduced him to "so real a fellow as Bailey".[7] Bailey was not a natural scholar, and won his intellectual battles the hard way by intense study of the things that he loved; his heavily-annotated *Paradise Lost* served as a model for

1. *Letters*, I, 153. Keats's letters to her at school are generally addressed to Miss Tuckey's or Miss Caley's. Miss Caley was an assistant mistress, with whom Fanny may have boarded. Adami, 46–47.

2. George, KC, I, 301, implies Tom took this alone, Brown, KHM, No. 104, that they both went, and at this time.

3. Haydon, I, 358–359, 364–365; "as you enter you feel a heated, whorish, pestilential air flush your cheek & clutch your frame."

4. KHM, No. 104.   5. KC, I, 33.

6. In his copy of Monckton Milnes's *Life, Letters, and Literary Remains*, Houghton Library, *EC 8, K 2262, W848(M)B.

7. *Letters*, I, 160.

Keats's later methods of reading. Even the platitudes acquired in his Evangelical training should not disguise the fact that Bailey also won through to a profound understanding of what was best in Keats, without in any way blinding himself to his character. He remembered that

The errors of Keats's character,—and they were as transparent as a weed in a pure and lucent stream of water,—resulted from his education; rather from his *want* of education. But like the Thames waters, when taken out to sea, he had the rare quality of purifying himself;

His appreciation of Keats's warm generosity, integrity and good sense, his distinction that Keats was "loveable" rather than merely "amiable" were arrived at, like everything he did, by patient loving study and thought; it was the opposite of Hunt's friendly but careless condescension.[1]

In reading, the friends were matched in enthusiasm. Bailey had the advantage of systematic method, Keats of insight. Wordsworth was the common starting-place, and Wordsworth at his greatest, the *Immortality Ode*, *Tintern Abbey*, the Lucy poems. With Bailey, Keats began to show critical taste toward even such favourite works as *The Excursion*, though only in small detail; he suggested that the passage in Book IV about Apollo, which he had told Haydon he preferred above all others,[2] would be more effective with a line cut.[3] The Shakespeare play they read together at this time was *Troilus and Cressida*. Keats quoted the great speeches of Ulysses on time and mutability not merely as theory but as practical wisdom. On the lyric side, he was still faithful to Chatterton, and used to recite to Bailey in his peculiar chant the minstrels' songs from *Aella*. Bailey introduced him to the Metaphysicals—he himself was a fervent admirer of Jeremy Taylor, and had a somewhat overpowering engraving of him in his rooms—and Keats became enchanted by "the matchless Orinda", the beautiful Katherine Philips, who had died of smallpox in 1664 at the age of only 33, leaving a book of verse of remarkable purity and distinction. Keats contrasted her modest but undeniable gifts with those of modern literary blue-stocking women, and was moved to copy out the whole of one of her poems *To Mrs. M.A. at Parting*.[4] He found in others "a most delicate fancy of the Fletcher Kind", and it is clear that among these he included her *Upon a Scandalous Libel made by J.J.* and her very fine and deeply-felt ode *Upon Mr. Abraham Cowley's Retirement*. The poem he copied had such an effect upon him that he borrowed a charming metaphysical conceit from it to expand into one of the most convincing and moving passages of this otherwise not very distinguished Third Book of *Endymion*. The last stanza of Katherine Philips's poem, which he sent to Reynolds on Sunday 21 September, ran

1. KC, II, 260–261.
2. Moorman, *William Wordsworth*, II, 315.
3. KC, II, 276.   4. *Poems* (1710), 94–96.

> A Dew shall dwell upon our Tomb
> Of such a Quality
> That fighting Armies thither come
> Shall reconciled be.
> We'll ask no epitaph but say
> Orinda and Rosannia.

In *Endymion* he had just reached his description of the ranks of the lovers drowned at sea:[1]

> Turn to some level plain where haughty Mars
> Has legion'd all his battle; and behold
> How every soldier, with firm foot, doth hold
> His even breast: see, many steeled squares,
> And rigid ranks of iron—whence who dares
> One step? Imagine further, line by line,
> These warrior thousands on the field supine:—
> So in that crystal place, in silent rows,
> Poor lovers lay at rest from joys and woes.

The armies reconciled by the tomb of love have become armies of lovers in death, a passage of Keats's poem which moved Bailey to write enthusiastically on the foldings of Keats's letter to Reynolds, "P.S. There is one passage of Keats's 3ᵈ Book which beats all he has written. It is on *death*. He wrote it last night."[2] As well as this lucky chance, Keats found on Bailey's shelves Milton and Dante, and his own instinctive Platonism put into words in Madame Dacier's abridged version of the Dialogues.

Bailey also directed Keats's attention to the philosophy of a living English writer. Though Keats had been attracted to William Hazlitt, both for his temperament and the quality of his mind, he had known his work solely through the essays Hazlitt contributed to the "Round Table" pages of *The Examiner*. Earlier this year these had been collected in book form, forty by Hazlitt and twelve by Hunt, and Keats and Bailey were reading Hazlitt's with fresh appreciation. They also may have read the even more recently published *Characters from Shakespeare's Plays*; Keats possessed a copy, and his annotations show how much Hazlitt confirmed his own intuitions about the plays. Yet without Bailey's prompting, it is unlikely that Keats would come to possess, as he did, a copy of Hazlitt's first book, the philosophic *Essay On The Principles of Human Action*. In this Hazlitt discusses the problem of human "identity". He shows the capacity of human beings to go beyond mere sensation and memory by an imaginative identification with the minds and feelings of others; against the mechanical determinism of self-love postulated

1. *Endymion*, III, 728–736.
2. KC, I, 7: but not (note 6) lines 766–806, which are not "on death".

by Hobbes and others, he shows that there is an instinct to identify oneself with every object of contemplation, forming a "natural disinterestedness of the mind".[1] He took the ideas of Locke, which regarded the human mind as a passive agent to be played upon by all impressions—a view which Keats later copied in his doctrine of the "chameleon" poet—and made the mind a more positive agent of sympathy. Hazlitt undoubtedly reinforced a thousand small examples Keats had noticed in his own life, his own tendency to instinctive mimicry, the ability Severn had noticed to take on the nature of everything he saw, even of inanimate objects typified in his own remark to Woodhouse about imagining the sensations of a billiard-ball.[2] The idea that he was acting out a living philosophy of human nature was perhaps slow-working with Keats, but it was fundamental; it came more and more to the surface of his thought in the next few months, and it stayed with him to the end of his life. It also crystallized now, perhaps even more clearly, through the discussions on religion which he had with Bailey.

Since Bailey was reading for the Church, it was inevitable that philosophy should lead to religion. Here Bailey showed a delicacy of touch that matched, and was perhaps called out by, the sweetness of nature he found in Keats, who, he said, "allowed for people's faults more than any man I ever knew". Bailey therefore respected Keats's confessions of scepticism in the long conversations they had about religion; indeed he regarded them as evidence of honesty. He believed that Keats was instinctively religious, and had only adopted a manner of disbelief toward religion. This he promised Bailey to modify, and Bailey was told, probably by Reynolds, that Keats's promise not to continue the scoffing manner of Hunt and Shelley was kept when he returned to London.

On the positive side of religious belief, Keats and Bailey had a great deal of earnest conversation. Bailey had not an original mind. He was disarmingly aware of its defects, "an odd and useless sort of mind . . . of no earthly use."[3] He took his religion, like many of his opinions, from the writings of others; his own writing over the next few months reveals its main source.[4] Joseph Butler's *The Analogy of Religion, Natural and Revealed, to the Constitution and Course of Nature* was a central text-book for the theological student at this time, and throughout the nineteenth century. Bailey's beliefs as a student were an unconscious summary of Butler's main theme. "I have seen" wrote

1. See Bate, 255–259 for the best account of this book. Ward, 262, places Keats's reading of it later, but see "disinterrested" in his letter of 14 September 1817. *Letters*, I, 160.

2. KC, I, 59. "He has affirmed that he can conceive of a billiard Ball that it may have a sense of delight from its own roundness, smoothness volubility & the rapidity of its motion."

3. KC, I, 8–9.

4. Ibid. and Bailey's *A Discourse inscribed to the Memory of the Princess Charlotte Augusta* . . . (December) 1817. Bodleian. G. Pamph. 1024.6.

F*

Bailey, "an analogy, conformity, & unity in all things; or, to speak more intelligibly perhaps, the last two are perceptible *by* analogy. I have thought that this principle is the governing one of the universe, and that I have equally perceived it in nature, external & internal." Butler's argument was primarily addressed to rationalists and deists, and was just what any young ordinand would use with a friend who, he believed, could be won from his position of scepticism. It was, in effect, an easy way into Christianity. The apparent contradictions and confusions of revealed religion, Butler argued, have their exact analogy in those of nature. Life itself is not fully comprehensible; therefore we should not ask that religion should be. Without converting him, this was the message that Bailey conveyed to Keats in their thoughtful discussions.

This period at Oxford was of immense formative importance for Keats. It led him both to clarify his own instincts, and to examine their basis in general thought. He even began to analyse his own verse, and to form theories of "the principle of melody in Verse", which, as Bailey noted, were to come to full fruition in the more deliberate composition of *Hyperion*. This month marked Keats's transition from what he later called the "infant or thoughtless Chamber" of life into the "Chamber of Maiden-Thought", an "awakening of the thinking principle".[1] The only temporary disadvantage of this growth of self-knowledge and wider apprehension was that it made him look on *Endymion* with disfavour, a healthy sign but a drawback to a poem he had not yet finished. This distaste did not come all at once; on 21 September he was apparently confident and pleased with the 800 lines he had just written, but a week later, with the Book finished, he read it over and was disillusioned. It seemed tired work and he was tired of it. Though he still had a quarter to finish, his mind was on "a new Romance" he wished to write, which would fulfil his awakened thought; this is perhaps the first mention of *Hyperion*, the philosophic or "abstract" poem his new development had made him desire. Some slightly malicious gossip from Reynolds had also unsettled him. Hunt, so Reynolds wrote, meeting him at the theatre, had claimed that *Endymion* would have been twice as long without his restraining influence.[2] Keats may well have been depressed by the mechanical nature of Book Three, and Hunt's claim, though unfounded, may have emphasized its longueurs. All the Books, as the poem progressed, were taking a rough pattern; an opening address before the narrative, and in the body of the book, a philosophic passage and a lyric digression.[3] In Book Three, the opening apostrophe was disastrous, the lyric interlude of Neptune's feast is poor stuff, the philosophic digression hardly exists. Keats's dispirited verdict was "all

1. Bate, 215.
2. *Letters*, I, 162, 169. Bate, 210–211, suggests that Hunt's wife and sister-in-law added wounding remarks, hence Keats's attack on literary women (*Letters*, I, 163).
3. The Bower of Adonis in Book Two was regarded as such a set-piece.

the good I expect from my employment this summer is the fruit of Experience which I hope to gather in my next Poem". Bailey, perhaps feeling his mood, took him off for a break of a day or two to Stratford-on-Avon; they visited Shakespeare's birthplace, where they wrote their names on the walls, and the church where they were pestered by a guide, and inscribed the visitors' book. Somewhat surprisingly, they decided that the Shakespeare bust was a true likeness of the poet. On Sunday 5 October, at the beginning of the Oxford Michaelmas term, Bailey saw Keats off to London with real regret.

After Oxford, it was a shock to pick up the tangles of London. "The web of our Life is of mingled Yarn", he commented, using one of Hazlitt's favourite quotations. Tom and George were back, the Hampstead rooms seemed cramped, and the Bentley children were noisy. Keats went out on 6 October to deliver a parcel for Bailey at the Reynoldses, and stayed out; he walked up the Marylebone New Road to see both Hunt and Haydon, for the painter had also just moved to the cheaper neighbourhood, and lived close to Hunt at 22 Lisson Grove North. He found everyone at loggerheads. Haydon's picture was at a standstill, and Hunt had made rude remarks about it. He had also tormented Haydon by attacking marriage, and extolling nations "where the Women have indiscriminate connection", just at the time when the susceptible painter was trying to fight his own desires about the maid in his new lodgings.[1] Shelley was with Hunt for what was to prove a two months' stay, distracted by the law, debts, ill-health, house-property, publishers and his father-in-law. However, his poem was finished, which Hunt pronounced very fine, while continuing to criticize *Endymion*; Hunt was also having a quarrel with Horace Smith. Keats, in a way very unlike his usual generous self, felt inclined to wash his hands of the lot of them: "I am quite disgusted with literary Men and will never know another except Wordsworth", he wrote to Bailey. In spite of all his independence, Keats thought bitterly, Hunt would claim him as a pupil of his school of poetry. Haydon too was proving a nuisance. Earlier in the summer, he had met at Oxford a young painter called Charles Cripps; in September he had written to Keats and Bailey offering to train Cripps free, if they would try to arrange support for him in London for a year. Now he seemed indifferent about the matter, though Keats and Bailey were trying to raise a fund for Cripps, whom they had sought out in Oxford.

Keats's mood of disillusion was increased by a fact to which he referred several times in the next six or seven weeks, and always with a certain air of mystery. While at Oxford, he had developed some infection which hung on over the next two months, and confined him to the house for a fortnight in October. The majority of biographers have hotly and even emotionally denied that this could have been a venereal infection; but the weight of

1. Haydon, II, 136, 137.

contemporary evidence seems to indicate that it was.[1] He first mentioned it while writing to Bailey on 8 October, where he said "The little Mercury I have taken has corrected the Poison and improved my Health". His health, however did not improve, and for the next fortnight he was "confined", as he says, at Hampstead. Since this is the word he only uses for doctor's orders,[2] he seems to have been under some sort of treatment during this period. Though he wrote to Bailey on 29 October that he was "like to be" well through his illness, he still spoke of it, in yet another letter to Bailey on 22 November. Two of these letters, including the first, Bailey sent to Taylor just after Keats's death,[3] for the publisher's projected biography; this, and the fact that Bailey was reading for Holy Orders, lead most modern writers to deny the possibility that the letters refer to venereal disease. Yet in the third letter, that of 29 October, Keats jokes with Bailey in sexual terms, and speaks in the slang of the day about having had some sexual experience,[4] not, apparently, a topic that would shock Bailey.

The idea that Keats might have been using mercury for a number of non-venereal infections, and that, at this time, mercury was recklessly prescribed for a wide range of these, is due to a total misreading of medical history.[5] In actual fact, in the first two decades of the nineteenth century, there was a strong reaction in informed medical circles against the indiscriminate use of mercury that had prevailed before. Writing in 1809, one of Keats's lecturers at Guy's, James Curry, an old-fashioned mercury user, pleaded vehemently against the increasing tendency of the time to use mercury only for venereal disease.[6] Another of Keats's lecturers, Astley Cooper himself, not only spoke approvingly of the sharp decrease in the use of mercury since the beginning of the century, but would only prescribe it sparingly and cautiously himself, and not even for some of the forms of venereal disease.[7] Keats, it must be remembered, was a "well-educated practitioner", lately trained in an up-to-date medical school. All his lectures, even Curry's, had stressed that mercury must only be used with extreme caution, if at all, and usually only when the disease was venereal. The danger, and even the criminality, of using it where there was any tendency to

1. No biographer seems to have consulted contemporary medical writings. Most rely on W. Hale-White, *Keats as Doctor and Patient*. This contains so many omissions and inaccuracies about medical practice and practitioners of Keats's time, that it should be treated with the greatest caution. Appendix 3.

2. Cf. *Letters*, I, 371.

3. Not to Lord Houghton in 1848, as stated Hewlett, 121.

4. See Appendix 4.

5. By Lowell, I, 515, followed by Hewlett, 121, and Bate, 219, n.

6. James Curry, *Examination of the Prejudices commonly entertained against Mercury* ... London, 1809.

7. *The Lancet* (1823–1824), II, 191–193, 399.

tuberculosis was strongly stated to him.[1] Whatever might still be done up and down the country by rural physicians and provincial doctors, a man of his training was only likely to use mercury for a venereal infection.

Yet it is quite unnecessary to assume, although controversy on the subject has always curiously turned on such assumption, that he had syphilis. Keats might have noted that Astley Cooper prescribed a very few weeks' course of a fairly mild mercury pill, the Pilula Hydrargyri or blue pill, for syphilis; but the strong likelihood is that he was following the prescription of another doctor for another form of venereal disease. This was Solomon Sawrey, of 27 Bedford Row, near Reynolds's home. He was already Tom Keats's doctor,[2] and if Keats was now "confined" under doctor's orders, it is practically certain he was his doctor also, as he continued to be for the next two years. Under him, Keats's "little Mercury" was not for syphilis, but for the less serious though much more common infection of gonorrhoea. Sawrey, only a few years older than Astley Cooper, held contradictory opinions. On the one hand, he was one of the earliest to attack the use of mercury for non-venereal infection. "When it is clear the complaint has a venereal cause", he wrote in 1802, "we give mercury to cure it. But if we should be of the opinion that its nature is not venereal, we should of course omit to use that remedy." Yet his horror of mercury, often forcibly expressed, was tempered by the fact that he believed one of the most damaging medical heresies of the day. This was the theory that gonorrhoea was the same infection as syphilis, only in an earlier stage. He therefore recommended, as firmly as Astley Cooper forbade, small doses of mercury for gonorrhoea, to prevent the infection or "poison" entering "the circulating blood" and becoming syphilis. The "pernicious effects" of mercury were more than balanced, so he believed, by the benefits of stopping the much more serious disease of syphilis from developing.[3] Such was the feeling of the time that neither Keats nor his friends would have experienced any moral revulsion at this infection, nor indeed treated it as particularly serious.[4] The general attitude was represented by Keats's lecturer, James Curry. "Without accusing the male youth of the present day of greater laxity than those of former generations, it may be asked,—how many arrive at the adult age without having occasion to use mercury? . . . few escape the necessity of using it."[5]

The treatment, which made Keats specially susceptible to damp and chills,

1. "It is lamentable to reflect on the number of lives that must have been destroyed by phthisis and otherwise, in consequence of the imprudent exhibition of mercury for a disease that did not require it", ibid. II, 191.

2. Three months later, Keats writes of him to Tom familiarly as "Sawrey". *Letters*, I, 196.

3. *An Enquiry into the Effects of the Venereal Poison* . . ., iv and 46–47.

4. Sawrey himself complained that people deceived themselves "by thinking too slightly of this disease", op. cit., p. 180.

5. James Curry, *Examination* . . ., 15.

certainly kept him indoors during the wet and cold fortnight up to Saturday 25 October,[1] and so helped him to progress with the fourth book of *Endymion*, though not so swiftly as at Oxford. He had written three hundred lines only, as he told Bailey; but these contained his longest and most effective set-piece, the lyric Song of the Indian Maid. The opening of the Book was a depressed and formal apostrophe of the native English poets and his own weak powers. Then, possibly taking a hint from Drayton's other version of the story, *Endymion and Phoebe*, he introduced for the first time a dramatic conflict into the poem by making his hero disloyal to Cynthia by falling in love with a mysterious Indian Maid, who identifies herself in a lyric with the sorrows of the world, and tells how she became a follower of Bacchus. This tremendous piece of word-painting, derived at least partly from Keats's visits to Titian's *Bacchus and Ariadne*, on public loan through this and the previous year, has the freedom and lyricism of another great poet he was now studying, Coleridge.

Coleridge had brought out his collection of poems, *Sybilline Leaves*, in which his *Ancient Mariner* appeared for the first time under his own name,[2] together with much of his finest work including the *Dejection Ode*. Keats had a copy of *Sybilline Leaves*, in which he was perhaps reading the *Ancient Mariner* for the first time. Not only verbal echoes, but a wildness of atmosphere and a flexibility of rhythm appear in his own free lyric, and many of the lines that follow owe their images to the Mariner's voyage. As he wrote on, in fact, much of his natural scenery contained reminiscences of both great Lake poets; Wordsworth's Skiddaw makes an unexpected appearance in classical Greece, as does a mountain tarn from the *Dejection Ode*.[3]

During his enforced seclusion, all the fruits of Keats's reading and discussion with Bailey were having time to mature; the concern with his problems of identity, started by Hazlitt, became a major one, and entered into his own poetic hero. Endymion, like Keats, ponders[4]

> What is this soul then? Whence
> Came it? It does not seem my own, and I
> Have no self-passion or identity.
> Some fearful end must be: where, where is it?

Keats's two intellectual gods were now Wordsworth and Hazlitt, and he was puzzled to find them in conflict, for in his new enthusiasm, he tried to accept Hazlitt's "depth of taste" in his ephemeral writings to be as important as his philosophic creed, though he was forced to realize Hazlitt sometimes

1. G.M. (1817), Vol. 2, p. 282.
2. "Frenzied Mariners" were lumped by Hunt into Wordsworth's work, and only acknowledged to Coleridge in a footnote.
3. *Endymion*, IV, 221, 250, 394, 405–406, 693.
4. *Endymion*, IV, 475–478.

should have "thought a little deeper and been in a good temper". Hazlitt in a footnote to a *Round Table* essay had attacked Wordsworth's poem, *Gipsies*. Keats recognized that it was one of Wordsworth's slacker poems, written in too "comfortable" a mood, but equally that the critic should have recognized this, and not attacked Wordsworth generally for it. Keats was now far enough advanced in his own taste and thought to be bold and criticize these giants, even when admiring them. His new enquiries into man's identity led him to attack complacency, the self-limited identity of the man who will not, in Hazlitt's words, "enter into the minds and feelings of others". He now began to see his own moods of depression as a positive sign of a necessary wider sympathy—"the Man who thinks much of his fellows can never be in Spirits". Only by shutting his eyes to the "vicious beastliness" in the world can a man be happy;[1] it is the poet's duty to keep his eyes open, not to ignore suffering, but to be "disinterested" and suffer with it. It is an ideal Keats returned to often, a touchstone of character, one, curiously enough, which he felt was a masculine prerogative: "Women must want Imagination and they may thank God for it—and so m[a]y we that a delicate being can feel happy without any sense of crime", he wrote later.[2]

These stirrings toward a philosophic rationalization of his own feelings were sent to Bailey at the end of October, with other news. Haydon had cut an appointment—he was on that very day[3] in the grip of an emotional crisis—had failed to produce a copy of Keats's life-mask for Bailey, and was behaving oddly about Cripps. Keats had seen much of Rice, and they had read poetry together. He had visited the Reynolds home, and John was just being articled to Fladgate's firm; but on 2 November, he heard from them that Bailey had been disappointed over a curacy in the diocese of Lincoln. He wrote him another letter of flaming indignation against the Bishop, and revealed some of his own troubles. A minor poet, Cornelius Webb, one of Hunt's set, had written some verses[4] on the conversation at the Vale of Health cottage:

> Our talk shall be (a theme we never tire on)
> Of Chaucer, Spenser, Shakespeare, Milton, Byron,
> (Our England's Dante)—Wordsworth—Hunt, and Keats,
> The Muses' son of promise; and what feats
> He yet may do.

1. *Letters*, I, 175; not a reference to the cause of his own illness, as Ward, 425, assumes.
2. *Letters*, I, 293.
3. Haydon, II, 137, entry of 19 October 1817.
4. This has not survived. Webb may have submitted his poem to *Blackwood's* in all innocence during its first innocuous editorship. J. R. MacGillivray, *Keats, A Bibliography*, xx. Like many in Hunt's set, he too was writing a long narrative poem during this year, *A Day in Winter*, from which he afterwards published (1820) an extract "Fairy Revels" which reminds one of the weaker parts of *Endymion*.

Blackwood's Edinburgh Magazine had just come out with an article 'On the Cockney School of Poetry' headed by these lines. The anonymous writer, 'Z', only attacked Hunt, but he did so in the most vicious terms; in fact, it was a collaboration by the new editors, John Wilson and John Gibson Lockhart, brought in by the proprietor to give the magazine more of an anti-Whig bite. What was ominous, as Keats noted, was that his own name, like Hunt's, had been printed in the motto in capital letters. Such unfortunate distractions followed Keats everywhere for the next weeks. London was a depressing place, with theatres shut and mourning everywhere after the death of the young and beloved Princess Charlotte Augusta on 6 November. Keats's time was frittered away on "little two penny errands" all over Town, connected with trying to raise a fund for Cripps. A deeper cause for anxiety was Tom. He now appeared very unwell; Keats, looking back, was to think that his still-secret love-problem was working on his spirits, but there were evidently physical signs of disease too, for Keats thought he should be shipped off to a warm climate such as Portugal for the winter, and even considered going with him. *Endymion* went on far too slowly, and was still a disappointment to him, as he admitted to Bailey, while promising him a better poem some day. His social life was too full. He went to Mableton Place, where the Shelleys had temporary lodgings, in company with Hunt and the journalist Walter Coulson, and met Godwin on 18 November; later in the week, at the Reynoldses, he met Jonathan Henry Christie, a friend of Bailey and a contributor to *Blackwood's*. Christie was of a different stamp from his editors, and he took to Keats greatly. There was for a time some talk of his reviewing Keats's *Poems* in *Blackwood's*, an event which, if it had occurred, might have changed literary history. To the end of his life, Christie remembered how Keats read on this occasion some lines from Chatterton "with an enthusiasm of admiration such as could only be felt by a poet".[1]

Meanwhile, there was only one way to finish *Endymion*. He must escape to the country, whose isolation he felt more fit to encounter than when he had begun the poem. All the same, this time he did not travel so far. The Fox and Hounds, at Burford Bridge under Box Hill, was a coaching inn, easily reached from London. The low white-washed building and stables, with a row of elms in front, had a large garden at the back, tucked under the hill, with sheltered walks and a hermit's grotto, or summerhouse. Keats lodged in the room overlooking the stable-yard, and at once felt at home. On the same evening he arrived, Saturday 22 November, he wrote off first to Bailey and then to Reynolds. His first letter shows how he had matured in the past difficult weeks. What set him off was a wounding letter Haydon had sent Bailey over the Cripps affair. Three weeks before, Keats had ranted at the Bishop of Lincoln for disappointing Bailey; now he preached universal tolerance, and went on to formulate his feelings about "Men of Genius"—

1. *Notes and Queries*, 24 August, 1872, p. 157.

for such he still sincerely believed Haydon to be.[1] "Men of Genius are great as certain ethereal Chemicals operating on the Mass of neutral intellect— by [for but] they have not any individuality, any determined Character." The progression of his thought is plain. If the truly feeling man or poet is one who has "kept watch on man's mortality", and entered into the nature and being of others, he finds his identity in having no individual character himself. He had achieved some answer to the problem of identity posed by his own Endymion. Once more, it is an idea that permeates the works of Hazlitt. In the *Round Table* essay "On Posthumous Fame", for instance,[2]

He seemed scarcely to have an individual existence of his own, but to borrow that of others at will, and to pass successively through 'every variety of untried being'.

Keats presses on further with the idea. Only by the sympathetic imagination, attracted by the power of beauty, can Truth be perceived:

I am certain of nothing but of the holiness of the Heart's affections and the truth of Imagination—What the imagination seizes as Beauty must be truth—whether it existed before or not—for I have the same Idea of all our Passions as of Love they are all in their sublime, creative of essential Beauty—In a Word, you know my favourite Speculation by my first Book and the little song[3] I sent in my last—which is a representation from the fancy of the probable mode of operating in these Matters—The Imagination may be compared to Adam's dream—he awoke and found it truth. I am the more zealous in this affair, because I have never yet been able to perceive how any thing can be known for truth by consequitive reasoning—and yet it must be—Can it be that even the greatest Philosopher ever arrived at his goal without putting aside numerous objections—However it may be, O for a Life of Sensations rather than of Thoughts! It is "a Vision in the form of Youth" a Shadow of reality to come—and this consideration has further convinced me for it has come as auxiliary to another favorite Speculation of mine, that we shall enjoy our selves here after by having what we call happiness on Earth repeated in a finer tone and so repeated—

These speculations, though ideas from Wordsworth and Hazlitt are interwoven, are largely a process of self-discovery by Keats himself. He had learnt, as he said, earlier, "humility and capability of submission", and this, once learnt, set the imagination free. Imagination, as he had just read in Coleridge's *Dejection Ode*, was a "shaping spirit", capable by its instinctive appreciation of beauty actually to create truth, "whether it existed before or not". To the task of being a maker, an actual creator, Keats was henceforward to set his poetry. He did not condemn logical reasoning. He realized that someone whose judgment he admired, like Bailey or his publisher Taylor, could be "a consequitive man", but he knew the way for him was through "sensations", which he used, as it was continually used by Hazlitt, in the sense of concrete experiences. This insistence on concrete experience, the readiness to draw a

1. *Letters*, I, 184, 203.
2. Muir, K. "Keats and Hazlitt", *John Keats: A Reassessment*, 153.
3. "O Sorrow", *Endymion*, I. 181.

larger meaning from actual incidents and things, corresponds with the significance Wordsworth found in his experiences from nature and human contacts. The necessity of actual experience in arriving at truth or in creating a poem becomes a prime creed with Keats. It is the beginning of the need he felt to experience everything "on the pulses".

His other letter, to Reynolds, which he wrote the same evening after a brief moonlit walk up the hill, is the first of many which associate this theme of self-effacing creative imagination with Shakespeare. Again Keats was in tune with Hazlitt,[1] though he had also arrived at the idea through his own close reading. This time he had with him not the plays, but the volume of Shakespeare's Poems. Here in Shakespeare he found scattered everywhere this power of summoning up the spirit of concrete things in the smallest instances: "He has left nothing to say about nothing or any thing". Keats even applied the doctrine of healthy experience to his recent troubles over what he called Heart-vexations; "They never surprize me—lord! a man should have the fine point of his soul taken off to become fit for this world".

The idea that the "fine point" should be taken off Endymion's soul before he became capable of real love with his immortal Cynthia also lay behind the confused symbolism of Endymion's adventures with the Indian Maid, as Keats pushed on with the poem. This final intense period of writing has two elements. On the one hand, Keats was exhilarated by the place, the superb natural scenery, the sense of freedom from worry and illness. All these permeate the poem. He rushed up the hill the first night "after the Moon . . . came down—and wrote some lines", the brilliant little picture owing equal inspiration to Box Hill and the *Ancient Mariner*:

> The moon put forth a little diamond peak,
> No bigger than an unobserved star.

By day, he slipped out of the little garden gate near the Hermitage, and walked up the sheer hill. After about twenty yards the path divided. One branch bore right, through heavy dark box trees, and wound parallel with the little gleaming River Mole in the valley beneath, looking down on it until finally bending back on itself to emerge at the top of the hill. The other, a chalk track, went straight up the bare down; about halfway up it plunged through a deep hanger of yew trees in full pale red waxy berry, some dropping as he brushed through them, and others pecked down at his feet by the birds. Once at the top, he looked into a quiet valley, where fallen beech leaves made a peaceful circle at the foot of their trees. Such a setting, in every detail,[2] he made Endymion imagine for his retirement in love with the Indian Maid.

The second over-riding element was to introduce more and more the theme of fulfilment of ideals through experience and suffering. This became

1. E. No. 389, p. 381.   2. *Endymion*, IV, 670–681, 763–769.

increasingly difficult to develop owing to the conventional mechanism of the set story. Keats made his greatest attempt at a philosophic realization of the theme in the Cave of Quietude, where Endymion finds himself at a moment when he has lost both Cynthia and the Maid. Here he describes, with no model but his own psychological self-experience, a state which he was continuously to explore all his writing life—the positive good that is to be had by accepting the very depths of despair: as Carlyle was to put it later, the Everlasting Yea that comes out of the deepest abysm of the Everlasting Nay. It is a universal experience, especially for the young:

> the man is yet to come
> Who hath not journeyed in this native hell.
> But few have ever felt how calm and well
> Sleep may be had in that deep den of all.
> There anguish does not sting; nor pleasure pall:
> Woe-hurricanes beat ever at the gate,
> Yet all is still within and desolate.
> Beset with painful gusts, within ye hear
> No sound so loud as when on curtain'd bier
> The death-watch tick is stifled. Enter none
> Who strive therefore: on the sudden it is won.
> Just when the sufferer begins to burn,
> Then it is free to him;

The importance of *Endymion*, at the last, was that it was an exploration into self-knowledge for Keats himself. The contrived ending, when the Indian Maid turns out to be Cynthia in another form, the perfunctory conclusion when Peona, reintroduced only a few hundred lines from the end of the poem, is left to ponder on her brother's final happiness, are hardly satisfying in themselves. What was deeply satisfying for Keats himself was the distance he had travelled since the First Book in the reconciliation of his own doubts and fears with the world as it appeared. For Keats in the character of Endymion, the early stages of the poem that summer had seen him at the mercy of those states of mind in which

> sunny glades
> Were full of pestilent light . . . If an innocent bird
> Before my heedless footsteps stirr'd, and stirr'd
> In little journeys, I beheld in it
> A disguis'd demon, missioned to knit
> My soul with under darkness;[1]

Now greater knowledge and thought into the nature of life had brought a complete and exact reversal of that horror. Looking out from his room

1. *Endymion*, I, 693–694; 698–702. See above, p. 136.

at the western sunset over the little stable-yard, he could write to Bailey

nothing startles me beyond the Moment. The setting sun will always set me to rights—
or if a Sparrow come before my Window I take part in its existence and pick about the
Gravel.

He could still say "I scarcely remember counting upon any Happiness", but
now, instead of his wounded early years throwing him at the mercy of that
"horrid Morbidity of Temperament" which had haunted him when he began
the poem, he had found an answer in the imaginative sympathy that enabled
him to live with life; he had found it, at least partly, in the long working-out
of his poem.

The poem itself was flawed in many parts, as he well knew. The reason was
his own extreme youth. He was only twenty-one when he wrote it, and he
had been writing poetry only three years. Yet the handicap of youth turns
out to be one of the poem's great advantages in the hold it has on the young.
What has always endeared *Endymion* to adolescent readers, even in the more
sophisticated stages of society, is that the poem seems to speak of their own
experiences and states of mind. The strongest impression the poem makes
on young people is that it is a poem about young people, caught in the first
and most natural complication of the world's adult dilemmas, the state of
being in love. To them, as to many older readers, *Endymion* is first and
foremost an account of what it is like to be in love, with all the uncertainty,
fears, surprise and joy of that condition. Even its vagueness is an advantage
to this end, for each person, imagining his or her love situation to be unique,
can fit its symbolism to self-experience. Keats, working out his own special
needs and problems in this poem, has provided for those still young and in
love his own sympathetic landscape, "a little Region to wander in where
they may pick and choose", and where each may gather an individual
reassurance and interpretation. His instinct provided him with an epilogue
summing up this message. This stands to *Endymion* in the same relation that
the lyric "My heart leaps up" stands to the *Immortality Ode*, where Wordsworth had now placed it as a miniature prologue. In a little lyric written by
the River Mole, as the last leaves came down from the "bare ruin'd choirs"
of which he was just reading in the Sonnets, Keats concentrated what he had
tried to say in *Endymion*, but what "was never said in rhyme" quite positively
in that poem. The tree and the river of the first two stanzas had found the
secret, of acceptance and of the use of change and loss, which human life,
in the last stanza, found so difficult, "the feel of not to feel it", which he
echoed from Coleridge's *Dejection Ode* in his own epitomizing lyric.

> In a drear-nighted December,
>   Too happy, happy tree,
>   Thy branches ne'er remember
>   Their green felicity:

The north cannot undo them,
With a sleety whistle through them;
Nor frozen thawings glue them
    From budding at the prime.

In a drear-nighted December,
    Too happy, happy brook,
Thy bubblings ne'er remember
    Apollo's summer look;
But with a sweet forgetting,
They stay their crystal fretting,
Never, never petting
    About the frozen time.

Ah! would 'twere so with many
    A gentle girl and boy!
But were there ever any
    Writh'd not at passed joy?
The feel of not to feel it,
When there is none to heal it,
Nor numbed sense to steel it,
    Was never said in rhyme.

Chapter 12

A MAN OF ACHIEVEMENT

"several things dovetailed in my mind, & at once it struck me,
what quality went to form a Man of Achievement."

– JOHN KEATS to George and Tom Keats, 27(?) December 1817

Endymion was finished, the place and date "Burford Bridge Novr 28.1817"
written at the end of the draft of Book Four.[1] In the dazed relaxation that
follows the completion of a large work, Keats stayed on for another week.
He could not bring himself to look much more at his manuscript, let alone
revise it, for the later stages show some curious images and clumsy expressions
which had to wait for correction until Keats made the fair copy for Taylor &
Hessey. Although the "sober gold" he had prophesied for this moment had
mostly fallen from the autumn trees, the dark evergreen hillscape of the
North Downs exerted its spell on him, and healed any nervousness he felt
about the poem. He came back to Town in intense high spirits, full of a
renewed intellectual liveliness that lasted him right over this winter.
Practically the first news he received there wrought up his feeling of excitement to the highest pitch.

William Wordsworth had just arrived in London, his first visit since the
summer of 1815. He stayed for the first half of December with his brother
Christopher, the rector of Lambeth, and then moved with his wife Mary and
her sister Sara Hutchinson to some West End lodgings in Mortimer Street.
These had probably been found for them by Mrs. Wordsworth's cousin,
Thomas Monkhouse, who lived close by at 28 Queen Anne Street, Cavendish
Square, and who made himself an unofficial channel of communication for
those who wished to meet the great man. One of the first of these was Keats.
A year before he had told Haydon how the idea of Wordsworth seeing his
sonnet "put me out of breath—you know with what Reverence—I would
send my Wellwishes to him—". This feeling had increased in the intervening
year with his serious reading and discussion of Wordsworth with Bailey at
Oxford. At some time he sent Wordsworth a copy of his 1817 *Poems*
inscribed touchingly "To W. Wordsworth with the Author's sincere
Reverence", though Wordsworth left most of the pages uncut. As Haydon

1. "In 1st copy—thus—" Woodhouse's note in interleaved *Endymion*, Berg Collection,
New York Public Library.

had been the intermediary for his poems with Wordsworth, he lost no time in telling the painter how anxious he was for a meeting. Haydon, he found to his delight, had already seen Wordsworth. Encouraged by painting the heads of Hazlitt and Keats into "Christ's Entry into Jerusalem", Haydon decided to embellish his picture by a remarkable group, consisting, in his own words,[1] of "Voltaire as a sneerer at Jesus, Newton as a believer, and Wordsworth, the living poet, bending down in awful veneration". Wordsworth sat and "read Milton & his Tintern Abbey & the happy Warrior, & some of his finest things", while Haydon painted, behaving with the gracious friendliness that he had shown to the artist on his previous London visit. At the same time, Wordsworth's impatience with criticism, which he had demonstrated by his refusal to meet Hazlitt, and his intolerance of the work of others, was reported to have reached alarming lengths. Haydon wrote to Monkhouse with extreme deference, asking whether Wordsworth might be willing to receive his young admirer, if only for a few minutes, at Lambeth, and Monkhouse was able to arrange an appointment, more conveniently, at his own house in Queen Anne Street. On the walk there from Haydon's studio at Lisson Grove, Keats behaved with the same mounting excitement as when he had walked with Clarke to meet Leigh Hunt; he expressed "the greatest, the purest, the most unalloyed pleasure at the prospect". The introduction was made, and Wordsworth seemed well-disposed. After a few minutes he asked Keats in a kindly way what he had been writing lately.

What followed, though often repeated in various forms, is still open to doubt. Haydon's account is as impetuous and emphatic as his own intervention at this point.

I said he has just finished an exquisite ode to Pan—and as he had not a copy I begged Keats to repeat it—which he did in his usual half chant, (most touching) walking up & down the room—when he had done I felt really, as if I had heard a young Apollo—Wordsworth drily said
"a Very pretty piece of Paganism"—
This was unfeeling, & unworthy of his high Genius to a young Worshipper like Keats— & Keats felt it deeply—so that if Keats has said any thing severe about our Friend; it was because he was wounded—and though he dined with Wordsworth after at my table—he never forgave him.

Circumstantial and vivid as this account may seem, it must be remembered that it was written nearly thirty years after the event, at a time when Haydon's megalomaniac tendencies were tipping over into the insanity, in which he destroyed himself a few months later. It was heightened too by one of his recurring desires to contradict Leigh Hunt, who had gossiped without knowledge of the affair. Haydon's own journals at the time of the meeting

1. Catalogue of the 1832 Exhibition at Philadelphia, Boston Public Library, 4074-19, No. 8.

say nothing of the incident, and when he recalls, in strikingly similar terms, the recitation of the *Hymn to Pan*, he does not say that Wordsworth was present. Moreover, though he is emphatic in saying that the incident did not take place a fortnight later, when Keats "dined with Wordsworth after at my table", that is, on 28 December, there is an entry in Haydon's Diary of that date which makes it clear that some sort of recitation of the part of *Endymion* containing the *Hymn to Pan* was made by Keats on that occasion in Wordsworth's presence, when "Keats's rich fancy of Satyrs & Fauns & doves & white clouds, wound up the stream of conversation". In fact, Haydon's anxiety to confute Leigh Hunt—"All Hunts assertions about it being said at my house is a mistake—as well as half his other sayings about both Keats & Shelley"—seems to have led him into some confusion.

Clearly some such incident did take place, on one or other of these two occasions, but, equally clearly, it did not have the effect on Keats's feelings towards Wordsworth which Haydon long afterwards attributed to it. Severn, the most inventive and unreliable witness of all, placed the incident at Haydon's, made himself present, and concluded his account of Wordsworth's remark, "with this cold water thrown upon us we all broke up". Yet nothing in Keats's attitude toward Wordsworth in the next month or so suggests that he took such a view of the remark, nor that it was said "drily" or even "coldly", as Severn has it. Keats's description to Cowden Clarke seemed to show, if anything, amusement rather than any other emotion, as may be shown by a joke about Wordsworth's pomposity which Keats perhaps added himself:

During that same interview, some one having observed that the next Waverley novel was to be "Rob Roy," Wordsworth took down his volume of Ballads, and read to the company "Rob Roy's Grave;" then, returning it to the shelf, observed, "I do not know what more Mr. Scott can have to say upon the subject."

Nothing in Keats's letters suggests hurt feelings or unforgiveness, and he went out of his way, early in the New Year, to let his publishers know that he had been seeing Wordsworth frequently. Wordsworth, for his part, had the habit of using the type of phrase which Haydon found so unfeeling in quite a different sense. "Pretty" with him, and indeed in common usage which has survived in sporting terms today, could be a synonym for "admirable" or "well-turned". The connotation afterwards given to it, however, undoubtedly reflects the bad impression made even on old friends and admirers like Crabb Robinson by Wordsworth on this seven-weeks' visit. From 1815 to 1820, the difficult second half of a man's forties, Wordsworth showed at his worst, and his emergence at fifty to something like his normal self was greeted by all with relief. It is an irony that his malaise coincided precisely with the whole of Keats's writing life.

For the time being, their ways parted. On Saturday 13 December,

Wordsworth went to stay at Sundridge in Kent, one of his brother Christopher's livings; on the same day, Keats saw his own brothers, George and Tom, off on the coach to Teignmouth. This had been decided three weeks before, for the sake of Tom's health, though it was not perhaps yet thought that his disease was tubercular. The romantic Miss Reynoldses seemed to put it down to an unhappy love-affair over the mysterious Amena.[1] Keats had wished to go with his brothers, but there was *Endymion* to be fair-copied and seen through the press; George, unemployed again,[2] undertook to accompany Tom. Their going left Keats free to satisfy the social demands of his friends, who had seen little of him since April. Now he relaxed among them to the exclusion of poetry; they occupied him nearly every day for the next four weeks, at the end of which he had to confess to Taylor that he had only just started revising Book One of *Endymion*. The strain and isolation of the long poem had left him with an appetite for society, which he was able to indulge with several varied sets. Every Sunday he had an open invitation to dine with Haydon, whose picture was progressing again under the stimulus of an advance from a rich banker.[3] Here he could meet Hazlitt and Haydon's favourite pupil, a young man of his own age, William Bewick. He enjoyed a very pleasant day there directly after George and Tom had gone. Haydon was now willing to be more helpful about Cripps, provided a premium of £150 to £200 could be raised. This task partly led Keats to cultivate a set of monied people who, he admitted, "will never do for me", but with whom he dined in the middle of the week, at Knightsbridge. These were Horace Smith and his curious but wealthy friend Thomas Hill, who had been at the Haydon–Shelley contest. There were also Smith's two brothers, James and Leonard, Edward Dubois, the fashionable editor of the *Monthly Mirror* and other magazines, and a senior Civil Servant, the deputy comptroller of the Stamp Office, John Kingston, whom Keats had met before. The touchstone of disinterestedness made these witty well-dressed men and their conversation seem vapid and empty. As Keats observed[4]

they only served to convince me, how superior humour is to wit in respect of enjoyment—These men say things which make one start, without making one feel, they are all alike; their manners are alike; they all know fashionables; they have a mannerism in their very eating & drinking, in their mere handling a Decanter—

and yet, he found, he had accepted a similar engagement for the following Wednesday, Christmas Eve.[5]

1. *Letters*, I, 186. Appendix 3.
2. Dilke, ann. I, 46, thinks he did not lose employment till now.
3. Haydon, II, 166–170.   4. *Letters*, I, 193.
5. Ibid, "yet I am going to Reynolds", where the "Reynolds" is almost certainly a mistranscription by Jeffrey, who also omitted something here. Reynolds was not a member of Smith's set but of Rice's.

A set much more to his taste was the "sort of a Club every Saturday even-ing", to which he had been introduced by Rice, the lively middle-class circle centred on Piccadilly. These were young men in their fathers' offices, Rice, Fladgate, and his cousin Squibb from a firm of auctioneers off Savile Row, or starting up businesses of their own like John Martin and his partner Rodwell, booksellers and publishers of Bond Street and Piccadilly. Neither artistic nor fashionable, they provided, with their racy slang and cheerful ways, a good mean of average society in which Keats always felt at home. He found himself using their private language, "getting initiated into a little Cant", as he told his brothers. Getting a girl with child was called knocking out an apple, staying at an inn was hanging out, a term still in use. With Shakespeare never far from his mind, he jokingly compared them with "all the good lads of Eastcheap" with whom Prince Hal became intimate, a comparison not at all far out for this eternal ingredient in English social life. The "little Cant" was embodied a few weeks later in a lyric[1] ending "O cut the sweet apple and share it!", and sent to Reynolds, who attended the circle whenever his love affairs in the west would let him.

The only drawback to this society was the long late-night journey back to Hampstead on a bad evening. There was, however, equally congenial society nearer home. All the autumn, the Keats boys had been in and out of the Dilke household on the edge of Hampstead Heath, which became a second home.[2] Maria Dilke was like an elder sister to them; Keats used his medical training to prescribe for her frequent ill-health. With Dilke he discussed the old plays he had edited, and began the serious study of *Paradise Lost* that Bailey had recommended. Notes and letters tell of books borrowed, left behind or returned. Dilke, his wife and his brother William, who also had a house nearby, became an accepted part of Keats's life, and by the New Year, Keats and he were "capital Friends". During the summer, Dilke's friend and neighbour in the adjoining house had not been visible. Like many Hampstead residents, who wanted to supplement a fixed income, Charles Brown was in the habit of letting his house during the holiday season, when many Londoners liked a breath of the country not too far from Town; he himself usually made tracks for his native Scotland. It was not until late August that Keats met this heavily-built, prematurely-bald man of thirty on the road leading up to Hampstead Village, and even then the meeting was brief, for Keats immediately left for Oxford. During the autumn, a friendship gradually developed.[3] Brown's life had been full and varied. The son of a broker, he had gone into business at fourteen, and at eighteen joined an elder brother trading in bristles in Russia. Like Keats's family, Brown's suffered a

1. "O blush not so", written 31 January 1818.
2. "three times a week, often three times a day", according to Dilke, KC, II, 104-105.
3. KC, II, 57. Brown's own account needs to be treated with circumspection, as pointed out by Dilke, KC, II, 104-106.

number of financial and personal disasters, including the Russian adventure;[1] but this at least left him with material for an unpublished novel and a musical play, *Narensky*, performed at Drury Lane early in 1814. The piece was worthless in itself, but it brought him a silver ticket, free admission for life, to the theatre which had put it on. Eighteen months later, a legacy from an elder brother gave Brown a small but assured private income, and cash enough for his share of Wentworth Place. The ups and downs of life had left him with a peculiar temperament, in which generosity and calculation played almost equal parts.[2] He was certainly as hearty as the "little circle of hearty friends" he noticed about Keats, but he was bookish too, and could hold his own in a religious or philosophic discussion.

One of Brown's contributions was to quicken Keats's interest in the theatre, if only by lending him his silver ticket to Drury Lane. The two great licensed theatres, Drury Lane and Covent Garden, had both been burnt down and rebuilt in the last ten years; each was a magnificent tiered and gilded structure which held about 3000 people. These huge and vocal audiences were an entertainment in themselves, often a riotous one. Keats was no stranger to the three-and-sixpenny Pit, where after 9 o'clock, halfway through the five-hour programme, he could get in for half-price, and he knew what it was to be "jumbled together at Drury Lane door" in the explosive crowd fighting for the best places on the benches. In these years, Drury Lane had the lead of its great rival, largely owing to the sensational emergence of Edmund Kean, who had taken the Town by storm with his Shylock in 1814. With this tiny dynamic figure, so like himself, Keats felt an instinctive kinship. He had seen him as Richard III, Hamlet, Macbeth, Othello and Timon, and he was totally enthusiastic about them all, especially the Othello, about which opinions varied.[3] Even the actor's private life, his brandy-drinking and the low-life claque that surrounded him, were to Keats another instance of the "light and shade" that made up existence. "They talked", he wrote of Horace Smith and his witty friends, "of Kean & his low company—Would I were with that company instead of yours said I to myself!" The talk had been occasioned by Kean's return to the stage on Monday 15 December after an absence of three weeks through illness. He played Richard III, "and finely he did it", commented Keats, who was there. Kean's performance in this part had both the virtue and the defect, noted by Hazlitt, his most appreciative critic, of exceptional attention to small details. When he spoke of his withered arm, he looked down at it with a bitter disgust; when he wooed Anne, he had a moment when he seemed to break off and laugh in sheer pleasure at his own wickedness. Such small touches, "immortal scraps" as he called them, which Hazlitt criticized as making a

1. Ruined by a substitute, fringed whalebone, which afterwards proved to be useless. Joanna Richardson, *The Everlasting Spell*, 9.

2. Dilke, ann. I, ix.   3. W. Robson, *The Old Playgoer*, 114.

sense of "a distinct effort in every new situation", were supremely attractive
to Keats, just in the same way as he had always been attracted by individual
embellishments in a long poem. He did not look for a "sum-total effect",
but rejoiced that "Kean delivers himself up to the instant feeling, without
a shadow of thought about anything else."

It was therefore with an evident sense of delight in every word he wrote
that Keats undertook this week to do the theatrical review in *The Champion*
in place of Reynolds. What he was supposed to review was the performance
on Thursday 18 December of *Riches*, an adaptation by Sir James Bland
Burges of Massinger's *City Madam*, in which Kean played Luke Traffic. What
he did was to write an article on Edmund Kean as a Shakespearian actor,
with only a few appreciative lines on his Luke. Like a good journalist, he
caught the tone of the paper he was writing for;[1] more to the point, he
caught that of his favourite critic. Though he disagreed with Hazlitt over
Kean's treatment of details, his description of the "indescribable *gusto*" in
Kean's voice echoed one of Hazlitt's highest and most characteristic terms of
praise. The whole cadence of his prose is that of Hazlitt, whose reviews he
seems to have had nearly by heart, though he turned them to his own uses.
Earlier in the year, Hazlitt had reviewed in the *Morning Chronicle* Kean's
Hamlet, which Keats also saw. The idea of Shakespeare's dramatic art and
nature, with which Hazlitt began this review, was one on which Keats was to
draw again and again; what he borrowed now was from a quotation used by
Hazlitt to described the difficulties of playing Hamlet:[2]

> Come then, the colours and the ground prepare,
> Dip in the rainbow, trick her off in air;
> Choose a firm cloud before it falls, and in it
> Catch, ere she change, the Cynthia of a minute.

Keats was always stimulated by a striking quotation. From this one, he developed the idea of the rainbow as the actor's art to apply it to all art in
general, symbolizing the evanescent quality of creative genius, which he saw
threatened by the materialism of the age, a theme hammered on weekly by
Hunt in *The Examiner*. He ended his review with an appeal to Kean to

Cheer us a little in the failure of our days! for romance lives but in books. The goblin
is driven from the hearth, and the rainbow is robbed of its mystery.

For good measure, he threw in a quotation of his own, which shows that he
was taking Bailey's advice and reading Dante's *Inferno* as well as *Paradise
Lost*;[3] he applied to Kean the line from Canto 4 in Cary's translation:

> And sole apart retir'd, the Soldan fierce.

1. Bernice Slote, *Keats and the Dramatic Principle*, 95.
2. Pope, *Moral Essays*, Ep. ii, *To Mrs. M. Blount*, 17–20, slightly misquoted.
3. His notes in *Paradise Lost* (KHM, No. 24) show him coupling the two.

The review appeared in *The Champion* on Sunday 21 December. Its quality gave Reynolds, who wanted to slip down to Devon, the chance to ask him to do the Drury Lane pantomime, *Harlequin's Vision, or, The Feast of the Statue*[1] and the new tragedy at Covent Garden, *Retribution; or, The Chieftan's Daughter*, by John Dillon. The latter was so bad, an "Eastern" counterpart to the modern "Western" film, that Keats, after once more invoking *Paradise Lost* and the *Inferno* in the opening of his review,[2] contented himself merely with giving the plot and the players, including the young and promising Macready as the villain.

He went to the traditional Boxing Day opening of the Drury Lane pantomime with Brown and Dilke. He had spent both evenings of the previous week-end with Dilke, and was finding him more and more interesting. Another "consequitive" reasoner, whom Keats could respect if not agree with, he based his philosophy on that of Godwin, who believed in the gradual improvement of man by the exercise of his rational faculties. Keats, with his belief in intuitive, instinctive art, was unwilling to admit the Godwinian premise, a feeling perhaps intensified by meeting that Christmas Day the philosopher himself, rational enough except where his own self-interest or dignity was concerned. Keats was applying the principles of his review of Kean to all arts. The previous Saturday, just after finishing the review, he had gone to see the huge allegorical picture "Death on the Pale Horse" by Benjamin West, the veteran President of the Royal Academy, probably led by Hazlitt's criticism of it in the *Edinburgh Magazine*, with which he agreed. The picture lacked the "gusto" he had found in Kean's acting, or "intensity" as he now called it, echoing the term he himself had used for Shakespeare a month before. He developed Hazlitt's and his own ideas further:[3]

the excellence of every Art is its intensity, capable of making all disagreeables evaporate, from their being in close relationship with Beauty & Truth—Examine King Lear & you will find this examplified throughout; but in this picture we have unpleasantness without any momentous depth of speculation excited, in which to bury its repulsiveness—

Keats's choice of *King Lear* to exemplify this theory of art is another instance of how far he had progressed both as an artist and as a person since he began *Endymion*. The play, when he had read it in the Isle of Wight in the spring, had haunted him unpleasantly, making him nervous and apprehensive for a month afterwards. Now he was able to resolve its "disagreeables" in a calmer manner, while still being stirred by its total grandeur. For this he had

1. Rollins (*Letters*, I, 37) incorrectly says it was the Covent Garden pantomime, *Harlequin Gulliver*. It is not certain Keats saw this.
2. Together with "the old dramatists", indicating the areas of his reading with Dilke at this time.
3. *Letters*, I, 92.

not only his own greater maturity, but an area of thought once more opened by Hazlitt in another book which he now possessed.[1] This was Hazlitt's *Characters of Shakespeare's Plays*, which the Olliers had brought out at midsummer.[2] Keats made a note in this book which shows his affection for the author and an appreciation of his social oddities, for at the end of the chapter on *The Tempest*, he wrote "I cannot help seeing Hazlitt like Ferdinand —'in an odd angle of the Isle sitting'—his arms in this sad knot." All his other notes and underlinings were in the chapter on *King Lear*; one in particular was written at the same time as his review of Kean's acting. In the review, he had spoken rather mysteriously of "one learned in Shakespearian hieroglyphics". That "one" is identified as Hazlitt in his *Characters*; against a passage about "the alternate contraction and dilation of the soul" in *King Lear*, Keats wrote, "This passage has to a great degree the hieroglyphic visioning." From the book, he took the idea "That the greatest strength of genius is shown in describing the strongest passions", a saying which he marked and developed in a long note.[3] This chimed with his critique of Kean, and what he had written to Bailey a month before—"What the imagination seizes as Beauty must be truth". There is a significant vigour in the word "seizes". Kean could make "disagreeables", irrelevant or discordant details, evaporate by the intensity of his playing them, which gave them a truth and a kind of beauty of their own, in close relationship with the greater themes of the play. This, Keats maintained, should be the principle in every art, creative or interpretive.

Either while walking back to Hampstead with Dilke after the Boxing Day pantomime, or on one of the many other occasions when he was now seeing him, Keats[4] found that

several things dovetailed in my mind, & at once it struck me, what quality went to form a Man of Achievement especially in Literature & which Shakespeare possessed so enormously—I mean *Negative Capability*, that is when a man is capable of being in uncertainties, Mysteries, doubts, without any irritable reaching after fact & reason— Coleridge, for instance, would let go by a fine isolated verisimilitude caught from the Penetralium of mystery, from being incapable of remaining content with half knowledge. This pursued through Volumes would perhaps take us no further than this, that with a great poet the sense of Beauty overcomes every other consideration, or rather obliterates all consideration.

The criticism of Coleridge, which has seemed to some untrue,[5] does not refer to his poems, which Keats had been reading in *Sybilline Leaves*, but to

---

1. Keats Collection, Houghton Library. Markings etc., printed in Lowell, II, 587–590.

2. Bate, 262, says "late in 1817", but it was noticed in *The Examiner* of July 6.

3. This note, with others, relates to his notes on *Paradise Lost*, indicating that he was reading the books simultaneously.

4. *Letters*, I, 193 is not clear on this point.   5. See Bate, 249 n.

his "true philosophical Critique" of Wordsworth's poetry, published earlier that year in his *Biographia Literaria*.[1] In this, Coleridge had deeply offended Wordsworth by carping at just such "isolated verisimilitudes" as Keats mentions. "At what time", Coleridge asked, questioning the whole idea of the *Immortality Ode*, "were we dipt in the Lethe, which has produced such utter oblivion of a state so godlike?", and on the same day that Keats was writing his comments, Saturday 27 December, the two older poets, estranged for years, had a singularly uncomfortable reunion at Monkhouse's.[2]

The various themes that had dovetailed in Keats's mind to produce his own theory can be fairly well followed. The acting of Kean, with its utter absorption in the isolated moment, "without a shadow of thought about anything else", as Keats had written, was allied with Shakespeare's nature as expounded by Hazlitt in his *Hamlet* review, in words which made the deepest impression on Keats. "The poet appears for the time being to be identified with the character he wishes to represent, and to pass from one to the other, like the same soul successively animating different bodies." Yet this lack of identity, of preconceived certainty, Keats found, was the mark of all great poets at their highest. He had just found it in a passage in *Paradise Lost*, against which he noted:

What creates the intense pleasure of not knowing? A sense of independence, of power, from the fancy's creating a world of its own by the sense of probabilities.

The intense pleasure of not knowing, or in the more famous expression he coined, of negative capability, was the perfect state for creation, since it left the imagination completely free to seize Beauty as Truth. Milton, he found, had achieved this momentarily in Books IV and VII of *Paradise Lost*, excelling even Shakespeare in "two specimens of very extraordinary beauty . . . better described in themselves than by a volume".

Finally, there was the slow-working underlying effect of the long religious discussions Keats had with Bailey at Oxford. Bailey, as a follower of Butler, held the opinion that since nature is mysterious, doubtful and uncertain, so, by analogy, the evidences of religion must be similarly obscure. Again Butler wooed the sceptic by not requiring full understanding and knowledge of all the Christian scheme. He could suppose people to have religion even though they remained "in great doubts and uncertainties about both its evidence and nature". Keats was no more a Christian than before, but he had adapted this view of Christian evidence into his own touchstone for the creative artist. With the pieces fitting together from every quarter, from the varied geniuses of Kean, Shakespeare, Milton and Hazlitt, from his religious and philosophical speculations, and above all from his own fluid and receptive nature, Keats had at last formulated a poetic creed by which he was to work

1. *John Keats: A Reassessment*, 143.
2. M. Moorman, *William Wordsworth*, II, 308–314.

for the rest of his life. From this moment he knew the kind of poet he had to be. Even his own slow and late development, which had driven him to suicidal thoughts in his teens, was now a positive hope, its uncertainties seen as a necessary part of genius on its way to creative freedom. As he wrote of the young artist Cripps a few weeks later, "I have the greater hopes of him because he is so slow in devellopment—a Man of great executing Powers at 20—with a look and a speech almost stupid is sure to do something." Applying the same idea to himself, he wrote, "Nothing is finer for the purposes of great productions, than a very gradual ripening of the intellectual powers."[1]

The ripening of his own powers can be seen by the way his friends now began to borrow thoughts from him, rather than he from them, and to rely on him for help in intellectual matters. Bailey had felt moved by the death of Princess Charlotte to write a discourse of Christian apologetic for the young woman's untimely end in childbirth. Keats promised to speak for it to Taylor,[2] with the result that this December the pamphlet appeared under Taylor & Hessey's imprint. An undergraduate essay, as its title announced,[3] it leaned heavily on Bailey's reading in Jeremy Taylor, Wordsworth and Butler. Yet it opened with a paraphrase of Keats himself, a prose version of the beginning of *Endymion*: "When we look upon beauty we cannot think of death . . . the object that thus presents itself before us cannot die." On its next page, Keats's recent "What the imagination seizes as Beauty must be truth" became "Every idea of beauty in the abstract associates itself with the imagination." Keats was taking his place as a leader of thought in his circle. Even Haydon, who claimed to find his conversation weak and inconsistent, learned more than he admitted.

In this great formative period of thought it was perhaps essential that Keats should not be writing; society was a solvent for the "continual burning" he had felt while trying both to think and write earlier in the year. The next day, Sunday 28 December, was the high point of his social activity, the famous "immortal dinner" given by Haydon.[4] In this, by delightful chance, almost the whole gamut of human nature was run through, from the solemn and poetic to the comic and even grotesque; it was a living instance of light and shade, "such" Haydon himself said, "as one sees in an act of Shakespeare". The dinner began at 3 o'clock in Haydon's large galleried painting-room at the back of the house. The table was set directly beneath Haydon's huge unfinished picture of Christ's Entry into Jerusalem; the firelight flickered on the heads of Keats and Wordsworth, which Haydon had painted into the crowd, in company with those of Hazlitt, Newton and Voltaire. Below sat

1. *Letters*, I, 210 and 214.   2. *Letters*, I, 187.
3. Not a sermon, as Keats called it, nor was it ever preached, as Ward, 170, supposes.
4. Haydon, II, 174–176. Writing this up for his autobiography in the 1840s, Haydon seemed to suggest the dinner was arranged for Keats to meet Wordsworth, but then contradicted himself. See p. 168, above.

Keats and Wordsworth themselves, who with Monkhouse and Charles Lamb made up the dinner-guests.[1] Wordsworth, perhaps in reaction after his unpleasant experience with Coleridge the day before, was splendidly relaxed, and in high good humour; it was difficult to be otherwise in the company of Haydon, whose laughs, as Leigh Hunt once wrote, "sound like the trumpets of Jericho, and threaten to have the same effect".[2]

At first they discussed Homer, Shakespeare, Milton and Virgil, with Wordsworth "repeating Milton with an intonation like the funeral bell of St. Paul's & the music of Handel mingled"; but Lamb, as he usually did, quickly got tipsy, and began to take the lead away from Wordsworth with the familiarity of an old friend, calling him a rascally Lake poet. He attacked him for saying, in The Excursion, that a novel by Voltaire was "the dull product of a scoffer's pen",[3] and though the rest defended Wordsworth and agreed that there was a state of mind in which Voltaire could appear dull, Lamb replied, "Well let us drink his health. Here's Voltaire, the Messiah of the French nation, and a very fit one." Still looking at the canvas above them he then attacked Haydon for putting in Newton, "a Fellow who believed nothing unless it was as clear as the three sides of a triangle". This drew Keats into the conversation; Lamb had seen Kean's Luke at Drury Lane, and, whether or not they met there, knew of Keats's review, for the two now applied the rainbow image to natural science and agreed that Newton "had destroyed all the Poetry of the rainbow, by reducing it to a prism". They drank, "Newton's health, and confusion to mathematics". It was a popular toast for Wordsworth too, with his own doctrine of the "meddling intellect", and his condemnation of the natural philosopher or scientist as

> One who would peep and botanise
> Upon his mother's grave.

The inspired talk, "an evening worthy of the Elizabethan age", Lamb's wit, and finally a recital from Endymion by Keats lasted for three or four hours, when they all moved into the front drawing-room for tea with some invited friends; among these were John Landseer, the deaf engraver, father of Haydon's pupils, and Joseph Ritchie, a young surgeon whom Tom Keats had met in Paris,[4] and who was being sent as an explorer by the Government to find a new route to the Niger. He was introduced as "a gentleman going to Africa", at which Lamb, now in the somnolent stage of drink, woke up and shouted, "Who is the gentleman we are going to lose?", an unhappily-true premonition. Ritchie took to Keats, and later praised him as likely "to be the great poetical luminary of the age to come",[5] while Keats made Ritchie

1. Bate, 269, says Reynolds was invited; the evidence suggests he was only asked to drop in later. Letters, I, 205.
2. CLH., I, 89.　　　3. The Excursion, II, 443.
4. Introduced by John Scott.　　　5. Lowell, I, 282.

G

promise he would carry his *Endymion* to the great desert of Sahara and throw it in the midst.[1]

The stage seemed set for some climax, and when it came it was overpoweringly comic. Earlier that day, John Kingston, the deputy Comptroller of the Stamp Office from Horace Smith's set, had called on Haydon, and asked if he might drop in that evening. Since 1813, to supplement his income for a growing family, Wordsworth had been a civil servant, Distributor of Stamps for Westmorland, Whitehaven and part of Cumberland. Kingston, whom he had never met, was his immediate supervisor from the London office. What followed is best told in Haydon's own familiar words:[2]

When we retired to tea we found the comptroller. In introducing him to Wordsworth I forgot to say who he was. After a little time the comptroller looked down, looked up and said to Wordsworth, 'Don't you think, sir, Milton was a great genius?' Keats looked at me, Wordsworth looked at the comptroller. Lamb who was dozing by the fire turned round and said, 'Pray, sir, did you say Milton was a great genius?' 'No, sir; I asked Mr. Wordsworth if he were not.' 'Oh,' said Lamb, 'then you are a silly fellow,' 'Charles! my dear Charles!' said Wordsworth; but Lamb, perfectly innocent of the confusion he had created, was off again by the fire.

After an awful pause the comptroller said , 'Don't you think Newton a great genius?' I could not stand it any longer. Keats put his head into my books. Ritchie squeezed in a laugh. Wordsworth seemed asking himself, 'Who is this?' Lamb got up, and taking a candle, said, 'Sir, will you allow me to look at your phrenological development?' He then turned his back on the poor man, and at every question of the comptroller he chaunted—

> Diddle diddle dumpling, my son John
> Went to bed with his breeches on.

The man in office, finding Wordsworth did not know who he was, said in a spasmodic and half-chuckling anticipation of assured victory, 'I have had the honour of some correspondence with you, Mr. Wordsworth.' 'With me, sir?' said Wordsworth, 'not that I remember.' 'Don't you, sir? I am a comptroller of stamps.' There was a dead silence;—the comptroller evidently thinking that was enough. While we were waiting for Wordsworth's reply, Lamb sung out

> Hey diddle diddle,
> The cat and the fiddle.

'My dear Charles!' said Wordsworth,—

> Diddle diddle dumpling, my son John,

chaunted Lamb, and then rising, exclaimed, 'Do let me have another look at that gentleman's organs.' Keats and I hurried Lamb into the painting-room, shut the door and gave way to inextinguishable laughter. Monkhouse followed and tried to get Lamb away. We went back but the comptroller was irreconcilable. We soothed and smiled and asked him to supper. He stayed though his dignity was sorely affected. However, being a good-natured man, we parted all in good-humour, and no ill effects followed.

All the while, until Monkhouse succeeded, we could hear Lamb struggling in the painting-room and calling at intervals, 'Who is that fellow? Allow me to see his organs once more.'

Although Haydon was supremely delighted by the comic denouement, he had some sobering reflections too. Kingston, he thought, "had a visible effect on Wordsworth. I felt pain at the slavery of office." If Keats had any such feelings, he did not show them yet. He accepted an invitation from Kingston to meet Wordsworth again at his house the following Saturday, though he excused himself later, "not liking that place," and also realizing he had an engagement with Rice's "Club". He managed to meet Wordsworth, apparently by chance, walking on a foggy day, the last of the old year, on Hampstead Heath, and so anxious was he still to see him, that he called round at Mortimer Street before Wordsworth went to dine with Kingston on Saturday 3 January. Here he did suffer a shock. Wordsworth first kept him waiting for some time; when he at last appeared, he was dressed formally, with frilled shirt-front, a stiff collar, knee-breeches and silk stockings, and seemed in a great hurry to go out and dine with his superior. Remembering the figure Kingston himself had cut at Haydon's, "frilled, dressed, and official",[1] Keats felt Wordsworth was lowering himself; it was this dinner-engagement, rather than any other occasion that he remembered painfully about Wordsworth and he referred to the incident afterwards "with something of anger".[2] For the moment, he met Wordsworth's wife and Sara Hutchinson, whom he at first took for his daughter, and received a kindly invitation to dine himself at Mortimer Street on Monday; he then went off to his Saturday night engagement with the Piccadilly set. This turned out to be another riotous occasion; if Haydon was convinced that nothing in Boswell was equal to what came out of the poets at his party, this one had its Boswellian touches too, those of Boswell's journals rather than his *Life of Johnson*. The occasion was a dance given by George S. Reddell, an elderly man in the sword-cutlery business at 236 Piccadilly, over his shop, soon to disappear in the new Piccadilly Circus.[3] Reddell, a comic old-fashioned little man, with one tall niece, one fat one, and one topic of conversation, his friendship with the engraver Bartolozzi, was unused to entertaining, and supplied far too much drink. The result was a splendid slice of Regency middle-class life,[4] at which Keats

drank deep and won 10.6 at cutting for Half Guinies there was a younger Brother of the Squibs made him self very conspicuous after the Ladies had retired from the supper table by giving Mater Omnium—Mr Redhall said he did not understand any thing but

1. Haydon, II, 175. 2. Dilke, ann. I, 86.
3. P.O. Directories, 1817, 1818. 4. *Letters*, I, 200.

plain english—where at Rice egged the young fool on to say the Word[1] plainly out. After which there was an enquirey about the derivation of the word C—t when while two parsons and Grammarians were setting together and settling the matter Wm Squibs interrupting them said a very good thing—'Gentlemen says he I have always understood it to be a Root and not a Derivitive.' On proceeding to the Pot in the Cupboard it soon became full on which the Court door was opened Frank Floodgate bawls out, Hoollo! here's an opposition pot—Ay, says Rice in one you have a Yard for your pot, and in the other a pot for your Yard—

It is one of the few glimpses we have of the behaviour of the English middle-class, as opposed to fashionable society, at this time. The future clergyman, Bailey, down for the Christmas vacation, was there enjoying himself; he presumably was one of the two parsons discussing the derivation of the four-letter word. As if this were not enough, Keats had his own home entertain-ment on the following day, Sunday 4 January. Putting off dining again with Haydon, he had Severn and Wells to dinner at Well Walk, drank claret and port, and "played a Concert", each one imitating some musical instrument for six hours after dinner, from four till ten. Keats's two reviews, of the tragedy and the pantomime, came out in *The Champion* this week-end, and his high spirits were shown in the latter, in which he imagined all the famous Shakespearian critics being learned on the subject of Punch and Judy.

That night he probably walked back with the other two, and slept at Wells's home at Holborn, where he wrote the next day, 5 January, to George and Tom. Their letters had held disquieting news. Tom was spitting blood. Keats went that morning to Sawrey in Bedford Row, and held a consultation. There was now no putting-down Tom's symptoms to his mysterious and unhappy love-affair;[2] tuberculosis, the "family disease" was manifest. Sawrey asked for a detailed report, but there was little he could do. The weather was bad; Keats at first hesitated about going to Wordsworth, but then decided to dine there, but come back to supper and another night with Wells's parents. Keats left no account of what happened when he dined with Wordsworth, "his beautiful Wife and his enchanting Sister"—that is, sister-in-law, as he now knew Sara Hutchinson to be—but as he afterwards referred to the ladies as Wordsworth's "fireside Divan",[3] and criticized the atmosphere of infallibility with which they surrounded him, an anecdote recalled by Clarke is probably true.[4] Keats disagreed with Wordsworth on some point, at which, according to Clarke, Mrs. Wordsworth put her hand upon his arm saying, "Mr. Wordsworth is never interrupted". There could have been great sympathy, in other circumstances, between Keats and Sara Hutchinson. Coleridge's beloved "Asra" was witty, shrewd, attractive, and not afraid herself to interrupt or criticize her powerful brother-in-law; yet on

1. Keats, by a slip, wrote "World".   2. *Letters*, I, 186. See Appendix 3.
3. *Letters*, I, 265.
4. C. Cowden Clarke, 'Recollections of Keats', *Atlantic Monthly*, Jan. 1861.

this meeting, she wrote off the younger poet merely as "little Keats". Her unspoken comment on *Endymion* was "I wonder anybody should take such subjects now-a-days."[1] It was good doctrine for a believer in *Lyrical Ballads*, and reflects the lack of esteem Wordsworth felt at the time for his own classical poem, *Laodamia*, but it cannot have made a sympathetic background for Keats's visit. Keats was perhaps too occupied with his own responsibilities to notice much at the time. Not only Tom but Fanny was ill, and on two visits to Walthamstow he had found her at loggerheads with the unpleasing Mrs. Abbey, who accused all the Keatses of being born lazy. He had to get "Kingston and Cº" to provide money for Cripps's training, and, most of all, he must start revising *Endymion* for Taylor & Hessey. On Saturday 10 January, he told Taylor he was well into Book One. It had been a month of intense spiritual and human growth, and it had made one significant change in his triumvirate of "great spirits" of just over a year before. This same Sunday, he wrote to Haydon, "I am convinced that there are three things to rejoice at in this Age—The Excursion, Your Pictures, and Hazlitt's depth of Taste." In his copy of Hazlitt's *Characters* he wrote and underlined "—he hath a kind of taste—", while now in Hunt's *Examiner* articles he could only find "so much egotism". Haydon and Wordsworth, at any rate up to this time, had survived the shocks administered to him by their own personalities, and were still on their thrones. The importance of this month without poetry had been the emergence of Keats himself, which Haydon at once generously divined: "allow me to add sincerely a fourth to be proud of— *John Keats' genius!*"

Chapter 13

NUMBERLESS POINTS

*"Minds would leave each other in contrary directions, traverse
each other in Numberless points, and all (for "at") last greet each
other at the Journeys end—"*

– JOHN KEATS to J. H. Reynolds, 19 February 1818

IN SPITE of his confession to his publisher—"I have been racketing too much,
& do not feel over well", in spite of the promise to hurry on with copying
Endymion Book One, Keats still found himself with a week of social engagements to fulfil. He spent the week-end in Town, probably again with Wells,
for he went theatre-visiting with him on Monday 12 January. Wells, a
smart young solicitor's clerk of Byronic good looks, seemed to have an
entry to all classes of society. He took Keats to a box in a small private theatre
near Drury Lane, a rather disreputable place "where the audience are admitted
gratis, and the performers pay for playing". Keats described it succinctly as a
"dirty hole", and took the precaution of bringing with him Brown's free
ticket for Drury Lane where Kean was on again in *Richard III* that night. In
the greasy oily atmosphere of the tiny auditorium, even George Colman's
ever-popular comedy *John Bull* palled after one act; Keats fled to the greater
theatre to enjoy "a Spice of Richard III", and did not return until the
interval between *John Bull* and its subsequent farce, *The Review, or, The Wags
of Windsor*. During this interval, Wells brought Keats backstage into the
minute green room, where the actors and actresses appeared in their fresh
costumes for the farce, swearing and quarreling. The evening ended in chaos
after the farce, which should have been followed by a burlesque comic opera,
Bombastes Furioso; but the curtain did not rise, although the orchestra played
the overture three times, after which they all adjourned to an ale-house,
where Keats observed "how they looked about, & chatted; how they did
not care a Damn; was a great treat". When he got back to Hampstead very
late that night, he found Haydon's complimentary letter waiting for him, but
he also found, paraphrasing ruefully his own early sonnet, "uproar's your
only musick". Not only had he still further social engagements to fulfil,
including two dances that week, one at Dilke's and one at the London Coffee
House on Ludgate Hill; there was also Cripps to be provided for. Keats was
beginning to think that the whole project of apprenticing him to Haydon

should be reconsidered, even if the "fat-purses", such as Kingston, should raise enough for his premium.[1] He had been shaken by two devastating quarrels in which Haydon was now involved with friends of his. Reynolds, who had been asked by Haydon to drop in and meet Wordsworth on 28 December, had neither come nor sent an apology, and a furious correspondence ensued. The near neighbourhood of Haydon and the Hunts had also, predictably, ended in a violent row, after Mrs. Hunt had borrowed Haydon's cutlery and not returned it on time.[2] "All I hope is at some time to bring them all together again", was Keats's comment. In this hope, he saw all three people involved, Reynolds on Friday 16 January, Hunt and Haydon, separately, on the following Sunday, but whatever efforts he made did not succeed. Reynolds was beginning to show the jealous possessiveness about Keats which other friends noticed.[3] He was in an emotional state himself over giving up literature for the Law in order to provide for marriage, though in fact, in spite of handing over his theatrical reviewing to Dilke, and bidding farewell to poetry, he continued to write poems and even take on fresh journalistic commitments. He had, as can be seen from his writing, a habit of praising by denigrating others, and he not only widened the gap between Keats and Hunt, an inevitable process, but also, more regrettably, contributed to the disenchantment which Keats came to feel over Wordsworth. Keats had already noticed the habit of carping which ran through the whole family, who had just moved to a "Master's House" near Christ's Hospital. Reynolds's mother and sisters at Little Britain were, understandably, on the look-out for young men with good prospects, but sour grapes embittered their tongues against those who chose elsewhere. In a few weeks George Keats would come into his inheritance, and Keats was quick to notice a tacit disapproval of him by the Reynolds girls, as his attachment to Georgiana Wylie became more obvious. They had, however, a rich prospect in Bailey, who during the Christmas vacation was openly courting Marianne in a manner befitting a future clergyman, "with the Bible and Jeremy Taylor under his arm", as Keats put it. All the same, the somewhat exclusive intimacy, which Reynolds pressed on him in the early months of this year, brought out some of Keats's finest thoughts and feelings on poetry, and it was in the Reynolds household on Friday 16 January that he wrote his first poem for several weeks. This was his sonnet *To Mrs. Reynolds's Cat*. Strangely dismissed by some critics as an unsuccessful joke, the sonnet has a great deal of interest, quite apart from being a quickening of his poetic pulse after such a long silence. It illustrates perfectly Keats's gift of sympathetic identification, reaching beyond his fellow men to the battered old feline who sat digging its claws into his knee. As he had done with the sparrow picking about the

1. There is no evidence Cripps ever became Haydon's pupil, though Haydon's Diary anticipates the event. Haydon, II, 177.

2. *Letters*, I, 205, 206, 210.   3. Sharp, 109.

gravel, Keats actually becomes the cat by the fire. In form, it is a successful parody of the manner of Milton's sonnets, from the onset of its Miltonic opening "Cat!", and marks his virtual farewell to the Miltonic sonnet, which he had used almost exclusively in his first book of poems. This fresh beginning was confirmed by another incident on Keats's peace-making rounds. When he visited Hunt on Sunday 18 January, or perhaps on a second visit the following Wednesday, Keats showed him Book One of *Endymion*, which he had at last finished fair-copying. In his casual manner Hunt skimmed through the pages, making objections at random, mostly on the conversations between Endymion and his sister, which he condemned as too high-flown, and not in the naturalistic, chatty style of his own *Rimini*. "Men should bear with each other", Keats wrote to Bailey, apropos of the quarrels of his friends. Generally he lived up to his own maxim; but here he was led into a suspicion that both Hunt and Shelley were prejudiced because he had not shown them *Endymion* before, a thought possibly put into his head by Reynolds, for it fell below his own standard.[1] Criticism had, however, the practical effect it always produced on Keats. He now wrote, as if in defiance of Hunt, in every form and on every subject under the sun.

The first was on an authenticated lock of Milton's hair, which Hunt himself showed Keats on 21 January, urging him to write a poem about it. Keats, perhaps chary of being tricked into another laurel crown episode, jibbed at the inevitable sonnet and began somewhat stiffly in ode form, writing in a notebook of Hunt's; then, taking up a spare sheet of paper, he began to expand and broaden the poem into something resembling the odes he so much admired of Katherine Philips, and with something of his new philosophy toward the creation of *Hyperion*, echoing his own markings in *Paradise Lost*:

> And by the kernel of thine earthly Love,
> Beauty, in things on earth and things above,
>   When every childish fashion
>   Has vanish'd from my rhyme
>   Will I grey-gone in passion,
>   Give to an after-time
>   Hymning and harmony
> Of thee, and of thy Works and of thy Life:
> But vain is now the burning and the strife—
> Pangs are in vain—until I grow high-rife
>   With Old Philosophy
>   And mad with glimpses at futurity!

1. Mrs. Shelley wrote an angry note about this suspicion by Keats in her copy of Milnes's *Life, Letters* etc. Keats Collection, Houghton Library, *EC 8, K 2262. W.848, m(c).

At the same time, the circumstances and the atmosphere at Hunt's jarred on Keats; on copying the poem for Bailey, he added "This I did at Hunt's at his request—perhaps I should have done something better alone and at home". The following day, at home, he not only copied the lines into his folio Shakespeare, but wrote in it another and much finer poem on an allied theme. Hunt's over-enthusiastic association with Milton had sent Keats back to Shakespeare, and Hazlitt's *Characters* had sent him back to *King Lear*. Sitting down to read the play again he felt its greatness now required from him the response which he had not dared make in the Spring, a sonnet actually on *King Lear*. He wrote it with his own coming ordeal by poetry in mind, the pangs he would have to endure in composing *Hyperion*, remembering the mental agonies of beginning *Endymion*:

> When I am through the old oak forest gone
> Let me not wander in a barren dream
> But when I am consumed with the Fire
> Give me new Phoenix-wings to fly at my desire.

"To paint from memory of gone self storm" he had described the task of the poet in his annotation to Hazlitt's remarks on *King Lear*, a phrase which might have formed a line in his own sonnet. This begins to give a clue to his intentions in the new poem, *Hyperion*, for "the old oak forest" through which he will have to wander is this coming poem, and not romance verse like the poem he had just finished, *Endymion*. Writing to Haydon about a proposal by Taylor that the painter should do a drawing as the frontispiece to *Endymion*, Keats advised him to wait for *Hyperion*, as "the nature of *Hyperion* will lead me to treat it in a more naked and grecian Manner—and the march of passion and endeavour will be undeviating." He had already announced in *Endymion* "Thy lute-voic'd brother I will sing ere long", and now on Friday 23 January in the letter to Haydon, he made clear the difference between the two poems:

one great contrast between them will be—that the Hero of the written tale [i.e. *Endymion*] being mortal is led on, like Buonaparte, by circumstance; whereas the Apollo in Hyperion being a fore-seeing God will shape his actions like one.

Yet it is also clear that in this "fore-seeing" God of healing and poetry, Keats, himself doctor and poet, will record his own experience and undergo the pains of Apollo himself in becoming a god. This identification of himself with the god who is both healer and poetic creator perhaps explains for the first time why the poem was called *Hyperion* and not *Apollo*. Hyperion, the moody, haunted and melancholy Titan of the Sun, whom Apollo supplants, is Keats's old self, which he had worked through to sanity and spiritual health in writing *Endymion*. When he came to write *Hyperion*, the horrors of the Sun Titan, so deeply dwelt upon, are so much like his own nervous imaginings, the "horrid Morbidity" of his old self, that the identification cannot be doubted.

G*

"But I am counting &c", he modestly added to Haydon. He was not yet ready for his epic, though he was sure of its general style and scope. There must be a long period of probation before he physically put pen to paper. He spent the evening, like many others, patiently working at the Dilkes, copying Book Two of *Endymion*, and beginning to make his drastic cuts and revisions in Book One. Although he did not admit Hunt's criticism, the cuts he now made, as the proof-sheets came in, all tended to remove the slacker passages and tighten the construction. He was looking forward to a new mental stimulus. The previous Sunday, after having Haslam to breakfast, he had taken him along to Haydon's studio, and found there, as well as Haydon's pupil, Bewick, William Hazlitt. Keats now learnt that Hazlitt had just begun a course of Tuesday lectures at the Surrey Institution, over Blackfriars Bridge, and that he had missed the first one, "On Poetry in General". He promised to come to the next, "On Chaucer and Spenser", but mistook the time. Arriving at eight instead of seven, he found everyone just coming out, Hunt's brother and nephew, Haydon's pupils—Bewick and the three Landseer boys—, Charles Wells, Harris, the Covent Garden manager, with whom he had some "curious chat" a few weeks before, and his old medical bookseller, Cox of St. Thomas's Street in the Borough.[1] Next Tuesday, 27 January, however, he did not mistake the time, and heard Hazlitt lecture "On Shakespeare and Milton". Pale, hectic, nervous, half-prepared, using scraps of old reviews or newspaper articles, often at odds with a very miscellaneous audience, Hazlitt, who had bolted in stage-fright at his first lecture, was now acquiring confidence. His lectures began to be the dramatic performances he usually reserved for the racquets court, and they fascinated Keats. He spoke on Shakespeare's universality ,and presented this idea, which ran through all his writings, in new and even more striking terms.

He was just like any other man, but that he was like all other men. He was the least of an egotist that it was possible to be. He was nothing in himself; but he was all that others were, or that they could become. He not only had in himself the germs of every faculty and feeling, but he could follow them by anticipation, intuitively, into all their conceivable ramifications, through every change of fortune, or conflict of passion, or turn of thought ... When he conceived of a character, whether real or imaginary, he not only entered into all its thoughts and feelings, but seemed instantly, and as if by touching a secret spring, to be surrounded with all the same objects ...

This was a definition of a poet that Keats was to accept all the rest of his writing life. So too was Hazlitt's account of Shakespeare's actual process of writing his characters:

In Shakspeare there is a continual composition and decomposition of its elements, a fermentation of every particle in the whole mass, by its alternate affinity or antipathy to other principles which are brought in contact with it.

1. "Rox" of *Letters*, I, 214, is one of Jeffrey's usual errors of transcription.

Hazlitt's quotations from *Troilus and Cressida* chimed with Keats's own favourite reading. Yet there was a disturbing note too. In an aside, Hazlitt attacked Wordsworth:

The great fault of the modern school of poetry is, that it is an experiment to reduce poetry to a mere effusion of natural sensibility; or what is worse, to divest it of both imaginary splendour and human passion, to surround the meanest objects with the morbid feelings and devouring egotism of the writers' own minds. Milton and Shakspeare did not so understand poetry. They gave a more liberal interpretation both to nature and art. They did not do all they could to get rid of the one and the other, to fill up the dreary void with the Moods of their own Minds.

There was more of the same sort in even stronger though veiled terms; but the contrast between Wordsworth and Shakespeare, "the least of an egotist", was made explicit by the biting reference to Wordsworth's unhappy sub-title in his 1807 edition of poems. Here, for Keats, was Hazlitt speaking on Shakespeare, a god speaking of a god, turning aside to denigrate another god, Wordsworth. Keats was left with much to ponder. He might have pondered more had he known that Hazlitt had waited for Wordsworth to have left Town just a week before delivering his onslaught.[1]

For himself, the way was clear. A Shakespearian universality, which he had admired before in poems and plays, must be added to his training for the great task ahead. It is no coincidence that this lecture ushered in a period of extreme trial and error, when Keats poured out poems in almost every conceivable form and mood, and even began to think of dramatic poetry. In his letter to Taylor on Friday 30 January, enclosing the vital revision of the "Pleasure Thermometer" passage from *Endymion*, Keats added that it was "my first Step towards the chief Attempt in the Drama—the playing of different Natures with Joy and Sorrow". The phrase is ambiguous, but the context, only three days after Hazlitt's Shakespeare lecture, points to play-writing being in his mind. It may also point the occasion when he composed the tripping light verse beginning "Welcome joy, and welcome sorrow" for as well as its likeness to his own words to Taylor, Keats heard Hazlitt fill up his next Tuesday's lecture "On Dryden and Pope" with a long quotation from George Wither, "describing the consolations of poetry in the following terms",

> She doth tell me where to borrow
> Comfort in the midst of sorrow;

Metre and sentiment were identical with his own little poem.

Meanwhile, a spate of poems was coming, in almost Shakespearian profusion, and with something of the Shakespearian lyric quality, for Keats was now re-reading not only Shakespeare's plays but his poems also. Before

1. He had left on Monday 19 January, after spending the week-end at Windsor, but Keats did not know this.

the end of January, he wrote his first fully Shakespearian sonnet. In the copy he shared with Reynolds, the most heavily-marked Sonnets were 60 and 64.[1] These are echoed strongly in his fine sonnet, "When I have fears that I may cease to be", but even more clearly in another sonnet "Time's sea hath been five years at its slow ebb", written a few days later on Wednesday 4 February. The image of time as a devouring sea, which ended one sonnet and began another, is taken from Shakespeare's great lines, but Keats gives it a personal application. His two sonnets are not written to any Mr. W.H. but somewhat surprisingly addressed to the memory of the mysterious lady, seen in adolescence one brief moment at Vauxhall long ago in the summer of 1814.

> Time's sea hath been five years at its slow ebb:[2]
> Long hours have to and fro let creep the sand;
> Since I was tangled in thy beauty's web,
> And snared by the ungloving of thine hand.

The high seriousness of these two sonnets contrasted with the light-heartedness of the rest of his verse. Keats seemed bent on celebrating the minor pleasures he loved so well, and which had filled his last month, in Shakespearian lyric style. The lines "O blush not so", which his friends afterwards called "on the mystery of the maidenhead", based on the slang of their West End set about "knocking out an apple", were sent to Reynolds on 31 January after seeing a pretty girl pass by with "a mere muslin Handkerchief very neatly pinned" in a fichu round her neck. He followed this lyric with some verses, "Hence Burgundy, Claret & port", extolling Apollo, and some more serious lines on the same subject, beginning "God of the Meridian". A visit early in the February to the Mermaid Tavern with the wit Horace Twiss, whose cousin had been at Clarke's School, and his fellow-wit Horace Smith, who had just lent Keats the manuscript of a new comic poem, led Keats to compose his *Lines on the Mermaid Tavern*, in which he addressed the "Souls of Poets dead and gone", who had drunk there. Getting two sonnets from Reynolds on Robin Hood, he capped them with a long poem in light-hearted metre on the same subject, sending both poems to Reynolds on the same day, 3 February. It is possible that Reynolds's letter, sending his own sonnets, contained some insinuating cue for an attack on Wordsworth, perhaps mentioning Hazlitt's onslaught, for Keats suddenly comes out with his own:

It may be said that we ought to read our Contemporaries. that Wordsworth &c

1. KHM, No. 22. The markings are by Reynolds, not Keats as Caroline Spurgeon, *Keats's Shakespeare*, 39, believes but they probably show the mutual taste of the two friends.

2. It was under four years, but "five" is a typically rhetorical verse-statement. Cf. Keats's sonnet beginning "This mortal body of a thousand days" and his jokes on "kisses four", *Letters*, II, 97.

should have their due from us. but for the sake of a few fine imaginative or domestic passages, are we to be bullied into a certain Philosophy engendered in the whims of an Egotist?

The words are practically those of Hazlitt; the reduction of Wordsworth's achievement to "a few fine imaginative passages" is startling in one who, only three weeks before, had pronounced the whole of *The Excursion* as a thing to rejoice at. Keats went on, in more general terms:

We hate poetry that has a palpable design upon us—and if we do not agree, seems to put its hand in its breeches pocket. Poetry should be great & unobtrusive, a thing which enters into one's soul, and does not startle it or amaze it with itself but with its subject.—How beautiful are the retired flowers! how they would lose their beauty were they to throng into the highway crying out, "admire me I am a violet! dote upon me I am a primrose!

The sneer against Wordsworth has returned in the last remark, and Keats makes it explicit by joining the older poet with Hunt, of all people: "I will have no more of Wordsworth or Hunt in particular—". Keats knows he is committing treason to one of his great poetic teachers, and this knowledge acts like an irritant on him; he cannot help enlarging by taking an individual poem to ridicule, Wordsworth's "The Two April Mornings":

> Matthew is in his grave, yet now,
> Methinks, I see him stand,
> As at that moment, with a bough
> Of wilding in his hand.

Keats exploded upon this last stanza:

The secret of the Bough of Wilding will run through your head faster than I can write it—Old Matthew spoke to him some years ago on some nothing, & because he happens in an Evening Walk to imagine the figure of the old man—he must stamp it down in black & white, and it is henceforth sacred—I don't mean to deny Wordsworth's grandeur and Hunt's merit, but I mean to say we need not be teazed with grandeur & merit—when we can have them uncontaminated & unobtrusive.

"Modern poets differ from the Elizabethans in this" was his general theme, as it had been Hazlitt's in contrasting Shakespeare with Wordsworth; but in his bitterness of tone, he went far beyond this thesis.

Keats's mind was now full of trial and error, as it may well have been when he had just heard a great critic attack a great poet. What was the touchstone for poetry? For himself, the process of experiment continued in an even more fevered bout of composition. On Wednesday 4 February, he not only wrote his second Shakespearian sonnet, "Time's sea", but was inveigled by Hunt, whom he had just denounced, into yet another sonnet competition, this time with himself and Shelley on "The Nile". Hunt, who stayed up all night to complete it, produced the best of the three sonnets. Keats's contribution, a poor effort, was significantly in the Miltonic form which he had practically discarded, a mechanical throw-back. That evening he discussed Spenser with Reynolds, and next day wrote a sonnet to Spenser, back again in the Shakespearian form. Another Shakespeare sonnet finished the week, a trivial affair for Reynolds about preferring blue eyes to dark ones. He also found time to see Macready in the new tragedy, *Fazio*, and get the fair copy of Book Two of *Endymion* off to his publisher.

The "many songs & Sonnets" Keats told his brothers he was writing were beginning to peter out, but now a new suggestion for a poetic exercise was presented to his mind. In recommending Dryden's modernizations of Boccaccio and Chaucer, Hazlitt had remarked:

I should think that a modern translation of some of the other serious tales in Boccaccio and Chaucer, as that of Isabella, the Falcon, of Constance, the Prioress's Tale, and others, if executed with taste and spirit, could not fail to succeed in the present day.

This, in Keats's present mood, seemed a desirable challenge—to write in the style of the old poets and on old themes, with the taste and spirit of a modern writer, but without the personal and ephemeral themes that seemed to engage modern poets. He chose Boccaccio's *Isabella*, and suggested that Reynolds should try one of the other tales. He found Reynolds eager to discuss the project. It would be a trial of poetical strength far removed from a Huntian sonnet-competition. Meanwhile, Hazlitt in his next lecture on 10 February had performed the sort of volte-face that was the despair and confusion of his friends. Arriving insufficiently prepared for a whole lecture, and unaccountably skipping most of the first half of the eighteenth century, this surprising man dealt with Thomson and Cowper mainly in long quotation from *The Seasons* and *The Task*, Cowper's domestic epic beginning "I sing the Sofa". After a brief look at Bloomfield, he "gave Crabbe an unmerciful licking", as Keats said, and then found that his lecture had turned into one on nature poetry, and was still short-weight. He therefore filled in with a disquisition on pastoral writing in general, in which he swept his audience backward in time nearly two hundred years, quoting in full Sir Thomas Overbury's prose study "A fair and happy milkmaid", and going himself into a prose essay on the renewing effect of nature on our feelings.

Not only did he quote Wordsworth with approval in this passage, and again before the lecture was finished; he completely reversed the implied criticism of his lecture a fortnight before, and made nonsense of Keats's echo of it. Instead of only "what was grand in the objects of nature" being the stuff of poetry, now "there is no object, however trifling or rude, that does not in some mood or other find its way into the heart". Admittedly, his next lecture, in which he hastily mopped up the rest of the eighteenth century, with a side-glance at Rabelais and Voltaire as satirists, reverted to two small sneers at Wordsworth, but these were balanced by two approving quotations. Once more Keats was left pondering.

His thoughts at this time had much to do with Reynolds, and were most fully expressed in letters to him. Reynolds, having been in a temperamental turmoil, was now genuinely ill, with what proved to be a severe attack of rheumatic fever. In this state, on 14 February, he wrote a curious kind of Valentine, a sonnet bidding farewell to the Muses. He inscribed this in the copy of Shakespeare's poems that he and Keats shared, and virtually handed the book over to Keats at this time.[1] In spite of this sonnet, he was just enjoying considerable success with a set of satirical articles in a new magazine, *The Yellow Dwarf*, and discussing with Keats Hazlitt's suggestion of new verse modernizations from Boccaccio. Keats had many other social engagements with what he called "a squad of people", including a call from Crabb Robinson, and a visit to Hunt, where he met Shelley, Peacock, Hogg and Claire Clairmont, but his thoughts were often at Little Britain, where Reynolds lay in bed. After a visit there on Wednesday 18 February, he sat down next day, a beautiful spring morning at Hampstead, to clarify his own conflicting impressions and thoughts in a long letter to his sick friend, intended partly to cheer him and "lift a little time from your Shoulders".

I have an idea that a Man might pass a very pleasant life in this manner—let him on any certain day read a certain Page of full Poesy or distilled Prose and let him wander with it, and muse upon it, and reflect from it, and bring home to it, and prophesy upon it, and dream upon it—untill it becomes stale—but when will it do so? Never— When Man has arrived at a certain ripeness in intellect any one grand and spiritual passage serves him as a starting post towards all "the two-and thirty Pallaces" How happy is such a "voyage of conception," what delicious diligent Indolence! A doze upon a Sofa does not hinder it, and a nap upon Clover engenders ethereal finger-pointings—the prattle of a child gives it wings, and the converse of middle age a strength to beat them—a strain of musick conducts to 'an odd angle of the Isle' and when the leaves whisper it puts a 'girdle round the earth. Nor will this sparing touch of noble Books be any irreverance to their Writers—for perhaps the honors paid by Man to Man are trifles in comparison to the Benefit done by great Works to the 'Spirit and pulse of good' by their mere passive existence. Memory should not be called knowledge—Many have original Minds who do not think it—they are led away by Custom—Now it appears to me that almost any Man may like the Spider spin from his own inwards his own airy Citadel—the points of leaves and twigs on which the Spider begins her work are few and she fills the Air with a beautiful circuiting: man should be content with as few points to tip with the fine Webb of his Soul and weave a tapestry empyrean—full of Symbols for his spiritual eye, of softness for his spiritual touch, of space for his wandering of distinctness for his Luxury—But the Minds of Mortals are so different and bent on such diverse Journeys that it may at first appear impossible for any common taste and fellowship to exist between two or three under these suppositions—It is however quite the contrary—Minds would leave each other in contrary directions, traverse each other in Numberless points, and all[2]

1. Although the gift is dated 1819, it contains MS work by Keats written in September 1818. KHM, No. 22.
2. For "at".

last greet each other at the Journeys end—A old Man and a child would talk together and the old Man be led on his Path, and the child left thinking—Man should not dispute or assert but whisper results to his neighbour, and thus by every germ of Spirit sucking the Sap from the mould ethereal every human might become great, and Humanity instead of being a wide heath of Furse and Briars with here and there a remote Oak or Pine, would become a grand democracy of Forest Trees. It has been an old Comparison for our urging on—the Bee hive—however it seems to me that we should rather be the flower than the Bee—for it is a false notion that more is gained by receiving than giving—no the receiver and the giver are equal in their benefits—The fower[1] I doubt not receives a fair guerdon from the Bee—its leaves blush deeper in the next spring—and who shall say between Man and Women which is the most delighted? Now it is more noble to sit like Jove that[2] to fly like Mercury— let us not therefore go hurrying about and collecting honey-bee like, buzzing here and there impatiently from a knowledge of what is to be arrived at: but let us open our leaves like a flower and be passive and receptive—budding patiently under the eye of Apollo and taking hints from evey[3] noble insect that favors us with a visit—sap will be given us for Meat and dew for drink—I was led into these thoughts, my dear Reynolds, by the beauty of the morning operating on a sense of Idleness—I have not read any Books—the Morning said I was right—I had no Idea but of the Morning and the Thrush said I was right—seeming to say—

> 'O thou whose face hath felt the Winter's wind;
> Whose eye has seen the Snow clouds hung in Mist
> And the black-elm tops 'mong the freezing Stars
> To thee the Spring will be a harvest-time—
> O thou whose only book has been the light
> Of supreme darkness which thou feddest on
> Night after night, when Phœbus was away
> To thee the Spring shall be a tripple morn—
> O fret not after knowledge—I have none
> And yet my song comes native with the warmth
> O fret not after knowledge—I have none
> And yet the Evening listens—He who saddens
> At thought of Idleness cannot be idle,
> And he's awake who thinks himself asleep.' . . .

Keats's philosophy of Negative Capability finds its most characteristic and perfect expression in this letter. His thought had been moving towards this point ever since he had written to Bailey three months earlier from the inn-room at Burford Bridge. It expresses in measured form his criticism of Words-worth and Coleridge—"let us not therefore go hurrying about and collecting honey-bee like, buzzing here and there impatiently from a knowledge of what is to be arrived at"—and at the same time realizes that the "wise passiveness" advocated by Wordsworth throughout his poetry was his own creative attitude too—"let us open our leaves like a flower and be passive and receptive". This great letter takes its style and tone, both in prose and poetry,

1. For "flower".   2. For "than".   3. For "every".

from what Keats had heard recently through Hazlitt's mouth, of Thomson, Cowper and the pastoral tradition. The gentle progress of the prose, owing something to the Overbury Milkmaid pastoral, takes its thought from Cowper's *The Task*, a poem itself engendered by "a doze upon a Sofa":

> Meditation here
> May think down hours to moments. Here the heart
> May give a useful lesson to the head,
> And Learning wiser grow without his books.
> Knowledge and Wisdom, far from being one,
> Have oft-times no connection. Knowledge dwells
> In heads replete with thoughts of other men;
> Wisdom in minds attentive to their own.

As Keats paraphrased it: "Nor will this sparing touch of noble Books be any irreverence . . . Memory should not be called knowledge—Many have original Minds who do not think it—they are led away by Custom." The message of the winter robin in Cowper's poem is that wisdom, distinct from knowledge, can be won "by slow solicitation" from those natural scenes, which form, as Hazlitt had noticed, "a link in the chain of our living being". The message of the thrush in Keats's poem, reinforcing his idea of the link between all humanity caused by all "budding patiently", is expressed in a blank verse that has the exact cadence of Cowper's,[1] and the little moralistic ending

> He who saddens
> At thought of Idleness cannot be idle,
> And he's awake who thinks himself asleep.'

is typical of both the eighteenth-century poets Hazlitt had been discussing. Keats's power of assimilating a recent experience and making it serve some long-standing process in his mind is nowhere better illustrated than in the prose and verse of this astonishingly perfect and balanced letter, written with special care for his ill and temperamentally-torn friend.

Keats's attention to Hazlitt's lectures was now as punctilious as his attendance at them. He turned to reading Voltaire after Hazlitt had praised him on 17 February, and it is likely his disappointment at Hazlitt's cavalier treatment of Chatterton at the tail-end of the same lecture reached the lecturer's ears, for next Tuesday Hazlitt announced: "I am sorry that what I said in the conclusion of the last Lecture respecting Chatterton, should have given dissatisfaction to some persons, with whom I would willingly agree on all such matters." Since Hazlitt then quoted in full the Minstrel's Song from *Aella*,

1. The "many Sonnets" he had written made him unconsciously break off at fourteen lines. There is no evidence that he intended an unrhymed Shakespearian sonnet (Lowell, I, 580–581), still less an imitation of the repetitive song of the thrush (HBF, II, 200).

which was Keats's favourite, it may be inferred that "some persons" meant Keats. This lecture, "On Burns, and the old ballads", contained the most blatantly unfair of all Hazlitt's attacks on Wordsworth, a total misrepresentation of the latter's moving and eloquent pamphlet *Letter to a Friend of Burns*; but Keats by now had accumulated enough material in his own mind to come to a comparatively balanced view. It was true that Wordsworth, in his recent visit to London, had shocked by his personal behaviour even close friends like Crabb Robinson, whom Keats had just seen; yet this should not take away from his greatness as a poet. "I am sorry", Keats wrote to his brothers on 21 February, "that Wordsworth has left a bad impression wherever he visited in Town—by his egotism, Vanity and bigotry—yet he is a great Poet if not a Philosopher." These words reflect his own state of balance and calm. He was steadily copying *Endymion*, Book Three, round at Went-worth Place with Brown and Dilke—he confessed "I don't think I could stop in Hampstead without their neighbourhood"—and for the past week, proof-sheets of the earlier books had come in. He was working extremely hard, but one moment of hilarious relaxation seems to have occurred about now. One Sunday, he went to dine with Haydon, taking with him a visitor whom Haydon afterwards dismissed as "a noodle". This unfortunate man was probably one of the Kingston and Horace Smith set, perhaps even Kingston himself, and the object of the visit connected still with raising money for Cripps's apprenticeship, since Keats otherwise would hardly have brought such a person to Haydon's.[1] Haydon too had been working full out at this time; "I painted 5 hours without breathing" he had just entered in his Diary.[2] After dinner, when the visitor, in true Kingston style, "expected we should all be discussing Milton & Raphael &c.", Keats, Haydon and Bewick, who was also there, hurled themselves into their favourite pastime of imitating instruments of the orchestra. Keats boomed away as the bassoon, Bewick took the flageolet, and Haydon the deep bass of the organ. Seeing the effect on the astonished visitor, they went on "deliberately",[3] as Keats afterwards said, swapping instruments and bursting with laughter, "while the Wise acre sat by without saying a word, blushing & sipping his wine as if we meant to insult him". Apart from such relaxation, he was refusing social invitations, including one with Horace Smith. He had somehow to get the double work of copying and correcting done. What he did not yet know was that Taylor was disappointed with Book Two. As a publisher, he also saw that the lush and effusive description of the hero's love affair might offend the conventional public, and he was nerving himself to say this to Keats. He did so the following week, under cover of suggesting some

1. Haydon, II, 198. The diary entry is May 11, but appears a reminiscence of a past occasion. On May 11, Keats had not been "working dreadfully hard the whole week", but "lounging" at Hampstead after his return from Devon with Tom. *Letters*, I, 291.
2. Haydon, II, 189.   3. *Letters*, I, 266.

alterations and improvements in the punctuation of Book One. His "after admonitions", as Keats called them, on the subject of Book Two, were very well taken by the poet, though his amendments can hardly have gone so far as Taylor might have wished. One specially fervid line

> By the moist languor of thy breathing face

was given a less passionate substitute, but nothing much else was altered, and Taylor's bracketed suggestions for cuts were ignored. Taylor had tactfully suggested that some readers might have to "overcome Prejudices" on reading such lines. Keats admitted that he would not wish this to happen, but side-stepped from the particular to the general in his reply to Taylor of Friday 27 February by giving him his definition of what poetry *should* be rather than any promise about his own verse in *Endymion*. The spirit of Hazlitt's definition of Shakespeare's genius was infused into his own axioms of poetry:

In Poetry I have a few Axioms, and you will see how far I am from their Centre. 1st I think Poetry should surprise by a fine excess and not by Singularity—it should strike the Reader as a wording of his own highest thoughts, and appear almost a Remembrance—2nd Its touches of Beauty should never be half way therby making the reader breathless instead of content: the rise, the progress, the setting of imagery should like the Sun come natural too him—shine over him and set soberly although in magnificence leaving him in the Luxury of twilight—but it is easier to think what Poetry should be than to write it—and this leads me on to another axiom. That if Poetry comes not as naturally as the Leaves to a tree it had better not come at all.

The measured, objective tone of these critical pronouncements, the effort to establish general principles for writing, may possibly show that, as some believe, Keats had just met and talked with the third member of the publishing firm, the eminence grise behind Taylor & Hessey, the lawyer Richard Woodhouse.

Woodhouse was the unofficial legal and literary adviser to Taylor & Hessey. From training and habit of mind, he was interested in the basic principles of both art and conduct, and the attempt to find a definition for them. Keats came to discuss with Woodhouse the general outlines of poems, his schemes for their development, his inspiration for them and his methods of work while actually composing. Keats valued not only his judgment but also his quiet sense of humour, whose tone of voice he was quick to catch. He thought him a good person, "because"—copying Woodhouse's own gift of understatement—"Woodhouse likes my Poetry—conclusive."[1] Not much taller than Keats—both were short enough to get a black eye from a cricket ball, even with under-arm bowling—the "little lawyer" was one of a large and intellectually-active family from Bath. They were connected with the wine-trade, inn-keeping and victualling, as the Jennings had been, and like

1. *Letters*, II, 180.

the Jennings subject to tuberculosis, the "family disease", of which Wood-house was to die in his forties. He was now twenty-nine; after going to Eton and spending two years in Spain and Portugal, he had settled as a lawyer in the Temple, while in 1811 he was introduced by West Country friends to Taylor and Hessey, and joined their literary club in the City. Precision and taste—including a taste for claret—marked everything he did. Keats res-ponded to his tactful pleasant manner; another fortuitous link was that Keats's old flame Mary Frogley turned out to be a cousin of Woodhouse, and later supplied him with copies of Keats's early poems. Keats's maxim about the natural composition of poetry intrigued Woodhouse, and he saw in two lines from his recent Shakespearian sonnet "When I have fears"

> And feel that I may never live to trace
> Their shadows with the magic hand of chance

an insight into his method of writing, by "the magic hand of chance", not by premeditation.[1] During this February, Woodhouse seems to have read for the first time Keats's book of *Poems*, and got Taylor to make him a special interleaved copy for annotation; he had also seen the early books of *Endymion*, and, most important of all, had discussed the theme of *Hyperion* with Keats. Woodhouse on 4 March put these confidences into a sonnet *To Apollo*, written after reading Keats's *Sleep and Poetry*, and announcing to Apollo the coming work by "Keats, thy last born".

Yet, as so often in Keats's life from now onward, huge schemes were to be interrupted or altered by personal events. This set the pattern for the next two years—that is, for all the rest of his writing life—a pattern which almost always concerned in one way or another his brother George. George had his share of the Keats fire and irrepressible temper; he was apt to take sudden and impulsive action, without warning even those closest to him. On Satur-day 21 February, Keats found in the post at Hampstead a letter addressed there to George from Georgiana Wylie. She was therefore expecting him back from Devon, the first Keats had heard of it. Within the next week George was in London, having persuaded himself that Tom, in spite of blood-spitting, had improved enough to be left alone. His plan was to realize, after his twenty-first birthday on 28 February, his inheritance from Mrs. Jennings. Financially, he could not have chosen to come of age at a more profitable time. The long-delayed post-war boom in Government stock was at its peak. For every £3 that Keats had received at coming-of-age, his brother would receive £4; and George, moreover, had kept his grand-mother's inheritance intact. Like Keats, he was ignorant of his grandfather's further fund in Chancery; but what he knew of, and now claimed, formed in itself a bright enough prospect for future plans. For the time, these absorbed him; he assumed that John, who had just finished copying Book Three of

1. KC, I, 128-130.

Endymion, would take his place with Tom when Book Four was done. Tom had other ideas; bored and feeling better, he wrote that he too was returning to London. Keats was trapped in his brothers' situation. He knew from Sawrey that Tom must finish the winter out at Teignmouth; he could not ask George, occupied with love and business, to go down again. To prevent Tom leaving, he hurriedly decided to go down to Devon himself, in spite of the inconvenience to his work and his publishers. He asked George to take Book Three to Taylor & Hessey, and left the rest of the proofs to be corrected, as they came in, by Charles Cowden Clarke, who was still in London.[1] Everything had to be cut short. A friendly meeting at the theatre with Peter Moore, one of the Drury Lane managers, which might have furthered Keats's dramatic ambitions, could not be followed up.[2] A preface to *Endymion*, which Taylor asked him to write, had to be postponed.

Among the confusion, one engagement was fulfilled. On Tuesday 3 March, Keats attended the last lecture of Hazlitt's course. This, "On the Living Poets", was perhaps Hazlitt's most curious performance. His dismissal of modern poetesses was brief indeed;[3] nor did he spend too much time on Rogers, Campbell, Moore, Byron and Scott. The Lake Poets, headed by Wordsworth, received lengthy but even more cavalier treatment. As if ashamed of his former sneers, Hazlitt paid tribute to Wordsworth as "the most original poet now living", of much of whose work "it is not possible to speak in too high praise". He actually read in full Wordsworth's poem, *Hart-Leap Well*. Then, as if under compulsion to attack, he turned on the Lake School, and delivered a long and violent broadside at a kind of composite figure of a Lake Poet, returning to his old abuse of Wordsworth. He ended by implying once more that English poetry ceased with Shakespeare and Milton, "like a play that has its catastrophe in the first or second act".

Some of the bitter phrases stuck in Keats's mind, but he was only superficially affected by them. Out of the experiment and trial of the past weeks, Keats had worked out fully the humble and passive role of the poet. "I have great reason to be content", he wrote,[4] "for thank God I can read and perhaps understand Shakspeare to his depths, and I have I am sure many friends, who, if I fail, will attribute any change in my Life and Temper to Humbleness rather than to Pride."

1. KC, I, 12.   2. *Letters*, I, 282.
3. For example, "Mrs. Hannah More is another celebrated modern poetess, and I believe still living. She has written a great deal which I have never read."
4. *Letters*, I, 239.

Chapter 14

SOLOMON'S DIRECTIONS

"I mean to follow Solomon's directions of 'get Wisdom—get understanding'."

– JOHN KEATS to John Taylor, 24 April 1818

TOM AND GEORGE had enjoyed themselves at Teignmouth. They lodged in the Strand,[1] a narrow street parallel with the waterfront and leading to the Den, the fashionable promenade where there was a bandstand. Over the last thirty years, Teignmouth had supplemented its dwindled deep-sea fishing industry by exporting china clay and importing visitors. There was plenty of fashionable life, theatres and dancing, and a newly-opened library, Croydon's, where Keats could get *The Examiner* every Sunday, and follow with indignation the passing of the Indemnity Bill to protect magistrates, ministers and informers from the consequence of any actions resulting from the suspension of habeas corpus.[2] Tom and George had found a couple of girls to flirt with, Marian and Sarah (Fanny) Jeffery. The Jeffery girls and their mother were kind to Tom, and found him a good doctor, William Turton, with a special interest in consumption. Now George was anxious to know what the girls would think of John. "How do you like John?", he wrote, "Is he not very original? he does not look by any means so handsome as four months ago, but is he not handsome?"[3] Marian may have thought so, for there was a local tradition that she fell in love with him; this was founded on her own later poems, published under her married name of Prowse, which seem both to copy his style and to refer to him. Keats had, however, much on his mind during the two months he was to spend there. He had set off cheerfully enough on the Exeter coach from The Swan with Two Necks, Lad Lane, on the evening of 4 March to be greeted by a hurricane. Though, as he said, "I escaped being blown over and blown under & trees & house(s) being toppled on me", the tempest can hardly have let him reach Teignmouth before Friday 6 March. His thoughts on leaving London were mixed. On the one hand, he had been impatient to see Tom and judge his progress for himself; on the other, his conscience troubled him over leaving the book in a critical state. When it came out, he wrote to Taylor, "I think I Did very

1. The identification as No. 20 is based on insufficient evidence.
2. *Croydon's Guide to Teignmouth*, 1817.   3. KC, I, 15–16.

wrong to leave you to all the trouble of Endymion", and there is even some hint of criticism of his brothers, who had forced him into this position. "Young Men for some time have an idea that such a thing as happiness is to be had and therefore are extremely impatient under any unpleasant restraining."[1] Since Keats had announced to Bailey long ago "I scarcely remember counting upon any Happiness", it seems likely that the young men of his apology were George and Tom, though he takes the blame for their self-centred actions. His whole intellectual life, stopped in its tracks, took a week or so to regain momentum; but during this time he managed to write another Shakespearian sonnet, "Four seasons fill the measure of the year". It is the most like Shakespeare's of any of his sonnets, notably in its ending

> to let fair things
> Pass by unheeded as a threshhold brook.
> He hath his Winter too of pale Misfeature,
> Or else he would forgo his mortal nature.

The well-worn idea of the seasons symbolizing mortal life may have been suggested by a speech of the Solitary in Book V of *The Excursion*,[2] but Keats had come across it more recently in the Winter section of Thomson's *The Seasons*, praised by Hazlitt:

> See here thy pictured life; pass some few years,
> Thy flowering Spring, thy Summer's ardent strength,
> Thy sober Autumn fading into age,
> And pale concluding Winter comes at last,
> And shuts the scene.

Yet it did not need literature to make the phrase "pale Misfeature" bite home, so that the word "pale" becomes an obsession in his writing over the next year or more.[3] He saw the pallor in Tom's face, evident after three month's absence, the worsening in health that George, either through familiarity or his own concerns, had been able to overlook. Keats began to admit to himself the possibility of Tom's death; he would have to accustom his mind to something as inevitable as the changes of season. The sonnet, he told Bailey, was "somewhat collateral" to his feelings about Bailey's discourse on the death of Princess Charlotte, which Keats had brought to Teignmouth with him;[4] religion, in which Bailey had found justification for the death of a young woman, was to Keats when he looked at Tom, "a nothing", though like all mental goals, "made Great and dignified by an ardent pursuit". To

1. *Letters*, I, 270.   2. Finney, I, 383–384.
3. See all the Odes of summer 1819, especially *Ode to a Nightingale*, III, 6.
4. It was a failure, in spite of the fact that Bailey sent it to Coleridge, and Keats lent it to Wordsworth, who neither returned nor commented on it. Keats then borrowed another copy from the Dilkes. *Letters*, I, 212, 214.

underline these feelings, on the very day Keats wrote to Bailey, Friday 13 March, Tom had a relapse with renewed blood-spitting. Keats had nearly copied Book Four of *Endymion*, but even poetry seemed to lose reality against the stark facts of life and death. "I am sometimes so very sceptical", he confessed, "as to think Poetry itself a mere Jack a lanthern to amuse whoever may chance to be struck with its brilliance."

Part of Keats's depression was due to the Devon weather. It was abnormally wet everywhere for the whole month of March, and just as rainy in Hampstead, but to Keats the rain seemed concentrated on the county he was visiting. He treated it to splendid invective:

it is a splashy, rainy, misty, snowy, foggy, haily floody, muddy, slipshod County—the hills are very beautiful, when you get a sight of 'em—the Primroses are out, but then you are in—the Cliffs are of a fine deep Colour, but then the Clouds are continually vieing with them.

Then he turned on the Devonshire men, "the poorest creatures in England":

I like, I love England, I like its strong Men—Give me a "long brown plain" for my Morning so I may meet with some of Edward Iron side's desendants—Give me a barren mould so I may meet with some shadowing of Alfred in the shape of a Gipsey, a Huntsman or as Shepherd. Scenery is fine—but human nature is finer—The Sward is richer for the tread of a real, nervous, english foot—the eagles nest is finer for the Mountaineer has look'd into it . . . but dwindled englishmen are not fine.

This odd outburst to Bailey echoed an even odder passage in Bailey's own discourse, where the Princess's death had been treated as a just punishment to the nation for its degeneracy.[1] "O Devonshire", wrote Keats, "last night I thought the Moon had dwindled in heaven." Yet neither what he called the "urinal qualifications" of the county, which made him, as he said "very peedisposed",[2] nor the fact he had caught a cold on his way down, were enough to account for Keats's mood of depression; nor was a somewhat galling incident when he was insulted, perhaps by a local man, in one of Teignmouth's several theatres. To make him "think Poetry itself a mere Jack a lanthern" deeper forces were at work. The deepest was the reality of Tom's condition; poetry like religion was "a nothing" to this fact. He finished copying *Endymion*, but the final task of writing a preface seemed distasteful; "I want to forget it and make my mind free for something new". Other family worries weighed on him during this month of March. About now, Tom told him something of his search for the mysterious French girl,

1. "Shall our rocks and green fields reproach us with the memory and virtues of our forefathers? Shall that Sun which rose upon the eagle-eyes of our Alfreds, our Sidneys, our Miltons, and our long train of heroes and patriots—shall that Sun send forth the same glories upon their faded posterity, their debased countrymen? . . . Let us call up the mighty shadows of the past." *A Discourse . . . to the Memory of the Princess . . .*, 23.

2. Needlessly edited to "predisposed". *Letters*, I, 255.

Amena, which made Keats feel uneasy. Then George wrote in the middle of the month on money matters, promising to make a rough calculation of the money he and Tom had borrowed from Keats, presumably for their French tour; but another letter, now lost, contained more serious news. He had obtained the consent of Mrs. Wylie to marry Georgiana, who was still under twenty-one, and, even more momentously, to emigrate with her to America. Taylor & Hessey had just published Morris Birkbeck's *Notes on a Journey in America*, in which the optimistic farmer wrote with enthusiasm of his experiences; in the previous August, Birkbeck had bought 1440 acres of virgin prairie in Illinois at two dollars an acre.[1] This, or something like it, was now George Keats's project, and the prospect distressed Keats alarmingly.

In Teignmouth itself, where the ancient streets away from the holiday quarter still stank of stale fish,[2] veterans of the traditional Newfoundland fishing-fleet spoke of the perils of their voyages out on the North American coasts for three-quarters of the year. One of the books Keats still re-read from his schooldays was William Robertson's *History of America*. In Book IV of this work, the historian gives a long and depressing account of the American continents, the difficulties of the terrain, the hardships of the climate, the brutalizing effects of the vast natural handicaps to civilized life. Images and ideas from Robertson occur throughout Keats's letters at this time, and serve as a clue to his feelings about George's venture, though he concealed them from George.[3] "I'll take to my Wings and fly away to any where but old or Nova Scotia" was Keats's unconscious contrast between himself and George. The world seemed full of menace; the savage and meaningless areas of unfriendly nature portrayed by Robertson were all of a piece with the disease that threatened Tom. Individual effort seemed doomed to failure. It was not a mood in which to write the preface to *Endymion*, but he attempted one in the middle of a short spell of fine weather on Thursday 19 March. Its opening had the ring of his recent thoughts; "in a great nation, the work of an individual is of so little importance." It went on in a strain of gloomy, muddled and defiant self-excuse, and he bundled it off to Taylor with Book Four two days later.

The brief spell of fine weather, however, brought Keats some country walks and a burst of light poetry, one snatch of doggerel, and two, to use his own term, of bitcherell about the Devon girls. These were contained in lively letters to Haydon and Rice, lovers of Devon. In the slang of their set, Keats suggested that Rice had also been a lover of the Devon girls, and had left a few bastards in those parts, who could be seen to resemble Rice physically and morally. The verses that followed about his own encounter

1. Gladys Scott Thomson, *A Pioneer Family*, 29–35.
2. G. D. & E. G. C. Griffiths, *History of Teignmouth*, 43.
3. A. D. Atkinson, *Notes and Queries*, 4 Aug. 1951.

with a girl on the way to Dawlish Fair, which he visited on Monday 23 March, are in the same vein of cheerful imaginative bawdy,[1] not necessarily to be taken literally. The over-riding pattern of his life is expressed in his half-quotation from *Henry IV*, Part One—"Oh! for a day and all well!" The Devon lyrics are in the metre of his favourite Chatterton, to whose memory he had just dedicated *Endymion*, and this itself was a reminder of Tom's destiny, a mere boy's appallingly early death. Keats's disillusion extended further than his own poetry; it embraced poetry generally, and fastened on the poetic models he had taken for himself. Disillusion with Wordsworth, fostered by Reynolds and by Hazlitt's lectures, returned for one last temporary spell. Hazlitt's final slashing attack, which had actually brought the lecturer three cheers and a round of applause,[2] was echoed in Keats's preface, in which he wrote of "men biggotted and adicted to every word that may chance to escape their lips". A day or so later, he wrote to Haydon a Hazlittian diatribe against people who "by associating themselves with the fine(st) things, spoil them—Hunt has damned Hampstead (and) Masks and Sonnets and italian tales—Wordsworth ha(s) damned the lakes—". There was more in this vein, ending "Hazlitt has damned the bigotted and the blue-stockined how durst the Man?! he is your only good damner and if ever I am damn'd—I shoul'nt like him to damn me." Keats was at a low ebb, full of fears for his own poetry with the uncomfortable threat from *Blackwood's* still hanging over him. He was shaken by circumstances out of the philosophic and poetic equilibrium he had gained that winter, and looked now on such a state with a kind of rueful despair:

What a happy thing it would be if we could settle our thoughts, make our minds up on any matter in five Minutes and remain content—that is to build a sort of mental Cottage of feelings quiet and pleasant—to have a sort of Philosophical Back Garden, and cheerful holiday-keeping front one—but Alas! this can never be:

On the next day, Wednesday 25 March, down came the rain again to add a final gloom. He had a conscience about owing a letter to Reynolds, for he knew from George how much the sick friend had enjoyed his last letter; yet he could not bring himself to write in any ordinary way. Still, as he wrote, "In hopes of cheering you through a Minute or two" he started a letter; it was in verse.

More than half of the couplets he wrote that evening were descriptions of various types of dream, nightmare or beautiful, catalogued in "careless verse" to interest or amuse Reynolds. They included a vision of a favourite picture by Claude, his so-called "The Enchanted Castle", mingled with other landscapes by the same painter,[3] and a classical description which anticipates that in the *Ode on a Grecian Urn*, which he was to write a year later. Suddenly,

1. Appendix 4.   2. E, No. 532, p. 174.
3. Ian Jack, *Keats and the Mirror of Art*, 127–130.

as he wrote on, the couplets became more serious. A Wordsworthian passage[1] announced this transition:

> O that our dreamings all of sleep or wake
> Would all their colours from the sunset take:
> From something of material sublime,
> Rather than shadow our own Soul's daytime
> In the dark void of Night.

He philosophized on his own self-confessed lack of a philosophy very much in the strain of a Hamlet soliloquy:

> Oh never will the prize,
> High reason, and the lore of good and ill
> Be my award. Things cannot to the will
> Be settled, but they tease us out of thought.
> Or is it that Imagination brought
> Beyond its proper bound, yet still confined,—
> Lost in a sort of Purgatory blind,
> Cannot refer to any standard law
> Of either earth or heaven?—It is a flaw
> In happiness to see beyond our bourn—

A moment later, the tone deepening even further, he gave the instance, which had been haunting him, of the perils "to see beyond our bourn". He had been down to the sea, in the calm evening time of quiet waters that he had previously found "so fulfilling" for himself and his poetry.[2] Now, with the realities of life beating in his mind, all was changed:

> I was at home,
> And should have been most happy—but I saw
> Too far into the sea; where every maw
> The greater on the less feeds evermore:—
> But I saw too distinct into the core
> Of an eternal fierce destruction . . .
> Still do I that most fierce destruction see,
> The shark at savage prey—the hawk at pounce,
> The gentle Robin, like a pard or ounce,
> Ravening a worm—

The philosophy "Of an eternal fierce destruction" is that of Hamlet, not of Wordsworth, whom he dismisses in the humorous epilogue to these lines with a reference to the stock joke of the reviewers, the unfortunate "Moods of my own Mind". It is also another turn, with sad and growing experience,

1. Bate, 308, notices the resemblance to *Tintern Abbey*.
2. *Letters*, I, 159.

to the recurring vision of the small bird that runs through his poems and letters. It is, indeed, no longer "a disguis'd demon" of the *Endymion* nightmare; yet he cannot "take part in its existence" with any comfort, as he could at Box Hill. The bird too is a symbol of the destruction which his new vision of the realities of life had brought, through Tom's declining health; it is also a reminder of the emptiness of a life without a philosophy or religion, harking back to Haydon's striking retort to Shelley at the Horace Smith dinner party.[1]

He tried to end this curious epistle to an invalid with an optimistic flourish:

> Do you get health—and Tom the same—I'll dance,
> And from detested moods in new Romance
> Take refuge—

but the poem into which he then plunged was hardly a comforting refuge. Following Hazlitt's advice, Keats had read Boccaccio's tale of Isabella in the *Decameron*, using the fifth edition of an early seventeenth-century translation. Reynolds, distracted by love, work and illness, had failed to keep his promise to start one of the other tales in friendly association; Keats had apparently managed a few opening stanzas before he left London, probably no more than half a dozen. He in turn had become too depressed for three weeks to write, and his picking-up of the story was full of painful hesitations. Once he got going, however, he wrote quickly, perhaps too quickly. *Isabella* was a working-out of his exclamation, "Let us have the old Poets". The stanza form he had selected was long familiar to him, the ottava rima of Fairfax's translation of Tasso, one of the first books he had read with Cowden Clarke. The style was a deliberate avoidance of the "bigotted" moderns, on the crest of his reaction from them. In a rhetorical address to Boccaccio, he disclaimed any intention of modernizing; his poem was

> no mad assail
> To make old prose in modern rhyme more sweet:

but an effort to reproduce an older mode of poetry itself. The poem it most resembles from this era, with only a small change in stanza-form, is Shakespeare's *A Lover's Complaint*. Keats and Reynolds read this poem with very special attention in the copy of Shakespeare's poems that Reynolds had lent or given him. Keats's simple presentation of the Boccaccio story, step by step, the rhetorical interludes, even some of the descriptions, such as the "lattice" both heroines peer through,[2] the whole style, even down to the dying fall at the end, heighten the resemblance to Shakespeare's poem. The

---

1. See above, p. 112.
2. In Shakespeare's poem metaphorical, "lattice of sear'd age"; in Keats's symbolic, the lattice of her brothers' house that keeps Isabella a prisoner.

unease over *Isabella*, which many critics have felt, and which Keats himself
was to feel a year later, is largely due to this conscious imitation which results
in an air of pastiche. It is the one serious poem of Keats where it is often
difficult to feel that he is whole-hearted. He himself came to condemn it for
naivety, but what is more apparent is a lack of sincerity, a sensation that it is
being written in a negative spirit. Its greatest successes are often when urgent
feelings, from which he was trying to escape in this "new Romance", assert
themselves. The medical and surgical details, which were never far from his
mind with Tom in view, even contain a harking-back to the old hospital
body-snatching days. The anger with the materialistic and murdering
brothers of Isabella, reduced from Boccaccio's three to two only, quivers with
vivid and painful images that seem to derive from his reading of Robertson
and the cruelties of the Spanish conquerors to the American Indians:[1]

> And she had died in drowsy ignorance,
>   But for a thing more deadly dark than all;
> It came like a fierce potion, drunk by chance,
>   Which saves a sick man from the feather'd pall
> For some few gasping moments; like a lance,
>   Waking an Indian from his cloudy hall
> With cruel pierce, and bringing him again
> Sense of the gnawing fire at heart and brain.

Stanzas such as this, and those about the merchant-capitalist brothers, praised
by Shaw as anticipating Marx, have a realism that contrasts uneasily with the
gentle sentimental approach of other stanzas, where Keats has overdone his
deliberate attempt to be uncontaminated and unobtrusive. Though his own
circle, Reynolds, Taylor, Woodhouse, Lamb, accepted and delighted in the
whole poem, though the nineteenth century tended to see it as the height of
his art, Keats's own view is more in line with twentieth-century criticism.[2]
The contrasts of *Isabella* have something of the contradictions in his own life,
something of the dilemma of the verse letter to Reynolds. It fails as a refuge
from reality, because reality keeps breaking in; yet he does not allow himself
in it to see too far into the "eternal fierce destruction". Yet it must be
remembered that it was Keats's first finished attempt to tell a story in verse;
Endymion had been much more like Wordsworth's *The Prelude*, the growth
of the poet's mind in the guise of a narrative. *Isabella*, for all its uneven faults,
begins, carries out, and completes its story.

None of this self-criticism occurred to Keats at the time, as he wrote
swiftly on. To him, it was a poem in the Shakespearian manner. His definition
at this time of the process of writing—"The innumerable compositions and
decompositions which take place between the intellect and its thousand

1. Woodhouse noted resemblances between this stanza and Katherine Philips.
2. Bate, 313–315.

materials before it arrives at that trembling delicate and snail-horn perception of Beauty"—not only echoes exactly Hazlitt's description of Shakespeare's way of writing, but draws its image from Keats's favourite stanza about the snail in *Venus and Adonis*, which Reynolds had triple-marked all down the margin of their copy. The effort of composition too had the salutary effect of clearing his mind for action, and he began to feel cheered. An isolated fine day gave him the chance of a long scramble over the rocks to Babbacombe Bay, and Tom seemed to be much better, and began to speak of their returning to London; but a much wider horizon suddenly opened before Keats. First, George's investigations into his own share of the inheritance from Grandmother Jennings had revealed a state of things far better than Keats's depleted account at his own coming of age. 3 per cent stock, in which most of the inheritance was invested, was maintaining its new post-war boom, and even increasing in value. Instead of the £1400 he had expected to be able to take to Illinois, George, if he cashed now, would have between £1600 and £1700. He decided eventually to take about £1100 and leave behind the remaining £500 to form "some means for my brothers".[1] This meant that Keats, whose own inheritance from his grandmother was exhausted, suddenly found his circumstances revived by this new transfusion of George's money. He at once began speaking of the plans to travel and see the Continent which he had had to abandon the previous summer. The second lucky chance at this moment gave Keats further plans for what he called "a sort of Prologue to the Life I intend to pursue". Each summer, Charles Brown let his portion of Wentworth Place, and set out on a cheap holiday in his native Scotland. He now suggested that Keats should be his companion on a walking tour this summer, through the Lake District and as far as they could get north of the Border. This seemed an admirable start to the new life for Keats, whose course he defined as "to write, to study and to see all Europe at the lowest expence".[2] This wide horizon of experience, he felt, would shake off the irritation he had felt at the suburban coteries of literary London, Leigh Hunt, Horace Smith, Kingston and the like—"to enlarge my vision—to escape disquisitions on Poetry and Kingston Criticism", with which he still felt Wordsworth had debased himself—"O that he had not fit with a Warrener that is din'd at Kingston's." This large scheme would be the physical foundation for his large vision of *Hyperion*; doubts about Tom's health were swept aside in this new optimism, and in any case it might be possible to arrange a visit to a southern climate for the invalid.

In this mood Keats wrote to Haydon on Wednesday 8 April. The very next day brought an irritating reminder of the life on which he intended to turn his back. The impossible preface he had written for *Endymion* three weeks before, in the depths of gloom, had naturally been rejected by his publishers. Knowing that Reynolds was in close touch with Keats, they gave

1. KI, 49 and 76.   2. *Letters*, I, 264.

him the task of saying that it would not do, and extracting a fresh one from the poet. Reynolds decided to achieve this by suggesting to Keats that the original preface was too much in the style of Hunt; he was able to indulge his own personal malice, and to produce an instant reaction from Keats when he got the letter on 9 April. "I am not aware there is any thing like Hunt in it, (and if there is, it is my natural way, and I have something in common with Hunt)" was Keats's retort, but he at once sat down to write another preface, which he sent to Reynolds the next day. He was conscious that this too was not quite right, but "one should not be too timid—of committing faults." With this his publishers would have to be satisfied. His impatience with Devon—"Rain! Rain! Rain! "—now extended to the whole of England. He travelled to Italy both in his own plans and in the poem he was writing; Italy was much in his thoughts, for Shelley had finally quitted Marlow and London, taking his ménage with him, and had just arrived in Milan. Keats had refused an invitation to go to Italy with Shelley, and was perhaps regretting it.[1] The beautiful background scenery of Lorenzo's ghost was, to do Devon justice, much more like Dartmoor, which Keats had intended to visit on Haydon's advice, and perhaps did;[2] the ghost appears,

> Saying moreover, "Isabel, my sweet!
> 'Red whortle-berries droop above my head,
> 'And a large flint-stone weights upon my feet;
> 'Around me beeches and high chestnuts shed
> 'Their leaves and prickly nuts; a sheep-fold bleat
> 'Comes from beyond the river to my bed:
> 'Go, shed one tear upon my heather-bloom,
> 'And it shall comfort me within the tomb.

Pieces of natural description, more in Keats's instinctive vein, carried through the somewhat artificial structure of the poem towards its conclusion, in stanzas of simple strength:

> And she forgot the stars, the moon, and sun,
> And she forgot the blue above the trees,
> And she forgot the dells where waters run,
> And she forgot the chilly autumn breeze;
> She had no knowledge when the day was done,
> And the new morn she saw not: but in peace
> Hung over her sweet basil evermore,
> And moisten'd it with tears unto the core.

Yet there was too much contrivance in the poem for it ever to be wholly satisfying. Keats again was his own best critic when he spoke of its having "an amusing sober-sadness about it". However, he pressed on now, though

1. C. Cowden Clarke, *Recollections of Writers*, 150–151.
2. See "Over the Dartmoor black", *The Eve of St. Agnes*, l. 351, cancelled.

not without doubts; self-conscious apologies to the reader for "all this wormy circumstance" of the story seem to show that, as with *Endymion*, he was dissatisfied with the poem before he had ended it.

The next fortnight was devoted not only to writing but to hard thinking. It was lightened by an unexpected week-end visit from James Rice, come to see how Keats was getting on in his own "favourite Devon". He brought Keats a splendid folio of the old Spanish romance *Guzman d'Alfarache*,[1] and Keats repaid him with a sonnet very much in the style of *Isabella*, which he was within a few days of finishing. Keats began to read and mark Rice's present with gusto, but after the first thirty pages his interest flagged. Now that *Isabella* was almost out of the way, his mind had reverted to its major task, the epic *Hyperion*, and his reading and thought were concentrated, as before, on Wordsworth and Milton. The power of these two authors brought him a sense of his own ignorance; his personal irritations with Wordsworth were swallowed up in renewed appreciation of his giant stature as a poet, still more as a thinker. He felt too clearly the lack of systematized thought as a stiffening element in his own poetry. On Friday 24 April, an advance copy of *Endymion* arrived from Taylor, and confirmed his feeling of inadequacy. His plans to travel and collect experiences seemed only to touch half the problem; what he needed was hard thought, intellectual exercise as well as the mere luxury of acquiring sensations. He wrote to Taylor in this self-critical vein: "I know nothing I have read nothing and I mean to follow Solomon's directions of 'get Wisdom—get understanding'— I find cavalier days are gone by. I find that I can have no enjoyment in the World but continual drinking of Knowledge—I find there is no worthy pursuit but the idea of doing some good for the world—". He wrote to George for books, but pure literature, he felt, was not enough. On Monday 27 April he wrote to Bailey, a letter which unfortunately has not survived, and to Reynolds, who was now convalescing at their friend Butler's near Kennington Common. He repeated his need for study and thought, spoke of learning Greek and Italian, and of asking Hazlitt's guidance in metaphysics. He showed indifference whether the finished *Isabella* should be published or not, though he encouraged Reynolds in his versions of Boccaccio. He still recognized that poetry must take chief place in his life but "there is something else wanting to one who passes his life among Books and thoughts on Books". This was in many ways a revolution against the whole tenor of his life since he was thirteen. He spoke in the same letter of the hell of recollecting "times past to our own blushing", and it is certain that his mind had been ranging over the whole of his past life; perhaps he alluded specially here to his own arrogance as a medical student, when he put poets and poetry before everything and had invited ridicule from the others at Guy's.[2]

1. Keats Collection, Houghton Library, Harvard. The gift is dated 20 April 1818.
2. KC, II, 208–209.

22   John Taylor, c. 1817, by William Hilton.

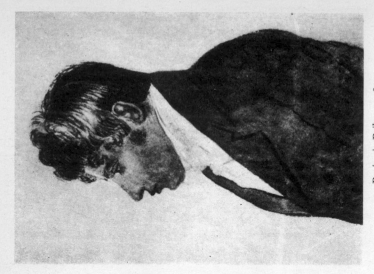

25 Benjamin Bailey, c. 1817.

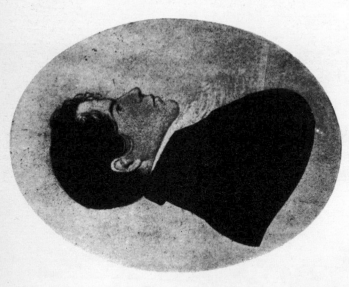

24 James Rice, c. 1817.

26 Magdalen Hall, Oxford, where Keats spent September 1817 with Bailey.

28 Maria Dilke.

27 Charles Wentworth Dilke.

29 Well Walk, Hampstead, where Keats and his brothers lived, 1817–1818.

30 Teignmouth, c. 1818.

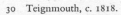

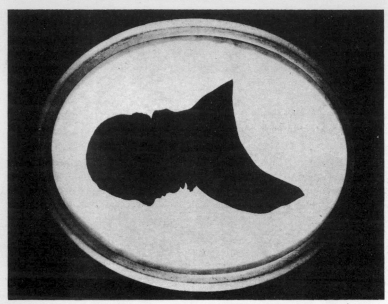

32　George Keats c. 1830.

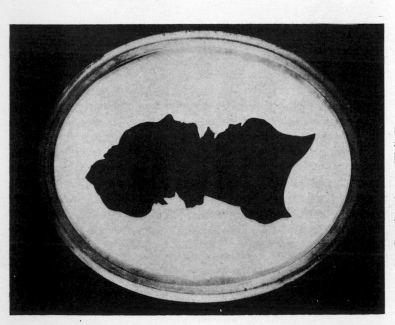

31　Georgiana Augusta Wylie Keats, c. 1830.

33 Windermere from above Bowness, looking north.

KEAT'S TWO VIEWS OF WINDERMERE

34 Windermere from above Ambleside, looking south.

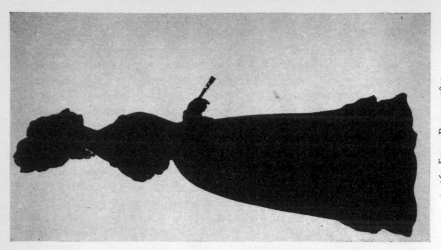

36 Fanny Brawne, 1829.

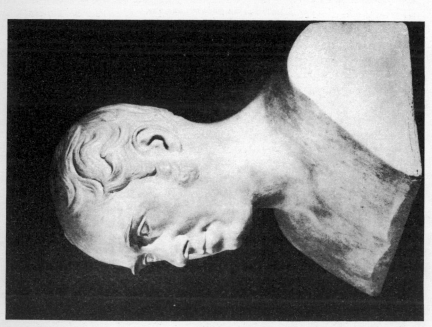

35 Charles Brown, 1828.

Isabella done, *Endymion* safely out, Keats was able to concentrate for a week more on reading, self-examination, and study. The fruits were seen in another, and most remarkable letter to Reynolds on Sunday 3 May. He had travelled through the whole of his past life, and emerged a decisive step onward toward a reconciling philosophy. Nothing, he saw, had been wasted, provided it tended to some sort of knowledge. This applied to his medical studentship as much as anything. "Every department of knowledge we see excellent and calculated towards a great whole. I am so convinced of this, that I am glad at not having given away my medical Books, which I shall again look over." He also spoke of being coached by Rice and Reynolds to become a sort of amateur lawyer[1] in order to extend his general information in that field also. He now saw the dangers of mere experience, mere unguided reliance on "Sensations", without the stabilizing power of knowledge. "The difference of high Sensations with and without knowledge appears to me this", he wrote, "in the latter case we are falling continually ten thousand fathoms deep and being blown up again without wings and with all horror of a bare shouldered Creature—in the former case, our shoulders are fledged, and we go thro' the same air and space without fear." His letter, shot through with quotations from Wordsworth and Milton, went on to a detailed comparison of the greatness of these two, but before this, he had not quite left the topic of his own self-exploration, and the true nature and use of experience. We can only judge a truth by our having actually experienced it to the full—"by larger experience—for axioms in philosophy are not axioms until they are proved upon our pulses: We read fine—things but never feel them to thee full until we have gone the same steps as the Author.—I know", he confessed to Reynolds, "this is not plain; you will know exactly my meaning when I say, that now I shall relish Hamlet more than I ever have done." This remark about Hamlet has been generally missed by critics,[2] intent on what comes after; but in its context it has startling implications. Keats is saying that he has lived through the experiences of Hamlet, "gone the same steps" as Shakespeare's tragedy in his own life, which he had just been reviewing in every aspect from its earliest days. The clear parallel between Keats and Hamlet is his mother's remarriage after only two months' widowhood,[3] and this implies something more if he has really proved upon his pulses, as he claims, the situation of Hamlet. Only five weeks later, he made, in a letter to Bailey, practically his only reference to his parents, in which he spoke of "the early loss of our parents and even . . .

1. This seems to be the most likely interpretation of the much-disputed expression "pip-civilian" which he uses. *Letters*, I, 277.
2. Including those who take the next remark—"No man can set down Venery as a bestial or joyless thing until he is sick of it"—to apply to Keats's own sexual adventures; but the Hamlet remark is as expressly personal as this is expressly generalized.
3. Ward, 11.

H

earlier Misfortunes". The last two words have been ignored, as if Keats never wrote them, but they mean quite precisely that he was conscious of "misfortunes" before his father's death. If Keats is Hamlet, as he claims, this may mean that he had noticed some disturbing element in his parents' marriage even before Thomas Keats's death. There seems to be some confirmation from Keats's own pen during this exact period of his own self-searching. The first thirty pages of the Spanish romance he was reading largely consist of the rogue hero, Guzman, describing his parentage. He is the son of a lively and attractive whore, who keeps two men on the go, a Knight and Guzman's "father". One passage which Keats marked in the book is typical of many:

I was between three and foure yeeres old: and by the recknings and rules of your feminine knowledge, I had two fathers: for my mother was so well learned in her Art, that she knew very well how to father me on them both. She had attained to the knowledge of working impossibilities, as plainely was to be seene, since she had the cunning to serve two Masters, and to please two husbands.

She persuaded each that he was the boy's father, and Keats put a cross against Guzman's comment on the next page:

And it is much better for me this way, than that people should say; that I am ill borne and the son of no man.

These markings,[1] made within a few days of his comparison of himself with Hamlet, seem to indicate without doubt one of the darkest passages of memory that he had set himself to traverse in the search for self-knowledge.

Keats had begun the search "in so uneasy a state of Mind" that he could not at first write down its results; but wider self-knowledge, and greater knowledge itself, he found, "helps, by widening speculation, to ease the Burden of the Mystery"; he had been led back to the same passage of Wordsworth's *Tintern Abbey* that he had discussed with Bailey at Oxford. He had been reliving his early appreciation of Wordsworth, and considering

how he differs from Milton.
—And here I have nothing but surmises, from an uncertainty whether Miltons apparently less anxiety for Humanity proceeds from his seeing further or no than Wordsworth: And whether Wordsworth has in truth epic passion, and martyrs himself to the human heart, the main region of his song—

Keats here returns to his study of Wordsworth's *The Excursion*; the quotation from Wordsworth's manuscript poem *The Recluse*

the Mind of Man—
My haunt, and the main region of my song.

can only have been read by him in Wordsworth's preface to *The Excursion*, the sole place where it was printed. He felt that his comparison of Words-

1. Reproduced by Lowell, II, 579–587.

worth and Milton was going to take some effort, and he put off expounding it to Reynolds until after dinner, when he sat down and resumed

I will return to Wordsworth—whether or no he has an extended vision or a circumscribed grandeur—whether he is an eagle in his nest, or on the wing—And to be more explicit and to show you how tall I stand by the giant, I will put down a simile of human life as far as I now perceive it; that is, to the point to which I say we both have arrived at—Well—I compare human life to a large Mansion of Many Apartments, two of which I can only describe, the doors of the rest being as yet shut upon me— The first we step into we call the infant or thoughtless Chamber, in which we remain as long as we do not think—We remain there a long while, and notwithstanding the doors of the second Chamber remain wide open, showing a bright appearance, we care not to hasten to it; but are at length imperceptibly impelled by the awakening of the thinking principle—within us—we no sooner get into the second Chamber, which I shall call the Chamber of Maiden-Thought, than we become intoxicated with the light and the atmosphere, we see nothing but pleasant wonders, and think of delaying there for ever in delight: However among the effects this breathing is father of is that tremendous one of sharpening one's vision into the heart and nature of Man—of convincing ones nerves that the World is full of Misery and Heartbreak, Pain, Sickness and oppression—whereby This Chamber of Maiden Thought becomes gradually darken'd and at the same time on all sides of it many doors are set open— but all dark—all leading to dark passages—We see not the ballance of good and evil. We are in a Mist—*We* are now in that state—We feel the "burden of the Mystery," To this point was Wordsworth come, as far as I can conceive when he wrote 'Tintern Abbey' and it seems to me that his Genius is explorative of those dark Passages. Now if we live, and go on thinking, we too shall explore them. he is a Genius and superior to us, in so far as he can, more than we, make discoveries, and shed a light in them— Here I must think Wordsworth is deeper than Milton—though I think it has depended more upon the general and gregarious advance of intellect, than individual greatness of Mind . . . He did not think into the human heart, as Wordsworth has done—Yet Milton as a Philosopher, had sure as great powers as Wordsworth—What is then to be inferr'd? O many things—It proves there is really a grand march of intellect—, It proves that a mighty providence subdues the mightiest Minds to the service of the time being, whether it be in human Knowledge or Religion . . .

This famous meditation[1] is a landmark in Keats's thoughts, a notable stage in his exploration into the "dark passages" of his own life; it is also a return to full acknowledgement of the genius of Wordsworth, the giant from whom he had been estranged in mind over the past months. Even the "simile of human life" which Keats adopts here, though verbally like the "many mansions" of the Gospel according to St. John, is taken from Wordsworth's description of his own epic plans in the Preface to *The Excursion*, just before the Recluse quotation which Keats had used. Wordsworth expounds the master-scheme of his own poetry, and explains that he has already written a long personal poem (*The Prelude*) in preparation for

1. Most fully discussed by C. D. Thorpe, *The Mind of John Keats*, 43–47 and elsewhere.

a much larger philosophical work (*The Recluse*), of which *The Excursion* is only a part. He goes on

The preparatory poem is biographical, and conducts the history of the author's mind to the point when he was emboldened to hope that his faculties were sufficiently matured for entering upon the arduous labour which he had proposed to himself; and the two Works have the same kind of relation to each other, if he may so express himself, as the anti-chapel has to the body of a gothic church. Continuing this allusion, he may be permitted to add, that his minor pieces, when they shall be properly arranged, will be found by the attentive Reader to have such connection with the main Work as may give them claims to be likened to the little cells, oratories, and sepulchral recesses, ordinarily included in those edifices.

The pomposity of Wordsworth's prose did not prevent Keats from eagerly adapting the simile to his own vision of life and poetry. On the philosophic side, he has found one place at least for the realities of suffering and destruction in human life, that of "sharpening one's vision into the heart and nature of Man". This is the essential business of poetry; Keats is restating, having now experienced it upon the pulses, his conviction that "the Man who thinks much of his fellows can never be in Spirits", but as a poet he views this with optimism. It is part of the training and development of a poet to explore these dark passages. Moreover—a great step—he sees this as a universal and evolutionary law. "There is really a grand march of intellect", and the greater sensitivity of Wordsworth to the human heart is partly explained by the development of civilization itself in the hundred and fifty years since Milton wrote *Paradise Lost*. This larger and more constructive view of human endeavour not only triumphed over the philosophy of his verse letter to Reynolds; it looked forward to a system of thought he was to incorporate in *Hyperion*.[1]

Two short poems Keats wrote on this new positive wave are themselves anticipations of the epic towards which he was growing. These were the sonnet to Homer and a stanza of an ode he wrote on May Day. Both are intensely Wordsworthian, and full of fresh but calm thought. The Homer sonnet epitomizes his own victorious quest through darkness back into light:

> Aye, on the shores of darkness there is light,
> And precipices show untrodden green;
> There is a budding morrow in midnight;
> There is a triple sight in blindness keen;

To live and feel human experience upon the pulses was now to be a necessary part of his whole conception of poetry. It is a poetic watershed, a great divide that marks off almost everything he wrote after *Isabella* both from that poem and what had gone before. He now felt the inner assurance that he

1. Bate, 334.

could achieve the type of poetry he foresaw in beginning his May Day Ode.

> Mother of Hermes! and still youthful Maia!
>   May I sing to thee
> As thou wast hymned on the shores of Baiæ?
>   Or may I woo thee
> In earlier Sicilian? or thy smiles
> Seek as they once were sought, in Grecian isles
> By bards who died content on pleasant sward,
>   Leaving great verse unto a little clan?
> O, give me their old vigour, and unheard
>   Save of the quiet Primrose, and the span
>   Of heaven and few ears,
> Rounded by thee, my song should die away
>   Content as theirs,
> Rich in the simple worship of a day.

Chapter 15

THROUGH THE CLOUDS

"I will clamber through the Clouds and exist"

—JOHN KEATS to B. R. Haydon, 8 April 1818

KEATS'S inward life hardly wavered from the certainty he had reached this May Day; yet his outward life was, as it continued to be, at the mercy of others. He had hoped to stay in Devon for some time more, to enjoy the fine weather, to read and prepare himself for his travels.[1] George would send him books for this purpose, and let him have the first stanzas of *Isabella*, which he had thrust into his folio Shakespeare, so that he could fair-copy the whole; Tom, he thought, was reconciled to staying a few more months under the care of Dr. Turton. In the event, none of this happened. George did not send the books, Tom, in spite of a return of blood-spitting, decided he must get back to Town. The journey, in the first ten days of May, was a portent of disaster. They sent a message for the Jeffery family from Honiton, where they joined the coach for London via Bridport and Dorchester;[2] but at Bridport, Tom suffered such a violent haemorrhage that they had to do the rest of the journey by very slow stages.[3] Keats was caught up in the needs and plans of his two brothers, one to marry, emigrate and buy his 1400 acres on the Birkbeck settlement, the other to travel, either by sea or down the Rhine, to Italy. Poems were put on one side; the May Day Ode was never continued, though Keats may also have been put off by Hunt's fulsome article "On Old May Day" in *The Examiner*.[4] He was also "very much engaged with his Friends", as Tom said, particularly with Brown in planning their northern expedition, which was to take four months and cover 2000 miles, mostly on foot. He tried to spend as much time as possible with George, and on one of their outings together an incident occurred which was in itself a tangled

1. Ward, 177, thinks "what Keats apparently intended was a period of retirement such as Milton had undertaken after leaving Cambridge", and points to his extensive reading of Milton. She also believes (427, n. 25) it was "the crystallization of George's plans" that caused Keats to leave Teignmouth.

2. There is no evidence they borrowed money from Mrs. Jeffery (Ward, 181). Keats borrowed from his landlady (Finney, II, 746), probably before receiving George's £20 of 18 March. His friends' mother was Mrs. Sarah Jeffery, not Margaret Jeffrey as often said.

3. Only "a hundred miles in the last two days", *Letters*, I, 284.

4. E, No. 541, pp. 289–291.

drama of friendship and perhaps something more. In one of George's last few days of bachelorhood, he and Keats went to the entertainment at the Lyceum Theatre, where, four times a week, the famous comedian Charles Mathews did a solo turn in which he parodied a number of living actors. On the way there, they met in the street the lady of Keats's Hastings encounter, Isabella Jones. Nothing seems to have happened except an exchange of recognitions;[1] Keats could not know that Isabella was already a close friend of his own publisher, Taylor.[2] At the beginning of the year, Taylor, who generally wrote poetry of a religious or domestic sort, struck a new vein for him; his stiff sonnets have a note of brooding passion, which he found prudent to alter when he printed some of them anonymously in the *London Magazine* four years later. One written on 7 January tells of a series of encouragements and rebuffs such as Keats had complained of in his lyric "You Say You Love", which he had written to Isabella at Hastings. April brought another sonnet with the publisher still engaged in a determined pursuit of his quarry, while as recently as May Day he had derived some hope, from a bust of Cupid the lady had sent him, that "gradual all we wish we gain". In this last sonnet he addressed the lady by name as Isabel; unless Taylor was lucky enough to know two very attractive women of the same name at the same time, there is no doubt that she was Keats's Isabella.[3]

The possible complications of this situation were in the future; for the present, Keats was occupied with thoughts of his brothers. He was in a state of numb depression; "if I were under Water I would scarcely kick to come to the top", he commented. Bailey, who had missed him in Town while he was down in Teignmouth, wrote inviting him for another stay at Oxford and offered to coach him in Greek "as much as so bad a scholar can"; he had read *Endymion* two or three times, was won over by all of it, and had written an appreciative account of the poem to be published in an Oxford paper.[4] Yet Keats could or would not go, and even Bailey's praise could not rouse him. He felt "almost stony-hearted" over George's wedding, which took place at St. Margaret's, Westminster on Thursday 28 May, Keats signing the register as witness. In spite of his settled gloom, he and the Dilkes were the only people in their set who encouraged George and Georgiana in their project.[5] Mrs. Reynolds had special reason to be caustic, for well-found young men were escaping from her daughters on every side. Bailey, far from following

1. Ward, who places the meeting in June, supposes (186) a party with her, George, Keats and Reynolds, misreading *Letters*, I, 402.

2. Her letter of 31 May 1819, partly quoted Blunden, *Keats's Publisher*, 96–97, and now lost, shows quite a long-standing intimacy.

3. For the printing and later MS of the two sonnets, made by Hessey, "The Authorship of 'The Poet' and other sonnets" by Mabel A. E. Steele, KSJ, Vol. V, 69–80. For the original dated MSS of Taylor's poems, I am indebted to Messrs. Quaritch, who allowed me to examine them.

4. KC, I, 25–26.   5. KC, II, 15.

up his understanding with Marianne, was remote in Oxford, where he had ceased to read for a degree, preparing for ordination by the Bishop of Carlisle. He seemed more interested in his room-mate, George Robert Gleig, and with good reason; for Gleig's father was the Primate of the Scottish Episcopalian Church, and well-known both sides of the border.

Some of the few flashes lighting Keats's gloom came through Haydon. On the Sunday before George's wedding, Keats dined with the painter, and had an amusing discussion on the Duke of Wellington with Hazlitt, Wilkie, and Thomas Barnes, the editor of *The Times*; on the Sunday after, Haydon managed to insert a quotation from *Endymion* in his *Examiner* article on a Raphael cartoon.[1] Keats, on second thoughts, felt he might be able to squeeze a week with Bailey between George's departure and his own expedition, though in the event there was no time to spare, and he never saw Bailey again in his life. Depression continued, though he dashed off a lively letter of thanks to the Jeffery sisters. He did not feel well, and the signs for *Endymion* were ominous. Hunt's collection, *Foliage*, containing the two laurel-crowning sonnets, had not passed unnoticed by the *Quarterly* or *Blackwood's*. The latter had just jeered at Hunt's ivy-crown, "fixed there by the delicate hand of young Mister Keats", and also referred to that "amiable but infatuated bardling, Mister John Keats". On 15 May, Taylor had tried to conciliate Gifford,[2] editor of the powerful *Quarterly Review*, with some tactful personal remarks about his young poet; but on 14 June, Leigh Hunt, justifiably hurt by the editor's onslaught on *Foliage*, but with inspired mistiming, printed a columnful of anonymous attack on Gifford himself. He also announced an *Examiner* review of *Endymion*, which was never to appear, for 28 June. Keats gloomily felt his own poem was damned already "for they have smothered me in '*Foliage*'". Taylor, for his part, had distinct doubts about *Endymion*, though he kept them to his own family. "Endymion does not by any means please me as I had expected", he wrote to his brother James, adding loyally, "but I can hardly allow others to find Fault with it." He was also full of kindness to the poet's brother, now living with his young wife at 28 Judd Street, Brunswick Square, Bloomsbury. He lent him a copy of Birkbeck's new book, just published, *Letters from Illinois*, gave him a letter of introduction to its author, and another to his own cousin, Michael Drury in Philadelphia. Tom he provided with a parcel of books, including J. C. Eustace's *A Classical Tour through Italy* to encourage him on his journey.[3] There was a certain feverishness in these preparations, which perhaps Keats felt when he remarked, "They say we are all (that is our set) mad at Hampstead". In the City, Abbey said they were all Don Quixotes. George was, by his own lights, prudent; on 4 June he had cashed his inheritance profitably, and deposited £500 at Abbey, Cock & Co. in Pancras Lane, to pay his debts and leave some money for John and Tom. He was able to do this since he had set his sights

1. E, No. 544, p. 349.   2. KHM, No. 63, f. 2.   3. KC, I, 29–31.

lower, and was now proposing to buy less than half the number of acres he had intended in America. In Bloomsbury he had become, without knowing it, a neighbour of Isabella Jones; she noticed him at a party, though he did not observe her.

Keats still could not stop brooding on the future of George and of Tom; he fought with himself to find some place in a world without them. The closeness of their orphaned lives, spoken of by Fanny Keats even in her old age, had an element that brought his thoughts to the brink of obsession. Yet the root obsession lay in his own heart. It was a crisis of the same sort as he had experienced just over a year before, when he separated himself from them to go to the Isle of Wight. At that time, he had hardly been able to bear the hundred miles distance between them. He had matured since then, but now he was faced with separation on a gigantic scale. "I have two Brothers", he wrote to Bailey, "one is driven by the 'burden of Society' to America the other, with an exquisite love of Life, is in a lingering state." In the event of George's emigration and Tom's death—he was now clearly facing this prospect—he alone would be responsible for their sister Fanny. "I have a Sister too and may not follow them, either to America or to the Grave."[1] This was not a mere romantic gesture in the face of death; he spoke of its reality throughout the letter. The highest triumph in poetry would be nothing, since he too was fated to die; one should embrace death "rejoicing", though he hoped to be allowed to die "for a great human purpose", a more sober version of his rhodomontade to Reynolds two months earlier—"I would jump down Aetna for any great Public good". Public service was perhaps in the fringes of his mind since on the day he wrote, Wednesday 10 June, Parliament was dissolved, and radicals everywhere were prepared to do battle for liberal principles in the General Election at the end of the month. Keats's basic philosophy was unshaken from the position he had reached at Teignmouth, that it is the poet's work to experience and explore the condition of human suffering. "Life must be undergone", he wrote, "and I certainly derive a consolation from the thought of writing one or two more Poems before it ceases." One of these was, of course, Hyperion, the major reason for this expedition to the North. Bailey had reminded him of the third prop of his reading for that poem, Dante's Divine Comedy, to add to his deep recent study of Milton and Wordsworth. Taylor & Hessey, by a happy chance and on Coleridge's recommendation, had just taken over Cary's complete translation, which had come out in 1814 in three tiny volumes, and reissued them under their own imprint. These were the right size to go into Keats's knapsack on his tour; his two-volume octavo Inferno was far too large.[2]

1. This refers to Fanny, not Georgiana Keats as Letters, I, 293 n. says.
2. It was among his books at his death, when one volume was given to Isabella Jones. MOK, 6–7.

H*

As usual with any long-planned expedition, the last few days and hours were a flurry of things forgotten. Taylor was left with a number of last-minute commissions, mostly to distribute promised copies of *Endymion* to friends. On 19 and 20 June, Keats and Tom drew a total of £170 from the £500 George had left behind for them. Some of this was to pay off George's own immediate debts, though a bill of £30 was left outstanding, which Tom drew for and paid when his brothers were gone; some was for Tom himself to pay Mrs. Bentley, who was to look after him at Hampstead, since it was now clear he was not well enough to travel alone to Italy. Some of the rest was to pay George's debts over past years to John. According to Brown, though prejudiced by his later dislike of George, Keats had a shock here; he himself reckoned that George owed him a substantial enough amount, from the French holiday and other advances, to set himself up well in cash for his own walking-tour. What George actually handed over to him in the haste of the final journey north, as they all travelled to Liverpool, was only £70 or £80.[1] Again we have only Brown's word for it, but it is evident there was some misunderstanding, since long before the tour was due to finish, Keats had to write asking for an extra £30 to be drawn from the money George had left with Abbey, to be forwarded to him in Scotland. Even Brown suggested no indignation on Keats's part at this, and with his habitual shrinking from any enquiry in money matters, Keats can hardly have known what George might really owe him. What he did know, was that even after these withdrawals, there was still about £300 of George's money, intact and accumulating interest in the custody of Abbey's firm, to be some security for any crisis of Tom's and to await his own needs when he got back to London.

On the morning of Monday 22 June, the company of four boarded the coach at the Swan with Two Necks, Lad Lane, near Guildhall, a stone's throw from where the Keats boys had lodged in Cheapside. The firelit domesticity they had enjoyed there, their understanding and affection, for good or ill, was at an end. They made an interesting sight, Keats and Brown with their knapsacks, George with his newfound efficiency and bustle, and Georgiana rather lightly dressed for such a long journey looking more girlish than her twenty years. She had brought some reminders of her child-hood, including a hunting scene in silhouette. George had some books from his brothers, including some of Keats's hard-won school-prizes. Early in the afternoon they reached Redbourn in Hertfordshire, and stopped at the inn for dinner. Keats, remembering that Henry Stephens was in practice there, sent him a note, and he joined them after dinner for a brief spell. He noticed

1. KHM, No. 104. Since the withdrawal of £170 (see above) was in two portions, £30 and £140, it is reasonable to suppose the £30 was for Tom, and the £140 originally intended for John's tour. George, however, in spite of a gift of £75 or £100 from Abbey (not usually noticed by the latter's detractors) may have found he had more outside debts to pay, and cut down John's portion to the sum Brown mentions.

that Georgiana had "something original" about her; though not strictly handsome, "she had the imaginative poetical cast", and he observed that John introduced her with evident delight and respect.[1] With his diagnostic instinct, he had divined the one factor that half-reconciled Keats to the break-up of his family. Keats had come to appreciate Georgiana as something he had never had, a sister near his own age. Not only was she pretty and lively, as Dilke noted,[2] and "piquant" as her own husband remarked after years of marriage,[3] but Keats applied to her one of his highest terms of praise, the Hazlittian adjective of "disinterested", able to sink her own interests in those of others, as she was certainly doing for George. It was this that made him look back on his brother's marriage, at one time an object of numb in-difference, with positive enjoyment. He felt that George would have with him a kindred link to keep their family feeling alive.

The short break over, the long journey continued, west and north in heavy, cloudy, showery weather,[4] though they caught one glimpse of the Welsh mountains; Liverpool was not reached till the following evening, when the weary travellers caught up their sleep at the Crown Inn, having first said their farewells to one another. Keats and Brown planned to skip the industrial district north of Liverpool by taking the coach very early the next morning to Lancaster, and starting their walk from that place. On Wednesday 24 June, they left George and Georgiana sleeping—their boat was not due to sail for a few days—and arrived in good time for dinner at Lancaster. It was the first manufacturing town Keats had experienced, and it was probably here that he heard for the first time what he described as "that most disgusting of all noises", the incessant shuttles of the crowded spinning mills.[5] There were other discomforts. For two hours dinner did not come, and even when it did, they were told the inn was full, and had to seek refuge for the wasted evening in private lodgings. The reason for all this disorganization was the General Election. Reflecting that a private house was better in such times than a public house, where votes were noisily being bought with drink, they went to bed prepared to start at dawn; but at four the next morning another disappointment met them—more rain. After three hours reading *Samson Agonistes* to help their patience, they walked four miles in a Scotch mist to breakfast at Bolton-le-Sands. There rain held them up again, but at mid-day it cleared, and they reached Burton-in-Kendal for a three o'clock dinner at the King's Arms, the Green Dragon being full of

1. KC, II, 212.

2. Dilke, ann. I, 142, adding, however, that she was ignorant and unaccustomed to society.

3. George Keats to the Rev. J. F. Clarke, unpublished letter of 17 January 1841, communicated personally by Miss Ella Keats Whiting.

4. Ward, 188–189, paints a picture of a golden sunny journey; but the weather records do not support this. See G.M. (1818), Vol. II, p. 574.

5. Ward, 189.

soldiers. Everywhere was crowded, so in spite of the returning rain they pushed on to Endmoor, where the landlady took pity on the two drenched travellers, although she was white-washing the inn, and all customers had to cram into the little parlour-kitchen. Keats and Brown were therefore thrust into the company of the local drunkard, Richard Radshaw, an old soldier who amused Keats by staggering bearlike up to Brown and asking if his spectacles were for sale. When they left Lancaster, they had looked like gentlemen with nothing to do, as a labourer scornfully remarked; but one day's bad-weather walking had made them more like travelling pedlars, and Radshaw was only the first of many to make this mistake.

The next morning was better, especially after they passed Kendal. The early mist gradually cleared, the larks were singing, and the high air of the fells freshened their steps. Suddenly above Bowness, the view opened out, and both stopped. To Keats it was a revelation like the explorer's vision of new ocean in his own first great sonnet. Windermere lay before them, mountains edged with silver cloud above it, a little green island floating in its midst, a Wordsworth poem. It was almost unreal. "How can I believe in that?—surely it cannot be!" exclaimed Keats. It was finer than anything Shelley could see in Italy, and every turn of the descending road brought some new and lovelier aspect. The fashionable inn at Bowness had fresh-caught fish for dinner; visitors were provided with a boat to fetch their own trout, and with a swim while they were waiting for it to be cooked. In the late afternoon, they walked along the ferny banks of Windermere to the Salutation Inn at Ambleside. The setting sun shot huge golden rays through the purple clouds that thronged the mountain. Leaving Brown with a talkative fellow-tourist, Keats disappeared to write. That evening, 26 June, he tried to combine in a letter to Tom his impressions of the lake, first from Bowness, and now from the north: "The two views we have had of it," he wrote, "are of the most noble tenderness—they can never fade away—they make one forget the divisions of life; age, youth, poverty and riches; and refine one's sensual vision into a sort of north star which can never cease to be open lidded and stedfast over the wonders of the great Power." It was a summing-up of intense experience that harked back to the opening of *Endymion*, and anticipated the third stanza of the Nightingale Ode and the sonnet "Bright Star".

His description was a prose homage to Wordsworth, returning, as so often, to the fourth book of *The Excursion*, with its image of "the polar star that never closed His steadfast eye". Next morning brought another set of Wordsworthian experiences. Brown and Keats rose at six, and went before breakfast to see the hundred-foot Stock Ghyll force. Missing their way, they found the water by its thunderous noise. Keats was lifted by the beauty and power of the falls to the imaginative identification with nature that Severn had seen him experience on their Hampstead walks, but this time on a giant scale. "To enlarge my vision" had been his object, and now this was achieved. "I never forget my stature so completely", he exclaimed in his letter to Tom, "I live in the eye; and my imagination, surpassed, is at rest." He tried to define his experience again in Wordsworthian terms, a prose *Prelude*:

At the same time the different falls have as different characters; the first darting down the slate-rock like an arrow; the second spreading out like a fan—the third dashed into a mist—and the one on the other side of the rock a sort of mixture of all these. We afterwards moved away a space, and saw nearly the whole more mild, streaming silverly through the trees. What astonishes me more than any thing is the tone, the coloring, the slate, the stone, the moss, the rock-weed; or, if I may say so, the intellect, the countenance of such places. The space, the magnitude of mountains and waterfalls are well imagined before one sees them; but this countenance or intellectual tone must surpass every imagination and defy any remembrance.

"I shall learn poetry here", he added, "and shall henceforth write more than ever". It was the physical prelude to much of his own great creative year.

After "a monstrous Breakfast", the Wordsworthian sunrise, in which everything was suffused, unhappily began to fade into the light of common day. Keats had been shaken the night before to find that Wordsworth was actively electioneering for Lord Lowther against the Whig Brougham, and that his house, far from being a philosopher-poet's retreat, was in a prominent place, pointed out as a fashionable landmark for tourists. He now called there to pay his respects, and found his worst fears realized. Wordsworth, and his family, had gone to await the poll at Appleby. Until this moment, Keats had reminded himself, though sadly, that the Lowther family were simply friends of the Wordsworths; now this rallying behind the Tory forces on the eve of the poll seemed, Brown noticed, an exposure of the elder poet's reactionary principles to the younger, who was bitterly disappointed. He wrote a note, propped it up in the frame of a picture which he took to be a portrait of Dorothy Wordsworth,[1] and made the best of a bad job by inspecting the waterfalls across the road in Rydal Park. He had at least seen that Wordsworth had a view from his parlour-window worthy of a poet; but disillusion stayed with him all along Rydal Water to Grasmere, and was only partly dispelled on seeing the dwelling of Wordsworth's humbler days, Dove Cottage. Here, looking back, Keats's spirits were lifted by identifying the landmarks of Wordsworth's poems, Kirkstone, Loughrigg, Silver How and "That ancient woman seated on Helm Crag". The poems, at any rate, lived visibly around him, however much their creator had distressed and disenchanted him.

They stayed the night of Saturday 27 June at Wythburn in the flea-bitten Nag's Head. Keats relieved the restless evening by writing to George and Georgiana. He assured them of his health; fourteen miles among such scenery left him less fatigued than the familiar four from Hampstead to

1. *Letters*, I, 303, though no such portrait is known.

London. Trying to bridge the vast gap of miles opening between them, he wrote a verse-acrostic for his sister-in-law on her new name, Georgiana Augusta Keats, which included an enigmatic line on the family surname

Enchanted has it been the Lord knows where,[1]

Weariness overcame flea-bites, and he slept. Eight miles before breakfast the next morning to Keswick, although in a drizzle, freshened him for better verse, an affectionate eight-line lyric to round off the letter before posting it. That Sunday, they did the entire circuit of Derwentwater, ten miles including a detour to see the Falls of Lodore. While dinner was being prepared, they managed to scramble another three miles up and down to a stone circle near the Vale of St. John, a prehistoric sight that strongly impressed them both. They went to bed tired, but rose at four the next morning to climb Skiddaw. They were already a thousand feet above sea-level, and were nearly at the top, another two thousand, by half-past six when a mist blotted the view. However, they had seen Lancashire to the south, Galloway to the north, and the Cumbrian hills, still snowy in midsummer, all round. Keats was exhilarated. "We went up with two others, very good sort of fellows," he wrote to Tom, "All felt on arising into the cold air, that same elevation, which a cold bath gives one—I felt as if I were going to a Tournament."

Ireby, where they stayed the night, provided another form of exhilaration. The Sun Inn had a big assembly hall upstairs, and that evening it filled with boys and girls, dancing like the Scots party in Burns's *Tam o' Shanter*. This was even better than scenery, Keats felt, the fresh faces, the fearless energy, the human beauty of the whirling figures. Tuesday 30 June saw the travellers at Carlisle. The unlucky fate that kept Keats from ever seeing Bailey again was displayed ironically here. Bailey was due to be ordained by the Bishop in Carlisle Cathedral, which Keats visited, but he had not yet arrived in Carlisle himself. At this moment, he was in London, seeing Keats's publisher, and leaving behind a copy of Livy's Roman History for Keats.[2] Even though missing him yet again, Keats was reminded of Bailey's advice about his reading, and got out the tiny volume of *The Inferno* from his knapsack. He read the early cantos on 1 July, when he and Brown, both having aching thighs and blistered feet, gave themselves the luxury of a coach ride over the Border to Dumfries. The descent into Hell in Canto Four struck him forcibly; so did the ceaseless icy pain of the carnal lovers in Canto Five. Both combined in his mind as he visited the tomb of Burns, a poet condemned by his own Kirk for sensual love. He tried a sonnet, "in a strange mood", whose setting

1. He first wrote "Enhanced", not "Entranced" as Garrod, *Works*, 566, has it, but altered it to "Enchanted", which he had evidently meant all along. It seems to indicate he did not know where his father came from.

2. KHM, No. 20.

is not really Dumfries, which he found antipathetic, but the half-world of
Dante's hell, at whose gate Minos the infernal judge sends the sinners to their
allotted torment, and where

All is cold Beauty; pain is never done.

The mood continued to haunt him as an undertone to the cheerful physical
excitement of the tour. Scotland struck him as a savage primitive harsh
country, inimical to full-blooded sensuous natures such as his own and
Burns's. "Poor unfortunate fellow", he wrote a week later, "his disposition
was southern." Joy seemed to have stopped with the dancers at Ireby, south
of the Border. Brown tried to argue him into liking Scotland; but the poverty
of peasant life and the domination of the Kirk over this hard-pressed people
obsessed him still. Hell could be literally here on earth in such a society, as it
had been at times for Burns. "A Poor Creatures pennance before those
execrable elders" must be something like the endless torture to which Dante's
stern vision had condemned Cleopatra and Helen. Keats began to imagine
himself, a poet of intensity and gusto, in Burns's position. He saw in Burns's
story his own life, menaced by frowning trouble.

Smaller matters kept him generally buoyant. He acclimatized himself to
drinking whisky, and had his coat neatly mended by a Scottish tailor. As
for Burns, he managed to persuade himself "we need not think of his misery
—that is all gone—bad luck to it", and he was delighted to find how everyone
spoke of their poet, though the verdict on him was usually the cautious one
"that he wrote a good *mony* sensible things". They reached Dalbeattie on
2 July, and stopped at a general shop kept by a man with a wooden leg. On
the next morning, walking their customary eight miles before breakfast,
Brown told Keats the plot of Scott's *Guy Mannering*. While they breakfasted
at Auchencairn, Keats wrote to his sister and to Tom. Brown noticed that
Keats was writing verse in Fanny's letter. It was an imaginative description
of Scott's character Meg Merrilies, in a ballad-form that Scott himself might
have admired. Brown copied it for Dilke, and Keats made a copy for Tom;
they set off again, ten miles to Kirkcudbright, with a two-mile detour
through charming country to see Dundrennan Abbey. Everywhere they
passed poverty; but Keats, imaginatively seeing it through the eyes of Burns,
was now full of sympathy rather than disgust. The bare feet of the girls,
which had seemed coarse and ugly at first sight, now made him expatiate on
"the beauty of a human foot, that had grown without an unnatural restraint";
at the back of his mind, the moral restraint imposed on these half-savage
native creatures still haunted him. His own disturbed but indulged childhood
now seemed a paradise, and he scribbled a doggerel reminder of it for Fanny.
At Creetown, where they walked on Saturday 4 July, the landlady was
surprised to have Southern visitors, and Gaelic was the general speech. After
reaching Glenluce on the Sunday, they trudged the next day toward

Stranraer. This was a diversion in order to make a quick trip to Ireland, and as the unexpectedly hot sun beat down, they began to regret it. A posthorn from the road behind, however, announced the coach making for the Irish mail-boat at Portpatrick. They stopped it gratefully, scrambled up, and by that evening they were in a pleasant inn across the water at Donaghadee at the head of Belfast Lough.

Human experience was pouring upon Keats in almost bewildering profusion. Here were two countries, speaking more or less the same tongue, divided by a few miles of sea-water, but utterly different. At first the freedom of the Irish, their ready smiles and engaging manners, filled him with relief after the dour, subdued, thrifty Scots, "regular Phalanges of savers and gainers." Two days' walking to Belfast and back made him change this opinion. Barbarous as the regimented life of Scotland seemed, the feckless poverty of Ireland threw him into absolute despair. The slums of industrial Belfast were a horror; the miserable ale-houses and peasant hovels made the humblest Scottish cottage seem like a palace. Hastening back to Donaghadee, they had an encounter on the road which was almost more than even Keats's taste for the human grotesque could stomach. It was

The Duchess of Dunghill—It is no laughing matter tho—Imagine the worst dog kennel you ever saw placed upon two poles from a mouldy fencing—In such a wretched thing sat a squalid old Woman squat like an ape . . . with a pipe in her mouth and looking out with a round-eyed skinny lidded, inanity—with a sort of horizontal idiotic movement of her head—squab and lean she sat and puff'd out the smoke while two ragged tattered Girls carried her along—What a thing would be a history of her Life and sensations.

"I can never forget", Keats added. Human misery was the same in all countries; it only took different shapes. There were evils in Scotland, Ireland, in the whole human condition, that no scenery or natural beauty could lift. Walking from Portpatrick to Ballantrae on Thursday 9 July, and following the coast, they had a sudden and wonderful view of Ailsa Crag; this brought a poem from Keats, a sonnet full of questioning. Entering Ballantrae, they met a Highland wedding, and Keats tried a pastiche of Burns; but even this impromptu had an underlying melancholy. Next day was unexpectedly fine after early rain; the effect of this was to make Ailsa, fifteen miles away, seem close at hand, and to follow them like a giant companion along the coast to the King's Arms at Girvan.

Here, and at Maybole the next day, Keats tried to take stock in letters to Tom and to Reynolds. He attempted to sum up his feelings about the Scotch and Irish natures, about Burns, and about his own tendency to see the dark side of all experiences. Just as he felt Shakespeare to be the presider over his expeditions the previous summer, he felt a self-identification with Burns in this summer's adventure, growing keener as they approached the poet's birthplace at Ayr on Saturday 11 July. Everything in the unexpectedly lovely countryside seemed to speak of the dead poet, meadows, trees, and ever-present mountains and sea. As he had done in the Wordsworth country, Keats counted the landmarks that he knew from Burns's poems, Kirk Alloway, the banks of the Doon river, and "the Brig across it, over which Tam o'Shanter fled". He reached the cottage in a wrought-up state, and vented his conflicting feelings on the garrulous and tipsy custodian, who claimed to have known Burns. As the man maundered on, Keats was filled with despair for the poet who had tried to live as a poet in such society. Significantly, the only remark he caught fully in these half-drunken reminiscences was a description of Burns's melancholy appearance near the end of his life. This misery of an over-generous nature degraded by circumstances oppressed Keats like a dead weight. "I tried to forget it—to drink Toddy without any Care—to write a merry Sonnet—it wont do—he talked with Bitches—he drank with Blackguards, he was miserable—We can see horribly clear in the works of such a man his whole life, as if we were God's spies." Keats destroyed the draft of his "flat sonnet", as he called it, an action which has led to the theory that he saw in its purely rhetorical opening line

This mortal body of a thousand days

a premonition of his own miserable death roughly a thousand days later.[1] There are signs that he felt the sonnet personally, but perhaps in a very different way. The experience certainly filled his mind during the walk to Kilmarnock on Sunday 12 July, and on to Kingswells on the 13th. The degradation of Burns and his consequent amours—"What were his addresses to Jean in the latter part of his life"—together with his early disease-ridden death gave Keats searching thought about his own strong passions and how to reconcile them with society. Not death but sex became the immediate topic of his letters. He assured Reynolds that though he had spoken at large against marriage, he was now at a point of accepting it as something more than a social necessity. George's happiness had made him realize it was a positive good, which he might one day embrace himself. "Things like these, and they are real", he exclaimed, using one of his highest terms of praise, "have made me resolve to have a care of my health." These words, in their context of the disastrous loves of Burns, point to Keats's own unfortunate experience the previous autumn; his doctor Sawrey was full of warnings not to take the disease too lightly because of the terrible effects it might have in marriage to an innocent partner. The fate of the Scots poet was an additional warning; meditations on this theme followed Keats long after the "Great shadow" of Burns was left behind.

His high spirits, however, broke through the clouds at a dinner encounter with a ridiculous traveller, who had seen Kean act but who had no idea of Shakespeare's plays; his healthy pugnacity had outlet as they entered Glasgow,

1. As Ward, 199-200, thinks.

where they were at once accosted by a drunk man so that, as Keats said, "I was obliged to mention the word officer and Police before he would desist." The weather too had taken a turn for the better as they spent the next few days walking up Loch Lomond to Tarbet; they went by easy stages as Brown was breaking in a pair of new shoes. Keats had more leisure for letter-writing. At Cairndow, on Friday 17 July, Brown relieved his feelings about the shoes by a string of bawdy puns on the names of places in the Lake District,[1] which Keats appreciatively copied as the beginning of a new letter to Tom, headed "Cairn-something". They had walked five more miles than usual before breakfast at the Cairndow Inn, having mistaken a stone seat marked on the map as "Rest and Be Thankful" for an inn. This had put them in a hilarious mood, and Keats capped Brown's sexual fantasy by writing a parody of Goldsmith's *Elegy on the Glory of her Sex, Mrs. Mary Blaize*. This too was largely indecent, concerned with the gadflies that had been biting Keats, and how and where they might profitably bite other people. One of the victims was to be Lord Lowther, now duly elected for Westmorland after a vituperative struggle; during this the Whig Brougham, while temporarily heading the poll, "pronounced an eloquent contrast between the character of Shakespeare's mind and that of Mr. Wordsworth",[2] who also came in for Keats's satire in the poem. Satire persisted all day. Reaching Inverary after a beautiful walk along the lakes, Brown was too knocked up to do more than rest; but Keats, with his insatiable human curiosity, found there was a local barnstorming performance of Kotzebue's heavy German tragedy, *The Stranger*, and went to it. The wretched company of actors had the added misfortune of a bagpiper playing interval music, and Keats wrote a mock-heroic Miltonic sonnet on the ludicrous effects of this combination.

Next morning, Saturday 18 July, began with a dramatic thunderstorm among the mountains. Brown was glad to rest, and Keats used the time to write to Benjamin Bailey, having picked up a letter from him at Glasgow. His serious underlying thought, concealed by the hilarities of the last twenty-four hours, came to the surface as he remembered their discussions late into the night at Oxford. There they had led to such questions as "Why should Woman suffer?", and Keats had always considered Bailey as a special audience for his own personal views about women. Burns and the fate of the carnal lovers in Dante had brought these to the forefront of his mind, and Bailey himself had just reminded Keats of Dante's message. "You say I must study Dante", Keats wrote, "well the only Books I have with me are those three little Volumes. I read that fine passage you mention a few days ago." What he wanted to say to Bailey was to discuss "in a sane and sober Mind" his own impulsive and passionate nature. His last letter, with its judgments about women, had pained Bailey; Keats now tried to elaborate, with a side-glance at his own vagaries of temperament. "I carry all matters to an

1. Appendix 4.   2. E, No. 549, p. 422.

extreme", he confessed, with a self-knowledge that matched his own school-fellow's verdict of "always in extremes". Now he tried to apply the same self-criticism to his feelings about women:

Is it not extraordinary? When among Men I have no evil thoughts, no malice, no spleen—I can listen and from every one I can learn—my hands are in my pockets I am free from all suspicion and comfortable. When I am among Women I have evil thoughts, malice, spleen—I cannot speak or be silent—I am full of Suspicions and therefore listen to no thing—I am in a hurry to be gone—You must be charitable and put all this perversity to my being disappointed since Boyhood—

"I must absolutely get over this", he confessed, "—but how? The only way is to find the root of the evil, and so cure it". With this anticipation of the methods of psycho-analysis, he dismissed the subject, but it was still very close to him. A week later he wrote to Tom, "With respect to Women I think I shall be able to conquer my passions hereafter better than I have yet done", and he now repeated to Bailey his promise to Reynolds that he would be prudent and take care of his health. Since he was exposing himself at this very moment to physical hazard in every other sort of way, this remark must once more apply to his relations with women and to the venereal scare of the previous autumn. The example of Burns was a potent argument, and the lines of poetry he added to Bailey's letter hinted at the tragic effects of an over-stimulated imagination. Its final passage had particular power:

O horrible! to lose the sight of well remember'd face,
Of Brother's eyes, of Sister's Brow, constant to every place;
Filling the Air as on we move with Portraiture intense
More warm than those heroic tints that fill a Painter's sense—
When Shapes of old come striding by and visages of old,
Locks shining black, hair scanty grey and passions manifold.
No, No that horror cannot be—for at the Cable's length
Man feels the gentle Anchor pull and gladdens in its strength—
One hour half ideot he stands by mossy waterfall,
But in the very next he read his Soul's memorial:
He reads it on the Mountain's height where chance he may sit down
Upon rough marble diadem, that Hills eternal crown.
Yet be the Anchor e'er so fast, room is there for a prayer
That Man may never loose his Mind on Mountains bleak and bare;
That he may stray league after League some great Berthplace to find,
And keep his vision clear from speck, his inward sight unblind—

The extremes that always threatened to rock the painfully-acquired stability of Keats's nature have hardly better expression anywhere in his works.

The weather improved though it was still treacherous; ironically, London, in the four weeks since they left it, had basked in a Mediterranean sunshine. The travellers spent the night of Saturday 18 July at Cladich, and on 19 July they walked twenty miles along Loch Awe, south and west down the narrow mountain-fringed water; every ten steps, as Keats wrote, created a new and beautiful picture, from the huge black bulk of Ben Cruachan at the beginning to the two islands at the southern base, each clad with its ruin, one of a convent and one of a castle. Next day their walk curving north-west to Kilmelfort was even finer. They were between the freshwater loch and the saltwater inlets of the sea, with mountains inland and the islands of the Hebrides on the other hand. Eagles swung lazily about the sky, while woodlarks sang from the sandy fern, as the travellers scuffed their way on a warm afternoon along the sea-shore tracks. They were now fairly in the Western Highlands, and it was virtually a foreign country. The inhabitants spoke and understood only Gaelic, and merely asking the way was a difficulty, with the visitors' English pronunciation of place-names. Food was primitive, and the only commodity in ready supply was whisky. Grey and gauzy veils of rain swept down without warning from mountain and sea; on Tuesday 21 July they walked fifteen miles to Oban in drenching weather. They were opposite the Isle of Mull, with Iona and Staffa beyond. These were fashionable places for the tourist, and the prices for the sea-excursion were high. Regretfully, they had decided to continue north the next day to Fort William, when a guide turned up who offered to take them cheaply by a direct track across the Isle of Mull instead of sailing round it.

This unlucky economy led them into the hardest two days of their walk. Keats slept the night of 22 July on the earth floor of a shepherd's cottage, after wading through bog and river all day. The next morning was another hard walk to the south-west tip of the island, though by a slightly better path, while the guide sang Gaelic songs to oblige the pair. Keats was exhausted, and even the sturdy Brown, who liked to think his ancestors came from these parts, found it by far the wildest and most taxing section of the whole tour. The next day, 24 July, buoyed their spirits with a reward beyond their hopes. It was after all, as Keats said in the letter to Bailey he now sealed, the main object of the expedition that it should "give me more experience, rub off more Prejudice, use me to more hardship, identify finer scenes load me with grander Mountains, and strengthen more my reach in Poetry." Iona and Staffa gave him more of the raw material of poems than any other places; in these islands lay for him the seeds of the full poetic growths of the following year, from the epic *Hyperion* to the ballad *La Belle Dame*, from the perilous seas of the Nightingale Ode to the moving waters of the Bright Star sonnet. Iona, where St. Columba had first brought Christianity, astounded Keats with its Cathedral ruins, cloisters and royal tombs, shown them by the local schoolmaster. Even more impressive than the man-made buildings was the superb natural architecture of Staffa, rising direct out of the swell of the crystal sea. "It is impossible to describe it", Keats exclaimed; but when he did so, it was in the terms of the epic poem he had been planning all year:

Suppose now the Giants who rebelled against Jove had taken a whole Mass of black Columns and bound them together like bunches of matches—and then with immense Axes had made a cavern in the body of these columns—of course the roof and the floor must be composed of the broken ends of the Columns—such is fingal's Cave except that the Sea has done the work of excavations and is continually dashing there— so that we walk along the sides of the cave on the pillars which are left as if for convenient Stairs—the roof is arched somewhat gothic wise and the length of some of the entire side pillars is 50 feet—About the island you might seat an army of Men each on a pillar—The length of the Cave is 120 feet and from its extremity the view into the sea through the large Arch at the entrance—the colour of the colums is a sort of black with a lurking gloom of purple therein—For solemnity and grandeur it far surpasses the finest Cathedrall—

He attempted verses on it, first catching some of the wonder of his prose, but then breaking down into doggerel about the tourist-boats that began to round the island in the afternoon; the experience needed weeks of quiet for its assimilation. In fact, the accidents of their journey were providing him with just that necessary respite. The thirty-seven-mile ordeal of Mull had given him a severe cold. Even a few days' laying-up at Oban did not prevent this developing into a severely ulcerated throat. He spent the next week travelling slowly, a victim to acute tonsillitis. On 1 August, when they had reached Fort William, he prepared for one more physical effort, and on Sunday 2 August, he climbed Ben Nevis. In spite of the immensity of the mists and chasms, partly reflected in a sonnet, his first comment was "I am heartily glad it is done". It was the finishing touch; he was too knocked up to do more than write some comic verse about a fat lady climbing the mountain. "Mr. Keats is gone to Scotland", wrote Marianne Hunt to Mary Shelley on Tuesday 4 August. In fact, he was just deciding to come back. The first doctor he saw at Inverness on 6 August found him thin, fevered and weary. He strongly advised a return to London, and persuaded Keats to catch a southbound vessel from the port of Cromarty, leaving Brown to continue alone. He wrote two stanzas on Beauly Abbey, on the way to Cromarty, and that was all. The pilgrimage, which had been as much spiritual as physical, was ended shortly after its highest point of experience. He was coming home to live with the poetic gains he had so deliberately sought to acquire.

Chapter 16

A MAN IN THE WORLD

*"As a Man in the world I love the rich talk of a Charmian; as an
eternal Being I love the thought of you"*

– JOHN KEATS to George and Georgiana Keats, 14 October 1818

KEATS sailed from Cromarty on the smack *George* on Saturday 8 August.
The ten days' trip, his first sea-voyage of any considerable length, was good
for his health and spirits. Although it was rough he was not sea-sick, and
though he could not manage the thick porridge, which the other passengers
ate with clumsy horn spoons, there was plenty of beef, which he had often
longed for during the tour,[1] to build him up after the scratch meals of the
last month. It was a fruitful interval for sorting out impressions before getting
down to work. Meanwhile at Hampstead, the worst was prepared for him.
Dr. Sawrey had called on Dilke. Tom's condition was now extremely
serious, and the doctor urged that his brother should be sent for. Dilke wrote
off at once, but on 14 August he got a letter from Brown announcing that
Keats had given up the tour and was on his way home. With any luck Keats
would at least be spared the distress of hearing about Tom while he was
hundreds of miles away. Mrs. Dilke wrote to her father-in-law, who had
already received the news himself from Brown, that Keats, "cheerful,
good-tempered, clever", would soon be on her doorstep. It was a less
unpleasant task in prospect than writing the letter had been; all the same, the
shock was bound to be cruel. Keats arrived in London in high spirits. It was
perhaps while waiting for the coach to take him to Hampstead that he
hurled himself into a cushioned chair, the first he had encountered for many
long weeks and exclaimed, in Shakespearian mockery, "O bottom, bottom!
thou art translated!"[2] When he got off at Pond Street, he could not resist
bursting into Wentworth Place, to surprise the Dilkes with the outlandish
get-up he still wore. Mrs. Dilke was an appreciative audience for the strange
apparition he made, "as brown and as shabby as you can imagine; scarcely
any shoes left, his jacket all torn at the back, a fur cap, a great plaid, and his

1. *Letters*, I, 360, 393.
2. KC, II, 137. Ward, 209, says this occurred at the Dilkes, but Severn, who tells the
story and was perhaps there, places it in "the City".

knapsack. I cannot tell what he looked like."[1] The Dilkes found what they had realized from Brown's letter confirmed by Keats's light-hearted behaviour; the news about Tom could not have reached him. They had to tell him themselves before he went up the hill to the lodgings. He left immediately for Well Walk, without, it seems, meeting their neighbours, Brown's tenants, who were to play so large a part in his life, the Brawne family.

Mrs. Frances Brawne was a widow, still in her thirties, with three children. The eldest, Fanny, was just 18, the boy Samuel just 14, and the youngest Margaret only nine. The Brawnes, like the Keates dynasty, were a family with extensive connections, and claimed to have come over with the Conqueror. They had, however, slipped recently in the social scale, and Mrs. Brawne's husband Samuel seems to have been a rolling stone, who left hardly any money.[2] His personal circumstances had been exactly like those of Keats's mother in two respects; his father had been an innholder and stable-keeper before retiring to a farm in Kilburn, and there was a family tendency to tuberculosis, from which he himself had died in his thirties. What money there was came from Mrs. Brawne's family, the Ricketts, West Indian administrators and City merchants. Her brother John had died in 1816, leaving her and her three children a small but sufficient income, out of which they rented in turn various Hampstead houses.

Even if he had met Dilke's neighbours, Keats would have been too distracted to notice them at this time. His main thoughts were centred on Tom at Well Walk, though he found time to write an attempted reassurance to his sister. This letter reveals what may have been another preoccupation during the next troubled month. From mid-August to mid-September he seems to have been dosing himself with mercury, taken orally in large enough quantities to produce the familiar effects of nervousness and aching gums. On 19 August he suffered from severe toothache, and on 21 September he spoke of "a nervousness proceeding from the Mercury", which he had evidently been taking for some time.[3] The most likely explanation is that he and Dr. Sawrey were taking precautions in case his severely ulcerated throat should turn out to be a syphilitic ulcer. Keats had been warned in his Anatomy and Physiology lectures at hospital not to mistake a bad sore throat for syphilis,[4] but the doctor had claimed to demonstrate in his book that an apparent cure of gonorrhoea by small doses of mercury could be followed in about ten or eleven months' time by a syphilitic outbreak needing large

1. *Papers of a Critic*, 5, Mrs. Dilke to C. W. Dilke senior.
2. P.P.R., Crickett 160. His estate was "Sub £100".
3. *Letters*, I, 369. Keats writes of the mercury treatment as something known to Dilke, who by 21 September had been away from Hampstead apparently for some time himself at Brighton.
4. Note-books of J. Waddington, 1815–1816, Wills Library, Guy's Hospital.

oral doses.[1] Modern medicine discounts this form of treatment, and has proved that the supposed connection between the two venereal diseases was a ludicrous error; nevertheless, that Keats was taking such precautions under doctor's orders is virtually certain. His frank mention of the treatment to his men friends, and his assurance to them that it was an "undangerous matter" was quite in key with the manners of the time, though when he made the last remark, on 22 September, he was beginning to realize, as perhaps he had suspected from the first, that it had been a needless scare.

This, and Tom's plight, were enough to keep him almost a prisoner at Well Walk for much of the next month,[2] especially as Sawrey frowned on his going out much during treatment. Keats was, as he said, confined to the house "by Sawrey's mandate".[3] For both these reasons he could not go and see his sister at Walthamstow, though he was also worried by her news that Abbey intended to remove her from the Misses Tuckeys' school now that she had passed her fifteenth birthday. He wrote to ask for Fanny to be allowed to come and see Tom, and ventured a day in Town himself on 1 September to see Abbey. Sometime about now, perhaps on the same day, he managed to call on the Reynolds family in Little Britain, and found them "in a sort of taking" about Mrs. Reynolds's niece, Jane Cox, whose father seems to have died in the service of the East India Company, leaving her the heir to her grandfather's property. Unfortunately she had fallen out with the old gentleman, and taken refuge with her aunt. Keats did not see her on this occasion; once again, it is probable he would hardly have noticed her if they met then, for perhaps on this exact day, another distracting event added itself to the unpleasantness of this whole disturbed month. The August number of *Blackwood's Edinburgh Magazine* came out, with the personal attack on himself which the previous Cockney School articles had foreshadowed. Keats had been long prepared to meet the familiar sneers of the anonymous Z, and had expected them to take the form of treating him as a young disciple of Hunt; "I shall have the Reputation of Hunt's eleve" he had written ruefully to Bailey, even before the articles began. He was totally unprepared for an article which treated his connection with Hunt comparatively lightly, but which lumped his work with the ignorant attempts at rhyme by characters in low life:

Of all the manias of this mad age, the most incurable, as well as the most common, seems to be no other than the *Metromanie*. The just celebrity of Robert Burns and Miss Baillie has had the melancholy effect of turning the heads of we know not how many farm-servants and unmarried ladies; our very footmen compose tragedies . . .

This reflection was soon applied to Keats in the most insulting and unexpected

1. S. Sawrey; *An Enquiry into the Effects of the Venereal Poison* . . ., 154–157.
2. Dilke seems to have believed that Keats took Tom down to Teignmouth again at this time, so little were the brothers seen about. Dilke ann. I, 241.
3. *Letters*, I, 371.

way; somehow Z had found out about Keats's medical training, and proceeded to reduce it to the lowest possible terms:

His friends, we understand, destined him to the career of medicine, and he was bound apprentice some years ago to a worthy apothecary in town. But all has been undone by a sudden attack of the malady to which we have alluded. Whether Mr. John has been sent home with a diuretic or composing draught to some patient far gone in the poetical mania, we have not heard. This much is certain, that he has caught the infection, and that thoroughly.

The review, which was of both the 1817 *Poems* and *Endymion*, then proceeded on the expected lines of picking on immature verses and "Cockney" rhymes, naturally choosing for special disapproval Keats's attack on Pope in *Sleep and Poetry*. Though it treated Keats as a mistaken follower of Hunt, as he had anticipated, it sneered even here at his social position, by saying that Hunt's praise in *The Examiner* "confirmed the wavering apprentice in his desire to quit the gallipots." It treated him throughout as a mere "boy", and Keats must have found the comparison with Hunt himself unutterably galling.

Mr. Hunt is a small poet, but he is a clever man. Mr. Keats is a still smaller poet, and he is only a boy of pretty abilities, which he has done everything in his power to spoil.

The final paragraph repeated the main theme:

It is a better and a wiser thing to be a starved apothecary than a starved poet; so back to the shop, Mr. John, back to the "plasters, pills, and ointment boxes," &c. But, for Heaven's sake, young Sangrado, be a little more sparing of extenuatives and soporifics in your practice than you have been in your poetry.

The *Blackwood's* writers, who had perhaps never originally meant to attack Keats so severely,[1] had been given this lead by what seemed to them a lucky chance. On 19 July, Benjamin Bailey was ordained deacon by the Bishop of Carlisle, to perform the office as curate of Orton, a small parish nearby.[2] He partly owed his ordination to the recommendation of Bishop Gleig, father of his Oxford room-mate, and he at once set off for Scotland, to stay with the Gleigs and to preach his maiden sermon in the Bishop's Chapel at Stirling, on Sunday 26 July, just when Keats's sore throat was beginning to trouble him at Oban. At dinner, a handsome young Oxford graduate was introduced; it was John Gibson Lockhart of *Blackwood's*, a friend of the younger Gleig. At first, Bailey and Lockhart found much in common, notably in their appreciation of Wordsworth. Although Wordsworth had been treated equivocally in *Blackwood's* by Lockhart's colleague, John Wilson,[3] Lockhart himself was a staunch admirer, and had been profoundly

1. The "main attack", Lockhart had announced, was to be on Hunt; that against Keats only "a diversion". *Blackwood's*, Jan. 1818, p. 415.
2. Bishop's Register, Record Office, Carlisle.
3. Moorman, *William Wordsworth*, II, 299–300.

moved by *The Excursion*. Unluckily the conversation then turned to Keats, and Bailey heard Lockhart refer contemptuously to his friend as being under the patronage of Leigh Hunt, and a mere copyist of Hunt both in poetry and in politics. Bailey, remembering Keats's letter to him in which he had feared such a verdict, felt himself bound to assert Keats's independence of Hunt. Unfortunately, and in a bout of well-meaning pomposity, Bailey overdid it.[1] He was so anxious to show that Keats owed little to Hunt, of whom Bailey himself disapproved, that he started to say what he knew of Keats's early life and upbringing. Conscious perhaps of the learned presence of the Bishop, who was providing him with a formidable list of books to help him read for a Scottish degree, Bailey blundered on about Keats's humble but respectable education and origins, his small inheritance and his apprenticeship to Hammond. This was intended to correct the idea that he was one of Hunt's bohemian coterie; but it gave Lockhart his cue for quite another line of attack. Bailey, also acutely conscious in this company that his friend's poem contained, as he put it, an inclination "to that abominable principle of Shelley's—that *Sensual Love* is the principle of *things*", painted such a picture of lower-middle-class commonplaces that Lockhart was halfway to his article already. Suddenly feeling this, Bailey pleaded with him not to use this personal information in any *Blackwood's* attack on Keats. Lockhart coolly replied that it would not be used by *him*, sheltering behind the anonymity and joint authorship of the Z series, though he later acknowledged he alone had written the article on Keats, and tried, though he was barely a year older than the poet he pilloried, to laugh it off as a youthful folly. The folly indeed was in Bailey's mistaken and clumsy loyalty.[2] In his innocence, he had provided a comic label for Keats, to which the *Blackwood's* reviewers reverted again and again, and for many years to come. While other unfavourable magazines, such as the *British Critic* that summer, merely printed a bad review and left it at that, *Blackwood's* continued to remind its readers every three months of the absurd apothecary's boy, "Pestleman Jack", whose admirers largely consist of "medical students, who chaunt portions of Endymion as they walk the hospitals, because the author was once an apothecary", while he himself "practises poetry and pharmacy."[3] Bailey had left Keats a legacy of caricature for the rest of his life. In nervous remorse, he posted a letter of warning to John Taylor on the same day that the magazine came out, promising, again over-importantly, that he himself would get an article into *Blackwood's* through Gleig, who was a contributor, if Keats should be grossly attacked. A month later he had to confess that this had been a vain hope. The only editorial response from Blackwood was to give Bailey an invitation for Keats to come and call on him if the walking-tour took him through

1. Ward, 214, suggests Lockhart led him on.
2. Bailey's three accounts are given KC, I, 34–35, 245–247, II, 286–288.
3. MacGillivray, xxv,

Edinburgh. Bailey forwarded this with an agitated recommendation that Keats should do so. Whether Keats ever knew of this invitation is doubtful; part of the trouble was probably guessed by Brown, when he called at Carlisle later in September, on his way back from Scotland.

Keats knew nothing of this at the time, and no one seems to have seen him during the first fortnight in September. On Monday 14 September, he emerged for a small gathering at 93 Fleet Street arranged by Hessey, while Taylor was on his usual long summer holiday with relations. Tom had a slight remission of illness, and Keats was able to spend the night and stay on for some time the next morning. He had agreeable company, for the small party consisted of relatives of Hessey, connections of the business, and authors. Richard Woodhouse was there before going off to his regular autumn holiday in the West Country. There were Hessey's two brothers-in-law, the Falkners from Bath, and Taylor's Nottingham friend, the Reverend John Percival, Fellow of Wadham. Above all there was Hazlitt, now a Taylor & Hessey author, since the firm had printed his *Lectures on the English Poets* that summer, and were negotiating for his forthcoming series. He too had been attacked in the same number of *Blackwood's* as Keats, with unsavoury remarks on his appearance, morals and habits. He was extremely angry and had just decided to sue the editors, which he did so successfully that his opponents settled out of Court, and John Murray the publisher, who had invested money in the magazine, hastily withdrew it. Hazlitt always had a stimulating effect on Keats, who, as Hessey observed, seemed to be in excellent spirits. The essayist regarded the *Blackwood's* attack as an incentive to more work, and Keats fell in with his ideas. He did not care about the article, he said, as it was so poorly done; all the same, it evidently had some effect on him, for later in the evening he launched into a rhetorical outburst about the future of his own writing.[1] He began by saying that he did not intend to publish any more at present, so the *Blackwood's* abuse did not really concern him. Then, becoming more excited, he developed a thesis, as Woodhouse understood it, that there was now nothing more original to be written in poetry. All its possible riches were exhausted, and its beauties forestalled. He would therefore write nothing new, but go back to his determination before the walking-tour, that is, to train his mind by getting more knowledge and experience, but without necessarily ever turning this into poetry. Woodhouse was pained and alarmed at this statement, which he pondered over all through his holiday. Hessey took a more philosophic view of Keats, and discounted it. He saw Keats's determination to concentrate on deeper study as a sign of maturity, and did not believe his interest in writing had diminished. He made a friendly and amused note on Keats's attitude:[2]

1. This outburst is so unlike his usual measured views on poetry that some emotional reaction to the review must be suspected.

2. E. Blunden, *Keats's Publisher*, 56.

He is studying closely, recovering his Latin, going to learn Greek, and seems altogether more rational than usual—but he is such a man of fits and starts he is not much to be depended on. Still he thinks of nothing but poetry as his being's end and aim, and sometime or other he will, I doubt not, do something valuable.

Either the next morning, or on a later visit this week, Keats called on the Reynolds sisters in Little Britain. With his reawakened enthusiasm for learning Greek, he probably wanted to hear news of Bailey, who had promised to teach him; but he found Bailey "not quite so much spoken of in Little Britain". The curate of Orton, who had been drawing large congregations in his little parish, was now thoroughly caught up with his benefactors the Gleigs; though renouncing his own ambitions for publication, he was approaching Taylor to see if he would accept translations by both father and son. There was a daughter, Hamilton Gleig, who was beginning to interest him; Brown had found him in high spirits at Carlisle,[1] and the Reynolds girls must have realized he was not missing them. They were also in a turmoil about their errant cousin Jane Cox. Though they had gushed over her romantic predicament when Keats had been there before, a few weeks of her company had changed their tune. They now had hardly a good word to say for her, and for a good reason; the young woman turned out to be extremely attractive to men. They accused her of flirting, and had now decided to hate her.[2]

Keats was introduced to her, and found her indeed just the sort of woman "apt to make women of inferior charms hate her". Jane Cox was a remarkable beauty with what Keats noticed as a much more cosmopolitan attitude towards men than was usual in their circle. "She is too fine and too conscious of her Self to repulse any Man who may address her", he noted. He added that from her experience of the world, she did not assume that every man who approached her was making advances to her—"from habit she thinks that nothing *particular*", he commented, using the word[3] in the sense it appears in Smollett, roughly "making passes at her". Her beauty too was exotic. "She is not a Cleopatra"; he decided, "but she is at least a Charmian. She has a rich eastern look; she has fine eyes and fine manners. When she comes into a room she makes an impression the same as the Beauty of a Leopardess." He summed up this impression she made upon him a few weeks later when he was writing to George:[4]

I always find myself more at ease with such a woman; the picture before me always gives me a life and animation which I cannot possibly feel with any thing inferiour—I am at such times too much occupied in admiring to be awkward or on a tremble. I

1. *Letters*, I, 369 and II, 139.   2. *Letters*, I, 395.
3. *Letters*, I, 395, n. 8, quoting Hewlett, 226, says "From Jane Austen's letters we know that 'being particular' was, in plain English, flirting"; but the sense is not so innocent as that.
4. *Letters*, I, 395.

forget myself entirely because I live in her. You will by this time think I am in love with her; so before I go any further I will tell you I am not—she kept me awake one Night as a tune of Mozart's might do—I speak of the thing as a passtime and an amuzement than which I can feel none deeper than a conversation with an imperial woman the very 'yes' and 'no' of whose Lips is to me a Banquet. I dont cry to take the moon home with me in my Pocket not (*for* nor) do I fret to leave her behind me. I like her and her like because one has no *sensations*—what we both are is taken for granted—

Keats's whole attitude to women had matured since he wrote to Bailey two months before. The "gordian complication of feelings" about them had been to a large extent unravelled, and he was able to speak about them for the first time in the straightforward and objective tone that he used for so many other human experiences. The insulting facetiousness of nearly all his early letters to and about women disappears almost for ever. There is the greatest possible contrast between his letter to Marian Jeffery in June 1818, with its coy naughtiness about handkerchiefs and garters, and his letter to her of exactly a year later, when he treats her as a person with whom he can seriously discuss his position as an English poet. The walking tour had achieved one of its main objects, to "rub off more prejudice", as effectively in this direction as any other. The months of isolation from both of his brothers had given him the chance, for the first time in his life, to consider his feelings toward women apart from the intense three-cornered relationship that he had enjoyed since childhood. George might never come back from America, and Tom's disease, he knew from Sawrey and the evidence of his own eyes, was mortal. He now moved among society in his own person, in a way he had been unable to do before, and it was inevitable that he would soon enter into some real relationship with a woman. He did not, as he said, quite fall in love with Jane Cox on this occasion, though she disturbed him for a few days; but his whole way of dealing with the experience shows him at once more capable of love and more vulnerable to it. He was now doubly impatient of the vapid conventional approach of the Reynolds girls, who used the meaningless clichés of their state of society, and whispered to him that their cousin was a mere flirt. "They do not know what a Woman is", he dismissed them, in the confidence of his own new knowledge.

At the same time, he had not matured beyond a certain point. From somewhere in his early days, he still retained the double standard of judging women, itself as conventional in its way as the Reynolds girls' petty objections. He tried to sum up in his mind the contrast between Jane Cox and his own "disinterested" sister-in-law; he still assumed that because Miss Cox was socially assured and sexually attractive, she could only be judged in what he called a worldly way. When he recounted the incident to Georgiana, he put this remaining prejudice in an extreme form. "As a Man in the world I love the rich talk of a Charmian; as an eternal Being I love the thought of you. I should like her to ruin me, and I should like you to save me." With this type of hard-and-fast distinction still in his mind, he was liable for trouble with women, however much his feelings had improved and broadened. He had also the typical capacity of the creative artist for endowing any woman he met with either virtue or vice, according to his mood.

Yet the dominant impression of Keats at this time is certainly that given by his kindly publisher—"altogether more rational than usual". This, as Hessey noted, did not mean that his capacity for poetry was in any way damped down, though in fact he had not written a single word for over a month. Haydon, who like most of Keats's friends was still on his summer holidays, wrote prophesying that if the walking-tour "has done as much good to the *inside* as the outside of your head, you will feel the effects of it as long as you live."[1] The walking-tour, for all its obvious effect, was only the culmination of a process that had been going on for the last two years. Keats, since his decision to give up medicine for poetry, had worked through the experiences, the trials and the vicissitudes of a lifetime. He had passed, in his own comparison, from the infant or thoughtless chamber into the Chamber of Maiden Thought, with its intoxication and joy, but also with its sharpened vision, in which, among the gradual darkening, many doors were set open for his future exploration, as a man and as a poet. The incidents and situations which had contributed to this position had been as varied and as multifold as human life itself, the trivial and the profound, the sordid and the inspiring jostling one another, each experienced, according to his own axiom, upon the pulses. Poetically, he had tried every possible form, from the huge but conventional attempt in *Endymion* to write what he had been taught was the "king" of poems, to the most light-hearted and occasional of lyrics. In reading, conversation and listening to lectures, he had been close to the greatest minds of his own and of all ages; at the same time, and not infrequently on the same day, he had mixed wholeheartedly in the low-life and backstage purlieus of Regency London, and taken the fine point off his soul in cheerful and ribald company. He had faced the mystery and tragedy of the impending death of his brother Tom, and he had treated himself for a venereal infection, which was almost a commonplace in the social life of a young man of his time, and which certainly did not carry the stigma and moral revulsion that later writers have assumed.[2] He had experienced the wild swings of his own temperament, isolated and recognized them, and found his individual remedies; he had seen and tolerated various changes and quirks of behaviour in his wide circle of friends. He had met and been disillusioned by a great practitioner of his own craft, without seriously wavering in his basic allegiance to him as a poet and a philosopher. His family circle, which had supported him in his adolescent days and reinforced his belief in himself as a poet, was now broken by distance and impending death. He was

1. *Letters*, I, 372.
2. B. W. Richardson, *The Asclepiad*, 143; Ward, 134–135.

on the threshold of having to deal with life as an individual, just at the stage when he had deliberately trained himself for this trial. As a poet, he had just seen the work, into which he had put the whole effort of youthful idealism, dismissed in the spirit of vulgar caricature, and taken no harm from it.

Knowing that Keats was about to enter into the most remarkable creative period of his life, it is easy to read back too much certainty into this moment. His friends would not have divined it from his day-to-day behaviour. He was still to them a creature of impulse, who, in Haydon's words, "cared not for himself, & would put himself to any inconvenience to oblige his Friends, and expected his Friends to do the same for him."[1] The inner preparation, which we now see as an inevitable creator of his great poetry, was unknown to all of them. It would be wrong too to read back from his physical collapse, only just over a year ahead, and to see in the coming year of achievement some kind of race against time: to think that Keats had some premonition of the short space allotted to him to fulfil himself in poetry.[2] In September 1818, he was still a healthy man. The sore throat, which was thought by Dilke to have been the beginning of tuberculosis,[3] and which was even treated by some biographers as the onset of laryngeal tuberculosis, was probably a comparatively unimportant illness. He was habituated to some discomfort after bathing, fatigue or getting wet from a very early stage in his life, and it seems likely that its outbreaks were merely those of tonsillitis.[4] Unlike the Jennings side of the family in every way, with a father who had been a vigorous man until death by accident, Keats showed no sign of any physical weakness that might make him open to tubercular infection, and his own insistence that his sore throats were unimportant, and indeed that his discomfort was in the throat and not in the larynx, rules out any question of a severe laryngeal infection such as tuberculosis. Both he and the more conventionally "tubercular" type, George, had so far avoided infection from the tubercular Tom during long spells of nursing him at Teignmouth. There is no evidence that Keats had tuberculosis of the lungs at this time; but weakened by fatigue, worry, and the unnecessary precaution of large doses of mercury, he probably caught it himself from the dying Tom, during the coming months when he hardly ever left his side at Well Walk. It is also probable that these months made an impression on his mind which certainly preyed upon him when his own turn came to be an invalid. In delirium or in extreme illness, Tom told him that he was dying because of his love for the mysterious Amena. Keats made some enquiries, and arrived at the truth. The French girl was a fiction, invented as a hoax by Tom's schoolfellow, Charles Wells, her letters patent forgeries, couched in the mock sub-Elizabethan language of their school-days. Keats never forgave Wells; in the emotional circumstances of these months, the clumsy consequences of a

1. Haydon, II, 316.   2. As Ward, 200, thinks.   3. KHM, No. 52.
4. Bate, 614–616, analyses admirably the medical theories of biographers of Keats.

foolish practical joke became one of those obsessions with him[1] that took on the stature, in his own words, of "a theme for Sophocles". It was to have, indeed, such poetical by-products as *La Belle Dame Sans Merci*; but it was also to poison his own love-relationship and the springs of many friendships when he himself became ill. In a sense, he caught this distorting psychological disease, as well as the actual physical germs of tubercle, from his close contact with the dying Tom.

Keats was therefore poised at this instant, ready for an extraordinary accumulation of experiences. It was not certain that these would result in great poetry. They might have destroyed a less inwardly-mature and singly-dedicated man. It was inevitable that he would soon have to face the experience of seeing his brother die an agonizing and distressing death, and perhaps as inevitable that he himself, isolated by that death and by other circumstances, would enter into some kind of serious and disturbing love-affair. As a minor but nagging accompaniment, it was also inevitable that unless good advice were offered, all these major themes of life would be played out against a background of quite unnecessary poverty and financial anxiety. All this, which might have distracted or blotted-out poetry in a lesser man, actually seems to have acted as a spur to Keats. The key was his great resource of character and aim, derived largely from the vicissitudes of his very early upbringing. His boyhood had been an almost exact rehearsal for just such a set of worldly assaults on his spirit. Misfortune, as he had said of others, would now be met by the self-comment which he had written to Bailey "Well it cannot be helped.—he will have the pleasure of trying the resourses of his spirit."[2] Leigh Hunt, in one of his casual moments of information, wrote that Keats "would look at his hand, which was faded, and swollen in the veins, and say that it was the hand of a man of fifty." What, in fact, marks Keats out from his contemporaries is that in any really essential matters of poetry, thought or human conduct, he behaved, until illness began to distort judgment, with the ripeness of a man twice his age. While still in his early twenties, he was beginning to assume the balance and range that his poetic mentor Wordsworth was just achieving in his late forties. Wordsworth's major work was already completed, summed and expressed in the published Poems of 1815 and in the unpublished and unrevised *The Prelude*. Keats's was just beginning; the great poems of the coming year, which found their public expression in the volume he published in 1820, left him ranking

1. Theodore Watts-Dunton (ed.), *Joseph and His Brethren with . . . a note on Rossetti and Charles Wells*, p. xlvi. "The poet believed—erroneously or not—that the hoax aggravated the malady." It is not clear whether or not Tom Keats ever knew that he had been hoaxed. Keats had had his suspicions, and communicated them to George before the latter left England, for he later wrote of "that degraded Wells", assuming that George would agree with the epithet. *Letters*, II, 82.

2. *Letters*, I, 186.

with both the older and the newer poets of the Romantic epoch as a major and eternal force. The trial, experiment and effort of the past years, with all their mistakes and misapprehension, saw him now ready to take his rightful place.

PART III

THE LIVING YEAR

Chapter 17

THE CLOUDY KINGS

"Meanwhile Love kept her dearly with his wings,
And underneath their shadow fill'd her eyes
With such a richness that the cloudy Kings
Of high Olympus utter'd slavish sighs"

– Translated from Ronsard, by JOHN KEATS

KEATS'S visits to the Reynolds household in Little Britain, to Fleet Street, and to the Dilke household at Wentworth Place, could only be brief respites from Tom's bedside. It seemed to him that he was caught in exactly the same trap that he had broken away from, nearly two years before, when he decided to give up surgery. Then he had felt the dangers of identifying himself too closely with the patient, in a self-destroying sympathy that should be reserved only for poetry. Now a sick brother's identity pressed on his own and pulled on his senses as if they were bell-ropes. This was worse even than the sympathy he might have felt for the struggling patient on the operating table under his surgical knife. Not only was Tom his own flesh and blood; for all his hearty and open commerce of thoughts and ideas with George, Tom was the brother who touched his deeper chords, and to whom he could speak, as Wordsworth had spoken to his own brother John, in the silent language of poetry. Besides, behind the thin mask of Tom's attenuated features lurked other faces—a mother who had returned home only to take to her bed and die, a tall uncle in uniform who had ceased to visit his small nephews at school.

It was no wonder that Keats's reaction to this was one of self-preservation, or rather the preservation of his poetic self. All poets in a crisis have this iron sense of values; in the long run, poetry must be served. It is a difficult decision to explain to non-poets, and Keats, though reviewing the situation frankly to Dilke, to whom he wrote on 20 September, felt some sort of apology necessary: "if I think of fame of poetry it seems a crime to me, and yet I must do so or suffer—I am sorry to give you pain—I am almost resolv'd to burn this—but I really have not self possession and magninimity enough to manage the thing othe(r)wise—" Quoting the 9th Book of *Paradise Lost*, which he was studying closely as material for *Hyperion*, Keats described his dilemma as "the hateful siege of contraries"; to the same passage in Milton's poem,

which he marked heavily, he had appended a marginal note, which, though
probably written earlier, includes words that sum up his own sensations at the
bedside of his brother: "Whose spirit does not ache at the smothering and
confinement—the unwilling stillness—the "waiting close"?"[1]

Keats himself knew that there was only one cure for this sensation. If he
allowed it to grow for a moment, he would be subject to one of his attacks of
"horrid Morbidity", and so, he may have argued, would be of even less use
to Tom. In the past, even from boyhood, he had eased the force of such
attacks by pouring out his feelings to Tom and George. Now Tom himself
was too ill, and George was in America. Keats was medically certain about
the benefits of poetic composition for his condition. He put his case perfectly
plainly in a letter to George three months later. "I feel I must again begin with
my poetry—for if I am not in action mind or Body I am in pain—".[2] To
Dilke, who did not have George's background of family insight into his case,
Keats now gave a more defensive explanation of his decision: "although I
intended to have given some time to study alone, I am obliged to write, and
plunge into abstract images to ease myself...".[3] A week before he had
announced in his rhodomontade to the astonished Woodhouse that he
intended to write no more; now his decision justified Hessey's description of
him on the same occasion as "a man of fits and starts".[4] The abstract images
into which he now plunged were the opening lines of the long-meditated
Hyperion.

In point of fact, the reluctance to start the poem which he expressed to
Dilke seems only half real. Keats had made extensive preparation for the
poem. For the last year he had soaked himself in *Paradise Lost* and for the
last few months in Dante's *Inferno*. A quotation from Dante's *Inferno*,
Canto 17, in the same letter to Dilke probably represents the point he had
reached in Cary's translation.[5] He had widened his dramatic scope by continual and intense reading of Shakespeare; he had enlarged his conception of
Wordsworth, in spite of personal disillusion, to appreciate "his more remote
and sublimer muse". He had studied Homer, Hesiod, Ovid and others in
translation. He also had received a recent stimulus in the copy of the works of
Ronsard, which Woodhouse had just lent him at Hessey's, with Ronsard's
classical ode to Michel de l'Hopital and its catalogue of the rebel Titans'
names; he had delved back into his schoolday reading, including Lempriére
and Tooke's *Pantheon*, to which he had added to some effect a book of the
same nature and title, the *Pantheon* compiled by William Godwin under the
pseudonym of Edward Baldwin. Even a curious book, Davies's *Celtic
Researches*, connecting the Greek Titans with the Druids, was pressed into
service. Nor was his agitation over Tom the sole spring-board from which
he launched this heavy load of preparation into the abstract space of poetry—

1. KHM, No. 24.   2. *Letters*, II, 12.   3. *Letters*, I, 369.
4. JKLY, 4.   5. *Letters*, I, 368; MOK, 19.

"abstract" is the word he always used to describe *Hyperion*, stressing the philosophic and not the merely narrative intent of the poem. He even confessed to Dilke, in a letter which is notably light-hearted when it leaves the topics of Tom and poetry, that his feelings might be due to nervousness from taking large doses of mercury. They were also due to another cause, which he did not mention to the married ears of Dilke. A day or so later, Reynolds, who had written Keats a letter from his fiancée's home in Devonshire, was allowed to hear more explicit details:[1]

I never was in love—Yet the voice and the shape of a woman has haunted me these two days—at such a time when the relief, the feverous relief of Poetry seems a much less crime—This morning Poetry has conquered—I have relapsed into those abstractions which are my only life—I feel escaped from a new strange and threatening sorrow.— And I am thankful for it—There is an awful warmth about my heart like a load of Immortality.

Poor Tom—that woman—and Poetry were ringing changes in my senses—

"That woman" was, of course, Reynolds's own cousin, Jane Cox.[2] Keats was careful not to name her in case news of his temporary infatuation should get back to the prying Misses Reynolds and add zest to their feud against their cousin. Yet short-lived as it may have been, the incident propelled him into poetry. He translated a sonnet of Ronsard, delighting himself[3] in the line

Love poured her Beauty into my warm veins

which echoed his description to Reynolds of Miss Cox's effect on him, while the first "Goddess of the infant world" to appear very early in *Hyperion* had the statuesque imperial eastern beauty of Miss Cox, and the deep rich contralto of her voice,

In solemn tenour and deep organ tone.[4]

It is an extraordinary concrete instance of the way Keats was able to sublimate the immediate personal physical experience into the abstract and general picture that he required for this type of poetry. "Poetry has conquered", he said; it would be more true to say "Keats has conquered".

The whole opening of *Hyperion*, in fact, shows Keats making all the elements of his conscious literary "study" entirely his own from the instant he sets pen to paper. The poetic setting for the defeated Saturn in the early

1. *Letters*, I, 370.
2. Ward surprisingly thinks it was Fanny Brawne, 216, 428, n. 8, and 429, n. 9, and therefore has to suppose that his temporary infatuation with Jane Cox (*Letters*, I, 395) took place *after* he fell in love with Fanny. In fact, the language of *Letters*, I, 370 and 395 clearly describes physically the same woman, one of quite a different type from Fanny.
3. *Letters*, I, 369.
4. Keats's MS has "tune". Cf. "she kept me awake one Night as a tune of Mozart's might do", *Letters*, I, 395.

lines of *Hyperion* is unmistakable; it is "the mournful wood" of Cantos 14 and 15 of the *Inferno*, which Keats had just been reading;[1] along the sandy margins, in Dante's epic, tread the restless ghosts whose sin was homosexuality, culminating in the brilliant and proud master of Dante himself, the teacher Brunetto Latini. A sense of unjust fate and noble defiance hangs about these "inhabitants of the Sulphur Kingdom", which Keats absorbed even through Cary's prosaic translation. It is a wonderful assimilation of atmosphere, which was hardly equalled until another great poet, in a totally different way, performed the same feat, from exactly the same source, in the famous second section of T. S. Eliot's *Little Gidding*; indeed, Eliot's "compound ghost" with the "brown baked features" is not perhaps even so fully realized as Keats's creation of the dispossessed Saturn.

Keats's eternal figure gains strength too from the fact that Saturn as well is a "compound ghost". If the old Titan's setting is transmuted Dante, his nature and appearance is transmuted Shakespeare. For sustenance for his work, for relief from immediate circumstances, Keats's instant resource was to go to the greatest of the tragedies. On Sunday evening, 4 October, he was reading *King Lear*, so overcome by the simple words "poore Tom" that he added the date beside them in the margin of his folio copy. The opening of *Hyperion* is permeated with echoes of the play, even with those of Keats's sonnet upon it which he had written earlier in the year. Once more it is completely transmuted into Keats's own style, but it serves as a reminder of the essentially dramatic nature of this poem, recognized unconsciously by Byron when he compared it with Aeschylus.

Although Keats felt he had been hurried by circumstances into starting the poem before he was fully prepared, it was easier for him to do so since his plan was not apparently as episodic as that of *Endymion*. Instead he plunged dramatically into the middle of events. The story of the legend, as he found it in his various sources, was the overthrow of the older Titans, led by Saturn, at the hands of the younger Gods, led by Jove. There then followed an unsuccessful counter-revolution by the Giants, as distinct from Titans, to restore Saturn. At the beginning of *Hyperion*, Saturn has already been dethroned; at the beginning of Book Two, his chief follower Oceanus has not only been supplanted, but has become reconciled to his new condition. Both Titans and Giants, whom Keats mixed indiscriminately, are lying subjugated by the new Gods. The main action of the poem was now to be concentrated on the one Titan still reigning, Hyperion, and his dethronement by a newly-created God, Apollo. Keats was therefore able to turn what might have been unwieldy and formal into another experience upon the pulses. It has been finely observed that "the theme of *Hyperion* is the struggle of spiritual growth itself."[2] Under this scheme, Keats was able to make it the record of his own spiritual development. To do this, he juggled the time-sequence of

1. MOK, 20-21.   2. Ward, 218.

the poem in opposite ways. To pass swiftly over the other Titans and Giants, he began the poem after their defeat; but in order to bring up the experience and nature of Apollo, he made this coincide with an earlier time when Apollo was not yet a God, so that he could show the pains of his assumption of Godhead.

By this concentration, Keats was able to make his main theme embody his own experience and thought since he had first conceived the poem. In a sense, both Apollo and, what is more, Hyperion too are Keats. Apollo is the new Keats of painfully-won experience supplanting the old Keats of morbid fears and forebodings. Hyperion is the old Keats, who had seen the small bird as a "disguis'd demon", only written large—

> But horrors portion'd to a giant nerve
> Oft made Hyperion ache.

The poem as we have it, up to the godhead of Apollo, is the record of Keats himself from the beginning of *Endymion* to the greater self-knowledge and development through suffering he had reached in May 1818. It is many other things as well, though it is limiting to see any one as dominant. Some see Apollo, some see Hyperion as the chief protagonist; others find a key in the idea of human evolution expressed by Oceanus in Book Two. All these were by-products of Keats's own evolution in the long preparation for the poem. In a sense, this preparation was too long, for Keats evolved beyond the scope of his poem, and was ultimately unable for this reason ever to complete it. The idea that it was deliberately left unfinished, and that its incompleteness was part of its design, is contradicted by the fact that Keats chopped bits out of it to fit into his last comic poem, *The Cap and Bells*, just as he used up ideas in the same way from another relinquished poem, *The Eve of St. Mark*.[1] To him, it became a poem he had failed to finish, and he did not want it published with his other poems; indeed, he was only prevented by Reynolds from allowing it to appear as a make-weight in a volume by Leigh Hunt.

Whatever uncertainty there may still be about the theme, there is no doubt whatsoever about the style; and though Keats himself, a year later, grew dissatisfied with the technique, it stands apart from everything he had written before September 1818, and reaches what a modern critic has called "a new level of writing".[2] Keats in the opening of *Hyperion* is true to every axiom he had expressed in the past two years about the nature of great poetry. From the first line, the poem illustrates the "great charm in the opening of great Poems", which he had looked for and found in *Paradise Lost* and Dante's *Inferno*. Saturn's deep, sad and shady vale adds a new creation to our literature, and though Keats had noted how "Milton has put vales in heaven and hell with the very utter affection and yearning of a great Poet",[3] his own initial

1. MOK, 121.   2. Bate, Chapter XVI.   3. KHM, No. 24.

I*

setting for the epic will always remain both individually his, and one of the highest points in all writing:

> Deep in the shady sadness of a vale
> Far sunken from the healthy breath of morn,
> Far from the fiery noon, and eve's one star,
> Sat grey-hair'd Saturn, quiet as a stone,
> Still as the silence round about his lair;
> Forest on forest hung above his head
> Like cloud on cloud. No stir of air was there,
> Not so much life as on a summer's day
> Robs not one light seed from the feather'd grass,
> But where the dead leaf fell, there did it rest.
> The stream went voiceless by, still deadened more
> By reason of his fallen divinity
> Spreading a shade: the Naiad 'mid her reeds
> Press'd her cold finger closer to her lips.
>
> Along the margin-sand large foot-marks went,
> No further than to where his feet had stray'd,
> And slept there since. Upon the sodden ground
> His old right hand lay nerveless, listless, dead,
> Unsceptred; and his realmless eyes were closed;
> While his bow'd head seem'd list'ning to the Earth,
> His ancient mother, for some comfort.

The contrast here with the almost jaunty openings of *Endymion* and *Isabella* comes like a physical shock; one is at once impressed with a sensation of sheer weight. One piece of poetic technique has been noticed by many observers. Keats has wiped from his new vocabulary the adjectives ending or created to end in the weak "y" sound, and has anchored nearly every line to a final "d" in one word or another. Springing partly from this, another dominant effect can be noticed. If Keats had studied musical composition, so he himself believed, "he had some notions of the combinations of sounds, by which he thought he could have done something as original as his poetry". With that in mind, and remembering how many musicians have composed on a set combination of notes, such as BAC, it is possible to see these opening lines of *Hyperion* as a deliberate play on the S and D of "sad", the theme-word announced in the very first line. A mixture of these two consonants dominates these lines, and keeps the original word continually tolling through them like a bell. There is no difficulty in supposing this process to be present in his mind, since it is recorded that "One of his favorite topics of discourse was the principle of melody in Verse". Bailey, who noticed this, added that "Keats's theory was worked out by himself"—that is, in his own verse—and he actually took these first lines of *Hyperion* to "illustrate his theory, as I understood him."[1]

What Bailey chiefly understood of Keats's theory was, however, how it applied to the interchange and variation of vowel-sounds, and modern prosodists have carried his observations further, using here again this same passage. There is no doubt that from these lines in *Hyperion* onward, Keats's use of contrasting and linked vowel-sounds and even more of a very subtle assonance give a consistent individuality to his work which has only been heard fitfully or fortuitously before. There is still the drive and spontaneity of his creative urge, the fever that he felt in himself all through this living and creative year that was just beginning; but the conscious preparation which he had steadily planned from early in 1818 was now beginning to bring its reward in a style at last suited to the height of its argument. Keats the poet has begun to equal Keats of the imaginative and philosophic prose as it had appeared in his letters over the past year.

There was an added reason why he should concentrate meticulously on technique at this exact moment. About 27 September, the long-awaited April number of *The Quarterly Review* appeared. The editor, William Gifford, had evidently been unmoved by Taylor's "Representations in Favour of Keats"; he had given *Endymion* for review to John Wilson Croker, the last critic to appreciate the poem's merits or to overlook its faults. This was a very different matter from the merely personal abuse of *Blackwood's* or the pointless vulgarities of *The British Critic*. A certain heavy-handed humour and wilful misunderstanding was the common stock of both the "Tory" school of literature and of the *Examiner* critics such as Hazlitt, however much they might claim to be free from prejudice. Croker's misrepresentation of Keats was nothing like as bad as Hazlitt's misrepresentation of Coleridge. The style, which could be discounted as common literary usage, was less damaging than the fact that Croker's opinions seemed intended as genuine criticism which would find an echo in a large audience. Many of the more old-fashioned readers of poetry at that time would echo Croker's plea for "a complete couplet inclosing a complete idea", which was still held to be a condition of the form Keats was using, and which they would find carefully observed whenever Byron used couplets. The deadly half-truth that "Mr. Keats had been amusing himself and wearying his readers with an immeasurable game at bout-rimés" is, though at several removes, a sneering version of Keats's own resolve at setting-out the poem—"I must make 4000 Lines of one bare circumstance and fill them with Poetry". What Croker denied was the powers of imagination and invention by which Keats had hoped to bring this task off successfully; indeed, he claimed not to have got through more than the first book, taking as part excuse Keats's own deprecation of his work in the unfortunate preface. What he did not deny—and

1. KC, II, 277.

this is a point in his criticism too often overlooked then and since—was that Keats had "powers of language, rays of fancy, and gleams of genius—he has all these". This was a remarkable admission by a critic of any stamp when applied to a modern, young and unknown poet. Unfortunately most readers would have any favourable impression they might gather from these words blotted out by the subsequent sentences, in which Keats was dismissed as mainly an inferior "copyist of Mr. Hunt". The Cockney token put in this scale would far outweigh any genuine though reluctant recognition of potential genius.

Probably because of this back-hander at Hunt, the review was generally thought to be by Gifford himself, and such was the editor's unpopularity that it earned Keats some support, and, hearteningly, even some mature and well-based notices. The first of these was probably by John Scott, in a long letter to *The Morning Chronicle* of 3 October, signed by initials. Keats had been wrongly led by Hunt to suspect that Scott was the originator of the "Cockney School" label, but he could have no complaint of the sensible and balanced criticism which this letter contained; his own comment was quick and generous. "J.S. is perfectly right in regard to the slipshod Endymion", he wrote to Hessey on 8 October, the same day on which an unknown R.B., probably a friend of Woodhouse, also defended the poem in the *Chronicle*. Keats's friends, as might be expected, did not take Scott's moderate and ultimately more valuable attitude. Reynolds wrote an indignant panegyric in a West Country magazine, to which Hunt gave wider circulation in *The Examiner* for 11 October, while even the sober Woodhouse was moved to dismiss Gifford, whom he believed to be the reviewer, as "a cobbling, carping, decasyllabic, finger-scanning-criticaster".

The most important by-product of this war of critics was the new maturity Keats showed toward it, matching the new strength of his verse. It would be difficult for some unfortunate seeds not to be sown in his mind; later remarks show that he was affected by Reynolds's intemperate and uncalled-for comparison with Byron: "Lord Byron is a splendid and noble egotist; ... he is liked by most of his readers, because he is a Lord ... Mr Keats has none of this egotism." Such a review, belittling most other modern poets, might in fact have tempted Keats to egotism, but his reactions showed immense commonsense. He wrote to Hessey, "My own domestic criticism has given me pain... beyond what Blackwood or the Quarterly could possibly inflict", and, as if to show there was no false modesty, he added, "and also when I feel I am right, no external praise can give me such a glow as my own solitary reperception & ratification of what is fine."[1] Moreover, while recognizing its imperfections, he had no false regrets about writing *Endymion* in the way he had done.

1. *Letters*, I, 374.

I have written independently *without Judgment*—I may write independently *& with judgment* hereafter.—The Genius of Poetry must work out its own salvation in a man: It cannot be matured by law & precept, but by sensation & watchfulness in itself— That which is creative must create itself—In Endymion, I leaped headlong into the Sea, and thereby have become better acquainted with the Soundings, the quicksands, & the rocks, than if I had stayed upon the green shore, and piped a silly pipe and took tea & comfortable advice.

Such a healthy attitude, reported to Taylor by Hessey, led the publishers to hope that Keats's next book would do all three of them full credit.[1]

The cornerstone of the new volume was still steadily being laid; for in spite of praise or blame, his own essential loneliness and Tom's illness, Keats went on writing *Hyperion*. Even the slow rate enforced on him, one-fifth of his normal writing-time for *Endymion*, benefited the massive and dense structure of the poem. With Shakespeare, Milton and Dante beside him, he assimilated all elements to give the first 150 lines the impress of his new struggle for individuality, the "identity" which he was so concerned to analyse for himself this autumn. He was doubly alone now, for the first time in his life. Keats, like Saturn in the poem, was questioning who and what he was. In the middle of October, the first letter from George in America gave him relief, and he plunged into a reply. He ran through the events of the last month or so, dismissing the *Blackwood's* and *Quarterly* affairs with the calm assertion, "I think I shall be among the English Poets after my death."[2] He gave news of acquaintances, George's relations-in-law, the Dilkes, and a frank account of his own two-days' attraction by Jane Cox. He then retailed for George's benefit a summary of the political news, at home and abroad, from *The Examiner* of the past few weeks,[3] and greeted the news that Georgiana was going to have a baby with a little ode of his own based on Milton's *Ode on the Morning of Christ's Nativity*, which he was reading together with *Paradise Lost*. He confessed his own sense of isolation, confined to what he called his own whims and theories, though on 16 October he broke off to have an evening's talk with Brown and Dilke, who had been away over a month; at Wentworth Place they discussed subjects ranging from metaphysics to fagging at schools. He felt a curious urge to offset the fever of poetry by writing a prose tale.

Restlessness and a certain weariness mark the letter, and are reflected in those parts of *Hyperion* that Keats was now writing. This was no bad atmosphere in which to introduce the Titan lord of the Sun, uneasy at the omens of his own dispossession by Apollo. Keats identified his own condition with that of Hyperion in a way that he was to expound to Woodhouse a week or so later. It is not only that Hyperion stands for the old "morbid" Keats. Quite trivial characteristics of his own recent life are translated into epic terms; for

1. KHM, No. 63.   2. *Letters*, I, 394.
3. *Letters*, I, 397; compare E, No. 561, p. 162 and No. 563, p. 646.

example, his self-induced mercurial poisoning took stature as the

Savour of poisonous brass and metal sick

experienced by the Sun God. The sense of brooding expectation, of struggling under some growing burden of inevitable loss, the day-by-day pressure of Tom's weakening state, enhanced the psychological portrayal of Hyperion's dilemma, and give a truth that is not merely external to the story. Hyperion suffers as Keats had suffered in the past, but also in terms of his present circumstances. There is, however, at this point, the beginning of a very slight decrease in the power of the verse, caused by his own distractions of spirit. Here Keats begins to slacken the masterly synthesis of epic styles he had managed to maintain, and falls back on the more artificial and direct imitation of Milton which he was afterwards to condemn in the poem; indeed when he finally gave up all attempts to revise the work a year later, it was at this precise point that he threw up the sponge. His mood over this passage has misled many later critics, who have compared the poem with *Paradise Lost*; for it is not until the second half of Book One and the very beginning of Book Two that the influence of Milton's blank-verse style is at all obsessive. It is only here that the extended and separate similes, so characteristic of Milton, are present in such comparisons as

> like anxious men
> Who on wide plains gather in panting troops,
> When earthquakes jar their battlements and towers.

or again, even more plainly,

> For as in theatres of crowded men
> Hubbub increases more they call out 'Hush!'

Here too, concentrated in the small space of a hundred or so lines, are the Miltonic inversions, repetitions and actual echoes which critics have pointed out, and which Keats himself finally repudiated without seeing how small a proportion of the poem they form. It is probable that the strain of this time in his life left a permanent bad taste for him about this section.

His natural and instinctive resource for any such feeling was to read Shakespeare. In his folio, he turned on from *King Lear* to *Troilus and Cressida*, marking and annotating it in the margin just as he had done with the former play. His life, when he could shake it free from the tragedy of Tom, was full this autumn of questioning about human relationships, most of all those between men and women; he was searching for some answer to these problems through his reading of this particularly haunting play. His letters at this time are packed with quotations and echoes of the play to an extent that precludes any memory from his 1817 readings in his other edition of Shakespeare; for such a thick concentration of images from the play, he could only have had it at his elbow as part of his deliberate "study" for

Hyperion, and this is borne out by the manuscript of that poem. Just as the start of Book One had been permeated, as far as concerns Shakespeare, with *King Lear*, so the end of that book, and most of the next, is shot through with *Troilus and Cressida*. The debates of the Titans are the play's debates of the Greeks and Romans. Ulysses's speech from Act I on Degree is echoed by the puzzled address of Saturn to his followers, while the famous reply of Oceanus, which many have seen as the key to the meaning of *Hyperion*, is once again an extension of the Act 3 speech of Ulysses, in which Keats at Oxford had found such "practical wisdom". Just as Ulysses stresses to Achilles the inevitable march of events which will push him on one side if he falters, so Oceanus develops to Saturn, using almost the same phrases and cadences, a doctrine of inevitable evolution of which they are a part and from which they are suffering:

> So on our heels a fresh perfection treads,
> A power more strong in beauty, born of us
> And fated to excel us, as we pass

Keats, speaking through Oceanus, in the philosophy of wisdom through suffering which he had been developing ever since the spring, counsels acceptance of the inevitable and even joy in it, since it is an essential part of nature. The protests, which follow in the rest of the book, through Clymene who is a kind of pathetic Cassandra, and Enceladus who is a kind of more vocal Ajax, are all based, even though remotely, on the central debate of Shakespeare's play—can we take positive action in the face of inevitable change and alteration, typified by Shakespeare in the conception of "Time", the monster with the devouring wallet?

The imagery of this part of *Hyperion* has in its purely physical descriptions another permeating literary influence, which also runs all through his letters. This is the imagery of three walking-tour letters from Keats to Tom which he now decided to make up into a parcel and send to George, since he had no time to copy them. These, the first three of his Lake District and Scottish tour,[1] abounded in natural description of the Lakes and the Lowlands, the view down Windermere, the Ambleside waterfalls, the prehistoric "Druid" stones on the Penrith road, the ascent of Mount Skiddaw, and the Kirkcudbright country. This was imported almost wholesale into the Titans' den of Book Two, elbowing aside the more epic reminiscences of Milton and Dante,[2] with no sense of incongruity. It had been part of Keats's deliberate purpose, in going on the walking-tour, to absorb mountain-scenery into his experience as the epic background for his poem. Less premeditated, but just as clear, were Keats's borrowings at this point from William Beckford's popular oriental tale, *Vathek*. From this romance, he transmuted the fiery palaces of Eblis, Lord of the Underworld, to be the glowing corridors of the Titan of the Sun:

1. JKLY, 24.   2. MOK, 25-26.

On he flared,
From stately nave to nave, from vault to vault,
Through bowers of fragrant and enwreathed light,
And diamond-paved lustrous long arcades,

The subterranean caverns of the mountain of Kaf, where Beckford described "the pre-adamite kings" stretched in torture, became the caves where Keats's Titans

Were pent in regions of laborious breath;
Dungeon'd in opaque element, to keep
Their clenched teeth still clench'd, and all their limbs
Lock'd up like veins of metal, crampt and screw'd;
Without a motion, save of their big hearts . . .

Yet the pain in this passage comes from more than literature; the sense of overwhelming strain is Keats's own, as he watched the tormented bed of his brother, and wrote it down in epic terms.

Something clearly had to break such strain. Somehow, perhaps through Haslam, who was alarmed at the effect on Keats,[1] some relief nursing was obtained. Keats was able to leave the close atmosphere of the small lodgings more often in the week beginning Monday 19 October than he had done ever since his return from Scotland. The week's visiting began inauspiciously in a row with Abbey over Fanny having called on the Dilkes when she had last come to see Tom; it is ironic that Abbey's prohibition of any further visits to Tom probably saved her life, though like Haslam he knew no more than the commonly observed fact that a person who nursed a case of tuberculosis often succumbed to the same disease. Abbey's refusal to let Fanny see Tom had, of course, nothing to do with her brother's illness, but sprang from his own suspicion of Keats's literary friends. Thursday 22 October was a more fruitful day, beginning with an encouraging letter from Woodhouse, who was back at the Temple. Keats dined in Town with George's mother-in-law and went on to Hessey in Fleet Street, perhaps hoping to meet Woodhouse. In fact, he met Hazlitt, who was there getting an advance on his next book. He and Keats walked up to Covent Garden, where Hazlitt was going to play racquets. On the next day he looked up Hunt, a visit damped a little by the presence of Ollier, who, Keats must have felt, may have been glad he was not the publisher of *Endymion*, though Hessey had hopefully thought the controversy had caused the book to "move". On Saturday 24 October, after scribbling these events into the letter to George, which was now becoming a journal after the style of his Scotch letters to Tom, he was able to leave the latter and dash off to Town again. He returned late that night to chronicle an adventure post-haste for George.

1. Sharp, 37.

Walking along Theobald's Road, Bloomsbury, towards Lamb's Conduit Street, he met Isabella Jones walking alone in the other direction. He passed her, hesitated, and turned back to join her. She seemed glad to see him, and allowed him to accompany her on the not very salubrious way, "sometimes through shabby, sometimes through decent Streets", to Islington. The friend on whom she called there was probably the wife of Lieutenant-Colonel Thomas Green, a retired Indian Army officer; she became, like Isabella, an admirer of *Endymion*, and remembered her meeting with the young poet with a kind of quizzical playfulness, which may have been caused by the equivocal situation in which she found him on her doorstep, escorting unannounced her attractive friend. After the call, Keats and Isabella retraced their steps till, a short way past where they had met, she led him in the direction of Queen's Square along Gloucester Street, where she lodged at No. 34,[1] close to the square. It was a fashionable address at the time for people of good taste and modest means, specially recommended for the pure air and open outlook to the heights of Hampstead and Highgate, and full of good-class furnished apartments. Keats had, as he frankly said, his "guessing" at work what this might lead to, as he went up to her well-furnished rooms, whose sophisticated interior, unlike the slightly threadbare middle-class surroundings in which most of his friends lived, provoked from him the exclamation, "a very tasty sort of place". The neatly-panelled walls, the books, pictures, piano, Aeolian harp, statuettes, caged-birds, above all the open display of expensive drinks which showed a familiarity with the habits of male visitors—did this suggest, as it seemed, the usual ambiance of an intelligent and well-protected kept-woman, or had he "in fancy wrong'd her", as he knew he was liable to do with women, by assuming that those who were not outwardly pure were necessarily unchaste. At all events, since he had felt a warm physical desire toward her seventeen months before, and kissed her then, he felt it would be "living backwards" not to kiss her now. She felt otherwise, and put him off with a tact which he appreciated, though it puzzled him. Her conversation hinted at a complicated situation. She now let him know that she had been "in a room"—that is, at a social gathering,— with Reynolds and George Keats himself. She added the wish which puzzled Keats, though he honoured it by not revealing her name even to George, that they "should be acquainted without any of our common acquaintance knowing it". Whether Taylor's passionate sonnet to Isabel was in her mind, or the irascible figure of her elderly friend Donat O'Callaghan lurked in the background of this prohibition is impossible to say; in any case, Keats apparently knew of neither's claim to her, and accepted her request as part of the "enigma" he had always felt her to be. She showed a close interest in him, asked about Tom, sent the invalid a grouse for dinner, and took down

1. Or possibly No. 4. The 3 and the 4 in Keats's hand (*Letters*, I, 402) are very widely spaced, and there seems to have been an attempt to cross out the 3.

the Well Walk address, which Keats had not given her at Hastings, for sending further delicacies. "She contrived" said Keats, "to disappoint me in a way which made me feel more pleasure than a simple kiss could do", though, he added to George, "I have no libidinous thought about her." He even paid her the compliment of comparing her with George's wife, his ideal of "disinterestedness" in women. "I expect to pass some pleasant hours with her now and then", he remarked.[1]

The exact nuances of a personal relationship are impossible to catch without closer evidence than we have here; all that can be said is that the encounter had a deep and almost symbolic meaning for Keats. It seemed chance and yet foreordained, like the vision of the unknown lady at Vauxhall which had haunted his poetic imagination for so many years. In fact, the precise nature of the pleasant hours Keats spent and continued to spend with Isabella is not so important as the stimulus her existence gave to his poetry and poetic thought. It is no coincidence that directly after this meeting, at this week-end, he sat down to pour out both to his brother and to Woodhouse his deepest feelings about his own essential character as a poet.[2] Isabella was like a visitant from another world, or rather from *the* world, the state of man's worldly existence which was the constant subject-matter for the poet, but of which he was not himself ever a real part, always remaining an outsider looking in. Her maturity, though she appeared of an age similar to his, her apparent material security and control over circumstances, contrasted in his mind with the ferment and material uncertainty of the poet's life as he understood it. In Platonic terms, she and her like, the majority of mankind, were in a state of being; he and his kind of poetical character (unlike what he termed "the Wordsworthian or egotistical sublime") were in a perpetual and unformed state of becoming. She was poetical, that is, fit subject for poetry, as were the sun, the moon, the sea and other men and women. They were fixed, "creatures of impulse", with formed and unchangeable attributes. "The camelion poet", by contrast, was "certainly the most unpoetical of all God's Creatures". That is, being unformed in personality, he was no fit subject for poetry. He had no identity, and only existed so far as he took on the nature of whatever he happened to be working on at the moment, "annihilated", as Keats said, by the varied presences of everyone else in society, even "in a room", a casual social gathering such as those that played such a part in Isabella's life.

In his letter to Woodhouse of the night of 26 October, Keats naturally stressed the characterless nature of his type of poet—"It has no character—it enjoys light and shade; it lives in gusto, be it foul or fair, high or low, rich or poor, mean or elevated—It has as much delight in conceiving an Iago as an Imogen." This emphasis was partly to excuse his exaggerated rhodomontade a month before when he had rashly said he would write no more poetry. "It

1. *Letters*, I, 402–403.   2. *Letters*, I, 386–388, 403–404.

is a wretched thing to confess; but it is a very fact that not one word I ever utter can be taken for granted as an opinion growing out of my identical nature—how can it, when I have no nature?" Woodhouse extracted the exaggeration from this statement, an exaggeration which he knew was meant to appease him, and produced from it what Keats really meant: "As a poet, and when the fit is upon him", commented Woodhouse to Taylor, "this is true . . . that he lives for a time in their souls or Essences or ideas—and that occasionally so intensely as to lose consciousness of what is round him." To George, writing on the same night, Keats went more deeply and perhaps a little more sincerely into the matter. He had begun the long journal letter in the middle of October with an affirmation of his close ties of feeling with George, made stronger now that Tom was dying; he ended it, in the last week of the month, with a personal confession that went beyond what he could write to a friend. He repeated his sense of annihilation by ideas, poetry and visions of beauty, which would always outweigh even a strong human relationship backed by the most propitious material circumstances—Isabella and perhaps even Jane Cox were surely in his mind here; but he told George what his brother must have already observed that as a poet, he was far from being blotted out by the company "in a room". He knew in himself the iron isolation of a poet, who would go so far in identifying himself with others, but always kept his unique personality intact—"there" he wrote, "they do not know me not even my most intimate acquaintance. I give into their feelings as though I were refraining from irritating (a) little child . . . because I have in my own breast so great a resource." This deeper account of Keats's involuntary loss of identity to great ideas, the stuff of poetry, and his secret and proud retention of it in human dealings, is more true than his more famous account of it to Woodhouse.

Unconsciously, though not for the first time, he was equating his own poetic nature with that of Shakespeare, whose "inate universality" he had just noted in the margin of *Troilus and Cressida*. Reading once more the scene between Ulysses and Achilles, he applied its wisdom to himself. The doctrine of human nature that Ulysses expounds is that no man really exists or can know himself except through others; he has, as Keats might have said, no self. Keats extended this idea to the self-loss of the poet during composition in a way that echoes this scene again and again.[1] Only twenty-three—he sealed his long letter to George on his birthday—and surrounded by every element of stress and tragedy, he felt in himself a Shakespearian confidence, in his own words,

> to bear all naked truths,
> And to envisage circumstance, all calm,
> That is the top of sovereignty.

1. MOK, 65–67.

Chapter 18

WHERE'S THE POET?

"Where's the Poet? show him! show him,
Muses nine! that I may know him!"

— Fragment, dated 1818

KEATS'S doctrine of the chameleon nature of the poet, and his knowledge of his own poetic integrity, expressed in his October letters, were put into a brief verse fragment which he wrote about this time:[1]

> Where's the Poet? show him! show him,
> Muses nine! that I may know him!
> 'Tis the man who with a man
>   Is an equal, be he King,
> Or poorest of the beggar-clan,
>   Or any other wondrous thing
> A man may be 'twixt ape and Plato;
>   'Tis the man who with a bird,
> Wren or Eagle, finds his way to
>   All its instincts; he hath heard
> The Lion's roaring, and can tell
>   What his horny throat expresseth,
> And to him the Tiger's yell
>   Comes articulate and presseth
> On his ear like mother-tongue . . .

Both the poor quality of the verse, and its abrupt ending, show the handicaps under which he laboured during the last month of Tom's illness. "The last days of poor Tom were of the most distressing nature" was how Keats described this month of November, and we may take the remark as an understatement. So too must be his comment that his studies and writing had been greatly interrupted. It is likely that a number of similar fragments, vaguely known to have been written in 1818, can be ascribed to this time, notably a curious piece of semi-dialogue entitled, though not by Keats, *Castle Builder,* possibly intended as a play, in more senses than one, on the initials and the habits of his hedonistic friend Charles Brown. All these have affinities, in one

1. It has affinities of imagery with *Hyperion,* Book 2, 68–72.

way or another, with *Hyperion*, Book 2, and all share the quality of hasty writing and lack of completion. The stray lyrics and pieces of blank-verse speech lumped together under the misleading title of *Extracts from an Opera* also have the same lack of concentration and purpose, though in these there is a glimmer of the theme of a great poem, a hint of the story of *The Eve of St. Agnes*, which may, in its turn, have been the subject of the mysterious prose-tale, much planned by Keats but never written. The wonder, of course, is not that there were so many of these bits and pieces unfinished or hardly begun, but that in a time of such stress he should write at all; most of all, that he should progress, however slowly, with *Hyperion*, and manage to bring Book 2 to a conclusion during this dark month. Admittedly, invention in the second half of this book begins to flag. Enceladus's speech falls back on conventional Miltonic phrasing, a sure sign of staleness, but the end of the book, the sudden reappearance of Hyperion, is rescued by an odd accident of inspiration. Keats found he had somehow overlooked one of his Scotch letters he had meant to enclose in his parcel to George. This was number seven in the sequence to Tom Keats, and specially important for *Hyperion*, since it was already associated with the poem in the description of Fingal's Cave beginning "Suppose now the Giants who rebelled against Jove had taken a whole Mass of black Columns . . ." The letter also went on to a verse description of the place, which Keats supposed haunted by the spirit of Lycidas. Both descriptions combine together in a scenery of rocky caverns and loud-meeting waters framing the huge and tragic figure with its golden curling locks.[1] Lycidas, "the Pontif priest, Where the Waters never rest" set the scene for what proved to be, in the epic, the final appearance of "the dejected King of Day".

It is difficult to dogmatize about the happenings of this month; Tom's final relapse and the need to struggle on with *Hyperion* left Keats hardly any time to communicate with his friends or even with his sister, except for a few brief notes. One may guess in it a culmination of a process of dissolution and rebirth which had been going on all autumn. It has been profoundly said that a part of Keats himself was dying before his eyes;[2] it was also a part of his poetic self, the last pulses of young naïve enthusiasm, which had been murdered by the reviews of the same autumn. Both these deaths led to a new life for him, as person and poet, but this could be only dimly guessed by him at the time. The strain of these weeks with every detail of death seen at close quarters was to dominate the rest of his own life and thought. At the time, there were minor flashes in the gloom; a complimentary sonnet and a gift of £25 arrived for him from an unknown admirer in Teignmouth. The name of the donor, "Mr P. Fenbank" did not strike Keats as genuine;[3] a possible

---

1. *Letters*, I, 348–350. 2. Ward, 221.
3. It was a local joke. Although a contemporary guide-book claimed that there had been "sanitary ventilation of the fens", much of Teignmouth still stood on the banks of a marsh.

guess, which he was too distracted to make, is that the gift and the poem were from Marian Jeffery. He also visited Rice, and had one or two other "rather pleasant occasions", which may have included some of the "pleasant hours" he had hoped to spend with Isabella Jones. Severn, himself recovered from a serious illness, came to see him and was shocked to see how much Keats's own vitality seemed to be absorbed by the dying Tom. He suggested Keats should rent a separate room nearby, to avoid continual contact, or get a nurse in; he even offered to take some night-duty himself, but Keats refused to allow any of these things.[1] Anxiety for Tom would have been ever present, and in the second half of the month everything he saw would have been a morbid reminder. The Queen had died on 17 November, London was plunged in mourning, and the theatres and places of public amusement were closed until 3 December.

This obscure month may conceal, and probably will conceal for ever, two highly-debated points in Keats's work and life. These are the writing of the sonnet *Bright Star* and his meeting with the person with whom that sonnet became most closely associated, Fanny Brawne. Briefly, what we know of the sonnet tells us that its first version could have been written early this November 1818, and that its final revised version was in Fanny Brawne's hands by the following April 1819.[2] This first version was more sensuous and direct than its better-known later form, though in parts more clumsily expressed:

> Bright star! would I were stedfast as thou art!
> Not in lone splendour hung amid the night;
> Not watching with eternal lids apart,
> Like Nature's devout sleepless Eremite,
> The morning waters at their priestlike task
> Of pure ablution round earth's human shores;
> Or, gazing on the new soft fallen mask
> Of snow upon the mountains and the moors:—
>
> No;—yet still stedfast, still unchangeable,
> Cheek-pillow'd on my Love's white ripening breast,
> To touch, for ever, its warm sink and swell,
> Awake, for ever, in a sweet unrest;
> To hear, to feel her tender-taken breath,
> Half-passionless, and so swoon on to death.

This version of the sonnet has, even more clearly than the later, close affinities with the style of his letters of the end of October; it echoes, as they do, *Troilus and Cressida* and the Scotch letters to Tom.[3] It chimes with much in *Hyperion* and in Keats's poetic thought at this time. In his letter to Wood-

---

1. Sharp, 37, though Severn's account of his own part, as always, is suspect.
2. See p. 299, below.   3. MOK, 54–68.

house, he had characterized the poet as the one person in the world who has nothing "unchangeable" about him; in the sonnet he hopes that in love at least he, as a poet, may be "unchangeable" like "The Sun, the Moon, the Sea and Men and Woman", to which he, in the sonnet, has added the symbol of the star. The wish for death, expressed more clearly in the last line of this sonnet than anywhere else in Keats, is also characteristic of this time when Keats told Severn "that not only was his brother dying, but that with the ebbing tide of life was going more and more of his own vitality."[1] The most evocative image in the whole poem, in its later version,

> The moving waters at their priestlike task

seems to have some close connection with

> the Pontif priest
> Where the Waters never rest

of the Scotch letter, No. 7 to Tom, which Keats had retained and used in *Hyperion*. No exact date can finally be given for the actual writing of this draft; it could have been written at almost any time between now and April,[2] when the revised and more decorous version was certainly in existence in Fanny Brawne's handwriting, yet the highest probability places it in November 1818.

The same obscurity attaches to Keats's first meeting with Fanny. Briefly again, the external signs point about equally to a meeting in this month of November, or one which had occurred earlier, perhaps in September. Her own account,[3] over twenty years later, is full of contradictions. She first stated that she did not know Keats when the review in *The Quarterly* appeared; but she seems to have thought the review was printed earlier in the summer than it was. She left it vague whether their meeting, at the Dilkes, was near the time of his return from Scotland or of his brother's death. Her description of Keats at the time of this meeting could be taken to apply to either period.

His conversation was in the highest degree interesting, and his spirits good, excepting at moments when anxiety regarding his brother's health dejected them.

She certainly seems to imply that she and her family were not still living at Wentworth Place when she met him, but visiting the Dilkes,[4] her actual

1. Sharp, 37.
2. The unusual word "Eremite", only used by Keats in *The Eve of St. Agnes* (composed 21 Jan.–4 Feb. 1819) and *The Eve of St. Mark* (13–17 February) may place it with these poems. Charles Brown dated it simply "1819", but his datings are not always accurate.
3. To Thomas Medwin in the 1840s. HBF, V, 184–186.
4. Confirmed by Dilke, ann. I, 241. It should be noted that first Dilke and then his wife were quite seriously ill from mid-August to the end of October, and both, at different times, were away recuperating. This would suggest a November meeting.

words being "at the house of a mutual friend, (not Leigh Hunt's)." As with the sonnet, one is left largely with probability, and on that score, there is one factor which makes an earlier time of meeting, before November, very doubtful. Keats makes absolutely no mention of her in his October letter to George. It has been argued that his feelings were too strong for him to do so; but since this letter began with the utmost protestation of faith and trust between him and George, echoing his earlier remark that the love between them was "passing the Love of Women", such a concealment seems unlikely. He went on, in the same letter, to describe to George with exceptional and detailed frankness every circumstance of his meetings in September and October with two other women, Jane Cox and Isabella Jones, and analysed his feelings for them at length. If he had really met Fanny Brawne before the letter was finished, it seems likely that he would have described her with equal frankness and detail. If, as has been claimed, he was so emotionally disturbed by her as to conceal her from George, it becomes almost incredible that his emotions should then run away with him so much about two other quite different women.[1]

All probability seems to point to the conclusion that he had not met Fanny in October, but did so soon after.[2] There is no doubt that the *Bright Star* sonnet has something to do with her; there also seems no doubt that it has something to do with the profound feelings on love and poetry called up by his encounter with Isabella Jones at the end of October. It is probably nearest the truth to regard the sonnet as addressed not specifically to one or the other, but as a summing-up of Keats's conflicting thoughts at that time on the claims of life and love on the poet's being.

During this November, an intimacy sprang up between Keats and Fanny, whose early progress was bound to be chequered. She afterwards reproached him for having been "an age" in showing his feelings; in fact, his duties at Well Walk left little time for visits to Wentworth Place or Elm Cottage, the house further up Downshire Hill, where the Brawnes had moved on Brown's return from Scotland late in September. However deep the first impression made on him by this striking young girl, he was quickly brushed off by a fancied rebuff from her, and burned, so he said,[3] a love-letter he had written. The huge reality of death was too close for him to respond to the minor manoeuvres and opening gambits of flirtation; Fanny went out of her way to flirt with Severn, who seems to have been present when they met, though she afterwards assured Keats "you must be satisfied in knowing I admired

1. "It is incredible, almost, that, in his affectionate frankness with his brother, he would ever have written thus of another woman, had he been already enamoured of Miss Brawne." H. Buxton Forman, *Letters of John Keats to Fanny Brawne*, xxxii.

2. Dilke, who believed Keats had taken Tom to Teignmouth again on his return from Scotland, thought that Keats came finally back to London and met her in October or November. Dilke, ann. I, 240–241.

3. *Letters*, II, 312.

you much more than your friend". Seldom, though, can a love affair have begun against a less propitious background, and neither can have known where it was to carry them.

On 18 November Tom Keats was nineteen; on 1 December he died, in the early hours. Keats at once wrote a note to their sister Fanny, posted it, and went on to wake Charles Brown in the half-light of morning. Keats took his hand, and Brown realized what had happened. He at once suggested that Keats should come and live with him, fearing a breakdown if he stayed alone among the associations of Well Walk. Keats's friends took over for him. Brown spread the news, Haslam wrote to George. The funeral was arranged on 7 December at St. Stephens, Coleman Street, under whose entrance-archway Keats had seen both his father and mother carried to burial. Every-one rallied round with a programme of social distractions, and for the next ten days a whirl of engagements and visits was arranged by Keats's friends to relieve his mind. "I have been everywhere". It was the Regency answer to grief, stoical and worldly. They took him to a bare-fisted boxing-match of thirty-four rounds down in Sussex, to see Kean in a new tragedy, and encouraged him to call everywhere, on the Reynoldses, the Dilkes, George's relatives-in-law, Hunt, Hazlitt, Haydon, Novello, Martin, and Charles Lamb. It was rough treatment for a threatened nervous collapse, but it seems to have worked. There is only one dubious anecdote that shows Keats feeling any tendency, at this time, to the depression and "morbidity" which his friends knew and feared for him.[1] His companionship with Brown and his sharing of the rooms at Wentworth Place was also on a practical and quite unsentimental basis. From the first, Brown's Scottish sense regarded Keats, though a friend, as "inmate", that is, paying lodger in his property; one of Keats's early calls after Tom's funeral was to draw some of the money George had left behind with Abbey, to meet the larger expenses of life with Brown, who expected a good rent and a contribution to the upkeep of a well-stocked cellar. The worldly Brown dominated, perhaps to good effect, the fortnight after Tom's death. The only signs of poetry in Keats's life were some mock-heroic lines of blank-verse, *Modern Love*, suggested by the lines on the She Dandy and the He Dandy, which had formed part of the Epilogue to the new tragedy of *Brutus* by John Howard Payne in which they had just seen Kean.[2] Brown was his constant companion everywhere, and never scrupled to use his caustic tongue about Keats's friends. Hunt took the two of them to Novello's, and Brown disliked the tinkling of Mozart on the piano and the endless facetious word-play so much that he communicated his

1. "After the death of Thomas Keats, a white rabbit came into the garden of Mr. Dilke, who shot the creature. Keats declared that the poor thing was his brother Tom's spirit." This anecdote was told by Dilke's nephew, John Snook, who claimed to have it from his uncle, and added further details. HBF, I, xxx.

2. E, No. 571, p. 773.

disapproval to Keats, who passed the unusually harsh judgment that Hunt was "disgusting in matters of taste and in morals". Hunt's gift of the recently-published Literary Pocket Book, containing two of Keats's own sonnets, brought an even harsher judgment on this latest literary effort—"full of the most sickening stuff you can imagine." The unlucky party inspired a splendid piece of comedy-writing by Keats for the benefit of Georgiana, in which he imagined Hazlitt at his most taciturn involved in one of these Hunt–Novello gatherings.[1] It was a sign of successful treatment that he could now write to George and Georgiana.

The letter began with the affirmation of a belief in immortality which had penetrated even the horror of Tom's death, and the statement of his own close sympathy with his remaining brother. It soon degenerated into a ragbag record of varied topics and events, matching his life at the moment, but in no way indicating that he felt out of touch with George.[2] Rather the reverse: Keats's letters to George now become the real diary of his life, a compendium of everything, momentous or trivial, just as it came along. There has seldom been such an unselfconscious stream of consciousness as this letter, marked B as the successor to his October letter, and the huge journal letter marked C, which Keats carried on for nearly three months, from mid-February to the first week in May, in which profound philosophy, self-revelation and the first drafts of poems alternate with gossip, trivial irritations or obsessions, and petty jokes. These letters, containing some of Keats's finest writing and thought, are as unpremeditated and spontaneous as life itself.

At the same time, it is worth noticing where exactly in the letters any event is placed. In part of this letter B, begun on 16 December, Keats gave a long description of a visit to the Brawne family at Elm Cottage with Brown on 11 December. Keats's picture of Fanny Brawne is in the section devoted to "a little quizzing" for his sister-in-law, and as part of his visit with Brown. Its light touch is the natural result of these two facts, its general impression perfectly sincere. Keats's physical description of Fanny at this time, small-built, delicate-featured, lively and unsentimental, with good figure and movements, and fashionably-dressed hair, is only a lighter version of his lines about her[3] nine months later:

> Deep blue eyes, semi-shaded in white lids,
> Finish'd with lashes fine for more soft shade,
> Completed by her twin-arch'd ebon brows;
> White temples of exactest elegance,
> Of even mould, felicitous and smooth;
> Cheeks fashion'd tenderly on either side,
> So perfect, so divine, that our poor eyes

1. *Letters*, II, 14.   2. As believed by Ward, 238, 246.
3. *Otho the Great*, V, v, 61-72.

Are dazzled with the sweet proportioning,
And wonder that 'tis so,—the magic chance!
Her nostrils, small, fragrant, faery-delicate;
Her lips—I swear no human bones e'er wore
So taking a disguise . . .

This young girl was a totally different type of woman from those of Keats's recent encounters. Jane Cox and Isabella Jones were formed and mature characters, the one "imperial" and self-assured, the other enigmatic and controlled. Fanny was, as he himself had been during his Byronic student days, unformed, fluid, and trying to work out a personality. She alternately repelled and attracted him, a dynamic combination; as he wrote

she is not seventeen—but she is ignorant—monstrous in her behaviour flying out in all directions, calling people such names—that I was forced lately to make use of the term *Minx*—this is I think not from any innate vice but from a penchant she has for acting stylishly.

"I am however tired of such style," Keats added, "and shall decline any more of it." Yet he had earlier indicated to George that he was not withdrawing from the contest, but had been drawn into the orbit of this new attraction. "We have", he said, "a little tiff now and then—and she behaves a little better, or I must have sheered off." On this visit, the rudeness was not all on Fanny's side. She introduced Keats and Brown to a clever but unattractive woman friend, Caroline Robinson, later the mother of a famous Latin scholar. Keats, egged on by Brown, behaved badly to Miss Robinson, teased her unmercifully, "and I think", he wrote with no apparent remorse, "drove her away". This mock-fighting reveals the unconscious sexuality of his early feelings towards Fanny, of which her own teenage bad behaviour was also a sign. Keats was more roused than he realized or allowed himself to say.

He was vulnerable to this mimic war because of Tom's death. All his senses, quickened by this experience, responded to her provocations. It was a natural rebound, and an extremely healthy one for the time. It helped his overstrained nerves and assisted his sanity. Whether he would have had such feelings for her under normal circumstances can never be known. Fanny Brawne's character has been endlessly debated, but at this heavily-charged moment in his life, it was a welcome and healthy element. The encounters in which every aspect seemed a symbol or portent gave way to one which had its feet firmly on the earth. Fanny was neither imperial nor enigmatic. She was a girl of her age; indeed she behaved as though she were younger than her age, which Keats underestimated by about a year and a half. Fanny at eighteen was a mixture of immaturity and precocious maturity. Her little sister Margaret, only half her age, was already showing the same qualities. Life had probably been hard for the children in the five lean years between their father's death and their uncle's will. Fanny had learnt to fight her own battles, and to make her own way; her aggressive tactics were part of this experience. Her talent in dressmaking extended beyond making her own clothes cheaply; it is clear she did this commercially for her friends and neighbours.[1] She may not have had much time for formal education, though she read intelligently, if not adventurously. Poetry did not feature much in her life; "I am not a great poetry reader", she confessed,[2] and when she wrote down a poem, she set it out awkwardly. She had, however, a quick wit and a quick ear, which gave her a talent for languages, and her opinions were pithily expressed. Her studied modish dress, her gift for repartee, and not least her brilliantly fair skin produced an effect described by several different people, at very different times of her life, as dazzling. All the same, she was still extremely young, and defensively conscious of her immaturity. Fanny capitalized some of the awkward edges of this immaturity by turning them skilfully to comedy, for which she had a natural theatrical bent[3]—"Comedy of all sorts pleases me", as she afterwards wrote. When Keats spoke of her "acting", he meant it literally, and showed it in the nickname he gave her, "Millamant", which was also suggested by her flair for fashionable dress. Above all, she was conscious of her effect on men, not in an assured but in an experimental way; she was trying them out, according to their own characters as she read them. If she spoke trivialities to Keats, it was a deliberate challenge to a clever young man. "Don't suppose", she again wrote, "I ever open my lips about books to men at all clever and stupid men I treat too ill to talk to at all."[4] She did not attempt, as Isabella was doing, to explore the literary interests of a young poet; she probed him for human weaknesses. He did not, according to Haydon, "bear the lovely little sweet arts of love with patience";[5] she soon found this, and set herself to try that patience. He gave as good as he got, although he saw through her with his slightly more mature insight; hence his comment that she did not behave like this "from any innate vice". All the same, he was intrigued, caught up and thoroughly taken out of himself. This was to prove a more serious diversion than prize-fights or shooting tom-tits on Hampstead Heath with Dilke.

Salutary as all this may have been for the ten days after Tom's funeral, it was exhausting, and had nothing to do with poetry. On Thursday 17 December, poetry literally knocked at the door. The postman Bentley staggered into Wentworth Place, after a frosty walk, with a clothes-basket of Keats's books from his old lodgings. Unpacking them was a reminder to Keats; he must begin to write again. "I live under an everlasting restraint—

---

1. See her pencil notes, KHM, No. 27.   2. LFBFK, 39.
3. She did not, however, inherit her acting talent, as sometimes said. Her aunt had married into a family with theatrical ancestors, and through this marriage Fanny was remotely connected with Beau Brummell.
4. LFBFK, 39.   5. Haydon, II, 316.

Never relieved except when I am composing—so I will write away." Brown had taken his rowdy nephews, who had added to the distractions of the past week, into the City to see the lions at the Tower, and the house was for once quiet. At last free from its forced damming-up, poetry poured out.

It was, in fact, of a far more fluid, less rigid kind than the monumental two books of *Hyperion*, whose manuscript Keats got out, and began to continue. The complete change in the third book from the "naked and grecian" style of the first two is remarkable. Though partly effective, as the introduction of a completely new character, Apollo, it was scarcely deliberate on Keats's part, but owed much to circumstances. Under the shock of death and his own nervous strain, reflected briefly in the opening lines of Book 3, his whole nature showed a regression to the themes and manner of his much earlier verse, which he associated with his boyhood and with his dead brother. This was reinforced by the arrival of their joint library of books, which they had read together by the fireside. Keats delved back into the romantic "Rowley" poems of Chatterton, who like Tom had died tragically and young. The lines of *Hyperion* on Apollo and the island setting of Delos have nothing to do with all his other sources for the poem, except perhaps with a half-remembered picture from Tooke's *Pantheon*; they are entirely in the manner and feeling of Chatterton's longer poems such as *The Battle of Hastings* and *The Story of William Canynge*,[1] and they mark the reappearance of Chatterton in Keats's reading and "study", which developed to such an extent that by next autumn he could actually say, again in part-reference to *Hyperion*, that Chatterton "is the purest writer in the English Language."[2] The first fifty lines of Book 3 are Keats's attempt to introduce that purity into his own verse, an attempt which culminated in *To Autumn*. It is unsuccessful here, not so much for itself, but because it does not marry with the style of the previous books.

In his new mood of release, Keats was not content with reaching his old standard of fifty lines of poetry a day. Picking out of the basket the Beaumont and Fletcher plays that George had given him,[3] he wrote in one of the volumes a little poem "on the double immortality of poets"

> Bards of Passion and of Mirth,
> Ye have left your souls on earth!

He did not stop there, but wrote a longer poem in the same metre. Here he seems to have been inspired by some more recent prose that had come his way, some of the "sickening stuff" Hunt had published in his *Literary Pocket-Book*. Hunt's essays on the seasons, which he thought well enough of himself to reprint in *The Examiner*, find a charming echo in Keats's lines on *Fancy*. The poem seems to contain too some echoes of his recent "sheering off" from Fanny Brawne. "Where's the eye, however blue", he wrote, "Doth not

1. MOK, 92–94. 2. *Letters*, II, 167. 3. KHM, No. 21.

weary?" The form of both these poems, which Keats called "a sort of rondeau", he borrowed from the "Dialogue between Pleasure and Pain", which he found at the beginning of *The Anatomy of Melancholy* by Robert Burton. Thus old memories, fresh experience, schoolboy reading and new "study" brought Keats back to the practice of poetry again after the sterile interregnum of life and death.

Once more he began to feel himself fully a poet, with poetry as his main concern. On the next morning he wrote, "look here Woodhouse—I have a new leaf to turn over—I must work—I must read—I must write—" and to George he added, "I cannot always be (how do you spell it) trapsing." Firmly, he turned down Woodhouse's suggestion that he should meet a lady novelist, Jane Porter, who had become a reader of *Endymion* through Keats's "old flame" Mary Frogley; he probably feared fresh complications in that direction. The only "trapsing" he allowed himself were several visits to his sister Fanny, three in ten days while she was on her Christmas holidays at Walthamstow; he took an interest in the pet livestock which filled her restricted life, and another delightful lyric, *I had a Dove*, was the result. The third visit, on 21 December, a bright frosty day, was a long one, and Keats had to rush back to Lisson Grove for a dinner appointment with Haydon. London was blanketed with fog that night and for the following two days, and Keats found, to his annoyance, it had brought on his sore throat again; however, even this fitted with the scheme of life he now proposed to himself, to work, to stay at home, and to let those who wished for his company come and see him.

They came, in more numbers than he may have wished, and partly for reasons which his good nature may not have divined. Hardly any of Keats's present acquaintance, except perhaps Haslam, knew much of his early background. What they did know led them to believe that there was still money in the family. George, after all, was known to have raised sufficient capital for his American adventure out of his inheritance. Keats was, of course, living on the surplus money George had been able to leave behind, but this fact seemed to be unknown to all Keats's present friends except perhaps Dilke. What they saw was a young man with apparent means of his own and generous habits, who would now surely have more from the same wealthy inheritance, as his share of Tom's property. The irony of the situation was that this would have been true, in a sense, if anyone had known of the Chancery Fund; for now, with Tom's death, over £1000 and considerable interest lay in Chancery as Keats's unclaimed share. The effect of Tom's death on Keats's friends was the same as if they had known of this fund, however, since Keats, with his habitual optimism about money, misunderstood and exaggerated what he might receive from Tom's share of the other fund, his grandmother's property administered by Abbey. Confusing capital with cash, he thought he should get about £700; the cash reality would have been about four-fifths of this, but he spoke to both Brown and Fanny Brawne as if the full £700 were already in his pocket, even planning with the former how to invest it.[1] To Haydon he wrote that he had enough private means to travel and study without employment for three or four years, that is at his habitual rate of about £200 a year.

It can hardly be wondered that nearly all his friends still regarded Keats as having great expectations in a material sense; it is no detraction from their genuine friendship to observe the quite objective fact that their interest in him quickened from this moment. There was some element of this in Brown's prompt assumption that Keats would be his paying guest; something of this must be suspected in the attitude of Mrs. Brawne to the "mad boy",[2] as she privately called him, when she displayed such affability to Keats, and encouraged his addresses to her elder daughter. There was also the curious reappearance of people whom Keats had not seen for years. A man named Archer, one of the Felton Mathew set, pestered Keats more than once at Wentworth Place, ostensibly with some business concerning Haydon. Shortly afterwards, Keats learned from Mathew's cousin, Kirkman, another visitant from the past, that the man had just jilted Caroline Mathew, giving the reason that he had not enough money for a wife. This inexplicable visitor—"Archer above all people" Keats wrote to George—was probably, as has been suspected, Archibald Archer, painter of religious and theatrical subjects. He was doing a picture of the interior of the Elgin Gallery at the time, which might explain his interest in Haydon, and he certainly changed his studios with great rapidity during these months, which might suggest he was running away both from debts and the Mathewses.

Archer was a small portent of what Keats might expect; the full omen was Haydon. Keats had let himself go in his company on 21 December. Some incident had occurred when Haydon was called away from the dinner-table, probably by an insistent dun. At all events, the painter summoned the young poet for another meeting after Christmas (to "bare" his "Soul"), and the request for money was not far off. Heavily in debt as usual, Haydon was about to incur further expenditure, in the cause of British Art, by putting on an exhibition of the work of his pupils Bewick and Charles and Thomas Landseer. He was scraping the barrel of all his friends, one of whom, an art-collector, came through with £200 early in the New Year.[3] Keats had indeed prudently advised Haydon to "ask the rich lovers of art first"; but he had less prudently offered his help when these ran out, and even more impulsively had spoken in terms of a loan of £500.[4] The newfound urge to get back to poetry again was once more being confounded by the ways of the world, and Christmas Eve actually saw Keats writing to borrow money from

1. KHM, No. 104. Its cash value deteriorated still further in the slump of 1819.
2. J. Richardson, *Fanny Brawne*, 30.   3. Haydon, II, 212.
4. KHM, No. 104.

his own publisher, as Abbey's business house was shut over the holiday.

It says much for Keats's unspoilt nature that he never realized the perils of being now an eligible young man, whose social assets might be exploited both by mothers of girls or by borrowers. One of his truly "disinterested" friends, the sweet-natured young Mrs. Dilke, commented on him at this time, "You will find him a very odd young man, but good-tempered and very clever indeed."[1] She was writing to her parents-in-law in Chichester, where Keats had been invited on a joint visit with Brown, which was to conclude with a stay with Dilke's married sister, Mrs. John Snook, just over the Hampshire border at Bedhampton. The idea was that Keats would be still further taken out of himself, "very much amused" by provincial life; Brown, who had gone on ahead, may have had his own ideas in introducing the attractive presence of a brilliant young friend to the old Dilkes, from whom he seems to have had financial expectations. Keats's life was tangled by this invitation, and by two conflicting ones for Christmas Day itself, one from Mrs. Reynolds, the other from Mrs. Brawne. He somewhat disingenuously chose the latter, and sowed the seeds of a lasting enmity between the Reynolds girls and Fanny Brawne, to say nothing of the respective mothers. It seems likely that this Christmas visit without Brown marked some emotional turning point in the sex-battle between Keats and Fanny, for she afterwards remembered it as "the happiest day I had ever then spent". This did not amount to an engagement, or anything like one. Fanny herself put their formal engagement much later; at this time he was still playing Mirabell to her Millamant, and their manoeuvres could still be summed up as "a chat and a tiff". Yet just as in Congreve's play, the two protagonists loosen the armour of wit, and let each other see their hearts, so some such shift occurred at this time to make Fanny remember it.

The renewed fine frosty weather tempted Keats further afield, and on 27 December he was dining with Haydon at the painter's urgent request. He lent him £30 to be going on with, which was probably not his money at all, but the sum he had extracted over Christmas from Taylor. The stage was set for a much larger loan, and Keats promised to see Abbey about his share of Tom's estate. The borrowing, in a sense, was not all on Haydon's side. His studio provided Keats with an experience which he chronicled as one of the most impressive of his life. "I do not think I ever had a greater treat out of Shakspeare" was his comment, and his idolatry of Shakespeare makes this a startling statement. It may seem even more startling that this experience was simply a folio of black and white prints, the recent engravings by Carlo Lasinio of the frescoes in the Campo Santo at Pisa,[2] but there were special

1. *Papers of a Critic*, 8.
2. *Letters*, II, 19, where Keats said they were "from the fresco of the Church at Milan". He may have glanced at the printer's name, Molini, to have got this impression. Haydon possessed a fine copy of the Lasinio engravings. Ian Jack, *Keats and the Mirror of Art*, 99.

reasons why Keats should be so susceptible to the subject of these pictures at this precise time. They are, in the main, an allegory of Pleasure and Life opposed by the reality of Pain and Death. It was this that sank so deeply into Keats's consciousness; matching his own experiences of the past months so exactly it became for him a new experience far more telling than a glance at the engravings would normally suggest. The black-and-white of the pages was coloured by Haydon's enthusiastic exposition of the principles of Italian art involved in them, but it was to receive an even richer colour in Keats's creative mind.

The immediate physical effect of the visit to Haydon was a less pleasant one. Not only did the sore throat return, causing Keats to postpone once more his journey to join Brown, but he was faced with the need, whenever well, to go into the City and investigate the financial affairs of his dead brother, an ordeal which he characterized himself as being "worse than any thing in Dante". The unhappy lawsuit had left a scar on his mind which winced at this mixture of money and family circumstances, and he found Abbey suspicious of proposals to realize large sums of capital quickly, before the bills of Tom's estate had been paid. What Keats wished was to be allowed to sit at home, seeing only Mrs. Dilke and her companionable cats,[1] writing to George, and occasionally visiting the Brawnes. His throat gave him part excuse for this in the first week of the New Year. He managed to copy for George his recent shorter poems, *Fancy*, *Bards of Passion*, and *I had a Dove*. He decided to keep George up to date with *The Examiner*, and copied from the issue of 27 December two passages from Hazlitt's lecture on the works of Godwin.[2] He may have been disturbed by the rough and ready state of American backwoods life painted by Birkbeck in earlier numbers of the paper,[3] for similar literary extracts now became a feature of his long journal letters to George and Georgiana; he intended also to copy George a political extract about Cobbett from *The Examiner* of 3 January, but had to send the letter quickly before he had time.

Keats was now anxious to get off to Chichester and Bedhampton, but on 7 January Haydon definitely took up his offer of a considerable loan, speaking in business terms of a two years' bond. More visits to Town ensued, and the whole matter began to irk Keats. On these visits, however, he was able to make one or two calls on Isabella Jones, and in her relaxed and indulgent atmosphere, he received a piece of inspiration which proved to be the complement to the "treat" he had received at Haydon's. Isabella's tastes tended to the fashionable quarter of the Gothic novel and the romantic

1. Robert Gittings, "Keats and Cats", *Essays and Studies*, 1962, Vol. XV.
2. There is no evidence that he copied from a manuscript of Hazlitt's, as conjectured (*Letters*, II, 24, n. 2). Both passages appear, exactly as he copied them, in E. No. 574, pp. 825, 826.
3. E. No. 558, pp. 563–566 and No. 559, pp. 579–581.

K

legend, and she had an eye for popular superstitions.[1] Looking for a topical theme, she suggested to Keats that they were approaching 20 January, the eve of St. Agnes. On that evening, according to legend, young girls could receive a vision of their true love. It was a theme which fitted the slacker or more romantic mood which had swept into Keats's poetry after Tom's death, a medieval, Gothic and Chattertonian conception, at the opposite pole from the stern classic architecture of the first two books of *Hyperion*. It was fanciful and imaginative in the same mood as the smaller poems he had just been copying for George.

It was, in fact, very closely allied with yet another small poem which he wrote about now. The playful love-lyric, *Hush, hush*, is a miniature dress-rehearsal in theme, atmosphere, and even in details of language and technique, for the narrative poem *The Eve of St. Agnes*. Like the much larger poem, it tells the story of a successful love-affair conducted under the noses of elderly and dangerous disapproval, though its summer setting is far from the topical winter scene of the great poem. Its heroine, true to the suggester of the theme, is called Isabel. Thus in a short space of time, both Keats and his publisher Taylor were found writing poems to an Isabel; it can hardly be doubted that their subject was the real Isabella, whose companionship they secretly had in common, especially as Keats's contribution resembles so closely the great work she brought to the forefront of his mind. The lyric suggests that she impressed it on him by conduct more like their first meeting at Hastings, when they had "warmed with" one another. At all events, she and the tumultuous events of the past weeks sent Keats off to Chichester in a ferment of suppressed creation.[2]

1. JKLY, 231–232.
2. Possibly on 21 January, St. Agnes Day itself (JKLY, 62), though perhaps more likely, as Rollins suggests (*Letters*, II, 58, n. 3), a day or so earlier.

Chapter 19

RICH ANTIQUITY

"Bertha was a Maiden fair,
Dwelling in the old Minster square:
From her fireside she could see
Sidelong its rich antiquity."

— *The Eve of St. Mark*

A WEEK or ten days before his long-deferred visit to Chichester, Keats had told Haydon, "I have been writing a little now and then lately; but nothing to speak of—being discontented and as it were moulting—." He was in a state of dissatisfaction with his poetry, though it did not provoke the violent reaction of his apprentice days when such a state made him think of suicide. Keats had learnt since then that such moods were often the prelude to a step forward. It is a measure of the distance he had travelled in the few years since he began poetry that he now made a joke of suicide. "Yet I do not think", he added to Haydon, "I shall ever come to the rope or the Pistol." He had learnt to make a medicine of his moods of depression. "I see by little and little more of what is to be done, and how it is to be done, should I ever be able to do it", and half-humourously he added, "On my Soul there should be some reward for that continual 'agonie ennuiyeuse'." Going through his box of books had reminded him of his early reading and his own early writing. The poets who had influenced him then, like Beattie and Tighe, now seemed nothing as he reread them; he himself, he felt, had progressed, but there was still so much to be done. It was a fruitful mood for a new leap forward in poetry, but so far he had been able to do nothing but tinker. He seems to have tried some revisions on *Hyperion*, but with Keats it was always difficult to restart a poem that had gone cold on him. In his present mood he needed a new shift of view to release the smothered poetic energy within him.

Keats was always affected by a change of scene. While writing the first book of *Endymion*, he had been oppressed by the isolation of the Isle of Wight, disturbed by the bleak landscape at Margate, and had dashed to Canterbury to strike inspiration out of its association with *The Canterbury Tales*. He deliberately exploited places for poetry—"to look into some beautiful Scenery—for poetical purposes"—and his epic mountain tour had been undertaken for the purposes of writing an epic. Neither Brown's

gossip nor Dilke's letters, however, could have told him how exactly
Chichester and what he found there would strike the note he was now
unconsciously seeking. The very approach, as the coach bumpily descended
the long chalk trackway from the South Downs, carried him into warmer
more welcoming climate than the bare cragginess he had sought in Scotland
and imported into the primeval background of the Titans. This coastal plain,
where corn ripens earlier than anywhere else in England, creates an instant
atmosphere of well-being. The city itself had risen from Civil War and siege,
which had left it still in an almost ruinous state only a hundred years before,
to an urbane prosperity. This was reflected in the warm red-brick Georgian
houses, "new-built", as their deeds described them, by the merchants who
derived their fat profits from the Government bounty on the export of
corn. From upper windows or belvederes, the owners could see their grain-
ships moving on the long haul out of the creeks of Chichester Harbour as if
they sailed along the flat fertile land. Elderly people who had profited in the
locality retired here, in solid comfort. Keats's hosts were such a couple in just
such a house. Charles Wentworth Dilke senior, during his career in the
Navy Office, had dealt with merchants and corn-factors of the coastal plain
between Chichester and Portsmouth. One of these, John Snook of Portsea,
acquired a mill at Bedhampton. Business naturally led to personal association,
for Dilke's daughter Laetitia had married Snook's son, John the second, who
had just taken over the mill on his father's death. The elder Dilke had by
now himself retired, and for the last five years he and his wife had lived among
the older society of Chichester, in a house looking out over the orchards
that still came up to the city walls. It was to these two households, the
elderly Civil Servant and his wife and the miller, a stout figure out of Chaucer,
that Keats was bidden. To someone who had been completely on his own,
fending for himself in the presence of death and continual doubts, this was a
warm refuge of relief.

When he got off the coach in the middle of the city, met by the ebullient
Brown with a torrent of provincial gossip, Keats instantly came upon a new
sight that seemed like an answer to his poetic mood. All his reading in the
past few weeks had thrown him back into the romantic and Gothic, to the
medieval rather than the classic, to Chatterton and Spenser rather than to
Milton and Wordsworth. As he walked through the streets with Brown back
to their hosts, the Cathedral sprang straight from the streets above them, on
the citizens' doorsteps, its separate bell-tower with the circling jackdaws
actually fronting the road itself. Unlike Canterbury, it was almost all as it
had been in the early middle ages, a building of one character hardly altered
in 600 years, except that clear glass showed where the Roundheads had
smashed the coloured diamonding with their pikes. For one in a romantic and
Gothic mood, here was a setting come to life; and as Keats was drawn by
Brown into the elderly card-playing circle of their hosts, "old Dowager card

parties" as he wrote to George, he found that these ancient ladies lived among even more ancient and medieval prospects, rooms dating from the middle ages with winding stone stairs and pointed windows, cellars with broad Norman supporting pillars. The Georgian facade, in houses in the midst of the city, often concealed a far older period of history.

So, as Keats sat and played cards with old Mrs. Lacy and old Miss Mullins,[1] while Brown, who had a way with elderly ladies, fluttered and teased their hostesses, the beginnings of the medieval setting of the new poem took shape. Yet this scene, though immediate and actual, and reproduced in early stanzas of *The Eve of St. Agnes* with their broad hall-pillars, lowly arched ways, and little moonlight room, was only an incidental spark to set light to the piled-up material within him. So too, for all the help that she undoubtedly intended to him, was Isabella Jones's suggestion that he should write, this St. Agnes Eve, a poem on the theme of the legend. Keats's mind was already prepared to go far beyond and behind the simple superstition

> how, upon St. Agnes' Eve,
> Young virgins might have visions of delight,
> And soft adorings from their loves receive
> Upon the honey'd middle of the night.

A much more tangible love-story was working below the surface of his mind. It was brought to light by Isabella—perhaps even by his own situation with her—and by the rich and evocative medieval ambiance which now surrounded him. Keats made the central part of his poem differ from the folk-lore tale. It was not a vision his heroine received, but the physical presence of her love, who had found his way into her room to see her sleeping. Either by design or by a lucky accident, he had been reading a small volume of tales in French, which all had the common property of a young man introduced, by varying means, into a beautiful young woman's rooms, a love-affair and an elopement. It seems probable that this was the volume on which he had hoped to base the prose story, never written, which he had promised to send George. The book consisted of three romances collected and written by M. de Tressan and published in Paris just over thirty years earlier, the ninth volume of the *Bibliothèque Universelle des Dames: Romans*. These romances were entitled *Flores et Blanche-Fleur*, *Cléomades et Claremonde*, and *Pierre de Provence et La Belle Maguelone*. Plot, setting and descriptive detail from all three combine to make them the undoubted source for the dramatic plan of Keats's poem.[2]

Although the first story of the group, in Boccaccio's Italian version and under the more familiar title of *Il Filocolo*, has been conjectured to have prompted

1. *Letters*, II, 34; JKLY, 69–72.
2. I am indebted for this suggestion to Dr. J. H. Walter, who has very generously placed his unpublished notes at my disposal.

Keats, it was a combination of all three stories, and especially the last-named on which he drew. Pierre and Maguelone become, as even their names might suggest, Keats's Porphyro and Madeline. Many small details in the story are the same, or similar. The setting is a palace or castle where festivities are taking place, with a small chapel adjoining; an old nurse helps the lovers to meet after satisfying herself on the hero's intentions; there is a reference to "un chanson de son pays"—that is, the hero's country of Provence—echoed by Keats's Porphyro when

> He play'd an ancient ditty, long since mute,
> In Provence call'd, 'La belle dame sans mercy:'

and finally when the lovers elope there is a storm, which, in the French romance, delays their story's happy ending by separating them. Other elements which Keats used as stage-properties come from the other two stories in the same little volume. The hero in the first story finds entry through a basket of fruits and flowers, in the second he wanders through a feast, both of which may have helped Keats to introduce the entirely new incident of a luxurious feast into the original legend of St. Agnes Eve. Similarly the immediate elopement, long-delayed in *Pierre et Maguelone*, is a part of the companion-piece of *Cléomades et Claremonde*, as is the sprawling figure of the Porter, which Keats transmuted into an unforgettable accompaniment to the escape of the lovers:

> They glide, like phantoms, into the wide hall;
> Like phantoms, to the iron porch, they glide;
> Where lay the Porter, in uneasy sprawl,
> With a huge empty flagon by his side:

These stories too, with their Mediterranean settings, which include adventures among the Moors of North Africa, foreshadow much of Keats's imagery in the poem, which contains a counterpoint throughout of Christian and pagan, such as his description of the sleeping Madeline

> Clasp'd like a missal where swart Paynims pray;

and the oriental luxuries of the feast Porphyro brings her.

Yet however much these romances may have settled Keats in the plot-form of his own love-story, the poetic texture of the poem is far too thickly woven to depend on any one literary source. More than perhaps in any other single poem, Keats brings to the actual working-out of the verse in *The Eve of St. Agnes* the fruits of an intense, though short lifetime of reading; he is his own poetic Porphyro, gathering together the most diversely-varied contributions to the feast, from Coleridge's *Christabel* to the romances of Mrs. Ann Radcliffe. A clear inspiration for the dramatic movement of the poem was, of course, *Romeo and Juliet*. Shakespeare is the "presider" over this poem to a larger extent than any other since the early passages of *Endymion*. Perhaps again his own love-passages had led Keats to "throw his whole being" into this play as he had done with *Troilus and Cressida* a few months before. The lovers in the poem play out their happier drama beset with the tremendous menace and danger of Shakespeare's warring families; "a hundred swords" are ready to put an end to their romance at the slightest false move. Old Angela the Beldam, who befriends the lovers, had much more of the character of Juliet's Nurse in Keats's own intended version of her speeches, before his publishers, careful to avoid religious as well as sexual offence in the poem, removed before publication some of her interjections of "Christ" and "Jesu". Moreover the story leaps from point to point in an entirely dramatic and Shakespearian way; even the climate points the drama, as Shakespeare's tempest does in *King Lear's* storm-scenes, which moved Keats so deeply. The frozen chill of the opening, the glowing warmth of the middle love-section, the wild and perilous storm of the ending, all make a dramatic sequence that develops with the actions of the characters in the story.

Yet the predominate feeling in *The Eve of St. Agnes* is not entirely literary, a piece of story-telling, nor merely dramatic, a play in stanza form. It is tangible, physical, and, above all, highly-coloured and pictorial. Keats used pictorial terms himself about the poem when, talking of his plans for future works, he wrote, "I wish to diffuse the colouring of St Agnes eve throughout a Poem", and he speaks of its "drapery". One reason why the poem seems like a series of medieval pictures, giving a fresh view of the same story from stanza to stanza, like some jewelled fresco from a church wall, is that Keats had literally such a series in mind. It was the fruit of his own creative imagination working on the black-and-white prints he had seen three weeks before at Haydon's. His remark on these—"I do not think I ever had a greater treat out of Shakspeare"—was not a casual exaggeration, but had the weight of fact. Next to *Romeo and Juliet*, the chief dramatic motif of the poem is provided by the Campo Santo frescoes. Keats went on to describe them as "Full of Romance and the most tender feeling—magnificence of draperies beyond any I ever saw." Already, in Haydon's studio, his eye was creating the colour of a poem, the "drapery" of *St. Agnes*. It is easy to see which of the frescoes had this great effect on him. Keats's general description, "Specimens of the first and second age of art in Italy" is accurate in that there are two sets, a fifteenth-century Biblical sequence by Benozzo Gozzoli, and a more primitive fourteenth-century series. Keats's further remarks are significant:

But Grotesque to a curious pitch—yet still making up a fine whole—even finer to me than more accomplish'd works—as there was left so much room for Imagination.

These make it certain that he is not referring to the far more finished and elaborate Gozzoli frescoes of the Old Testament, which have the brilliance and sophistication of that artist's famous *Journey of the Magi* at Florence.

Keats's imagination had been stirred by the Primitives, and the way he commended them showed how great the effect had been. They were grotesque; that was, for him ever since childhood, a term of admiration, a sure way of arousing his interest. They "left so much room for Imagination" that they were the proper and almost inevitable material for poetry. Moreover, though he did not perhaps know, one in particular of these primitives was a masterpiece of its kind, one of the most individual paintings in the world.

This was *The Triumph of Death* by an unknown master of the mid-fourteenth century. The fresco is in two halves, the left dramatic and vivid. A medieval hunting-party of lords, ladies and grooms is suddenly confronted by the reminder of the grim physical facts of death; three corpses burst out of their coffins in horrible detail, one bloated, one decayed, one fleshless. Horror is dramatically conveyed by the faces and gestures of the party. The right hand part of the fresco is a group of lovers, at court, with musical instruments. Yet even here is horror; devils swoop about their heads conveying lost souls to hell while angels try ineffectively to save them. The moral is pointed out by a series of composite pictures of the lives of hermits, one of whom leaves his cell to show these appalling sights to the revellers, and present to the hunting party a scroll reminding them that even in the pride of life man must die. Though the idea that in the midst of life we are in death is a common medieval pictorial conception there is an urgency and reality about this example that makes it far from a formal traditional exercise. It is, in historical fact, a terrible and accurate reflection of its own time, painted by someone who, as an adult, had actually experienced the Black Death, the most horrible plague to sweep across Europe. This is a picture of that time by a survivor, and its corpses that burst reeking from their coffins distorted by disease are no parable but the substances of death.

Keats had just come from a death-bed "of the most distressing nature"; his whole being for the rest of his days was suffused by this fact. Love, for him, never evades the background of death. This was why he bodied out the engraving of *The Triumph of Death* into the moving stanzas of a narrative poem in which the sense of death is ever-present. The sombre figure of the Beadsman, who begins and ends *The Eve of St. Agnes*, is the pervading hermit of *The Triumph of Death*, who is shown, like the Beadsman, praying with his rosary in his little austere chapel, setting the whole tone of the poem from the first stanza:

> St. Agnes' Eve—Ah, bitter chill it was!
> The owl, for all his feathers, was a-cold;
> The hare limp'd trembling through the frozen grass,
> And silent was the flock in woolly fold:
> Numb were the Beadsman's fingers, while he told
> His rosary, and while his frosted breath,
> Like pious incense from a censer old,

> Seem'd taking flight for heaven, without a death,
> Past the sweet Virgin's picture, while his prayer he saith.

In the fresco, even the small detail of the hare is shown, crouching with other animals near the little door of the Beadsman's chapel, in the focal centre of the engraving that Keats saw. The revelry of the poem in the midst of the icy chill of death that seems to encompass it, the literal picture

> Amid the timbrels, and the throng'd resort
> Of whisperers in anger or in sport;

is taken from the right-hand panel of the fresco, the gossiping courtiers with instruments in their hands, oblivious of the destruction just above their heads. The tragic and sinister end of the poem is full of the atmosphere of the dramatic left-hand panel.

> And they are gone: ay, ages long ago
> These lovers fled away into the storm.
> That night the Baron dreamt of many a woe,
> And all his warrior-guests, with shade and form
> Of witch, and demon, and large coffin-worm,
> Were long be-nightmar'd. Angela the old
> Died palsy-twitch'd, with meagre face deform;
> The Beadsman, after thousand aves told,
> For aye unsought for slept among his ashes cold.

In the nightmare experience of the hunting-guests, large worms crawl out of the bursting coffins before their eyes, plain even in the uncoloured engraving, while the ever-present demons wait close by to snatch the living to a like horror. This aspect of Keats's poem shows one of the most extraordinary and genuine cross-fertilizations of one artist and one medium by another; the unknown fourteenth-century painter and the Romantic poet are joined by chance in a common realization of actual death, and the underlying reality and full physical quality of the poem is the result.

The contrast between love and death had been the actual experience of Keats's childhood and adolescence. It was brought back to him now by Tom's death, and he reverted to the love-dreams of his own early days. As a schoolboy, dreaming of women, he said "my mind was a soft nest in which some one of them slept though she knew it not." Madeline, "trembling in her soft and chilly nest" was an extension of this adolescent day-dream, her discovery while sleeping a further version of the Chattertonian fragment about a sleeping beauty attributed to Keats in his student days. Yet now, his own tumultuous and mixed sexual feelings brought a need for adult reality in the love theme of the poem. He later revised some verses to show that the love-affair between Porphyro and Madeline was physically consummated. Even the most explicit alteration,

K*

> See while she speaks his arms encroaching slow
> Have zon'd her, heart to heart

seemed mild enough, though it nearly pushed Taylor out of publishing the whole poem, but Keats felt it vehemently and personally. He would despise, he said "a man who would be such an eunuch in sentiment as to leave a maid, with that Character about her, in such a situation."[1] With the death of Tom had died the last vestige of the hazy mock-Elizabethan common language they had about women; and though Madeline, "so pure a thing, so free from mortal taint", is not in the least like the women Keats had been meeting, imperial, enigmatic or flirtatious, they had aroused in him an underlying sexuality that pervades the whole poem.

Still, for all the adult realism behind it, the poem succeeds in capturing an energy of youth that goes back to the earliest springs of his poetry, released once more by Tom's death. In it, he drew on every experiment in poetry he had made since his initial Spenserian stanzas. It was, of course, his first lengthy attempt in that stanza, to which the poem owed a freedom that had never before appeared in his narratives, and it reached back to his apprentice reading, just as details reached back to his newly-awakened boyhood memories: as he told Clarke, the sounds of distant music that come and go throughout the poem were suggested by the sounds heard by himself and Holmes from the Headmaster's house at school. Besides Spenser, the eighteenth-century Spenserians he had just re-read, even though he now condemned them, Tighe, Beattie and others, played their part. *The Minstrel* of the latter poet contributed to the new poem many echoes, and even one character, the Beldam—the same word used by both Beattie and Keats— who in both poems instructs the young hero in traditional superstition and folk-lore. Even a memory of poor Felton Mathew's verse helped the advent of the lovers' storm.[2] Keats's recent return to Chatterton was also present, though he rejected the more Chattertonian stanzas, to the poem's final benefit. Yet the technical tour-de-force of the poem is that it applies to all these early and essential groundworks of Keats's verse the recent hard labour and thought he had put into *Hyperion. The Eve of St. Agnes* is a poem where all this massive interplay of vowel and consonant finds a free unhampered narrative movement. It did not come easily, as his scored manuscript showed; this was not evidence of weakness in composition, but of the higher standards

1. KC, I, 92.
2. Compare

> Hark! 'tis an elfin storm from faery land (*The Eve of St. Agnes*, l. 343)
> and
>
> Against the casement dark (l. 324, draft)
> with Mathew's
>
> Mark! while the squally wind and torrent rain
> Against the rattling casement (*The Garland*, p. 154, Finney photostat).

he was now applying to his poetry. Again and again, he begins a stanza with an idea or expression which would have seemed adequate to him six months before in *Isabella*, only to reject it, and try perhaps half-a-dozen radical variations before he is satisfied. The beautiful line "A chain-droop'd lamp was flickering by each door" appeared in no less than five different versions before the adjective "chain-droop'd" gave him the exact picture he wanted. *The Eve of St. Agnes* is the first and perhaps greatest fruit of his determination not to produce any more slipshod work for the critics; it is the most striking result of the application of his "own domestic criticism". The final impression of this poem, when all the elements of suggestion, local impression, artistic and literary influence have been assimilated, is that it is the first poem in which Keats speaks sustainedly and at full length in a voice entirely his, and in a medium over which he has complete and ample control.

Accident and chance played their part, of course, on a mind in which everything was absorbed into the web of creative agitation. On Saturday 23 January, Keats and Brown took leave of their elderly hosts in Eastgate Square, Chichester, and walked along the gusty exhilarating coast road to the waterside millhouse down by the harbour, thirteen miles away at Bedhampton. A letter wildly punning on the first syllable of the village told the Hampstead Dilkes of their arrival at the Snook house. There was also a postscript for "Millamant"—Fanny Brawne, from whom Keats had perhaps received a letter at Chichester.[1] In the same light-hearted mood in which the week-end had been passed, Keats and Brown went on an expedition on Monday 25 January to the dedication of Stansted Chapel. This was a great local event. The owner of the chapel and the estate of Stansted was Lewis Way, a rich man who had made his life work the conversion of the Jews. Ribald stories were told of his Jewish guests at Stansted, where he hoped, unsuccessfully, to found a College for them; more seriously, he had actually persuaded the Powers at Aix-la-Chapelle in 1818 to add a clause to their protocol promising tolerance to the Jewish race.[2] Way had chosen the Feast of the Conversion of St. Paul, 25 January, for the dedication of the building which he had raised from a former hunting-lodge to a house of religion that bore the marks of his own extremely individual character. The Regency Gothic design was of great delicacy. The owner's taste showed everywhere, from the stained glass of the triple-arched windows in the nave, embellished with scutcheons of the Fitzalan family, to the unique painted East window, the only window in a Christian place of worship that is wholly Jewish in design and symbolism. Texts everywhere pointed to conversion and baptism, and as Way's own daughter put it, "The idea throughout is the Gospel Dispensation shadowed forth in the Law, or 'Moses a schoolmaster leading to Christ'."

1. *Letters*, II, 137, suggests this, though the sense is obscure.
2. Bodleian MSS Eng. Lett. c. 139. f. 38.

Keats certainly did not go for religious reasons; but as he sat through the long service with Brown and John Snook's small son and namesake, he absorbed yet another version of the Gothic which added to the crowded scene-painting of his poem. The triple windows, the rosy shields, the diamond panes and the coloured light shining on the congregation helped to make a picture transmuted by the silver moonlight drench of imagination into

> A casement high and triple-arch'd there was,
> All garlanded with carven imag'ries
> Of fruits, and flowers, and bunches of knot-grass,
> And diamonded with panes of quaint device,
> Innumerable of stains and splendid dyes,
> As are the tiger-moth's deep-damask'd wings;
> And in the midst, 'mong thousand heraldries,
> And twilight saints, and dim emblazonings,
> A shielded scutcheon blush'd with blood of queens and kings.

Magnificent carvings by Grinling Gibbons, their motifs repeated in the Chapel, were seen afterwards in the house, which was thrown open to the public, and which contained, again in the words of Way's daughter, "the great tapestry rooms, the wainscotted saloon, the oak room with its fine panelling". Just as Keats was equally affected and inspired by the genuine archaisms of Spenser and the fake Middle English of Chatterton, so the medieval Gothic of Chichester and the Regency Gothic of Stansted fused in the setting of his poem, where, it has been noticed, properties of a much later date insinuate themselves into the bleak historical realism of the opening. In the pressure of composition, every impression was swept in, and it took the publishers' cautious proof-correction to remove the hero's expletive "By the great St. Paul!" which signposts the Stansted visit, and its new impetus to the poem.[1]

Keats was lucky in every small detail of composition during this poem. Brown, stimulating but distracting, left, the day after their Stansted visit, for Wentworth Place. Keats's sore throat returned, so he was not tempted by walks over the Downs, and did not go past the garden gate. His hosts were quiet, homely and friendly, not intellectuals; he had mild discussions on religion and politics with the miller, who kindly promised to put on paper some of his experience in farming to help George in America. Moreover, the large thin blue sheets of paper Haslam had found, so that they would fold in a small packet for his own letters to George, proved to be ideal for the composition of a poem where there was a lot of crossing-out and marginal alteration. The poem had its difficulties and hesitations mainly at strongly human moments. Keats found it hard to undress his heroine convincingly in front of the concealed Porphyro, and the consummation of their love

1. JKLY, 78–81.

dissatisfied him so much that he afterwards tried to make it more explicit; yet it is a mark of his new poetic conscience that just those places eventually show his master-strokes. The touch in Madeline's disrobing

Unclasps her warmed jewels one by one

has been picked out for praise by many later critics; it is typical of the care he now gave to every small turn that the slack original "bosom jewels" was rejected from a poem that never once loses its grip.

He stayed long enough at Bedhampton to finish the poem in draft. The situation in London, when he returned in the first week in February, was much as he had left it, except that for a time Haydon was off his hands. The painter had opened on 30 January the exhibition of his pupils' drawings of the Elgin Marbles and the Cartoons of Raphael, and was busily occupied fighting their battles and, incidentally, his own. The cares of a young man in society crowded in upon Keats, in contrast with the last fortnight in which he had been allowed simply to be a poet, engaged in a relationship between artist and work. Now the cross-currents of human behaviour began their inevitable tow. Brown, though a welcome companion against depression, was also a complicating force. If he resented Keats's intimacies with other men, he was even more likely to resent the influence of women. He resorted to strange methods, while proclaiming the purest motives, to "protect" Keats; he even, so he himself said, put indecent verses of his own making among Keats's manuscripts to prevent female prying. In Fanny Brawne he seems to have recognized a lively and shrewd appraisal of masculine tactics that needed a different approach. If he could not beat her, he would at least attempt to join her, and he carried his scheme out by pretending to be attracted and to flirt with her. A somewhat feverish three-cornered relationship thus developed, which Keats was later to think actually did him physical harm, and which certainly did his peace of mind little good. Another disturbing visitation came from the Reynolds girls, who were having a short stay with Mrs. Dilke. They had suspected their own cousin of flirting with Keats, and now formed the worst possible view of Fanny Brawne. Brown wrote Fanny a valentine, in which he said she deserved to be "whipped for being naughty", and the artificial sexual badinage and fencing so much infected Keats that he too began to act strangely. It is very probable that the whole of this uneasy and equivocal three-cornered impasse found its way into a piece of charade-writing, which has been attributed to Keats. This curious piece of work, known as the Gripus fragment, is a comedy-scene in rough blank verse which describes a bald-headed houseowner, his pert housekeeper and smart Cockney valet, between whom there is just such a triangle of vaguely improper double-entendre as appeared to be going on at Wentworth Place. Gripus the householder has Brown's lecherous propensities, the housekeeper makes notes on fashionable dress, like those which still exist in Fanny's hand,[1] while the Cockney valet, like Keats, breaks into light verse extempore. It is a charade based on life.

Perhaps in order to escape these pressures, Keats decided on Saturday 13 February that his sore throat, which he had been nursing, was well enough to let him go into the City; in fact, he spent much of the next week there. A good deal of the time was passed, unpleasantly enough, with his ex-guardian at Pancras Lane. Abbey had now taken his guardianship of Fanny to lengths of which Keats strongly disapproved. He had removed her from school at the age of fifteen and a half, and he had objected to her getting letters from her own brother. Keats saw him several times and wrote him a "plain spoken" letter, which removed the embargo on correspondence, though it did not put her back to school. The letter also dealt with money; here he was in an awkward position, since he needed to conciliate Abbey and get his share of Tom's estate quickly, before the inevitable demand came from Haydon. An added complication was the missing trustee, by now in Holland, leaving Abbey the sole authority.[2] Abbey, correctly but unhelpfully, referred Keats to Walton as the lawyer who had drawn up Mrs. Jennings's deed of inheritance. Here, if only Keats had known, was a chance to be told of the other fund, in Chancery, owing to him; but, although he visited his office, it is doubtful if he ever saw Walton. The lawyer himself was out at his home in Epping Forest, in what proved to be a dying state, drawing up codicils to his own will in a condition of mind that suggests senility.[3] Keats was frustrated at every turn; no one would produce the deed to him, and Abbey even suggested from memory that it contained a clause preventing any share of Tom's inheritance until all three survivors including Fanny were twenty-one—that is, for nearly another six years. Keats in exasperation suspected what he called a "bam" or hoax,[4] though it is quite possible there was such a clause. He was reduced to drawing £20 from the money left by George, to meet his own housekeeping expenses with Brown.

His other meetings were less frustrating. A chance encounter with Woodhouse led to them splitting a bottle of claret, over which Keats told the lawyer some intimate facts about his early sonnets, those to his grandmother and the Vauxhall lady. "There is a great deal of reality about all that Keats writes", Woodhouse had noted, "and there must be many allusions to particular circumstances in his poems: which would add to their beauty & Interest if properly understood." He now copied every detail he could gather about Keats's poems into his large note-books. Keats's spirits rose with the claret, which he celebrated in a piece of Falstaffian prose:[5]

it fills the mouth with a gushing freshness—then goes down cool and feverless... and the more ethereal Part of it mounts into the brain, not assaulting the cerebral apartments like a bully in a bad house looking for his trul and hurrying from door to door

1. KHM, No. 27.   2. KHM, No. 104.   3. KI, 37.
4. *Letters*, II, 40.   5. *Letters*, II, 64.

bouncing against the waistcoat; but rather walks like Aladin about his own enchanted palace so gently that you do not feel his step—Other wines of a heavy and spirituous nature transform a man to a Silenus; this makes him a Hermes—and gives a Woman the soul and imortality of Ariadne.

His other main visit during this week, he celebrated in poetry. He naturally went to Isabella with the poem he had finished, since she had suggested its subject; she continued her role by suggesting yet another subject with a medieval and superstitious trend, *The Eve of St. Mark*. Keats laughed at these "fine mother Radcliff names", adding "I did not search for them", but they agreed with his present romantic and Gothic mood. He had by him the little leather-bound notebook[1] in which he had fair-copied *Isabella*; he may even have been showing Isabella Jones the poem, which, by coincidence, bore her name. Flipping over two pages, he began another Gothic poem, this time not in the metre of Spenser but of Chatterton, from whom he even borrowed his new heroine's name, Bertha.

So began what he described to George as "a little thing call'd the 'eve of St Mark'." Like the larger *St. Agnes* it was a series of brightly-designed medieval pictures. This time the paintings were not fused together, and he did not draw on such deep resources. They are separate, gem-like, a turning of the pages of a portfolio; they do not stretch far back into his consciousness, but recreate each one a facet of recent experience. The first picture is of the rain-drenched Cathedral streets of Chichester; in the next, Bertha looks at an illuminated manuscript. What she sees there are the unique symbols of the strange East window at Stansted, transformed all the more naturally by Keats to decorations in a book, since he had even seen at Stansted the marble book placed by Way just beneath the window.[2] Keats filled that book with

> The stars of Heaven, and angels' wings,
> Martyrs in a fiery blaze,
> Azure saints in silver rays,
> Aaron's breastplate, and the seven
> Candlesticks John saw in Heaven,
> The winged Lion of Saint Mark,
> And the Covenantal Ark,

mostly recalled from his Stansted vigil. The next picture shifts back to Chichester Close and Cathedral, its quiet sheltered ways, its drowsy chimes and circling jackdaws; then, as he begins to describe his heroine, the picture shifts again, from the "old Dowager" surroundings of Chichester, to something far more like Isabella Jones's own London rooms, with their square-panelled walls, cage-birds, and detail so naturalistic that Keats seems almost

1. B. M. Egerton 2780. *The Eve of St. Mark* shows every sign of fresh composition.
2. JKLY, 87–89. The book, removed to the west end, is now a war memorial.

to have written on the spot. His heroine reads a fragment of Chattertonian verse in a firelit interior that feels as if it were drawn from life:

> Down she sat, poor cheated soul!
> And struck a lamp from the dismal coal;
> Leaned forward, with bright drooping hair
> And slant book, full against the glare.
> Her shadow, in uneasy guise,
> Hover'd about, a giant size,
> On ceiling-beam and old oak chair,
> The parrot's cage, and panel square;

Keats's two Gothic poems show an extraordinary fusion of pictorial realism and attention to externals with an underlying sense of unbounded internal emotion. In both, the warm firelit world of personal feeling is threatened by the huge and dark forces of the world at large. They reflect his inmost preoccupations, and, almost miraculously, find perfect expression for them in simple and childlike legend, embellished by all the poetic force at his disposal. Nowhere else did Keats more successfully tell stories in verse, and though the second story ended almost before it had begun, both have been of equal inspiration to poets and artists of other generations.

Chapter 20

IN THRALL

" 'La Belle Dame sans Merci
Hath thee in thrall!' "

WHY, it has been asked, did Keats drop writing *The Eve of St. Mark* in the middle of a line on Wednesday 17 February, and never take up the poem again? It has been suggested that he found the legend forbidding, the superstition that a watcher by the church door on the eve of St. Mark will see the ghosts of all who are to die during the following year; yet he inserted at some time another piece of Chattertonian verse to make this legend explicit. A more plausible suggestion is that he felt both *St. Agnes* and *St. Mark* trivial. However much he had jumped at the chance offered him in the simple folklore tales suggested by Isabella, they were distractions in a minor vein from the real work of *Hyperion*.[1] He spoke of them both as "little" pieces, a strange term for over forty stanzas of *St. Agnes* unless the comparison with an even larger scale work was in his mind. When he at long last copied *St. Mark* for George, six months later, he referred to the poem's carelessness, and merely said "I think it will give you the sensation of walking about an old county Town in a coolish evening." At the same time, he made a comparison between himself and Byron which may be significantly related to this poem: "He describes what he sees—I describe what I imagine." *St. Mark* as far as it went had been a series of pictures of what Keats had seen; the creative imagination, as he understood it, had hardly worked on the material at all. He simply seems to have felt that it was not his sort of poem, and he first mentioned sending it to George with the ominous proviso "if I should have finished it".

The dropping of *St. Mark* heralded an intense and complex period of depression for Keats. Many causes can be traced, though the record of his life at this time suggests nothing momentous in the first few days of what proved to be a poetic silence of about a month. On the 17th itself, he seems to have visited Isabella again, bringing home some of the game she still provided although Tom was dead, a present which inspired a piece of prose on food to match his panegyric on claret. On the 18th there was a birthday party for

1. Ward, 254.

289

the Dilkes's nine-year-old son, and the Brawnes were present; on the 19th he called on a Hampstead neighbour, Mr. Lewis, who had been kind to Tom. The next day he dined at the Dilkes on a pheasant from Isabella with Rice and Reynolds as guests. With a twinge of conscience he wrote to Haydon on the same day, more hopefully than the facts justified. Owing to Abbey's obstinacy and Walton's disorganization, they had missed the chance of selling Tom's shares profitably; a steep slump was just beginning, and Brown came back from the City reporting panic and bankruptcies. Luckily the painter was in one of his moods of manic exaltation thanks to the success of his pupils' exhibition: "by Heaven I'll plunge into the bottom of the sea, where plummets have never sounded, & never will be able to sound, with such impetus that the antipodes shall see my head drive through on their side of the Earth to their dismay & terror".

Yet behind these characteristic and sometimes amusing trivialities of daily life, there was a sensation of great uneasiness, which emerges in the third long journal letter to George, marked C, which Keats had begun on 14 February. Its opening at once points sharply to one cause for his state of anxiety: he had not heard from George for four whole months. "How is it we have not heard from you from the Settlement yet?" While Keats had been nursing his throat at Hampstead, two old schoolfriends[1] had written to him, both doubtless asking after George; one of them, Peachey the lawyer, had friends going out to the Birkbeck settlement in Illinois, who would see that a letter was personally delivered. A sense of strain from the long silence pervades the beginning of this letter, and Keats reveals his troubles more by implication than by direct statement. They were similar to the difficulties he had faced in October and chronicled in Letter A; what was disquieting was the difference in attitude he now displayed. Then he had met the critics and his own disappointment with the stoic and confident "This is a mere matter of the moment." Now, four months later, he harped on failure. Jealousy of other poets peeped out; he commented gloomily on Byron's sale of 4000 copies of the last canto of Childe Harold. He was touchy of anything like a joke on his status as a poet. When kind Mr. Lewis said to gossiping Mrs. Brawne, "O, he is quite the little Poet", Keats burst out, "You see what it is to be under six foot and not a lord", a phrase that recalled Reynolds's untimely attack on Byron in his defence of Endymion. He kept returning to Gifford, the supposed author of the review in the Quarterly, and eventually copied for George whole pages of Hazlitt's superb invective diatribe "Letter to William Gifford Esq". He was more capable of concealing these feelings in some company than in others. According to Haydon, Keats "became morbid and silent, would call and sit whilst I was painting for hours without saying a word".[2] Fanny Brawne, however, later recorded that she saw nothing "to give the idea that he was brooding over any secret grief or disappointment".

1. *Letters*, II, 37 and 58.   2. Haydon, *Autobiography*, 354.

All the same, a general bitterness of outlook took the place of the level magnanimity Keats had shown under much more trying circumstances the previous autumn. Its most open sign was his uncalled-for censure of someone to whom his poetry and thought owed much, Benjamin Bailey. The unfortunate Bailey had just severely blotted his copybook with the whole of the Rice-Reynolds circle. Since his summer visit to the Gleigs at Stirling, an understanding had ripened between him and the daughter of the house, Hamilton. Bailey, in an awkward and unresolved position with Marianne Reynolds, had behaved clumsily, but, according to his own lights, honestly. Before asking for Miss Gleig's hand, he had shown her father his letters to Marianne, which he had got her to return. The situation was apparently above-board enough to satisfy the Bishop, who gave his blessing to Bailey as a sufficiently well-endowed son-in-law, and an official engagement took place. Mrs. Reynolds, however, saw Bailey as yet another well-off young man who had defaulted; indeed, she clearly regarded both George Keats and John himself in something of the same light, and Keats was satirical about her and her daughters—"It will be a good Lesson to the Mother and Daughters— nothing would serve but Bailey—If you mentioned the word Tea pot— some one of them came out with an a propos about Bailey—noble fellow— fine fellow! was always in their mouths." Yet, with a lack of self-perception quite unusual in him, Keats forgot that he himself had applied the expression "noble" to Bailey, and now expressed his utter disgust with him. "I do not now remember clearly the facts", he wrote to George,[1] though he was prepared to enlarge on them to the extent of accusing Bailey of playing fast and loose with a number of girls, one at least of whom, the publisher Martin's sister, was his relative-in-law. Although admitting that Marianne herself had never intended to marry Bailey—"She liked Bailey as a Brother—but not as a Husband"—he could see no excuse in Bailey's turning to Hamilton Gleig "except that of a Ploughmans who wants a wife".

The independence of judgment and loyalty to friends, on which Keats prided himself, the tolerance which had helped him to bear with Haydon and Hunt at their most trying, and which he had preached to Bailey himself, had temporarily vanished; he was prepared to take the worldly-wise view of James Rice, who, as a lawyer, was bound to see Marianne cheated of her chance of Bailey's £3000 marriage settlement. For such a reversal of principle, some other cause must have been at work. It seems that Keats, at the same time that he heard from Taylor of Byron's phenomenal sales, had received a hint from the publisher about Bailey's unhappy handling of Lockhart at Bishop Gleig's dinner-table. The whole topic of Bailey and the Gleigs would be associated in his mind with intimate family details of his own life, which Bailey had let slip and which had been so travestied in the *Blackwood's*

1. The facts were perfectly clear and known to Dilke, who was prepared to accept them impartially without assigning blame. Dilke, ann. II, 11.

review. Keats's remarks at this time about "an ideot parson", though ostensibly caused by his experience among the clergy at the Stansted dedication, have a violent and personal ring.[1] His attack on Bailey follows, in the letter to George, almost immediately after an attack on the literary reviews, introduced by the comment, "my poem has not at all succeeded". He could perhaps have forgiven Bailey for clumsiness over Marianne; he could not forgive a friend whose self-importance or nervousness had betrayed the poetry of *Endymion* to the destroyer.

Brooding over past grievances made Keats, as he said, suspicious over everyone's motives; thinking ahead at this time made him seriously question his own. At the birthday party at the Dilkes, on 18 February, he had heard some news, trivial enough, but of deep importance to his peace of mind. Dilke, an over-anxious father, had decided to send his son to Westminster, and since the journey to school would be a long one, he was preparing to go and live in that part of London himself. The Brawnes, who had liked Wentworth Place when they rented Brown's half of the house, were now ready to rent Dilke's, and would move in early in April. In six weeks Keats would have to make up his mind about Fanny; there could be no ambiguity in their relationship if she and her mother were to live next door. Mrs. Brawne, like Mrs. Reynolds, he must have thought, would want to know the exact motives of a young man who saw her daughter every day. He could offer no hopeful answer to any enquiry she might make. There was no question of making any money out of poetry, and he could only look for success, if at all, "in a course of years". These were staggering problems, and it is no wonder Keats found them almost too much to bear stoically. Haydon, who was watching him anxiously during the next six weeks for a sight of the promised loan, recorded, undoubtedly of this time, that "For six weeks he was scarcely sober." Haydon added the dramatic and much-disputed legend that Keats covered his throat with pepper in order to enjoy his claret;[2] but even discounting Haydon's habitual exaggeration, there are signs that Keats was drinking more heavily than usual at this time. He could conceal this, and did, notably to Cowden Clarke, who visited him after a long absence, and found him still the manly schoolboy character of the Enfield days, who had just fought and beaten a butcher's boy for tormenting a kitten, and who illustrated the famous one-two blows of Randall the prizefighter by drumming briskly with his fingers. Both Haydon and Clarke saw what they wanted and expected in Keats, one the dramatic maker of gestures, the other the natural gentleman. Both views of Keats had their truth, as well as reflecting their holders' very different natures; but there is no doubt that

1. Ward, 250–251 and 431, n. 17.
2. Haydon, II, 317. It must be remembered that Haydon recorded this in his private diary shortly after Keats's death, as something told him by Keats himself, and that there was no later writing-up of the incidents.

Haydon's, stripped of the picturesque detail with which the painter coloured it, seems nearer the facts at this time. Nothing, however, could have a simple solution in such a complex nature, and in such an intractable situation. Keats's own words, before he plunged into a fortnight of silence, were a warning that his own depths could not easily be fathomed. They were a hint of corresponding deepening of thought in himself to deal with the new problems:

A Man's life of any worth is a continual allegory—and very few eyes can see the Mystery of his life—a life like the scriptures, figurative—

He paused for one of his bitter remarks about Byron, then ended in the wiser vein of former letters, "Shakspeare led a life of Allegory; his works are the comments on it—."

Keats himself said that he did not find "one thing particular" to write about this fortnight, but there are signs that it was a time of thought and decision, from which he emerged, if not yet with any certainties, at least with some lines to follow. Its actual events are a blank, except that on 24 February he was caught by a late snow-storm while in Town, and stayed two nights with Taylor in Fleet Street. It is possible that something occurred during this stay to alter his relationship with Isabella Jones; for though he had intended to go on visiting her, he never mentions her again for the rest of his life. Keats hated an equivocal situation, or the sense that he was being played with. Her wish that he and she should meet without Taylor, Reynolds and the rest of their common acquaintance knowing was specially difficult for a man of his out-going nature to keep. Her short notes to Taylor showed more than a trace of sexual banter, and his sonnets to her had sexual overtones. Whether she was at any time the publisher's mistress, or whether there was only, as she expressed it, a close "coincidence of ideas" between them, her enforced secrecy must have irked Keats even more at this time, when he was trying to straighten the complications of his own life. He had announced to George four months before that he had himself "no libidinous thought" about her, but he had been seeing her frequently since in an atmosphere of provocation, and their original encounter had suggested such thoughts to him. What may have been even more disturbing was a feeling that she was trying to run his life as a poet. Several resentful phrases over the next few months suggest that he had suffered such an experience at the hands of a woman; in the most outspoken of these, he specifically stated, "I have met with women whom I really think would like to be married to a Poem and to be given away by a Novel." No woman in Keats's circle in any way fits this description except Isabella. His remark to Haydon about this time, on 8 March, "that in the height of enthusiasm I have been cheated into some fine passages" may be connected with the same feeling, and in the same letter occurs a judgment on the type of gathering Isabella encouraged, which he also echoed during the next few months—"that most vulgar of all crowds the literary". There is never likely to be any final certainty about a relationship hedged in by her enigmatic prohibition; but every sign shows that Keats found it necessary, whatever the reason, to break away from it in this fortnight of decision. Whether he was influenced by any crystallization of his feelings about Fanny Brawne must remain equally uncertain. Perhaps ultimately the most important result was that it helped him to come to a decision about his own future poetry:

I have come to the resolution never to write for the sake of writing, or making a poem, but from running over with any little knowledge and experience which many years of reflection may perhaps give me—otherwise I will be dumb.

Characteristically, Keats did not keep, even remotely, to the letter of this decision; the next six months show more verses written "for the sake of writing, or making a poem" than at almost any time in his life—light, occasional verse of every sort, dramatic verse for stage production, narrative verse in order to make up a book. Yet there is no doubt that the spirit in which he approached poetry showed a change from this time. It was a step he had prophesied exactly in May 1818 when he spoke of seeking out "in about a year's time the best metaphysical road I can take".[1] He did not mean the philosophic poets, the epic-makers such as Wordsworth, Milton and Dante, nor the great humane principles running through the works of Shakespeare. Now, faced with the insolubles of life, he felt a need to go beyond poetry to the sources of thought itself, to study philosophy as a philosopher. Forty-eight hours with Taylor, who had a wide-ranging philosophic mind, may have helped this decision, but it also revealed an urgent inner desire. Keats needed, as he again expressed himself to Haydon, the exercise of "trying myself at lifting mental weights, as it were". Taylor, who had taken the place of Bailey as someone with whom Keats could discuss intellectual matters, had interested him again in Plato, but Keats in his new mood was not prepared to confine himself to Greek philosophy as formerly. He read the parallel in Rousseau's Emile between Socrates and Christ, concluding that the latter was God. Although at the height of his anti-clerical phase, echoing with approval Hazlitt on the clerical character and Hunt on the corrupt London clergy, Keats could still see the "splendour" of Christ, in spite of "the pious frauds of religion"; his desire for an all-embracing philosophy led him to forget even these prejudices, and to read Church history. Everything he now thought and read seemed to contain a hint that he had perhaps concentrated too exclusively on poetry rather than the thought behind poetry. He pondered on Hazlitt's dictum

that Poetry, that the imagination, generally speaking, delights in power, in strong excitement, as well as in truth, in good, in right, whereas pure reason and moral sense approve only of the true and good.

1. *Letters*, I, 274.

When writing to Woodhouse in the autumn, Keats had been "ambitious of doing the world some good", and had seemed to regard poetry as a preliminary to this final end. This position was a halfway stage in his thought, after the great revolution at Teignmouth the previous April, when he had first realized that "thoughts on Books" were not enough to equip him as a poet. By the autumn of 1818, he had developed this to the extent of admitting that poetry might only be a stepping-stone to better things. Now, nearly a year later, in March 1819, after the experience "on the pulses" of Tom's death, he carried revolution a stage further. Not only would poetry never reach the heights he hoped for without serious study of the good toward which it tended; the study of the good, the "continual drinking of Knowledge" he had set himself as a task a year before, might itself lead him to regard poetry as "not so fine a thing", and to compare a life of poetry unfavourably with a life of well-doing.

Like many deep revolutions this had periods of slow and painful groping, and these weeks of late February and March 1819 seem to have been one of them. The time spent on thought elbowed out poetry itself, and seemed to Keats entirely unproductive, "annihilated" in idleness. "I do not know what I did on monday—nothing—nothing—nothing—I wish this was any thing extraordinary". Time was consumed, in spite of the inner life he was leading, in meaningless outward trivialities. Social events, scandals, puns, dinners, parties, theatres, the British Museum, having his miniature painted by Severn, all seemed equally boring and pointless. When, at the end of March, Severn suggested putting the miniature in for the Royal Academy Exhibition, Keats wrote him a disillusioned letter[1] advising against it and suggesting that the artist's oil-painting, Hermia and Helena, exhibited two years before at Spring Gardens, and praised then in the New Monthly Magazine,[2] would be a better choice. Severn entered both, and the miniature fulfilled Keats's gloomy prophecy by remaining unnoticed, "a drop of water in the ocean". Yet for all his disillusion, fresh, serious growth was working below, and only needed some chance event to bring it to the surface. This came when on Thursday 18 March, he filled up an idle day by playing cricket on the Heath with Brown; even under-arm bowling brought the ball up to Keats's height, and a bumper gave him a black eye. Brown applied leeches to decrease the swelling, Keats slept late the next day, perhaps under laudanum, and in this relaxed state felt his mind free. Half-dreaming of something he had seen lately, an etching in Piranesi's Vasi e Candelabri, he had a vision of three figures, two women and one man, on a Greek vase. They seemed to represent Poetry, Ambition and Love, and to sum up the personal side of his present dilemma, though they may also have been, with himself as the man, the three dramatis personae of his situation. Their contemplation gave him a

1. Letters, II, 48, 68, 70, 77.
2. Sharp, 18; New Monthly Magazine, Vol. 7, pp. 352–353.

curious pleasure, broken only when he was handed a note to say that his friend Haslam's father was expected to die. Keats was lifted into a philosophic mood by this reminder that, while he was bounded by his own problems, the great inevitabilities of life and death went on. It made him realize how far he fell short of the "humble standard of disinterestedness" he set up as an ideal. His thought continued; self-interest seems the order of the world, from smallest to largest animal, Man included. Man has the same animal instincts as the hawk, whose predatory image had haunted Keats since the religious argument at Horace Smith's. Yet there is always something "in human nature tending to purify". He himself felt in this state—"straining at particles of light in the midst of a great darkness"—and his religious reading and musing led him to a hopeful thought, relating to poetry:

May there not be superior beings amused with any graceful, though instinctive attitude my mind m(a)y fall into, as I am entertained with the alertness of a Stoat or the anxiety of a Deer?

He thought perhaps of his own recent encounter with the butcher's boy, and his defence of a lesser animal against him:

Though a quarrel in the streets is a thing to be hated, the energies displayed in it are fine; the commonest Man shows a grace in his quarrel—By a superior being our reasoning(s) may take the same tone—though erroneous they may be fine—This is the very thing in which consists poetry;

Again he returned to his previous thought that nothing is real until experienced; all his recent experiences came before him, and he wrote a poem which fulfilled the theme he had just encountered, that "While we are laughing the seed of some trouble is put into the wide arable land of events."

> Why did I laugh tonight? No voice will tell:
> No God, no Deamon of severe response
> Deigns to reply from heaven or from Hell.—
> Then to my human heart I turn at once—
> Heart! thou and I are here sad and alone;
> Say, wherefore did I laugh? O mortal pain!
> O Darkness! Darkness! ever must I moan
> To question Heaven and Hell and Heart in vain!
> Why did I laugh? I know this being's lease
> My fancy to its utmost blisses spreads:
> Yet could I on this very midnight cease,
> And the world's gaudy ensigns see in shreds.
> Verse, fame and Beauty are intense indeed
> But Death intenser—Deaths is Life's high mead.[1]

1. *Letters*, II, 79–81.

The relief afforded by writing this sonnet can be felt in Keats's remark following it: "Sane I went to bed and sane I arose." He needed this "Ode to Darkness", which he had just told Haydon he would not write, to clear his mind, and there is no doubt that it did more than that. Until this moment, his mood that nothing was worth while had extended to *Hyperion*, "being in a sort of qui bono temper, not exactly on the road to an epic poem". Now the question of "Cui bono" was partly answered; might it not be for the interest of "a superior being" that he should make one more effort? In the same mood as the sonnet, Keats took up the great poem where he had left it off, with Apollo about to be initiated into his godhead. At once the words, as he delightedly found, "seemed to come by chance or magic—to be as it were something given to him".[1] As his pen raced over the unblotted manuscript, he put into Apollo all his own confused search for and part-achievement of a wider knowledge:

> Knowledge enormous makes a God of me.
> Names, deeds, grey legends, dire events, rebellions,
> Majesties, sovran voices, agonies,
> Creations and destroyings, all at once
> Pour into the wide hollows of my brain,
> And deify me,

As "with no Agony but that of ignorance" he had written the sonnet, so he made Apollo approach and achieve divinity

> In fearless yet in aching ignorance

Yet in achieving this, Keats had perhaps destroyed the poem itself; he could not proceed to complete this book and go on to show the new god taking over from the moody Titan of Books One and Two. He had thought himself to a creative standstill. His description of Apollo's godhead is the final contradiction of his theory of Negative Capability, which he had once seen as necessary for the creator. Apollo only becomes the god of poetry by complete and painful knowledge. It is Hyperion who remains in the state of half-ignorance and half-knowledge which Keats had once seen as the creative state. Thus in more senses than one, Hyperion is the old Keats and Apollo is the new Keats, but the knowledge with which he invested his hero, and toward which he was darkly striving himself, posed a problem for the continuance of the poem. Apollo had been a poet of the Keatsian nature, able to take the identity of "any one particular beauteous star". Now, to be a god of poetry, absolute knowledge of good and evil, life and death, was required. In arriving at this thought, Keats perhaps made it certain that the poem broke off there. He could not yet face the pain of absolute knowledge, necessary for his continuance as a poet.

1. KC, I, 129.

That problem, the most important for his artistic and spiritual life, was still to be solved; all that thought could produce about his outward life was a series of sign-posts pointing in conflicting directions. Where and how he should live was an incessant problem, many-sided. The Brawnes were coming to live next door, his life with Brown was costly, he had no money of his own, and the £700 he had optimistically hoped from Tom's estate was receding daily as shares fell and lawyers muddled: Keats in exasperation even accused Walton's firm of systematically cheating the estate, but there is no evidence of this. He fell back on drawing an even larger sum than usual from George's money on 15 March (one of the many days when, he complained, nothing happened to him) but clearly this could not go on. He still had his medical books; as a potential physician, he could at least not appear to the Brawnes as a totally unprincipled wooer, but he would have to make show of increasing his qualification. The M.R.C.S. was now out of the question, with his aversion from surgery; the best, quickest and easiest way to obtain a further physician's qualification was to become a "Scotch doctor" and take the L.R.C.P., Edinburgh, where his room-mate, Tyrrell, had gone. A course there would get him away from Hampstead and postpone decision, and for a time he played with the idea; but try as he would, he could not see himself as a family doctor, coming into the sick-room with a hand held out for fees. Meanwhile, time advanced relentlessly, bringing fresh crises. As quarter-day approached, Haydon's demands became insistent. "Before the 20th if you could help me it would be nectar and manna and all the blessings of gratified thirst." Early in April, a bachelor claret-feast saw Dilke off to Westminster. "We all got a little tipsy—but pleasantly so—I enjoy Claret to a degree." On 3 April Fanny and her family moved in next door,[1] and some decision must be made.

Its outward sign was, in all probability, two more sonnets. One was an existing sonnet revised, which he gave her, and which became for ever afterwards associated with their love. This was *Bright Star*. In revising it, Keats removed its more physical and sensuous aspects:

> Cheek-pillow'd on my Love's white ripening breast

became, with less emphasis on touch and sight,

> Pillow'd upon my fair love's ripening breast

Yet it was none the less a declaration of love, and the sign of at least an understanding between them. Keats began to give Fanny books and to read them with her, notably those parts which dealt with the deepest love. One of these was the Fifth Canto in Dante's *Inferno*. On the fly-leaf of this tiny volume, she inscribed the *Bright Star* sonnet. Reading with her the lines which describe how Paolo and Francesca were also reading a love-tale when they

1. Dilke, ann. I, opp. p. 288.

fell in love, the story of Lancelot, and "How him love thrall'd", Keats became obsessed by this picture of the fated lovers. At night, in the same dreaming state in which he had visioned the three figures of the Darkness sonnet, he now had a vision of himself "being in that region of Hell". Only one figure was with him now; he floated with her, above the cold of other lovers in a sensuous warmth, with his lips joined to hers. In the symbolism of the dream, all his desires were concentrated on Fanny. When they met, to read again, he took back the little volume from her, and impulsively began to write another sonnet at right-angles across the fly-leaf; recalled, by her or by his own eyes, to the fact that he was "crossing" her own writing-out of *Bright Star*, he turned to the end of the book, and after false starts, he succeeded in writing a sonnet; at least, as he said, "there are fourteen lines but nothing of what I felt in it". Much of the feeling, however, remains, and the two sonnets taken together mark a crisis in their relationship; henceforward, as much as the lovers in Dante, "him love thrall'd".[1]

The conflicts and intensity, in this mid-April, remained. Keats was still "in a great darkness", though the pressure of experience was maturing him. There was, of course, one pressure of which he may not have been aware. His dreams, his lassitude and depression, his sensation of "stifling" even on a cold day, all point to the temperatures and night-sweats of a tubercular infection, caught from Tom while nursing him. It is not certain that Keats allowed himself to know this, still less, as has been thought, that his anxiety over his sister Fanny was also connected with their "family disease". Keats put his medical knowledge into the recesses of his unconscious mind, whence it emerged as poetry, as in the Darkness sonnet; for his sister, he was chiefly anxious that, removed from school, she should not be the Abbeys' drudge, paying for this doubtful privilege out of her own legal income. In his letters, written once a fortnight at her request, he now regarded himself as her true guardian, criticizing the Abbeys, advising her on her reading, games and hobbies, providing her with plants, jewellery, and books, even including one to help her prepare for confirmation. These letters form a human counterpoint to the dark stirrings of the rest of his thought, and show that he underestimated his "disinterested" care for other people.

Disease and death were banished into his inner mind; there they became symbols lurking just below the level of consciousness virtually for the rest of his life. When they emerged, through the accident of poetry, they now came with an effect unlike anything he had written before. Such was the most famous of all poems of this hardly conscious sort, *La Belle Dame Sans Merci*. So much went into this almost fragmentary poem, so much has been interpreted from it, that any examination must start with the warning that nothing one says either about its origins or its effects can fully explain it. All that can be said in a general way is that in this magical poem the identification

1. The volume, with the two sonnets, is now in the Library of Yale University.

of Love and Death, implicit in the Darkness sonnet, the end of *Bright Star*, and the Dante sonnet, is made explicit, and that this is a theme to which Keats returns all through the rest of his writing life. It marks a huge shift in thought. In *St. Agnes* and *St. Mark*, Love and Death are dramatically opposed. Now they are seen as one. It is a new reading of his own life. Almost everything that occurred to Keats in the first three weeks of this April found its way into the poem. Trivial or momentous, they all made their mark.

On 2 and 3 April, he drew the last £100 or so that George had left behind. The Brawnes were moving in, and it was necessary to appear to have some money in his pocket. Some he used to pay the debts of his social life—it was the exact time of the claret-feast—some he put aside for his summer lodgings, since Wentworth Place would be let, following Brown's usual custom. Clearly there was nothing for Haydon, and he nerved himself to tell the painter. A letter of rebuke, to which he wrote a stiff little reply, accused him of holding out "delusive hopes" and leading Haydon on. Keats was wounded by this accusation, and in turn accused Haydon of disturbing his own peace of mind. That it was disturbed was shown by another incident a few days later. On 15 April, Keats went and collected from Bentley's the last of Tom's belongings. Here, for the first time, he read the actual letters Wells had sent to Tom in the name of the fictitious Amena. As he read them, Keats began to see his dead brother as the victim of a delusion, cruelly fostered by his mischievous schoolfriend; this faked love, as he suspected, had helped on Tom's death. He also saw, very unpleasantly, that the letters contained cunning parodies of phrases from his own early Spenserian poems, in a sequence where Tom was addressed as a Knight, with the false Amena to soothe and lull him as his companion.[1] He wrote murderously to George of this, in a tone of voice hardly sane. "I will harm him all I possibly can" was the mildest of his phrases for Wells. At the same time, such were the contradictions of his nature, he himself jotted some light verse for George, made out of a family joke in which the three brothers appeared, George as an Ape who had "picklocked a faery's boudoir" i.e. got married, Tom as a Fool (Tom-Fool) and Keats himself as a rhyming dwarf, all serving a Princess—Georgiana. Indeed his poetry at this time is entirely light-hearted, whatever went on in his heart. Parodies were the order of the day—a parody in the style of Spenser on Brown, a parody of Wordsworth's *Dover* sonnet, possibly helped by Woodhouse during a visit to Town. Both are comic catalogues of opposites; Brown was described as the reverse of himself, the sonnet took Wordsworth's list of things he liked and produced a list of dislikes. Visits to the theatre, to the panorama of Arctic exploration in Leicester Square, an all-night card-playing party at Wentworth Place with Taylor, Woodhouse and Reynolds as guests—nothing could have seemed more trivial; yet suddenly, on the evening of Wednesday 21 April, his pen

1. JKLY, 120–122.

traced to George the words "La belle dame sans merci", followed by the draft of the poem.

O what can ail thee, knight-at-arms,
   Alone and palely loitering?
The sedge has wither'd from the lake,
   And no birds sing.

O what can ail thee, knight-at-arms,
   So haggard and so woe-begone?
The squirrel's granary is full,
   And the harvest's done.

I see a lilly on thy brow,
   With anguish moist and fever dew,
And on thy cheeks a fading rose
   Fast withereth too.

I met a lady in the meads,
   Full beautiful—a faery's child,
Her hair was long, her foot was light,
   And her eyes were wild.

I made a garland for her head,
   And bracelets too, and fragrant zone;
She look'd at me as she did love,
   And made sweet moan.

I set her on my pacing steed,
   And nothing else saw all day long,
For sidelong would she bend, and sing
   A faery's song.

She found me roots of relish sweet,
   And honey wild, and manna dew,
And sure in language strange she said—
   'I love thee true'.

She took me to her elfin grot,
   And there she wept, and sigh'd full sore,
And there I shut her wild wild eyes
   With kisses four.

And there she lulled me asleep,
   And there I dream'd—Ah! woe betide!
The latest dream I ever dream'd
   On the cold hill side.

I saw pale kings and princes too,
  Pale warriors, death-pale were they all;
They cried—'La Belle Dame sans Merci
  Hath thee in thrall!'

I saw their starved lips in the gloam,
  With horrid warning gaped wide,
And I awoke and found me here,
  On the cold hill's side.

And this is why I sojourn here,
  Alone and palely loitering,
Though the sedge has wither'd from the lake,
  And no birds sing.

The record of light-hearted days, even allied to the dark nightmares and repressed thoughts of death by night, would not alone account for the supreme poetic quality of the simple-looking stanzas. With Keats, poems were always partly begotten by poetry. Here, the begetters of the most lyrical poem he ever wrote were, in indirect ways but appropriately enough, the great authors of *Lyrical Ballads*. Ten days before he had actually met Coleridge, walking in Millfield Lane, Hampstead Heath, with Joseph Green, one of Keats's demonstrators at Guy's. Keats joined them, and Coleridge afterwards claimed to remember, with a hindsight not perhaps so inaccurate, how his handshake felt like that of a dying man.[1] What Coleridge chose not to remember, but Keats amusingly recorded, was that he himself delivered one of his famous monologues lasting about an hour. In Keats's resumé to George, the dominant topics are dreams and the unconscious, of which Coleridge was a connoisseur and Keats, unknown to him, a living example. Keats was a reader of Coleridge, both earlier and more recently, for elements of the critic-mangled *Christabel* had appeared in *The Eve of St. Agnes*. Both the subjects of the older poet's monologue, and his own presence, must have recalled the nightmare atmosphere of *The Ancient Mariner*, with its incantatory power.

  Wordsworth came into the picture less directly. One of the reasons for Keats's addiction to parody at this moment was that he had just read one of the most brilliant parodies of all time. This was Reynolds's parody of Wordsworth's poem, *Peter Bell*, a scoop by Taylor and Hessey, which they brought out in anticipation of the real poem. Its devastating likeness even amused Coleridge, who felt bound to defend Wordsworth, but had to admit that "the preface and notes are very droll and clever", while Keats recognized in

1. Coleridge, *Table Talk*, 14 August 1832. He described Keats as "loose, slack, not well-dressed", a description copied by Horace Smith, though it had been contradicted by Hunt in the *Book of Gems*, Vol. III, 1838.

the verse "an inveterate cadence" of the real Wordsworth. He had been asked by Reynolds, at their card-party on 19 April, to write a short review for *The Examiner*. He did this on the morning of the 21st and, searching for a graceful way of pleasing Reynolds and being fair to the "half of Wordsworth" he always admired, he hit on the device of comparing the parody to the "false Florimel" of Book III of *The Faerie Queene*, the double of the real heroine. Spenser, never far from his mind, came in by way of this comparison, as yet another literary element on the verge of *La Belle Dame*, especially the lines

> Girlonds of flowres sometimes for her fair hed
> He fine would dight; sometimes the squirell wild
> He brought to her in bands, as conquered
> To be her thrall . . .

At the same time, Burton's *Anatomy of Melancholy*, which Keats now seemed to be reading and marking almost as if with a personal application to himself, provided a picture of the melancholy man, wandering alone and pale by the waterside, the knight-at-arms of Keats's poem.[1]

Wordsworth for the cadence of the poem, Coleridge for its nightmare quality, Spenser for its medieval setting, Burton for the melancholy of its hero, all contribute to, but none account for the intensity and underlying depth of a poem which brought Keats's darkest and most fundamental experiences to the surface. Much can be attributed to his identification of the knight with Tom, deceived by the false Amena, deluded, as Keats believed, by Wells's phantom lady, and betrayed to death, the whole horror of that death recalled by finding Wells's mocking letters. La Belle Dame is not only Love but also Death, and Keats is reliving "on the pulses" Tom's death. Yet she was also much more to Keats himself. She was clearly connected with the dream of the Dante sonnet, and with the eternally tormented lovers of the *Inferno*. Even what has been called the metrical secret of the poem, the short last line of each stanza, chimes here with the breaks in Cary's blank-verse translation which produced half-lines like "How him love thrall'd", and "All trembling kiss'd" and which are echoed unmistakably in the first draft of Keats's poem.[2] The pale knight of *La Belle Dame* has the paleness of the lovers in this canto and in his own Dante sonnet. Yet the sonnet had expressed some-how the strange happiness of the dream that caused it; there is no happiness in the knight's dream. In it he sees the vision of the pale dead kings and princes. That these are dead, and not merely in thrall, is made clear by Keats's source for them; for these are the dead Kings of Scotland, from his letter to Tom about Iona, which he had just fetched with Tom's other letters. Speculation has been spent on whether the Lady is Fanny Brawne, or even Isabella, but she is more archetypal than that. On the other hand, the Jungian claim that

1. JKLY, 117.   2. MOK, 32.

she represents the "false" poetry, from which he was now turning away towards philosophy, is an over-simplification too. She is, when all literary hints from other sources, when all the accidental events of Keats's day-to-day life are exhausted, the symbol of the eternal fusion of Love and Death. Keats from now onwards instinctively knew that these two for him were coupled together. In a month he had progressed from the halfway position held in the Darkness sonnet, that Death was "intenser" than verse, fame and beauty, all the things he loved. Death, he realized in the vision of *La Belle Dame*, was a part of all those loves; they held their nature from the fact that all contained in them the seeds of the death they were all to experience. Whether this was heightened in him by any conscious knowledge that he himself, as much as Tom or the Knight, had entered into love and yet was full of the germs of imminent death, is impossible to say. It was certainly not revealed by any process of reasoning, though it may lurk between the lines of this poem which, for all its complicated and circumstantial ancestry, is, in the final result, a pure expression of the deepest instincts of mortal nature.

37   Wentworth Place, Hampstead

38 Chichester Cathedral and the Vicars' Hall, which was visited by Keats,
and which provided some of the medieval setting for *The Eve of St.
Agnes*, 1819. Just previous to Keats's visit, it was occupied by a wine-
merchant and postmaster, Joseph Redman.

IL TRIONFO (DELLA MORTE)

39   The Triumph of Death from the Campo Santo at Pisa, the engraving by

LE (TRIOMPHE) DE LA (MORT)

Giovanni degli Alessandri

delle belle Arti &c &c &c

...sinio, which Keats saw in B.R. Haydon's studio, 27 December, 1818.

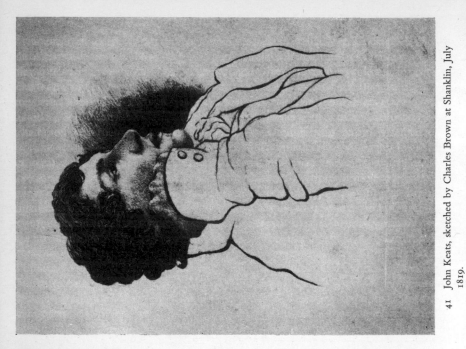

41 John Keats, sketched by Charles Brown at Shanklin, July 1819.

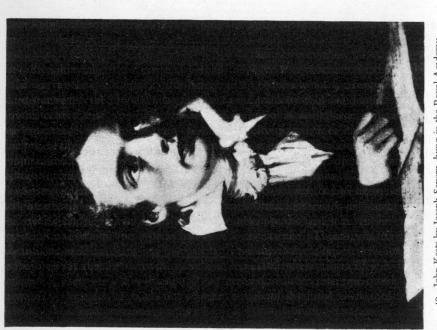

40 John Keats by Joseph Severn, hung in the Royal Academy Exhibition, Somerset Home, 1819.

Chapter 21

SPARKS OF THE DIVINITY

*"There may be intelligences or sparks of the divinity in millions—
but they are not Souls till they acquire identities, till each one is
personally itself"*

– JOHN KEATS to George and Georgiana Keats, 21 April 1819

WHATEVER else it represented, the writing of *La Belle Dame* formed part of
an immense release in Keats at this time. The indolence, gloom and brooding
of the past months gave way to action, strong feeling, real thought.
Exceptionally early and beautiful spring weather in the first half of April was
a simple cause; as he had hoped earlier, it roused him up, and helped to give
him "the great shake" which, he told his sister, his life needed. From the
middle of April, ideas and poetry poured from him. The second half of his
long letter to George has a liveliness quite absent from the first, as can be seen
by comparing his bits of "quizzing" for his sister-in-law. In March he had
only been able to manage some rather stale repartee about her brother's
fiancée and a mock petition to a pauper madhouse for himself, signed
ironically "Count de Cockaigne"; now he made brilliant fun in imagination
of her backwoods life, following the lines of Cobbett's attacks on Birkbeck's
Settlement.[1] The arrival of the Brawnes next door added to his sense of
day-by-day exhilaration, in spite of his dark unconscious forebodings about
the consequences of his love for Fanny. Her beauty was an inspiration to him,
and if he had been, as she complained, "an age" in declaring his love, it was
because the by-play of her social manner put him off. Meeting now naturally
and under ordinary conditions, his feelings deepened. There was still no
formal engagement. With George's dwindling money in his purse, Keats
turned a blind eye to the future. The physician's course at Edinburgh went
into limbo, and so did a plan to join the Dilkes at Westminster; he was glad
to find that Brown did not intend to let the house any earlier than last year,
and that they could stay at Wentworth Place till the end of June. There was
also a sense of relief that he had handed over to Woodhouse, at the card-party
on 19 April, the manuscripts of the unfinished *Hyperion*, and *The Eve of St.
Mark*, together with *The Eve of St. Agnes*. In poetry too, out of sight was out
of mind, and he could concentrate on the new phase of his work, the

1. *Letters*, II, 92–93; E. No. 585, p. 168.

illustration of a philosophy of life by the writing of poems. *La Belle Dame* is Keats's last poem conceived without conscious thought. From henceforth his poems are meditations, and his meditations poems.

This was made clear as he went on writing to George immediately after the last haunting lines

> And this is why I sojourn here,
> Alone and palely loitering,
> Though the sedge has wither'd from the lake,
> And no birds sing.

He dismissed the poem with a joke which suggests he never valued it highly; in fact, his unfortunate revision of it for publication by Hunt a year later was probably not due either to his ill-health or Hunt's bad taste, but simply to the fact that he never saw in the poem the importance others have done. To him it was a piece of light occasional verse, which he followed with another, a fragment of dialogue between symbolic spirits recalling closely the opening of *Manfred*, the only part of Byron's works that Keats quoted and mentioned with approval.[1] Indeed, from now onward, the obsessive criticism of Byron drops out of Keats's writing, another sign of stability and the "abatement of my love of fame", as he afterwards put it. Writing on,[2] Keats left verse, and turned to thought. He had been reading lately, he told George, two contrasted books. One was, once again, Robertson's *The History of America*, which he still got out from time to time to try and recapture "identity" with George overseas; the bleak primitive landscape of Robertson's prose had even penetrated a little into *La Belle Dame*. The other was a book about sophisticated society, Voltaire's *Le Siècle de Louis XIV*. Viewing thus the whole gamut of Man, from Robertson's savages, "less improved than in any part of the earth", to Le Roi Soleil, Keats sought for a whole philosophy of life. He did not believe in the noble savage, nor in the perfectibility of earthly life; indeed, perfect happiness in life, he saw, would make death intolerable. In any case, it was unattainable; the same natural disasters overcame savage and civilized man. Yet the Christian idea that the common hardships of this world were only a miserable interlude before the blessed state of another struck him as "a little circumscribed straightened notion". It did not square with the observable facts of the natural world.

In seeing Man against the huge and often violent and disastrous manifestations of Nature, Keats was following closely another book of Voltaire, which

---

1. *Letters*, I, 279.
2. *Letters*, II, 95–104. Ward, 432, n. 9, states that since the MS shows breaks after *La Belle Dame* and *Chorus of Four Fairies*, this part of the letter was written on three different occasions. However, the MS in the Keats Collection, Houghton Library, shows no breaks.

he possessed, the French philosopher's *Essai sur les mœurs*.[1] His admiration of Voltaire had shown itself in more ways than one since he had drunk Lamb's toast to Voltaire at the dinner-party at Haydon's. Recently, after one of his periods of silent brooding in Haydon's painting room, Keats got up and stood before the picture where the figures of Wordsworth and others were now fully painted as worshippers of Christ. Looking at the figure of Voltaire, placed there in contrast by Haydon as an unbeliever, Keats put his hand on his heart, bowed his head, and announced "there is the being I will bow to".[2] Voltaire, in the opening of his *Essai*, saw Man as subject to the giant forces of Nature, the shifting sands of Africa, the whirlpools of Messina, the volcanoes of Vesuvius and Etna. Keats repeated this idea almost exactly:

Look at the Poles and at the sands of Africa, Whirlpools and volcanoes—Let men exterminate them and I will say that they may arrive at earthly Happiness—The point at which Man may arrive is as far as the paralel state in inanimate nature and no further—

Yet although Keats also used the precise words of Voltaire in describing orthodox religion as a "pious fraud",[3] he could not be satisfied with a complete and negative scepticism. Somewhere he must find a faith.

What he had just written reminded him of his religious discussions at Oxford with Bailey, who had formed his beliefs on *The Analogy of Religion* by Joseph Butler. Butler, from the Christian standpoint, had made just the same statement. "Every species of creature is, we see, designed for a particular way of life ... Our nature corresponds to our external condition", or, as Keats put it, "the inhabitants of the world will correspond to itself". Man, as Keats had also observed, "is left, by nature, an unformed, unfinished creature", corresponding with the state of the natural world in which he finds himself. Instead of seeing this condition as a cause of despair and scepticism, Butler viewed it as a reason for faith and hope. He did this by drawing an analogy between childhood and our present life, and then between the maturity, toward which we grow in this world, and the life to come: "our being placed in a state of discipline throughout this life, for another world, is a providential disposition of things, exactly of the same kind, as our being placed in a state of discipline during childhood, for mature age". This world is a place of probation, or proving, through which we develop so as to become capable of a future world. It is not, in the phrase which Keats contemptuously rejected, "a vale of tears", from which we are released by divine intervention, but all part of a necessary and natural process for the education of the soul.

How much Keats remembered of Bailey's exposition of Butler is hard to

1. Stuart M. Sperry, Jr., "Keats's Skepticism and Voltaire", KSJ, Vol. XII, Winter 1963, 75–93.

2. Haydon, II, 317.   3. *Letters*, II, 101 and 80.

say; various phrases suggest that he may even have included Butler among his recent reading of religious books. He wrote on to George[1]

Call the world if you Please "The vale of Soul-making" Then you will find out the use of the world ... I say "*Soul making*" Soul as distinguished from an Intelligence— There may be intelligences or sparks of the divinity in millions—but they are not Souls till they acquire identities, till each one is personally itself. I(n)telligences are atoms of perception—they know and they see and they are pure, in short they are God—How then are Souls to be made? How then are these sparks which are God to have identity given them—so as ever to possess a bliss peculiar to each ones individual existence? How, but by the medium of a world like this? ... I will call the *world* a School instituted for the purpose of teaching little children to read—I will call the *human heart* the *horn Book* used in that School—and I will call the *child able to read, the Soul* made from that *school* and its *hornbook*. Do you not see how necessary a World of Pains and troubles is to school an Intelligence and make it a soul? A Place where the heart must feel and suffer in a thousand diverse ways! ... As various as the Lives of Men are—so various become their souls, and thus does God make individual beings, Souls, Identical Souls of the sparks of his own essence—This appears to me a faint sketch of a system of Salvation which does not affront our reason and humanity.

Far from intelligence being a touchstone, reason must be sent to suffer with the heart before it can become a soul. This suffering, which Keats observes everywhere in the world, is a creative and not a destructive process. He tried to sum up for George:

I began by seeing how man was formed by circumstances—and what are circumstances?—but touchstones of his heart—? and what are touchstones?—but proovings of his heart? and what are proovings of his heart but fortifiers or alterers of his nature? and what is his altered nature but his soul?—and what was his soul before it came into the world and had These provings and alterations and perfectionings?—An intelligence—without Identity—and how is this Identity to be made? Through the medium of the Heart? And how is the heart to become this Medium but in a world of Circumstances?

Keats put this scheme forward, he wrote to George, as a grander system of salvation than the Christian religion, "or rather", he added, "it is a system of Spirit-creation". This was its essential difference from the Christian scheme expounded by Butler, from whose analogies Keats seems to have borrowed his own. Butler, with orthodox Christianity, assumed that the soul in each individual was already created by God before it came into this world. To Keats, there was specifically no such pre-creation. God creates souls in the world, indeed, through the trials and probations of the world. The idea of Christ as mediator between God and Man which formed a great part of Butler's argument was also rejected by Keats; for though he could see the splendour of Christ, as he had said earlier in the same letter, he could not accept any idea of a divine personal intervention. Soul-making seemed to

1. *Letters*, II, 102–104.

him perhaps the parent of all known religions. It was the belief he himself had reached, in just over a year after his vision at Teignmouth of the destructive forces of/the world, and it provided a faith that his positive nature needed. "There now", Keats added, "I think what with Poetry and Theology you may thank your Stars that my pen is not very long winded." The mammoth evening of writing, on which he jokingly looked back, had indeed released him into inspiration. When he took up his pen, nine days later, it was to copy an ode of nearly seventy lines and four sonnets. The *Ode to Psyche* he somewhat strangely introduced as "the first and only one (poem) with which I have taken even moderate pains". In enlarging on this remark, he seemed to be comparing it not only with the fugitive sonnets, but even by implication with all he had written before—"I think it reads the more richly for it and will I hope encourage me to write other things in even a more peacable and healthy spirit." The "great shake" that Keats was now giving to himself applied not only to his life and thought but to his whole verse technique. Listening to Hazlitt's praise of Dryden's tales in verse from Chaucer and Boccaccio just over a year before, he had produced *Isabella*; but in that poem he had not attempted Dryden's verse-technique. Now, with Croker's criticism of the couplets in *Endymion* deeply-bitten into his mind, he recalled Hazlitt's favourable verdict on Dryden generally as "a bolder and more varied versifier than Pope". To study Dryden's verse-style would not be to give in to the camp of Pope, and the strength and masculinity of that style, also praised by Hazlitt, commended itself to Keats. According to Brown he made "much study" of it; Dryden, like Spenser, is a poet's poet, and lends himself to technical study. Already, strong signs of Dryden had appeared in verses as different as the family-joke *Extempore* couplets for George and the Dante sonnet for Fanny, whose imagery is taken as much from Dryden's translation of Ovid as from the *Inferno*. He read Dryden at this time wholesale, even the Odes which Hazlitt found less successful, and his own long irregular *Ode to Psyche* has the marks of this reading. In shape and technique it derives from Dryden's *Ode to Mrs. Anne Killigrew*, and shows Keats somewhat at odds with the new form and the fresh poetic stimulus; this explains why the "pains" Keats said he had taken did not yet produce a highly-finished work. Yet the *Ode to Psyche* was another turning-point in Keats's earnest and strenuous self-development as a poet. In it he was also trying to assimilate his new thought, to write poems "running over with . . . knowledge and experience". The story of Psyche, enduring trials of "a world of circumstances", the story taken, as he found in Lemprière, as a symbol of the soul itself, attracted him as an allegory for his own philosophic soul-making; he probably read more than one translation of the story as told by Apuleius, and even reinforced his own soul-making theory from the introduction to the translation by Thomas Taylor, the Platonic philosopher.

Much of the disappointment critics have felt with this ode is because it has been associated too much with the other odes of this early summer. Neither in form nor in method does it resemble them in any way. As a poem of ideas, it sticks to its brief of simply stating that Keats will be the poet-priest of this hitherto hardly-recognized deity, the soul. If the soul, taught by experience of this world, as Psyche was by her trials, is a perfected spark of God, then the poet should celebrate it. As a verse counterpart of the soul-making doctrine it falls short, as Keats's verse often does, of the sweep of his prose. It is for incidentals that *Psyche* is chiefly memorable—the Miltonic vision, like the bower of Adam and Eve in *Paradise Lost*, Book IV, of Cupid and Psyche sleeping, and the repetitive Miltonic echoes of the *Nativity Ode* as Keats claims to be the new divinity's priest. These incidentals themselves are a summary of his life and thought in the disturbed and dark months before. Even the beautiful image.

With the wreath'd trellis of a working brain

recalls, in anatomical detail, some taking-up of his medical text-books when he had considered training professionally again. The myriad flowers, the "casement ope at night To let the warm Love in" are like his dream of Fanny in the Dante sonnet and their present situation in the shared garden at Went-worth Place. Keats had not yet assimilated either his new reading nor the thought he hoped to express in it.

The same confusion of aims and techniques was seen in the sonnets, or "sins" as Keats wryly called them, that accompany the ode. Two on *Fame* are awkward workings-out of his repudiation of Ambition; the first beginning

Fame, like a wayward girl will still be coy

is still pure Dryden, and all have a strong connection with his other great reading-source at this time, Burton's *The Anatomy of Melancholy*. Burton's *Remedies Against Discontents* for the melancholy man struck a particular chord for Keats just now; he echoed phrases of the book in these sonnets, and marked his copy copiously, and often humorously. It was perhaps after some un-successful visit to the City that he added the note, "Precious stones are certainly a remedy against Melancholy: a valuable diamond would effectually cure mine." Keats began to be weary of the sonnet-form itself, that dangerous arm-chair for so many poets' tired thought. Neither of the two main sonnet-forms seemed adequate for what he wanted to say. The Miltonic was too automatic with what Keats called its "pouncing rhymes"; the Shakespearian was too elegiac, the final couplet often unmanageable. Keats tried an experimental arrangement of rhymes with a sonnet *On the Sonnet*, but he was still dissatisfied, and apart from two intensely personal and private poems, he never tried the sonnet-form again. On the other hand, he had found the Pindaric type of ode used by Dryden, and also attempted by himself in the lyric interludes to *Endymion*, far too diffuse for philosophic argument. As he sealed his immense letter to George at the beginning of May, hoping now to send it to the Settlement by Birkbeck's son Richard,[1] Keats had probably already at least sketched some of the poems that were to embody all his new aspirations in both form and thought.

The four poems he now wrote in the next few weeks frame the most coherent block of verse that Keats achieved, and they are rightly the most widely known of his works. They are bound together by a unity of form and theme. All four are written in ten-line stanzas, whose scheme, with small variations, is identical: a Shakespearian quatrain, followed by a Miltonic sestet. The thought of each of the four is not identical, but the themes of all are related. The four—*Ode on Indolence*, *Ode on Melancholy*, *Ode to a Nightingale*, *Ode on a Grecian Urn*—may be said to make an Ode-sequence with a great deal more unity than many sonnet-sequences normally contain. It must be said at once that no one knows in what order the odes were composed.[2] Brown, who had conceived what Keats charitably called "one of his funny odd dislikes" to Woodhouse at the card-party on 19 April, was now assiduous in making copies of Keats's poems, and dating them. Though he afterwards overcame his jealousy, and handed his jottings over to Woodhouse, he now saw himself as Keats's true Boswell, even claiming to have rescued the scattered first draft of the *Nightingale Ode* from oblivion.[3] Yet even he only dated the four poems as written in the year 1819, specifying the month of May but no exact date for the *Nightingale Ode*, with which he was most concerned. The order does not matter greatly; there is no progress of thought from one ode to the other. Rather each is an attempt at the same theme from a different viewpoint, just as the Socratic dialogues deal with the same philosophic ideas from some different starting-point. They are attempts to answer the agonized questions of Keats's Darkness sonnet, and the long months of self-examination, in the light of the soul-making philosophy Keats had just achieved. Whatever their order, these May odes were composed, perhaps within a few days, as a unity. All four are saturated in the natural surroundings which now matched Keats's mood, and which he had sketched in the April *Ode to Psyche*. There is a sense of homecoming in all of them. They are filled with the garden setting of fruit, flowers, undergrowth, green lawns, and birdsong, which had been the geography and climate of his verse from earliest days, an ideal world conceived in the gardens at Enfield and Edmonton. Now, his first summer at Wentworth Place, this ideal was

1. It must have found its way by other means, for Richard Birkbeck did not eventually sail to join his father until July 16. Gladys Scott Thomson, *A Pioneer Family*, 61.

2. See Ward, 432, n. 12.

3. KC, II, 65. His whole account was doubted by Dilke, KHM No. 203. The state of the MS, in fact, suggests that he confused the composition of *Indolence*, whose stanzas have always been jumbled, with that of the *Nightingale Ode*.

actually all about him, so that he could walk out into it each morning, and linger in it every evening. For all their questionings, there is a sense of security in the midst of storm about the May Odes. There was too the inspiring and lovely presence of Fanny Brawne, and the material well-being spread by Brown with his diligent bachelor housekeeping, which led Keats to a little panegyric in prose, written on May Day to his sister—"please heaven, a little claret-wine cool out of a cellar a mile deep—with a few or a good many ratifia cakes—a rocky basin to bathe in, a strawberry bed to say your prayers to Flora in—".[1] His cheerfulness broke out into a parody of nursery rhyme for Fanny at Walthamstow, with a cheeky shared joke about Mrs. Abbey.

> Two or three Posies
> With two or three simples
> Two or three Noses
> With two or three pimples—
> Two or three wise men
> And two or three ninny's
> Two or three purses
> And two or three guineas
> Two or three raps
> At two or three doors
> Two or three naps
> Of two or three hours—
> Two or three Cats
> And two or three mice
> Two or three sprats
> At a very great price—
> Two or three sandies
> And two or three tabbies
> Two or three dandies—
> And two M^{rs}———mum! , . .

In everything he wrote there was a feeling, perhaps for the first time since his mood of acceptance in the May Ode of a year ago, that the light and shade of his own life could be reconciled. He now reasserted the value of those moods of negative capability, which he had seemed to abandon in facing, with Apollo, the assumption of godhead through total knowledge. Half-joking, he recognized this in June, when, looking back, he said, "the thing I have most enjoyed this year has been writing an ode to Indolence". The *Indolence* and *Melancholy* odes, in fact, show diffuseness, repetition, and cancelled stanzas. It may not be wrong to regard these two as Keats's earlier essays in this form, and the great *Nightingale* and *Grecian Urn* as his more finished and later works. *Indolence* and *Melancholy*, too, borrow much of their

1. The likeness to *Ode to a Nightingale*, stanza 2, has often been pointed out.

ideas and imagery from the particular wording of the part of Keats's letter to George which had resulted in his *Darkness* sonnet. The sonnet, as he said, had given him relief at the time. Now, in the more philosophic mood which he derived from the doctrine of soul-making, he was able to re-read this passage before closing his letter to his brother, and see in it the germs of his two minor odes:

Neither Poetry, nor Ambition, nor Love have any alertness of countenance as they pass by me: they seem rather like three figures on a greek vase—a Man and two women —whom no one but myself could distinguish in their disguisement. This is the only happiness; and is a rare instance of advantage in the body overpowering the Mind.

The news that Haslam's father was dying then arrived, and he continued

This is the world—thus we cannot expect to give way many hours to pleasure— Circumstances are like Clouds continually gathering and bursting—While we are laughing the seed of some trouble is put into the wide arable land of events—while we are laughing it sprouts is [*for* it] grows and suddenly bears a poison fruit which we must pluck—

The first passage has naturally been recognized as the origin of *Indolence*; but it is just as natural to recognize in the second passage much of the imagery of the last two stanzas of *Melancholy*. The image of Melancholy itself being a cloud that gathers, "sudden from heaven" as the Ode puts it in its second stanza, the whole idea of pleasure "turning to poison while the bee-mouth sips", in the striking image of the third stanza, links this part of the letter closely to the poem.

There can be little doubt that *Indolence* was written on Tuesday 4 May, since it describes a May morning between showers. This was the only day of such weather in a three weeks' fine spell.[1] Putting together the scattered papers of his immense letter to George on 3 May, Keats had been struck by the indolent vision he had described in March of the three figures on a Greek vase, which he identified as Poetry, Ambition and Love.[2] He borrowed phrases for the Ode from his recent reading about Psyche in Apuleius,[3] and even imported one expression "my idle spright" wholesale from his mid-April Dante sonnet. The whole ode, in fact, has a borrowed air, and he acknowledged its lack of success by not printing it with the others. He could seldom fully recapture a mood once it had gone cold on him, still less an image, and the events and feelings of a month and a half before now seemed a world away. Yet with its acceptance of the numb, dull and indolent mood as something creative, it set the scene for all the odes that followed. He recognized, as he had often done throughout his life, the worth of such a fallow period as opposed to a life of apparent activity and achievement as the

1. G. M. (1819), I, 494.
2. Ward, 280 and 423 n. 15, is correct, not my JKLY, 145–146.
3. Colvin, 412, n. 1.

L*

world knows it, "the voice of busy common-sense". The Ode contained his final and most emphatic repudiation of Fame or Ambition or the sensation of being made to behave as others thought a poet ought to behave:

> For I would not be dieted with praise,
> A pet-lamb in a sentimental farce!

He liked this phrase about himself [1] so much that he repeated it in a letter; this suggests he now felt free from some situation which he knew to be false to himself and to his work.

The *Ode on Indolence* looks forward to the explorations of his soul-making doctrine in the following odes. In each one he takes the "World of Pains and troubles", questions it, analyses it, and resolves it in some sort of conclusion. Although the questionings are dark, the explorations full of doubt, the general effect of the conclusion in each ode is positive and hopeful. The "visions", to which he looked forward in the last stanza of *Indolence*, are, in the last resort, creative and happy in their fulfilment. As has been shown, it is natural to take the *Ode on Melancholy* next; [2] many features in it, too, including a cancelled first stanza, suggest that Keats was still feeling his way in the ode form. It was also natural for him to take an early chance to discuss, as one of the problems in a world of pains and troubles, his own innate tendency to melancholy, suspicion, with the profound and sudden disquiet which his friends noticed, and which he had himself made so many attempts to resolve in poetry and in thought. Critics have regarded this ode in various lights, ranging from an expression of the highest, realistic knowledge of life to an indulgence in the conventions of decadent romanticism. [3] The poem must always be viewed against Keats's whole history; in that view, it is his most complete attempt to describe, explain and reconcile his own tendencies, harking back to many other attempts, such as the Cave of Quietude passage in *Endymion*, but with even more self-knowledge and self-revelation. Keats naturally turned for this topic to Burton's *The Anatomy of Melancholy*, which he had been reading earlier in the year in the two-volume edition given him by Brown, and to the section on which he had already drawn for the Fame sonnets and the Indolence Ode, the various cures for melancholy to be found in the first 150 pages of Vol. 2. [4] He dismissed the traditional cures of this

---

1. Woodhouse's one editorial fault was to see uncomplimentary references to Byron in Keats's poetry; not knowing Keats meant himself (Letters, II, 116), against this "pet-lamb" line he noted "q allus[n] to Lord Byron" (last two words in shorthand). Keats Collection, Houghton Library, H 4.

2. Generally regarded as the last of this group in most works, including my own JKLY, 142–143, mainly because it was printed last (Ward, 433, n. 23). Its position in the 1820 volume, however, is arbitrary, since there it follows *To Autumn*.

3. E. C. Pettet, *On the Poetry of Keats*, 298–315.

4. Ward, 289, argues that Brown did not give Keats these volumes until June. Keats's markings (KHM, No. 25) in Vol. 2 do, however, parallel the order of his poems

compendium in his first stanza, just as he had cancelled a preliminary stanza which echoed some of Burton's more grotesque descriptions of the disease. What Keats chiefly repudiates is his former philosophy of the Cave of Quietude in *Endymion*, a state that now seemed to him mere escapism, "where anguish does not sting", and the soul drugs itself with the familiar symbols of oblivion, Lethe and the muffled tick of the death-watch beetle. The soul must keep itself awake to accept its anguish, the depressions of spirit Keats knew so well, and to whose almost clinical descriptions he added another, more telling than them all, in the opening of the second stanza:

> But when the melancholy fit shall fall
> Sudden from heaven like a weeping cloud,
> That fosters the droop-headed flowers all,
> And hides the green hill in an April shroud;

In this state, he now believes, the sufferer must remain open-eyed to everything around him, take an extra enjoyment in the symbols of beauty, the rose, the peony-flower, "the rainbow of the salt sand-wave". It is the solution he had not been able to accept a year before at Teignmouth, when by the "untumultuous fringe of silver foam", he had been appalled by his vision "Of an eternal fierce destruction". Now, with the philosophy of soul-making through a world of trial to support him, he can bear that vision, and even use it for good. Even destructive anger can be assimilated

> Or if thy mistress some rich anger shows,
> Emprison her soft hand, and let her rave,
> And feed deep, deep upon her peerless eyes.

Perversity, masochism and sadism have been found in these lines,[1] and if they are isolated, this can certainly be read into them. In the sense of the whole poem, though, it seems certain that Keats is not speaking of a physical mistress, but of the personified figure of Melancholy herself,[2] immediately addressed as "She" in the next stanza, and, incidentally, in the preliminary stanza which he cancelled. He is echoing in this form of address the passage in Burton which he marked—"if we melancholy men be not as bad as he that is worst, 'tis our dame Melancholy kept us so", and his whole solution is like that accepted by Burton at this point. Since Melancholy runs through everything,

---

from late April on. His original manuscript of the Ode shows strong parallels with Burton. "Wolfsbane" of line 2 was originally "henbane" (cf. Burton, Part 2, Sec. 5, Mem. 1, Subs. 6) while the original spelling of "pionies" in line 16 parallels that in Burton.

1. See Pettet, op. cit, 307–308; Leavis, *Revaluation*, 260.
2. Keats's original manuscript shows that he wrote "Mistress" with a capital M, which strongly suggests that the word personifies Melancholy herself. Facsimile reproduced T. W. Higginson, *Book and Heart*, opp. p. 18.

it must be faced as a part of life, and even embraced willingly. The final stanza, with its companion personifications of Beauty, Joy, Pleasure, reinforces this doctrine in strong, physical terms. The kinships of Melancholy and Delight, the twin shrines of Melancholy and Pleasure, can only be appreciated by one

> whose strenuous tongue
> Can burst Joy's grape against his palate fine;

Anguish is accepted, not avoided as in the Cave of Quietude; and so the Ode, for all its darker symbolism, ends in a positive way.[1]

The *Ode to a Nightingale* seems to have been written with *Indolence* and *Melancholy* in one very short space of time. The "drowsy numbness" of its opening line echoes the same words in *Indolence*, while its whole beginning has much in common with the mood of *Melancholy*. It must in any case, like all these Odes, have been written in the beautiful spell of fine weather that lasted from 26 April to 18 May; it seems probable that he composed it fairly close to his letter to Fanny Keats of May Day, since that contains so many phrases used in the second stanza. Though it has been thought unlikely in view of the mass of other composition,[2] it is just possible that he drafted it in some form as early as 30 April, and even ran its composition in double harness with the two lesser Odes. Brown said that on the day Keats wrote the *Nightingale Ode*, he himself was given permission by Keats to retrieve and copy the manuscript of any other poems he could find about Wentworth Place; it was on Friday 30 April that Keats observed Brown "rummaging up" and copying some of his past sonnets.[3] Brown believed that the nightingale had already built her nest as well as singing, which suggests a later date,[4] but he was no ornithologist; what is certain is that nightingales in Highgate had combined with indigestion to keep Coleridge awake early in May,[5] and that all nature was forward that season. Roses, as Keats noted, were out on 3 May; "mid-May's eldest child", as he called it in the Ode, was in the garden already.

The Ode, in any case, has a double setting; the Hampstead garden mingles with a more literary scene. Brown wrote that in that spring—he too placed it early in the season—a nightingale had built near the house, and that Keats felt "a tranquil and continual joy" in the bird's song. One fine morning, he

1. Though Middleton Murry, *Keats and Shakespeare*, 129, perhaps exaggerates it as "triumph through despair", he seems right to regard it as essentially a poem of acceptance of good and ill.
2. By Ward, 433, n. 19.
3. Brown's date of "May" would then refer to the time of copying.
4. To Ward, 433, n. 19, mistaking H. F. Witherby, *Handbook of British Birds*, II, 188.
5. Coleridge, *Letters*, IV, 941. "Ah! PHIlomel! Ill do thy strains accord with those of CALomel!" He may have heard them as early as 11 April, when he discussed them with Keats. H. W. Garrod, *Keats*, 124.

took his chair from the breakfast table to the grass-plot under a plum-tree, and wrote continuously for two or three hours. Yet if the morning's work was begun in the small garden, secluded by its hedge of laurustinus, it soon strayed from that "melodious plot", as Keats's imagination worked on it, into a wider landscape of deep forest and woodland ways. In his reading of Dryden, intensely cultivated this spring, Keats had come upon one favourite poem of his younger days in a new version. This was Dryden's modernization of *The Flower and the Leaf*. Keats two years before had written a sonnet on the original poem; now he wandered like the medieval poet, but in Dryden's phrases, through the woods of hawthorn and eglantine where the dancing festal troops of Flora appear. In his own imagination's country of

> White hawthorn, and the pastoral eglantine

he listened to the nightingale of his imagination

> pouring forth thy soul abroad
> In such an ecstasy

just as the poet of *The Flower and the Leaf* heard his nightingale "with Extasy of Bliss", in a setting of hawthorn and eglantine.[1]

For the most magical parts of the poem, it is also clear that Keats, just as he did in *La Belle Dame*, owed much to the authors of *Lyrical Ballads*. His nightingale is, like Coleridge's, a happy bird, not another of the conventions of melancholy, and its verdurous woodland setting also harks back to Coleridge's poem on the same subject. To the "sad embroidery of the Excursion", to which Keats had been recalled in his *Peter Bell* review, the deeper parts of the poem are implicitly dedicated. Wordsworth's vision of mortal life

> While man grows old, and dwindles, and decays;
> And countless generations of mankind
> Depart, and leave no vestige where they trod.

becomes Keats's vision of mortality's decay in stanza 3 and the beginning of stanza 7. Yet the poem is very closely allied to Keats's own life and meditation. Its likeness to Wordsworth at this point comes from an exactly like cause, the death of a deeply-loved brother in tragic circumstances.

"Where youth grows pale, and spectre-thin, and dies" alluded directly to Tom's death,[2] and the living song of the nightingale is everywhere contrasted with the dying generations of mankind. It might even seem "rich to die" in its presence, just as the "rich anger" of Melancholy in the other ode was something to be accepted and embraced. The theme of the song's eternal quality throughout man's decay is matched by Keats's delicate use of his one technical innovation in the pattern of this poem, the short eighth line. This

1. JKLY, 133–135.   2. Haydon, II, 318.

reached its highest effect in the freedom with which he used it in the last-but-one stanza, with its haunting associations of Wordsworth's Solitary Reaper and of Keats's own recurring vision of Claude's Enchanted Castle:

> Thou wast not born for death, immortal Bird!
> No hungry generations tread thee down;
> The voice I hear this passing night was heard
> In ancient days by emperor and clown:
> Perhaps the self-same song that found a path
> Through the sad heart of Ruth, when, sick for home,
> She stood in tears amid the alien corn;
> The same that oft-times hath
> Charm'd magic casements, opening on the foam
> Of perilous seas, in fairy lands forlorn.

Yet reality breaks in upon the vision for the following and final stanza. The eternity promised by the nightingale's song is only another illusion, a wishful creation of the fancy. The bird's song retreats down the valleys, no longer hopeful but plaintive. Keats is left once more with his "world of circumstances", in which the soul must grow through its pains of experience, helped by such inklings of eternity, but not in the end able to depend upon them.

The *Ode on a Grecian Urn* was another attack on the same problem from a different starting-point: not the eternity promised by nature, but that promised by art. It can hardly have been written much before the middle of this productive month of May, for it leans heavily for its ideas and their expression on two articles written by the high-priest of eternal art, Haydon, in *The Examiner* of 2 and 9 May.[1] In the same issue in which Hunt dismissed the real *Peter Bell* as "another didactic little horror", Haydon discussed Raphael's cartoon, *The Sacrifice at Lystra*. Although the sacrificial animal in the cartoon is a white bull, Haydon gave a great deal of information about the Greek ceremonies, in which a heifer, garlanded, was the victim, and the worshippers were often loose-robed, with dishevelled hair. In the particular sacrifice of this cartoon, he drew attention to the figure of the boy flute-player, "wholly absorbed in the harmony of his own music", and he described in detail the crowds from the city, where "all classes were crowding to sacrifice". In his second article a week later, he went on to contrast Raphael with those artists who seemed above human passion. Michelangelo's creations "look as if they were above the influence of time; they seem as if they would never grow old, and had never been young". Even he is outdone by some medieval sculptures, which have in their "immoveable stillness a look as if the

---

1. E. No. 592, pp. 285–287; No. 593, pp. 300–301. The likeness between these articles and the Ode was first noticed by J. R. MacGillivray, "Ode on a Grecian Urn", *Times Literary Supplement*, 9 July 1938, pp. 465–466.

figures were above the troubles of life, and saw through the imbecillity of appetite or passion".

Keats had been seeing Haydon again at this time. In spite of the cool letters they had exchanged in April, he had been moved by the painter's necessity, and had lent him £30 from his final withdrawal of the money George had left. Brown had prudently extracted from Haydon a signature to a bond making this loan repayable at three months; Keats and Haydon went, as in their earlier days, for a walk in the Kilburn Meadows, where Keats recited the recently composed Nightingale Ode, "with a tremulous under tone",[1] which moved Haydon. Visits to Haydon's studio were resumed, and it was almost certainly there that he looked into the various books of prints, from which the composite image of a Grecian urn began to form in his mind; two different engravings of the Louvre Sosibios Vase seem to be combined in the tracing which exists in his own hand[2]. The Elgin Marbles were also recalled to him by the man who claimed to have rescued them for England.

Haydon, both by his articles and his print-books, had an immediate effect, but he had only revived in Keats a train of thoughts that ran through all his life. The "immortal youth" of the Greek spirit, which he had taught to Severn, and found himself in The Excursion, was always in Keats's mind. He now applied this idea as a touchstone to his own recurrent problem of the impermanence of human life. The rondeau he had written shortly after Tom's death "on the double immortality of Poets" pointed some of the way;[3] could it be that the work of the artist, in any form, has an eternal message from which the soul may learn and profit? The new ode, itself written with much greater artistic certainty than all the rest,[4] explored this question. Beginning by invoking not only the permanent quality of a great work of art, but also its stillness and serenity, Keats, in Socratic style, went on to question its essential meaning. What are these scenes of love or joy or festival meant to convey to us? The answer he proposes in the next two stanzas is that they satisfy us in a way which life itself cannot. They are permanent, while life changes and passes. As he said to Severn there is "no Now or Then" for them. Even in their incomplete moments, they are more satisfactory than life itself; the lover on the urn, fixed in his attitude, may never reach his mistress, but he and she will never grow old and fade, like Beauty and new Love in the earthly setting of the Nightingale Ode. They are for ever in a state

1. Haydon, II, 318; his statement that Keats also recited Ode on a Grecian Urn (KC, II, 142) does not appear in his earlier journal version, but near the end of his life, and is therefore suspect.

2. Noel Machin, "The Case of the Empty-Handed Maenad", Observer, colour supplement, 28 Feb. 1965. James Dickie, "The Grecian Urn: An Archaeological Approach", Bulletin of the John Rylands Library, Vol. 52, No. 1 has the best account.

3. Bate, 518.

4. Bate, 510; Ward, 433, n. 22, on the other hand, finds a technical advance in the Nightingale Ode.

of "immortal youth". The stillness, the timelessness of great art, of which
Haydon had written in his articles, is contrasted with the inevitable
disappointments of human experience:

> All breathing human passion far above,
>   That leaves a heart high-sorrowful and cloy'd,
>   A burning forehead, and a parching tongue.

Yet just because this ideal scene is not human, not imperfect, at the core of it
all there is not satisfaction but desolation. This seems to be Keats's turn of
thought in the deceptively simple fourth stanza, where he leaves the urn for
wider scenes of classical life, suggested by pictures such as Claude's *Sacrifice to
Apollo*, sculptures such as the Elgin Marbles, and even perhaps the original
subject of the Raphael cartoon, quoted in Haydon's article:

Then the Priest of Jupiter, which was before the city, brought bulls and garlands to the
gates, and would have done sacrifice with the people.

The world of art is perfect but empty, in a way that the actual "World of
Pains and troubles" is not. Nor does it fail to remind us of that actual world.
It is not only that the inhabitants of the city cannot return to their town
because they are the fixed figures of an artist's conception; they also cannot
do so because they are dead in some remote past, and only exist for us now in
their sculptured form. Art contains reminders of the world of inevitable
decay, even in its most ideal and unforgettable moments:

> Who are these coming to the sacrifice?
> To what green altar, O mysterious priest,
> Lead'st thou that heifer lowing at the skies,
> And all her silken flanks with garlands drest?
> What little town by river or sea shore,
> Or mountain-built with peaceful citadel,
> Is emptied of this folk, this pious morn?
> And, little town, thy streets for evermore
> Will silent be; and not a soul to tell
> Why thou art desolate, can e'er return.

It is a picture repeated from his questioning lines to Reynolds of over a year
before; like them, it arouses meditations that "tease us out of thought",[1] for
the mood of this stanza is carried over into the next and final one, where the
urn is once more addressed and makes its own famous statement. Critics
have perhaps rightly stressed Keats's recognition of the limitations of the urn
in this stanza,[2] though it is unnecessary and even a little absurd to treat the last
two lines as a dramatic and unprepared-for remark by the urn to the poet.[3]

1. *To J. H. Reynolds, Esq.*, l. 77: *Ode*, l. 44.
2. Bate, 517-519.   3. Ward, 282.

The stanza is more of a piece than these interpretations would suggest. "O Attic shape! Fair attitude!" does not necessarily suggest that the vase is now for Keats a mere empty form; the Elizabethan delight in the pun in the chiming syllables would seem to rule that out, nor does the exclamation "Cold Pastoral!" bear the reproachful tone that has been invented for it. The urn in this stanza is openly "a friend to man", something that has an existence in the midst of human woe, a part of life and not merely a remote symbol. Its message

> Beauty is Truth,—Truth Beauty,—that is all
> Ye know on earth, and all ye need to know.

is no surprise, nor any contradiction of what has gone before. Beauty in art and the truth of life are seen as complementary to each other in Keats's "World of Pains and troubles". In this new world of soul-making, Beauty and Truth do not make "all disagreeables evaporate" by their relationship, as Keats had once thought. Far more important, they make it possible to live with the disagreeables of human existence, and even to see them as part of an eternal process. The May Odes are philosophic poems based on Keats's April thought. Shot through with phrases and cadences from Keats's philosophic master, Wordsworth, they express a complete philosophy of his own, and in a style entirely his own. Wordsworth himself traced here his kinship with the younger poet, and acknowledged it. He felt, he said, "a peculiar satisfaction" in having anticipated in his own sonnet "Praised be the art", printed in his 1815 volumes, the thought of Keats's *Ode on a Grecian Urn*; he hastily and generously added "not that he suggested any borrowing of the idea on the part of Keats."[1] This tribute from Wordsworth, who himself paid Keats the compliment during Keats's lifetime of borrowing for a sonnet of his own from the *Ode to a Nightingale*,[2] indicates the unique value of the Odes, seen and distinguished by the greatest poet of Keats's own time. They are the poems in which Keats's thought and essential nature find totally their own poetic expression.

1. R. P. Graves, *The Afternoon Lectures on Literature and Art*, Dublin, 1869. Lecture VIII, "Recollections of Wordsworth and the Lake Country", 300–301.
2. M. Moorman, *William Wordsworth*, II, 377–378.

Chapter 22

GORDIAN SHAPES

"a gordian complication of feelings"

– KEATS to Bailey

"She was a gordian shape . . .

– *Lamia*, I, 47

SUCH a period of calm and fruitful peace as that in which the May odes were conceived was never to come to Keats again. The deep disquiet, which he was able to resolve for a time through the philosophy of these poems, was a natural part of his soul; it was not this, but the intractable weight of outside events that now began to destroy him. From May Day of the previous year, every advance in poetry had been followed by some crippling reminder from life. This time it was the long-awaited letter from George, which arrived on Wednesday 12 May 1819. The contents have not survived, but they were more ominous than Keats cared to tell his sister or his friends. According to Fanny Brawne, they caused Keats at once to dash off a letter, which also has not survived, promising George all the financial help he could give. George had not joined the Birkbeck Settlement in Illinois, as everyone had thought. After a long journey over the Alleghannies and down the Ohio, he had landed up at Louisville, Kentucky,[1] and had decided not to put his money into farmland but into a trading concern on the Mississippi river. He was doubtless confident he could get more capital for this from England, since he had left John and Tom £500 and reckoned on a share of Tom's estate. Keats knew the £500 was all but gone, and he had experienced the legal difficulties over Tom's estate. Even the news that George had found an old schoolfriend of theirs in Louisville, the merchant Charles Briggs, did not make the rest of his letter less disconcerting. Keats showed it to Mrs. Wylie and George's brothers-in-law; in his heart he did not trust his brother's business ability, nor his own capacity as an agent for his affairs in England. His comments on the news were guarded, and he could not help remarking " 't is a queerish world in which such things are call'd good". It is also probable that at this time he

1. He first stayed at Henderson, Kentucky, though it is not known for how long. HBF, IV, 381.

heard another piece of news to disquiet him; Isabella Jones was ill, and had gone for a cure to Tunbridge Wells, where she wrote Taylor a letter mentioning her "favourite *Endymion*". At Somerset House he was reminded of her beauty by her miniature painted by A. E. Chalon, which hung close to his own painted by Severn.[1] The world, like the weather, had lost the sunshine of early May, and turned to grey—"taken on a quakerish look".

A deterioration had also taken place in the love that had been his new security. It seemed more than flesh could bear to live next door to such an attractive girl, and resign oneself to the prospect of an indefinitely long engagement; as Keats said, later that summer, "I am not one of the Paladins of old who livd upon water grass and smilcs for years together." Marriage was the only solution in their class of society, and by that same society's rules, before marriage must come steady employment and an income; by appalling irony, the fact that Keats had enough capital to produce a small private income still in Chancery was unknown to Mrs. Brawne, as it was to him. To Mrs. Brawne and her Hampstead friends it now appeared that Keats could not support a wife. To add to his troubles, the change in weather had brought back his sore throat. To provide health and money and get him away from the agonizing temptations of Fanny, Keats for some weeks considered engaging himself, like his student friend Newmarch, to the East India Company; as a surgeon on one of their ships he would need no more qualification than he had already, and the voyages might do him good. A less practical scheme of a Shelley-like idealism was that he might emigrate to South America and join the wars of liberation, much publicized in *The Examiner*. His moods swung to many extremes, among which was a self-disgust at his own lack of sexual control in his thoughts of love. He wrote against a part of Burton's *The Anatomy of Melancholy*, which contained the remark, "Love, universally taken, is defined to be *desire*", the following words:

Here is the old plague spot: the pestilence, the raw scrofula. I mean that there is nothing disgraces me in my own eyes so much as being one of a race of eyes, nose and mouth beings in a planet called the earth who all from Plato to Wesley have always mingled goatish, winnyish, lustful love with the abstract adoration of the diety.

Even Burton's attempt to divide the two still left him disturbed and uneasy. In another note, only a few pages before, Keats had compared the love-knowledge of old men, "innocents", with that of old women, "herodesses", that is the murderers of innocence in such matters. Keats kept no secret diary of these disquieting thoughts; but they may be traced all this summer in many other similar marginal notes and underlinings which he added to Burton's disquisitions on Love-Melancholy.[2] A disgust with sex, with the

1. E. Blunden, *Keats's Publisher*, 97.
2. Ward, 312, does not believe the markings quoted above were made until much later in the summer. She constructs a scheme whereby Keats began reading at the Lamia story in June, then went back to read and mark earlier sections. Parallels with his letters

artificiality of women, their vanity and fashion shows through these markings; Keats was not merely noting the curious and grotesque in Burton, but applying the worldly-wisdom of the bachelor don to his own situation. Woman is seen as a hunter, marriage as a trap, baited by physical desire. Statements supporting this view are heavily underlined, and even come to have such remarks as "good" or "aye, aye" written against them.

Keats's abnormal feelings toward women, which he had frankly analysed in his letter to Bailey nearly a year before, had not been completely solved. "I am certain I have not a right feeling towards Women", he had then confessed; he had gone on to recognize that it was only in the company and physical presence of women that the worst of these feelings occurred: "I . . . think insults in a Lady's Company—I commit a Crime with her which absence would have not known." His self-analysis seemed to have made his attitude better. His encounters with Jane Cox and Isabella Jones showed no signs of this strain. His early love-passages with Fanny Brawne in December 1818 showed simply the superficial antagonisms and mimic warfare of two young people who are quite normally sexually attracted to one another. Now, after a delighted spell, the horror of being in close relationship with a woman returned. It was not a horror of sex; but his strong and natural sexual feelings found themselves in collision with a deeper and more complex distrust. He still made a distinction between good women and those who were sexually attractive. Fanny, by being both, now filled him with suspicion. There was also the disgust caused by Wells's hoax on Tom. The markings in Burton were the first open sign that these suspicions were getting out of hand; in tone, they echo his mad threats of revenge on Wells the previous month. They indicate a jealous and vindictive neurosis, against which he fought with all the healthier side of his being, but which was deep-laid. Its origins lie buried in his total silence about his early years.

Now, faced with a situation in which he would have to make some permanent decision about his future, Keats threw himself with relief into a mood of restless efficiency. He called on his sister at Walthamstow to reassure her about George, and found the Abbeys surprisingly gracious. Since Brown was going to let the house at the end of June to a Jewish summer visitor, Nathan Benjamin, Keats decided at the end of May to tidy up by returning to their owners the many books he had borrowed, sending back a parcel to his generous publishers, and by destroying a mass of old letters. He held back a packet which gave him a twinge of conscience. Although he had written a facetious letter to thank the Jefferys at Teignmouth, they had not had another

---

and poems, however, confirm a continuous if sporadic reading and marking of Vol. 2 from April onwards. Compare his phrase on 1 May, "an amulet against the ennui" (*Letters*, II, 56) with the passage he marked in Burton on amulets as a cure for Melancholy, which occurs much earlier than the Lamia story, and only twenty to thirty pages before the markings quoted above; they were therefore probably made in May.

word from him for nearly a year. Now he tried to put this right by writing to Marian, the elder of the two, asking her for some advice. Could she recommend a cheap lodging near Teignmouth where he could stay for the rest of the summer? The relief of writing to someone unconnected with the stormy vicissitudes of the past year led him to tell her some of his difficulties, and to confess that George had always stood between him and worldly decisions—"Now I find I must buffet it—I must take my stand upon some vantage ground and begin to fight—I must chose between despair & Energy —." He added, "I choose the latter", but already, as he confessed, the idea of becoming a ship's surgeon was beginning to pall. She wrote back, giving her vote against the East India job, and suggesting lodgings where he could write in a village near Teignmouth called Bradley, but by this time, on 9 June, he had changed his mind about that too. Devon might remind him too much of Tom. The day before, James Rice had called and had suggested they took a holiday together at Shanklin in the Isle of Wight. Keats, with happy memories of the place from his springtime visit while starting *Endymion*, impulsively accepted. He wrote off a disquisition to Miss Jeffery on the theme that difficulty was good for a writer, and she heard no more of him. His discourse on the English ill-treatment of their writers—"They have not been treated like the Raphaels of Italy"—was an echo of Haydon's argument on the matter;[1] England was the place where, "trampled aside into the bye paths of life", one could become "a miserable and mighty Poet of the human Heart".[2] Haydon did more than provide Keats with some sturdy sentiment about continuing to live and practise his art in England. He had been so impressed by Keats's reading of the Nightingale Ode that he recommended the poem to his friend James Elmes, who edited *Annals of the Fine Arts*; the encouraging result was a request by the editor to print the poem, which appeared in July.

Keats's renewed friendship with Haydon was short-lived; as in the Spring, money was the stumbling-block, but this time the circumstances were very different. Keats had now spent the last of the money he had drawn on George, having probably handed it over to Rice, who was going to engage the lodgings and do the housekeeping at Shanklin. He was penniless unless he touched Tom's estate; encouraged by Brown, he saw Abbey on 16 June. After telling Keats that Georgiana's baby had been born, a girl, the conversation took a less pleasant turn. Abbey produced a solicitor's letter, written on behalf of Captain Midgley John Jennings's widow. After a silence of ten years, Keats's aunt was threatening a Chancery action of a similar nature to that she had undertaken in 1809. This time it did not refer to Keats's money still in Chancery, which everyone had by now forgotten, but to the capital bequeathed by old Mrs. Jennings to her grandchildren. The younger Mrs. Jennings's claim must have been that since her children had shared in this bequest, this gave them a claim on the estate of the dead Tom. Thus, although the suit was quietly dropped later in the year, and never reached Chancery, a second obstacle was put in the way of any of Tom's capital being distributed.[1] Keats returned to Brown at Wentworth Place as empty-handed as he set out, and talking of finding a junior partnership in a medical practice at once.

It was at this point that Brown decided to organize Keats's business affairs; ironically again, if the methodical Dilke had been consulted, he might have uncovered Keats's fund in Chancery, and the crisis would have been averted. Brown's first remedy was to extract from Keats what he had already admitted to Haydon; over the years he had lent sums to friends amounting to more than £200. Brown urged him to write at once to all of these, and promised to lend him money against that security. One of these debtors was Haydon himself, with the £30 Keats had lent him; in spite of Keats's letter, he made no attempt to pay,[2] and the friendship plunged finally to an end. Brown's second suggestion, like his first, was not without a side of self-interest.[3] He proposed that he and Keats should collaborate in a play, for which he should supply the plot and dramatic interest in return for a half share of the profits, while Keats did the actual verse-writing. He knew Keats's ambition to do something in the drama, and especially to write for Kean, would set him off, and he suggested a lurid story of intrigue set in the reign of Otto the Great, first of the Holy Roman Emperors, with a hero who performs noble deeds, suffers dark betrayal, goes mad and dies. Keats could see Kean in the part, and they sat down to rough out a scheme for the opening scene before Keats left for the Isle of Wight. It must have occurred to Keats that a verse-play would be publishable. Great interest had just been aroused by *Dramatic Scenes and other poems*, written by B. W. Procter under the pen-name of Barry Cornwall. Isabella Jones wrote to John Taylor about the author's identity, comparing the style to *Endymion*. Hunt had devoted two reviews in *The Examiner* to praising *Dramatic Scenes*, quoting long stretches of dialogue. He too was reminded of Keats, for he used one review[4] to recall to his readers "the young poet Keats, who burst suddenly upon them like a shape out of the old world of imagination, and threw the mere party critics into all their flattering convulsions of rage". Keats himself paid Procter the unconscious compliment of copying his dialogue-style in a first sketch for *Otho the Great* though he soon rejected it for a vigorous and rough style, in the manner of Philip Massinger, whose works he was reading extensively at the time, and in one of whose plays he had actually seen Kean perform.

Hunt's generous praise of his own past work, Brown's persuasion "to try the press once more", his own assiduous study of Dryden's tales in verse,

---

1. KI, 44.
2. On 7 July, he entered in his own journal "My pecuniary difficulties are now more dreadful than ever." Haydon, II, 226.
3. KC, II, 105.   4. E. No. 595, p. 333.

and the nagging need to write something popular and immediately successful led Keats to look round at the same time for a new subject for a narrative poem. By great good luck, he had now come upon[1] this passage in Burton's *Anatomy*:

Philostratus, in his fourth book *de vita Apollonii*, hath a memorable instance in this kinde, which I may not omit, of one Menippus Lycius, a young man 25 years of age, that going betwixt Cenchreas and Corinth, met such a phantasm in the habit of a fair gentlewoman, which taking him by the hand, carried him home to her house, in the suburbs of Corinth, and told him she was a Phoenician by birth, and if he would tarry with her, *he should hear her sing and play, and drink such wine as never any drank, and no man should molest him; but she being fair and lovely, would live and die with him, that was fair and lovely to behold.* The yong man, a philosopher, otherwise staid and discreet, able to moderate his passions, though not this of love, tarried with her a while to his great content, and at last married her, to whose wedding, amongst other guests, came Apollonius; who, by some probable conjectures, found her out to be a serpent, a lamia; and that all her furniture was like Tantalus gold, described by Homer, no substance, but meer illusions. When she saw herself descried, she wept, and desired Apollonius to be silent, but he would not be moved, and thereupon she, plate, house, and all that was in it, vanished in an instant: *many thousands took notice of this fact, for it was done in the midst of Greece.*

The surface attraction of the story was irresistible for Keats, though in working it out he delved perhaps deeper into human life than anywhere else in his poems; superficially, he too was a young man who had recently set philosophy above all else, and who was also deeply in love. Moreover the tale of the mysterious lady had a whiff of topicality, which might catch public taste if he wrote quickly enough. Even the serious papers had lately carried long articles on a "fair Circassian", brought over by the new Persian ambassador, who watched the goings-on of London from behind drawn blinds and who was attended by Persian eunuchs;[2] Keats was enough influenced by this to make his secretive lady Persian and not, as in the story, Phoenician in her illusion of human form. He set to work with an extraordinary concentration of all his faculties so as to produce something far nearer the realities, as he now saw them, of day-by-day human life.

He had also forced himself further into coming to terms with the facts of his own life. Some time before the end of June, he at last arrived at some sort of understanding with Fanny. This was far from a formal engagement; he still had too little to offer Mrs. Brawne for that. He regarded Fanny as free in a way that would have been unthinkable in an engaged girl at that time, and could even contemplate "the worst that can happen"—that is, that she might

1. Ward, 289, assumes that Brown found the passage for him, and then gave him the book; but if this had been so, Brown would not have failed to claim the credit in his own MS Life of Keats (KC, II, 52–97), as he did for *Otho the Great* and *The Cap and Bells*.
2. E. No. 590, pp. 241–242; No. 592, p. 281; No. 594, p. 315.

fall in love with and accept someone else.[1] For all his wish to stay near her, and her natural expectation that he would, he had to tell her that, for any hope of marriage, he must go away, live cheaply in the country, and concentrate on writing until he had produced something that would improve his fortunes. He would not return to London until he had done that, and he seemed to contemplate staying away for a whole year. It was a harsh decision to make, and a difficult one to explain to her, but Keats, as he wrote to Reynolds a fortnight later, had been learning to "make use of my Judgment more deliberately than I yet have done". It was certainly a more planned approach to life than he had ever shown before, part of the energy with which he now must act; he wished Fanny not only to be married but to be married well, to himself as a success, living "among those amusements suitable to your inclinations and spirits". On the night of 27 June he caught the Portsmouth coach, travelling outside for lack of money in a violent storm of icy rain. Nothing shows better how Keats had altered and developed as a person than the difference between his description of this journey and the other coach ride which began his previous visit to the Isle of Wight in 1817. Two years before, he had been full of literary references and Shakespearian quotation; the human figures in the passing landscape were stylized, conventional types. Now his interest was almost wholly in character and human touches; he shared the journey with some poorly-dressed French émigrés, noting their good manners in contrast with their ragged clothes, and recording how one of the men plucked a wild-rose from the hedge and gave it to a woman with a flourish "more gallant than I ever saw gentleman to Lady at a Ball".

This was one sign of his new energy of purpose. Another and less healthy sign was that composition now threw him into a fever of which he speaks continually during these summer months. It is possible that he was in fact running a temperature; his sore throat had returned after the wet coach journey, he felt too unwell to bathe, he found the climate in Shanklin oppressive, and everything got on his nerves. The summer visitors, the harsh voice of an old lady across the way, the cramped coffin-like cottage rooms, all piled up to irritate him in a way that suggests a slight fever. Rice was in the same state and this too was an irritant to Keats: "He was unwell and I was not in very good health: and I am affraid we made each other worse by acting upon each others spirits. We would grow as melancholy as need be."[2] Whether or not tubercular infection was fuelling Keats's powers, it is clear that he was composing poetry in an entirely different way from the calm and fruitful indolence of the May Odes. It was now a set task to be hammered out, with control and detachment but also with a restless driving force unlike anything he had known before. He and his doctors later believed this work had harmed him; it was more likely a symptom than a cause of

1. *Letters*, II, 123.   2. *Letters*, II, 134.

breakdown, but it had signs of abnormality about it. The rate of writing was prodigious, even for Keats, far more than the fifty lines a day of *Endymion*. In a fortnight, he wrote an act of the play and the first part of *Lamia*, the poem alone being 400 lines. Even allowing for some start on both before he left Hampstead, this was one of the greatest feats of concentrated work in his life, especially as in both he was working in what was virtually a new medium. The couplets of *Lamia* were as taut and dramatic as those of *Endymion* had often been lax; the poem started in the vein of his conscious model Dryden, with a fable of Hermes and a Nymph which echoed Dryden's translations from Chaucer and Ovid, as Hazlitt had recommended; but it soon broke away into a glittering, pliant yet steel-sinewed line that was a new acquisition for Keats. Luck held with him in the reading that had been the original inspiration of the poem; twenty pages on in Burton, he came upon this magnificent example of prose in a passage describing the immediate effect of external beauty:

Whiteness in the lilly, red in the rose, purple in the violet, a lustre in all things without life, the cleer light of the moon, the bright beams of the sun, splendor of gold, purple, sparkling diamond, the excellent feature of the horse, the majesty of the lion, the colour of birds, peacocks tails, the silver scales of fish, we behold with singular delight and admiration.

Keats marked this passage heavily down the margin; coming just when he wanted to produce his own first great effect it must have seemed like an omen as he proceeded, with sparkling objectivity, to recreate it in the appearance of his own snake-heroine:

> She was a gordian shape of dazzling hue,
> Vermillion-spotted, golden, green, and blue;
> Striped like a zebra, freckled like a pard,
> Eyed like a peacock, and all crimson barr'd;
> And full of silver moons, that, as she breathed,
> Dissolv'd, or brighter shone, or interwreathed
> Their lustres ...

Nor when later in the story Lamia becomes "a real woman", and is extolled for being so in a passage which has led Keats to be accused of vulgarity, is he doing more than following the tales of instant effects of woman's beauty, catalogued in Burton, and chiming with his own sympathies.

The letters Keats was now writing to Fanny Brawne also show a dramatic sequence that progresses like the poem, though its themes are often very different. The first letter he wrote from Shanklin was too passionate to send; the second spoke of how she had "entrammelled" him and destroyed his freedom, but showing himself overcome by the recollection of her beauty: "I want a brighter word than bright, a fairer word than fair." Her answer came teasing him for dwelling so much on her physical attractions; he replied, echoing a passage he had marked in Burton—" 'T is beauty in all things which pleaseth and allureth us"—with a spirited defence of his own obsession—"I cannot conceive any beginning of such love as I have for you but Beauty". The new realism in his life included an honesty in his love affair, which she, brought up in the social habits of their time and class, may well have found disconcerting.

Keats had more to face than the pressure of composition and the conduct of a long-distance love affair. On 6 July, another letter from George followed him to Shanklin. Now his brother in the boldly speculative atmosphere of a new society had been talked into a fresh scheme. John James Audubon, backwoods merchant, painter and naturalist, had persuaded George to invest in a Mississippi steamboat; George urgently wanted not only his share of Tom's estate but a loan of John's share, since he himself had helped out John and Tom when he left England a year before. Keats wrote to Abbey on the next day, and a short letter to George, telling him about the hold-up due to Mrs. Jennings's threatened action. He also wrote to the missing trustee in Holland for power of attorney to deal on behalf of his brother; he had not obtained this before, since George's previous letter had not suggested any urgency.[1] At the same time, he was able to take these material worries in his stride and continue writing; after all, as he remarked in a letter to Reynolds, he had got used to the idea that he himself was to write poems for money: "the very corn which is now so beautiful, as if it had only took to ripening yesterday, is for the market: So, why sho^d I be delicate." All the same, the distraction weakened his resolve in love and work. On 13 July he felt in an "irritable" state of health, and when, on 14 July, he took the next letter from Fanny to bed with him, and found in the morning her name on the seal obliterated, all his tendency "to bode ill like the raven" returned. He told her that these moods "proceeded from the general tenor of the circumstances of my life"; George's financial difficulties had reminded him of his earliest family crises. His determination to forge ahead with profitable work slackened. He reverted to his "three or four stories half done" as if he feared *Lamia* might be another, and confessed "I cannot write for the mere sake of the press" in contradiction with his statement to Reynolds. He even played with the idea of returning to Town and Fanny within a month; Abbey had not replied to his urgent letters, and the need to see him would be an excuse. In this unsettled mood he contemplated anything, even London with its "hateful literary chitchat".

The curtain rose after a week's silence on quite a new scene, the little cottage crowded with people. Brown had arrived, bringing as usual his own ebullient atmosphere, and also John Martin the publisher, who had come to take Rice away. Martin in his turn had brought his sister, and she had brought

1. *Letters*, II, 228–229.

three friends to lodge in a cottage over the way. The whole tempo and scheme of Keats's life had gone back to what he had originally planned. The swings of temperament, usual to him, were now often provoked by Brown's influence. Brown read and approved of the first part of *Lamia*, and inspired him with a new confidence. He also brought first-hand news of Fanny, and as soon as Keats could shake himself free from the card-playing and the social parties he wrote to her. On 25 July, when Martin had taken Rice and the ladies away, the little cottage was at last quiet. Brown had brought down papers and books from Hampstead. One of the most important of these from Keats's point of view was probably the manuscript of the unfinished *Hyperion*, which Woodhouse had now copied and returned. Perhaps as some token from Fanny, there seems to have been also the little volume of Dante's *Inferno* in which she had copied the *Bright Star* sonnet and he had written the sonnet *On A Dream*. At all events, his letter echoes many phrases and ideas from the sonnets, in an upsurge of his early love for her, of which they reminded him so poignantly. Once again, the idea of the consummation of love at the same time as death breaks into his thought, from which his brisker mood had banished it; "I have two luxuries to brood over in my walks, your Loveliness and the hour of my death. O that I could have possession of them both in the same minute." He ended the letter, "Your's ever, fair Star". The other reminder from the past, *Hyperion*, set him deeply brooding on this unfinished poem; could he perhaps finish it now, as Brown had given him confidence to finish *Lamia*? He spent a day in thought about it, though Brown was clearing the decks for a serious attack on their tragedy.

Keats had put *Hyperion* out of his head for the past three months. When he handed it to Woodhouse at the card-playing party on 19 April, he had meant to make a final gesture. He told Woodhouse that he was dissatisfied with what he had done of it, and that he would not complete it. Woodhouse was deeply disappointed. Even skimming through the fragment, he realized that here was something beyond anything else he had seen by Keats. "It has an air of calm grandeur that is indicative of true power", he commented, and he compared its effect as a poem to that of the Elgin and Egyptian Marbles in sculpture. Keats was firm before all his pleadings; he had abandoned the attempt. Part of the trouble was the huge scale on which he had planned. Although he had begun dramatically with the overthrown Titans, it was still his intention[1] to show their overthrow individually, Oceanus by Neptune,

---

1. De Selincourt's theory (*Poems*, 486–489) that, though this had been Keats's original scheme when he first discussed it with his publishers, he had already altered and shortened it, unknown to them, seems disproved by the date "April 1819" given by Woodhouse in explaining Keats's scheme. Annotated *Endymion*, pp. 196 and 212, Berg Collection, New York Public Library. Woodhouse's lengthy notes on *Hyperion* here bear all the marks of recent conversation with Keats, who, he says, "is qualified for such a task", i.e. the full-length scheme for *Hyperion*.

Saturn by Jupiter: as well as the main conflict between the new god, Apollo, and Hyperion, he planned to show the second war of Giants against Gods. The scheme of the poem was like that of *Paradise Lost*, where in Books V to VIII, Raphael relates to Adam and Eve the war in Heaven and all that had passed before their creation. The scale alone was daunting; with only two and a half books done, he was perhaps only a quarter of the way through the poem. If it had been a mere matter of showing Apollo supplanting Hyperion, the main theme, he could have pushed on to a finish, in spite of the painful difficulties of Apollo assuming his complete knowledge of life and death.

Yet now a new idea for revision occurred to him. In his mood of actuality, the allegory seemed too "abstract", as he called it, the personages of the legend too remote, the whole mythological apparatus too long-winded and clumsy. In the assumption of godhead by Apollo, he had drawn on his own agonies of thought and experience while becoming a poet. Should he not remove the mask, frankly introduce himself into the poem, and explore his own poetic character? He had exact precedent for this at hand; here, in the little volume of the *Inferno* which he was reading again, he found Dante introducing himself, with Virgil as his heavenly guide, into the mysteries of the after-life. It was this human touch, the personal presence of the poet, that gave the work its moments of brief pathos which appealed to Keats. Somewhere about this time was born the idea of recasting *Hyperion* in the mould of the Divine Comedy into a new shape of personal vision.

For the moment, however, everything was absorbed by the money-making *Otho the Great*. "Brown and I are pretty well harnessed again to our dog-cart", wrote Keats on the last day of July. His wry reference to the play whose plot Brown fed to him was not a good augury for its quality; yet as its "Plots speeches, counterplots and counter speeches" began to work him to a fever of composition, he began to put more and more of himself into it. "The Lover is madder than I am", he announced to Fanny Brawne. It would be more true to say that he projected much of his own irrational and suppressed feeling into the hero Ludolph. Even quite idiosyncratic obsessions of his were repeated in the play.[1] "I begin to dislike the very door-posts here", he wrote, in his disgust with Shanklin; "Even the senseless door-posts", he wrote in Act IV of *Otho*, "Are on the watch". This was partly forced on him by the speed of writing in which everything had to be utilized; by the middle of August he had written four out of the conventional five acts. Brown apparently tried to counteract any strain or morbidity by a round of other pursuits. Seeing Keats's interest in Dante, he encouraged him to learn Italian. The two men had sketching competitions, Shanklin Church being one subject; Brown, who had made a silhouette of Keats in Hampstead, for him to give to his sister, now tried his hand at a head and shoulders of him in

1. See Ward, 434, n. 5, for parallels between the play and expressions in Keats's letters.

pen-and-ink. Brown was no artist, but a very exact copyist; his study, with its relaxed yet energetic look and fist doubled under the cheek, is closer to Keats as he usually was than any of the idealized portraits from more accomplished artists. Brown had other activities in an island where, as Keats had noted on a previous visit, there were signs that girls were "a little profligate" owing to the barracks, a legacy of the late wars. There is no proof that Keats joined him in these; a little bit of sexual punning on the subject was habitual with them, as it had been in their letters from Scotland and Bedhampton.[1]

Keats's sexual problems were of a kind peculiar to his situation with Fanny, the understanding that was not yet a binding engagement. His passionate letter of 25 July had been answered by a flirtatious one which aroused all his old suspicions of the trivialities of conventional marriage. "No my love, trust yourself to me and I will find you nobler amusements", he wrote, and for the first time a real hint of jealousy breaks in. She had mentioned going out late; where had she been? It was a curious letter for Fanny to receive on her birthday, when, from his previous letters, she had perhaps half-hoped he would pay her a flying visit; now he spoke quite casually of a visit, very short if at all "for as I am in a train of writing now I fear to disturb it". Her answer seems to have been, in not unreasonable pique, to tell him of the dances she had been enjoying, especially those at the Royal Artillery Mess at Woolwich, which were a great feature of that season. Since there was no formal engagement, Fanny was fully within her social rights, but she added evident fuel to the holocaust of jealousy and destruction which Keats was now stoking for the last act of *Otho*. He had other reasons for restlessness. As soon as he finished the play, he would have to get back to *Lamia*, and prepare the climax of that poem. The story required a wedding-feast in Ancient Greece; for this Keats needed factual information that could only be found in books, notably absent in a holiday-resort. Looking at the map, he and Brown fixed on Winchester as the nearest centre likely to have a good library; though they were wrong about this, they found the Cathedral city full of useful bookshops. They moved there on 12 August. Keats, in his mood of observant realism, noted the imperturbable behaviour of officers and men on board a naval craft which nearly collided with theirs on the crossing to the mainland. He also described with detached accuracy the beautiful sight of the Prince Regent's new yacht at Cowes. Winchester delighted him, a setting like Oxford but among hills. There were trees, streams, old buildings, "the pleasantest Town I ever was in". Sitting down to work, he rejected Brown's scheme for the last act of *Otho* as too elaborate and far-fetched, and proceeded to write it according to his own scheme.

Though the action is hardly plausible, the feelings in it are intensely real. It is likely that Ludolph's picture of his unfaithful bride is a picture of Fanny Brawne, drawn in exact physical detail. The mad Ludolph himself is not far

1. Ward, 301, 313, thinks otherwise.

off Keats's own sensations at this time, which he himself described as a succession of "day-night mares". One passage is significant. He borrowed some lines in Ludolph's ravings from a description in Burton, which he marked. At the foot of the page he annotated "Beware of the rustling of silks and the creaking of shoes". What was uppermost in his mind was the correct and full quotation from *King Lear*—"Let not the creaking of shooes, Nor the rustling of Silkes, betray thy poore heart to woman." Only when he had finished the Act could he bring himself to write to Fanny, and when he did it was, in his mad hero's words, to

> Put on a judge's brow, and use a tongue
> Made iron-stern by habit!

His own heart, he now said, seemed made of iron. He was deeply offended by her tone and her news of the military balls, which she had been enjoying. "I am no officer in yawning quarters", he commented. She had told him that he too might do as he pleased; he replied coldly that he could not, since his life was ruled by lack of money. It was, as he said, an unloverlike, ungallant and flint-worded letter. Ostentatiously, he put his work before her. "I would feign, as my sails are set, sail on without an interruption for a Brace of Months longer." He would not visit Hampstead, and his love-letters apparently stopped.[1] Instead, he wrote to people who would appreciate his views on poetry and philosophy, which poured back into his letters from which they had been absent since April. He even tried awkwardly to pick up his friendship with Bailey, who had now left his Carlisle parish in order to seek at a Scottish University the degree that he had failed to get at Oxford. Thoughts of Bailey reminded Keats of a phrase from Katherine Philips,[2] which they had read at Oxford, "Honour . . . cannot descend, To beg the suffrage of a vulgar tongue." He wrote to Taylor and Reynolds rejecting the idea that he should "beg suffrages" in the world of literature. He poured scorn on "the poisonous suffrage of a public", though he now felt it in his power to become what he had never imagined he might be, a popular writer. To Bailey he wrote, "I am convinced more and more every day that (excepting the human friend Philosopher) a fine writer is the most genuine Being in the World", and to Reynolds, "I am convinced more and more day by day that fine writing is next to fine doing the top thing in the world". Shakespeare and Milton returned as his heroes, and such was his satisfaction at having written a whole play that he decided to press on and "make as great a revolution in modern dramatic writing as Kean has done in acting".

His new play, suggested by Brown and by the history of Winchester, was to be about King Stephen. "Stop! stop!" he cried, when Brown tried to

1. Though it must be remembered that some were apparently later destroyed by Sir Charles Dilke. Richardson, *Fanny Brawne*, 169.
2. Katherine Philips, *Upon a scandalous libel made by J.J.*

outline a plot for him, "I have been already too long in leading-strings. I will do all this myself." He wanted to write in unfettered style the play he felt was in him, designed expressly for Kean, and based on the actor's great Richard the Third. The few scenes he wrote have a tremendous sense of physical action; he was seeing the actor in the part, filling it in return with human interest gathered from all the impressions of that summer. The verse too was not merely Shakespearian, but had the rough vigour he had learnt from Dryden and Massinger, and assimilated so well into the first part of *Lamia*. Above all he was writing with confidence and gusto, personal problems set aside. Three scenes were complete,[1] and then the blow fell. Some time just after 24 August, Brown and Keats learned from the press that Kean intended to go on an American tour; he was not likely to consider even the finished *Otho* until next season, and there was less than no point in going on with *King Stephen*. No one could play either part at the rival Covent Garden, of whose company Keats shared Hunt's low opinion.[2] As Keats had written to Fanny, he was ruled by lack of money. Brown's supplies were running out, and they had just written a joint letter to Taylor, asking for an advance. The publisher would expect at least the promise of a completed book, not a lot of half-finished poems. In spite of the dislike of writing expressly for publication, which had overcome Keats again ever since finishing the first part of *Lamia*, he at once set himself resolutely and as quickly as possible to write the second part of the poem.

1. Bate, 568, doubts Brown's statement that this took place at Winchester; but images from *Otho* recur in *Stephen*, suggesting one followed the other. For the number of scenes, see Ward, 434, n. 8.

2. E. No. 598, p. 381; *Letters*, II, 149.

Chapter 23

A QUIET POWER

"Some think I have lost that poetic ardour and fire 't is said I once had—the fact is perhaps I have: but instead of that I hope I shall substitute a more thoughtful and quiet power"

– JOHN KEATS to George and Georgiana Keats, 21 September 1819

.

TO WRITE the second part of *Lamia* in the next ten days was in many ways the greatest achievement of this whole remarkable year. In it Keats showed all the confidence he had just expressed to Taylor and Reynolds in his power to be a popular writer. He himself was pleased with the result, and put the poem first in his published book; here was, he realized, the key poem his collection needed. Technically, the process of completing *Lamia* was something he had never been able to do before; if he stopped in a poem, he habitually left it unfinished. Now, after a six weeks' gap, he wrote a conclusion that hammered home the poetic narrative in an even more decisive style than its opening. These powerful last 300 lines were an outlet for his dammed-up dramatic writing. Keats's mistake in abandoning *King Stephen*—for the news about Kean was a false alarm—meant that all the tension and conflict prepared for that play went into *Lamia*. Scenes, speeches, situations have a dynamic quality, which, though it does not quarrel with the first part, carries it a dimension further. His mastery of the couplet form was thorough enough for him to take it up where he left off. His move to Winchester had, as he planned, provided him with the one book he needed for background colour, the *Archaeologia Graeca* of John Potter, quoted as an authority by Haydon earlier in the summer. His renewed reading of Dante's *Inferno*, evident in the descriptions of the demonlike Stephen, now added an unearthly tone to the unmasking of the poem's serpent-heroine.[1] Everything he looked at, felt or read added its weight and depth to the poem. In all this accumulated concentration, there was only one flawed passage, which he was wise to drop later, a would-be humorous description of a Glutton at Lamia's feast. Hunt was running a ponderous comic series in *The Examiner* called *Praeter-natural History*, which amused Keats, and from which he borrowed his own incongruous idea.[2]

1. MOK, 37–38.   2. E. No. 606, pp. 506–508.

That he introduced this passage, and even sent it to his publisher as part of "a good sample of the story", is itself a minor clue to what the poem meant to him, and what he intended by it; for *Lamia* on the whole has been the critics' puzzle. Many have felt what one called "the bewilderment . . . as to the effect intended to be made on our imaginative sympathies".[1] While acknowledging its strength, the "sensation" Keats felt sure it would give any reader, some have found its message or philosophy confusing and full of warring elements. In trying to resolve this, they have over-simplified and assumed that Keats was led by the tangled circumstances of his own life to identify himself with his hero, Fanny with Lamia, and Charles Brown with Apollonius; they base this on Keats's additions to Burton's story, in which he made Apollonius the friend and tutor of Lycius, who dies when the philosopher reveals Lamia's true nature. Yet Lamia, dignified, mysterious, passionate, and adult, seems to have nothing in common with the girl who had just been carrying on the teasing but innocent sex-war with Keats in terms of dances, officers, and flirtatious remarks about Keats's friends. Lamia is "a lovely graduate . . . in Cupid's college", that is, an unmarried woman with full sexual experience.[2] Though again this solution is far too simple, one might more easily think of her as Isabella Jones, enigmatic, full of pro-hibitions and reasons for not admitting the outside world to their relation-ship; the highly evocative passage, at the end of Part One, of the lovers' evening walk through the suburb streets and their arrival at Lamia's mysterious house has all the atmosphere of Keats's long prose description of his meeting with Isabella in October. Yet the chief over-simplification is to assume that Brown was now playing the part of a cynical adviser against Fanny's or any other woman's charms. Keats knew that Brown thought Fanny had many faults; but to elevate Brown to a moral philosopher who had guarded Keats from evil, and would not now see him overcome by sexual infatuation, seems the most unlikely view of this cheerful woman-hunter that anyone could take.

In fact, *Lamia* is perhaps the most consciously artistic of all Keats's produc-tions; he was in control of the poem, and if he used autobiographical details, it was in a much more deliberate sense than these immediate explanations suggest. He himself judged that it was entirely free from what he called "inexperience of life, and simplicity of knowlege". In other words, it looked at life, and not merely at the limited area of his own life, as a whole, with all its essential contradictions. These contradictions have puzzled thoughtful critics. Why, if Lamia is false, evil and destructive are we asked to sympathize with her and pity her dilemma? If Apollonius vindicates truth against falsehood in his exposure of her, why is he presented so

1. Colvin, quoted Pettet, 228.
2. Graduate was the slang term for "an unmarried woman who has taken her degree in carnal love".

M

unsympathetically, and why is his philosophy belittled? Some critics have objected strongly that in the love of Lycius for Lamia, presented as in some senses ideal, there is a strong element of sadism on his part and of masochism on hers; the cynical opening to Part Two on the relation between love and money, which echoes Burton, has also been condemned.

Yet these are only contradictions if one forgets that Keats was trying in the poem to show "experience of life". It is part of his attempt to come to terms with the whole of life, not a selected interpretation of it, which had absorbed him from the spring. Just as he tried in this poem to insert, though unsuccessfully, a piece of vulgar humour into high tragedy, so the scheme of the poem was that in representing life nothing should be omitted. It was part of Keats's rapidly-increasing dramatic skill to leave all the contradictions in, as he would have done in a play. Love is full of destruction, and yet one pities and loves the destroyer; truth can be a murderer, and yet the truth must be spoken. Ideal love can be full of material considerations and of sexual violence.

> Besides, for all his love, in self despite
> Against his better self, he took delight
> Luxurious in her sorrows, soft and new.
> His passion, cruel grown, took on a hue
> Fierce and sanguineous as 'twas possible
> In one whose brow had no dark veins to swell.
> Fine was the mitigated fury, like
> Apollo's presence when in act to strike
> The serpent—Ha, the serpent! certes, she
> Was none. She burnt, she lov'd the tyranny . . .

or, as Keats frankly translated the passage to Woodhouse, "Women love to be forced to do a thing, by a fine fellow."[1] Keats knew his own life was made up of violent contradictions. He now faced and related its pattern to life itself, not with his previous moods of revulsion, confusion and boding, but with what he himself had called "a healthy deliberation" and acceptance. Accepting a world often contradictory, with human nature capable of any inconsistency, Lamia attempts to record all sides of its characters, just as Keats at least realized, though he could not control, all sides of his own nature. Even in a literary sense Keats used his total experience, incorporating memories of very early reading, Wieland's Oberon and Hunt's The Feast of the Poets, with his latest mental stimulus.

It is in a purely literary sense, however, that Lamia falls short of the total effect Keats intended to achieve. It somehow holds off and repels the reader just where it should most attract and impress. For all its power, there is something about it which puts us on our guard. It is the opposite of the didactic poem, of which Keats had written "We hate poetry that has a palpable

1. KC, I, 93.

design upon us", and yet it has a similar effect. This is almost entirely a technical matter, yet it corresponds with something in Keats's own life at this time. Twice in his recent letters he had compared his words to the strokes of a hammer,[1] and had drawn a distinction between "hammering" and writing. Some such distinction can be drawn between *Lamia*, for all its force and assurance, and the May Odes. The iron which, as Keats told Reynolds, had entered into his mental processes, had also taken a hand in his verse, with mixed benefits. Yet at its best, and where the story requires it, this continuous terse dramatic repetitive attack produces something hardly heard anywhere else in Keats:

> 'Lamia!' he cried—and no soft-toned reply.
> The many heard, and the loud revelry
> Grew hush; the stately music no more breathes;
> The myrtle sicken'd in a thousand wreaths.
> By faint degrees, voice, lute, and pleasure ceased;
> A deadly silence step by step increased,
> Until it seem'd a horrid presence there,
> And not a man but felt the terror in his hair.

The confidence Keats felt in *Lamia* reflects the confidence he felt at this time about himself. For one of the few times in his life, Keats believed himself to be in control of his own destiny, "My own being which I know to be", as he wrote to Reynolds. There is no evidence that this outward control and certainty masked any lasting moments of brooding doubt, disgust, or self-disillusion over the broken course of his own love-affair.[2] He himself said that he was "becoming accustom'd to the privations of the pleasures of sense", but his one considerable letter now showed him full of appreciation for the minor pleasures of life. This was one of the letters to his sister, in which his mind always reverted to the family surroundings of their early years. Keats picked up the tone of the letter he had written her on 1 May, in the fruitful time of the Odes, repeating his simple enjoyment of health, fine weather, reading and relaxation:

Give me Books, fruit, french wine and fine whether[3] and a little music out of doors, played by somebody I do not know—

He went on to a catalogue of the garden delights of their childhood, ending with an ideal picture of ease and summer contentment:

I admire lolling on a lawn by a water-lillied pond to eat white currants and see gold fish: and go to the Fair in the Evening if I'm good—

1. *Letters*, II, 141, 144.
2. As suggested by Ward, 312–313, who believes Keats's annotations in Burton, showing sexual disquiet, were made at this time, and even refer to supposititious sexual adventures in the Isle of Wight.
3. His own spelling: *Letters*, II, 149.

He had, he knew, faults of what he called "temper". He confessed himself annoyed with Haslam for having mishandled two letters from George, one of which he had accidentally destroyed, and in asking Fanny about the rumour that Abbey was intending to retire from business, he had no compunction in referring to Hodgkinson as one "whose name I cannot bear to write" and hoping that he would be out of a job. His general tone, however, was calm and deliberate, as was his method of preparing a volume to be headed by *Lamia*. *Isabella* seemed mawkish and remote from life, but *The Eve of St. Agnes*, he felt, could be brought up to his new standard of realism. He added an early stanza and wrote the lines at the climax of the story that make it clear the love of his hero and heroine was sexually consummated. In the same mood of all-inclusive "experience of life", he altered the dignified final lines to make the old woman and the beadsman die in grotesque and realistic detail. The grotesque, one of the ruling passions of his life, was not now to be excluded from his poetry; it was a part of life, just as were the real and far from ideal deaths he had seen in the pauper ward of Guy's. He got out the Odes and arranged them, rejecting his previous favourite, *On Indolence*, whose weakness was now apparent. The book was shaping for his publishers. Meanwhile they themselves were playing a minor comedy behind Keats's back. On 23 August, Keats and Brown, completely out of money, had written to Taylor asking for an advance on the security of *Otho*. Keats had added a harangue against writing for the public taste, not calculated to please Taylor, who did not answer. Keats wrote again a week later, more tactfully and uneasily. On the same day, Woodhouse was writing a letter of special pleading to Taylor, who was ill and staying in his native Nottinghamshire. Keats's first letter had followed Taylor there; his reaction had been, as Keats anticipated, "How a solitary life engenders pride and egotism!" He sent it to Woodhouse and Hessey in London with some scathing comments. The loyal Woodhouse put himself out to absolve Keats to Taylor—"It is not in my opinion personal pride, but literary pride which his letter shews". He then offered to scrape together £50 of his own money to help Keats, with the generous words:

Whatever People regret that they could not do for Shakespeare or Chatterton, because he did not live in their time, that I would embody into a Rational principle, and (with due regard to certain expediencies) do for Keats.

As the result of these moves, Keats got, on 5 September, a much kinder letter than he might have expected from Taylor, and £30 out of the £50 from Hessey. News came too that Haslam, assuming like most of their friends that they had moved not to Winchester but to Chichester, had repaid a debt of £30 to Keats at the old Dilkes. Brown had borrowed money from the Snooks, and the pair were in funds. Keats wrote off in high spirits, not, of course, to his real and unknown benefactor, but to both Hessey and Taylor.

Exuberance again getting the better of tact, he harangued Taylor on the unhealthiness of his native county, comparing its inhabitants, by implication, with "the imbecillity of the Chinese", and he sent him a section of *Lamia* containing the Glutton passage, not yet removed. The publisher's uneasiness about his young poet was not allayed. Keats, however, was still at the peak of confidence. There was nothing to hold him back. The dry chalky air of Winchester, "worth sixpence a pint", had improved his health. He lodged in a quiet side-street between the north of the Cathedral and the High Street, where nothing but the genteel tapping of door-knockers and walking-sticks disturbed him. The view was not distracting, a blank wall in a side-passage, and the room was large. Moreover, on 6 September, Brown slipped off to Chichester, Bedhampton, and on errands of his own. He would be away for some weeks, and would not return, as he had in the Isle of Wight, to break in upon Keats's routine "like a thunderbolt". Keats had money, and had somehow managed to put his love into cold storage. He felt in "the only state for the best sort of Poetry".

The magnet which always drew his attention in such a state was the unfinished *Hyperion*. The plan of making it a personal vision had already occurred to him. In search of a setting appropriate to the defeated Titans and their dejected leader, he had begun his first version in the gloomy wood of the *Inferno*. Now, with an eye more close to the original, which he was beginning to read in the Italian with Cary as a crib,[1] he began a first canto where he himself, like Dante in the first canto of the *Inferno*, was in a mysterious wood; like Dante's, this canto was to be devoted to the poet meeting his guide. As Dante was to meet Virgil, so Keats was to meet Moneta, the Goddess of Knowledge. The poem was to take up almost where the first *Hyperion* had left off, with Apollo's cry

"Knowledge enormous makes a God of me."

It substituted Keats himself for Apollo, the poet for the poet-god, both having drunk the "elixir"—the word used in both poems—of Knowledge: the new poem stated in the first fifty lines

That full draught is parent of my theme.

Even more than in *Lamia*, the actual writing was an epitome of a whole life. In the opening to the new poem, Keats ranged through the best of all his hard-won poetic experiences, from youthful Spenserian freshness to the tempered finality of his latest work, bringing all to an essential harmony. There are clear traces from all of the four great odes he had just decided to keep for his book; the imagery of a feast enjoyed before some decisive experience was repeated, as it had been in every narrative poem since *The*

1. John Saly, "Keats's Answer to Dante: The Fall of Hyperion", KSJ. XIV, Winter 1965, 65–78.

Eve of St. Agnes. Milton adds Keats's often-recurring image from the Eden of his imagination, while the new humanizing effect of Dante is felt everywhere. Some of the furnishings of his reading for *Lamia* are incorporated.

The familiar pattern of a feast, a sleep, and an awakening to some new mode of being, which begins the poem, can have many interpretations. Whatever its psychological implications, it is clear here that it meant for Keats an awakening to truth. In this poem, he intended to face the truth about himself as a poet, and penetrate to a verdict attainable only by death:

> Whether the dream now purposed to rehearse
> Be Poet's or Fanatic's will be known
> When this warm scribe my hand is in the grave.

He therefore had to feel in this poem

> What 'tis to die and live again before
> Thy fated hour.

It is in this experience that he naturally comes nearest Dante, though the staggering scenery in which the trial takes place derived from a lucky accident. Keats discovered that he had still failed to send to George the Scotch letter describing Fingal's Cave. Getting this out of his luggage to copy, he drew from its landscape a region whose gigantic columns and arch lead now in the new poem to a mysterious altar and priestess at the top of steps which Keats must climb. The altar and the agony of his ascent, more reminiscent than anything else of Keats's heavily-marked passages in the *Inferno*,[1] have a fearful intensity that may well come from his own physical symptoms, a sense of icy suffocation which may not be entirely a creation of imagination. When, by effort, "one minute before my death" he manages to ascend, he is met by the veiled priestess, whose answers to his questions echo all his thought for the past six months. "Do you not think I strive—to know myself" he had asked six months before. Now he faced in poetry the answer; in the terms of the opening theme of the poem, he might be a mere fanatic, not a poet. In any case, he is maimed; his share of human agony has given him access to the altar of knowledge, but he will never, as poet or as dreamer, be one of those who see the world and its problems clearly, "those to whom the miseries of the world Are misery, and will not let them rest". Keats at this point not only doubts his powers as a poet; he seems to be doubting the power of poetry to benefit mankind, just as a year before, writing to Woodhouse, he had separated even "as high a summit in Poetry as the nerve bestowed on me will suffer" from the maturer ambition "of doing the world some good".

---

1. They have generally been compared with passages in *Purgatorio* and *Paradiso*, but there is no evidence Keats read those. He, however, read and marked *Inferno*, Canto XXIV, which describes a similar experience. MOK, 39.

So for four or five days, Keats wrote with extraordinary assurance and a self-knowledge beyond anything he had achieved before. It is impossible to say where this would have led him, if his exploration of his own function as a poet had been allowed to progress unhindered. The poem has the air of setting off into quite uncharted tracts of apprehension, in a way that resembles nothing else except perhaps Coleridge's *Kubla Khan*. Like that poem, it was fated to fortuitous interruption. By one of the most ironic timings in the history of literature, Keats received on 10 September a desperate letter from his brother George. What had happened to George's capital in America is still uncertain; what is certain is that the man who had persuaded him to invest it, Audubon, was at the time being sued by five creditors himself, and eventually bankrupted six partners. Possibly George, who had been so lucky financially in England, was caught in the Panic of 1819, when so many western pioneer banks collapsed.[1] From whatever cause, George was in a crisis, and relied on Keats to raise every penny he could in England, and forward it immediately. Whether the crisis was really acute or not— George managed to subsist for three months more by borrowing money in Louisville —the tone of his letter was so urgent that Keats at once put down his work, and took the night coach to London. His first thought, he said, was to get a substantial advance for a poem from Murray, Byron's publisher, but he must have quickly realized this was impracticable, quite apart from its disloyalty to Taylor & Hessey. He burst into their Fleet Street office, where he found Hessey, on Saturday 11 September, with an impetuous plan. They must publish all his poems, except *Isabella*, at once, before Christmas. Hessey tactfully temporized, falling back on Taylor's absence from Town. Indeed, if Keats had thought, a week-end in the summer holidays was not the best time to come and do business in London. All his friends were out of Town. Haydon, who owed him money, was down at Hastings again, sea-bathing for his health.[2] Abbey could not see him till Monday evening. Yet he had one piece of luck, though it did not affect his financial prospects; at Fleet Street, he just caught Woodhouse, who was setting off for the West Country the next afternoon. The lawyer invited him to a Sunday breakfast at the Temple, which lasted for six hours of animated talk. They ran through the poems, and Woodhouse was delighted with *Lamia*, which Keats read to him in full, though the lawyer did not catch all he heard in the author's chanting mumble. A full hour was taken over the alterations to *The Eve of St. Agnes*. Defending the new realism of the death episodes, Keats took Woodhouse's disgust as evidence he had succeeded, but on the sexual stanzas, mild as they now seem, the two had a battle which led, as Woodhouse said, to a "Keats-like rhodomontade . . . that if in the former poem there was an opening for a doubt what took place, it was his fault for not writing clearly & comprehensibly".[3]

1. M. Smelser, *American History at a Glance*, 65.
2. Boston Public Library, Ch. 1, 4. 43.   3. KC, I, 92.

Woodhouse's suggestion that it would offend women readers was treated with contempt; but the last thing Keats did, as he saw Woodhouse off on the Weymouth coach, was to promise him, a little contritely, some poetry to his taste, meaning the new *Fall of Hyperion*.

Keats went straight on to dine with George's mother-in-law at Westminster. There he had to play a part, for he could not bring himself to show her George's disastrous letter, nor hint at the horrors that might be facing her daughter and tiny grandchild, a lock of whose hair she proudly showed him. He got through the evening with gossip and "quizzing", in which he was joined by Georgiana's two brothers. Next morning he went from Fleet Street, where Hessey had let him sleep, to visit Fanny Keats at Walthamstow. His action in turning his back on the other Fanny at Hampstead was deliberate, though he could hardly explain his motives to himself. "Am I mad or not?" he asked her in a letter which he carried about all day, not daring to post it. "I love you too much to venture to Hampstead, I feel it is not paying a visit, but venturing into a fire." He tried to reason with her, though really with himself. "Knowing well that my life must be passed in fatigue and trouble, I have been endeavouring to wean myself from you: for to myself alone what can be much of a misery?" He was back in the inescapable dilemma that had sent him to the Isle of Wight. Luckily for his peace of mind, Keats found himself caught up in a national event. He returned that afternoon from Walthamstow just as Henry Hunt the Radical orator was making his triumphal entry into London. A crowd of nearly 300,000 lined the streets from Islington to the Strand; red flags and red cockades were everywhere. Hunt had been arrested four weeks before at the mass meeting in St. Peter's Fields, Manchester. Panic action by the local Yeomanry, backed by a troop of Hussars, had led to eleven deaths and hundreds injured, adding the word Peterloo to history. Its permanent effect was to unite rival parties in the movement for constitutional and economic reform so that it became a nation-wide cause; its temporary effect was to elevate Hunt from an embarrassment for the Radicals into their hero. His propaganda procession included a youth still bearing the sabre-wounds of Peterloo. Cheapside was seething with cheering crowds as Keats made his way to Abbey; but if his own political feelings were stirred, he had the good sense to suppress them for the moment. Abbey indeed had sent Keats a kindly letter during the summer about George's affairs, and he now seemed disposed to be helpful, as they sat down to tea. He read the note George had enclosed for him, promised to raise some money on Tom's estate to send to George, and also to get Walton's partner, Gliddon, to deal quickly with Mrs. Midgley Jennings and her solicitors. He even seemed anxious about Keats, though he could not resist a dig at his poetry. Picking up a magazine, he read out with heavy humour a quotation from Byron's *Don Juan* on the folly of literary ambition:

Some liken it to climbing up a hill,
Whose summit, like all hills, is lost in vapour:

These lines, with their mocking parallel to his own symbolic climb in *The Fall of Hyperion*, brought back all Keats's envious disgust at Byron and his "flash poem", as he dismissed *Don Juan*. He even introduced a reference to Byron's "proud bad verse" into his own poem, though he apparently intended later to cancel it. For the moment, he was glad to get out of his interview with Abbey fairly agreeably. He left him, walked up Cheapside, then remembered the letter to Fanny Brawne in his pocket, and returned to the General Post Office in Lombard Street, perhaps glad to have missed the last post. Cutting back through Bucklersbury, he again fell in with Abbey, who had shut the warehouse and was walking to the Poultry, where he again brought up the topic of investment in a hat-maker's business—"I do believe if I could be a hatter I might be one", as Keats commented.

Nothing more could be done; it only remained for him to go back to Winchester and get on with his work, yet for a day he waited, indecisive. He probably visited the newly-engaged Haslam, and perhaps slipped into the second half of the entertainment at Covent Garden, where the dramatic romance of *Blue Beard: or, Female Curiosity* was being performed. Wednesday 15 September found him back at Winchester, and on Friday he poured his unsettled thoughts into a long letter to George, calming himself by writing. He spoke of both their failures, his in particular. "My name with the literary fashionables is vulgar—I am a weaver boy to them". One of the Peterloo demonstrators, Samuel Bamford, had just had naive poems printed in *The Examiner*, from his collection "Weaver Boy".[1] Keats felt bitterly that he himself had been treated like a freak, labelled as an apothecary-poet, one of the lowlife literary amateurs with whom Lockhart had classed him, taken up as some sort of working-class phenomenon, then dropped. In his strained state, it was a relief to indulge in his fancy for the grotesque. He took a ludicrous idea from Burton, about a city or army composed entirely of lovers, and turned it into mock-heroic blank-verse. He pounced on one bravura passage of Burton's prose beginning "Every lover admires his mistress, though she be very deformed of herself", a catalogue of grotesque description, which delighted him so much that he underlined every word, made an appreciative note, and copied it, note and all, into his letter to George. Significantly he added, "I would give my favourite leg to have written this as a speech in a Play." His dramatic ambition was by no means finished, nor, when he had recovered from the break in composition, was the great design of the new poem that he had set himself. Some time during these days, he wrote the lines that show the farthest reach of his new style and vision, the unveiling of the face of Moneta:

1. E. No. 607, p. 528.

> But yet I had a terror of her robes,
> And chiefly of the veils, that from her brow
> Hung pale, and curtain'd her in mysteries
> That made my heart too small to hold its blood.
> This saw that Goddess, and with sacred hand
> Parted the veils. Then saw I a wan face,
> Not pin'd by human sorrows, but bright blanch'd
> By an immortal sickness which kills not;
> It works a constant change, which happy death
> Can put no end to; deathwards progressing
> To no death was that visage; it had pass'd
> The lily and the snow; and beyond these
> I must not think now, though I saw that face—

The extraordinary vision of these lines has had many interpretations. Nor is it entirely certain when Keats wrote them, though everything points to their having been written at Winchester, at least before he left for London in October. The chilling line

> That made my heart too small to hold its blood

sounds like a reminiscence of his favourite stanza from Chatterton, beginning

> Comme, wythe acorne-coppe and thorne,
> Drayne mie hartys blodde awaie;

and Chatterton was very much in his mind during this third week of September. This in itself might support the Freudian theory that the vision is in some way connected with a constant return of Keats's thoughts to the death of his mother; the reading of Chatterton was itself, as it had been after Tom's death, a regression in his mind to an earlier and more adolescent way of life. There may be much also in the rival view of the Jungians, that the vision represents the true Self with which Keats can at last integrate his ego, or more limited selfhood. Whether it is the discovery of beauty in the face of death, the ultimate solution of the "Beauty that must die", or the death of the soul into a greater Soul, it seems certain that the vision represents death in some way.

These unconscious elements may well underlie Keats's writing in this passage; it still remains to be asked what it meant to him. Here all is again conjecture, since he left no comment or parallel in his letters; but, considering his aim in all his poetry at this time, it seems likely that he intended at last to face and portray the complete reality of death. Hitherto he had softened and romanticized the idea, spoken of Death as "Life's high mead", and

> Call'd him soft names in many a mused rhyme,

He had linked Death with the ultimate fulfilment of Love:

O that I could have possession of them both
in the same minute.

Now, not with love but with terror, and a draining away of his heart's blood,
he forces himself to look on and describe death as it really is. There is a
difference from the crude realism, itself perhaps a half-evasion, that he had
injected into the close of St. Agnes, for here he finds himself able, with an
effort, to stay with the vision of reality, as the passage continues

> But for her eyes I should have fled away.
> They held me back, with a benignant light,
> Soft-mitigated by divinest lids
> Half-closed, and visionless entire they seem'd
> Of all external things—they saw me not,
> But in blank splendor beam'd like the mild moon,
> Who comforts those she sees not, who knows not
> What eyes are upward cast.

How far his foreknowledge of his own illness and death, how far the many
deaths he had known in his own family contributed to this vision it is
impossible to gauge; but his purpose in his new poetry is clear, to give death
its reality "pass'd The lily and the snow", the common similes for it. In the
scheme of the poem, only by this realistic vision can he share the "Shade of
Memory" and see, through Moneta, the whole state of life.

In the soft Autumn days at Winchester, Keats looked back over his whole
life, though he did not hesitate to give George some topical politics, which
showed that he divined what a watershed Peterloo had been, modestly adding
"I know very little of these things". He summed up his own life as Autumn
and the familiar shapes of field and tree restored his broken calm. He went for
a daily walk, strolling down by the west front of the Cathedral, past the
clergy buildings, down College Street where Jane Austen had died two years
before, along "a country alley of gardens" to the monastery of St. Cross, set
in its beautiful water-meadows. Calmer aspects also entered into his reading.
He marked in Canto 26 of the Inferno one of the brief passages of natural
description by which Dante threw into relief the attendant horror.[1] He laid
aside the cynicism of Burton, and delighted in the innocent naiveties of
Chatterton, whom he always associated with autumn. He had always admired
the beginning of the Third Minstrel's song in Aella, describing autumn "with
his goulde honde guylteynge the falleynge lefe".[2] It found an echo in his
situation now. It was one of those magical times in Keats's life when, against
all odds, his surroundings, his reading, and his own inner resources seemed to

1. MOK, 40.
2. Leigh Hunt, MS annotation to Warton's History of English Poetry, 1840 edition, II,
343.

give him all that he needed for the greatest poetry. "I am surprized myself at the pleasure I live alone in", he commented. In this mood, on Sunday 19 September, he wrote *To Autumn*.

> Season of mists and mellow fruitfulness,
> Close bosom-friend of the maturing sun;
> Conspiring with him how to load and bless
> With fruit the vines that round the thatch-eves run;
> To bend with apples the moss'd cottage-trees,
> And fill all fruit with ripeness to the core;
> To swell the gourd, and plump the hazel shells
> With a sweet kernel; to set budding more,
> And still more, later flowers for the bees,
> Until they think warm days will never cease,
> For Summer has o'er-brimm'd their clammy cells.
>
> Who hath not seen thee oft amid thy store?
> Sometimes whoever seeks abroad may find
> Thee sitting careless on a granary floor,
> Thy hair soft-lifted by the winnowing wind;
> Or on a half-reap'd furrow sound asleep,
> Drows'd with the fume of poppies, while thy hook
> Spares the next swath and all its twined flowers:
> And sometimes like a gleaner thou dost keep
> Steady thy laden head across a brook;
> Or by a cyder-press, with patient look,
> Thou watchest the last oozings hours by hours.
>
> Where are the songs of Spring? Ay, where are they?
> Think not of them, thou hast thy music too,—
> While barred clouds bloom the soft-dying day,
> And touch the stubble-plains with rosy hue;
> Then in a wailful choir the small gnats mourn
> Among the river sallows, borne aloft
> Or sinking as the light wind lives or dies;
> And full-grown lambs loud bleat from hilly bourn;
> Hedge-crickets sing; and now with treble soft
> The red-breast whistles from a garden-croft;
> And gathering swallows twitter in the skies.

The poem goes far beyond the landscape in which it was conceived, and which Keats described in a letter two days later:

How beautiful the season is now. How fine the air. A temperate sharpness about it. Really, without joking, chaste weather—Dian skies—I never lik'd stubble fields so much as now—Aye better than the chilly green of the spring. Somehow a stubble plain looks warm—in the same way that some pictures look warm—this struck me so much in my sunday's walk that I composed upon it.

The first intention then was to compose a poem like a set of warm pictures of the season, just as *The Eve of St. Mark*, which he was just now reading through before sending it to George, had been a series of vignettes beginning with the "chilly green of the spring", when

> The chilly sunset faintly told
> Of immaturd, green vallies cold.

The poem retains this pictorial quality, especially in the brief one-line pictures of its last stanza, but it goes far beyond externals. It also goes far beyond its sources, though the passage of Dante describing the fruitful vine-clad Italian countryside watched by the reclining peasant coloured the personified figures of the second stanza; direct borrowings from the minstrel's song of Autumn in Chatterton's *Aella* are apparent in the first draft, but alter under Keats's hand to more rich and positive form, though he retained the essential simplicity of Chatterton.

Yet the poem throughout is an application of the new calm style of *The Fall of Hyperion* to the form and thought of the earlier odes, and the contrast is striking. The May Odes, for all their magnificence, are full of rhetorical question and answer, written in what Keats had now come to regard as a fever, a beating at the bars of life. This is a poem of acceptance, and it was written in a style of acceptance, in which the poet has lost himself in the poem. It recalls his own first axiom of poetry, the rise, progress and setting as natural and as inevitable as that of the sun. There is no striving, either in thought or technique. It has been well said that "the poet himself is completely lost in his images, and the images are presented as meaning simply themselves: Keats's richest utterance is the barest of metaphor".[1]

For a day or two he hung on the threshold of a new era in his poetry. More poems like this and like the new *Hyperion* were, he knew, his right path. There is no evidence that *To Autumn* was even a half-conscious gesture of farewell, as it has been called. All his thought for the next few months showed him actively concerned with the problems of poetry, and especially of his whole new conception of poetry, demanding a much more acute critical sense. He looked to poetry continually in the long letter to George, which he took up again on Monday 20 September. "The great beauty of Poetry", he wrote, "is, that it makes every thing every place interesting." He copied at last *The Eve of St. Mark*, and perhaps added some more Chattertonian verses to it. The next day found him deepening more and more his ideas of poems to come, and of the character needed in composing them: "Quieter in my pulse . . ., exerting myself against vexing speculations—scarcely content

1. Ward, 322.

to write the best verses for the fever they leave behind. I want to compose without this fever. I hope I one day shall."

Looking to the future involved looking at the past; from the moment Keats got up this day, he looked back at himself, up and down the years, particularly the last one, a year to the day since he had started the first version of *Hyperion*. Dimly he felt he must come to some decision about his life and work, as he considered how far he had gone. He wrote to George, "From the time you left me, our friends say I have altered completely—am not the same person—", and his thought continued to hark far back to his apprentice days when he had had the quarrel with Hammond. As he wrote on all through the morning to his brother, including a description of his daily walk in a style mildly parodying a local guide-book, two main themes began to emerge. One was their financial difficulty. Although Keats promised to remit his brother any sum he could, he had to confess that his own debts now probably equalled all he could hope to get from Tom's estate. The other, which kept returning, was the future of his poetry. He had received letters from Woodhouse and Reynolds, who were staying at Bath, pressing him to get his narrative poems ready for publication; on the other hand, apart from *Lamia*, which he liked on re-reading, he felt these did not match his new conception of what poetry was. Nor, trying to weld the beginning of the old *Hyperion* into the vision of the past shown him through Moneta's memory, could he be happy with a style that now seemed artificial beside the new purity of what he had just written. He felt it to be too Miltonic, in its inversions and elaborate similes, the complete reverse of what he now reckoned the Chattertonian purity of *To Autumn*. He even borrowed Chatterton's own criticism of Milton as too Latinate, but what clearly worried him was the difficulty of marrying the old *Hyperion* with the new. "I wish to devote myself to another sensation", he wrote, thinking of the quiet feverless verse he intended to be his future. He put down George's letter and wrote to Reynolds, who would want to know his latest poetic plans. "I wish to give myself up to other sensations", he repeated. This involved the decision his mind had been slowly reaching all through the morning. He must give up *Hyperion* itself, both versions. He could not separate in it the false beauty proceeding from art and the true voice of feeling. To mix the two together would be to botch the work.

The decision made him realize how confused his mind was after a long morning's writing and thinking, so he broke off for his calming afternoon walk. His thoughts continued as he did so, his own character, his own obstinacy in the face of events. He stooped under a fence in the meadows. Why not get over, he asked? Because no one tried to make you get under, he told himself. The weather was colder, and he lingered by a blacksmith's fire, the first chill of the year increasing his mood of remembrance and stock-taking. That evening he wrote on to Reynolds

To night I am all in a mist; I scarcely know what's what—But you knowing my unsteady & vagarish disposition, will guess that all this turmoil will be settled by tomorrow morning. It strikes me tonight that I have led a very odd sort of life for the two or three last years—Here & there—No anchor—

"I am glad of it", he added, half-jokingly; but already another serious decision faced him. He had given up *Hyperion*, and he had little faith in most of the other poems prepared for his book. How was he to manage his life now, both so as to get through it at all, and to write his new poetry? He must reason it out with fresh self-knowledge. "I would give a guinea to be a reasonable man—good sound sense—a say what he thinks, and does what he says man." With a humorous echo of the poet's trial on the altar of Moneta, he added, "They say men near death however mad they may have been, come to their senses." Finishing off the letter, he embarked on a companion-piece for Woodhouse, giving him, as well as *To Autumn*, three extracts from *The Fall of Hyperion*. His phrase about its opening, "Here is what I had written for a sort of induction", confirmed that the poem was to be given up. The year of tremendous achievement that began with one *Hyperion* had ended with another, both unfinished. The progress his poetry had made in that exact year is symbolized by the differences between the two. It had been the greatest year of living growth of any English poet.

PART IV

THE LAST YEAR

Chapter 24

UNMERIDIANED

"I have been so very lax, unemployed, unmeridian'd, and object-less these two months"

– JOHN KEATS to Joseph Severn, 10 November 1819

ON WEDNESDAY 22 September, Keats wrote to Brown, finished his letter to Woodhouse, and then wrote, though he did not post, a letter to Dilke. All three announced his new decision and his practical hopes. It was something comparable in his mind with his decision to give up medicine and surgery nearly three years before; indeed, as he now looked at it, this was the first time since that occasion when he had really made an act of will-power about his own life. It bore out his conviction that doing was even superior to writing, expressed to Reynolds in August, implicit in *The Fall of Hyperion*; he resolved to become one of those who, in Moneta's words, do benefits to the great world, no longer merely one of the tribe of dreamers. Yet he realized his own limitations; he would not plunge into any profession for which his past life had unsuited him. "My occupation is entirely literary", he wrote to Brown,[1] "I will do so too." Reading his own nature, he strove to find a compromise for himself between dreamer-poet and man of action, with a stress on the word "do", but on a type of doing that best suited his abilities. "I will write, on the liberal side of the question, for whoever will pay me." A month before he had disclaimed any interest in politics, "Fat Louis, fat Regent, or the Duke of Wellington." Now—and it is not without some meaning that Peterloo had come in between—he would strike out a career as a political journalist. His only journalistic experience, however, was not in politics but in his *Champion* reviews of the theatre; for the time, he would make a start by getting a foothold in dramatic criticism for some paper. While existing on that, he went on to explain to Woodhouse and Dilke, he would train as an all-round journalist, living cheaply in Westminster, getting up subjects by reading at the British Museum, until, as he remarked with a flick of cynicism, he could "shine up an article on any thing without much knowlege of the subject, aye like an orange".[2] For all the latent uneasiness in such comments, there was no lack of idealism too: "I hope sincerely", he added, "I shall be able to put a Mite of help to the Liberal side of the Question

1. *Letters*, II, 176.   2. *Letters*, II, 174–175; 178–180.

before I die." Anything would be better than remaining "a dead lump". There was another consideration, which he revealed only to Brown, and even then in guarded terms: "If you live at Hampstead next winter—I like Miss Brawne and I cannot help it. On that account I had better not live there." This was still the major problem. Keats, in his copy of Burton, put a cross against the remark that "St. Austin . . . would not live in the house with his own sister."[1]

Just as eighteen months before, he had proposed seeking the help of Hazlitt in his new life of thought, so now he proposed taking the older writer as his new guide to journalism. Hazlitt, he hoped, might recommend him for a job on the *Edinburgh Review*, as he had done for Reynolds. Poetry was, for a time, to be pushed into the background, though not forgotten. The new deliberate poetry he wished to write, without stress, without fever, might indeed gain from the consideration such a way of life would entail. The resolve he had failed to follow in the Spring, "never to write for the sake of writing, or making a poem", might, forced on him by necessity, purify his whole poetic output. As for the dubious prospect of the play, his eyes were fully open to the long months of waiting involved in dealing with theatrical managements; if it at last succeeded, no harm would have been done by earning some money in the meantime. Keats's disillusion with poetry at this point has been exaggerated;[2] in spite of the preoccupation with action, with doing, in spite of remarks to Dilke and Haydon showing contempt for the poetry-reading public, poetry itself never loses its place for him. In a second letter to Brown, he spoke still of poetry as "a high tone of feeling", and talked of himself as only "prosing for awhile".[3]

He had intended to slip up to London and lodge with Rice till Dilke could find him quarters in Westminster; but on Friday 24 September, a letter from Brown persuaded him to stay on at Winchester until the latter returned in person to thrash the whole matter out. Brown would not easily acquiesce in a scheme which seemed to put the money-making potential of *Otho* on one side. So Keats waited, filling in time with even longer and more circumstantial details of his life for George and Georgiana, written in an easy vein of humour that relieved the stress of the decisions he had just taken; in these pages, one can almost catch his exact tone of voice, his gift for friendly mimicry, the charm he extended over all his friends. Two long stories he told them, two humorous situations, one he perpetrated and one of which he was the victim, have all the marks of an assured and made-up mind. The discomfiture of Brown and Brown's tenant, Nathan Benjamin, by Keats's practical joke, his own discomfiture in a misunderstanding with another pair of tenants in the Winchester lodging, have a sparkle of comedy and a turn of dramatic writing, "I must first give you the scene and the dramatis Personæ" was how

---

1. Probably annotated next month, after his return to Hampstead.
2. By Ward, 326–328.　　3. *Letters*, II, 181.

he introduced the latter account. Monday 27 September brought yet another letter from George, more "bad intelligence", though Keats now was in a state to take it calmly. Better news had come in the last *Examiner* Dilke had forwarded; the report of Kean's American tour, like other stories about the actor, might after all be false.[1]

Keats sealed the long letter, hopefully though anxiously, with a few lines from *Otho*. The end of the month brought Brown and a discussion; it also brought the next *Examiner*, with the news that Kean, who had been performing at Manchester to audiences shouting "Peterloo", still intended to go to America, and was defying the Drury Lane management to hold him to his contract.[2] Keats therefore stood firm to his intentions, and wrote on 1 October a decisive letter to Dilke, announcing his return to Town in a week's time, and asking for two rooms to be engaged for him in Westminster "A Sitting Room and bed room for myself alone", he added swiftly, in case the Dilkes, not knowing how affairs stood at Wentworth Place, might jump to the conclusion that he planned an elopement. To Haydon, two days later, he reaffirmed his faith in poetry; it was, as always, only self-criticism about the quality of his work that gave him doubts. He did not believe, in spite of what Brown might say,[3] that genuinely great work would ever go unrecognized by the public, for all its obtuseness. If he had written anything as fine as Shakespeare had done in *Othello*, he would have had as big and as enthusiastic a reception as Henry Hunt obtained in the streets of London after Peterloo. He allowed himself a hint of envy for poets with more freedom of life than his own, thinking of his past plans for travel. He would like to be writing letters "from my Palace in Milan", as Shelley had done on arriving in Italy the year before; that was all.

On 8 October, Keats moved back to Town. Dilke had found him quiet lodgings overlooking the Abbey gardens at 25 College Street, near his own house in Great Smith Street. The Abbey Library was at hand, and the British Museum, for which Keats had asked Haydon to get him a ticket, was not far distant. He had, of course, books and belongings to fetch from Wentworth Place, where the indignant victim of his practical joke had just moved out, and where he would inevitably meet Fanny. Should he venture into the fire? On Sunday the 10th he did. The result was overwhelming. As he had feared, knowing himself, three month's abstinence from even seeing her had made her unbearably desirable to him. "You dazzled me"; he was completely dazed by the encounter. There is no knowing how she behaved to him,[4] but he at once wrote of threats she made that, if carried out, "would hurt my heart—I could not bear it". One cannot tell if these exchanges had anything to do with his new resolve for life and work, but it is certain that he

1. E. No. 612, p. 603.   2. E. No. 613, pp. 615 and 619.
3. KC, II, 71.
4. Ward, 329, says "she welcomed Keats with . . . passion".

returned to College Street with all his plans unsettled and his life in a turmoil. All he could think about was Fanny. "When shall we pass a day alone?" was his main concern. Early on Monday morning, he saw the friendly Mrs. Dilke, to ask her to accompany him soon back to Wentworth Place, so that his visit should have the colour of convention. He dropped all other plans. He did not apparently attempt to see Hazlitt.[1] Severn, who in later years made increasing and obsessive claims to have been present at every major crisis in Keats's life, does seem to have called on him at College Street. His muddled recollections were that Keats was in high spirits though not much improved in health by his summer out of Town, confirmed in his resolution to give up *Hyperion* and very much taken up with *Lamia*. If there is any value at all in Severn's account of this visit, it sounds as if it took place before Keats had seen Fanny. Now his whole life was absorbed by her with a sense of almost physical dissolution. "I have a sensation at the present moment as though I was dissolving", he wrote on 13 October. It was the sensation he had described at the foot of the sacrificial steps in *The Fall of Hyperion*. In both, one may guess the dramatic changes and emotional extremes of a constitution already infected with tuberculosis. These extremes he now poured into a series of poems for Fanny; she had absorbed his poetry too. He had ended his previous letter to her with a quotation from Chaucer's *Troilus and Criseyde*. Chaucer had seemed to him an example of the new realistic poetry he himself wished to write, the type of future poetry he had planned to produce with deliberation in the intervals of his new life. Now, with those schemes shattered, he still clung to Chaucer's wisdom and his way of summing up the human situation. Keats saw himself as Troilus, Fanny as Criseyde. All the poems he wrote her have the emotional atmosphere, and even the expressions, of the Trojan lover whose mistress is now parted from him in the Grecian camp.[2]

Oh herte myn, Criseyde, oh swete fo!
Oh lady myn, that I love and no mo!

In all his poems to her, Fanny appears as the "sweet foe", an exact expression of Keats's complicated feeling toward her at this time. His whole being was torn apart by contradictory stresses. In his first *Lines to Fanny*, written an hour after his visit, he wrestles with love and tries to get back to serenity and poetry. There are even more confusing emotions. With all his apprehensions quickened by the new situation, he cannot rid his mind of the sickening fears he has for George and Georgiana in America; all his morbid reading, ever since their journey, about the horrors of the vast interior of the continent, came to the surface in this poem, prompted by the disturbance of his own life:

1. Though Ward, 330, argues he did, there is no evidence of this.
2. MOK, 69–78.

Where shall I learn to get my peace again?
To banish thoughts of that most hateful land,
Dungeoner of my friends, that wicked strand
Where they were wreck'd and live a wrecked life;

He tried to blot out all thought, as Troilus does in Chaucer's poem, by the image of the "dazzling breast" of his love, and the poem disintegrates in a way matching his whole life.

Keats's four poems to Fanny Brawne, these lines, an ode, and two sonnets were almost certainly written during the ten days from 11 to 21 October, when he was separated from her and struggling against the overwhelming temptation to throw up all his resolve, and return to Hampstead. The Ode, with its chilling reference to the wintry air, into whose icy grip his love beckons him, may well be the last of the sequence, written during the abnormally early fall of snow on the 21st,[1] which ushered in one of the most fatally cold seasons for many years. They are part of Keats's attempts, as he told Fanny in a letter, quoting from John Ford, "to reason against the reasons of my Love", and all, even the one calmer sonnet, show him succumbing to a power stronger than reason. This power was not only love, but its black obverse, jealousy. Fanny may well have matured during his apparent in-difference to her all through the summer; on the other hand, she was still young enough to take revenge. All Keats's letters to her during these ten days speak of her threatening to be cruel to him; all the poems have a note of apprehension. Even in the calm sonnet, "The day is gone", her beauty vanishes from him "unseasonably", just when their love should come to fruition. The Ode and the other sonnet were as wild and disturbed as Chaucer's portrayal of their literary begetter, the lover Troilus hurling him-self upon his lonely bed. Yet the special imagery of Keats's own poems suggests a dilemma peculiar to himself, and quite foreign to the accepted Christian world with which Chaucer had surrounded his pagan lovers. Keats packs his poems with phrases that suggest the ceremonies of the orthodox established Church—"a heresy and a schism", "love's missal", "the Holy See of Love", "the sacramental cake"; in his letter of 13 October, he burst out, "My Creed is Love and you are its only tenet", and he spoke of Love being now his religion. All these terms can only mean one thing; he was contem-plating a formal engagement leading to the sacrament of marriage. Yet Fanny was a Christian believer, and Keats was not. However close he might come to Christian doctrine in his philosophy of soul-making, he would never accept orthodox Christianity, "the pious frauds of religion". Later he wrote to Fanny "by the blood of that Christ you believe in", marking the total difference in their spiritual outlook. He told her now, "I could be martyr'd for my Religion—Love is my religion", but his real feeling broke out when

1. G.M. (1819), II, 382.

in his copy of Burton he wrote against the word "martyrs" the note "The most biggotted word ever met with"; he even proposed to "decapitate", as he said, the large letters in which the name "Christ" was printed. The real crux of a formal engagement to Fanny was that he would have to be intellectually false to himself; yet he could not hope to have her without it.[1] This agonizing dilemma was heightened by another factor. All through the year, Keats's feelings about the Church and the clergy had become wilder and less rational. If his had been a straightforward intellectual doubt, the scepticism he shared with many in the deistic circle, he might well have accepted marriage for the sake of making Fanny happy with some sort of half-amused shrug, as even Shelley had done. There was, by contrast, an increasing and abnormal violence in Keats's attitude. It was not only that he repeated with relish a discreditable story about Samuel White, the Vicar of Hampstead, who would have to marry them, nor that he applauded Hunt's clumsy satires in *The Examiner*. To be so obsessed with anti-clericalism that he wished to avoid staying in a place whose name contained the word Bishop, Bishop-steignton in Devon, seems hardly sane.[2] This obsession, which appears clearly in his markings in Burton, resembles one other strand in his life. It is like his insane outbursts against Charles Wells, who, he believed, had harmed Tom's chances of recovery by his hoax. He still reverted to this topic; "I'd rather have died", he said, and added menacingly, "Wells should have brothers and sicker than I even had."[3] The connecting link between these two types of obsession is the death of Tom; it is from Tom's death that his emotional fury against the clergy gets out of control. It seems likely that some cleric, perhaps the Vicar of Hampstead himself, had made unfortunate remarks. Keats's own words, "I will not enter into any parsonic comments on death", indicate that some had been made. Yet his violence was out of all proportion to such a cause. It was an emotion he could not control, and its irrational obsessive quality joined with his deep neurosis about women to blacken the whole idea of marriage. Against nine of the twelve reasons in favour of marriage set out in his copy of Burton, Keats took the trouble to pen laboriously and distinctly the letters "Qᵛ" to express his querulous disagreement. "Aye aye" he wrote against the corresponding list of reasons against marriage, and proceeded to underline one of them—"The band of marriage is adamantine; no hope of loosing it; thou art undone." "Cogliam la rose d'amore *ubique*", he had written a few pages earlier, with hungry underlining.

How much Fanny knew of all this, or what, if anything, she made of it, is impossible to say. These were matters going far back in Keats's history, over which she had no control and perhaps very little real knowledge. Her view of

1. JKLY, 196–197.   2. *Letters*, II, 70–71; 115.
3. Finney, II, 746. Woodhouse's note, shorthand. It is not certain to whom Keats made this remark.

him at this time, and in the months that followed, was given many years after his death, and actually in answer to an opinion that in the later stages of his life, "Keats might be judged insane". She wrote of him[1]

That his sensibility was most acute, is true, and his passions were very strong, but not violent, if by that term violence of temper is implied. His was no doubt susceptible, but his anger seemed rather to turn on himself than others, and in moments of greatest irritation, it was only by a sort of savage despondency that he sometimes grieved and wounded his friends. Violence . . . was quite foreign to his nature. For more than a twelvemonth before quitting England,[2] I saw him every day, often witnessed his sufferings, both mental and bodily, and I do not hesitate to say that he could have never addressed an unkind expression, much less a violent one, to any human being.

This deeper analysis of his nature was something that the years brought to Fanny; at the beginning of the eleven months they now were to spend together, he must have been puzzling in the extreme for any normal young woman. What was she to make of a tenderness, an admiration and a devotion that had such savage undertones? Keats was living out the diversities of love which had formed part of his satisfaction with his treatment of *Lamia*, a love which included every possible element. Fanny could hardly know in what monstrous forms the commonplaces of her life might appear to him. They had doubtless laughed together at his own practical joke on Brown's tenant, which had an unkind robustness typical of its time. Yet when she teased, joked and flirted, she found herself accused of cruelty and threats. When Brown told her a made-up story against him, probably a suggestive one, Keats told her he would die if she believed it. With all this and a watchful mother to contend with, Fanny seems to have kept her head remarkably. From 15 to 17 October, Keats was allowed a three days' stay next door at Wentworth Place, a "three days dream" as he called it, to sort out their future. He returned to the Dilkes with his mind made up; he sent Mrs. Dilke to tell Fanny he was coming back to live at Hampstead, and on Wednesday 20 October, he told her so himself, together with several other things. These seem to have included the final decision for a formal engagement. On the next day he moved back with Brown, under the same roof as Fanny; he probably gave her a garnet ring as a sign of betrothal, though as their prospects of marriage were so far off, she did not wear it openly. Like all semi-secret arrangements, the situation was probably better-known to friends than has been thought,[3] and their verdict on it was not encouraging. "It is quite a settled thing between John Keats and Miss Brawne", wrote one of

1. HBF, V, 184–186.
2. Actually almost exactly eleven months. Like all Keats's friends, Fanny tended to lengthen the time of association with him.
3. Ward, 332, believes that Keats did not tell Brown till 14 Aug. 1820 (*Letters*, II, 321, n. 4) but the letter hardly bears this out.

them,[1] "God help them. It's a bad thing for them. The mother says she cannot prevent it and that her only hope is that it will go off. He don't like anyone to look at her or speak to her." This was the general tone of their circle. Only the Dilkes seem to have remained loyal, as they had over George's marriage, though Dilke's younger brother William heartily disliked Fanny. As for the Reynolds family, their fears that yet another eligible young man had escaped them were now confirmed. Reynolds himself found the engagement unaccountable; his family's disparaging opinions must have reached Fanny, for two years later she expressed her delight that Mrs. Dilke had quarrelled for ever with them.

Keats himself went back to Hampstead with no illusions about the difficulty of his position. An indefinite engagement would be almost more than he could bear physically. "I must impose chains upon myself", he wrote to Fanny before taking the plunge. One of these restraints he imposed on himself at once. He left off eating meat so that, he joked to his sister, "my brains may never henceforth be in a greater mist than is theirs by nature". It has been said that the only conceivable reason he can have had for this was that he already treated himself as tubercular,[2] though as he was found eating beefsteaks three months later, this seems unlikely. What appears more likely is that he put himself on a low diet to try to lessen physical desire during the first few weeks of adjustment to living near Fanny. In his copy of Burton, which he was now marking with personal avidity, he found blood-letting and a vegetable diet recommended to damp down physical desire and quieten jealousy. "Physician Nature, let my spirit blood", he cried in his Ode to Fanny, and he wrote the exclamation "good" against Burton's remark that fasting keeps the body in subjection so that "concupiscence is restrained". These restraints were acutely hard to bear. Severn, who called on him on Sunday 24 October to hear him read Lamia, found him greatly changed; he did not seem to be well either in mind or in body. Encouraged by his Hermia and Helena having at last been hung during the summer at the Royal Academy, Severn was painfully painting away in the cold weather and his icy studio at the set subject for the Royal Academy Gold Medal that year, Una and the Red Cross Knight in the Cave of Despair from The Faerie Queene, Book I, Canto ix.[3] He was delighted when Keats quoted from memory the stanza most relevant to his picture, in which Una snatches the dagger from the knight, who has almost been tempted into suicide by the horrors presented to him by Despair. He did not realize how nearly this

1. The Papers of a Critic, ed. Sir Charles Dilke, I, 11. Ward, 332, and even Richardson, 62, surprisingly give the remark to Mrs. Dilke, who remained a lifelong friend to Fanny. In the original source it is not given to her, and is totally unlike her tone.

2. Ward, 338, Bate, 620, and generally.

3. Sharp, who gives the wrong canto, also (24–27) gives a totally confused account of this picture, but his description of Severn's privations from cold seem to fit this time.

approached to Keats's own mental state until four weeks later, when Keats added to a letter the grim joke, "You had best put me into your Cave of despair."

Brown, robust, busy, full of financial schemes that seemed more practical than they were, tried to rouse him up. Kean had just publicly announced that, in spite of differences with Elliston's management, he bowed to the wishes of the public, and would remain at Drury Lane for the winter season, which had opened with spectacular brilliance.[1] Brown's optimism bubbled up. He persuaded Keats to tidy their play and send it to Elliston; Keats did, but he would not put his own name to it for fear that the ridicule of his poems would damage its chances. Brown was glad to see Keats back at Wentworth Place, and pleased to lend him the money he had got from his summer tenant, while at the same time keeping strict account of all that Keats cost him and stipulating for half any profits on the production of *Otho*. He was also genuinely disturbed by the turmoil of Keats's mind, which was completely plain to his eyes.[2] All the same, he added to the strain under which Keats was living in his own very characteristic way. Some time earlier in the year, Ann, the maid who looked after them at Wentworth Place, had left; Brown had installed a sturdy, handsome, ignorant Irish girl called Abigail O'Donaghue as living-in housekeeper. By now he was sleeping with her, and she soon became pregnant. Normally, with the manners of the age, this would be something that Keats would have no difficulty in accepting. Even the righteous Haydon seems to have behaved like Brown in a similar situation, and Keats had joked quite recently about Severn either getting a bastard or being cuckolded into accepting one as his. Now his reactions were not so balanced. Here was Brown, a wall away, doing what he was denied by society and convention the right to do with Fanny. The fact that Brown could gather the rose *ubique*—everywhere—and was happily doing so, threw his own deprivation into relief. Later he was to speak to Fanny of these "indecencies" of Brown as something that complicated his feelings towards her,[3] quite unbearably.

One cure for the strain of living was to plunge into business and work. George's affairs were urgent enough excuse for him to put them first. At the end of October, he called on Mrs. Wylie in Romney Street to reassure her, though this was a call he avoided making too often. "I am there in the character of a Prevaricator", he wrote to George, "I must not tell the truth." He went several times to Abbey, and the financial position began to clear. In September, Abbey had heard from Fry, the missing trustee to whom Keats had written in July; early in November, Keats himself received from Fry in Holland the long-delayed power of attorney to act in his place with Abbey as joint trustee, and sell out some of the stock George had now

1. E. No. 615, pp. 651 and 653. 2. KC, II, 71, 105.
3. *Letters*, II, 312.

inherited as his one-third share of Tom's portion from Mrs. Jennings.[1] Keats immediately put this into effect. On Abbey's advice he did not cash all George's portion. It was still a bad time for selling. Since February, stocks had remained low. Keats's publisher Taylor commented on the low state of Consols,[2] and even Keats realized he would be doing George a disservice to realize the whole of his share. He sold enough to raise £100, and forwarded it through Capper and Hazlewood, George's London brokers, to Warder's, an agency in America[3] acting for George. In actual fact, with, as Keats said, "the Posts so uncertain", and, he might have added, the winter weather so bad, the ship on which the money travelled, the *William*, was driven far north out of her course, and did not make landfall till well into the New Year.[4] George was forced to borrow money from American sources to tide him over. It was lucky that Keats, acting partly also in the fear that his aunt still meant to press her Chancery claim to Tom's inheritance, did not commit more money to the high seas. He suffered the fate of all who take responsibility, by receiving an angry letter from Fry, furious at being ferreted out in his exile, and telling him and George to go to hell.[5]

Keats also collected £100 of Tom's inheritance for himself, the first of it he had been able to touch since Tom died,[6] eleven months ago. This enabled him to pay off his outstanding debts, including one recently contracted to Haslam, for in spite of having lived all the earlier part of the year on the fund George had left behind, the expenses of his mode of living and his long holiday had been so high, that he actually still had some debts owing from last Christmas. Abbey had finally despaired of trying to get Keats, any more than George, to take an interest in anything so commercial as a hat-making business; he now came up with a proposal that he may genuinely have thought nearer Keats's taste. As Keats did not seem to be making any attempts in the field of journalism, Abbey suggested he should chance his arm in another trade allied to literature, bookselling. Keats brushed this aside, annoyed at the caution Abbey had shown in releasing Tom's money, but it was probably kindly meant. Keats was in a mood which made him disposed to quarrel. Calling on Dilke at the Navy Pay Office, in Somerset House, he disagreed strongly with the latter's opinion that George should have stuck to his original plan and joined the Birkbeck settlement. Dilke noted later

1. *Letters*, II, 228, 231.   2. KHM, No. 63.
3. Not "of London", as indexed by Rollins, *Letters*, II, 437. They were probably a Philadelphia firm.
4. *Letters*, II, 228, n. 1.
5. It is suggested (*Letters*, II, 185, 231) that this was Thomas Fry, a London stock-broker: but George Keats's stockbrokers are known, and only the missing trustee remains to fit this transaction.
6. This explains Keats's statement that he had not had money *from Abbey* for ten months (*Letters*, II, 230). The money he had drawn from George's fund earlier in the year was merely deposited with Abbey's firm. See KI, 50.

that "The very kindness of friends was at this time felt to be oppressive to him." Dilke also observed that "from this period his weakness & his sufferings, mental & bodily, increased—his whole mind & heart were in a whirl of contending passions—he saw nothing calmly or dispassionately."[1] Keats had always been amusedly irritated by Dilke's logic and coolness; now irritation conquered amusement. There is no foundation, however, for the often-repeated statement that Dilke was critical of Keats's attachment to Fanny;[2] like his wife, he seems to have been consistently a loyal friend to her, even helping her with her own money affairs.

If money was now temporarily easier for Keats, the problem of what to do with his own life and poetry was gradually spinning out of control. He told his sister he was in an industrious humour, but to Severn he confessed on 10 November that he had been "very lax, unemployed, unmeridian'd, and objectless these two months", ever since he had written *To Autumn* and given up *Hyperion*. The first flush of sending *Otho* to Drury Lane seems to have set him on to add another scene to *King Stephen*, and make some tentative notes for it, but by 12 November nothing had still been heard from Elliston, and his hopes, unlike Brown's, were cooling. A week earlier, Hazlitt had begun another series of lectures at the Surrey Institution on the dramatic literature of the Age of Elizabeth. A year before, Tom's illness had prevented Keats from attending the series on English Comic Writers. Now his own disturbances of mind and body kept him away; there is no evidence he went to a single one, although Hazlitt had quoted, or rather misquoted from *Sleep and Poetry* in the opening lecture. The seven miles from Wentworth Place and the lateness of the hour in the cold evenings now were enough to form a barrier between him and one of his most constant sources of intellectual inspiration.[3] Poetry seemed quite in abeyance as a part of his life, unless one counts a cheerful quatrain about the pox, sent to him by James Rice;[4] readings and literary exchanges between Keats and his circle of friends were now, as he noted, a thing of the past.

All the same, he kept up with one small set. For the past two years, on his way to and from Taylor & Hessey's bookshop in Fleet Street, Keats had been in the habit of calling on a pleasant household at 10 Percy Street, just off Rathbone Place. Here the artist Peter De Wint shared the house with a fellow-artist William Hilton, whose sister Harriet he had married. The two men were well-known as the David and Jonathan of English art. De Wint, a water-colourist, had more talent, but Hilton was more successful, and had just been elected to full R.A. Their home was friendly, a meeting-place for artists and literary men, and Keats had been introduced into their circle by Taylor and Hessey. About this time, Hilton made a chalk drawing of Keats's head. He was a plodding traditional technician, and the likeness is wooden. Yet it is

1. KHM, No. 52.   2. *Letters*, I, 73.   3. *Letters*, II, 227.
4. *Letters*, II, 230.

not romanticized, and may give a fair impression of Keats at this time of disillusion and stress. Its dulled and dogged expression seems an illustration of his words this mid-November: "Nothing could have in all its circumstances fallen out worse for me than the last year has done, or could be more damping to my poetical talent."[1]

Possibly Taylor thought of the sketch as a frontispiece for the new poems, for he invited Keats and Hilton to dine with him on 15 November at the Fleet Street office. Taylor, who had not been well all the summer, had lost patience with his young poet at the end of September, and had written to Woodhouse to tell him so. Keats's views seemed to him absurd. The crowning folly, in his opinion, was Keats's insistence on the revisions of *The Eve of St. Agnes* to show that the love-affair was consummated. To Woodhouse's objection that this would make the poem unsuitable for ladies, Keats had retorted that he did not want ladies to read his poetry. This infuriated Taylor when he heard it. The publisher saw the better half of his public gone at a blow by "This Folly of Keats", and he even threatened that if Keats persisted in this attitude, he must bring out his poems under some other imprint. He had also not been impressed, quite rightly, by the fragment of *Lamia* Keats had sent, and, again rightly, criticized its sentiments. These judgments by Taylor[2] have surprisingly been taken by all Keats's biographers to show that the publisher was a prude. In fact, he was first and foremost a publisher, and probably knew very well what he was talking about. Much as he admired Keats's genius, he knew the public's reaction to the sexual passages in *Endymion*, and he could not afford to take risks a second time. This had nothing to do with his own character, as was known to all his friends. On his return to London this autumn, Isabella Jones invited Taylor to her housewarming at a new set of rooms a few streets away in Bloomsbury, 57 Lamb's Conduit Street. She offered him, among other attractions, the best liqueur whisky and pretty women to look at.[3] During October and November, he was taking a great deal of trouble to get the rights of a first book of poems by John Clare. Taylor knew that Clare liked drink and women, one of whom was a local whore, while another was with child by him; he also had had venereal disease. This did not prevent Taylor believing in his genius and wanting to publish his poems, provided this side of his private life did not get into print; he merely suggested that such a reputation would not help Clare if he tried to be a village schoolmaster.[4]

At all events, Taylor was now reconciled to his former good opinion of Keats, probably through the tact of Woodhouse, who was present at the dinner on 15 November.[5] *The Eve of St. Agnes* was evidently discussed

---

1. *Letters*, II, 231.   2. KC, I, 96–97.   3. JKLY, 230 and n. 2.
4. John and Anne Tibble, *John Clare*, 51–54, where Taylor's advice on schoolmastering is taken as showing him a poor judge of men, though it seems common sense.
5. KHM, No. 63.

amicably, for Keats wrote about it to Taylor two days later in quite a normal manner. They had talked about publishing, and Keats went away and did some hard thinking. He came up with his own somewhat startling decision; the firm, remembering his declaration at Hessey's that he would never write again as a piece of bravado that had ushered in his great creative year, probably put the same value on this statement. It was that he would not publish anything he had written up to now, but would write a new poem for publication that would outdo all the rest. What he meant no one knows,[1] but his intention was to delve even deeper into all sides of human nature and feeling. "I wish to diffuse the colouring of St Agnes eve throughout a Poem in which Character and Sentiment would be the figures to such drapery." He still doubted his powers in drama, but he knew, with *Lamia* in mind, he had enough skill for a dramatic poem. If he wrote two or three such poems with his new deliberation in, say, the next six years—now he was looking far ahead—he might end as a playwright, which he now felt to be his highest ambition. This was of a piece with the progress of his work through the year toward a greater experience of life. "I am more at home amongst Men and women", he remarked, "I would rather read Chaucer than Ariosto." The new ideal of poetry with emphasis on reality, the poet who wrote without fever, who could see the workings of Moneta's mind, was now his goal. His thoughts were once more with Shakespeare and his universality, and he was now tinkering with a subject from Shakespeare's own time. This was the story of Elizabeth's Earl of Leicester. He had talked about this with Taylor earlier in the year, and the publisher had promised to lend him some books on it; meanwhile he was reading up the reign in Holinshed's *Chronicles*. He asked Taylor for the books, so that he could set out selfishly—that is, perhaps, neglecting both Fanny and George—"on this Poem that is to be". The letter had its ominous proviso: "if God should spare me", he wrote.

1. Certainly not *Hyperion*, which bears no relation to the description that follows.

Chapter 25

THE DEATH WARRANT

"That drop of blood is my death warrant"

– JOHN KEATS to Charles Brown

KEATS'S next actions could hardly have justified more aptly his publisher's contention that he was "such a man of fits and starts". He not only did none of the things he had outlined in his letter to Taylor; he did the exact opposite. On the day after writing, he managed to fit in a visit to Fanny Keats at Walthamstow; for the next month he was very busy,[1] but not at all in the way he had told Taylor he would be. In spite of his determination not to publish anything already written, he prepared his poems for spring publication. Nothing more was heard of the "Poem that is to be", written in a new deliberate and dramatic style. The poem he began to write, far from being in the manner of Chaucer, with an emphasis on the real character of men and women, was a fanciful satire in the style of Ariosto, whom he was now reading fluently, having far outstripped Brown, who, according to Dilke, could not read ten lines of Italian without a dictionary.[2] Keats's inconsistencies, of course, may have been more apparent than real. His publisher may have written back insisting that he got his existing poems ready for the press,[3] while Charles Brown certainly claimed to have encouraged Keats to write "a comic faery poem in the Spenser stanza".[4]

This poem was *The Cap and Bells*; Keats, with perhaps a dark hint at his own private life, preferred to call it *The Jealousies*. Keats was also reading Burton's sections on love-jealousy, several expressions from which occur in the early stages of the poem. What he intended by this poem has, from the first, been subjected to a great deal of confusing comment. Brown himself, often wrongly regarded as a collaborator in it, as he had been with *Otho*, made two contradictory statements. In a note appended by Monckton Milnes to the poem's first publication in 1848, Brown was quoted as saying

1. *Letters*, II, 237.   2. Dilke, ann. II, 50: HBF, II, 73.

3. Ward, 341, believes that Taylor waited until mid-December before he "decided to take the risk of bringing out the new collection of poems", but cites no evidence.

4. KC, II, 72.

This Poem was written subject to future amendments and omissions: it was begun without a plan, and without any prescribed laws for the supernatural machinery.

On the other hand, in another note to Keats's own letter about the poem, Brown spoke of "the intended construction of the story" and claimed that "I knew all, and was to assist him in the machinery of one part".[1]

Brown further spoke of the poem being written chiefly for amusement and relaxation,[2] while Keats always seems to have thought of it commercially as a poem for publication. This obscurity and confusion has been continued by all critics except, to his credit, Milnes himself, who printed the poem without any misleading speculations on its subject, and praised it as an example of Keats's artistic versatility. The general verdict has been that the poem is a political satire; but the two stanzas on George IV and his politicians were, in fact, added later.[3] The poem is not concerned in the main with public matters, but with domestic personalities. Its story is simple, and its characters plainly set out with a number of small personal details, as if they were meant to be recognized. Elfinan, fairy Emperor, is in love with a mortal named Bertha Pearl, but to please his people is betrothed to a fairy princess, Bellanaine, daughter of Pigmio of Imaus, who is herself in love with a mortal named Hubert. His Chancellor, Crafticanto, leaves Panthea, capital of Elfinan's Empire, to bring him the princess; meanwhile, Elfinan, dreading his marriage, summons his dark slave, Eban, to fetch the magician Hum, who is in the town. Hum, an engaging rascal, arrives at the palace and, while consuming a great deal of drink, supplies Elfinan with a magic book, which, he assures him, will enable him to carry off Bertha Pearl. Elfinan leaves for Bertha's home, Canterbury, just as Crafticanto's embassy returns, escorting the princess and her maid Coralline. After a digression giving Crafticanto's diary of the journey, they enter the palace, to find Elfinan gone and everything in confusion. Crafticanto discovers Hum, drunk, and at that point the poem breaks off. One point at once emerges, although, as Brown said, the poem has many inconsistencies, which Keats intended to revise. Panthea is London, a large capital city with spreading northern suburbs, recently beginning to be lit by gas, and in which the transport is by hackney coach.[4] Moreover, it is literary London, where booksellers live in Scarab Street—that is, Grub Street—literary parties are held, and all the talk is of memoirs, poetical style and publications.

This alone would provide the clue to the poem's intention as a topical

---

1. KC, II, 79.   2. KC, II, 99.
3. Garrod, *Works*, xlvii. Brown instanced these stanzas as "failures in wit", KC, II, 99. The matrimonial affairs of the Prince did not become news until next year, with the death of his father and the return of his wife after six years' exile. All biographers, from Colvin to Ward, antedate this in attempts to make the poem refer to George IV's matrimonial affairs.
4. MOK, 121–122.

N

satire. The marriage affairs of the Prince Regent, which have been seen as the theme of the poem, were not topical.[1] If we regard the poem as a political one with some literary allusions, it is unintelligible. If it is regarded as a literary satire with some later political insertions, it at once becomes full of meaning. Moreover, this was topical. The tide of literary satire had been rising this year; in prose, Hazlitt's *Letter to Mr Gifford*, in verse, Reynolds's parody of *Peter Bell* had attracted great attention. Now Byron, in the introduction and in a coda to Book One of *Don Juan*, had just satirized the contemporary poetic scene, and his verses were in every mouth. A wholly literary satire might catch public taste and be a popular success; meanwhile, it would exactly suit his talents, which, as Keats said in September, were "entirely literary". As further confirmation, the work was to have been supplied with literary footnotes by the arch-parodist Reynolds himself, who perhaps was the author of the two such notes that exist.[2]

In this light, the fairy personages of *The Cap and Bells* are fairly well traceable as figures of Keats's literary world. The most obvious is Eban, the dark slave, who closely resembles William Hazlitt. Hazlitt, of course, had been much in Keats's mind this autumn, and in his long descriptions of Eban he draws a picture of the writer's appearance and habits. Eban, like Hazlitt, has the habit of only saying "Yes" and "No" in company, which Keats had satirized in a friendly way in his prose parody of a party at Hunt's. At the same time, Hazlitt's brilliant turn for invective when roused is exactly caught by Keats in Eban's outburst on the hackney-coachman, which Hunt thought good enough to print separately in *The Indicator*. Eban is even given the personal details of Hazlitt's long black curly hair, and his habit of stopping to look in a mirror and admire his own features. "Swift of look, and foot", he is the counterpart of Hazlitt, who had "a quick restless eye" and was a dashing racquets player; Amorio, a name that Keats tried for his fairy character before finding it would not fit the metre, also suggests Hazlitt, whose pursuit of village maidens in the Lake District had permanently offended the Wordsworths. Not all the other fairies are characterized so clearly; some of them are composite figures, standing for schools of poetry. Byron had repeated the now-familiar satire on the Lake poets, Wordsworth, Coleridge, Southey, in *Don Juan*. Keats combined them in the person of Crafticanto. His name, which Keats wrote Crafty Canto, echoed the puns, common even among his friends, which were made on the two syllables of Wordsworth's name. The usual target of satires on Wordsworth and Coleridge, their obviousness and their habit of philosophizing over the small

---

1. Ward, 334, believes that proposals to try the Princess for adultery "had been rocking the kingdom since August", but these hardly became news till she arrived in England in June 1820.

2. *Letters*, II, 268. Rollins, n. 7, says the notes were never written but does not explain who wrote the notes that exist.

manifestations of nature, is quickly hit by Keats in lines early in the poem:

> Show him a mouse's tail, and he will guess,
> With metaphysic swiftness, at a mouse;
> Show him a garden, and with speed no less,
> He'll surmise sagely of the dwelling house,

while later there is a satirical echo of *The Leech Gatherer*. The chief satire in this character, however, pointed strongly to the pet aversion of the liberal press, the Poet Laureate, Robert Southey. Crafticanto's state-office and his toadying to authority is at once announced,

> He's Elfinan's great state-spy militant,
> His running, lying, flying foot-man too,—

in the precise manner of Hunt's *Examiner* attacks on Southey, one of which appeared as his first leader for the New Year.[1] His grey hairs, his alleged hypocrisy, his moral criticisms

> Against the vicious manners of the age

were all taken by Keats from the stock-in-trade of the accusations made against Southey by liberal opposers such as Hazlitt, but his literary style, naturally, is chiefly parodied. Crafticanto is represented as immensely long-winded in everything he writes, his works divided into endless books, chapters, sections and subsections. When he writes his diary, it describes the aerial flight of the fairy embassy over Asia in exactly the style of *Thalaba* and *The Curse of Kehama*, Southey's two very long oriental poems, both of which have mysterious aerial journeys over Asiatic landscapes, full of exaggerated portents and happenings, on a would-be epic scale. Deserts, huge volcanoes in eruption, fabulous beasts and shooting stars make Crafticanto's journey like that of Southey's Ship of Heaven in *The Curse of Kehama*, which, after a similar set of experiences, lands on the peak of the sacred Mount Meru.

If poetic style points to Crafticanto being representative of the Lake Poets, with special regard for Southey, the same test makes his rival and enemy Hum into Leigh Hunt; for Hum is avowedly a poet. "Tit-bits for Phoebus" he calls his work, with a false modesty that again recalls Keats's earlier parody of Hunt sitting at the piano and talking about his own poems Hum is allowed his own poetic version of the fairy embassy;

> See, past the skirts of yon white cloud they go,
> Tinging it with soft crimsons! Now below
> The sable-pointed heads of firs and pines
> They dip, move on, and with them moves a glow
> Along the forest side! Now amber lines
> Reach the hill top, and now throughout the valley shines.

1. E. No. 627, pp. 1–2.

"Why, Hum", comments Elfinan, "Those *nows* you managed in a special style." It is, in fact, the style of Hunt's *The Story of Rimini*, and a direct parody of passages when the wedding-embassy arrives in that poem too:

> And now his huntsman shows the lessening train,
> Now the squire-carver, and the chamberlain,
> And now his banner comes, and now his sheild . . .

while Hunt's scene reaches its bathetic climax with the moment

> When some one's voice, as if it knew not how
> To check itself, exclaims, "the prince! now—now!"

When Hum manages his "Nows" in a special style, he is the Hunt of *Rimini*.

The kingdom of these fairies then is the kingdom of poetry, and that being so, its king is obvious. Elfinan is Lord Byron. Speaking of Reynolds's parody of Wordsworth in April, Keats had written "I(t) would be just as well to trounce Lord Byron in the same manner." This was included in the general literary satire of *The Cap and Bells*. Elfinan is celebrated for his amours. He is out of love with his bride before he even marries her, and ready to deceive her before and after marriage. All this follows the pattern of Byron's disastrous marriage with Annabella Milbanke, while Elfinan bids mocking farewell to Bellanaine in a direct quotation from Byron's farewell stanzas to his own wife, which had been printed in *The Examiner*.

Keats's satire ranged Byron and Hunt on one side and the Lake Poets on the other, with Hazlitt as a sardonic outsider. One point suggests that its bias was to have been against the Lake Poets; he wrote it under the feigned name of Lucy Vaughan Lloyd, recalling the lecture where Hazlitt had attacked the Lake School and modern women poets, "the blue-stockined". The authoress's name, which Keats often used as the name of the poem itself, carried on the association; Lucy suggests Wordsworth, while the poems of Charles Lloyd, Wordsworth's close and distressing neighbour, had just been reviewed in *The Examiner*.[1] "Lucy", the supposed writer, is crudely handled in one of the notes to the poem, where she is said to have "copied a long Latin note" from Bayle's Dictionary; the implication was that what she copied, being given by the lexicographer in Latin, was indecent, though she set it down in all innocence.[2] "The bigotted and the blue-stockined" were the chief literary targets. Even with the revisions he admitted were necessary, Keats's satire as a whole is a failure. The hard exactness of true satire was foreign to his nature. Even in imitation, for which he had such talents, Severn noted at this exact time that Keats's gift was for "imitating the manner to increase your favourable impression of the person he was speaking of". *The Cap and Bells* was

---

1. E. No. 617, pp. 685–686.

2. This explains why Keats thought "Lucy Vaughan Lloyd" would offend the "squeamish stomachs" of lady readers. KC, II, 79.

doomed by his own temperament; it is also confused by some elements of personal obsession, for the early stanzas have affinities with his own strained feelings for Fanny. Yet it sometimes catches the "light and shade" of ordinary life that his prose creates; we can see him, as in his letters, walking along Cheapside after the dusk had descended on the City, picturing commercial London:

> It was the time when wholesale houses close
> Their shutters with a moody sense of wealth,
> But retail dealers, diligent, let loose
> The gas (objected to on score of health),
> Convey'd in little solder'd pipes by stealth,
> And make it flare in many a brilliant form . . .

In his poetry generally, humour and grandeur are in separate compartments; here, however unsuccessfully, they jostle each other as they do in Keats's letters.

As Keats wrote on into December, he was also revising his poems for Taylor. He cannibalized for *The Cap and Bells* those which he did not wish to publish. The borrowings from the fragmentary *The Eve of St. Mark* are obvious; it is also significant that he chopped out pieces of *Hyperion* for his comic poem, so it is clear he did not intend to publish that fragment either. He and Brown were back in a routine that at least did his nerves good, their "old dog trot" as he called it. In the morning, he wrote *The Cap and Bells*, while Brown, sitting opposite, copied it, sometimes as many as twelve stanzas a day; in the evenings he sat alone with *Hyperion*, brooding. He also tinkered with *Otho*. Elliston had at last accepted it, but with the proviso it could not come out this season, during which the manager was pinning his faith on comedy. Brown advised threatening to send it to the rival Covent Garden. With poems, tragedy and hopes for the satire, Keats had flashes of optimism. "My hopes of success in the literary world are now better than ever" he wrote on 20 December to his sister. Even Abbey seemed anxious to help. Hodgkinson, who had married earlier in the year, was looking out for another firm which would offer partnership; Abbey put out feelers to Keats about coming into the tea brokerage himself. The idea did not stick, as Abbey had second thoughts, and Keats did not like the scheme on obtaining more details of the work; he had only considered it so that he might be able to keep the job warm for George, if the latter should give up America. The exceptionally bleak winter was making Keats more than ever conscious of his health. Some of the money he had drawn from Tom's estate was spent, on Dr. Sawrey's orders, on a warm greatcoat and thick shoes to combat his ever-threatening sore throat. He was cheerful enough to send James Rice a long story, whose theme has the crudities of an old country ballad. He visited Leigh Hunt at York Buildings, where the editor, in financial difficulty, was finding himself unable to keep up his four-year lease.[1] Keats championed to Hunt the idea of a poet as a creator; if a poet added to a familiar legend, he was to be regarded as a classical authority. He instanced Dante's account of Ulysses' death at the end of *Inferno*, Canto xxvi, which he had marked in his own copy, and said that Dante's invention here should be treated as authentic.[2] He also made the remark, whose critical acumen delighted Hunt, that John Home, author of *Douglas*, was "a curious old fellow poking about".[3] He was regaining his equilibrium as a poet and as a person, in yet another violent swing of temperament after the tragic moods of October. He picked up again with the Dilkes, went to Charlie Dilke's Westminster speech day, and dined with his parents in Great Smith Street on Christmas Day. As Brown was there, and *The Cap and Bells* in full progress, the conversation naturally turned on fairy tales, and ended in a bet of a beefsteak supper between Dilke and Brown as to which could write the better tale; Keats was appointed one of the judges, with Reynolds, Rice, and also Taylor to give his independent view as professional publisher.[4] The circle, which Keats had gloomily felt a month before to be broken, was renewing itself. Best news of all for their set, Severn, against all the odds, was awarded on 10 December the Gold Medal at the Royal Academy. Keats too learnt about this time that James Elmes, who had printed his *Ode to a Nightingale*, was also printing the *Ode on a Grecian Urn* in *Annals of the Fine Arts*.

Work, hope, friendship had advanced Keats from the desperate state of his sonnet to Fanny two months before, when he had feared he might

> Forget, in the mist of idle misery,
> Life's purposes,—

Yet the razor-edge on which he still stood was perilous. *The Cap and Bells* represented a compromise between his idea of earning by topical writing and his real resolve to give his whole being to a new and finer poetry; mixed in its motives, it was to achieve neither. The bluff, which Brown wrongly advised, of coercing Elliston by hinting they would offer *Otho* to his rivals if it were not put on that season, was an unworthy, dangerous, and, as it proved, unsuccessful manoeuvre. Health, in spite of the comforts of greatcoat and thick shoes, was still precarious, and the New Year began a season of the most horrible weather, when intense cold and snow alternated with freezing fog. Most of all, the two essential and interlocked problems, George's finances and Keats's long engagement to Fanny with its wear and tear on his whole system, were not being resolved at all. Here he tried to blind himself

---

1. CLH, I, 119; *Letters*, II, 230.   2. KHM, No. 172.
3. Leigh Hunt, MS, ann. to Warton; *Letters*, II, 238.
4. *The Papers of a Critic*, I, 14. They were not all present at the original dinner as implied by Ward, 342, nor was Fanny Brawne as implied by Rollins, *Letters*, II, 237, n. 3.

to the real situation. When a letter arrived from George for Mrs. Wylie, Keats almost superstitiously tried to tell himself that the firmness of George's hand in addressing and sealing it indicated good news.

It did not; in fact, it heralded the most fatal of all George's interventions of his own necessities into Keats's affairs. He was still in difficulties, and Georgiana was expecting another child; he had set sail for England, at all costs to obtain more money quickly. He arrived at Wentworth Place at the end of the first week in January, where he sat eating home-made twelfth-night cakes with John and the Brawnes, and sizing up the situation he found there. He was not altogether in the dark about Fanny.[1] John had written to him from Shanklin about his desire to enjoy "what the competences of life procure",[2] and it seems probable the letter contained at least some hint of the prospect of marriage. With his family possessiveness, it was inevitable that he should be suspicious of her, and he shared the doubts of most of Keats's friends. Some of these had been quick to get his ear, and he was soon told, perhaps by the Reynoldses, that Fanny was nothing better than "an artful bad hearted Girl". In all fairness, he did not form the judgment himself; in his affection for John, he trusted that there must be something in her, since his brother was in love with her. All he could find to criticize was her manner toward her pretty and precocious younger sister, which seemed hard, and toward her mother, to whom she seemed rude.[3] Fanny obviously felt herself to be on trial, and a brittle sharpness was still her nervous reaction, as it had been a year before. She was much harsher about George than he was about her. "He is no favourite of mine and he never liked me", was her sweeping verdict. At the same time, she was the only one of Keats's friends to see exactly the position George was in, and his feelings on this journey to England. She wrote to Keats's sister only a year or so later

when his affairs did not succeed and he had a wife and one child to support, with the prospect of another, I cannot wonder that he should consider them first and as he could not get what he wanted without coming to England he unfortunately came—By that time your brother wished to marry himself, but he could not refuse the money.

Yet neither she nor anyone else gives a clue how the two brothers felt towards each other at this meeting after eighteen months apart. Could they, as Keats had hoped in September, take up their existence from the time they last met? George had, as Keats had anticipated, altered, and he was ridden by the nightmare of his financial set-back and his growing family. Yet the affection between the brothers was still strong enough for Keats to tell his sister-in-law that if there were enough money available for the two of them, he "could almost promise" to come back with George to America for a few months, and think it no loss.[4]

1. Though Ward, 344, thinks the engagement was concealed from him.
2. *Letters*, II, 128, quoting from a lost letter. 3. MLPKC, 20.
4. Severn remembered this as a serious plan by Keats.

For all the high spirits at his brother's arrival, there was a constant note of disillusion. Keats's nature had taken another of its abrupt swings. The swiftness with which these now succeeded each other, sharp changes of outlook each month since he had left Winchester, suggest the restlessness and fever of growing tubercular infection. The targets of his dislike were much as they had been at other times—Hunt's puns and piano-playing, Haydon's grandiose art-talk, Dilke's Godwinism, the dullness and sentimentality of the Reynolds girls—but his weariness with society was now much more general. "All I can say is that standing at Charing cross and looking east west north and south I can see nothing but dullness." He felt he hated England and Englishmen, especially City men, mainly because he had been baulked of all his chances to travel, and he took a dislike to two Scotsmen he met, one of them Charlie Dilke's tutor. Things annoyed which at other times might have amused him. When Abigail O'Donaghue said her father in Ireland looked like Keats's engraving of Shakespeare, "only he had more color", he felt piqued. Possibly about now there was an open outburst of rage. Dining with De Wint, Hilton and other artists in Percy Street, someone mentioned Severn's Academy Gold Medal, and said the painting was a bad one, but the painter was an old man who had entered so often that the medal had been awarded out of pity. Keats waited for Hilton or one of the others to deny this scandal. When they did not, he got up, exposed the story, and left saying he would not sit at table with snobs and liars.[1] Brown's ill-advised gambit with their play was probably another source of disillusion. Elliston would not be rushed, and sent it back; they made some alterations and sent it to Covent Garden, for Macready to play Otho. It was returned swiftly, apparently unread.[2] Keats did not blame his friend, but in fact Brown had been too clever by half, and their theatrical chances were gone.

"Upon the whole I dislike Mankind", he wrote to Georgiana. Quite a large part of his denigration of England and English society was meant, in a back-handed way, to comfort his sister-in-law in America, "settled among people you hate". He was intent to point out how much she might find to dislike in her own country. It is risky to use his remarks as complete evidence of his own state of mind, still more to see in some of their generalizations a veiled criticism of George.[3] The brothers had long and intimate discussions during this visit, and continued to write to each other after George had gone.[4] At times, when they were alone together, George found Keats extremely melancholy; but this was a state he was used to ever since their schooldays, and he responded with the optimistic treatment that had always worked before.

The long letter Keats wrote to Georgiana covers nearly all the events of his brother's three-weeks' stay in England. There was a round of parties. They went to Mrs. Wylie's, and George took her to the theatre. George went on

1. Sharp, 65–66.   2. KC, II, 67.   3. As Ward, 345, suggests.
4. Bate, 633, says Keats never wrote again, but see MLPKC, 16.

his own to Haslam at Deptford, and stayed two days, for Haslam had made himself responsible for the correct forwarding of all George's correspondence and business matters, and there was much to discuss. There was a "pianoforte hop" at the Dilke's, and a dinner at Taylor's, where the publisher gave his decision on the fairy-tale competition between Brown and Dilke; Dilke had won, a verdict in which Keats and the other judges agreed. There was a meeting of the old lively London set of two years back, Rice, Reynolds and Richards, all of whom Keats brilliantly characterized in his letter to Georgiana. Finally, on Saturday 22 January, there was the beefsteak dinner paid for by Brown as the loser of the competition, and held at the house of Dilke, the winner. As well as the competitors and judges, Thomas Richards was probably asked to join. Six days later, Keats saw George off at six in the morning on the coach to Liverpool for his journey back. The brothers parted promising frequent letters to each other. George took with him a notebook full of Keats's poems which he had found time to copy; Keats gave him Hazlitt's recently-published *Political Essays*.

The tragic misunderstanding that now occurred was one for which no blame can be attached to anyone. Although it has been obscured by the partisan emotions of friends, and confused by later accounts, it is clear what happened. The crux of the matter was Keats's attitude to money. "It was so painful a subject" to him, as his brother commented; the far-off lawsuit of his childhood days had left him with a morbid reluctance to enquire into any financial matter. Nor was George by any means completely experienced in such things. The result was that the two brothers were faced with a situation which ought never to have occurred. Since Tom's death, their grandfather's fund, still in Chancery, amounted to over £1000 for each surviving brother and over £300 each of interest. Either one, by simple application to Chancery, could have got his share; George, indeed, need never have come to England, since Keats could have acted as his representative. Neither knew about it. Walton, the sole connection with the Chancery suit, had died that summer; his partner Gliddon was slowly taking over the reins of a tangled business. Over the negotiations of the brothers hung this appalling irony that both really had enough money for their immediate needs, George to retrieve his business, Keats to put better colour on his prospects as a husband. Of this, neither, and no one else, had at this time the least inkling.[1]

The brothers were therefore left solely with Tom's portion of their grandmother's trust fund, their own portions having been by now cashed and spent.[2] The market was still low, and Tom's total inheritance, when

---

1. KI, 51.
2. *Letters*, II, 40, where Keats wrote to Haydon, "What I should have lent you . . . was belonging to poor Tom". See also Dilke, ann. II, 40, who remarks that George now raised capital "by recovering his share of Tom's property" and adds "where was he to, or where did he raise other capital?"

N*

cashed, was only £1350, three hundred pounds less than George's had realized in the 1817–1818 boom year. Moreover Tom had run up debts, which had to be paid; George estimated these at £250, but even if he were mistaken, the cash available must have been only between £1100 and £1350. John, using his power of attorney, had already drawn three lots of £100 from this, one for himself, one to send to George (and still on the high seas) and one, to keep their accounts level, to be held for the third survivor Fanny Keats. The remaining cash was between £800 and £1000, of which a third part, about £300, belonged to Fanny. Keats took only £100 of his third and let George have the rest. It would therefore seem to him that he had lent George about £200 when he was himself in very great financial need, and that George had taken the offer Keats had made earlier in the summer literally, perhaps even selfishly.

This was certainly how it appeared to Keats's friends when they got to know about it, and how, for all her fairness, it appeared to Fanny Brawne. Yet it is quite clear that George never for one moment regarded this as a loan, but as his own money, a simple squaring of accounts between himself and his brother. This confusion between the two brothers, inherited by anyone who has ever discussed the subject, arose solely from the £500 cash which George had been able to leave behind in June 1818 after the successful sale of his own securities, and which had been drawn on by Keats in the year following. To George, the greater part of the £500 was intended as providing "some means to my Brothers". There is no sign he regarded it as a gift; it was a loan. Keats, he reckoned, had used about £300 of this for himself, so George's appropriation of the larger share of Tom's money was no more than a fair settling-up. To Keats, however, it is likely that the £500 seemed not a loan but a gift; it was some compensation for the way both George and Tom had drawn on him for their own purposes after he was 21, for the trip to Paris and the Palais Royal, for instance, and for the debts that George had spoken of owing him in the spring of 1818.

This was one of those unspoken tragedies, where both felt in the right. Financially, George seems to have acted correctly; when all possible factors are weighed, it was an approximate but just settlement of their affairs. George, even while ultimately paying all Keats's posthumous debts, always maintained that he did not really owe his brother a shilling,[1] and he was almost certainly right.[2] Yet the manner and timing of the transaction laid George open to question, and on this point most of Keats's friends were much

1. KC, I, 279.
2. Abbey, the sole acting trustee for Tom's estate, estimated the sum at issue between the two brothers as £350 to £400. He at first regarded this, like Keats, as a loan to George, and advised Keats strongly against it (KHM, No. 88). Going more closely into the matter later, he confirmed George's contention that it was a just settlement (KC, I, 285–286).

less charitable and understanding than Fanny Brawne. It must be remembered that the sum at issue was thought to be much greater than it was, owing to his own over-estimate, a year earlier, of its cash value, when he could at the most have had barely £700 capital.[1] The moral indignation of such friends as Brown and Haslam was inflamed by the large sum they thought involved, "about 800£ according to the best Estimate his friends can make", his publisher afterwards wrote. Yet in their friendship they all felt that a principle was violated which had nothing to do with the amount of money.[2] George should not have chosen this moment even for a just settlement. They too felt themselves right in judging him harshly, and, like everyone else in the matter, they had the best possible motives.

"You, John, have so many friends, they will be sure to take care of you!", George had remarked in parting; he could hardly guess in what spirit his words would be taken up. According to Brown, the sole witness to Keats's behaviour at the time, John repeated these words with bitterness to him at Wentworth Place, and handed over £70, all that George had left him. Keats's unpaid bills, Brown said, were also handed to him for payment, and amounted to £80, so that he was left £10 in debt.[3] Keats added "That was not fair, was it?",[4] and commented on George taking the money, "Brown, he ought not to have asked me." To Fanny Brawne he was more philosophical. "George ought not to have done this", he said, "he should have reflected that I wish to marry myself—but I suppose having a family to provide for makes a man selfish."[5] When Brown complained he had been kept in the dark about the offer to help George, Keats explained that he knew Brown would have opposed the idea, but that he would have had to stick to it whatever his friend said.

No one knows when all this took place, though it was so deeply burnt into Brown's memory that he repeated much of it word for word thirty years after. It does not seem to have been on the day of George's departure.[6] When George was going off, Keats found that he had left behind at Wentworth Place the journal letter he had so carefully prepared for George to take back to Georgiana. Returning to Hampstead, he dashed off a long postscript of another two pages. This was in his liveliest style, and in it he spoke, as he had done earlier in the letter, of leaving London and staying for a long time in the country, as he had done last summer. His financial straits were not perhaps clear to him for a day or so, and there was no hint of estrangement from George; he only regretted his short stay, and promised another letter

1. His share of the full amount was approximately £670 capital.
2. Brown, after finding in 1822 from Abbey that much less was involved, still continued his strictures on George, KHM, No. 104.
3. KC, I, 217–218.   4. KC, II, 102.
5. Woodhouse's note, Morgan MS, Finney, II, 746; LFBFK, 26–27.
6. As assumed by Ward, 346, though Brown did not say so, and Taylor said it was the day after that Keats handed over the £70 and the unpaid bills.

to them both in a few days' time. The strain and disillusion with life that had peered through the lines of the letter were confirmed by something quite different. In the next day or two, it seems, someone at Wentworth Place, probably Abigail O'Donaghue,[1] stumbled on the fact that Keats was taking small doses of laudanum.[2] Brown was told, and he extracted from Keats the promise that he would stop at once before it became a habit. Brown, though relieved, was disturbed at this further sign of Keats's melancholy; he had noticed that Keats had given up writing *The Cap and Bells* and no longer made any pretence of revising *Hyperion*.

Worse soon came. The long cold spell broke, and February set in warmer, with a general thaw. Keats left off his greatcoat but the nights were still cold. On the night of Thursday 3 February, he came back at eleven o'clock from Town, travelling outside on the stage-coach for cheapness, full in the cold wind which chilled him to the bone. He staggered the few hundred yards from the stop at Pond Street in a fever, and stumbled into Wentworth Place as if he were drunk. Brown saw at once that he was seriously ill, and said he should go upstairs to bed, which he did readily. As Brown came into the bedroom with a glass of spirits, Keats was just slipping between the sheets. As he did so, he coughed; it was only a slight cough, but Brown immediately heard him say "That is blood from my mouth". He was examining a single drop of blood upon the sheet. As Brown came forward, he said, "Bring me the candle, Brown, and let me see this blood." They both stared at it; then, looking up with a steady calm which Brown could never forget, he said, "I know the colour of that blood; it is arterial blood. I cannot be deceived in that colour. That drop of blood is my death warrant. I must die."

---

1. KC, II, 73. Brown's reticence seems to suggest it was she.
2. Brown thought Keats took it as a stimulant "to keep up his spirits". On the other hand, the symptoms of pain and tightness in the chest, from which Keats afterwards suffered, may already have appeared, and he may have been taking it as a normal pain-killer.

Chapter 26

PATIENT IN ILLNESS

"I will be as patient in illness and as believing in Love as I am able—"

– JOHN KEATS to Fanny Brawne, June (?) 1820

BROWN'S simple and dramatic account exactly describes a small lung haemorrhage. Tubercle bacilli in the lungs having destroyed the wall of a blood-vessel, it gives way over one specially-weakened area after coughing. Keats's own account[1] makes it clear that this first warning, during which he could comment calmly and courageously on the situation, was followed that same night by a second massive haemorrhage, a familiar and sometimes immediately fatal pattern in tubercular cases.[2] Further coughing enlarged the area of bleeding, and such a rush of blood came into Keats's mouth that he thought he was suffocating then and there. His earlier words seemed to be coming instantly true. He felt he was dying, and this time he could only gasp out to Brown the prosaic but equally moving remark, "This is unfortunate." It was one of his typical understatements; it bore no relation to his depth of feeling, as he seemed anxious to assure Fanny Brawne in the first long note he wrote to her after the attack. In the moment of speaking, he said, he had thought instantly of her, and of her only. In the same note he spoke of their "Love which has so long been my pleasure and torment". Now this love was to be put to its cruellest test. Lying in bed, or on the sofa which had been made comfortable for him in the front parlour, looking at the wall-paper or out of the window, trying to guess whether she were at home or not, when she was coming to see him, when the stage-coach would bring her back from a visit to Town, Keats's world had suddenly contracted to one person. It was a frightening burden for a girl of nineteen to carry. No wonder he found her "a little silent" when she came to see him.

It was true that, as he told her, after the first shock was over, "other subjects" had entered his head. The chief of these was his own sixteen-year-old sister. If he had died that February night, as he had feared he might,

1. *Letters*, II, 254.
2. W. Hale-White, *Keats as Doctor and Patient*, 52–53, confuses the two accounts, and makes the further confusing suggestion that the severe haemorrhage occurred first, while Keats was in the coach. Keats, however, writes of speaking to Brown during it.

what would she have thought of the brother who always promised to visit her, and hardly ever came? "My Conscience", he had written to her in the autumn, "is always reproaching me for neglecting you for so long a time." Now, the fright had made him determine, it should not reproach him again. He actually wrote her three letters in eight days, and continued to send her odd scribbles of comfort on any scrap of paper he could find to hand. Unlike George, who had not even been out to Walthamstow to visit Fanny, Keats sympathized with her about the petty tyrannies of Abbey at home, his portentous manner which struck her dumb at meals, his meanness over pocket-money. Perhaps his own conflicting feelings about George caused a renewal of the responsibility he had expressed exactly a year before—"You have no one in the world besides me who would sacrifice any thing for you —I feel myself the only Protector you have."

After the first day or two, friends began to call, Mrs. Reynolds, Mrs. Wylie and her two sons. Keats's fever returned, and he was kept on a low diet and bled, according to the practice of the time, by G. R. Rodd, the surgeon of Hampstead High Street, whom Brown had fetched on the night of the first haemorrhages, and whose wife was a friend of the Brawnes. Keats commented on the unnecessary weakness this produced, though he himself subscribed to the current medical theory of a starvation diet in such cases. He sent his sister vivid and amusing letters about the country scenes that still surrounded their isolated little settlement on the edge of the Heath, the gipsies, the tradesmen and workmen on their errands, the foreigners and Jews who already made up a sizeable proportion of the Hampstead population, and such oddities as "a fellow with a wooden clock under his arm that strikes a hundred and more". He tried to console himself that everyone, Brown included, had been affected by the bad weather that winter, and that his case was nothing out of the ordinary; on the first really fine day, Wednesday 9 February, he ventured a quarter of an hour in the garden. Yet he knew, as he began to view the situation with professional objectivity, that there must be serious damage to his lungs. His deadening weakness was due to something more fundamental than diet, fever and medicine; it seemed organic. In such a mood, he wrote to Fanny Brawne "on a certain unpleasant subject". This was, that she should feel herself free to break their engagement. This, he must have known, was now doubly impossible for her to do, and he showed his relief and grateful joy when she refused the offer. "How hurt I should have been had you ever acceded to what is, notwithstanding, very reasonable!" All the same, there were anxious consultations going on all around them, and no lack of friends and relatives to give opinions and advice. It seems to have been thought that both Fanny and Keats might harm each other by too frequent meeting. She might expose him to the agitation which his doctors said should be avoided, he might expose her to the infection which was seen to come from too close contact. Brown was, moreover, a possessive nurse, and Keats had to face his friend's dislike of Fanny at a difficult time for all three of them. He seems to have taken the situation fairly philosophically. He argued with himself that he could not expect to monopolize Fanny, and stop her ever going into Town, or seeing anyone else. He even tried to quiet her suspicions of their friends' motives and advice. "Our friends think and speak for the best, and if their best is not our best it is not their fault." He himself found that if he was a little strained and nervous during the day, it upset him to see her at night, and he had to ask her not to come then. As a reassuring substitute, they initiated a private system by which she sent him a note every evening, sometimes just the words "Good night" to put under his pillow, sometimes a short message, without which he felt he could not face the night; they also arranged that he should watch from his front parlour to see her receive his notes at her front door.[1]

To Reynolds, who had called on him on 13 February, and to Rice, both of whom had faced the realities of severe illness, Keats wrote longer and more explicit letters about himself. His thoughts were most fully expressed to the sympathetic Rice:

How astonishingly does the chance of leaving the world impress a sense of its natural beauties on us. Like poor Falstaff, though I do not babble, I think of green fields. I muse with the greatest affection on every flower I have known from my infancy—their shapes and coulours are as new to me as if I had just created them with a superhuman fancy—

"It is because", he added, thinking perhaps of the garden days at Enfield and Edmonton, "they are connected with the most thoughtless and happiest moments of our Lives." He was still not too ill to think like a poet, and to Reynolds, at the end of the month, he wrote proposing to take up *The Cap and Bells* again soon, with Reynolds providing the comic prose notes. Yet he knew he was not getting better, as he sat surrounded by the pots of jam and preserves which all the ladies sent him. He tried to find some modest comfort in philosophic reasoning with himself. If the worst came to the worst, he had served poetry faithfully: " 'If I should die', said I to myself, 'I have left no immortal work behind me—nothing to make my friends proud of my memory—but I have lov'd the principle of beauty in all things, and if I had had time I would have made myself remember'd.' "

The incentive to feel himself a poet again came from an unexpected quarter. B. W. Procter ("Barry Cornwall") had caught the implications of Hunt's review of his first book, *Dramatic Scenes*, with its hint that he himself was of the school of Keats, another of Hunt's young poets, and had given Hunt a copy of the book for Keats. In Keats's long absence from Town in the summer of 1819, Hunt had completely forgotten about his promise to deliver

1. *Letters*, II, 223, 225, 226, 227, 230, 231, 232, 233, 235. These notes are, of course, all undated.

Procter's book, and the author had now brought out a second book, *A Sicilian Story* and other poems. Not trusting Hunt this time, he sent the new volume direct to Keats, who may well have been surprised at the accompanying note, which spoke of a gift he had never received. He had another cause for surprise, and perhaps thought. The title poem was a very different treatment of his own subject of Isabella and the Pot of Basil, still unpublished. He had been overtaken and anticipated, and though he now valued *Isabella* less than more recent poems, this was a warning of what might happen to the others. A note of thanks to Procter brought a copy of *Dramatic Scenes*. Keats found them teasing with their prettified commonplaces, but their trivialities stimulated him to do something about his own work. Taylor was urging him to get it ready for the press, while Woodhouse had shown copies of some of the new poems, for interest, to Cary, the Dante translator.[1] Keats sent to Fanny,[2] to whom he had lent his own manuscripts, for the collection he now wanted to prune and improve, and even spoke of starting something new. He wrote to Dilke on 4 March quite in his old vein, full of anecdotes, of Reynolds, of Rice, of Hunt's typical conduct in not forwarding Procter's gift, and of Brown's amateur attempts at art, a constant joke between them all. Brown had purchased some Hogarth prints, including the grotesque *Sleeping Congregation*, in order to copy them. Keats, who had always loved the grotesque, was now disturbed by it, a sign of his nervous state since his collapse, and in the first few weeks of his illness, the print had given him nightmares. "I know I am better, for I can bear the Picture", he now joked to Dilke in a flash of his old form, and he even improved on that cheerfulness by chaffing Dilke on another favourite subject, his crabbed classical handwriting. "If the only copies of the greek and Latin Authors had been made by you, Bailey and Haydon they Were as good as lost." He had also taken to reading his weekly copy of *The Examiner* again, and shared Hunt's over-optimistic forecast that William Cobbett might be elected to Parliament in the General Election that had followed George III's death.[3]

This phase of hopeful normality did not last. With the swings of his own temperament now accelerated by the ebb and flow of fever, he was plunged almost overnight into extreme stress and tension. The immediate cause seemed to be his poems. The hopeless distance between the mastery he had felt while writing them, and his new helpless state, may indeed have thrown him into despair. There were also personal tensions near at hand, which set him off; the basis of his illness was, of course, physical, but he began more

1. Keats Collection, Houghton Library, *59M—159.

2. *Letters*, II, 257, conjecturally dated April by Rollins, but surely earlier, with its references to low diet and sitting by the fire. HBF, IV, 168, n. 1 points out its resemblances with the letter to Dilke, and dates it the first week in March.

3. *Letters*, II, 271–278. Rollins conjectures the title of the Hogarth print, whose name Keats never actually mentioned.

than usual to display quick alternations of mood which led many people to think his disease a psychological state. Though their undated notes can only be read in a conjectural order, it seems from Keats's correspondence with Fanny that Brown's dislike of her was now open. Brown, in his turn, had his reasons for disliking female visits into his household; Abigail's pregnancy must have been obvious, and she could not always be kept shut in the damp little basement. Fanny was quick-witted and little could have been kept from her, either of Brown's predicament or his disapproval. She began to stake claims to Keats, bringing her dress-making to do while she sat with him, though he tactfully suggested she should always wait until Brown himself was out. She also refused to believe her anxious mother's idea that writing Keats a nightly note might be bad for him, and she began to put more of her mind into these missives; one at least of them Keats found "not so treasurable as former ones". Like all people in intense personal relationships, they shared a private world of their own. The thrush singing on the Heath was their thrush, its life invested with their own emotions. "I hope he was fortunate in his choice this year", wrote Keats, in an echo of his own thwarted desires. Anxieties began to appear. In one longer note, when he had compared Rousseau's *Correspondence . . . avec Mme. Latour de Franqueville* with their own, and concluded sturdily "Thank god that you are fair and can love me without being Letter-written and sentimentaliz'd into it", he suddenly added, less assuredly, the hasty words "love me for ever—". In a letter blessing her for sending him a ring, and full of grateful love, he had to add another sudden and anxious postscript, "You had better not come today". It is hopeless to guess too much of a pattern into this one-sided duet—none of her notes has survived—but the tensions were there, even for a man in perfect health, when suddenly a new symptom of his basic illness sapped Keats's nerve. On Monday 6 March, in the evening, he was assailed by violent palpitations of the heart. He took to his bed for two days, too agitated by this set-back to see anyone or even open a letter. Brown too was thrown into despair, and hastily wrote to Taylor saying that the revision of the poems would now have to be put off indefinitely. Rodd, both physician and surgeon, was now Keats's regular attendant, as it was a long way for Sawrey to make frequent visits at each crisis, and it was probably Rodd who suggested calling in a specialist.

The authority chosen was Dr. Robert Bree, an Oxford M.D. with a distinguished record. He was the leading expert on asthma, from which he himself had suffered while in general practice, and he had written the standard book on the subject, which had gone into five editions. He was now about 60, and at the top of his profession. His treatment of Keats has been roughly handled by modern writers, but his book, on a still-obscure subject, is a sound one, and he was only following one of his own lines of observation, which he thought applied to Keats. In it, he had devoted one whole section to psychosomatic or hysterical symptoms, "instances of mental impression operating upon the body, and inducing morbid motions".[1] This was his diagnosis of Keats's palpitations; he did not, as has been thought, dismiss his former blood-spitting and phthisic symptoms, but believed that Keats had induced the further appearance of them by anxiety, and presented a condition of nervous asthma by association. This is the meaning of Brown's relieved reassurance to Taylor that the doctor had said "there is no pulmonary affection, no organic defect whatever,—the disease is on his *mind*." With no stethoscope, Bree had little means of knowing whether there was organic disease, but he observed Keats's mental agitation, though he could not probe its cause. In fact, on hearing that his patient was a poet, and doubtless being told by Brown that the work of revision had been disturbing Keats, he seems to have made the jocular medical remark that Keats would do better to study mathematics. His visit was by no means wasted, for it gave back to Keats the confidence he had suddenly lost. He got up, went out in the garden, and went on with his poems. Bree, moreover, took Keats off starvation diet; he believed in meat and light wine for his patients,[2] and Keats soon found he was building up his strength again, which must have been sorely weakened by what he called the "pseudo victuals" he had been prescribed until now. Although Keats had further palpitations Bree believed, and seems to have made him believe, that this frequently happened while a patient was regaining strength. He also prescribed sedatives for the type of self-induced asthma he thought Keats had, and some of the pain and tightness Keats felt in his chest was probably eased from now on by doses of opium, "to abate sensibility of slight irritations".[3] All in all, it is probably owing to Bree that Keats passed two fairly quiet and calm months, in March and April, and was able to prepare his 1820 volume of poems for the press. By some time in March, *The Eve of St. Agnes* at least was in his publishers' hands.[4]

Keats wrote during this time in a much more objective and resigned way about himself and his situation. To Fanny, who had apparently made some playful comment on a fancied lack of love, he wrote one of his most charming and devoted letters. "You are always new", he told her, a recantation of the poem he was just running through for his book, *Fancy*, with its rhetorical question, "Where's the maid, Whose lip mature is ever new?" His words were those of a poet, only just prose: "the last of your kisses was ever the sweetest; the last smile the brightest; the last movement the gracefullest". His self-criticism became sane and wise. "My Mind", he wrote in the same letter, "has been the most discontented and restless one that ever was put in

1. Robert Bree, *A Practical Inquiry into Disordered Respiration*, 213–222.
2. Ibid., 294. Keats's wine bill (KHM, No. 104) was considerable.
3. Robert Bree, *A Practical Inquiry into Disordered Respiration*, 347.
4. Its revisions were "before March". Woodhouse's shorthand note, Keats Collection, Houghton Library, H 4.

a body too small for it. I never felt my Mind repose upon anything with complete and undistracted enjoyment—upon no person but you." Now he was, for the moment, stronger, the lovers were happy, seeing more of each other, no longer dependent on notes or snatched meetings. He even joked about surprising her by running round and knocking on her door, instead of her coming to his. He felt only a little tiredness and tightness in the chest, and was actually at his best at about 8 o'clock in the evening. He went ahead with the poems, and at this time seems to have preferred *The Eve of St. Agnes* to head the volume, though *Lamia*, which he revised next, soon took its place. Above all, he now felt he had a future. "Let me have another oportunity of years before me and I will not die without being remember'd", he told Fanny. He could joke mildly at the death he had thought might part them: "I fear I am too prudent for a dying kind of Lover. Yet", he added, with a reminiscence of his horror at the first night of blood-spitting, "there is a great difference between going off in warm blood like Romeo, and making one's exit like a frog in a frost."

Keats's interests revived, and ceased to be centred on himself. He remembered to congratulate Fanny on her new black dress, probably home-made, and he wrote Mrs. Wylie a kind letter of comfort about George and Georgiana. He was even well enough to leave Hampstead. On 14 March, he went to Town, and dined with Taylor. Though he could not see her, he had always special time to spare for his own sister. The Abbeys objected to her keeping a pet spaniel, and Mrs. Abbey had threatened to turn the dog loose. Keats promised that the dog would always find a kind home, but to save her any unnecessary distress, he had it brought over to Hampstead, and found an owner for it in Mrs. Dilke's brother.[1] He had also the simple pleasure of demonstrating to an old friend, Haydon, that the coolness between them over money could be bridged by the loyalty of one creative artist to another. At last, the picture which had occupied so much of their lives, and in which Keats's vehement head appeared, was to have its private view at the Egyptian Hall, Piccadilly, on Saturday 25 March. The weather was warmer, and Keats determined to go, and even to walk the four or five miles there, a stupendous effort of will and perhaps wilfulness, since his doctors' advice, though optimistic, was still against too much exertion till the new normal diet had given him strength.[2] What might have been a disaster turned out to be a triumph for everyone concerned. Piccadilly was blocked with carriages, everybody of rank was there, and whispers that the figure of Christ was weak, as Haydon silently confessed it was, were totally stilled by the voice of Mrs. Siddons pronouncing in her best Lady Macbeth tones, "It is completely

1. *Letters*, II, 289. "Brother" may mean "brother-in-law", William Dilke of Wentworth House, their nearest neighbour.
2. *Letters*, II, 280.

successful".[1] As for Keats, he found William Hazlitt in a corner of the crowded room, and was seen with him in high spirits. He was, in fact, so exhilarated that he walked all the way back to Wentworth Place with no apparent ill effect. "I am getting better every day", he wrote a week later, and shortly afterwards, "I still continue on the mending hand."

Meanwhile Brown, who had faithfully if possessively performed his function of male nurse for the last two months, began to consider his own situation. For various reasons he wanted to let Wentworth Place earlier than usual this year; in particular he needed more money for the child he would soon have to support. As usual in the later years of Keats's life, lack of money complicated every action; it is impossible to measure what relief would have been afforded to him and everyone around him if his inheritance in Chancery had been known and obtained. "I never heard of his having any hopes from Chancery", Brown exclaimed years later; but the fact is, he was obsessed by the idea that George should and could pay the debts Keats had contracted in the last two months for board and lodgings to himself, together with the doctors' bills. Up to this quarter day, 25 March, Keats had covered these, as Brown's own account shows. Three days after the haemorrhage, Keats had either found George had left him more, or had recovered one of his own many loans, or had been given money by someone now unknown. At all events, he had an extra £40, which he at once handed over to Brown on 6 February, clearly in case the attacks should return and he should die. Brown had now spent almost exactly this amount, taking a fully commercial board and lodging allowance of £5 a month, excluding drink bills.

Brown's eye, however friendly, was always for the main chance. He had proposed taking Keats down again to Chichester, to see old Mr. Dilke, who had also suffered from the severe winter. The possible significance of this move was not lost on his quick-witted neighbours, and Sam Brawne was caught whispering to Fanny how anxious Brown was to be at the old man's bedside. Brown was huffed by the hint, and had not the face after it to go to Chichester; but it was still urgent for him to leave Wentworth Place soon, and Keats from now on must be provided for. Brown had already written to Abbey, and received a calculated silence, for the merchant had now no Keats capital left in hand, except for Fanny's portion. Seeing Keats return so cheerfully from Haydon's triumph, Brown now persuaded his friend to let him write a letter, as from Keats, to George, from whom no one had heard since he left Liverpool. This letter, written with Keats's approval and knowledge,[2] painted a more optimistic picture for George than it could have done at any

1. Haydon, *Autobiography*, 377. There are many versions of this decisive remark. Haydon at first wrote "decidedly" for "completely".

2. Keats says it was written "as from me." *Letters*, II, 284; Ward, 356, believes it mentioned matters without his knowledge, but he would be unlikely to let it be sent without reading it through. George did not receive it until mid-June. *Letters*, II, 295–296.

time since he had parted from his brother. It did not conceal that his condition had been dangerous, but it reported that he was now eating, drinking
and sleeping, under Bree's new regime, quite normally, and, of course, that
he had just performed the feat of walking five miles in one day without
fatigue. Keats then broached through Brown a subject which had been in his
mind for two years, a holiday for himself in Italy. In former years it had
merely seemed desirable for him to go; now it was the standard prescription
for a medical case such as his, and Rodd had probably already advised it.
Could George afford to finance the trip? It is not certain that any sum was
mentioned, but the expense of a journey and a winter abroad would be at
least £200.[1]

This was, of course, looking ahead to the winter. Brown's own immediate
concern was to let his house early and profitably for the summer, while he
went off for another stay in his native country, travelling this time by boat.
By the middle of April he had arranged a let from the second week of May,
at which time Keats would have to turn out of Wentworth Place. Brown
later said that Rodd had recommended Keats to go on a walking-tour of the
Highlands with him, but that he himself advised Keats to stay behind for his
health. Since Keats had been advised by Rodd to avoid any undue exertion,
and felt himself unable to risk "the casualties of rain and sleeping out" of
a mere walk to Walthamstow, Brown's attempt to transfer responsibility to
the doctor was a lie, forced by his own urgent necessity. What Rodd had
said, according to Keats, was that he might try the sea-voyage up the east
coast on the Scottish smack with Brown, to give himself a change of air; he
would perhaps then either come back, or stay in Scotland for a while.

None of this was pleasant for Keats to contemplate. Everyone, for their
own reasons, seemed engaged in a game of pretending he was better than he
actually was. He himself could not bring his mind to dwell on anything that
disturbed or depressed it. He shut out thoughts of his brother, his sister, the
future, even perhaps of Fanny Brawne, since he was going to be parted from
her neighbourhood. He managed to push ahead, and finish revising the rest
of his poems, which he presented to Taylor & Hessey on 27 April. He made
one or two visits to Town, but could not face the City for the unhopeful
errand of trying to raise a loan from Abbey. Brown encouraged him to take
up *The Cap and Bells*, with the idea that it might be publishable and make
money; Keats, knowing what his doctors called "the too great excitement of
poetry", never seems seriously to have considered even this mild exercise,
though he spoke of sending Brown some stanzas to read in Scotland. Even the
sea-voyage with Brown seemed, as May drew relentlessly nearer, a terrible
and pointless effort in his nervous state. Uncertainty swung his moods

1. Ward supposes that the prospect of an Italian journey was not discussed with Keats
at all. It was, however, something Keats had wished to do even before his breakdown in
health. *Letters*, I, 269.

back to darkness again, after the brief sunshine of the past few weeks.

A compromise appeared from an unexpected quarter, and Keats snatched at it. This was, to rent lodgings within easy walking distance of Wentworth Place, though not in Hampstead itself with its inflated summer prices. In search of just such an economy, Leigh Hunt had broken his four-years' agreement in York Buildings, and moved early in the year to 13 Mortimer Terrace, Kentish Town. It was, he explained,[1] "a sort of compromise between London and our beloved Hampstead." At about this time, Hunt, making up for past carelessness, brought over Procter, whom Keats had expected before, but who had also been ill with pleurisy. Procter was impressed by Keats's delightful personality, as people always were on a first meeting: "I never encountered a more manly and simple young man", he wrote. Leigh Hunt, who had had his share of hard times, and whose wife was herself a consumptive, saw Keats's difficulties, or some of them. He undertook to find Keats cheap lodgings for the summer near his new home. He would be just as near Town for the publication and proofs of his book, only a mile away from Fanny, and with the good-hearted Hunt as neighbour. Something in Keats's distress stirred Hunt to an unwonted promptness and efficiency. By the beginning of May, he had arranged for lodgings at 2 Wesleyan Place, only a few doors away from his own home, and at a rent much less than Keats had been paying Brown. Keats moved there on 4 May, on which day Brown paid the few shillings for the expenses of moving and a guinea, the first week's rent, in advance. He did not press Keats for the month and a half of rent he himself was owed since last quarter-day, nor the bills for the wine which had gone to build Keats up on Bree's prescription. In fact, in a burst of responsibility, he borrowed on Saturday 6 May £50 from his lawyer, Robert Skynner, and lent it to Keats to cover the summer's living expenses. He sailed that weekend, Keats accompanying him on the smack as far as Gravesend. It was the last time they were to see one another.

The compromise solution, like all such remedies, was only good so far as it went, as Keats realized when he came down the village street, and turned into his quiet, pleasant but at once unbearably empty lodgings. It only worked by omitting or ignoring the thing most important to him, the sight and sound and near presence of Fanny whenever he wanted her, whenever the mood of depression should come sweeping over him out of a clear sky, as he had described it in his own *Ode on Melancholy*. It was not rational, but it was real, and no reasoning that she was only a mile's walk away would serve. By the rules of society she could not call at his bachelor lodgings without a chaperone, and Hunts's house, full of wild young children and gossiping women, was hardly one into which he would wish to introduce her. Hunt himself was busy with two weekly papers to edit, now that he had started *The Indicator*, sometimes ill, often worried. He showed his friendship in the first week that

1. CLH., I, 147.

Keats was his neighbour by printing *La Belle Dame Sans Merci* in his new publication, but he was too rushed to see much of him, though the two sometimes had discussions on literary subjects. In one of these Keats showed his appreciation of Scott's novels, but the instance he chose was significant. He "touched especially on Balfour of Burley and the scene in the cave", from *Old Mortality*. This scene is introduced by lines from Spenser's Cave of Despair, and describes a man at the end of his tether. When Keats took a book in his hand, intending to read it on the Heath, his thoughts always returned to Fanny. What was she doing, where was she going, did she still love him? Her mother called to see how he was in his new surroundings, but there is nothing to show that Fanny herself came. He only went once himself to Wentworth Place,[1] for the effort of meeting here there and then parting again was worse and worse. He went to Town, but could not feel easy in the society which now held so many reminders for him of his healthy state. At one house, probably Dilke's, something irritated him and he behaved badly, as he realized. "I forsee I shall know very few people in the course of a year or two", he commented gloomily. Severn, who lived in North London, and had only a short way to come to him through Islington, seems to have seen him more than anyone. They went for their old walks on the Heath, but Keats was out of tune with his light-hearted talkative friend; by the end of May his moodiness had increased so much that their meetings grew shorter and shorter.

Keats's mind slowly darkened in solitude to growing suspicion. In spite of the new love and affection Fanny had given him in the spring, his deep-rooted distrust of women began to return. Just a year before, he had been haunted, in his own words, by the throng of jealousies that he felt while brooding over her, but he had only revealed this abnormal feeling in the secret notes in Burton. Then he had found relief by plunging into what he called "imaginary interests", the poetry of *Lamia*, *Otho*, and *The Fall of Hyperion*. He was too weak and shattered for this relief now, and his self-control had begun to disintegrate through illness. For the first time, this distortion and flaw in his personality, hinted in so many ways earlier in his life, burst to the surface in two, or much more probably three[2] long and impassioned letters to Fanny Brawne. Undated, they seem to be connected with a period at the end of May when some incident had brought weeks of brooding ferment to sudden explosion, perhaps at Dilke's. Fanny Brawne had much in common with Mrs. Dilke, the only one of Keats's friends with whom she felt completely at home. Maria Dilke liked to entertain at

1. *Letters*, II, 298. He went to pick up letters for Brown. Though the name of the place is deleted, this must be Brown's house, not (as suggested by Bodurtha and Pope, 113) Dilke's.

2. *Letters*, II, Nos. 261, 262 and also 271, which MacGillivray, xxxv, plausibly dates at this time, not later.

Westminster much as she had done at Wentworth Place, with small intimate parties and dances. To one of these Fanny Brawne seems to have gone unchaperoned. This was permissible since her hostess was a young married woman and a close friend; but it meant that she, an engaged girl, was going about in society without her fiancé, and this, with her lively social behaviour, might be misconstrued by any man she chanced to meet. Unfortunately Keats, visiting the Dilkes soon afterwards, heard about this, perhaps through the Reynolds girls, and at once put the most jealous construction on it, and even on the Dilkes's part in encouraging it. Whatever he did and said at Great Smith Street, he returned to Kentish Town to write a batch of jealous letters, two of which oddly but significantly echo *Othello*.[1] The letters were deliberately written, he said "because I wish you to see how unhappy I am for love of you". Her going to Town alone had been a shock, perhaps not unexpected, but—and he underlined the request so that it became a command —"promise me you will not for some time, till I get better". He armed himself against the possibility that Mrs. Brawne, who was due to call on him, would pretend her daughter had not been to the Dilkes, by letting her understand he knew all about it. His anger burst out, not only against her but all their friends, who had made their love a subject of gossip, as the Reynolds girls had done, perhaps another idea he had picked up at the Dilkes; yet he felt what seemed to him her betrayal more than anything else. "I cannot forget what has pass'd. What? nothing with a man of the world, but to me deathful." He rounded on her for flirting with Brown in their first uneasy days, and he swept Brown too up into the general condemnation; "though he has done me many services, though I know his love and friendship for me, though at this moment I should be without pence were it not for his assistance, I will never see or speak to him until we are both old men, if we are to be". A phrase half-remembered from the poems of Katherine Philips welled up in him. "I *will* resent my heart having been made a football", he exclaimed. His imagery for their love took on a lurid romanticism. "You must be mine to die upon the rack if I want you", and continuing in another letter the same metaphor, "I have been a Martyr the whole time, and for this reason I speak; the confession is forc'd from me by the torture." He saw her as his torturer, who made him endure "the agonies and uncertainties which you are so peculiarly made to create", and he appealed to her "by the blood of that Christ you believe in". He saw her simple enjoyment of society as evidence that she could no longer love him, of being, as he had once said, like Shakespeare's and Chaucer's Cressida. This suspicion now seemed to be fact, unless she could whole-heartedly deny it; "if you still behave in dancing rooms and other societies as I have seen you—I do not want to live".[2]

1. *Letters*, II, 290, 292.
2. All these quotations come from *Letters*, Nos. 261 and 271, and seem connected, though without dates this can only be guessed.

In the dubious sequence of their letters, it appears that Fanny wrote back to him with spirit. Any rumour he had heard of her conduct had been due to the gossip of their so-called friends, and as she later singled out the Reynoldses for her dislike, she probably had them in mind. Keats got her letter on a calmer morning, and was contrite though he did not withdraw. "You complain of my illtreating you in word thought and deed—I am sorry,—at times I feel bitterly sorry that I ever made you unhappy—my excuse is that those words have been wrung from me by the sha(r)pness of my feelings." He could not, however, quite recant his suspicions, though he sympathized with her fully about what he now regarded as the bad faith of their friends in gossiping about their love and her conduct. He was able now to reaffirm his love, which "has ever been greater than my cruelty which last(s) but a minute whereas my Love come what will shall last for ever". He still thought of her perhaps as Cressida, for he thought of himself as Shakespeare's Troilus, whose love was "true as truth's simplicity"; but he now saw himself and her in a more philosophic spirit. He had spoken, he said, "not in the spirit of a Threat to you—no—but in the spirit of Wretchedness in myself." He added, pathetically, "do not believe me such a vulgar fellow. I will be as patient in illness and as believing in Love as I am able—".[1]

1. *Letters*, II, 292–294.

Chapter 27

MR. KEATS LEAVES HAMPSTEAD

"Mr Keats left Hampstead"

– Pencilled note by Fanny Brawne, Keats House Museum,
No. 27

THOUGH Keats could no longer compose new poetry to lift him out of his depression, the poems he had already written saved him from its worst effects; for at the beginning of June, the proofs of his book began to come to him for correction, and he was able to plunge into them for some distraction from his brooding. One whole poem, *Lamia*, was already in print by the end of May. On 6 June, Taylor wrote to John Clare that Keats's poems would appear in about three weeks. Keats worked on them during the first half of June, including one session with Taylor himself at Fleet Street. It has been said that Taylor altered and even bowdlerized[1] Keats's poems for the press, as he did so extensively with Clare's. In fact, apart from a few tentative suggestions for *Isabella*[2] and one passage in *Lamia*,[3] he seems hardly to have touched them. The main editorial work was done by Woodhouse, who spoke himself of "my revise of Lamia".[4] For all their explosive disagreement with Keats the previous autumn, the publishers' concern was not to remove suggestions of sex, or they would hardly have passed the darkly passionate love-struggles of *Lamia*. They were chiefly on the watch for any technical looseness, obscurity or slackness in the verse, which *The Quarterly*, still the main enemy, had censured. Quaint or coined words, which would put Keats again into the school of Hunt, were another bugbear; so were actual lapses of tact or taste. The Glutton passage in *Lamia*, with its belching and farting, had already been removed by Keats.

Though these were his general principles, Woodhouse's methods varied with each of the major poems. Since George had taken to America Keats's fair-copy of *Isabella*, this poem was set-up from Woodhouse's own transcript,[5] after Keats had made some alterations, mainly prompted by

1. Ward, 361.
2. Keats Collection, Houghton Library, H 3.
3. Garrod, *Works*, xxxv.
4. Keats Collection, Houghton Library, H 5, f. 41.
5. Keats Collection, Houghton Library, H 3.

Taylor's queries. Keats's notes show indifference to the poem over punctuation and even some lines. "Stop this as you please", he wrote, and again, "Please point this as you like"; "you may use your judgement between your line and mine", he commented in one instance. His main interest was that the poem should not be printed first in the book, a wise precaution, since lazy reviewers, following Croker's lead in reading only the early pages of *Endymion*, might have applied the verdict Keats imagined them using about *Isabella* to the whole book—" 'A weak-sided Poem' with an amusing sober-sadness about it."[1] It was printed with little alteration, and the publishers' faith was justified by critics like Charles Lamb, who quoted and praised it as the finest thing in the volume.

For *The Eve of St. Agnes*, Woodhouse had before him two versions. One Keats had given him on 19 April 1819, the other Keats had revised and copied by March 1820, including the episode where, in Woodhouse's words, the hero getting into bed with the heroine "winds by degrees his arm around her, presses breast to breast, and acts all the acts of a bona fide husband".[2] Here too Keats was now so indifferent that he left it to his publishers, as Woodhouse noted, "to adopt which they pleased, & to revise the whole".[3] He only intervened when there was an actual mistake—Woodhouse nearly ruined the first line by a slip in copying "cold" instead of "chill"—or when the revisions destroyed meaning and syntax. The seventh stanza was altered on the un-imaginative assumption that Keats used the word "train" as a stale poetic cliché for "concourse of passers-by", which, as Keats said, would quite destroy his much more concrete meaning of ladies' skirts trailing unnoticed past the self-absorbed Madeline.[4] Apart from this, the revisions were sound if predictable. They went back to Keats's first version for its very mild sexual passages, also for the death-bed scenes of the Beadsman and Angela, and in both they simply substituted good poetry for bad; Keats's second thoughts, after a lapse of several months, were seldom happy. Less justifiably, Angela's tendency to swear by Christ went out, softening her character, while the hero was denied his oath "by the great St. Paul", though more to avoid quaintness than impiety, since he was allowed to invoke instead all the saints, to signify his chaste intentions towards the heroine. Otherwise not a great deal was done to the poem, which benefited on the whole by being restored to the broadly romantic style in which Keats had first conceived and carried it out.[5]

Lamia was another matter. Keats wished it to head the volume, and Taylor and Woodhouse agreed,[6] though realizing that this would draw the attention

1. *Letters*, II, 174.   2. KC, I, 92.
3. Keats Collection, Houghton Library, H 4.   4. *Letters*, II, 294–295.
5. It is sometimes forgotten by those who wish to restore Keats's second version (Brit. Mus. Egerton, 2780) that Keats gave his publishers the authority quoted above, saw what they had done in proof, and made no protest.
6. Two sketches of the title page, one in Taylor's, one in Woodhouse's hand, both put *Lamia* first. Keats Collection, Houghton Library, H 3.

of the critics. So would the fact that it was the only poem in the book in the same form as *Endymion*, heroic couplets. Any lapses here would be fatal. Woodhouse was on the look-out for correct prosody, scansion and rhyme. When the first proofs arrived,[1] he had a shock. No one had noticed in Keats's fair copy that he had given wrong quantities to most of the Greek names. Some of the lines would not scan, others would not rhyme. Keats, who must have wished he had taken Greek lessons with Bailey, was told how to pronounce the names. He wrote a list on the half-title page of the proof, with the correct stresses marked, and then set about altering the lines where they occurred, cutting-out and adjusting words and syllables. In Part One of the poem he also attempted some small improvements, not always successfully. Woodhouse followed him closely, with an eye to technical flaws. Sometimes he found Keats's corrections had led to worse trouble. Originally, Keats had written as one couplet

> She fled into that valley they must pass
> Who go from Corinth out to Cencreas

To correct the false quantity of the Greek name, Keats had substituted a false rhyme

> She fled into that valley they must skirt
> Who go from Corinth out to Cenchrea's port

Woodhouse, realizing the rhyme would never pass the critics, made his own version for publication:

> She fled into that valley they pass o'er
> Who go to Corinth from Cenchrea's shore

Woodhouse had a sound if conventional ear for prosody, and most of his emendations, like this one, though seldom poetical, would appease the critics. After Keats had juggled the stresses into place in the line

> The rugged paps of the Perean rills

Woodhouse substituted "founts" for "paps", to avoid the heavy alliteration rather than for decency, while a few lines further on, finding the line

> Ah! never heard of, delight never known

with what seemed a forced stress on the first syllable of delight, he came up with

> Ah! rapture rarely heard of, never known

though the couplet was abandoned altogether in the final printing. In fact,

1. Keats Collection, Houghton Library, H 53. Discussed by William A. Coles, "The Proof sheets of Keats's 'Lamia' ", Harvard Library Bulletin, viii (1954), 114–119, but unfortunately with incorrect attribution of some of the handwriting. No corrections are in Taylor's hand; the two hands are those of Woodhouse and Keats himself.

Keats did not always accept Woodhouse's ideas, altering some of them back, and the proof got into such a state that a fresh agreed copy was made for the printers.[1]

Generally, however, Keats seems to have acquiesced in this doctoring of his work, and Taylor was happy to leave it to Woodhouse's tact. Only in one instance was there a sign of any serious disagreement, when all three found themselves at odds, and this, happily, showed how a clash of opinion between poet and publisher might be fruitful for the poem itself. At the very climax of the story, where some critics still find the tension weakens, Woodhouse had passed without comment this description of the confrontation of Apollonius, Lycius and Lamia, which appears in the first proof as Keats wrote it:

> 'Fool!' said the sophist in an under-tone
> Gruff with contempt; which a death-nighing moan
> From Lycius answer'd, as he sank supine
> Upon the Couch where Lamia's beauties pine.
> 'Fool! Fool!' repeated he, while his eyes still
> Relented not, nor mov'd; 'from every ill
> That youth might suffer have I shielded thee
> Up to this very hour, and shall I see
> Thee married to a Serpent? Pray you Mark,
> Corinthians! A Serpent, plain and stark!'

When he came finally to print, Taylor had natural misgivings about this passage. There was the false rhyme of "supine" and "pine", the awkward run-on of "see Thee", the rhetorical repetition of "Serpent", and the odd "stark", a weak rhyme for "Mark" and liable to be misconstrued as meaning "naked". In his Fleet Street office, Taylor put this to Keats, who responded then and there by scribbling a new couplet to eliminate "supine" and "pine" on the nearest scrap of paper, which happened to be a letter from John Clare.[2] As for the rest, Woodhouse, when consulted, produced some alternative versions of his own, and justifications for "stark" from the *Faerie Queene* and from Shelley; but Taylor was not gainsaid, and the lines finally read:

> 'Fool!' said the sophist in an under-tone
> Gruff with contempt; which a death-nighing moan
> From Lycius answer'd, as heart-struck and lost,
> He sank supine beside the aching ghost.

1. Woodhouse kept the first proof copy, had it interleaved, and copied on the interleavings other variant readings such as the rejected Glutton passage. See Keats Collection, Houghton Library, H 53, as above.

2. Garrod, *Works*, xxxv, who, however, goes on to confuse the incident by relating it to quite a different emended couplet in *Lamia*, Part One.

'Fool! Fool!' repeated he, while his eyes still
Relented not, nor mov'd; 'from every ill
'Of life have I preserv'd thee to this day,
'And shall I see thee made a serpent's prey?'

The added compression and dramatic tension, the heightening of suspense by
delaying the word "serpent" are happy results of Taylor's intervention. The
final result is so unlike the neat poetic platitudes of either Taylor or Woodhouse that Keats clearly roused himself to a fresh and successful act of
composition.

The enthusiasm of proof-correcting whipped up his spirits for a week or so,
but it did not last. By the second half of June, he had sunk back into his former
deep depression. "My book", he wrote to Brown, "is coming out with very
low hopes, though not spirits on my part." His inner obsessions continued.
He told Brown of his resentment at the kindnesses of friends. "Fact is, I have
had so many kindnesses done me by so many people, I am cheveaux-de-
frised with benefits which I must jump over or break down." Brown himself
with his £50 loan seems to have been among these, for the tone of the letter
is colder than usual, and it ends abruptly. About this time, Abigail
O'Donaghue was presenting the absent Brown with a son. A scribble in
Keats's hand on the back of a note from Woodhouse to Taylor concerning
Lamia poses a fascinating though unanswerable question about his state of
mind. "Shore Shore Shore Shore Jane Jane", he wrote.[1] Jane Shore was the
famous courtesan, much spoken of in the first act of Richard III, and herself
the subject of a play which Keats probably saw. Did he, as has been suggested,
see a connection between her and his own Lamia,[2] or was this an unconscious
expression of his irrational suspicions about Fanny? He felt ill and lonely.
Some time in the third week in June, when the rainy weather turned to a
brilliantly warm spell, he found enough energy to visit the British Institution
exhibition in Pall Mall. He met Monkhouse, and learned that Wordsworth
was again in London with his wife and sister, preparing for a long tour on the
Continent. Wordsworth had heard from Haydon of Keats's call on him two
years before. He kept a close interest in the younger poet, and in January
1820 had asked how he was, remarking, "he is a youth of promise too great
for the sorry company he keeps"—a reference probably to Reynolds, whose
parody of Peter Bell still rankled. In April, Haydon had told him that Keats
was "very poorly, I think in danger".[3] Wordsworth had just paid Keats two
unconscious tributes. In his River Duddon sonnets, published in May, he had
echoed the last stanza of the Nightingale Ode, and this June, listening himself

1. The suggestion of William A. Coles, op. cit., 119, that Keats was doodling the
word "shore" from Woodhouse's correction to the false rhyme in Lamia is just possible
though it seems over-ingenious.
2. Bernice Slote, Keats and the Dramatic Principle, 154.
3. KHM, No. 163; Dove Cottage MS.

to the nightingales at Richmond, he had written a sonnet which takes its final idea from the same poem. A fresh meeting might have been a happy one, and Monkhouse suggested it, at a supper where Southey, Lamb and Haydon were also invited. Keats would not risk the night air, though he might have done so had he known the temperature was rocketing into the eighties, and a notable opportunity was lost.

In any case, Keats, though he also did not know it, was already heading for another crisis, pitifully at the mercy of every small accident. At the end of the third week in June, a letter from George at last arrived; he was safe home, but any such letter was now a source of agitation. It was followed on 22 June by a disturbing letter from Fanny Keats about the Abbeys. Hastily Keats went to catch the City coach. He returned without catching it. His mouth was full of blood. The small haemorrhage of the first February night had been repeated. He could no longer disguise his fears with Bree's diagnosis; this was no hysterical symptom but actual blood-spitting again. He went to Hunt's, but said nothing. Shelley's friend, Mrs. Maria Gisborne, came in, and was introduced. *Endymion*, she noticed, was never mentioned. The Hunts and she talked of music, and how a famous Italian singer controlled his breath, "alternately swelling and diminishing the power of his voice like waves". Speaking in a low voice, with his own secret fear constraining him, Keats observed "that this must in some degree be painful to the hearer; as when a diver descends into the hidden depths of the sea you feel an apprehension lest he may never rise again". That evening, the premonition of this image came true; just as in February, a violent and heavy haemorrhage followed the slight warning. His landlady, who had spoken anxiously of his health one day to Haydon when Keats was out, probably told Hunt; at all events, Keats was moved to 13 Mortimer Terrace, where he continued to cough blood. George Darling, a doctor recommended by Haydon, and who attended many of Keats's literary friends, was now called.[1] He had little doubt what was wrong with Keats, though he later consulted a second opinion. Like Rodd, he believed in copious blood-letting, and Keats, who had at least recovered some strength through Bree's lighter treatment, was once more subjected to this depressing regime. He lay helpless in Hunt's hot and noisy house. Hunt, busy and suffering himself from migraine, did his best, and tried to provide light distraction. Monday 26 June was an exceptional day. By noon the shade temperature in London was 87 degrees. Hunt, always behind with copy for *The Indicator*, tried to write a topical essay, and, to amuse Keats, sat with him and read it to him as he wrote. Keats, as he had hoped, joined in the spirit of the exercise, and began to suggest passages. These passages in Hunt's *A Now, Descriptive of a Hot Day*, printed in *The Indicator* of 28 June, may be

1. Hewlett, 300, believes Dr. William Lambe was first consulted, but Hessey wrote to Clare on 30 June "A Blood Vessel in his Lungs broke last week, and he has been under Dr. Darling's care ever since." Lowell, II, 423.

guessed; two at least seem certain to be Keats's own. There is surely a memory of his small sister Fanny at Edmonton in the sentence, "Now the little girl at her grandmother's cottage-door watches the coaches that go by, with her hand held up over her sunny forehead." An even more certain attribution to Keats's hand is the sentence, "Now rooms with sun upon them become intolerable; and the apothecary's apprentice, with a bitterness beyond aloes, thinks of the pond he used to bathe in at school." There was indeed bitterness beyond expression in Keats's thoughts at this moment. His book was coming out any day now, and he was dying. In this mood his sickened disgust began to accuse the *Blackwood's* review of contributing to his illness. This is the time when Hunt spoke of his suffering from "critical malignity" and when Bailey was told by Reynolds "that poor Keats attributed his approaching end to the poisonous pen of Lockhart".[1] Two notes written by Hunt about now certainly fostered this impression; one was to Severn, and the other, without much doubt, to Shelley.[2] The legend that Keats was murdered by reviewers had its seeds in the bitter obsessions of his sick-bed, though with curious obtuseness most of his friends still took the guilty party to be *The Quarterly*.

Other griefs too weighed on his mind. He could not bring himself to see Fanny Brawne, though he wrote her a short note, and continually looked at her ring on his finger. She sent him flowers and a note, in which she asked for some books he had left behind at Wesleyan Place. One was the copy of Dante's *Inferno* that meant so much to them. If he should die suddenly—this seems to have been her thought—this precious relic of their love, with the *Bright Star* sonnet in her handwriting and the *Dante* sonnet in his, might be lost for ever in a Kentish Town lodging. Keats, looking at the little book when it came, may have had other thoughts before he sent it on to her. The *Dante* sonnet was yet another reminder of promise unfulfilled. As a weary return for Hunt's kindness, he allowed it to be used to fill up that number of *The Indicator*, over the signature "Caviare", which he had used for *La Belle Dame* when it appeared earlier. This sidelong reference to Hamlet was no accident; in a letter to Fanny not long after, his self-identification became complete:

Shakspeare always sums up matters in the most sovereign manner. Hamlet's heart was full of such Misery as mine is when he said to Ophelia "Go to a Nunnery, go, go!" Indeed I should like to give up the matter at once—I should like to die. I am sickened at the brute world which you are smiling with.

These words, and probably many like them which have not survived,[3] formed a ghastly spiritual legacy for a girl to inherit on the eve of her twentieth birthday.

1. KC, I, 232.
2. As convincingly argued by MacGillivray, xxxvi and note.
3. In other letters burned by Dilke's grandson, Sir Charles Dilke. Joanna Richardson, *Fanny Brawne*, 169.

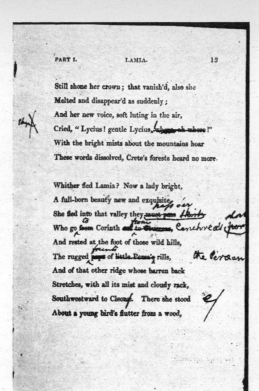

Still shone her crown; that vanish'd, also she
Melted and disappear'd as suddenly;
And her new voice, soft luting in the air,
Cried, "Lycius! gentle Lycius, ~~where, ah where!~~"
With the bright mists about the mountains hoar
These words dissolved, Crete's forests heard no more.

Whither fled Lamia? Now a lady bright,
A full-born beauty new and exquisite,
She fled into that valley they ~~must pass thirty~~
Who go ~~from~~ Corinth ~~out to Cenchreas~~,
And rested at the foot of those wild hills,
The rugged ~~pays~~ of ~~little Panac's~~ rills,
And of that other ridge whose barren back
Stretches, with all its mist and cloudy rack,
Southwestward to Cleone. There she stood
About a young bird's flutter from a wood,

42   Page-proof of *Lamia*, with corrections by Keats
and Woodhouse. The larger hand is Keats's.

43   The Mill House, Bedhampton, where Keats spent his last night in England.

44 Keats's sonnet 'Bright Star', written by Fanny Brawne in his copy of Dante's *Inferno*. The words 'Amid a thousand', written in Keats's hand across this, are a rejected opening for his Dante sonnet (mid-April 1819) and give a date by which 'Bright Star' existed in this, its final version.

45 The sonnet 'Bright Star' in Keats's hand, written in his copy of the Poetical Works of William Shakespeare on the blank page opposite the opening of 'A Lover's Complaint'.

46 No. 26 Piazza di Spagna, 1819.

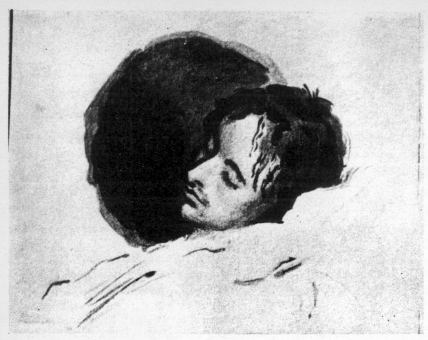

47   Keats, sketched by Joseph Severn, 28 January, 1821.

48   The Protestant Cemetery, Rome, 1819.

Calmer moments also came to him. Among his other books was *The Faerie Queene*, and he spent a week marking the most beautiful passages in it for her, "intending it for you, and comforting myself in being somehow occupied to give you however small a pleasure". By now, the first week in July, his fate was decided. Dr. Darling wished him to winter in Italy, and Dr. William Lambe, Shelley's vegetarian consultant who had written on consumption, concurred that it was the only hope. This was a far different thing from the vague talk of taking an Italian vacation, earlier in the year. Now it was a last resort. "Keats, under sentence of death from Dr. Lamb", wrote Maria Gisborne, when she saw him again on 12 July, and the day after Reynolds wrote, "He is advised—nay ordered—to go to Italy; but in such a state it is a hopeless doom." Only Reynolds's sister could find anything to rejoice at, in her hatred of Fanny Brawne, to whom Keats was, in her brother's words, so unaccountably attached; "poor fellow!" she wrote, "His mind and spirit must be bettered by it; and absence may weaken, if not break off, a connexion that has been a most unhappy one for him."[1] Otherwise, consternation spread. Severn saw him, and was shocked, though he refused to believe Keats's own conviction that he was going the same way as Tom.[2] Mr. Gisborne wrote to Shelley in Italy, telling him of Keats's wasted appearance and his plight. Taylor, who had left London in the hot weather to stay with Hessey's relatives in Bath, was anxious; Hessey wrote round to their friends telling them the bad news.

They had no doubts, however, that the book was going to be a success. Abandoning an earlier plan to issue it in the form of five separate pamphlets at half-a-crown each—Lamia, Isabella, The Eve of St. Agnes, other Poems, and Hyperion[3]—they now saw what an impressive collection it made at 7s. 6d. for the volume—"cheap in my Opinion", as Taylor remarked.[4] "Next week Keats's new Volume of Poems will be published", Taylor wrote to his father on 24 June just before leaving London, "and if it does not sell well, I think nothing will ever sell again—I am sure of this that for poetic Genius there is not his equal living, & I would compare him against any one with either Milton or Shakespeare for Beauties". Reynolds wrote to Hessey, "His book looks like an angel & talks like one too." Loyal Mrs. Dilke wrote "the devil take the public" if it did not recognize a great poet. This time, and for the first time, the chorus of acclaim was a public one, not confined to a small circle of friends and well-wishers. The reviewers were won over, some grudgingly, but all to a measure of admiration, and without any dispiriting delays. The book came out in the last week of June,[5] and on Saturday 1 July,

---

1. *Papers of a Critic*, 11.　　　2. *Letters*, II, 306.
3. Keats Collection, Houghton Library, H 9. Wrongly transcribed in Lowell, II, 426.
4. KHM, No. 63.
5. Mary Cowden Clarke, "A Friend of John Keats", *Illustrated London News*, 15 February, 1896.

O

The Literary Gazette printed the *Ode to a Nightingale*, the *Mermaid Tavern* lines and *To Autumn* as the best commendation they could give it. Lamb gave it warm praise in *The New Times* of 19 July, and next day *To Autumn* was reprinted in *The Chronicle*. *The Monthly Review* for July, more guarded and agreeing with Keats in disliking *Isabella*, quoted admiringly from *Hyperion* and in full from *To Autumn*, a general favourite. *The Sun* of 10 July recognized the unfinished *Hyperion* as a masterpiece, "the greatest effort of Mr. Keats's genius", while *The Literary Chronicle* of 29 July, though not joining in the universal praise and keeping up the old complaints of obscurity and affectation, quoted the *Ode on a Grecian Urn* in full. In August, Hunt, who had reprinted Lamb's *New Times* review in *The Examiner*, added two reviews of his own in *The Indicator* of 2 and 9 August. In this month, the biggest fish that any publisher could want was caught by the book. Jeffrey, the editor of *The Edinburgh Review*, came out with a long article, not only on the *Lamia* volume, but also on *Endymion*, which he had hitherto ignored, praising both, and by implication dispraising Croker's review of the latter book in *The Quarterly*. September brought further reviews, and even a half-ashamed reference in *Blackwood's*. Altogether, it was as good and as swift a response as any author could expect or demand.[1] Keats had at last the consolation of being fully reviewed, recognized, praised and extensively quoted and reprinted in his lifetime, a success by no means accorded to all poets.

"My book has had a good success among literary people, and, I believe, has a moderate sale", wrote Keats in the middle of August. One hundred and sixty had, in fact, been subscribed at the first week-end before any of the reviews or extracts had appeared. Yet in the collapse of his life and health, this meant little to him. The unfinished *Hyperion* now seemed a symbol of that collapse, and he had asked for it not to be included. It had gone in, however, with a hasty note probably written by Woodhouse in Taylor's absence, saying that the publishers took sole responsibility for printing it. The note added, representing Woodhouse's belief, "The poem was intended to have been of equal length with ENDYMION, but the reception given to that work discouraged the author from proceeding." In a copy given to the Hampstead banker, Burridge Davenport, who had befriended him and Tom, Keats crossed the whole note out, with the comment "This is none of my doing —I was ill at the time." He marked off the final statement, and scrawled after it, "This is a lie." Yet for all his disillusion, the book and the reviews, when they came in, set Keats thinking about poetry again. After all, he was marking Spenser, his first love as a poet, for Fanny Brawne. His first verses had been an imitation of Spenser; now he tried another, which he wrote in his copy at the end of Book V, Canto 3. It was to be his last; according to Brown "the

---

1. Hewlett, 322–336, has the best summary of these reviews.

last stanza, of any kind, that he wrote before his lamented death".[1] With this stanza, for there was only one, he ended the poetic career which had begun only six years before. It is a half-serious allegory of the spread of learning through printing. The Spenserian stanza also made him take up *The Cap and Bells* again, and show some of it to Hunt, though there is no evidence he added a word to it. All the same, it is possible that poetry flickered in him for one brief moment more. He had the manuscript of *The Cap and Bells* in his hands. There was a gap on the page where he had written stanza 51; in it there appear in his handwriting these lines.

> This living hand, now warm and capable
> Of earnest grasping, would, if it were cold
> And in the icy silence of the tomb,
> So haunt thy days and chill thy dreaming nights
> That thou wouldst wish thine own heart dry of blood
> So in my veins red life might stream again,
> And thou be conscience-calm'd—see here it is—
> I hold it towards you.

Though it can never finally be said when these lines were written, their tone is like his letters to Fanny Brawne before his second haemorrhage. It is even more like a letter he wrote to her at this time.[2]

If my health would bear it, I could write a Poem which I have in my head, which would be a consolation for people in such a situation as mine. I would show some one in Love as I am, with a person living in such Liberty as you do.

"Do not write", he had written earlier to her, "unless you can do it with a crystal conscience."[3] The idea that she would somehow have his death on her conscience runs through both the letters and the lines, and may indicate that they were part of the "Poem which I have in my head", laying this terrible burden upon her. This marks the lowest depths of his disease-ridden repudiation of both love and poetry. He was now at the opposite pole from his calm statement of the spring, when he had said that his love for Fanny shared, with his confidence that he had "lov'd the principle of beauty in all things", the whole of his reflection. Brooding, staring from Hunt's house on the noisy street toward the cool green garden he knew at Hampstead, coughing, bleeding, propped uneasily on two chairs, an attitude in which one of Mrs. Hunt's silhouettes caught him, he was hardly recognizable as the

---

1. *The Plymouth and Devonport Weekly Journal*, 4 July 1839, where the stanza was printed with this comment. Both stanza and comment came from Brown, who copied it into the same place in his own Spenser, and added "John Keats 1820". KHM, No. 106.
2. *Letters*, II, 312.   3. *Letters*, II, 304.

Keats of the living year that had produced his great book, though when the Novellos called he was pleased and managed to talk calmly.[1] He had looked back on that year itself with despair; now he added the year that had just followed to write them both off with disgust. To express to Fanny his total negation, he used images from the symbol of himself, *Hyperion*. "The last two years taste like brass upon my palate." The "horrors portion'd to a giant nerve" were now "the horrors that nerves and a temper like mine go through". He had built up self-mastery over his passionate temperament through a life of conscious control. Now, tragically, the obsessive suspicions and emotional crises, which form part of tuberculosis, swept away the self-discipline of a lifetime.

To his mind in this state, everything was a conspiracy of ironies. The weather at the end of July was fine and hot again, another mockery when he was too ill to enjoy it. The wealthy Horace Smith, who had probably heard the news from Hunt, sent his coach to Kentish Town to bring Keats over to the summer arbour of his charming new house in the aptly-named Elysium Row, Fulham. Under the vines through which the afternoon sun glinted, he pointed out to his daughter the sad shabby emaciated young man. "Do you see that man?" he whispered to her. "That's a poet." The other guests arrived, Smith's brothers and the absurd but kindly Thomas Hill, who had brought from his cellars at Sydenham a dozen of Keats's favourite drink, "some quite undeniable Chateau Margaux". After an early dinner suited to an invalid, they drank through the long and exquisite evening in the open air.[2] These men, whose manners Keats had satirized with proud independence a few years before, were now playing the patron to him, and he was too feeble to protest. Friendship on such, or indeed on any terms, now seemed a blight. A visit from Dilke was a mockery, and gave "more pain than pleasure". Haydon kept both pestering him with advice, and asking anxiously for the return of a book that he had lent Keats, another mockery from an inveterate borrower who still owed him money. On Saturday 12 August, Keats had an even more galling example of being "cheveaux-de-frised with benefits". A letter from Shelley arrived at Kentish Town, via *The Examiner* offices. It was immensely generous, offering to be his host in Italy, and suggesting that Keats should come straight by boat to the port of Leghorn, which was only a few miles from the Shelleys at Pisa. He had not yet read the *Lamia* volume, which Keats was going to send him by the Gisbornes, soon on their way back to Italy, but he had re-read *Endymion*, which he now praised; he added unfortunately to the praise some just but patronizing criticism. His conclusion was well-meant but condescending: "In poetry *I* have sought to avoid

1. Mary Cowden Clarke, "A Friend of John Keats", *Illustrated London News*, 15 February 1896. Mrs. Cowden Clarke thought her future husband was also there, but Charles Cowden Clarke does not mention it in his recollections.
2. Arthur H. Beavan, *James and Horace Smith*, 134–135.

system & mannerism; I wish those who excel me in genius, would pursue the same plan—".

Consideration of this generous but lordly offer was momentarily swept aside by an accidental upheaval which, in Keats's overwrought and suspicious state, was bound to come from one cause or another in Marianne Hunt's chaotic household. Two days before, a note from Fanny Brawne had arrived, and the harassed Mrs. Hunt had asked a servant to give it to Keats. The girl, like most of the Hunt's servants, had given notice, and left the next day without having delivered the note. It was not produced until Saturday by Hunt's small son Thornton with the seal broken. It needed only a small incident like this to set light to the whole fire of Keats's irrational misery with the world. He wept for several hours, as Hunt had seen him do once before when they had taken a coach and stopped in Well Walk. Then, sitting on the familiar bench of happier days, he had shocked Hunt by saying his heart was breaking.[1] Now, with heartbreak returning a hundredfold, in spite of Hunt's entreaties and ill as he was, he left the house and crawled painfully toward Hampstead. Approaching Well Walk, the agony increased even more; he could not go to the lodgings where Tom had died, and the last two terrible years had begun. He was seen at the end of the road, sobbing into a handkerchief.[2] That evening he appeared on the Brawnes' doorstep at Wentworth Place, so spent and exhausted that Mrs. Brawne abandoned discretion and took him in. He was to remain there for the next month, his last real home in England, and, as he afterwards said, his happiest.

That week-end he wrote a spate of notes, to his sister as always in any crisis, to Hunt with a gentle and graceful apology, to Taylor who had just returned to Town. He asked Taylor the cost of a passage to Italy and a year's residence there, with any information about boats sailing, and he enclosed a small unofficial will, leaving all his assets to Taylor and Brown as first creditors. He felt, as he wrote in another note to Haydon, that he might "pop off" at any time.

The next task, each one heavier and increasing the nervous tightness in his chest, was to do something about Shelley's generous but embarrassing offer. He had already asked Taylor to look out specially for a passage to Leghorn, the port for Pisa. He wrote, on 16 August, a letter to Shelley reflecting his helpless state—"is this not extraordina(r)y talk for the writer of Endymion? whose mind was like a pack of scatter'd cards—I am pick'd up and sorted to a pip." He struck back at Shelley's attempted criticism of that poem by some of his own on Shelley's published work, which the author had been sending him through the Olliers ever since the previous autumn: "You I am sure will forgive me for sincerely remarking that you might curb your magnanimity and be more of an artist, and 'load every rift' of your subject with ore."

1. HBF, IV, 294.
2. William Hone, *The Every-Day Book and Table Book*, III, Pt. I, col. 810.

Using a metaphor that now occurred again and again in his letters, he confessed that the thought of going to Italy was to him like the sensations of a
soldier marching up against an enemy battery; yet he would not now take the
hospitality Shelley held out, and, as Leigh Hunt wrote through the Gisborne's,
only hoped to see him in the spring, if he was not prevented, in his own
words, "by a circumstance I have very much at heart to prophesy"—that is,
his own death.

Meanwhile Taylor, refreshed by his own holiday, busied himself to set up
a scheme to get Keats to Italy, well provided with money and in good hands.
He had already found out that Rome was the best place for medical care, and
that there was a good doctor there, James Clark. The success of the new
volume made the publisher ready to advance money for the stay in Italy.
On Friday 18 August, Taylor left his office early for Hampstead to see Keats.
The discussion took longer than he thought.[1] Keats's nervous dread of even
imagining the journey to Italy was still great. He was also haunted by the
crowd of new obsessions that had grown while at Hunt's. At some stage of
their talk, he exclaimed, "Taylor, if I die, you must ruin Lockhart."[2] Painful
as their discussions had been, Taylor came away with firm arrangements that
Keats would go to Rome.

Something else was weighing heavily on Keats's mind. A few days before,
he had written to Brown in Scotland a letter which his cautious friend edited
with many omissions. It contained a mysterious confession, which Brown
called "the secret", and refused to reveal to the world. This has been universally thought to be the news of Keats's engagement to Fanny; but this
cannot have been news at this time to Brown, when, many months before,
friends had noticed that the matter was "quite a settled thing". The secret
was written down after the remark, "I think there is a core of disease in me
not easy to pull out", and Brown himself connected it with "his physician's
urgent advice".[3] It probably therefore refers to some physical state, real or
imagined. He may now have convinced himself, as he did of Tom, that his
love-affair had hastened tuberculosis, a distortion of ideas partly caused by
his feelings about the hoax that had been played on his brother. It may be that
he was referring to some more secret physical or medical cause, connected
with his naked confession later, "My dear Brown, I should have had her
when I was in health, and I should have remained well."[4]

Now, after Taylor's visit, with the die cast for Rome, Keats wrote the
further letter he had promised Brown. In it, he asked his friend to accompany
him to Rome. Brown has been represented as concealing this request, and

1. KHM, No. 65.
2. Ward, 369, assumes the remark was written in a letter to Brown, who was in no
position to influence Lockhart's ruin. Woodhouse's note in the Pierpont Morgan MS
reads, "T. if I die you must ruin Lockhart," and T. can only refer to Taylor.
3. *Letters*, II, 321.   4. *Letters*, II, 351.

staying on his tour till it was impossible to fulfil.[1] In fact, he actually made a note on the letter to say that Keats had asked him, and hurried back from Scotland much earlier than he had done from his previous visit, only to find that his friend had already left England. Keats, still at the nadir, spoke quite unjustifiably of the unpopularity of his book, and blamed it on the lack of interest by women readers. All sales of books were hit, at this time, by the sensational news of the indictment by George IV of his wife. Keats was finished with literature, off, as he said, to escape the cold winds that began to blow at the end of August. Health was now his only goal, and the money to provide it. As a last resort, he wrote to Abbey, suggesting a loan on the security of George's remittance, which had still not arrived. Abbey refused, but offered a small personal gift if Keats would call in. He displayed his usual heavy-handed timing by reminding Keats that he had never approved of George taking both brothers' share of Tom's inheritance, and remarking that Keats's bête noir, Hodgkinson, had injured the firm by giving George £50 too much, a little trouble that Keats had already learnt from his sister, and rejoiced at. Keats also commissioned Haslam to let George and Mrs. Wylie know he was off to Italy. The arrangements for his journey, whether successful or unsuccessful, were only just made in time. At the end of August, he had another very severe haemorrhage—they were now getting more frequent—and lay in bed for most of the time, nursed by Fanny and in danger of his life.[2] Haydon called and found him obviously very ill. He seemed, the painter thought, "to be going out of the world with a contempt for this and no hopes of the other." When Haydon attempted to be both optimistic and Christian, Keats muttered that if he did not get well soon he would cut his throat.[3] The adolescent urge toward suicide had returned to him in full horror.

September sped on to his departure. He was too nervous to see anyone, to think deeply, to write. On 11 September, he got Fanny Brawne to write for him to Fanny Keats a letter which was to pave the way for friendship between the two. Brown was not back, and the question of a companion for Italy was still undecided. On the next day, 12 September, Haslam, who had been enlisted by Taylor to be the main agent of Keats's journey, as he had been of George's, called on Severn. "Our oak friend", as Severn named him, put the matter squarely. Would the painter be the man to go with Keats? The responsibilities would be great, but as the winner of the Academy Gold Medal, he could apply for a travelling fellowship, and the winter in Rome

1. Ward, 369. What Brown concealed was another reference to "the secret". Letters, II, 327.

2. Hewlett, 342, imagines he went for walks with Fanny. There is no evidence; he was ordered to avoid "every sort of fatigue".

3. Haydon, II, 318; though doubted by Hewlett, as above, and others, there is no evidence this is not a true picture.

might benefit not only Keats's health but his own painting. Severn, impulsive in all things, at once answered, "I'll go."[1] Then the question; how long would it take him to get ready? Severn said three or four days. They had five; the boat, on which Keats was booked, was now due to sail on Sunday 17 September. Haslam hurried off to Hampstead to tell Keats, and slept the night there. Next day in the City he booked a second passage for Severn, who was hastily making his own arrangements, and telling his startled family. When he had packed his trunk, after five days of hectic preparation, Severn's father, a man of erratic passions, who had a violent relationship with his beloved elder son, struck him to the ground in his baffled emotion, and had to be restrained by the rest of the family from doing worse.

Keats's farewell from Wentworth Place can only be guessed at. On Wednesday 13 September, Fanny briefly but poignantly pencilled in the copy of *The Literary Pocket Book*[2] he had given her the words "Mr Keats left Hampstead". She already had several of his other books; now he gave her his miniature by Severn. They exchanged locks of hair. Each wore the other's ring. She gave him a pocket diary and a pen knife, for the letters she hoped he would write, but which he never did. She had lined his travelling-cap with silk, her chief skill set to make some small remembrance for him.

Everything seems to show how much her nature had matured and her love had deepened. For the past month she had been with him and had nursed him every day. To see him helpless, and to be able, however little, to bring help to him, had given her a profound understanding and tenderness. It had brought a reality into their relationship, far removed from the play-acting of their first meetings. The day-by-day physical task of nursing a sick man in that age was something that could have destroyed a conventional love-affair. With Fanny it was a challenge to which her strong and practical nature responded. It put their love once and for all on a real footing. The clarity of this new position included her mother, who shared with Fanny in nursing Keats. She was no longer the conventional, watchful guardian of her daughter's interests, but someone involved in the whole future of them both. She became some part at least of the mother Keats said he had never had. He even wished she could go to Italy with him, though there is no knowing whether the plan was ever seriously discussed.[3] One thing became positive; if Keats returned, he and Fanny would marry at once, and live with Mrs. Brawne. With memories of her own penniless and ailing husband, this was a tremendous gesture by Fanny's mother. Fanny too made her own small last characteristic gesture, a mixture of sentiment, affection and practical sense.

1. Sharp, 48, though Ward, 372, supposes him to have waited a night before deciding.
2. As it was for 1819, she wrote it against 8 September, the second Wednesday in September for that year.
3. Ward, 370, thinks it was, and even that Fanny asked to go too; Fanny herself says nothing of this. LFBFK, 25.

She put into Keats's hand what was afterwards described as a beautiful, large, polished, oval, white cornelian. It seems likely that this was a marble object, still seen in museums, for cooling the hands while doing needlework.[1] Her present was both an intimate personal gift, something that she had touched every day, and a practical source of relief for a fevered patient.

Keats travelled alone,[2] first to Taylor at 93 Fleet Street, to stay there a few nights in case wind or tide should alter the ship's sailing. He also had to make a final business settlement with Taylor. He assigned to the firm the copyrights of his three books for £200, the exact amount they were still out of pocket on *Endymion* and the *Lamia* volume. Taylor had also guaranteed him £150 at a Rome banking firm, on the dubious hope, as he privately thought, that something would soon turn up from George. Keats's friends, all in various ways, took a farewell they must have known would probably be the last. Hunt, who had printed some of *The Cap and Bells* in an essay in *The Indicator* three weeks before, now sat down to write a florid but sincere tribute for the same pages. He alone, with his own wife spitting blood and still no nearer death, was optimistic up to Keats's last hours. Now he was confidently elegiac. "Thou shalt return", he wrote, "with thy friend the nightingale." Taylor contrived a fortuitous boost for Keats's morale. At the end of August, he had had a call from Blackwood, the proprietor of the *Magazine* itself. Remembering Keats's urgent words, Taylor did not mince matters with Blackwood, and gave him a thorough gruelling over Lockhart's review. When the owner weakly claimed that it was done in the spirit of fair criticism, Taylor roundly told him, "It was done in the Spirit of the Devil, Mr. Blackwood." If Taylor was not quite able to "ruin Lockhart", he had at any rate taken a step in that direction by his forthright words to Lockhart's employer. The shamefaced tone of the next number of *Blackwood's*, though it did not last, may show that the message was passed on. Reynolds, with mean-spirited volatility, saw in the voyage, as he wrote to Taylor, a chance to separate Keats from "one or two heartless and *demented* people", among whom he went on to include Fanny Brawne.[3] In his shallow way he expressed hopes for recovery, forgetting that he had thought Keats as good as dead, voyage or no voyage, only a month before. Chief among the circle of friends, Woodhouse kept character as the best and most generous sympathizer any poet could wish. He sat down on the evening of Saturday 16 September to write a last note to Keats from his rooms in the Temple. In the next six months, he hoped, he could supply Keats, as he had always wished, from his

1. Ward, 237,400, believes it was the Tassie seal of the broken lyre; but this was neither oval nor large, measuring only ½ by ⅜ inches, while Severn testified that the object, whatever it was, bore no crest and was unset. *Letters of Joseph Severn to H. B. Forman*, 14 and 18.
2. Ward, 372, believes he left Hampstead with Haslam; but see *Letters*, II, 333 where Taylor tells Haslam that Keats has come to Fleet Street that day.
3. KC, I, 155, 156.

own small income. The modest friendly letter shows the best that Keats could inspire in a sensitive mind.

Keats's gift of arousing affection extended to people quite unknown to him. A young Scotsman of his own age, John Aitken, who had offered him hospitality and a fine library at Dunbar a month before, now wrote a protest to Lockhart. The last few months left to Keats, though barren of poetry, a time when he felt he had lost his vocation for ever, have nevertheless a living poetry of their own. Even in the distorting mirror of extreme illness, he kept the power he showed all through his life to reflect everybody around him at their best. Fanny Brawne summed up this gift when she wrote her first letter to Fanny Keats on the Monday when he finally sailed. Speaking of Keats's friends, she drew on her deep and most recent understanding of his own profoundest nature to write

I am certain he has some spell that attaches them to him, or else he has fortunately met with a set of friends that I did not believe could be found in the world.

She knew that the first part of this explanation was the real truth. Now he was leaving them all; the spell was to be broken for ever.

Chapter 28

LATE OF THE CITY OF ROME

*"Administration of goods, chattels, credits of John Keats, formerly
of Hampstead in the County of Middlesex, but late of the City of
Rome, Bachelor, deceased, granted to Frances Mary Keats"*

– Principal Probate Court, Administrations, 1825

ON SUNDAY 17 September the weather had began to break, and the morning
was overcast and grey. Keats had few friends to see him off; he had himself
looked in at Dilke's office at Somerset House during his last days at Fleet
Street, but had found his friend out, and was unable to erase the bad impression he had given at their last meeting. In the carriage came an apprentice
of Taylor's, William Smith Williams, for any last-minute errands. Taylor,
Haslam and Woodhouse went on board with Keats at Tower Dock. The
vessel was the *Maria Crowther*, a brigantine of 127 tons, whose master was
Thomas Walsh. Keats quickly settled into the small cabin, which he was to
share with three other passengers, "with 6 beds and at first sight every
inconvenience" as Severn, who had joined them, put it. The two others
were both ladies; one, Mrs. Pidgeon, who seemed middle-aged and motherly,
was already there, and her younger companion, Miss Cotterell, was to join
them next day at Gravesend. A screen divided the sexes in the cabin, but the
quarters, even with one bed empty,[1] were cramped. They dined with the
Captain on the way to Gravesend, as did Taylor, Woodhouse and Haslam,
who left the boat there, the latter to expedite Severn's passport, which had
still not arrived. Tea, with Mrs. Pidgeon doing the honours, saw Keats,
refreshed by the sea air, cracking jokes in quite his old form; but the strong
breezes and the early start had also made them sleepy, and after dozing off
more than once they all went to bed.[2] The morning found Keats a little
hoarse but well. Severn went on shore with the Captain, who was buying

1. Captain Walsh slept with Keats and Severn. *Letters*, II, 355.

2. Sharp based his *Life of Severn* on four manuscripts written by Severn in the last
twenty-one years of his life. These were *Incidents from my Life* (1858), *On the Adversities
of Keats's fame* (1861), which Severn used for his *On the Vicissitudes of Keats's Fame* in
The Atlantic Monthly, April 1863, *Adonais . . . with notes by Joseph Severn* (August 1873)
and *My Tedious Life* (September 1873). The first is in private hands, the three latter in the
Keats Collection, Houghton Library, *54 M–195. They are here designated IFML,
OAKF, AJS and MTL respectively.

supplies, and visited the chemist at Keats's suggestion, to buy medicines for the voyage, including a bottle of laudanum. Dinner was a cheerful meal again, and at six Severn's passport arrived, but two hours later came a shock. Miss Cotterell, who arrived just in time for the boat to catch the evening tide, proved to be eighteen, pretty, but very obviously consumptive, on the same search for health as Keats. The coincidence, with perhaps the added irony that she was practically the same age as Fanny Brawne, set him back noticeably; then, in the bustle of the ship's setting sail, he hurled himself into distracting both her and himself from any sinking of heart with another stream of jokes. Exhausted, he fell into a sound sleep, while Severn sat up on deck till midnight, sketching the moonlight on the water as they proceeded down the Kentish coast in a freshening wind.

Next day the storm had come in earnest, though the wind was favourable, driving them past Margate and on to Dover. All four passengers were seasick after breakfast, and could take nothing more than a cup of tea all day; more ominously, Miss Cotterell fainted. All went to bed, and thought it better to keep their clothes on all that day and the following night. Keats, spurred as usual by practical difficulties to forget his own feelings, made himself their doctor, and prescribed for the party from his bed, "like Escalapius of old in baso-relievo". On Wednesday 20 September, off Brighton, the weather was deceptively bright and calm; in fact, as Keats was able to anticipate from his knowledge of the South Coast, the wind was swinging round into the real tempest quarter for the English Channel, blowing into the teeth of the vessel's course, directly from the south-west, just as it had done during the whole of his last visit to Sussex. That afternoon the ship was pounded by mountainous seas, and the cabin flooded, just as dusk came, from a leak in the side, much to the terror of the ladies and of Severn, who exclaimed, "Here's pretty music for you". "Water parted from the sea", was Keats's reply, calmly quoting a popular song by Arne.[1] The Captain, however, seeing the state of the damage, stopped trying to beat up against wind and tide, and went about to run with the wind and retrace their course. By dawn, after a shattering night, they were twenty miles back off Dungeness and New Romney. For the next day or two, by contrast, they were becalmed, and even went on shore along the sandy dunes of Dungeness, tramping along miles of bare shingle and arousing the suspicions of an exciseman.[2]

Keats had made no complaint or shown any weakness throughout the last few days' adventures, but for all his forced cheerfulness, they had told upon him. As they lay in the Channel, becalmed now, Severn began to see a change for the worse. He grew irritable at the close quarters, the dull food, the unaired beds in the tiny cabin, and fell into frequent fevers. His state was

1. *Letters*, II, 343; Severn's memory later transferred this incident to the Bay of Biscay.
2. MTL.

made much worse by the fact that in Miss Cotterell he had an inescapable mirror of his own complaints. Every symptom of tuberculosis that she exhibited was a reminder of his own. He felt she was wearing him out, as the presence of the invalid Rice had done a year before in the Isle of Wight. Severn marked these changes with horror, and half-determined to return to London with him if he got any worse before leaving the English coast. Slowly they drifted in the light airs past Brighton again, taking nearly a week now to do the journey for which a day's favourable wind had sufficed before. On Thursday 28 September the *Maria Crowther* reached Portsmouth, where Captain Walsh decided to put in for twenty-four hours, to refit and revictual the ship. Anything was better than staying on board, where everyone was ill-tempered and exhausted, and Keats and Severn set off from Portsmouth Harbour to the neighbouring harbour of Langstone, where the Snooks had their mill-house, seven miles away. Here, in the beautiful setting of trees and water where he had written most of *The Eve of St. Agnes*, he burst in upon the surprised miller and his wife, who had a surprise in turn for him. Charles Brown had returned to England. Though Keats did not yet know it, the smack, in which he had sailed from Scotland, had actually passed the *Maria Crowther* as she left Gravesend, ten days before. To add to this irony, Brown was himself staying with the elder Dilkes now in Chichester, only ten miles away. Here was the chance to return to London, which Severn secretly hoped Keats would take; a visit to Brown might make his mind up for him. Yet the conviction began to grow on Keats that everything he now did was fated to disaster. Suppose he should return to London, what good would it do? He would still take with him his tubercle-riddled lungs and fevered, diseased body, to say nothing of what he called "other worse things". These, worse even to his mind than the disease which was killing him, were un-doubtedly the intolerable stresses of his love-situation with Fanny. To return with Brown to Wentworth Place, to take up the whole hectic cycle of their relationship there, would be certain death for him. Sick as he was of the voyage, and doubtful of any good that the journey might do, he decided to press on and not alter his plans. He returned to the *Maria Crowther*, which sailed from Portsmouth with a fair wind on the afternoon of Friday 29 September. Next morning, he poured his thoughts about the decision he had made into a letter to Brown.

"The time has not yet come for a pleasant Letter from me", he began; yet he wrote on, for fear that he might later become too ill for writing. He soon reached the crux of the matter. Even if he were restored to bodily health, he believed the conflicts of his love for Fanny would make him fatally ill again; his deep-seated neurosis about women had taken the final form that love was an actual cause of his death.

Even if my body would recover of itself, this would prevent it—The very thing which I want to live for most will be the great occasion of my death. I cannot help it. Who can help it? Were I in health it would make me ill, and how can I bear it in my state? I dare say you will be able to guess on what subject I am harping—you know what was my greatest pain during the first part of my illness at your house. I wish for death every day and night to deliver me from these pains, and then I wish death away, for death would destroy even those pains which are better than nothing. Land and Sea, weakness and decline are great seperators, but death is the great divorcer for ever. When the pang of this thought has passed through my mind, I may say the bitterness of death is passed...I think without my mentioning it for my sake you would be a friend to Miss Brawne when I am dead. You think she has many faults—but, for my sake, think she has not one—if there is any thing you can do for her by word or deed I know you will do it. I am in a state at present in which woman merely as woman can have no more power over me than stocks and stones, and yet the difference of my sensations with respect to Miss Brawne and my Sister is amazing. The one seems to absorb the other to a degree incredible. I seldom think of my Brother and Sister in america. The thought of leaving Miss Brawne is beyond every thing horrible—the sense of darkness coming over me—I eternally see her figure eternally vanishing. Some of the phrases she was in the habit of using during my last nursing at Wentworth Place ring in my ears—Is there another Life? Shall I awake and find all this a dream? There must be we cannot be created for this sort of suffering.

Illness had now beaten to its knees his splendid and sane philosophy of the world as a place of soul-making. The trials of life, far from developing his soul, now threatened to blot it out altogether. He longed to believe in a future life as a release from the pains of the present, an idea he had strongly rejected when in full health. Poetry took no place in his thoughts, which were now totally centred on his unattainable love for Fanny, "the very thing which I want to live for most".[1]

Keats brooded on this single thought as the ship sailed slowly past Yarmouth and the Needles, left Hampshire and edged its way along the Dorset coast. Still waiting for the favourable wind, Captain Walsh found it wise to let his disheartened passengers go on shore at intervals. One such landing seems to have been at Studland Bay. Either on this, or at another point a few miles along the coast, traditionally Lulworth but more likely the neighbouring Holworth, Keats suddenly became like his old self. He showed Severn "the splendid caverns and grottos with a poet's pride, as tho' they had been his birthright".[2] When they returned to the *Maria Crowther*, the wind was freshening from the right quarter to take them down the Channel and out to the open sea at last. It was their final sight of England. Keats was thrown back again on his thoughts of Fanny, "eternally vanishing" now perhaps for eternity.

1. Bate, 662–663, thinks that these words refer to "The writing of poetry", though "the incurably sentimental" may assume they refer to Fanny. See, however, *Letters*, II, 350 for similar phrases which undoubtedly refer to her.

2. MTL. Sharp, 54, added "He was in a part that he already knew", which has led to theories (see my own MOK, 83–87) of a Dorset origin for Keats's family. This may, however, have been merely Sharp's imaginative extension of the term "birthright".

Then occurred an incident obscured from truth by the shifting mists of Severn's memory and the vagaries of his imagination. According to the painter, Keats first scribbled in pencil, and then, at Severn's request, wrote out fair in ink the *Bright Star* sonnet.[1] This famous story, which has been interpreted in different ways by various biographers, has a number of inconsistencies, and it is most improbable that it is literally true. The pencilled version, which led Severn to claim the poem had been composed in his presence, has not survived; it is doubtful whether it ever existed. Still less likely is Severn's statement that Keats then read the poem to him; for it was associated intimately with Fanny, a topic that Keats concealed from Severn throughout the voyage. The final turn of unlikelihood is Severn's statement that at his request Keats copied the poem in ink "on a blank leaf in a folio[2] volume of Shakespeare's 'Poems', which had been given him by a friend, and which he gave to me in memory of our voyage". He refers, of course, to the volume Keats and Reynolds had shared, which, he says elsewhere, Keats gave him "a few days before".[3] The book was not given to Severn until the following January, as the inscription on the fly-leaf records;[4] there was no handing over of it on board ship. The copy of the sonnet, written on a blank page opposite the opening of *A Lover's Complaint*, shows no signs of having been written down by Keats at this late date, when the handwriting of his letters was beginning to deteriorate. It appears in his firm earlier hand. Moreover, it hardly seems to have been written from memory. In all but minor points of punctuation, including peculiarities of spelling and even one mistake, it is absolutely identical with the copy of the sonnet Fanny Brawne had made in the pocket Dante sometime before the middle of April 1819, and which he had left behind in England with her.

This provides a clue to what is probably the truth. Keats and Fanny had copied the sonnet each in a book, she in the Dante, he in the Shakespeare, some time when they reached their first real understanding in April 1819. Now, in his utter despair in leaving the shores of England, Keats got out the book, and brooded over the poem. Severn, observing him, made the very natural mistake of thinking that he was composing the poem he pored over, and he told Brown just a year later that Keats wrote it down in the ship.[5] Time and the painter's highly imaginative memory did the rest. Yet the legend of Keats's "last poem", however incorrect, has a symbolic truth. It was his farewell to England, to Fanny and to life; as Dilke's grandson was quick to point out, it ended with the word "death".[6]

1. Sharp, 54 and 55. 2. It was, in fact, in quarto.
3. Joseph Severn to the Editor, *The Union Magazine*, 21 January, 1846.
4. KHM, No. 22.
5. Sharp, 110. Severn seems to have known the sonnet was composed earlier (Ward, 438, n. 3) but grew to persuade himself that "it seemed inspired by our recent visits to the sea coast" (MTL).
6. MS note, KHM No. 22.

The three-weeks' voyage that followed was the final blow to Keats's health. Several times Severn thought that his friend was bound to die before they reached Italy;[1] a slight improvement as they passed through the Straits of Gibraltar was followed by a severe haemorrhage, and fever that persisted all the way across the Mediterranean. It was a nightmare ship with the two consumptive passengers making demands which the kindly but puzzled Captain was quite unable to meet. If the portholes were closed, Miss Cotterell fainted for several hours at a time, while if they were open, Keats coughed until he spat blood. Mrs. Pidgeon kept herself as far away as she could from the two invalids, while Severn was continually seasick, though he felt his own health improving, and sat up on deck painting. Keats tried to sit with him, reading *Don Juan*; but Byron's cynical account of the shipwreck affected his nerves so much that he threw the book aside in disgust, and condemned Byron's "paltry originality, that of being new by making solemn things gay & gay things solemn."[2] He was in the blackest depression, and to Severn's horror, he now revealed his real reason for getting his friend to add the bottle of laudanum to their medicine chest at Gravesend. He had deliberately planned to kill himself, once he was sure in his own mind that he could not recover. Both his own medical knowledge and the experience of nursing others made him dread the extended misery of a long illness. He saw all too clearly the nights without hope, the growing weakness of the body, the increasing dependence on other people. He was determined to escape all this by suicide, and he told Severn to give him the bottle so that he could swallow the draught. Severn was not a strong character, but he was a confirmed Christian. Somehow, pleading and persuading, he managed to head Keats off his purpose.[3]

So the monotonous and weary voyage went on, relieved only by an incident in the Bay of Biscay when two Portuguese men-of-war made the *Maria Crowther* heave-to, on the suspicion that she was carrying Liberal revolutionaries to Spain. Bad weather, cramped quarters, poor food narrowed Keats's life. His only escape, now that Severn had denied him what he planned, was to fix his thoughts on the parting gifts he had from Fanny, and consider how they should be preserved for her before his death, the knife in a silver case, her hair in a locket, and the pocket book in a gold net. Of Fanny herself he dared not even trust himself to think. He clung like a child to making these small tokens a memorial of their love as soon as he should reach land. On 21 October, at sunrise, the *Maria Crowther* entered the Bay of

1. KHM, No. 133.

2. KC, II, 134–135. He later compared Byron's depravity with that of the crew, who sang indecent songs in the hearing of the two ladies.

3. Bate, 686, and Ward, 391, following Sharp, 84, place this incident much later when Keats had his relapse at Rome; but see *Letters*, II, 372, which makes it clear it occurred "3 Months since—in the ship".

Naples. After the drab, frowsty cabin it was like a dream, the shimmering water, the darting brilliant boats, the great curve of the harbour and the purple cone of the volcano, with its plume of smoke edged golden by the morning sun.

Even this dream was to turn into nightmare. The harbour was unnaturally crowded, and the little boat slid in between tier upon tier of ships. They soon learnt why. The Bourbon authorities in Naples, masters of red tape and all too conscious of the dangers of epidemics, had heard of an outbreak of typhus in London. Every ship from the Port of London was refused landing until six weeks from the start of voyage; the *Maria Crowther* had ten more days of quarantine. Shut in with two thousand other ships, unable to land or to see much but masts and decks, they were denied more than a tantalizing view of the magical city.[1] Keats tried to conjure up the past for his companions, talking of the Greek galleys and Tyrrhenian sloops that had once crowded these waters. It was a despairing fling of imagination. As he looked out at their modern descendants, poling between the stranded ships, selling grapes, melons, figs and peaches, pulling up little fishes like anchovies, Keats felt like someone in another world. "Every man who can row his boat and walk and talk seems a different being from myself." One of the crews hailed them in English. It was a Lieutenant Sullivan, rowed over by ten naval ratings from the British squadron anchored out in the Bay. Sullivan and six sailors came aboard, and instantly the Neapolitan officials pounced. The Lieutenant and his men had broken quarantine and must stay on the *Maria Crowther*. The appalling inconvenience of seven more men now quartered on them was balanced for Keats by the cheerful presence of Sullivan, anxious to make up for his blunder. Although these ten days did Keats more harm than the whole voyage, he hurled himself into a forced gaiety, summoning up, he said, more puns than he usually made in a whole year. His sense of humour, however, was tinged with bitterness. One of the Italian boatmen jeered at the *Maria Crowther's* cabin-boy, who, he said, laughed "like a begger". Hearing this, Keats said indignantly, "Tell him he laughs like a damned fool". When the phrase could not be translated, he exclaimed moodily that the boatmen themselves were "not worth a damn".[2] Somehow he managed to write a letter to Mrs. Brawne, the nearest he could bring himself to addressing Fanny. He told her of the hardships of the voyage and quarantine, the oppressive effect of the other invalid, of his numbed sensations—"O what a misery it is to have an intellect in splints!" He sent formal love and messages to Fanny, her brother and sister; but before sealing the letter, his real feelings overwhelmed him. In a cramped little scrawl at the bottom of the page he added, "Good bye Fanny! god bless you". It was his final cry to her.

1. Severn's later accounts of the quarantine are exaggeratedly rosy; but see *Letters*, II, 353.
2. KC, II, 136.

On his birthday, Tuesday 31 October, the passengers were at last allowed to go on shore. Severn and Keats lodged at a small trattoria with a view of Vesuvius, the Villa di Londra in the Vico S. Giuseppe, a narrow noisy street. They were, however, comfortably settled into these lodgings by Miss Cotterell's brother, a banker in Naples, who had voluntarily joined their quarantine, and who showed them every possible kindness. The weather was now cold, wet and foggy; in these depressing surroundings, they sat down next morning to write letters for the courier to England, Severn to Haslam, and Keats to Brown. Keats tried to make it what he called "a short calm letter"; after only two sentences, his resolve broke down. "As I have gone thus far into it, I must go on a little;—perhaps it may relieve the load of WRETCHEDNESS which presses upon me." The word was in capitals as if to express the weight of misery. He went on, "The persuasion that I shall see her no more will kill me. I cannot q—". He could not finish the word, which was, Brown thought, "quit", a memory of his attempted suicide. Then his obsession gathered into one sentence. "My dear Brown, I should have had her when I was in health, and I should have remained well." Now he was utterly convinced, as he had been over Tom, that unsatisfied love was the real cause of his illness. He could not live with Fanny, and he could not bear to live without her. "If I had any chance of recovery, this passion would kill me." He ran through the miserable hours his love had caused him, all the time from his first haemorrhage, both at Wentworth Place and in Kentish Town. Again and again, his agonized thoughts returned to Fanny, although he knew Brown did not like her. "My dear Brown, for my sake, be her advocate for ever." He ended with an echo of his letter off the Isle of Wight, which he still carried with him, unsent. "Oh, Brown, I have coals of fire in my breast. It surprised me that the human heart is capable of containing and bearing so much misery. Was I born for this end?" Once more, the world of pains and trials, which he had seen as creating the soul, overwhelmed him in agony. He was reduced to groping for the explanation which he had denied himself by his rejection of Christianity. Nothing but hopeless misery remained.

His suffering and despair communicated itself to Severn. Keats had complained enviously that Severn's nerves were too strong, and the painter was perhaps protected by an incurably light-hearted disposition and triviality of interest. Now his companion's horror impinged on him; he left the room and gave way to tears, congratulating himself that he had concealed this weakness from Keats. Keats, however, his normally acute sympathies abnormally sharpened, had perhaps suspected that Severn was affected too; for after dinner he interrupted Severn at his writing, and showed he wanted to talk. What Keats told him that evening is uncertain, but according to Severn it was "much—very much—and I dont know wether it was more painful for me or himself." There is no doubt that he spoke of Fanny, though it remains unsure how much he revealed of what Severn later called "the seriousness & solemness of his passion".[1]

Whatever he told Severn, it relieved his feelings. He slept well, woke late, and made an Italian pun, which Severn took as a good sign. They were anxious to get to Rome,[2] where Keats had written in advance to the doctor recommended for him, but spent a few days before setting out, entertained by the friendly Cotterell, who drove them to see the sights of the smiling bay, though their stay was probably less idyllic than Severn's later memory made it; he recorded at the time that the rain was coming down in torrents.[3] As an indoor entertainment, they went to the San Carlo opera. It was a time of political unrest, with the Bourbon King of Naples conspiring to betray his new constitution to the demands of the Austrians. Soldiers were posted at each side of the proscenium arch, in case any disturbance should break out. When Keats realized their purpose, having at first taken them for a novel scenic effect, he was, according to Severn, filled with disgust. He made further contemptuous remarks on the soldiers at a military review, and hurried his departure for Rome. He did not wish to die among such people. He got his visa from the British Legation on 6 November and from the Papal Consul General on the next day; on one of these days, Cotterell gave a farewell party, where Keats appeared in high spirits, making a special effort for his kind host. The following morning, he and Severn set out for Rome in a small hired carriage. In the effort to live cheaply before using the credits arranged by Taylor and Hessey in Rome, they had a long and uncomfortable journey, taking a week over the 140 miles, staying at poor inns with poorer food. Keats sank back into listless apathy. Severn made him more comfortable by walking most of the way beside the carriage, and tried to cheer him by plucking armfuls of wild flowers, and filling the carriage with them, so that Keats could see their bright colours and breathe their scents. They reached Terracina on 12 November, passed through the wastelands of the Campagna, where they met a red-cloaked Cardinal shooting birds, and arrived at Rome on 15 November.

While they travelled, George was writing to his brother from Louisville. It was a letter full of anxiety. He had not been able to send Keats any money, and therefore assumed that the journey to Italy had not yet started. He had so far been unable to sell his steamboat, while the saw-mill, in which he had invested his new supply of capital, was only just built, and required constant supervision. Although a second child had been born, he was not even in a house of his own yet, and he and Georgiana lodged with a family called

1. *Letters*, II, 354; KC, II, 130. In view of Severn's own words, Bate, 669, is surely wrong to say "Keats showed little to Severn of what he was really feeling."
2. Severn imagined Keats received a letter from Shelley, but this, in fact, was not written till long after Keats left Naples. Jones (ed.), *Letters of Shelley*, II, 268.
3. *Letters*, II, 355.

Peay,[1] with whom they became close friends and, later, relatives by marriage. Just as Keats's recent letter to Brown had been full of anxious and affectionate thoughts of George, so this letter was full of affection for Keats. Brown kept both brothers in ignorance of the other's feelings, and in his summary of George's letter, which he gave Severn, said that George was "a canting, selfish heartless swindler". George, not knowing the virulent campaign being waged against him in England, was naturally puzzled that no one seemed to be writing to him. All he wanted to do, having re-established his fortunes, was to get back to England, and live "with those who understand us and love us", of whom the chief would be his brother. He did not realize that Keats was far from England, and already too ill to write.

In Rome, Dr. James Clark was sitting in his rooms in the Piazza di Spagna, writing to a friend in Naples for news of his patient, when the carriage containing Keats drew up at his door. He hurried down to meet the new arrivals, and was at once impressed by Keats, though he did not form a favourable view of Severn as companion for a sick man; "I suppose, poor fellow", he thought, "He had no choice." He had already engaged the travellers their rooms on the other side of the piazza, just beside the famous broad stone stairways up to the Church of the Trinità dei Monti, known to generations of later tourists as the Spanish Steps. No. 26 Piazza di Spagna was already well-established as a lodging house for foreign visitors to Rome. As Keats moved with difficulty up the steep marble staircase, he passed on the first floor the rooms of an elderly Englishman, Thomas Gibson, and his French valet. On the top floor was a young Irishman, James O'Hara, with his Italian servant.[2] The rooms on the second floor had been occupied earlier in the year by an English doctor on his own, but they were particularly suitable, the landlady said, for a family or for two friends, and were very well furnished. Their only disadvantage, as Severn was to find later, was that they communicated with her own rooms on the mezzanine floor between first and second, and that, like most landladies in a district that catered for visitors, she charged a high price for them, nearly £5 a month per head. However, after the depressions of Naples and the weary journey, the rooms seemed worth it. The front door, on the left[3] of the little second-floor landing, led into the lightless and shut-in hall, usual in Italian town houses, but out of this, and overlooking the piazza, was a fine sitting-room, more than fifteen feet square. Out of it, again to the right, was a small bedroom, only eight feet wide, but with two good windows, one over the piazza and the other looking out on the Steps. At the back of this, yet another communicating door led to a tiny

1. Statement by Fannie T. Arnold, quoted by John Anderson, bookseller, N.Y., Yale University Library.

2. Stato dell'Anime dell'Anno 1821 (S. Andrea delle Fratte).

3. Now blocked up.

box of a room,[1] but with a window over the Steps; Severn soon adopted this as his painting-room.

Clark had found the right situation for Keats, who soon let the doctor know that he greatly preferred Rome to Naples. The view from the windows, as he rested in the little bedroom, was a constant delight. The piazza was full of small workshops, mosaic-makers, engravers, sculptors and plaster-moulders. On the Steps lounged a continual crowd of artist's models in local costumes, waiting for hire; their bright colours mingled with those of huge stalls of flowers, brought in for sale from the Campagna, whose scent floated up to Keats. By day, the Steps were alive with song, conversation, and the shuffle of innumerable sandals. By night, when the thronging people and the flocks of goats or cattle had departed, the fountain in the piazza came into its own, Pietro Bernini's broken marble boat, the Barcaccia, with lion heads at prow and stern. Its quiet music sent Keats to sleep, until the early morning voices of the passers-by woke him gently again.

Moreover, as he settled down, Rome itself began to exert its spell, the feeling of welcome and timelessness it gives to all travellers. The late autumn made it still possible for Keats to climb the Steps to the Pincio, and look out over the dome of St. Peter's, a dark grape colour in the lemon-tinted dusk. Loitering under the ilexes, he met another young consumptive, Lieutenant Isaac Marmaduke Elton of the Royal Engineers, and struck up a friendship; they strolled the tree-lined walks, and visited the Villa Borghese, where they saw the semi-nude statue of Pauline Buonaparte, which Canova had just executed. Her notorious accessibility prompted Keats to call her rather vulgar likeness "The Aeolian Harp", presumably because every wind could play upon it. The lady herself, however, had her unconscious revenge. She met the young men on the Pincio, and stared so hard at Lieutenant Elton, who was extremely good-looking, that it upset Keats's nerves, and he tried to avoid her usual walks. He found plenty to amuse him in the other direction out of the piazza, past the goldsmiths and his banker, Torlonia, down to the Corso, the main artery of the busy commercial life of the city.

Keats was lucky too in the doctor who had been found for him. James Clark was a well-qualified Scotsman, thirty-two years old, well-read and fond of music. He took *The Edinburgh Review*, had noticed Jeffrey's favourable article on Keats's work and himself possessed copies of *Endymion* and the 1820 poems.[2] He had a comforting bedside manner, which he later carried to excess as Royal physician, but at this time he was cautious in his diagnoses and commonsense in his treatment. A great believer in simple diet and fresh air, he had written a youthful thesis on their good effects. He observed Keats carefully over the first fortnight, and noted that he was having trouble with his digestion, the tubercle having apparently spread to the stomach. Sur-prisingly, he thought the lungs little affected; his own *post-mortem* examination

1. Now the entrance hall.   2. Sharp, 106.

was to prove him wrong here. He noticed particularly Keats's mental distress, and diagnosed rightly that he had something on his mind. Knowing that Keats's publishers had arranged a credit for him at Torlonia's, he guessed wrongly that this might be due to money worries. He saw how well Keats was responding to his gentle walks and his interest in things about him, and proposed to extend both. Probably owing to his suggestion, Keats and Severn hired a horse some time after 27 November and a piano on 29 November. Clark lent them music. The most encouraging sign of all was that Keats, for the first time since last February, began seriously to plan a poem. It was, Severn said, to be about Sabrina the river-nymph, goddess of the river Severn. This idea may have started as part of the usual joke on the painter's name—Keats had inscribed a copy of his first book, "The Author consigns this copy to the Severn with all his Heart"—but it was a subject he had already discussed. On board the *Maria Crowther* he had read the Sabrina passages from *Comus* to Severn,[1] and he now felt himself willing to begin the poem. The calm life and creative spirit of Rome could, of course, have no effect on him physically; but it could offer him one last respite from mental suffering in a way that doctors, friends and well-meant remedies had failed to do. On 30 November, Keats wrote to Brown. The tone of the letter, in contrast with the last two he had written to his friend, was calm and philosophical.[2]

'Tis the most difficult thing in the world to me to write a letter. My stomach continues so bad, that I feel it worse on opening any book—yet I am much better than I was in Quarantine. Then I am afraid to encounter the proing and conning of any thing interesting to me in England. I have an habitual feeling of my real life having past, and that I am leading a posthumous existence. God knows how it would have been—but it appears to me—however, I will not speak of that subject. I must have been at Bedhampton nearly at the time you were writing to me from Chichester—how unfortunate—and to pass on the river too! There was my star predominant! I cannot answer any thing in your letter, which followed me from Naples to Rome, because I am afraid to look it over again. I am so weak (in mind) that I cannot bear the sight of any hand writing of a friend I love so much as I do you. Yet I ride the little horse,—and, at my worst, even in Quarantine, summoned up more puns, in a sort of desperation, in one week than in any year of my life. There is one thought enough to kill me—I have been well, healthy, alert &c, walking with her—and now—the knowledge of contrast, feeling for light and shade, all that information (primitive sense) necessary for a poem are great enemies to the recovery of the stomach. There, you rogue, I put you to the torture,—but you must bring your philosophy to bear—as I do mine, really—or how should I be able to live? Dr Clarke is very attentive to me; he says, there is very little the matter with my lungs, but my stomach, he says, is very bad. I am well disappointed in hearing good news from George,—for it runs in my head we shall all

1. Sharp, 110.
2. Ward, 388, however, thinks that in this letter, "Keats kept carefully to the surface of things".

die young. . . . Write to George as soon as you receive this, and tell him how I am, as far as you can guess;—and also a note to my sister—who walks about my imagination like a ghost—she is so like Tom. I can scarcely bid you good bye even in a letter. I always made an awkward bow.

God bless you!
John Keats.

This touching letter was, as its ending hinted, his last. It was full of a new-found and constant fortitude, which impressed everyone around him. Dr. Clark had just exclaimed, "he's too noble an animal to be allowed to sink".[1] It is remarkable for one of his deepest definitions of poetry, and the sense it gives that poetry is once more in his mind. Indeed, the words "I ride the little horse" do not refer to his rides in Rome,[2] which he had hardly yet had time to take, but to the "little Pegasus" of stanza 71 in his own *Cap and Bells*, an allusion Brown would recognize. They meant that Keats was once more letting his mind play with the idea of a poem. He felt how difficult it would be to get back the prime sources of inspiration—"the knowledge of contrast, feeling for light and shade, all that information (primitive sense) necessary for a poem". The physical sources for poetry have hardly been better expressed, their primitive and deep-seated nature. All these were around him now, in the open human commerce of the streets of Rome, the light and shade of life, which he had always looked for in men and women, and which had come to inspire him more and more. If he should plunge into these now, as a poem would demand, his whole precarious respite of calm might be shaken. "There is one thought enough to kill me"; it was perhaps this thought, or some expression of it now, that led Severn later to say that Keats felt his greatest misfortune was "being cut off from the world of poetry". Yet even in his "posthumous existence", he managed this last comment on the nature of the poetic vocation, to add to the many for which his letters have been a living inspiration to later poets.

So for ten more days, Keats enjoyed a brief Indian summer of self-renewal. All the stories of this time sound like his old self. When Severn played him piano arrangements of Haydn symphonies, Keats exclaimed delightedly that Haydn was like a child "for there is no knowing what he will do next".[3] His sense of humour and prompt action returned. Their dinners, for which they paid extra, were sent up from a trattoria in the square.[4] They were badly cooked, and his stomach could not stand them. One afternoon when the food came in, Keats rose with a mischievous smile,

1. *Letters*, II, 358.
2. As supposed in *Letters*, II, 360, n. 4, though he soon afterwards "went out on horse-back every day", LFBFK, 12.
3. MTL.
4. Severn later said it was in the same building; there is no sign of this in the *Stato dell' Anime*.

took the dishes, and quietly emptied them one by one out of the sitting-room window on to the pavement below, fowl, cauliflower, macaroni and rice pudding. "Now you'll see", he told Severn, "we'll have a decent dinner." He pointed to the basket, and the porter and the landlady laughed in appreciation; in less than half an hour an excellent dinner was brought at no further charge, and the food after that was well-cooked. He even made a lavatorial joke, in the style of his old Piccadilly set, on one of the Roman customs, commenting that a certain corner fountain on the Pincio "was a corner watering out of revenge for watering in a corner".[1] Yet if the old humour and light were coming back into his life, he was the more affected, as he had feared, by the shade. He had learnt enough Italian to begin Alfieri's tragedies; but on the second page, he translated to himself two lines: "Unhappy me! No solace remains for me but weeping, and weeping is a crime." He broke down, and could not read on. He discussed Tasso, his favourite reading as a boy, but sadly commented that he had no chance of becoming as great a poet, as he was going to be cut off before he had completed anything.

On 10 December the respite ended, as it was bound to do. Severn went for an early morning walk, to post a hopeful letter to Haslam. Keats woke on his return, looking cheerful; then suddenly a cough brought heavy vomiting of blood, two cupfuls. Clark came and let more blood. Keats's brain, confused by the lack of blood, had only one thought. When the doctor had gone, he leapt out of bed, stumbling about the little room crying, "This day shall be my last." Severn, forewarned by what had happened on the boat, took every means of self-destruction from his reach, knives, scissors, razors, and, of course, the bottle of laudanum. For twenty-four hours Keats raved, until another haemorrhage and blood-letting weakened him so much that Severn was able to talk him into a little calmness, and even persuade him to read the newspapers. In nine days he had five haemorrhages, and his tortured mind gave him no rest. With staring glassy eyes, he horrified Severn into believing that his brain was permanently affected: "How he can be Keats again from all this I have little hope." Clark, who came over four or five times a day, put him on starvation diet, mostly fish cooked by the doctor's wife; Keats raved that they were conspiring to starve him. At length he fell into an exhausted sleep. By the second half of December, his blood-spitting was less, but his mental condition was at its worst.[2] He ran through all his past life, his friends, his love-affair. Tom's death, as always, obsessed him. Again and again, he returned to the notion that he too was dying of a broken heart. Memories of Tom led him into insane delusions of persecution. Long before, in one of his less sane moods, he had himself threatened to poison Wells for what he considered the fatal hoax. Now, by a ghastly distortion of

1. MTL. Severn comments elsewhere on the free-and-easy sanitary customs of the Roman inhabitants. IFML.
2. KC, I, 179–180.

his own threat, he seemed under the firm conviction that poison was administered to him by someone in London.[1] In his delirium, he may have thought that Wells had used his own threatened means of revenge.

Above all, he horrified Severn, who had been at his bedside for all but two hours of the past fortnight, by raging against the comfort of Christian consolation which his friend had, and which was denied him by his own unbelief. On the night of 23/24 December, as Severn sat writing to Taylor, Keats said, "I think a malignant being must have power over us—over whom the Almighty has little or no influence—yet you know Severn I cannot believe in your book—the Bible." Denied, so he felt, "this last cheap comfort —which every rogue and fool have", he exclaimed, "Here am I with desperation in death which would disgrace the commonest fellow."[2] He had already given Severn a list of books he would like. These harked back to his religious and philosophic discussions at Oxford with Bailey, the works of Jeremy Taylor, Dacier's Plato, and also *The Pilgrim's Progress*. Severn wrote all night, and when Keats woke on the morning of Christmas Eve, it was to make a macabre bookish joke for his publisher. "Tell Taylor I shall soon be in a second Edition—in sheets—and cold press." That afternoon,[3] Keats said it was his last request that no mention should be made publicly of him in any newspaper or magazine, and that no engraving should be made of any picture of him.

Dr. Clark could hold out no hope to Severn, nor could even his practised manner conceal from the patient that he was dying. The Italian physician he summoned for consultation on Christmas Eve also gave no hope, and diagnosed a malformation of the chest. Clark believed that, apart from any organic disease, Keats's state of mind alone would soon kill him. Keats, in fact, returned all through the next month to the idea of suicide. At first, he tried to persuade Severn to let him have the bottle of laudanum by appealing to the painter's own interests. He set out, with full medical details, in what Severn called "the most dreadful scene",[4] the horrors of his own lingering death. It would involve loss of all bodily control, constant diarrhoea, which would need continuous nursing, and which would cut Severn off from all the artistic prospects of his visit to Rome. "Why not let me die now?" he pleaded.[5] When Severn refused to give him the bottle, Keats swung to the other extreme. For a time he lost all self-respect, and in childish rage would throw away the coffee Severn prepared, bitterly abusing him for keeping him alive against his will, and pouring every sort of mad reproach upon his

1. KC, I, 180. The conjectural reconstruction by Ward, 391, seems likely, though her reading of "terrible delusion" should clearly be something like "firm conviction". MS in Keats Collection, Houghton Library, torn.

2. MTL.   3. KC, I, 184.

4. OAKF. Altered in *The Atlantic Monthly*, April 1863, to "the most touching scenes".

5. MTL.

friend.[1] To keep him quiet, Severn even made a pretence of promising he should have the bottle; in fact, not able to trust himself, the painter had already put it into Clark's safe keeping. When Keats knew this, he transferred his reproaches to the doctor. Fixing Clark with his penetrating sunken eyes, he asked him at every visit, "How long is this posthumous life of mine to last?"

So the shadows deepened in the tiny cramped room, while outside fruit trees began to blossom in the warmth of the Roman New Year. When Severn reported a rose in bloom, Keats wept at the news. Everything that reminded him of his past life was now an agony for him. On Christmas Day, three letters had arrived for Keats, from Hessey, Brown and Fanny Brawne. He could not bear to read them, and handed them back to Severn, the one from Fanny unopened, saying, "No more letters for me." This, and further letters from Fanny, set him off on the old topic that she had denied him sexual satisfaction, and that this had been a prime cause of his illness. Severn, who now heard much that his later memory glossed over, wrote to Brown early in February that Keats "found many causes of his illness in the exciting and thwarting of his passions, but I persuaded him to feel otherwise on this delicate point."[2] He was now entering into the last stage of illness, a total weakness, with terrible night sweats, teeth chattering uncontrolled, a hard cough, and thick expectoration instead of blood-spitting. Severn sat by him day and night, stringing up a set of candles, so that as one guttered it lit the other. At 3 o'clock on the morning of 28 January he drew a sketch of Keats to keep himself awake, and wrote on it "a deadly sweat was on him all this night". Keats's head, the hair matted with sweat, cast a shadow on the wall in the light that flickered from the little fireplace with its decoration of marble lions. Immense exhaustion filled his weary sleeping features.

At all events, he was now mostly calm. Severn had managed through Clark to get some of the books Keats wanted, Taylor's *Holy Living* and *Holy Dying*. He not only read them to Keats, but he prayed beside the friend who had no prayers to make.[3] In this, Severn afterwards felt himself to have been an instrument of Providence. Among all Keats's freethinking friends, it seemed to him, there was a divine purpose that he, a simple Christian, should be chosen to comfort the dying poet. Yet nearly forty years afterwards, he was still deeply puzzled why Keats should be "hurried down a sea of troubles to death, without looking back to the rainbow of hope or clinging to the actual ways of Providence."[4] The thought became too painful, and a few

1. *Letters*, II, 373, shows this phase lasted at least until 26 January when Severn wrote, "His mind is bordering on the insane." See also Sharp, 85.

2. KC, II, 92. Ward, 397, thinks Severn wrote these words "in mystification", but Keats's deliriums must have left him little doubt what to think.

3. It took Severn over fifty years to persuade himself that Keats prayed too. "Prayed by him" (OAKF, 1861) becomes "prayed with him" (MTL, 1873).

4. IFML, 1858. Sharp, 106, truncates this passage.

years further on he managed to persuade himself that Keats had died a
Christian.[1] Keats certainly grew more reconciled to his end as the month of
February wore on. He began to look on the hope of death as his only
comfort; there is no sign that he accepted any of the comforts of his friend's
Christianity.

Severn himself had matured through the devastating experience of the
past two months. Perhaps the greatest service he gave Keats was to protect
him from those material worries which seemed fated to dog him even on his
death-bed. Torlonia, the banker, had advised Keats and Severn to draw
most of their credit in one large amount, so as to save commission on small
withdrawals; Taylor in London had thought he would only need to meet
regular small bills. When Torlonia's invoices reached him, the publisher
withdrew further credit in alarm, and in the middle of January Torlonia
stopped payment to Severn. Dr. Clark promptly wrote to London, and the
matter was cleared up without Keats knowing anything of it. A further
disaster had been hanging over them since Christmas Eve. Anna Angeletti,
their landlady, was a brisk Venetian lady in her forties, with a talent for
engraving, like her unsatisfactory husband, who had just died. Solely
responsible for the property, where her younger daughter also lived with
husband and small baby, she naturally had to keep a sharp eye for regulations.
Probably advised by the Italian physician, who had visited the house on
Christmas Eve, she reported Keats's dying condition to the police. Under the
laws for contagious diseases, this meant that each room the patient had lived
in would have to be fumigated and redecorated after his death, and its
furniture burnt. Severn was faced not only with this horrible reminder of his
friend's expected end, but with an unknown expense, which he had no means
to meet. Understanding little Italian, and assuming, perhaps quite wrongly,
that the landlady was out to make money from their misfortune, he determined to trick her into thinking that Keats had been confined all through his
illness to the single small bedroom. In a letter of unfounded optimism on 11
January to Mrs. Brawne, he told her how he had locked the connecting door
to the landlady's apartments, and moved Keats into the sitting-room for a
change of air without being discovered. The unknown debt hung over him,
but it was eventually reduced, again by Clark, to a very small amount. The
doctor, seeing in Severn's small obsessions, a sign of the strain he was under-
going, managed on 26 January to get an English nurse. Severn at first protested no one else could care for Keats, but Keats's own liking for the nurse
persuaded him. He not only took time off to chalk out pictures in the little
back-room but went out sketching in the Roman spring, and made several
friends in the artists' colony there. One of these, a young sculptor named
William Ewing, also came frequently to help at Keats's bedside during these
last weeks.[2]

1. OAKF, 1861 and MTL, 1873.   2. Sharp, 103.

Not everything could be kept from Keats. In the second week in February, Severn opened for him a letter in Brown's hand, having had another the week before; but out of this one fell an enclosure in Fanny Brawne's thin delicate handwriting. The incident tore Keats's new calm to pieces for several days. Unable to read it, he first asked for it to be put in his coffin, and then countermanded the request. On 14 February, however, a last calm began to suffuse everything he said and did. The nightmares of his fever ceased, and his dreams were easy as he prepared for death. He made Severn go to the Cemetery for those not of Catholic faith, just outside the Aurelian Wall, under the Pyramid of Caius Cestius, where he knew he would be buried. Severn described the flocks of sheep and goats there, and the early daisies and violets among the grass. Keats asked that Fanny Brawne's letters should be placed in his grave, together with a purse made by his sister, and a lock of hair —not his sister's, as Severn thought, but the fair curl given him by the other Fanny at their parting. On the night of 14 February, after a long talk about these matters, he asked Severn that his gravestone should bear simply the words "Here lies one whose name was writ in water". The quotations that may have suggested this phrase[1] are many; but the gentle sound of the fountain, which had been his companion for so many nights as he lay in the narrow room above the square, may have seemed the right symbol for his end. He woke in continuing calm, delighting in simple things, tasting his morning milk with pleasure. Remembering Severn's description of the meadowy graves, and looking up at the yellow-and-white flowerlike pattern on the ceiling, he murmured that already he seemed to feel the daisies growing over him. In his hands he kept continually the large white oval cornelian stone, given to him by Fanny Brawne, shifting it from one fevered palm to the other, but never putting it down. It seemed, thought Severn, "his only consolation, the only thing left him in this world clearly tangible".[2]

About 19 February a further calm came over him, astonishing Severn. The ideal of disinterestedness, at which he had aimed all his mature life, seemed achieved. As he had done in the crises of life, he now found comfort in the face of death by identifying himself with another person. Suffering had laid cruelly bare his abnormally passionate nature, unbalanced since his boyhood, always in extremes; yet the philosophy he had always sought, and had embodied in his doctrines of negative capability and soul-making, came to his rescue at the last. Still rejecting Christianity, he found his final consolation in losing his own nature in that of others. His essential belief in the poet's view of life saved him now in death.

His thoughts now were almost all of Severn's ordeal at seeing him die: "did you ever see anyone die?" he asked, "well then I pity you poor Severn":

1. KC, II, 91, n. 72.
2. OAKF, where this statement first appears, and *Letters of Joseph Severn to H. B. Forman,* 18.

then, reassuring, "Now you must be firm for it will not last long." He specially cautioned Severn not to inhale his dying breaths. His horror and disappointment when he woke from sleep to find himself still alive was great, and he cried bitterly; but he soon became calm again. On the night of 21 February he seemed to be going, and asked Severn to lift him up to ease the pain of the coughing that racked him. Still he lingered for a day or two more. Throughout Friday 23 February, the nurse stayed in the house for Severn to snatch some sleep; but at four in the afternoon, Keats called to him, "Severn—Severn—lift me up for I am dying—I shall die easy—don't be frightened—thank God it has come."[1] It had not quite come yet. For seven hours he lay in his friend's arms, clasping his hand. He breathed with great difficulty, but he seemed calm and without pain. Only once, when a great sweat came over him, he whispered, "Don't breathe on me—it comes like Ice." At eleven o'clock that night he died as quietly as if he were going to sleep.

1. Draft of letter, Severn to Brown, Keats House, Rome. In the completed letter (KC, II, 94), according to Brown, Severn added the words "be firm" after "don't be frightened", probably transferring them from Keats's earlier talk with him.

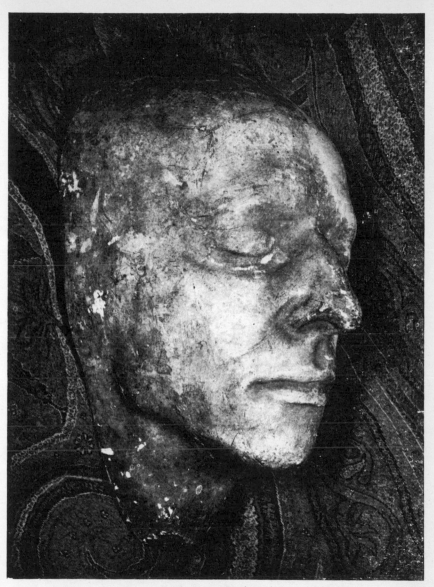

49   John Keats: Death Mask.

51 Fanny Keats in her forties.

50 Fanny Brawne in 1833, just after her marriage to Louis Lindo.

EPILOGUE TO LIFE

DR. CLARK took charge of the overwrought Severn. On Saturday 24 February, casts were made of Keats's face, hand and foot. On Sunday, Clark performed an autopsy in the presence of two other doctors. Keats's lungs, he found, were entirely destroyed. Just before dawn on Monday 26 February, Keats's coffin, with the gifts and unopened letters of his sister and Fanny Brawne, was taken to the Cemetery; in another carriage, Severn followed, with Wolff the English chaplain at Rome, and two young architects from the English colony, Henry Parke and Ambrose Poynter.[1] At the Cemetery they were joined by the faithful William Ewing, Richard Westmacott the sculptor, and Clark, accompanied by another doctor. It was Clark, remembering Keats's last wishes, who made the Italian gravediggers put turfs of daisies on the grave. Back at the Piazza di Spagna, the police had already taken over, scraping walls and burning furniture. When the landlady produced a table covered in broken crockery and tried to present à bill for it, Severn relieved his feelings by smashing it to atoms with his stick.[2] It was some weeks before he could recover his calm, soothing himself by visits to Keats's grave. The daisies had grown all over it, and nothing disturbed the quiet but the gentle bells of sheep and goats. Once he found a young shepherd sleeping by moonlight, his head on the gravestone. It seemed the poet of *Endymion* had at last found a fitting place.[3]

The news took three weeks to reach England. During Keats's last months, his friends had shown by letter how much they dreaded the inevitable. Brown swung from jocularity to rage against George. Both Taylor and Hessey counselled recourse to religion—"it is not Cant believe me", wrote the latter, excusing their pietistic phrases. The unbelieving Hunt showed at his best in words of stoic philosophy. "Tell him", he wrote to Severn, "he is only before us on the road, as he was in everything else." Only Fanny Brawne, who had nursed him, seemed totally prepared to face the truth. "I believe he must soon die", she had said to her mother, "When you hear of his death, tell me immediately. I am not a fool!"[4] She thought Fanny Keats should be prepared for the worst; "I shall never see him again", she told her.

1. Copy of letter by Poynter, c. 1850, sent to Colvin by Mrs. Mackail, 25 Oct. 1921
Severn's "Henderson" (*Letters*, II, 379) is probably a mistake for "Henry Parke".
2. MTL.   3. IFML.   4. Sharp, 75.

P   433

When Brown broke the news, he was amazed at his young neighbour's firmness of mind. Yet forced gaiety had already indicated strain. Now, in widow's weeds, her brown hair faded, her face alarmingly thin, she pored over Keats's letters in her room, or walked late at night across the Heath. Against the word "Finis" at the end of *As You Like It* in Keats's folio Shakespeare, she pencilled "Fanny April 17 1821". A month's stay with Mrs. Dilke at Westminster made Keats's friends think that, like them, she was over the first shock, "but", she wrote to Fanny Keats, "I have not got over it and never shall". She continued to wear mourning for several years.[1]

Taylor raised a subscription, paid Keats's debts and death-expenses, and exacted repayment in full from George. Brown, as co-executor, drew up a list of Keats's friends and relatives to divide his books among them. He included Isabella Jones, but omitted Haydon and George Keats, judging they owed Keats money. George was bitterly hurt by both executors' transactions, especially Brown's. He did not receive even Keats's print of Shakespeare, which his own wife Georgiana had embroidered with silken tassels.[2] In 1823, he discovered and obtained his legacy in Chancery, which might have averted tragedy. Fanny's portion fell due next year.[3] The quarrels, which only Keats's life had kept in check, time and distance soon disintegrated the circle held together by his magic. A dozen years after his death it was practically all gone. Rice too was dead, Woodhouse dying, Bailey in Ceylon, Severn in Rome, becoming himself a legend, Brown in Florence. In that year, 1833, even greater divisions occurred. Fanny Keats had married Valentine Llanos, a young Spanish liberal, who had actually seen Keats in Rome three days before the end. Now, with a political amnesty, he took her to Spain, from which she never returned for the rest of her long life. A few months later, on 15 June 1833, Fanny Brawne, who had lost her mother and brother, married one of a Sephardic Jewish family, Louis Lindo, nearly twelve years younger than herself. She and her sister Margaret, who married a Portuguese diplomat five months later, lived largely abroad for the rest of their lives, though Fanny returned to England for the last six years, and was buried in Brompton Cemetery in December 1865. Her tombstone bears the name Lindon, which her husband had adopted.

Meanwhile, Keats's own tombstone bore a misleading inscription. Severn had designed an emblem, a Greek lyre with half its strings broken or untied. He first said this was Keats's wish, "a long time back in England", but then

---

1. Accounts differ between three and six. Joanna Richardson, *Fanny Brawne*, 176.

2. Brown, for unknown reasons, gave it, with one of Keats's books, to Bailey. KC, II, 280.

3. She obtained legal administration of the estates of John and Tom on 21 May 1825, applied to Chancery, and was granted her portion before the end of that year. KI, 40. Abbey tried to detain her legacy from Mrs. Jennings, but was sued by Dilke and Rice, who obtained it for her. KI, 52–53.

treated the idea as his own,[1] This was quickly agreed, but he found Keats's executors completely opposed on the inscription. While Taylor wished only for the words Keats had requested, "Here lies one whose name was writ in water", Brown wanted a preface, "This Grave contains all that was Mortal, of a YOUNG ENGLISH POET Who, on his Death Bed, in the Bitterness of his Heart at the Malicious Power of his Enemies, Desired these Words to be engraven on his Tomb Stone." Severn hesitated, until Brown's own arrival in Italy in autumn 1822 clinched matters, and the inscription was cut late in the year.[2] By now, Shelley's ashes lay in the same cemetery. Drowned with a copy of Keats's 1820 volume thrust in his pocket, Shelley had confirmed the tombstone's legend by his own *Adonais*, whose picture of Keats,

> Like a pale flower by some sad maiden cherished,

succumbing weakly to the reviewers, far outweighed the splendid strength of its conclusion, and invited Byron's gibe

> 'Tis strange the mind, that very fiery particle,
> Should let itself be snuffed out by an article.

Hunt's reminiscences in 1828 completed the legend; yet the very next year, Fanny Brawne herself protested that they gave Keats "a weakness of character that only belonged to his ill-health". She was writing an appallingly difficult and often-misinterpreted letter to Brown, who had asked permission to publish poems and a letter referring to her. She believed Keats's character could and should be rescued from obscurity and misrepresentation, but by asking anxiously, "Will the writings that remain of his rescue him from it?" revealed her own doubts. For this she has been extravagantly attacked, and, later, extravagantly defended. It was simply an honest mistake on her part; in fact, Keats's writings had just begun their long, slow but triumphant battle against the Keats legend. Brown's letter to Fanny had been prompted by the first collected edition of Keats's poems, published in 1829 with those of Coleridge and Shelley by Galignani in Paris. Successive collections of poems, and the letters as more and more came to light, built up a true picture of strength and creative achievement. Yet Keats's biographers, while using and quoting the writings, still subscribed to various aspects of the legend. Dilke, who remembered the real Keats, greeted the first official biography by Richard Monckton Milnes in 1848 with the sarcastic quotation,[3]

> Appearances to save his only care;
> So things *seem* right, no matter what they are.

His words remain true of much that has been written since.

1. He wrote of having drawn the lyre at Keats's request in Brown's copy of *Endymion* (KC, I, 242; KHM, No. 54), but took the final design from drawings he had made in the British Museum (Sharp, 119).
2. Brown later admitted this was an error. Sharp, 178.
3. Dilke, ann., title-page.

Yet although misunderstanding continued to cloud certain facts of Keats's life, gradually his position as a poet and writer became clear. The sentimental commendation of the Victorian age strengthened his reputation, though in limited directions, and the sterner criticism of our century found equally admirable, though different, qualities to praise. His best poems have the individual power to draw on, and yet transcend tradition, which we have come to expect in a great poet. His letters, undervalued or even regretted by the Victorians, now seem the counterpart of his poems. They are handbooks of poetical thought and practice; they show him as a man of ideas, a professional in technique, and a human creature whose tragic view of life was accompanied by stoutness of heart and a resilient sense of humour.

These attributes are the common stock of poets, and Keats shares them with other great poets; the comparison with Shakespeare has often been made. What makes him different from any other poet is his extraordinary sensitivity to the impression of the moment, and his use of the day-by-day circumstances of life for poetry. He could, and did, transmute almost any experience into poetry, in an instantaneous and instinctive process. The initial value or nature of the experience did not matter to him; it could be the most trivial incident or piece of reading, the most casual sight or sound. In this sense, he put the poetic precepts of his great contemporary, Wordsworth, into practice, without any of the self-conscious deliberation that marred much of Wordsworth's own verse. It is true that he deliberately set himself to improve and extend this poetic faculty, and that his life was spent on this task;[1] but the vital force behind all his verse was his power to apply imagination to every aspect of life, so that the result far transcended its origins. This is why no part of Keats's life should be neglected, and every incident, once truly recorded, may have immense value in interpreting his poetry. With no other poet are the life and the works so closely linked. With difficulties of temperament and background that might have disabled him, Keats dedicated his life to almost continuous creation; in doing so he was for ever creating himself for fresh advances. The Genius of Poetry, as he himself put it, worked out its own salvation in him. His life was a living illustration of his own summing-up—"That which is creative must create itself."

---

1. Ward, 415.

APPENDICES

APPENDIX 1

THE JENNINGS AND SWEETINBURGH FAMILIES

The information about these families, first given in my article "Mr. Keats's Origins", *The Times Literary Supplement*, 5 March 1964, has been contested by Phyllis Mann, "Keats's Maternal Relations", KSMB, XV, pp. 32–34. A study of the original registers, however, does not bear out Miss Mann's three main points, which are

1. *John Jennings*. Miss Mann states that since John Jennings, Keats's grandfather, is entered in the burial registers, St. Stephen's, Coleman Street, as aged 73 on 14 March 1805, he was not the John Jennings, son of Martin and Mary Jennings, baptized in the same parish on 13 October 1730, since the latter would be 74. Errors in age in burial registers of a year or two, or even more, are a commonplace of genealogical research. Keats's medical friend Henry Newmarch was announced as being 68 at his death; he was in fact 71. Even today the age on a burial register is entered on the unsupported word of the next-of-kin.

2. *Mary Jennings*. The entry in the baptismal registers, St. Botolph, Bishopgate, for 10 October 1733, reads

Child's Christian name: Mary
Surname: Jennings
Father's Christian name: Todd Martin
Mother's Christian name: Mary

Miss Mann argues that this indicates the baptism of a bastard daughter of a Mary Jennings and a Todd (Christian name) Martin (surname). Apart from the improbability of Todd as a Christian name, this is not the way in which bastard children were entered in this particular register. A typical entry of this sort, for 4 February 1747, reads

Child's Christian name: James
Surname: Holl
Father's Christian name: James Holl
Mother's Christian name: Margaret Jordan

As with other entries of this nature, the full names of both father and mother are given, and the father's name entered under Surname. A more likely explanation of the word "Todd" being inserted before the father's Christian name Martin is that Mary Jennings was a posthumous child, and her parents of Baltic or Germanic origin. Martin Jennings wrote his name "Jennigs" (G.L., MS. 10091/65), his wife's name was Clementson, and "Todd" may have been the clerk's misunderstanding of the word "Todt" = dead. This, however, can only be conjecture.

3. *Charles Sweetinburgh.* Usually appearing as Sweetingburgh, his name is given, as he writes it in his marriage allegation of 1768 and his will of 1790, "Sweetinburgh". In the marriage register of St. Botolph, Bishopsgate, 1768, he writes it "Sweetinburg", (G.L., MS. 4520/2), and in the entry of his first marriage to Elizabeth Holt, widow, in 1759 at St. Luke's, Old Street (G.L.C. Record Room, P76/Luk/27) he signs the register "Sweetinbourg". This has led Miss Mann to believe that the St. Luke's entry is not by him, and does not refer to his first marriage; but the signature is clearly in the same hand as all the others, and the variation of one letter not significant, since there is also a one-letter variation between the signature of the allegation and that of the register, both in 1768, and obviously referring to the same marriage. The unusual name of Mary Jennings's second husband and his uncertain spelling may also indicate Baltic or Germanic origin, and perhaps tend to strengthen the conjecture in 2, above.

APPENDIX 2

KEATS'S FATHER

Various accounts and claims have been made relating to the origins and family of Keats's father, Thomas Keats, who died on 15 April 1804 at the age of 30, and who was therefore born in 1773 or early in 1774. These may be tabulated:

1. "His daughter, Mrs. Llanos, tells me she remembers hearing as a child that he came from the Land's End." Colvin, *Keats*, (1887), 2, n. 2.

Mrs. Llanos (Fanny Keats) was by no means accurate in her memories of her family, as may be seen by her letters to Harry Buxton Forman, 1877–1889, KHM, No. 85, though when only 30, she registered her child Rosa Mathilde as grand-daughter of Mr. Thomas Keats, Land's End, Cornwall, England (Fernando Paradinas, "Evidence in Spain", KSMB, XVIII, 23).

No Cornish parish shows a baptism of Thomas Keats in or about 1773/74 (Bishops' transcripts, County of Cornwall Record Office and Devon Record Office). Nor has any record of a Nonconformist baptism survived in the Public Record Office.

In the neighbourhood of Land's End, there was a marriage at Madron, Penzance, on 7 June 1767 between Shilson Keate and Ursula Stokes of that parish. The couple were apparently childless. However, in a nearby parish, Gulval, there is an entry for 24 December 1780 naming Shilson Keate as the reputed father of a girl baseborn child. It might therefore perhaps be argued as a remote possibility that Thomas Keats was a similar baseborn child, not registered under his father's name, but later taking a variant of it. This, though, can only be conjecture.

At Sennen, the parish immediately adjoining Land's End, on 21 January 1776, Thomas Keast was baptized, the son of Thomas and Bridget Keast, the father being of the neighbouring parish of Phillack, in which subsequently other children were born. If this were Thomas Keats, he would be considerably under 30 at his death. Moreover, though Colvin states that Keast, a specifically Cornish name, might suffer a phonetic change into the commoner Keats, there is no documentary evidence of this, though there are many other variant spellings of the name Keast. To accept this Thomas Keast as Keats's father one would have to assume (a) an incorrect entry of age at death, (b) that he married, in 1794, while under age, and (c) the phonetic change of name.

2. "His father was a native of Devonshire". Charles Brown, KC, II, 54. "The father was a Devonshire man." C. W. Dilke, KHM, No. 52.

No Devon parish shows a baptism of Thomas Keats in or about 1773/74. There is no record of a Devon Nonconformist baptism in the Public Record Office.

3. Thomas Hardy informed Colvin and Mrs. Thomas Hardy informed Amy Lowell (Lowell, I, 6–7) that a family called Keats in the East Dorset village of Broadmayne bore a facial and temperamental likeness to the poet.

No Thomas Keats was baptized in any Dorset parish in 1773 or early in 1774 except one in Fordington (Dorchester) very early in 1773. See also 4 below.

4. On 25 December 1917 at 129 Wirtemberg Street (Clapham) died Mrs. Amelia Spicer, in her 104th year, who claimed to be related to John Keats (*Clapham Observer*, 28 December 1917). She said she was a "step-sister" of the poet, and had his portrait over the fireplace in her sitting-room (personal communication, E. E. Smith).

According to the registers of St. James's, Poole, Dorset, Amelia Elizabeth Keats, afterwards Spicer, was born on 28 June 1820. Her elder sister Eliza was born on 12 August 1814. They were the daughters of Charles and Elizabeth Keats, the father being a victualler (Bishops' transcripts, Diocesan Record Office, Salisbury).

In some unexplained way, Amelia Spicer seems therefore to have appropriated the age of her own sister. Whether this should invalidate her claim to relationship with the poet is a matter of opinion. According to the registers of St. James's, Poole, a Thomas Keats, son of Thomas and Sarah Keats, was baptized on 30 December 1774, but died in infancy and was buried on 14 May 1775. There is no evidence that he was related to Amelia Elizabeth Keats.

5. In September 1858, B. W. Procter ("Barry Cornwall") made the acquaintance at Brighton of a bookseller named Keats, who claimed to be a second cousin of the poet, and to have talked about him more than once with Leigh Hunt. Hunt, however, replied to Procter on 16 September 1858 (CLH, II, 261) that "well as I recollect Keats, I have no remembrance whatsoever of his cousin". Since Hunt's memory retained many small anecdotes about Keats, it therefore seems likely that the bookseller's claim to have spoken to Hunt about the poet was false, and may perhaps invalidate his claim to relationship. He himself was Joseph Henry Keats, who from 1839 to 1857 had been bookseller and stationer of 142 Sloane Square, Chelsea, where he had carried on business as Keats's Cadogan Library and produced a *Hand Book for Chelsea*. He was born c. 1815–1816 in Chelsea (1851 Census Returns, PRO), the son of Joseph Keats, linendraper of 47 Paradise Row, Chelsea, who was born somewhere outside the county of Middlesex in the late 1770s (1841 Census Returns, P.R.O.). No connection has ever been established between either the bookseller or his father and the poet.

6. Joseph Henry Keats also claimed relationship with Frederick Keats (1807–1865) who was Sheriff of London 1856–1857, and therefore implied a connection between the Sheriff's family and the poet.

Frederick Keats's grandfather was John Keate(s), vintner of Newport Pagnell, Bucks, who lived c. 1744–1788. On 7 January 1777 he married at St. George's, Hanover Square, Ann Mower of that parish, one of the witnesses being Mary Keats (also born c. 1744). He was the father of Thomas Mower Keats (born 2 April 1778) and Joseph Keats (1783–1819).[1] Both boys served apprenticeships in the City of London, and by the years 1808–1809 both are described as hatters (Registers of Christ Church, Blackfriars Road and Feltmakers Company Court Minutes, G.L., MS. 1570/6).

Thomas Mower Keats, father of Frederick Keats, was in partnership as a hat-manufacturer at 14 Poultry from 1817 to 1819, in which year he became bankrupt.

---

1. There was a third son, John, born 19 March 1779, of whom nothing is known.

Joseph Keats had a hat-manufacturing business at 12 Pancras Lane and 74 Cheapside from 1810 to 1819, in which year he died apparently without issue. His widow Betsy (née Thornley) carried on the business at 74 Cheapside until her remarriage, c. 1835. (Post Office Directories).

No connection has ever been established between these hat-manufacturing Keatses and the poet. The fact that Richard Abbey appears to have had a commercial interest in some hatter's shop in the vicinity of Cheapside or Poultry, and attempted to get Keats and his brother George to join him in it (*Letters*, II, 77 and 192) has led Jean Haynes, "Keats's Paternal Relatives", KSMB, XV, 27–28, to assume a relationship for which there is no direct evidence. That none of Keats's friends, who passed both hat-shops while visiting Keats at 76 Cheapside, ever speaks of a relationship tells heavily against one.

There are, however, two small pieces of circumstantial detail which may leave the relationship with the hatter Keatses still an open question. Keats writes (*Letters*, II, 192) of "the coffee-german", who attempted to strike up a close acquaintanceship with him at Covent Garden Theatre on 14 September 1819. This cryptic term, evidently a familiar one to George, to whom Keats was writing, may indicate a first-cousin (cousin-german) connected with coffee; the parents of the hatter Keatses are described at various times as keeping what is termed a "Coffee house" (Victuallers' registers, Newport Pagnell). In its context, however, it seems more likely to refer to some cousin of Richard Abbey, connected with the latter's tea and coffee business, since Keats couples this person with Cadman Hodgkinson, Abbey's apprentice and junior assistant.

The second circumstantial hint of a relationship lies in an apparent coincidence between John Keate(s) of Newport Pagnell and the witness to his marriage, Mary Keats, and the Keats family at Stratfield Mortimer, Berkshire (see below).

None of these claims shows any certainty of a relationship with the poet's father. The sole document known to mention a relative is the register of the Poor Rate, St. Stephen's, Coleman Street, for the first and second quarters of the year 1804 (G.L., MS. 2433/12). In this, the rate is shown as being paid after Thomas Keats's death not by his widow but by someone called Elizabeth Keats (see Jean Haynes, "Elizabeth Keats", KSMB, IX, 21), presumably a close relation.

The origin of a very great number of the Keate or Keats families of South-West England and of London can be traced to the county of Berkshire.[1] Baptisms for this county (Bishops' transcripts, Diocesan Record Office, Salisbury) show two baptisms of a Thomas Keats in the year 1773. These were

Sparsholt. On 7 May 1773 in this parish was baptized Thomas, son of John and Ann Keats. There were apparently a cousin and an aunt, both named Elizabeth. The family, mostly of labouring folk, has survived to this day. There is no tradition of any link with the poet.

St. Mary's, Reading. On 21 July 1773, in this parish was baptized Thomas Keats,

---

1. J. L. Vivian, *Visitations of Cornwall*, 250–251; C. S. Gilbert, *An Historical Survey of the County of Cornwall*, 11, 168–169.

son of Thomas and Elizabeth Keats. At his marriage in the same parish (23 August 1770), the father is described as a baker. There was also a sister Elizabeth, baptized 12 April 1775.

It seems likely that Thomas Keats the father was born in the nearby village of Stratfield Mortimer in the year 1742, son of Thomas and Sarah Keats, since these latter were also married at St. Mary's, Reading, on 6 December 1739. The Keats, Keates, or Kates family[1] occurs in the Stratfield Mortimer parish registers from 1692 to 1786, after which there is no mention, suggesting that they left the parish.

There is an interesting possible connection between these Stratfield Mortimer Keatses and the hatter Keatses (see above). On 12 May 1745 was baptized John Keats, who thereafter does not appear in the parish records. John Keate(s) of Newport Pagnell, in whose parish records there is no previous mention of the Keats family, the father of the hatters, was married on 7 January 1777, aged 32 (Bishop of London, Marriage Allegations), which would make him the same age as John Keats of Stratfield Mortimer. His marriage was witnessed by Mary Keats, also, as her own marriage allegation shows, born c. 1744. Mary Keats of Stratfield Mortimer, apparently a cousin of John Keats, was baptized 10 July 1743. It is therefore possible that John Keats, father of the hatters, came originally from Stratfield Mortimer.

This may in its turn strengthen the probability that Thomas Keats (baptized 1773) of St. Mary's, Reading, was the poet's father. He is the only Thomas Keats to be born in the right year, and to have the closest possible female relatives named Elizabeth.

If this Thomas Keats of Reading were the poet's father, it may be asked how the strong tradition that he came from the West Country arose. The two facts are not, however, incompatible. Many families of Keate, Keates or Keats in the West Country originated from the Berkshire Keatses, and their armigerous members bore the arms of the Berkshire family, three wild cats passant in pale sable (College of Arms).

One of these families was the Keate, Kates or Keates family of Wells, Somerset. The apparent founder of this branch, Dr. William Keate(s) was born c. 1708–1709. He first appears as resident in the High Street, Wells, in 1733, and is described as apothecary. He was Mayor of Wells in 1740, 1746 and 1757.[2] After the death of his wife in 1781, he retired to Reading, where he lodged in the Forbury, and died on 10 September 1790. He was buried at his own request, as the memorial tablet records, in the church of St. Lawrence, Reading.[3] The fact that the Doctor, although always described as "of Wells", both retired to Reading and wished to be buried there, may suggest that he had strong family connections with Reading and Berkshire. His younger son, Thomas Keate (1745–1821), married as his first wife a Maidenhead (Berkshire) girl, Ann Powney, which may also suggest an original Berkshire connection for this family.

This son, and other descendants of the Doctor, show strong physical, temperamental and vocational characteristics, similar to those of the poet. Thomas Keate began a medical career as house surgeon at St. George's Hospital on 24 June 1767. He had great ability, which he did not always use in his hospital work, and was immensely successful, being Surgeon to George, Prince of Wales, afterwards George IV, Surgeon

---

1. Spellings vary for the same people, according to the parish clerk. I have here standardized as "Keats" for convenience.
2. Somerset Record Office, Taunton; Town Clerk's Office, Wells.
3. *Reading Mercury*, 11 September 1790; Berkshire Record Office.

General to the Army, and three times Master of the Corporation of Surgeons. His sketch by Rowlandson,[1] though satirizing him, seems a fair likeness, and shows him to have been small-built, with reddish hair, a long straight nose, and quite a long upper lip, all characteristics of the poet. He is reported to have shown a quick temper in criticizing the first amputation by his nephew, Robert Keate (1777–1857), whom he took as apprentice in 1790.

Robert Keate, also a distinguished and successful surgeon, showed even more clearly the temperamental and physical characteristics of the poet. A letter from his own apprentice, signed "Berks" (*Medical Times and Gazette*, 21 August 1869) describes him as

> a square and compact little man . . . In conversation at odd times, or when wiping his hands in the wards after the usual preliminary scour, with his head well thrown in the air and one foot well planted forwards, and talking very aptly and intelligently you could not mistake in him the gentleman.

This may be compared with Severn's statement (Sharp, 19) that Keats

> though small of stature . . . seemed taller, partly from the perfect symmetry of his frame, partly from his erect attitude and a characteristic backward poise (sometimes a toss) of the head.

Compare also Cowden Clarke's remark on Keats (*Recollections of Writers*, 146), "Had he been born in squalor he would have emerged a gentleman."

Robert Keate is described elsewhere as below the middle height, exceptionally quick tempered, and looking and behaving like a sailor, expressions also used in describing the poet. Robert Keate's brother John (1773–1852) was the notorious Head Master of Eton, well-known for his reddish hair, quick temper, and short stature, "having been early 'set', for I do not think he grew in height after 15."[2]

These likenesses to famous surgeons of his day[3] may certainly explain why Keats seems to have been favoured in his early training at Guy's. Whether there was a family connection between the Thomas Keats of Reading, who may have been Keats's father, and Dr. Keate of Wells, who was buried at Reading, is uncertain. The resemblances, in temperament and physique, of the Doctor's descendants to the poet, who in turn strongly resembled his own father, may be thought to heighten the probability.

It is therefore not impossible that Keats's father may have been born in Berkshire, but may have been brought up, or spent some of his youth with West Country relatives, and so produced the impression that he came from the West Country. It should be emphasized that there are many other possibilities—e.g. an illegitimate birth, a baptism not registered or not surviving—Nonconformist baptisms are often very incomplete—, or a baptism occurring several years after birth.

---

1. Print Room, British Museum, George, Catalogue of Personal Political Satires, Vol. VIII, No. 11536.

2. Christopher Bethell to the Rev. Edward Coleridge, 14 May 1852, King's College Library, Cambridge.

3. The portrait of Robert Keate by J. P. Knight, of which an engraving by Richardson Jackson exists in the Wellcome Historical Medical Museum, is unfortunately said to be valueless as a likeness ("Berks", *Medical Times and Gazette*, 21 August 1869).

APPENDIX 3

KEATS AND VENEREAL DISEASE

ON 8 OCTOBER 1817, a few days after his return from Oxford, Keats wrote to Benjamin Bailey (*Letters*, I, 171):

> The little Mercury I have taken has corrected the Poison and improved my Health—though I feel from my employment that I shall never be again secure in Robustness—would that you were as well as
>
> your sincere friend & brother
> John Keats

In *The Asclepiad* of April 1884, 143, B. W. Richardson (1828–1896) expanded and interpreted this passage, reprinted in HBF (1883), III, 83, as follows:

> Returning to the last volume[1] of the Forman edition, and rapidly reviewing the life presented there, we find that . . . in the autumn of the same year, 1817, he visits a friend, Bailey by name, at Oxford, and in that visit runs loose, and pays a forfeit for his indiscretion, which ever afterwards physically and morally embarrasses him.

In his *Life of John Keats* (1887) W. M. Rossetti repeated Keats's statement, which, he said, "speaks for itself", and also Richardson's interpretation of it.

In 1925, Lowell, I, 512–513, provided her own muddled and confusing statement, quoting Keats's letter and adding:

> W. M. Rossetti was, I believe, the first to read into this the suggestion that Keats had contracted syphilis at Oxford.

In point of fact, neither Richardson (whom Lowell ignored) nor Rossetti had ever mentioned syphilis nor indeed any form of venereal disease. The invention of the syphilis interpretation was entirely Miss Lowell's own. She then proceeded to refute her own invention, and was followed by Hewlett and Bate, both in the refutation and in attributing the syphilis theory to Rossetti.

Ward, 134, accepted Lowell's syphilis invention with slight reservation—"probably syphilis"—and proceeded to argue that it was true, going back to the original source, Richardson. She, however, further confused the issue by stating that Richardson had the information from Keats's friend Henry Stephens, with whom Richardson had conversations about Keats from 1856 to 1864. In context, however (see above), Richardson's statement is a straight interpretation of Keats's own words quoted by Forman. In *The Asclepiad*, it bears no relation to the reported conversations with Stephens.

---

1. It should be "last but one".

It would therefore seem that the hotly-debated point whether Keats had or did not have syphilis is a pure invention of his biographers. W. Hale-White, *Keats as Doctor and Patient*, 44, in a passage which shows a curious ignorance of the medical history of Keats's time (see below), only discussed the matter in terms of whether or not Keats had syphilis, and did not mention or consider any other venereal infection.

Two other passages from Keats's letters to Bailey have been used by biographers in support or refutation of this theory.

1. *Letters*, I, 175

> You ask me after my health and spirits—This Question ratifies in my Mind what I have said above—Health and Spirits can only belong unalloyed to the selfish Man—the Man who thinks much of his fellows can never be in Spirits—when I am not suffering for vicious beastliness I am the greater part of the week in spirits.

"Vicious beastliness" has been interpreted by Ward to mean syphilis. The whole passage, however, refers explicitly to "what I have said above", i.e. earlier in the letter. Keats has been arguing that men ought to "volunteer for uncomfortable hours" and "be self spiritualized into a kind of sublime Misery" by opening the sensations of their hearts to all the trouble that there is in the world. The man who suffers, in imagination, the wrong and evil that there is in the world can never be "in spirits". Taken in the context of the whole letter, Keats's last remark can be paraphrased "when I am not allowing my imagination to realise what viciousness and beastliness there is in the world, I am selfishly in good spirits".

2. *Letters*, I, 186

> I think Jane or Marianne [Reynolds] has a better opinion of me than I deserve—for really and truly I do not think my Brothers [Tom's] illness connected with mine—you know more of the real Cause than they do—nor have I any chance of being rack'd as you have been—

The interpretations made by biographers of the above passage are impossible to summarize, but none seems to have read it carefully.[1] It is often assumed that "my Brothers illness" refers to tuberculosis; but Tom Keats had not yet started spitting blood, and how it would be "a better opinion" of Keats for the Misses Reynolds to think that he himself had tuberculosis is unexplained. The clue seems to lie in what was *thought* to be the matter with both Tom and Bailey. Both were thought at this time to be suffering from unrequited love. Keats thought Bailey "was in a dying state" about Miss Leigh (*Letters*, II, 66) and Tom had just searched France in vain for his Amena. Keats is simply saying in this passage that his own illness is not due to the pangs of unrequited love as the romantic Reynolds sisters suppose.

One should therefore consider solely Keats's statement to Bailey of 8 October 1817, and interpret it in the medical terms and practice of the time, though it is worth noting

---

1. e.g. "An examination of the passage given above makes it clear that if Keats had contracted syphilis so had Bailey". Hewlett, 121. The point of the passage, however, is that Keats is not suffering in the same way as Bailey.

the air of mystery with which Keats surrounds his disease, and his cryptic reference to a similar illness suffered by a member of Rice's Piccadilly drinking-set, John Martin: "He is ill—I suspect—but that's neither here nor there—all I can say I wish him as well through it as I am like to be" (*Letters*, I, 172). The main statement by Keats, "The little Mercury I have taken has corrected the Poison and improved my Health", has been subjected to various inaccurate and unhistorical interpretations, mostly by Hale-White. These are:

1. That when Keats wrote "Mercury" he meant "Calomel" or mercurous chloride, a mild compound of mercury prescribed for many illnesses. W. A. Wells, *A Doctor's Life of John Keats*, 167, and Hale-White, op. cit., 45.

Keats, however, distinguished in his own *Note Book*, 64, quite distinctly between Calomel and Mercury, as do all the leading medical writers of his time (cf. Astley Cooper's Surgical Lectures, *The Lancet*, 1823).

2. That mercury was prescribed for syphilis "always in considerable doses for a long period; no doctor in his senses would use 'a little Mercury' for syphilis." Hale-White, op. cit., 44. This is untrue. Astley Cooper prescribed small doses of mercury for a few weeks as a cure for syphilis, and summarized "Syphilis should be cured by a slight, and not a violent mercurial action" op. cit., II, 399.[1]

3. That in the first third of the nineteenth century, mercury was used recklessly for a great number of diseases (Lowell, I, 515). During almost the exact period of Keats's lifetime, however, this excessive use was attacked in a succession of authoritative works, e.g. S. Sawrey, *An Inquiry into Some of the Effects of the Venereal Poison . . .*, etc. (1802), A. Philips Wilson, *Observations on the Use and Abuse of Mercury, and on Precautions Necessary in its Employment* (1805), William Fergusson, *Observations on the Venereal Disease in Portugal* (1813), James Bedingfield, *A Compendium of Medical Practise* (1816), and Joseph Swan, *An Inquiry into the Action of Mercury on the Living Body* (1822).

Keats, in fact, lived at a time when there was a strong reaction against the indiscriminate use of mercury, and when many doctors tended to confine its use solely to the cure of venereal diseases. One of these was the doctor who attended both himself and Tom, Solomon Sawrey (see above). It is significant that Hale-White, who gives biographies and publications of all other medical men concerned with Keats, merely mentions Sawrey by name briefly (op. cit., 46) and suppresses the existence of his treatise on venereal disease listed above.

From Sawrey's *An Inquiry into the Effects of the Venereal Poison. . . .* etc. three main points are relevant to Keats's statement.

1. Sawrey believed that mercury should only be used for venereal diseases. "When it is clear the complaint has a venereal cause we give mercury to cure it. But if we should be of opinion that its nature is not venereal, we should of course omit to use that remedy and depend upon others", p. iv.

---

1. James Bedingfield, *A Compendium of Medical Practise*, 293, also recommends specifically a slight mercurial action.

2. He believed that gonorrhoea or clap should be treated with small doses of mercury and syphilis with large doses. "I am persuaded that a small quantity will prevent the clap contaminating the blood: and a great deal is often necessary to cure that disease (i.e. syphilis)", p. 47.

3. He believed, erroneously with Hunter, that gonorrhoea or clap was an early stage of syphilis or lues venerea, and therefore that a small quantity of mercury, by curing gonorrhoea, would prevent syphilis taking place (p. 45). On the other hand, if it failed, for instance by leaving off the treatment too early, he believed that syphilis might ensue from an apparently cured case of gonorrhoea (pp. 153–157).

It therefore seems clear that Keats, in taking his "little Mercury" with Sawrey as his doctor, could only be taking it for the venereal infection of gonorrhoea. A further incident in Keats's medical history seems to confirm this. Nearly a year later, in August and September 1818, while under "Sawrey's Mandate"—that is, Sawrey's treatment— he is found taking mercury in large enough quantities to cause nervousness and apparently toothache (*Letters*, I, 364, 369). Sawrey only used large doses of mercury for suspected syphilis, and then only with extreme reluctance (*An Inquiry . . .*, 122– 123). With his views, this implies that he believed that he had treated Keats previously for a gonorrhoeal infection, which was in danger of developing into syphilis. He was probably taking this precaution because of the severely ulcerated throat, with which Keats returned from his Scottish walking-tour, fearing that it might be a syphilitic ulcer.

This later treatment has considerable psychological implications in Keats's still-further medical history. Whether or not the heavy dosage of mercury at this time predisposed Keats to catch tuberculosis from Tom, Keats would believe, by medical theory of the day, that he had hastened tuberculosis in himself by taking mercury. All text-books emphasize that mercury should not be taken if there is any danger of tuberculosis. Keats may have had this physiological reason for the self-blame that so many people noticed him displaying during the course of his tubercular illness. This indeed may have been the physical "secret" he confided to Charles Brown shortly before leaving England (*Letters*, II, 321, 327).

It has never before been suggested that Keats in October 1817 was suffering from gonorrhoea, since all biographers who mention the "little Mercury" have debated the fallacious syphilis theory invented by Lowell. A gonorrhoeal infection, however, seems the only answer that fits contemporary medical evidence, and particularly the work and belief of Keats's own doctor, Sawrey. Four conjectural objections, which have been raised from time to time to the idea that Keats was treated for a venereal disease, should, however, be mentioned.

1. That Keats, both in October 1817 and September 1818, was treating himself, not under Sawrey's direction, and might have prescribed mercury for other diseases.

This is unlikely, since Keats shows great respect for Sawrey as a consultant (*Letters*, I, 196). His lectures from Astley Cooper at Guy's taught him to use mercury very sparingly for any disease other than the venereal.

2. That Keats had no sexual experience, and therefore could not have contracted any form of venereal disease.

The lyric "Unfelt, unheard, unseen" speaks explicitly of sexual experience (Appendix 4). It was written by 17 August 1817. This may, indeed, indicate that Keats contracted the infection just before going to Oxford, not at Oxford as originally assumed by Richardson, and that it developed during his stay there.

3. That Keats would not have written to Bailey, a future clergyman, about venereal disease.

Keats certainly used sexual terms and terms denoting sexual experience (Appendix 4) in his letter to Bailey of 30 October 1817 (*Letters*, I, 175). Bailey is found a few months later using sexual terms (*Letters*, I, 200), when he was presumably one of the "two parsons" discussing "the derivation of the word C——t." The worldliness of the Regency clergy, in spite of their Evangelical phraseology, is evident in all contemporary literature, and has not been appreciated by Keats's biographers.

4. That Bailey would not have sent John Taylor the letter containing the "little Mercury" remark.

When Bailey sent the letter after Keats's death, on 8 May 1821, he was intent on justifying himself for having defended Keats to Lockhart as not being closely connected with Hunt, a defence that had led to Lockhart's personal attack on Keats in *Blackwood's*. He endorsed the letter, "I think this letter will be a groundwork for a defence of poor Keats's having had *Hunt for a Patron*.—which is so shamelessly insisted on by the writers of Blackwds. BB—". He was therefore drawing Taylor's attention to the main body of the letter, not to its ending, though there is no reason to believe (see 3, above) that he would have seen anything wrong in Taylor reading the whole letter.

APPENDIX 4

KEATS'S USE OF BAWDY

Considering the manners of his time, Keats's letters and poems are remarkably free from sexual slang. There are, however, some half-dozen passages, some of which were omitted by editors such as Colvin, or ignored by editors such as Rollins, who in at least one instance printed a misreading through not recognizing the meaning of a word. In the following summary, the definitions are all taken from *The Slang of Venery and its Analogues* (by Henry Cary), privately printed, Chicago, 1916, unless otherwise stated.

1, *Letters*, I, 175.

When you are settled I will come and take a peep at your Church—your house—try whether I shall have grow(n) two (*for* too) lusty for my chair—by the fire side—and take a peep at my cordials[1] Bower.

chair, penis, or flesh. Exactly the same pun on this meaning of the word is made by the friend of Keats's publishers, William Robson, *The Old Play-Goer*, 119.
cordial, the semen.
Bower, the vagina.

2. *Letters*, I, 200, 201.

there was a younger Brother of the Squibs made him self very conspicious after the Ladies had retired from the supper table by giving Mater Omnium . . . On proceeding to the Pot in the Cupboard it soon became full on which the Court door was opened Frank Floodgate bawls out, Hoollo! here's an opposition pot—Ay, says Rice in one you have a Yard for your pot, and in the other a pot for your Yard.

Mater Omnium, Mother of all Saints (or Souls), the pudendum.
Yard, penis.

3, *Letters*, I, 256

. . . a secret she gave you on the nail . . . I have met with a Brace or twain of little Long heads—not a kit[2] o' the german—all in the neatest little dresses, and avoiding all the pudd(l)es—but very fond of peppermint drops, laming ducks, and seeing little Girls affairs. Well I can't tell!

---

1. Rollins prints "cardials". The vowel is doubtful in the MS.
2. Rollins prints "bit". The MS appears to read "kit".

451

secret, general, applied to the vagina or copulation.
nail, penis (John Cleland, *Fanny Hill*).
kit, male parts.
puddle, the female pudendum.
pepper, the clap (*peppered*, clapped).
drops, the clap (*dropping member*, penis affected with gonorrhoea).
affair, the vagina.

4. *Letters*, I, 333

Here's Brown going on so that I cannot bring to Mind how the two last days have vanished—for example he says 'The Lady of the Lake went to Rock herself to sleep on Arthur's seat and the Lord of the Isles coming to Press a Piece and seeing her Assleap remembered their last meeting at Cony[1] stone Water so touching her with one hand on the Vallis Lucis while he (*for* the) other un-Derwent her Whitehaven, Ireby stifled her clack man on, that he might her Anglesea and give her a Buchanan and said.

Piece, prostitute.
Ass, arse.
Cony, the female pudendum.
stone, testes.
Water, semen.
Vallis Lucis, valley, sluices, the female pudendum.
haven, the female pudendum.
stifled, choked, sexually occupied (John Cleland, *Fanny Hill*).
clack, the clack-valve of a pump, pump and pump-handle being commonplaces of sexual slang.

5. *Letters*, II, 36

and beat him with a $\left\{ {k \atop c} \right.$ertain rod . . . Ah! he may dress me as he likes but he shan't ticlke me pillow the feathers.

rod, penis.
feathers, the female pubic hair.

6. *Letters*, II, 205

Severn has got a little Baby—all his own let us hope—He told Brown he had given up painting and had tu(r)ned modeller. I hope sincerely tis not a party concern; that no Mr.—or **** is the real *Pinxit* and Severn the poor *Sculpsit* to this work of art— You know he has long studied in the Life-Academy.

concern, the female pudendum.
Academy, brothel.

---

1. Rollins prints "Corry". The MS shows "Cony".

Keats's lyric "Unfelt, unheard, unseen" has in its draft form the line

                    And stifling up the Vale

whose meaning can be inferred from *Letters*, I, 333 above.
Line 17 of the same poem reads

                    I'll feel my heaven anew,

To feel one's heaven, or, more often, to feel one's way to heaven, is defined "to grope a woman".

INDEX

Abbey, Eleanor, 33, 181, 312

Abbey, Miss, 33

Abbey, Richard, 340, 443; and Taylor, 3–4, 124; character, 3–4; his evidence as to Keats family's lives, 14–15, 19, 20–1, 22, 25; Alice Jennings's trustee, 32, 34, 44, 71, 270; background and early life, 33; and Fanny Keats, 43, 149, 256, 286, 382; maligned by posterity, 91–2; and George Keats, 136, 141, 344, 363–4, 378; opinion of the Keats boys, 216; and Brown, 388

— and J.K.: 33, 232, 330, 343; financial affairs, 34–5, 48, 71–2, 91–2, 265, 273, 286, 290, 325, 363–4, 389, 407; guardian and ward, 85; suggests occupations for J.K., 97, 345, 364; strained relations with J.K., 98; on J.K.'s *Poems*, 123–4; suspicious of J.K.'s friends, 256; guardianship of Fanny, 256, 286, 387; kindlier attitude to J.K., 344–5, 373

Angeletti, Anna, 420, 427, 433

Apuleius, Lucius (2nd cent.), 309, 313

Archer, Archibald, 271

Ariosto, Ludovico (1474–1533), 367, 368 ·

Audubon, John James (1785–1851), 330, 343

Babington, Dr., 49

Bailey, Benjamin, 144, 447, 450; background, appearance, character, 145, 148, 234; attitude to religion, 153–4, 175; and death of Princess Charlotte, 176, 199, 200; at Reddell's party, 180; and Marianne Reynolds, 183, 216, 236, 291; and the Gleigs, 216, 233, 234, 236, 291; ordained, 233; and Lockhart, 233–4, 291; and *Blackwood's*, 234–5; in Ceylon, 434

— and J.K.: J.K.'s reading, 145, 217, 222; invites J.K. to Oxford, 146, 215; J.K. at Oxford, 148–55; on J.K., 151, 153; and sexual matters, 156; influence of

J.K. on, 176; tells Lockhart of J.K.'s origins, 234–5; on J.K.'s theory of poetry, 250–1; J.K. censorious of, 291–2; J.K. tries to renew friendship with, 334

Bamford, Samuel (1788–1872), 345

Barnes, Thomas (1785–1841), 216

Bate, W. J., vii, 446

Beattie, James (1735–1803), J.K. influenced by *The Minstrel*, 37, 40–1, 43, 282; and Reynolds, 90; Shelley's *Alastor* and, 107; J.K. grows out of, 275

Beckford, William Thomas (1760–1844), 255, 256

Benjamin, Nathan, 324, 356

Bentley (Keats brothers' landlord), 124, 268

Bentley, Mrs., 124, 218

Bewick, William (1795–1866), 169, 186, 194, 271

Birkbeck, Morris, 118, 201, 273, 311

Blackwood, William (1776–1834), 409

Boccaccio, Giovanni (1313–1375), 190, 204, 277

Brawne, Frances (Fanny) (1800–1865), 231; and the Dilkes, 263, 362, 391–2, 434; and Severn, 264; appearance, 266; character and personality, 267–8; and the Reynolds girls, 272, 362, 393, 401; Brown and, 285, 385, 434, 435; and *La Belle Dame Sans Merci*, 303; and *Ode to Psyche*, 310; and George Keats, 375; and Fanny Keats, 375, 407, 410, 433, 434; and the Keats finances, 378, 379; and death of J.K., 433; marries, 434; protests against the Keats legend, 435

— and J.K.: and *Bright Star*, 262, 264, 298, 415; first meeting, 263–4; early love, 264–5, 272; behaviour between, 266–8, 333–4, 361; on J.K., 263, 290, 361, 410; J.K. on, 267; relationship between J.K., Brown and, 285; J.K.'s difficult position over, 292, 323, 344;

455